THE COMPLETE
UP NORTH

ALSO BY DOUG BENNET AND TIM TINER

Up North
Up North Again
Wild City

THE COMPLETE UP NORTH

A Guide to Ontario's Wilderness from Black Flies to the Northern Lights

DOUG BENNET · TIM TINER

Illustrated by MARTA LYNNE SCYTHES

McCLELLAND & STEWART

Library and Archives Canada Cataloguing in Publication

Bennet, Doug
The complete up north : a guide to Ontario's wilderness from black flies to the
northern lights / Doug Bennet and Tim Tiner ; illustrated by Marta Lynne Scythes.

ISBN 978-0-7710-1141-2

1. Natural history – Ontario, Northern. 2. Ontario, Northern – Miscellanea.
3. Natural history – Outdoor books. I. Tiner, Tim II. Scythes, Marta III. Title.

QH106.2.O5B44 2009 508.713'1 C2009-905021-8

We acknowledge the financial support of the Government of Canada through the
Book Publishing Industry Development Program and that of the Government of Ontario
through the Ontario Media Development Corporation's Ontario Book Initiative. We
further acknowledge the support of the Canada Council for the Arts and the Ontario Arts
Council for our publishing program.

Typeset in Bembo by M&S, Toronto
Printed and bound in Canada

ANCIENT FOREST
FRIENDLY

This book is printed on acid-free paper that is 100% recycled,
ancient-forest friendly (40% post-consumer waste).

McClelland & Stewart Ltd.
75 Sherbourne Street
Toronto, Ontario
M5A 2P9
www.mcclelland.com

1 2 3 4 5 14 13 12 11 10

TABLE OF CONTENTS

ANIMAL KINGDOM

PLANT KINGDOM

THE HEAVENS

MOTHER EARTH

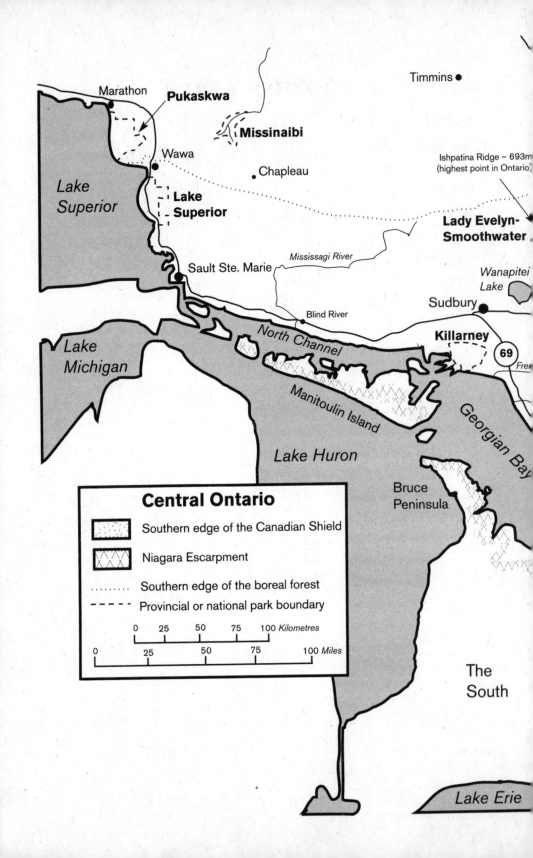

Timmins •

Marathon

Pukaskwa

Missinaibi

Wawa

• Chapleau

Ishpatina Ridge – 693m
(highest point in Ontario)

*Lake
Superior*

**Lake
Superior**

**Lady Evelyn-
Smoothwater**

Mississagi River

Sault Ste. Marie

*Wanapitei
Lake*

Sudbury •

Blind River

Killarney

*Lake
Michigan*

North Channel

69

Fren

Manitoulin Island

Georgian Bay

Lake Huron

Bruce
Peninsula

Central Ontario

Southern edge of the Canadian Shield

Niagara Escarpment

. . . . Southern edge of the boreal forest

– – – – Provincial or national park boundary

| 0 | 25 | 50 | 75 | 100 *Kilometres* |

| 0 | 25 | 50 | 75 | 100 *Miles* |

The
South

Lake Erie

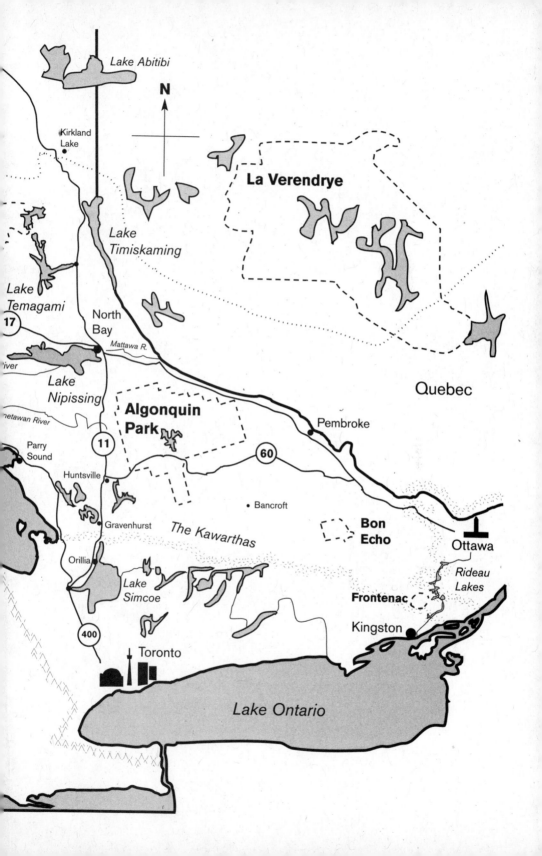

INTRODUCTION

Who would have thought a 1989 conversation around a campfire in Algonquin Park would lead to this, *The Complete Up North,* the fifth book in a loose series sparked by simple curiosity about the world around us "up north."

This book is both a compilation of the best from the first two books, *Up North* and *Up North Again,* and also an update based on the many natural changes and scientific advancements since those titles were published in the 1990s. Just two examples: in our early books, there was nary a mention of double-breasted cormorants. But the waterfowl's population has since exploded, and now the black bird – love it or hate it – merits its own entry. And in our Night Sky section, many entries have been updated to reflect mind-bending advances in astronomical research and even bureaucratic redefinitions: Pluto's not even a planet anymore, technically speaking.

But the basic premise of *The Complete Up North* remains the same: it is an attempt to answer, from a sense of wonder, a good number of the questions prompted by our experiences in the woods and wilderness when we go up north.

As much as possible, *The Complete Up North* aims to incorporate the whole outdoor experience – from the bugs that pester to the northern lights that dance across the night sky. We have concentrated on the most commonly seen or experienced species and phenomena in central Ontario, as they are what occupy your immediate attention most of the time when camping or visiting the cottage.

By central Ontario, we refer to the vast, mixed-forest hinterland from the Rideau Lakes, Kawarthas and Bruce Peninsula on to the rocky Canadian Shield as far as the Temagami and Mississagi Provincial Park areas – the "up north" for millions of Ontarians. Although much of the guide's information applies as well to other parts of the country, including far northern Ontario and much of Quebec, we have sought, by concentrating on this specific region, to give as complete a picture as possible within the space of the book.

As in the earlier books, we have arranged the entries in a way that we hope is useful to readers. There are four main chapters: Animal Kingdom, Plant Kingdom, The Heavens, and Mother Earth. Each chapter is further divided into subsections, such as Birds within the Animal Kingdom. Finally, within each subsection, individual entries are arranged alphabetically. An index is also included.

Being journalists ourselves, rather than scientists, we have endeavoured to be accurate while avoiding a strict scientific or academic tone in these pages. Our intent is to answer the many questions of campers and cottagers in the same spirit in which they are asked. If we anthropomorphize, it is because that is what people tend to do when they talk about and relate to nature around them. We have tried, however, to ensure that a sense of fun does not distort the true nature of the subject.

We hope *The Complete Up North* informs and entertains a new generation of cottagers, campers and hikers – while replacing our first readers' dog-eared copies with a fresh, updated edition.

Doug Bennet
Tim Tiner

To learn more about *The Complete Up North* and other books by the authors, please visit www.upnorthguides.com.

ANIMAL
KINGDOM

BIRDS

Birds are *the most conspicuous variety of wildlife in the wilderness. Some 482 species of birds have been confirmed sighted in the wild in Ontario. Almost 300 of them nest in the province. Most species fly primarily by day, adding music and bright splashes of colour to the forest and waterfront.*

The majority of birds – more than 75 per cent of all North American species – are migratory. An estimated five billion fly south from Canada and the northern U.S. every fall. Hardy chickadees, ravens, gray jays and ruffed grouse remain behind to tough it out through the winter. But before the snows are even melted, a parade of migrants begins, heralding the return of spring and reaching a crescendo with waves of wood warblers in mid-May. Some come all the way from South America to raise a new generation on the bugs, berries and seeds of a Canadian summer.

Over the past 20 years, many of Ontario's bird populations have experienced considerable change. Species once pushed to the brink by DDT, such as peregrine falcons, bald eagles and cormorants, have made considerable comebacks. Others, such as turkey vultures and Canada geese, have pushed their nesting ranges farther northward, while ravens have moved into southern Ontario. Unfortunately, human actions continue to have major negative impacts as well. Climate change is probably affecting most birds in ways that are still not well understood, though the gray jay's range is clearly retracting northward. Many tropical migrants, including Canada warblers, wood thrushes, kingbirds and bobolinks, are in steep decline, faced with habitat loss in both north and south. By some estimates, there are only half as many songbirds around today as 40 years ago. Thankfully, central Ontario still hosts a rich abundance of birds, and hopefully growing appreciation of them will inspire their preservation.

As in the other sections of this book, some single-species entries include information on related or similar species, whose names appear in **bold**.

BARRED OWL
Voice in the Night on Silent Wings

"Who cooks for you?" is probably the most persistent question of central Ontario's woodlands at night. The phrase, when hooted through cupped hands, is the approximate sound of the barred owl's call, which may be heard throughout the year. Though infrequently seen, the barred owl is one of the loudest and noisiest of Ontario's hooters. Its March-to-April mating season is known as the months of madness, for hoots, hisses, screams, barks and cackles are all part of the owl's courtship repertoire. Later, when they are nesting and their eggs or young are vulnerable to predators, barred owls enter their quietest period.

Calls: Slightly muffled, but resonant, hollow, rapid hoots that sound like "Who cooks for you, who cooks for you all" or "hoohoo-hoohoo, hoohoo-hoohooaw," with the first hoot sounding like a dog bark and the last uttered in a drawn-out, fading gargle that is not always audible from afar; also screams, barks, whistles, whoops, cackles

Accolades: Owls have the largest ear drums, relative to their size, of all birds, and can hear the faintest sounds and the widest frequency range

Length: 43–51 cm (17–20 in)

Wingspan: 1–1.2 m (3.3–4 ft)

Weight: Males 0.5–0.8 kg (1.1–1.8 lb), females 0.6–1 kg (1.3–2.2 lb)

Markings: Both sexes grey-brown; vertical light and dark bars on whitish chest, white spots on back; round, puffy, ghostly-looking head with grey facial disc around dark brown eyes; feathered legs

Alias: Northern barred owl, wood owl, crazy owl, *la chouette rayée*, *Strix varia*

Name origin: Anglo-Saxon *ule*, meaning "howler"

Name for a group: A parliament of owls

Whereabouts: Mature, unfragmented coniferous and mixed forests, especially near swamps, rivers or lakes

Food: Voles, mice, shrews, squirrels, chipmunks, young hares, frogs, snakes, salamanders, grouse, smaller owls and other birds, crayfish, fish, insects, spiders

Home range: 1–4 km² (0.4–1.5 sq. mi)

Nest: Usually in tree cavity with an opening of at least 15 cm (6 in), an average of 5–10 m (16–33 ft) above the ground; sometimes in ravens,' crows,' hawks' or squirrels' old nests

Average clutch: 2–3 spherical, white eggs, about the size of chicken eggs

Incubation period: 28–33 days

Fledging age: About 10 weeks

Lifespan: Up to 18 years in wild, 23 years in captivity

To many Eastern Woodland peoples, owls represented the female moon spirit. They were thought to have beneficial, healing powers, and to be messengers between living and dead relatives. Owl feathers were hung from tobacco pipes as prayer offerings to the Earth and moon. Owls were similarly associated with the moon and with female deities in the Old World. Athena, the Greek goddess of wisdom and war, was usually depicted with an owl at her side. Sometimes, though, the owl's persona was more ambiguous. To the Chinese, it was both a thunderbird and a stealer of souls. It was a symbol of death in ancient Rome and an evil night hag – a witch in bird form – in the Christian world. When her husband bumps off the king of Scotland, Shakespeare's Lady Macbeth hears an owl call and says,

It was the owl that shriek'd. The fatal bellman, Which gives the stern'st good night.

But to be as wise as an owl is an axiom that has survived from ancient Greek times. The image was probably fostered by the bird's huge, serious eyes, with lids that close downward like a human's rather than with the bottom lids rising up, as with most birds. Owls' eyes are also set flat on their faces like those of humans, giving them binocular vision – each eye's view overlaps to enhance depth perception and faraway details. A large number of light-sensitive retinal rods at the back of their eyes make owls see small objects in the dark up to six times more accurately than do people. Their eyes are so large that owls can barely move them up, down or sideways in their sockets, while their broad face narrows their view to 110 degrees, compared with 180 degrees for humans. They make up for it by being able to turn their neck 270 degrees, sometimes so quickly that their heads appear to turn completely around.

Despite their sharp, long-range sight, owls do not see as well close up. They don't give a hoot about farsightedness, though, because highly specialized hearing allows them to pinpoint small prey exactly. In experiments conducted in absolute darkness, they have no trouble catching mice.

An owl's ear openings are even bigger than its eyes, but are hidden by large, movable flaps of skin and feathers at the sides of its head. The ears are at the edge of rings of feathers spreading from around the eyes, forming a facial disc that acts like a radar dish in picking up sounds. The disc feathers move to help direct the sound, and the skin flaps over the ears can be raised to deflect noises coming from behind the head. Each ear is in a slightly different shape, size and position, enabling the owl's brain to detect noises at two different angles at the same time — high-tech stereophonics. The two sound lines target the prey precisely, with the owl snatching it up where they meet. Owls can hear and locate prey even beneath the snow. Deep or crusted snow makes hunting difficult, leading to good times and population explosions for mice.

Even while it is using noise as its meal ticket, the owl itself is silent, swooping down without warning on fluffy, serrated wing feathers that make no sound. Their puffy feathers always make owls look bigger than their real size. A

Predators: Great horned owls, goshawks and other large raptors; nests also raided by raccoons and crows

Pellets: Average less than 1 cm long

Droppings: Like melted candle wax

Nesting range: Mainly south-central Ontario to the southern boreal forest, though sparsely scattered farther north and south; also found in all other provinces and territories except island of Newfoundland and Nunavut

Population density: Usually 2–10 pairs per 100 km^2 (39 sq. mi)

Winter whereabouts: Stays on breeding range; flies into southern Ontario some winters when food is scarce

Owl capital of Ontario: Wolfe and Amherst islands, near Kingston

First appearance of owls: Up to 65 million years ago

Canada's most northerly wintering bird: Snowy owl

Northern owls making cyclic winter irruptions into central and southern Ontario: Snowy, great grey, boreal, short-eared and northern hawk owls

Ontario owls at risk: Barn owl (endangered), short-eared owl (species of special concern)

Number of owl species nesting in Ontario: 10

Number of owl species worldwide: About 130

Also see: Deer Mouse

light body, in relation to their large wings, makes them particularly buoyant, with less need of flapping. Owls usually hunt from perches on dead trees. Since they eat small animals whole, pellets of regurgitated bones, fur, feathers, claws and beaks often mark the spot beneath a regular perch or nest.

Though they are mainly nocturnal, when they're raising families, barred owls sometimes hunt during the day, like moonlighting humans. They're a settled lot, and from one generation to the next often use the same nest for one or two decades.

Unlike smaller birds, the downy white young hatch separately, a couple of days apart, because their mother starts incubating each egg as she lays it in April or May, rather than waiting till all are together. If food is in short supply, only the oldest – the biggest and first to eat – will survive. When they are four or five weeks old, usually in June, the young begin hanging around on branches outside the nest, though it is several more weeks before they fledge, and they continue to live off the folks until about four months old. In late summer or fall they set out into the world to establish their own territories and make something of themselves.

Barred owls occasionally make a meal of Ontario's smallest nocturnal hooter, the **saw-whet owl**, which is also quite common, especially in evergreen woods. The hand-sized saw-whet gets its name from its short, high-pitched whistles, likened to the sound of a saw being sharpened with a whetstone, repeated in triplets 100 to 130 times per minute in March and April by courting males. Deer mice are the tiny owl's primary fare. Saw-whets are one of the few resident owls in the province that regularly migrate, moving south of the Canadian Shield and into the northern U.S. in October and November, though many stay put in the north year-round. Males often stake out breeding territories in autumn and stick with them through the winter, while females tend to roam once they've raised their young. Among the early birds of spring, migrants begin returning in March.

BLACK DUCK
Falling for Mallard Magnetism

Once reputed to be the most common quacker in Ontario, the darkly mottled black duck has hit a lot of turbulence in the past 50 years. Though still the fowl most likely to turn up in weedy Canadian Shield backwaters, it's declined by 40 per cent in central Ontario and nearly disappeared farther south in recent decades, beset by hunting, habitat loss and even sex and assimilation.

Blackies are the most wary of ducks, flying straight up from the water at the slightest whiff of trouble. The challenge of their fast, elusive flight and the fact that they are a large, tasty eating duck have long made them an autumn shotgun favourite. They fell from the sky in numbers approaching a million birds in the U.S. and Canada up to the early 1980s, halving their breeding population from three decades earlier.

Top flying speed: More than 40 km/h (25 mph)

Wingbeats per second: 5

Black duck wing loading: 1.4 g/cm^2 (0.3 oz/sq. in)

Red-winged blackbird wing loading: 0.3 g/cm^2 (0.07 oz/sq. in)

Length: Females 53–56 cm (21–22 in), males 57–61 cm (22.5–24 in)

Wingspan: 84–94 cm (33–37 in)

Weight: Females 1–1.2 kg (2.2–2.7 lb), males 1.1–1.5 kg (2.5–3.3 lb)

Markings: Both sexes are mostly dark brown, with sandy face and neck, violet-blue wing patch, white inner-wing undersides and orange-red or olive feet; bill yellowish on male, greenish and often mottled on female

Alias: Dusky duck, blackie, black mallard, brown duck, blackjack, redleg, American black duck, *le canard noir, Anas rubripes*

Scientific name meaning: In Latin, *anas* is "duck," *ruber* is "red" and *pes* is "foot"

Name origin of *duck*: From Old English *ducan,* meaning "to dive" or "to dip"

Name for a group: A paddling or raft of ducks

Calls: Females quack like mallards; males make a low croak

Whereabouts: Beaver ponds; sluggish alder-lined streams; shallow, weedy lakes; marshes; swamps; bogs

Home range: Up to 13 km² (5 sq. mi)

Food: Pondweed, water shield, water lily, sedges, wild rice and other grasses and aquatic vegetation, seeds, berries, acorns, mussels, crayfish, frogs, toads, tadpoles, insect larvae, snails and worms

Nest: Depression in grassy vegetation, filled with leaves and stems, lined by down, hidden in brushy stands of sweet gale or other shrubs or sedge along shorelines and islands

Average clutch: 8–10 creamy white or greenish eggs, about the size of large chicken eggs

Incubation period: 26–29 days

Stricter hunting regulations have since tempered their overall decline.

But compounding the black duck's problems is an apparently irresistible, well-known green-headed waddler: the ever-popular **mallard** duck. Native to both the prairies and Eurasia, mallards are the ancestors of most domestic ducks and are genetically almost identical to black ducks. The two probably separated only during the past Ice Age, with black ducks becoming camouflaged for a wooded setting. After forest barriers fell, however, western mallards moved east, reaching Ontario in the 1930s. Some 1.7 million mallards were also released from game farms in northeastern North America in the mid-20th century and expanded into northern waters wherever black duck numbers were falling. Under such conditions, the two species interbreed, with the brightly coloured mallard drakes seeming to win out over the less glamorous local males. Their hybrid descendants, which invariably tend to look like mallards, are fortified with black duck genes that make them fairly resistant to a blood parasite, avian malaria, spread by black flies on the Canadian Shield. The parasite normally causes mallards to go duck up.

One reason blackies and mallards mate so readily with each other is that their courting customs are virtually the same. Drakes cruise by females while shaking their heads and tails and holding their chests high. On their wintering grounds, small groups of males often circle around the hens, whistling catcalls, making nasal quacking small talk, and flicking water at the hen that takes their fancy. For their part, a female may goad a drake to attack an interloping male, to test his mettle. Just before mating, pairs get in the mood by facing each other and rapidly raising and lowering their heads in tandem.

Once they begin nesting, females binge on protein-rich invertebrates to nourish egg production, eating nearly twice as much as their closely guarding mates. Black ducks are "dabblers," gleaning their food from the surface of the water or dipping their heads down to forage off shallow bottoms, mooning observers in the process. Their bills are highly sensitive and efficient food processors, tipped with 28 nerve endings per square millimetre (human fingers have only 20 per square millimetre). Thin, closely spaced ridges inside their bills filter food from the water.

Once egg-laying begins, males usually paddle off within one to three weeks to larger lakes, some flying as far as the coast of Hudson Bay, to hang with the boys while they moult, rendering them flightless for about 10 days. Their single-parented offspring hatch between mid-May and early June. Females escort the downy ducklings out of the nest usually within a day of hatching and tend them up to a week or two before they fledge in midsummer, when the mothers seclude themselves to moult. Later, everyone joins the groups of dads on the big lakes, where pairing off for the following spring's mating season begins.

Fledging age: 58–63 days

Age at first breeding: 1 year

Average annual adult survival: 60–70%

Lifespan: Up to 26 years in wild

Predators: Goshawks, harriers, red-shouldered hawks, great horned owls, foxes, raccoons, coyotes; eggs also eaten by crows, herring gulls, skunks, mink, fox snakes and rat snakes; ducklings taken by snapping turtles, pickerel, pike and muskies

Nesting range: All of Ontario to the tree line; also in Quebec and the eastern and Prairie provinces

Spring migration in central Ontario: Early Apr. to early May

Fall migration in central Ontario: Oct. to late Nov.

Winter whereabouts: Most along U.S. Atlantic coast; others from Great Lakes to Gulf of Mexico

Continental midwinter population: About 270,000

Number of duck species nesting in Ontario: 25

Number of duck family species worldwide: 148

Also see: Common Merganser, Black Flies, Beaver

BLUE JAY
Smart, Loud, Bold and Brash

Flying speed: Avg. 33 km/h (20 mph); 37–42 km/h (23–26 mph) in migration

Length: 25–30 cm (10–12 in)

Wingspan: 41–42 cm (16–16.5 in)

Weight: 70–100 g (2.5–3.5 oz)

Markings: Blue back, white undersides, black necklace, blue crest

Average number of feathers on a songbird: 1,500–3,000

Alias: Blue coat, common jay, jay bird, northern jay, nest robber, corn-thief, *le geai bleu, Cyanocitta cristata*

Calls: Wide variety, including short, loud, harsh screams, a "queedle" sound like a

Among other birds, blue jays are not nearly the favourites they are of humans. Jays have a nasty habit of eating other birds' eggs and even their nestlings. Though nest robbing accounts for less than one per cent of their fare, it's enough to make them terrors. Small birds often gang up and mob a jay to drive it away, noisily diving at and sometimes striking it in the air. For their part, jays mob hawks, owls, crows, weasels and foxes, which can threaten them or their nests. The jay's loud, harsh alarm call also commonly warns other birds and animals that a potential predator is entering the area.

Blue jays in general are considered bold, brash, alert and intelligent. They can adapt quickly to a wide variety of habitats, though they favour evergreen trees for nesting and roosting, and oak and beech trees for feasting on acorns and nuts.

When oaks have bumper acorn crops, about once every other year, far more blue-jay young survive and remain through the winter.

A single jay can bury, or hide in the nooks and crannies of tree trunks, up to 5,000 nuts and acorns in one autumn, retrieving them later through the winter. Many commonly fly one to two kilometres (0.6 to 1.2 miles), and sometimes up to five kilometres (three miles), to a fruitful stand, cram their throats and beaks with up to five acorns or 15 beechnuts, and then return to their regular haunts to hide the loot. Those they forget about often germinate, making the birds important agents of long-distance nut dispersal. Experts studying buried pollen records believe blue jays may have played a big part in the rapid advance of oaks into southern Ontario after the glaciers retreated 11,000 years ago.

In early spring, loose winter-feeding parties of jays begin to break up. Males try to out-shout, intimidate and trounce each other as they pursue unattached she-jays. After the roughest, toughest customer finally wins and settles down with his new mate, the raucous brigand actually whispers softly whistled love songs to her. A pair usually remain together for life. By late April or May, unlike most other songbirds, a hitched male jay clams right up and becomes inconspicuous as he helps his spouse build a well-hidden nest, usually within the dense inner branches of an evergreen. He also fetches food and feeds his partner, strengthening their bond and providing her with the energy and protein needed for producing eggs.

Blue-jay young, like many other birds, hatch featherless, blind and unable to generate enough

squeaky clothesline and whistles

Origin of name: Old German *gahi*, meaning "quick"

Name for a group: A party of jays

Whereabouts: Mixed and deciduous forest edges, especially stands with oak or beech

Food: About 80% of diet is acorns, beechnuts, hazelnuts, pine seeds and berries; also caterpillars, beetles, grasshoppers and other insects, their eggs and cocoons, spiders, frogs, mice, minnows, small birds, their eggs and nestlings

Nest: Bulky construction of sticks, grasses, bark and mud, lined with moss, feathers and rootlets, wedged between a forked branch, usually 2–15 m (6.5–49 ft) above ground

Average clutch: 4–6 cherry-tomato-sized light green, blue or buff eggs, with brown specks

Incubation period: 17–18 days

Fledging age: 17–21 days

Age at first breeding: 2 years

Annual adult survival: About 50%

Lifespan: 6 years common; up to 18 years in wild, 26 years in captivity

Predators: Hawks, owls, ravens, shrikes; nests also raided by raccoons, squirrels, crows and grey rat snakes

Estimated Ontario population: 700,000

Accolades: Provincial bird of
  Prince Edward Island
Nesting range: Southern
  Ontario to the southern
  edge of the boreal forest;
  also in all other provinces
Winter whereabouts: Central
  Ontario to the southern U.S.
**Number of blue jays pass-
  ing Holiday Beach in fall:**
  Up to 440,000
**Number of jay species
  nesting in Ontario:** 2
**Number of jay species
  worldwide:** 42
Also see: Chickadee, Gray
  Jay, Beech, Red Oak

heat to warm their blood to normal survival temperatures. For their first two or three days, they are closely brooded and not fed, instead living off the yoke absorbed from their eggs. After those first critical days, their circulatory systems rev up, their blood warms and they acquire downy insulation. Their bright red, opened mouths trigger an automatic feeding response in their parents, who nourish them with a rich soup of regurgitated caterpillars and other juicy insects. By June, four-week-old fledglings accompany their parents in regrouping flocks of foraging jays.

In autumn, some blue jays, especially those hatched earlier in the year, gather in larger flocks and head south. Unlike many passerines, they migrate by day, from treetop level up to 300 metres above the ground. As many as 54,000 in a single day, spread out in long, loose lines, have been counted in steady flights past the Holiday Beach hawk watch on Lake Erie in late September and early October. While many stay in Ontario all winter, they sometimes all but vanish from some areas on the Shield, probably due to poor nut and seed crops.

BROAD-WINGED HAWK
Secretive Mid-storey Sentinel

As birds of prey, hawks have the advantages of size, deadly striking power and remarkable eyesight. They peer downwards with eyes that can make out long-distance details far smaller than anything human beings can distinguish. On their breeding grounds, crow-sized broad-winged hawks use their powers of vision to detect minute moving prey from mid-canopy hunting perches above small clearings, beaver ponds, stream sides and other forest edges. Transparent, side-closing lids let them moisten their eyes without blinking so they don't miss a thing.

On the fresh, breezy days of mid-September, eagle-eyed hawk watchers at strategic locations scan billowy white clouds and deep blue skies for large flights of migrating broad-wings. The raptors they admire so much face a daunting task when migration time comes around. Their

Ability to distinquish details at a distance: 2½ times as good as humans

Migrating altitude: Most at 300–800 m (1,000–2,600 ft), up to 3,000 m (9,840 ft)

Height at which a hawk disappears from view: 1,100 m (3,610 ft)

Total migration distance: 4,500–10,000 km (2,800–6,200 mi), covered in average of 40 days

Average daily migration distance: 100–400 km (62–250 mi), covered in 6 hours

Flying or gliding speed: 30–67 km/h (19–40 mph)

Average glide performance: 12 m forward for every 1 m drop

Length: Males 33–44 cm
(13–17 in), females 38–
48 cm (15–19 in)
Wingspan: 80–100 cm (2.6–
3.3 ft)
Weight: Males 310–400 g
(11–14 oz), females 390–
560 g (14–20 oz)
Markings: Adults have black-
edged white underwings,
mottled reddish bars on
breast, wide black and white
tail bands and brown back;
young birds are more
streaked, less distinct
Alias: Broad-wing, broad-
winged buzzard, *la petite
buse, Buteo platypterus*
Origin of *hawk*: From Old
English *haf,* meaning
"seize"
Name for a group: A cast of
hawks
Call: Very high, thin, 2-note
whistle, 2–4 seconds long
Whereabouts: Near streams,
beaver meadows, bogs and
other openings in dense deciduous or mixed woods and
forest edge
Food: Toads, frogs, snakes,
chipmunks, mice, voles,
squirrels, baby hares,
shrews, small birds, salamanders, grasshoppers,
dragonflies, crickets, caterpillars, earthworms, crayfish
Daily food helping: 14–23 g
(0.5–0.8 oz)
Breeding territory: 2.5–
5 km² (1–2 sq. mi)
Nest: Loose sticks lined with
leaves, moss and bark, 30–
60 cm (1–2 ft) wide, usually
6–12 m (20–40 ft) up in

winter homes are in dense rainforests in Central America and the Amazon. Broad-wings must conserve their energy as much as possible because their bodies are heavier in proportion to their wings than smaller migrants'. They also don't get a lot to eat along the way.

To make it, broad-wings harness the energy of the sun on clear days, soaring upwards in tight circles on rising columns of warm air, called thermals. Because rock faces and patches of open ground heat up more quickly than the atmosphere, the air just above them expands and rises like a bubble as it warms. Broad-wings rise as high as 2,500 metres (8,200 feet) before the thermal weakens, its moisture condensing and forming small cumulus clouds. Then, launching off on wind currents, they glide for up to six kilometres (four miles), losing altitude slowly until they reach the next thermal, marked by groups of other hawks drifting upwards. The amount of flapping required throughout is kept to a minimum.

Because they have farther to migrate than most other hawks, broad-wings return to Ontario later and head south earlier, when the sun is high and yields six or seven hours of good thermals. The cold-blooded prey that make up a big portion of their grub are abundant only during the year's three or four warmest months anyway. Draining from forests across the province, broad-wings pour into southern Ontario in mid- to late September, bunching up along the Great Lakes, which they can't cross for lack of thermals over water. Cold fronts of northwest winds can pepper the skies with huge, rising kettles, or "boils," of broad-wings over hawk watches near Windsor and Port Stanley. Flights of up to 97,000 in a single day have occurred. In April, the returning hawks move along the southern sides of the lakes, with large numbers seen at Grimsby's hawk watch on top of the Niagara Escarpment.

Although broad-wings appear to migrate in flocks, they are really travelling as individuals following the same highway. Even mates, which may return to the same nest site every year, journey separately and remain single in their winter resorts. Their lifelong relationship is purely seasonal, bound by a common nesting site. Some ornithologists believe that they may not even recognize each other in the spring: they engage in courtship flights and mating calls as soon as they return. Broad-wings may spend two to four weeks building a large new stick nest or, less often, refurbishing an old one. Mothers add fresh evergreen sprigs daily, many containing natural bug-repellent substances, until their young leave the nest around late July or August.

crotch of a deciduous tree or near trunk of a conifer

Average clutch: 2–4 spotted white eggs, about the size of small chicken eggs

Incubation period: 31 days

Fledging age: 5–6 weeks

Mortality rate in first 6 months: 50–75%

Lifespan: Up to 16 years in the wild

Predators: Great horned owls, raccoons and crows raid nests

Estimated Ontario population: 200,000

Population density: Usually 2–10 pairs per 100 km² (39 sq. mi)

Nesting range: Most of Ontario, except Hudson Bay lowlands; also in all other provinces except British Columbia, Prince Edward Island and island of Newfoundland

Spring migration in central Ontario: Mid-Apr. to mid-May

Fall migration in central Ontario: Mid-Aug. to late Sept.

Winter whereabouts: Southern Florida to Bolivia

Number of day-hunting birds of prey nesting in Ontario: 14

Number of day-hunting birds of prey worldwide: About 292

Also see: Barred Owl, Sharp-shinned Hawk, Sun, Thunder and Lightning

CANADA GOOSE
Fabled Honker Taking to the Shield

Flying speed: 65–85 km/h (39–51 mph)

Wingbeats per second: 2

Canada goose wing loading: 2 g/cm² (0.5 oz/sq. in)

Herring gull wing loading: 0.4 g/cm² (0.09 oz/sq. in)

Migrating altitude: Average 300–1,000 m (1,000–3,280 ft); up to 3,350 m (11,000 ft)

Length: 56–114 cm (1.8–3.7 ft)

Height: 63–102 cm (2–3.3 ft)

Wingspan: 1.1–2 m (3.7–6.7 ft)

Weight: Females 4.1–5.2 kg (9–11.5 lb); males 4.4–5.1 kg (9.7–11.2 lb); up to 10 kg (22 lb)

Markings: Both sexes have black neck and head, white

Every hitchhiker ever stuck in Wawa knows the wanderlust symbolized by the fabled giant Wawa goose. It is an emotion stirred in human hearts all across the Canadian Shield each fall and spring by the enormous, shifting V formations of honking Canadas passing over in migration. When the geese drop down to rest and refuel, the deep, steady sound of rushing air from each wingbeat betrays the essence of power in flight.

Geese fly in a V formation because it cuts wind resistance, and the suction created by the powerful downstrokes of one bird helps carry the one following it, like a bicycle behind a truck. Migrating flocks are made up of several family groups that merge in the air, with adults, according to some experts, taking turns leading the way, since they're the strongest and know the route.

Migrating geese keep track of each other by honking, but young making their first journey south are especially noisy. They have not had time in their four months of life to build up as much fortifying fat as adults have and are generally ravenous, nagging constantly, like kids in the back seat on a long car trip, for their parents to land for refreshments below. After flying continuously for 300 kilometres (180 miles) or more, geese commonly land in small lakes or large old beaver ponds near the southern edge of forested areas, where they can rest and spread out into nearby fields to forage.

Geese mate for life, though adultery is common

While Canadas may migrate during the day, they also take advantage of clear nights to fly by the light of the moon. Winds often drop after sunset, making progress easier. Impending winter weather sends each group south towards its traditional wintering ground. It is said that their passing generally forecasts snow up to two weeks in advance. Biologists theorize that geese may be acutely sensitive to air currents, barometric pressure or weather-activated biochemical changes in their food.

The Cree and Inuit called the full moon of late April or early May the Goose Moon, for that was when the big birds returned to their nesting grounds. It was salvation on the wing for northern hunters, ending the leanest, hardest time of the year, when winter food supplies were running out and other game was scarce.

chin strap, light brown back, off-white breast and tail
Alias: Honker, wild goose, Canada, white-cheeked goose, grey goose, *la bernache canadienne, Branta canadensis*
Goose name origin: From the proto–Indo-European *ghans,* probably an imitation of the honking call
Name of a group: A gaggle of geese
Call: Honk; females higher-pitched than males
Whereabouts: Marshes, beaver ponds, lakes, rivers, fields
Food: Sedges, grass, aquatic vegetation, willow buds, seeds, berries, grain, insects
Number of daily droppings per goose: Up to 150
Nest: Sticks, reeds and down, lining a ground depression 75–90 cm (2.5–3 ft) wide, near water, sometimes on beaver or muskrat lodges
Average clutch: 4–6 dull white eggs, about the size of average potatoes
Incubation period: 27–30 days
Fledging age: 9–11 weeks
Age at first breeding: 2–3 years for most; less than 10% at 1 year
Portion of goslings that survive to fledge: 60–80%
Lifespan: Up to 23 years in wild, 33 years in captivity
Predators: Wolves, coyotes, foxes, eagles; nests also raided by ravens, crows, gulls, raccoons; goslings

also taken by hawks, owls, snapping turtles

Accolades: Unofficial symbol of Canada, emblem of the Canadian Wildlife Federation, featured on Canadian $100 bill (1990–2004) and on 1967 Centennial silver dollar

Famous geese: Mother Goose, Goosey Gander, goose that laid the golden egg

Goosisms: Goose egg (zero), goosebumps, goose step, silly goose, wild goose chase

Nesting range: All of Ontario, though thinly scattered in northern Shield; also in all other provinces and territories

Spring migration in central Ontario: Mid-Apr. to late May

Fall migration in central Ontario: Mid-Oct. to early Nov.

Winter whereabouts: From southern Georgian Bay and Ottawa south to Georgia and Texas

Winter population in southern Ontario: 50,000–60,000

Hudson Bay lowlands fall population: About 1.25 million

Number of Canada and cackling geese shot each fall in Ontario: 150,000–180,000

Age of oldest waterfowl fossils: 80 million years old

Close cousins: In 2003, small, short-necked tundra

Until relatively recently, Canada geese were largely drifters in the Canadian Shield, bypassing the region's deep, rocky, sterile lakes in favour of the vast, rich fens and marshes of the Hudson Bay lowlands and other northern areas. Prized game birds, they were virtually extirpated as a nesting species from southern Ontario by the 1920s, save for some remnant flocks on Lake St. Clair. Strict hunting regulations and conservation measures later allowed North America's Canada goose population to rise from about 250,000 around 1935 to probably more than five million – before the fall hunt opens – in recent years. Ontario's Ministry of Natural Resources began a captive nesting program with birds from small scattered surviving populations of a particularly large subspecies, known as the giant Canada goose, and started releasing their offspring in the south in 1968, hoping to both increase their numbers and provide big trophy birds for hunters during migration. They flourished, and by the 1990s were spreading into the southern Shield in a big way. Late-summer numbers now swell to more than half a million in Ontario south of the French River.

Many adolescents and unsuccessful breeders from southern and central Ontario, however, also migrate to the wetlands of James and Hudson bays to moult in early summer, when they are flightless for several weeks. Though the young birds initially return to the breeding grounds with their parents in spring, they're soon sent packing to join flocks of other one- and two-year-olds as nesting begins. They usually rejoin their moms, dads and new siblings later in the summer.

Geese mate for life, though adultery is common. They differ from ducks in family values (in addition to both sexes appearing identical), with males sticking around to help raise their offspring. A gander closely guards his spouse while she remains almost constantly on her nest for a month, losing considerable weight, before her eggs hatch in May. Afterwards, while she rebuilds her strength grazing with her new downy yellow goslings, her mate continues to stand sentinel, keeping other geese away from their turf. The largest families claim the best grazing sites, with their parents given the highest deference by the other geese. Extended families, usually consisting of the adult breeding offspring and an older dominant pair and their broods, also sometimes pool their goslings together, forming "crèches" of 20 or more youngsters that are looked after communally.

nesters previously regarded as several subspecies of Canada geese were deemed to form a single separate species, known as the cackling goose, which ranges from 1 to 3 kg (2.2 to 6.6 lb), about a quarter the size of southern Ontario's giant Canada goose.

Number of geese species nesting in Ontario: 4

Number of geese species worldwide: 15–90, depending on species definition

Also see: Common Merganser, Beaver, Wind and Weather Systems, Lakes

CEDAR WAXWING
Fruit-flocking Late Nester

Flying speed: 34–50 km/h
(21–31 mph)
Length: 15.5–20 cm (6–8 in)
Wingspan: 28–31 cm (11–
12 in)
Weight: 28–38 g (1–1.3 oz)
Markings: Both sexes have a
black mask, brown breast,
back and head crest, yellow
bar at tip of black tail, waxy
red tips on secondary feathers of black wings
Alias: Cedarbird, cherry bird,
southern waxwing, Carolina
waxwing, cankerbird, *le
jaseur des cèdres,
Bombycilla cedrorum*
Call: High, dry, reedy "zeee,"
frequently repeated
Whereabouts: Around berry-
bearing trees in open
woods and forest fringe;

Cedar waxwings are the most fruit-focused birds in eastern North America. Roving bands of the genial, black-masked fruitarians wander widely from one ripening crop of berries to another. They run on sugar like no other bird, shunning the fattier fruits, such as poison ivy and viburnum berries, sought by robins, thrushes and white-throated sparrows. In spring, when there's not much fruit around, returning migrants turn to sweet blossoms to provide almost half of their sustenance. Courting couples are often seen perched side by side, daintily passing flower petals or berries back and forth, hopping sideways along the branch, bowing and calling softly as they do so. After dining together, mates affectionately touch bills and ruffle one another's feathers.

Because there are seldom enough varieties of berries in any one spot to last the whole nesting period, waxwings don't keep breeding territories or sing territorial mating songs like most other passerines. Rather than relying on voice and real estate appraisal, they choose their mates by sizing up each other's wings for the sealing-wax-like red dabs for which they're named. The dabs are much more prominent on birds that are two years of age and older, marking them as experienced, dependable partners. Waxwings nest in loose clusters of up to half a dozen pairs around the edges of small groves of pine, cedar or hawthorns, with nests as close as eight metres (26 feet) from each other. Flocks of males commute as far as two kilometres (1.2 miles) to forage. After gorging himself, one of these providers may fill his throat and beak with up to 30 chokecherries to bring back home to the missus, who almost never leaves the nest while incubating her eggs.

Waxwings nest in loose clusters of up to half a dozen pairs

The sleek, pointy-crested nomads don't settle down to nest until late June, when egg-laying females can fatten up on the first fruits of the year, such as serviceberries and strawberries. When the hatchlings emerge, they're initially plied with a high-protein insect mash that allows them to grow very quickly. At this time of year, waxwing parents are often seen hunting from tree perches, snatching insects from the air like flycatchers. But within a couple of days, the nestlings are weaned onto regular waxwing fruit fare.

above shorelines and wetlands

Food: Flowers, beetles, flying ants, caterpillars, crane flies, mayflies, dragonflies, other insects and spiders in spring; raspberries, strawberries, serviceberries and fewer insects in early summer; dogwood berries, wild cherries, blueberries and elderberries later in summer; red cedar, mountain ash and pokeweed berries, hawthorn fruits, wild grapes, crabapples, sumac and alder seeds in fall and winter

Average full passage of food through digestive tract: 7–30 minutes

Community density: 5–44 nests/ha (2.5 acres)

Nest: Bulky cup, 10–13 cm (4–5 in) wide, of grasses, twigs, rootlets, bark and lichens; usually wedged in a forked branch 1–4 m (3.3–13.3 ft) up in a cedar, pine or hawthorn tree

Average clutch: 3–5 olive-sized blue, grey or greenish eggs with black spots

Incubation period: 11–14 days

Fledging age: 14–18 days

Portion of eggs that hatch: 54–75%

Portion of eggs that produce fledglings: 39–57%

Average annual survival: About 45% for adults

Lifespan: Very few live more than 3 years; up to 8 years in wild, 14 years in captivity

Predators: Sharp-shinned, Cooper's and red-tailed

hawks, merlins, grackles; nests also raided by red squirrels, raccoons, blue jays and house wrens

Estimated Ontario population: 4 million

Average population density: 1–10 pairs per 10 km² (4 sq. mi)

Nesting range: All of Ontario to the tree line; also in all other provinces

Spring migration in central Ontario: Mid-May to early June

Fall migration in central Ontario: Mid-Aug. to late Sept.

Winter whereabouts: From about Sudbury, Sault Ste. Marie and Ottawa south to Central America, with most going to the southern U.S.

Also see: Goldfinch, Robin, Yellow-rumped Warbler, Blueberry, White Cedar

Some successful parents – fewer than a third – nest again after their first brood takes wing around early August. As the breeding season ends, flocks resume their nomadic ways. Some groups begin flying south in mid- to late September, migrating by day and sometimes at night, amalgamating into larger loose flocks as they go. If they can find enough food, others choose to stay behind, taking shelter with over-wintering robins in shrubby streamside thickets, especially in areas of southern Ontario with scraggly red cedar trees, which bear powdery, dark blue, berrylike fruits that are a winter waxwing mainstay. Sometimes waxwings have an unplanned winter bash, when fermented fruits, such as clusters of black pokeweed berries, actually make them drunk, causing them to sway and even topple from their perches. Sloshed waxwings can be oblivious to the point of allowing themselves to be picked up, a dangerous prospect when winter predators lurk nearby.

CHICKADEE
Big Vocabulary and Expanding Mind

Patrolling the woods in their grey, black and white uniforms, tame chickadee troops communicate with a kind of rudimentary language, one of the first discovered among wildlife. Their namesake, a buzzing "chick-a-dee-dee" call – which is uttered in innumerable different combinations, key shifts and repetitions that some researchers liken to human sentence structure – carries a wide variety of distinct messages, allowing flock members to keep contact, announce food discoveries and warn of danger. They also have a wide repertoire of tweets, twitters, gargles and hisses – 15 types of vocalizations in all, used in love, war and other social interactions.

Black-capped chickadees begin distilling their most hopeful of calls on sunny midwinter days, when males start laying claim to breeding territories by whistling their high, lingering

Average territorial flock: 6–8 birds

Body temperature: 42°C (108°F), dropping to 30–32°C (86–90°F) during regulated hypothermia on cold winter nights

Approximate number of feathers: 2,000

Flying speed: Avg. 20 km/h (12 mph) (dense plumage yields warmth but slows flight)

Wingbeats per second: 27–30

Chickadee wing loading: 0.16 g/cm² (0.035 oz/sq. in)

Song sparrow wing loading: 0.25 g/cm² (0.06 oz/sq. in)

Heartbeats per minute: 500–1,000

Length: 12–15 cm (4.5–6 in)

Wingspan: 15–22 cm (6–8.5 in)

Weight: 10–14 g (0.3–0.5 oz)

Markings: Black cap and beard, white cheeks and belly; grey wings, back and tail; rusty buff wash on lower sides

Alias: Black-capped chickadee, common chickadee, *la mésange à tête noire, Parus atricapillus*

Calls: Nasal, buzzing "chick-a-dee-dee"; whistled song with the first note much higher than the second, commonly rendered as "fee-bee"

Name for a group: A chatter of chickadees

Whereabouts: Mixed and deciduous woods, especially near forest edges with white birch or alder; swamps

Food: In spring and summer, mostly caterpillars, spiders, beetles, katydids, plant lice, insect eggs and pupae; in fall and winter, about 50% hemlock and other conifer seeds, poison ivy and other berries, cherries, acorns, maple sap

Flock territory: 8–23 ha (20–56 acres)

Breeding territory: 1–7 ha (2.5–17 acres)

Nest: Cavities in rotted tree trunks, limbs or stumps, especially birch, most often 1–4 m (3–13 ft) above ground; entrance about 2.5 cm (1 in) wide; lined with moss, fur, grass, pine needles and feathers

Average clutch: 6–8 reddish-brown-spotted dull white eggs, the size of pistachio shells

mating song. The simple two- or three-note verse can be heard into early summer, but its debut bears the promise of spring. After spending the early winter in small foraging flocks, the birds disperse over a wider area in March. The dominant one or two males reserve choice territories within the flock's winter foraging area, often pairing up with their previous year's mate. Younger or meeker chickadees are pushed out to less favourable sites. On average, only one couple per flock survives from one breeding season to the next, most often the dominant pair with the best feeding and sheltering locales.

In place of chocolates, courting males offer the opposite sex large insects, which have lots of protein to help produce eggs. If a pair can't find an old woodpecker hole or other tree cavity, they peck one out in a week or two. Lower-ranking females sometimes fly to the realm of a dominant male for an illicit liaison then return to their nests on the wrong side of the tracks to have their cuckolded husbands help raise their blue-blooded broods. From when eggs are laid, usually one a day, until the young fledge, parents become quiet and secretive. Fathers bring food while mothers incubate. Like most songbirds, the chicks hatch helpless and blind. But stoked with a rich protein diet of insects, they are 50 to 75 per cent heavier after their first 24 hours, and 10 times their birth weight in 10 days.

In late summer and fall, the bearded sprites reform into small, inquisitive flocks, often joined by migrating species also foraging for seeds, insects and bug eggs. Chickadees specialize in searching through the bark crevices of low outer branches, hanging upside-down from the tips and hovering under leaves. Young-of-the-year birds that join the flock are usually from other areas, not the offspring of the resident dominant pairs, ensuring the gene pool is mixed.

Each troop fiercely defends its borders from neighbouring chickadee bands. The stakes are high, since each bird in autumn may stash hundreds of seeds, berries, cocoons, egg sacs and insect bodies a day under strips of bark and inside knotholes or tufts of pine needles and curled dried leaves. Studies suggest that chickadees remember not only where they've hidden things, but which caches contain select entrees, which they break into first during winter. Neuroscientists have also found that to handle all this data, black-caps actually expand their memory banks around October, growing new neurons in the hippocampus, the part of the brain that deals with spatial recollection. Human brains are incapable of such a feat.

Quick access to winter grub is essential for the tiny birds. While roosting, they often burn all of their body fat shivering their muscles to produce heat and must replenish it every day, meaning they need far more food than in the summer. To save fuel on particularly cold nights, they shiver less and enter a state of regulated hypothermia, allowing their body temperature to drop by 10–12°C (18–22°F).

Incubation period: 11–13 days

Fledging age: About 16 days

Dispersal: Young join unrelated flocks when 5–6 weeks old

Age at first breeding: 1 year for most

Average annual adult survival: 60%

Lifespan: Adults avg. 2.5 years; up to 12 years

Predators: Sharp-shinned hawks, saw-whet owls, kestrels, northern shrikes; nests also raided by red squirrels, raccoons, weasels

Estimated Ontario population: 5 million

Accolades: Official bird of New Brunswick, Maine and Massachusetts

Often seen with: Nuthatches, juncos, downy and hairy woodpeckers in winter flocks; also kinglets, brown creepers, warblers and vireos in autumn

Nesting range: All Ontario, except the far northwest; also in all other provinces and territories except Nunavut

Winter whereabouts: Most stay put; flocks of young birds sometimes migrate to northern U.S. mid-Sept. to Nov., especially during food shortages about every 3–5 years; return Apr. to May

Number of chickadee and titmouse species nesting in Ontario: 3

Number of chickadee and titmouse species worldwide: 65

COMMON MERGANSER
Tree-nesting Fish Duck

Top flying speed: 70–
85 km/h (42–51 mph)
**Fastest level flight of any
bird:** 161 km/h (100 mph),
by a red-breasted merganser
**Common merganser wing-
beats per second:** 4.6
Deepest dives: 6 m (20 ft)
Dive duration: Usually 18–
30 sec; up to 2 min
Length: 55–68 cm (1.8–
2.2 ft)
Wingspan: 86–91 cm (2.8–
3 ft)
Weight: Females 0.9–1.8 kg
(2–4 lb); males 1.2–2.2 kg
(2.7–5 lb)
Markings: Reddish-brown
head and crest, grey back,
white breast, throat and
square wing patches on
female; green-black head,

The common merganser is the premier duck of the clear, rocky lakes of the Canadian Shield, readily recognized by its signature rusty, ragged-crested hairstyle. Unlike the dabblers of weedier waters, it's primarily a fish-eating diver. Like those of loons, a merganser's feet are placed far back on the body for maximum underwater propulsion, which makes walking on land difficult. The bird's long, pointy, serrated bill is designed to hold on to its slippery supper, which it mostly catches in knee- to head-deep shoreline shallows.

Their fishing prowess sometimes gets mergansers in trouble. Though loons usually fish in deeper waters, they occasionally balk at merganser competition, especially in small, secluded bays used for loonling nurseries. Irate loons sometimes speed underwater like torpedoes, their long beaks trained on the transgressing ducks. While not considered tasty hunting prizes, mergansers were once also persecuted by cottagers who, after fishing out and fouling lakes, concluded that the long-time resident mergies must be responsible for the disappearance of fish. In truth, the big ducks concentrate on slow-moving species rather than sport fish, and they're usually too thinly spread out to have a significant impact on populations. In more recent years, they've prospered wherever there's not too much waterfront development or boat traffic to disturb them, recovering even in lakes around the Sudbury area, where fish were decimated by acid rain before industrial emissions were curbed in the 1980s and '90s.

As soon as the ice breaks up on smaller inland lakes in early spring, mergansers, after gathering in large flocks in sheltered bays along the Great Lakes, hurry north. They're often already paired up when they arrive on their breeding grounds, having begun air- and water-courtship chases at the southern staging sites. Sporting striking iridescent dark green heads, male mergansers have the distinction, along with other ducks, geese and swans, of being among the few birds with a penis. Most birds merely have cloacas − orifices combining all excretory functions − which are rubbed together during mating in what's known as a "cloacal kiss." Male ducks, however, inflate a fold of skin from the cloaca to do the job.

'Males' usefulness in the continuance of the species does not extend far beyond their penis. Soon after their rusty-crested mates settle onto their eggs in tree-cavity nests and are no longer

black back, white breast, neck and sides on males; orange-red feet and saw-edged bill on both

Alias: Goosander, fish duck, American merganser, flapper, saw-bill, sheldrake, *le bec-scie commun, Mergus merganser*

Name origin: Latin *mergus anser,* meaning "diving goose"

Calls: Though usually silent, males make low, raspy croaks, females a guttural call

Whereabouts: Forest lakes, rivers, ponds

Usual depth of hunting grounds: 0.5–1.8 m (1.5–6 ft)

Food: Minnows, suckers, sculpin, sticklebacks and other small or slow-moving fish, most 10–30 cm (4–12 in) long; aquatic insects, fish eggs

Nest: Usually a down-lined tree cavity with an opening 12 cm (4.7 in) wide, often in dead aspens; sometimes in a crevice, beneath rocks, stumps, roots or bushes; within 180 m (200 yd) of water

Average clutch: 8–12 light brown eggs, about the size of large chicken eggs

Incubation period: 28–35 days

Fledging age: 60–75 days

Age at first breeding: 2 years or older

Average annual adult survival: 50–70%

Predators: Mink, martens, raccoons, skunks, squirrels, snakes eat eggs; barred owls, hawks, pike, muskies, pickerel prey on young

Ontario Canadian Shield population: About 75,000 breeding pairs

Nesting range: Most of Ontario, though scattered thinly north of Temagami and Lake Superior and south of the Shield and Bruce Peninsula to about Kitchener; also in all other provinces and territories

Winter whereabouts: Great Lakes, Atlantic coast from the Maritimes to North Carolina, Mississippi Valley

Spring migration in central Ontario: Early Apr. to early May

Fall migration in central Ontario: Mid-Sept. to late Nov.

Other Ontario tree-cavity-nesting ducks: Wood ducks, common goldeneyes, buffleheads, hooded mergansers

Number of diving duck species nesting in Ontario: 15

Also see: Black Duck, Loon, Pileated Woodpecker, Lakes

interested in mating, the dashing drakes hit the road, heading to larger water bodies, such as the Great Lakes or Lake Nipissing, to lie low while they moult, when they become flightless for about three weeks. Some go as far as Hudson Bay or to wintering grounds on the Atlantic coast.

Within a day or two of hatching, usually in June, merganser ducklings bail out like tiny paratroopers from tree nest holes up to 15 metres (50 feet) high, their scant bodies fluttering to the ground without injury. Hatchlings waddle behind their mother to the water and swim immediately, learning to dive in another day or two. They also hitch rides on their mother's back. But the most common summer merganser sight is a hen with a long line of paddling ducklings behind her, tracing the indentations of the shore. Often there may be 20 ducklings or more in tow.

Such large broods are sometimes the result of saw-billed mothers laying their eggs in the temporarily unoccupied nests of others when tree cavities are in short supply. Hens also often amalgamate their broods, allowing one mother to go off to feed alone while another stays to babysit the whole crèche. Combined broods become especially common a month or two after hatching, when mothers drift off to moult, leaving the still-flightless youngsters for good.

COMMON YELLOWTHROAT
Black-masked Balladeer

"Black-masked warbler" would probably be a better name for the common yellowthroat, its Zorro mask being the male's most distinctive feature by far. Many other warblers also have yellow throats; one – a foreign, grey-backed bird nesting no closer than southern Ohio – is even confusingly called the "yellow-throated warbler."

The bird is quite deserving of the epithet "common," though, being perhaps the most abundant warbler in North America, divided into some 13 subspecies. Ontario certainly has plenty, chanting their well-known "witchety, witchety, witchety" song loudly from shrubby watersides and forest fringes from May to July. Initially, males sing an average of 125 songs an hour until they win a wife, after which they let it slide to about 20 to 40 songs an hour. They

Length: 11–13 cm (4–5 in)

Wingspan: 17–19 cm (6.7–7.5 in)

Weight: Average 9–11 g (0.3–0.4 oz)

Markings: Olive-brown back and sides, yellow throat and breast, whitish belly; males have a wide black mask trimmed with white or grey above

Alias: Yellowthroat, black-masked ground warbler, northern yellowthroat, olive-coloured yellow-throated wren, *la paruline masquée, Geothlypis trichas*

Name for a group: A yellowing of warblers

Calls: Loud, rapid, rolling song, usually written as "witchety, witchety, witchety,

33

witchety, witch" or a 2-sylla-
ble "whichy, whichy, whichy,"
lasting 1–2 seconds; also a
sharp, raspy "chip" call

Whereabouts: Shrubby
swamps, bogs, marshes and
streamsides, wet thickets,
forest fringes, black spruce
woods, old fields

Food: Caterpillars, grasshoppers, dragonflies, mayflies,
beetles, grubs, aphids,
moths, butterflies, ants, flies,
spiders and some seeds

Breeding territory: 0.1–3 ha
(0.3–7 acres)

Nest: Loose, bulky cup, 7–
11 cm (3–4 in) wide, of
grass, sedge, stems, bark
and leaves, lined with fine
root fibres and hair; on
ground or up to 10 cm (4 in)
high in shrubs or a dense
clump of tall dead grass,
sedge or cattails

Average clutch: 3–5 cherry-
sized white or creamy eggs
speckled brown, grey and
black

Incubation period: 12 days

Fledging age: 9–10 days

**Nests parasitized by cow-
birds:** 20–50%

**Average annual number of
eggs laid by a cowbird:** 40

**Average annual adult war-
bler survival:** Less than
50%

Lifespan: Few live more than
2 years; up to 11 years in
wild

Predators: Sharp-shinned
hawks, harriers, kestrels and,
when perching near water
level, snapping turtles, large

also sometimes hurl themselves high into the sky
to perform carolling "ecstasy flights." Passionate
orators quiver as they sing and climb three to 10
metres (10 to 33 feet) in the air, occasionally
shooting to 30 metres (100 feet).

When not performing, common yellowthroats seek anonymity, skulking low in deep
vegetation, flitting from branch to stem, seldom
offering a clear, lingering view of themselves.
Their leaf-to-leaf insect-collecting speed is
legendary. By one count, a yellowthroat picked
off 69 aphids in a single minute. They are,
however, eminently pishable: a human "pissssh!"
quickly summons them into the open to investigate the noise.

Females spend four or five days building their
well-hidden nests and do all the egg-tending
themselves. Common yellowthroats, however, are
one of the most frequent victims of **cowbirds**,
which lay their eggs in other species' nests so that
they don't have to raise their own young. Upon
finding a cowbird egg, yellowthroats sometimes
abandon their nest or build a new nest layer over
it, dooming it not to hatch. But if they've already
laid two or more eggs of their own, they most
often settle down on and tend the alien egg as
well. The cowbird chick typically hatches a day
before the other eggs in the clutch and begs more
loudly and persistently than its step-siblings,
elbowing them aside at feeding time. The warbler
nestlings usually end up starving to death. Driven
by instinct, the foster parents continue feeding
the impostor even after it grows monstrously
larger than themselves.

Yellowthroat young normally hop out of the
nest when only eight or nine days old. They take

their first leaps into the air within a day or two after that, and once fledged stick around home longer than most warblers, keeping adults busy for about another three weeks. Music goes out of their lives in early August, when fathers begin their moult and stop singing. Once their new set of sturdy fall migration feathers is complete, the males begin flying south a week or two ahead of their spouses and offspring. Family units probably dissolve in mixed flocks of southbound songbirds, which swell to contain thousands passing in vast unseen fronts high overhead in the night sky. It's a gruelling, perilous journey, with the tiny birds losing 1.6 per cent of their body weight for each hour of flight. Large numbers often perish in storms and cold weather. Once they reach the Caribbean and Central America, males and females, like most tropical migrants, live separately in closely defended individual feeding territories, 50 to 100 metres (55 to 110 yards) wide. Mates meet again, however, on the same breeding territory the following spring, provided they both make it safely back.

fish and bullfrogs; nests also raided by chipmunks, red squirrels, mice, snakes, raccoons, skunks

Density in prime wetland habitat: Up to 335 pairs per km² (0.4 sq. mi)

Estimated Ontario population: 2 million

Nesting range: All of Ontario except the far northwest; also in all other provinces and territories except Nunavut

Spring migration in central Ontario: Mid-May to early June

Fall migration in central Ontario: Mid-Aug. to early Oct.

Winter whereabouts: Atlantic seaboard from North Carolina to Panama and the West Indies

Number of wood warbler species nesting in Ontario: 36

Number of wood warbler species listed as threatened, endangered or of special concern in Ontario: 8

Number of wood warbler species worldwide: 115

Also see: Red-eyed Vireo, Yellow-rumped Warbler, Bullfrog

CORMORANT
Riding Wheel of Fortune

Dive Duration: Average 20–25 seconds, up to 70 seconds

Depth of hunting grounds: Usually less than 8 m (26 ft)

Underwater swimming speed: 90 m/min (98 yd/min)

Flying Speed: 52 km/hour (32 mph)

Wingbeats per second: 5

Length: 70–90 cm (2.3–3 ft)

Wingspan: 1.2 m (4 ft)

Weight: 1.8–2.1 kg (4–4.6 lb)

Markings: Black or dark brown body, head, wings and feet, sometimes with a greenish or bronze sheen; yellow-orange beak, face and upper throat; young have greyish-brown back and mottled brown and whitish undersides

Bill length: 5–8 cm (2–3 in)

Alias: Double-crested cormorant, sea crow, crow-duck, shag, *le cormoran à aigrettes, Phalacrocorax auritus*

Name origin: From the Latin *corvus marinus*, meaning "sea crow"

Name for a group: A gulp of cormorants

Calls: Low, guttural grunts, but usually silent

Whereabouts: Lakes, slow-flowing rivers

Food: Minnows, sunfish, sticklebacks, perch, alewife,

The double-crested cormorant is the new bird in town on many cottage-country lakes. The glistening, dark diver's piscivorous appetite and rapid spread from thronging Great Lakes colonies have raised alarm bells from the Kawarthas to Muskoka, Lake Nipissing and beyond. Flying from dense waterside rookeries, groups of cormorants may be seen in tight formation, often low over the water, on fishing grounds up to dozens of kilometres away.

At a distance the large birds resemble loons, but they sit lower in the water and have longer, snaking necks. Up close, they're remarkably colourful, with striking blue-rimmed, emerald eyes and an orange-yellow bill that contrasts sharply with the bright blue insides of their mouths, which are held agape in solicitations and greetings between mates. Their eponymous double crest refers to small tufts of back-swept nuptial feathers above each eye which drop off by June.

Contrary to common belief, cormorants are not alien invaders. There is good evidence that there have always been at least small numbers of the hook-beaked fish fanciers on the Great Lakes. But upheaval of the lakes' ecosystem put the birds on a roller-coaster ride over the past two centuries. Though persecuted and pushed back throughout their range in the 1800s, they began advancing eastward in the 1930s from redoubts on Lake Superior into the rest of the Great Lakes. At the time, lake trout and other large predatory fish were in steep decline due to overfishing, the spread of sea lampreys and destruction of spawning grounds. With little to keep them in check, exotic alewife and rainbow smelt were also spreading exponentially in the Great Lakes, providing an immense feed stock for cormorants.

The storied bird's fortunes reversed again, however, during the postwar pesticides boom. Cormorants came to be the cross-billed poster birds for the ravages of DDT. Together with other contaminants, the pesticide produces both deformations and eggshells so thin they're crushed by nesting parents. After DDT was banned in the early 1970s, Great Lakes cormorants rebounded from near oblivion, from fewer than a hundred nesting pairs to 115,000 by century's end. In the 1990s, they began moving into inland water bodies on the southern Shield. More recently, their population has stabilized on the Great Lakes and expansion has slowed.

Despite oft-vented angling angst, countless studies show sport fish usually constitute a very

rainbow smelt, round gobies and other fish usually less than 15 cm (6 in) long; also crayfish, aquatic insects

Average daily food helping: 300–600 g (0.7–1.3 lb)

Foraging flights: Usually within 10 km (6 mi) of nesting colony; up to 62 km (38.5 mi)

Nest: Bulky, untidy mass of sticks, twigs, plant stems, bones and other diverse debris, 45–90 cm (1.5–3 ft) wide, 10–45 cm (4–18 in) high, lined with grass and rootlets, cemented on outside by droppings; in a tree or on the ground on a small, rocky or sandy island or peninsula; old, reused ground nests become basketlike structures up to 2 m (6.6 ft) high

Space between nests: Avg. 65–70 cm (26–28 in); some nests may touch

Average clutch: 3–4 light blue eggs, sometimes with chalky coating; size of large chicken eggs

Incubation period: 25–28 days

Fledging age: 6–8 weeks

Age at first breeding: 3 years for most

Annual survival: Avg. 50% in first year, 75% in second year, 85% for adults

Lifespan: Adults avg. 6 years; up to 22 years in wild

Predators: Bald eagles, great horned owls; nests also raided by gulls, ravens, crows, grackles, foxes, coyotes, raccoons

Ontario Great Lakes population: About 60,000 nesting pairs

Number of Ontario colonies: More than 200; more than 40 on inland lakes

Ontario's largest colony: About 7,000 nests, on Toronto's Leslie Street Spit

Nesting range: Mainly on large lakes from southern Ontario to Lake Abitibi and northern edge of Canadian Shield in northwest, plus one spot on James Bay; also in all other provinces

Spring migration in central Ontario: Late Apr. to late May

Fall migration in central Ontario: Mid-Aug. to early Oct.

Winter whereabouts: Atlantic coast from Long Island to Mexico's Yucatán Peninsula, and south-central U.S.

Other birds that nest in cormorant colonies: Gulls, herons, pelicans, egrets

Closest Ontario relation: White pelican

Number of cormorant species worldwide: 39

Also see: Herring Gull, Loon, Osprey, Minnows

small portion of cormorant fare. In the Great Lakes, alewife, rainbow smelt and round gobies, another recent foreign invader, fill most of the birds' diet. In the interior, they mostly go after minnows, sunfish and other small or slow-swimming shallow-waters quarry. However, their living style, in tightly packed, jostling, smelly colonies, has gotten them into trouble. Copious quantities of droppings, or guano, often kill long-used nest trees and the vegetation beneath within 10 years, prompting periodic government culls of thousands of cormorants on small islands in Lake Erie and Lake Ontario with rare plants and fragile ecosystems. On barren islands off the coast of Peru, timeless guano deposits up to 50 metres (164 feet) thick, left by millions of cormorants, were mined in the mid-19th century to provide nitrates for fertilizer and much of the world's gunpowder.

Most cormorant rookeries on inland lakes are much smaller than those on the Great Lakes, usually holding no more than a few dozen bulky nests. Males claim their digs and once paired collect most of the material for their mates to build a nest. Mates later take turns at the nest, effusively caressing as they meet to take their turn cradling and warming the eggs atop of their webbed feet. Their charges hatch naked, blind and helpless, but can fly, swim and dive within six to eight weeks and gain independence when about two and a half months old. Flocks of young birds often visit new lakes to fish and roost before starting new colonies there in subsequent years.

EVENING GROSBEAK
Robust, Gregarious Newcomer

The prospect of a bone-chilling winter sends most Ontario avifauna winging south for the season. Other species, without the need, desire or Club Med reservations, will stick around, however, and batten down for a long, cold blow. And there are a few for whom the winter is a time of boundless wandering and sometimes even opportunity. Robust, gregarious evening grosbeaks are among the most familiar in this group of wintry rovers, flocking wherever bountiful conifer cones yield their nutritious seeds. They're also attracted to roadside salt, and they often mob bird feeders. The burly finches knock one another off feeder perches and platforms as if they were brawling in a hockey game, each bumped bird eager to rejoin the melee, like a little feathered Boston Bruin in its black and yellow and white uniform.

Sunflower seed-eating record: 96 in 5 minutes

Length: 16.5–18 cm (6.5–7 in)

Wingspan: Avg. 33–35 cm (13–14 in)

Weight: 53–74 g (1.8–2.6 oz)

Markings: Male has yellow breast, undersides and eyebrow, with brown head blending to yellow above black and white wing; also black tail and greenish or off-white beak; female is grey above, with brownish head and touches of yellow, black wings and tail with scattered white markings

Alias: Eastern evening grosbeak, American hawfinch, *le gros-bec errant, Coccothraustes vespertinus*

Calls: Loud, sharp "chip-chur" notes; a warbled whistling song is seldom heard

Whereabouts: Coniferous and mixed forests, especially more open woods

Food: Cherry pits; conifer, maple, ash, dogwood and sumac seeds; conifer, birch, ash and aspen buds; hawthorn fruit, serviceberries and mountain ash and juniper berries; birch catkins, maple flowers, maple sap; caterpillars, beetles, aphids and other insects during nesting season

Mating duration: 3–5 sec

Nest: Usually a shallow bowl, 12–14 cm wide, of loose twigs and rootlets towards tops of spruce or other evergreens

Average clutch: 3–4 peach-pit-sized blue or turquoise eggs with brown, grey or purple marks

Incubation: 11–14 days

Fledging age: 12–14 days

Lifespan: Often 4–9 years; up to 15 years in wild, 17 years in captivity

Predators: Sharp-shinned hawks, Cooper's hawks, goshawks, northern shrikes; ravens raid nests

Estimated Ontario population: 250,000

Nesting range: Mainly from the southern edge of the Canadian Shield to Lake Abitibi and Red Lake; scattered south to Lake Ontario and the base of the Bruce Peninsula and into the

Originally nesting in western boreal forests, wayfaring evening grosbeaks seem to have found Ontario so much to their liking that they began staying year-round in the 1920s, annually drawing hordes of naturalists to Camp Billie Bear on Muskoka's Bella Lake, one of the first spots they inhabited in summer. Bird feeders and shade-tree plantings of Manitoba maples, whose seeds are a grosbeak staple out west, are credited with helping to lure the birds east. Logging, forest fires and grosbeaks' love of cherries probably have more to do with it, however. Vast numbers of pin cherry and chokecherry, which thrive in open sunlight, popped up across the province wherever forests were felled. In late summer, flocks of evening grosbeaks can be heard noisily devouring the wild fruits, cracking open the pits to eat the stones while discarding the sweet flesh. Each 60-gram (two-ounce) bird exerts 11 kilograms (25 pounds) of pressure with its hefty, vicelike beak to burst open a cherry pit. The industrial-strength bill gives grosbeaks both their common name – *gros* meaning "big" or "thick" in French – and their genus designation *Coccothraustes*, "kernel cracker."

Once established, evening grosbeaks really began to prosper in Ontario during periodic spruce budworm outbreaks. In such times of superabundance, the thronging moth caterpillars can supply up to 80 per cent of a grosbeak's grub, though the bird usually eats mostly seeds and fruit. The highest grosbeak densities usually reflect where budworms are most locally abundant. When the caterpillars disappear, so too can the birds. The finch's numbers, in fact, have declined considerably since the last provincewide spruce budworm outbreak began to abate in the early 1980s.

Though they may nest in loose colonies wherever the eating's good, wandering grosbeak flocks generally dwindle as the birds pair off in late April or May. Males challenge each other by wrestling with their stout bills locked together, and both sexes sway and posture for each other's attention. Rapturous males seem to sing only directly to their mates during the most climactic moments of pair bonding. The rarity of the song helps perpetuate the fallacy that evening grosbeaks sing only at night, hence their name.

As the heat of first passion cools and relationships solidify, females build nests. The restless birds still frequently forage far from home, however. Females incubate eggs, but males help feed the chicks, stoking them with pulverized cherry-stone meal, budworms or whatever is plentiful. After the nestlings fledge, several or more families leave the nesting grounds to tour the countryside in flocks of usually about 10 to 50 birds, descending where they find lots to eat. Come winter, though, the merry bands become more segregated, with males tending to stick closer to the breeding grounds and more females roving farther afield. In years when food is scarce, the mostly female flocks, sometimes numbering in the hundreds, may move in late autumn into southern Ontario and beyond, migrating by day as far as South Carolina and northern Louisiana. They return in early spring as melting snow uncovers the fallen maple keys and other seeds on the forest floor, filling woods with a loud racket of "chip-chur" calls. They also employ their powerful beaks – which shed their

northern boreal forest to Moosonee; also in all other provinces

Other big eaters of spruce budworms: Cape May warbler, bay-breasted warbler, Tennessee warbler

Other songbirds that migrate by day: Blue jay, robin, chickadee, cedar waxwing, goldfinch, crow, swallows

Number of bird species that have expanded nesting ranges into Ontario in the past 150 years: At least 16

Alien birds introduced into Ontario: Starling, house sparrow, rock pigeon, ring-necked pheasant, grey partridge, mute swan

Number of cardueline finch species nesting in Ontario: 9

Number of cardueline finch species worldwide: 122–137

Also see: Goldfinch, Balsam Fir, Chokecherry, Red Pine

whitish coatings to reveal a fresh green shade underneath – to snap off maple twigs to tap the sweet flowing sap.

During winters with big crops of conifer seeds, the evening grosbeak's northern finch relatives may arrive in central Ontario to join them in the feasting. Because many tree species produce bumper crops erratically, finches that specialize in them are true nomads, moving widely from one region to another in search of bounty. When a flock drops out of the sky, it can turn somnolent winter woods into an exotic theatre of song.

In particularly bountiful years, crossbills may even nest in the dead of winter. These rugged boreal finches construct large, well-insulated nests for their young. **Red crossbills** use their odd, crossed-over upper and lower beak tips to pry open tough red and white pine cones to get at the seeds. Another species, the **white-winged crossbill**, has a similarly designed but smaller beak suited to flimsier, unopened spruce, hemlock and tamarack cones. Brown-streaked, loquacious **pine siskins** use their pointy, slightly curved bills to harvest seeds from already opened spruce, birch and alder cones. Plump, red **pine grosbeaks** mostly eat tree buds. **Redpolls**, with their bright red caps and black goatees, also migrate from the arctic tundra to devour birch, cedar and alder-cone seeds by the bunch.

FLICKER
Head-in-sand Woodpecker

To the untrained eye, this woodpecker, spending so much of its time on the ground probing ant holes, might be mistaken for some sort of tawny thrush. It is, in fact, the supreme anteater of the avian world, known to fill its stomach with as many as 5,000 of the tangy-tasting insects, snagging them with a barbed, sticky tongue that darts the length of a human pinkie beyond its bill. Similar foraging habits of the European green woodpecker earned it a place in Greek and other Indo-European mythologies as the father of the inventor of the plough.

When at a tree trunk, however, the northern flicker assumes the classic woodpecker posture, its body parallel to the trunk, looking up. Woodpeckers maintain the position with parrotlike claws — most with two toes stretching backwards instead of one like other birds — and

Tongue: Extends 7.5 cm (3 in) beyond beak

Flicker drum roll: Loud, even, 21–24 beats/sec, lasting up to 1.5 sec

Downy woodpecker drumming rate: 16–18 beats/sec

Machine-gun shots/sec: Up to 17

Flicker flying speed: 32–40 km/h (20–25 mph)

Average number of wing-beats between dipping "bounds": 1–5

Length: 28–31 cm (11–12 in)

Wingspan: 42–52 cm (16.5–21.5 in)

Weight: 110–160 g (4–5.6 oz)

Markings: Dark brown bands across tan back and wings; tan neck and face with grey cap and a red, arrowhead-shaped patch on the back of the neck; wide black bib at top of the breast; black spots covering a white belly and sides; white rump; blackish-brown pointed tail is yellow on the underside, as are the wings; male has a black "moustache" across cheek

Alias: More than 130 names, including northern flicker, common flicker, yellow-shafted flicker, golden-winged woodpecker, antbird, yellowhammer, wood pigeon, wick-up, heigh-ho, Tarzan bird, *le pic dor, le pic flamboyant, Colaptes auratus*

Name origins: Imitation of "flicka" call; may also have

roots in Old English *flicerian,* meaning "to flutter" or "fluttering of birds"; *Colaptes* comes from the Greek word for "hammer"; *auratus* means "gilded" in Latin

Calls: Song a rapid "wick, wick, wick, wick" or "yuck, yuck, yuck, yuck," sounding like a car trying to start, continuing up to 6 seconds; also a "wicka" call, a creaky "clear" call note and several other vocalizations

Buzzing babies: A unique buzzing noise made by flicker nestlings when anything comes near them is suspected by some biologists to trick predators into believing the nest cavity is occupied by angry bees

Whereabouts: Open and patchy woodlands, forest edge, beaver ponds; especially in areas with sandy ground

Food: Ants, their eggs and larvae about 50% of diet; acorns, nuts, berries and seeds about 25%; also beetles, grasshoppers, crickets, wasps, wood lice, caterpillars, grubs, worms

Breeding territory: About 300 m (330 yd) wide

Average width of flicker nest entrance hole: 6–7 cm (2.4–2.8 in)

Width of downy woodpecker hole: 3–4 cm (1.2–1.6 in)

Nest: Round cavity 11.5–25 cm (4.5–10 in) wide and 25–100 cm (10–39 in)

stiff tails braced against the tree. During the mating season, both flicker sexes also drum like the rest of their kin, hammering beaks against anything sufficiently resonant, from dead trees to TV antennae, to mark territories or attract mates. Strong head bones and neck muscles act as shock absorbers. Each woodpecker species is cued to its own unique drumming rate and cadence. Unlike most other woodpeckers, however, both male and female flickers additionally proclaim their territories with a loud, repetitive, urgent cry reminiscent of a car engine turning over without starting. The call's jungle-like quality inspired the nickname "Tarzan bird."

Migrating by night, males usually begin returning north in mid-April, a few days ahead of the females. They're the real workers in any flicker marriage. Two females will even face off against each other to win a devoted mate, flaring their wings and tails, bobbing their heads and circling their haughtily upturned beaks in an attempt to intimidate. Contentious males deal with each other in a similar manner. Strangely enough, this pugnacious behaviour between two birds of the same sex becomes seduction between two of the opposite sex. And the only way the blue jay–sized lovebirds can actually tell each other's gender is by the male's black moustache. A clever biologist proved this by painting a moustache on a mated female. Hubby quickly rejected the cross-dressed flicker, but took her back when the moustache was removed.

After pairing, males choose a nest site in a soft, rotted tree. In 1995, one pair of fervent flickers forced the last-minute cancellation of a space-shuttle mission after drilling more than

100 exploratory holes in the foam insulation cover of the multi-billion-dollar craft's fuel tank. When they find a good site, both mates usually spend one or two weeks excavating with their long, subtly curved beaks, though sometimes they simply renovate an old hole. Occasionally all their work comes to naught as they're evicted by scrappy, cavity-nesting red squirrels, kestrels or, in more settled areas, the reviled starling. Though flickers can still carve out another nest and lay a second batch of eggs if a suitable tree is available, the delay decreases their chances of nesting success. Sometimes they don't show very good manners themselves, taking over the sandbank burrows of kingfishers or bank swallows to secure a place for their young when there are no other options.

Males are the chief incubators and brooders, sitting on the nest through the night and doing most of the feeding by day. Nestlings are plied with heaping helpings of regurgitated ants about twice an hour. After they fledge, the raucous young continue to demand food with loud, high-pitched calls. But within two weeks, they join their parents in ravaging ant cities, flashing golden yellow beneath their wings and tails as they dip through the air. As the season wears on, they increasingly turn to nuts, seeds and berries.

Long before most flickers turn up in Ontario, the late-winter woods echo with the drumming of their smallest relatives. Sparrow-sized **downy woodpeckers** remain on their territories in deciduous and mixed forests with their mates year-round. The black and white birds search for insects, spiders and their eggs along branches and tree trunks, tapping erratically

deep; entrance usually facing south or southeast; bottom lined with fresh wood chips; usually 4–19 m (13–62 ft) high in snags or trees dying of heart-rot, often aspens; also uses poles, posts, banksides

Average clutch: 5–8 peach-pit-sized, glossy white eggs

Incubation period: 9–13 days

Fledging age: 24–28 days

Age at first breeding: 1 year

Lifespan: Up to 9 years in wild; 12 years in captivity

Predators: Sharp-shinned, Cooper's and other hawks; nests also raided by crows, blue jays, red squirrels, flying squirrels, chipmunks, raccoons, weasels and bears

Estimated Ontario population: 700,000

Average population density: 1–10 pairs per km^2 (0.4 sq. mi)

Nesting range: All Ontario; also in all other provinces and territories except Nunavut

Spring migration in central Ontario: Mid-Apr. to mid-May

Fall migration in central Ontario: Late Sept. to mid-Oct.

Winter whereabouts: Most Ontario flickers go to the southeastern United States; a few linger as far north as Pembroke and Parry Sound

Appearance of first woodpeckers: 55–67 million years ago

Birds that nest in old flicker holes: Wood duck, tree swallow, kestrel, bluebird, saw-whet owl
Number of Ontario bird species that usually nest in tree cavities: 36
Number of mammal species that den in tree cavities: At least 7
Number of woodpecker species nesting in Ontario: 9
Ontario's threatened woodpecker: Red-headed woodpecker, in southern Ontario
Number of woodpecker species worldwide: 214
Also see: Kingfisher, Pileated Woodpecker, Tree Swallow, Yellow-bellied Sapsucker, Trembling Aspen

and listening for the reverberations of tiny tunnels and the sound of hidden creatures munching away. **Hairy woodpeckers**, which also stay the winter, are almost identical to downies but are about as big as robins. They also have proportionally bigger beaks, about as long as the width of their heads, for uncrating more deep-lying quarry. The hefty bill adds decibels to their tapping and drumming, and they have a much louder, more piercing call than their smaller cousins.

Another year-round resident, the **black-backed woodpecker**, is sparsely scattered in most of central Ontario but becomes more common around Temagami and the boreal forest beyond. Black-backs, which are also robin-sized, nest in evergreen tracts near bogs, beaver ponds and lakeshores but are most abundant in areas with lots of burnt standing timber left by forest fires. They specialize in the beetles and other burrowing insects that feast on the sudden bounty of dead and dying trees. Males sport a yellow crown on top of their heads, rather than red like most woodpeckers. Along with their relatives that stay put, by escaping the perils of migration they generally live longer than flickers.

GOLDFINCH
Ontario's Wild Canary

Bouncing through the air in deeply dipping flights, goldfinches sputter and twitter over tangled riversides and meadows throughout summer. They're often called wild canaries, for both their song and their coat of bright yellow feathers. Goldfinches are indeed closely related to the long-domesticated cage birds originally from the Canary Islands, off North Africa. Another species, the European goldfinch, was also tamed as a cage bird long ago and widely admired for its beauty; it's often depicted in medieval manuscript illuminations with the child Jesus and was also widely associated with Easter.

Ontario's goldfinch was far less common before European settlement greatly expanded

Calls: Song is a long, musical, canary-like series of high, squeaky chips, twitters and trills; also a flight call in 3 quick, repeated "per-chicory" notes, and a long, springy call that drops and rises, sounding like a cork twisting in the neck of a wine bottle

Flying speed: 30–62 km/h (19–39 mph)

Length: 11–13 cm (4.5–5 in)

Wingspan: 21–23 cm (8–9 in)

Weight: 11–13 g (0.4–0.5 oz) in summer, 13.5–20 g (0.5–0.7 oz) in winter

Markings: Males yellow with black wings, tail and cap and a white rump; females olive-green back, dull yellow breast, black wings and tail and white wing bars; in autumn both sexes turn more olive-brown, with buff breasts; juveniles light brown above and dull grey-yellow below

Alias: American goldfinch, wild canary, yellow bird, thistle bird, shiner, willow goldfinch, common goldfinch, *le chardonneret jaune, Carduelis tristis*

Name for a group: A charm of goldfinches

Whereabouts: Forest borders, meadows, shrubby river bottomlands, open woods, scrubby young forests

Food: Seeds of thistles, grasses, willow, birch, alder, spruce, cedar, hemlock, tamarack, elm, goldenrod, aster, burdock, teasel, mullein, chicory, evening primrose; in spring, cherry and elm flower buds, birch and alder catkins, tender bark from twig shoots and maple sap; small amounts of insects and berries

Nest: Tidy, tightly woven, rounded cone, 6–10 cm (2.4–4 in) wide, 4.5–11 cm (1.8–4.3 in) high, with thick walls of grass and bark strips; lined with thistle and milkweed down, bound with spiderwebs; usually wedged between upright forked branches in bushes, hawthorns, willows, service-berries or saplings near wa-ter; so well made and cozy that they are often taken over as winter quarters by deer mice

Average clutch: 4–6 kidney-bean-sized, pale blue eggs, often with light spotting

Incubation period: 10–14 days

Fledging age: 11–17 days

Lifespan: Up to 11 years in wild, 13 years in captivity

Predators: Sharp-shinned hawks, kestrels, shrikes; nests also raided by blue jays, garter snakes, weasels

Estimated Ontario popula-tion: 4 million

Classical homage: Antonio Vivaldi's Concerto No. 3 in D, opus 10, *Il Cardellino* (*The Goldfinch*)

Nesting range: Southern Ontario to the southern edge of the Hudson Bay lowlands; also in all other provinces

the open-area and forest-fringe settings in which it prospers. The seed connoisseur's breed-ing season does not even begin until the first field "weed" seeds of summer start ripening, in late June and July. Fresh, pulpy seeds are more palatable for nestlings than old, dry leftovers. Parents make them further digestible by munch-ing them first, often mixing in a caterpillar or some aphids, and then serving up the fortified gruel. Thistle seeds are especially favoured and their downy fibres line the nest. In fact, the sci-entific name for the goldfinch genus derives from the Latin word for "thistle," *carduus.*

Ever gregarious, goldfinches nest as close as three or four metres (10 to 13 feet) from each other in small groups, often into September. After the young fledge, families forage together for a while. Then, gradually, the drably coloured youngsters drift away and form large, wandering flocks of adolescents. Adults hunker down in their own groups in the shelter of streamside thickets and cedar woods until late September or early October while they moult, becoming less buoyant and agile during the transition, like other moulting songbirds. Studies have shown that, once outfitted in their warmer, heavier grey-green winter plumage, goldfinches can withstand temperatures of −70°C (−94°F) for up to eight hours.

Still, as it grows colder in autumn, most adults head south in large flocks, the females tending to fly a little farther than males and returning about two weeks earlier in spring. Mobs of juvenile birds, on the other hand, don't seem to know enough to retreat. Goldfinch young stick it out in the land of their hatching for their first winter, subsisting on seeds from dead standing stalks of goldenrod and aster, or from birch and conifer cones while sheltering in the woods. Winter flocks of more than 200 are common, often mixing with chickadees and northern finches such as redpolls and pine siskins. Adult goldfinches present in central Ontario during the months of snow are generally birds that have migrated from even colder breeding grounds farther north. More and more have been braving Ontario winters in recent decades, probably because of the buffets on offer at bird feeders across the province and perhaps also because of a warming climate. The birds will fly up to seven kilometres (four miles) from roosts to well-stocked feeders. In mid-March, over-wintering males put on their bright yellow spring jackets and become recognizable to those accustomed to the goldfinches of summer.

Spring migration in central Ontario: Early May to mid-May

Fall migration in central Ontario: Late Sept. to early Dec.

Winter whereabouts: From about New Liskeard and Lake Nipigon to the Gulf of Mexico

Origin of canary: According to the Roman writer Pliny, the Canary Islands were called Canaria, "Land of Dogs," because of the very large canines reputed to roam the archipelago

Also see: Cedar Waxwing, Chickadee, Evening Grosbeak, Goldenrod

GRAY JAY
The Friendly Camp Robber

Length: 25–33 cm
  (10–13 in)
Wingspan: 38–43 cm
  (15–17 in)
Weight: 62–82 g (2.2–2.9 oz)
Markings: Both sexes have
  dark grey back, wings and
  tail; lighter grey undersides;
  off-white face, crown and
  throat; black on back of
  head and neck extending to
  the eyes; juveniles are a
  darker, sooty grey
Alias: Whiskeyjack, Canada
  jay, moose bird, meat bird,
  grease bird, Labrador jay,
  carrion bird, Alaska jay, *le
  geai du Canada, Perisoreus
  canadensis*
Whereabouts: Black spruce
  bogs, coniferous and sometimes mixed forests, beaver
  meadows, clearings

Gray jays are legendary in the northwoods for
their intelligence, industry and amazing tame-
ness and curiosity. They are the chipmunks of
the bird world, complete with cute, beady black
eyes, fluffy feathers, and a penchant for frequenting campsites. Gray jays sometimes even land on
human hands and shoulders when coaxed with
tasty morsels, yet they don't commonly come to
call until September. In late winter, they also hop
onto the backs of tick-infested moose to pluck
the grape-sized, juicy parasites from the beasts.

For Native peoples, the plump grey bird was
a well-known, whimsical rascal. Wisakedjak, the
culture hero of Cree and Ojibway lore, often
took the form of the crafty jay. "Whiskeyjack" is
still a common name for the gray jay. The bird's
familiar presence in winter logging camps,
sidling up for dinner along with everyone else,

led to stories of the jays as souls of dead lumber-jacks, perhaps killed tragically in one of the grisly accidents common to the trade. Even today, the lumberjack staple of baked beans is said to be a gray jay favourite, along with cheese.

Gray jays are compulsive hoarders, as implied by their scientific name *Perisoreus,* Latin for "heap up." They work from June to autumn like feathered beavers, storing away enough food to let them live comfortably through winter. Drawing from unique enlarged saliva glands, the jays cover insects, berries, seeds and mushrooms in gluelike bird spit, then paste them behind curled strips of birchbark, beneath lichen on tree trunks and in the needles and forks of evergreen branches. Studies suggest that a gray jay can remember precisely where each of its thousands of hidden snacks is located over its square kilo-metre (0.4 square miles) or so of turf.

Their food storage system is so efficient that the vast majority of jays easily survive the winter and even begin nesting in February or early March, the leanest and deadliest time of the year for most forest creatures. Native hunters from Labrador to Alaska reported that it was bad luck to see or disturb a gray jay nest. The aboriginal people of northern Scandinavia – the Sami, or Lapps – believed the same about the Siberian jay, probably the gray jay's closest relative.

Three or four weeks after both mates begin building a nest, in March or early April, female jays usually lay just three eggs. After a month of happy family life, foraging with their parents, many sooty gray jay fledglings encounter tougher times. In early to mid-June, intense sibling rivalry sets in, culminating about 10 days

Calls: Main call often written as "whee-ah"; also a raspy "chuckle," whistles, squeaks, scolds; sometimes imitates hawks
Food: Caterpillars, beetles, grubs and other insects, moose ticks, spiders and their eggs; berries, seeds, mushrooms, carrion, birds eggs and nestlings, mice
Average family territory: 0.6–1.7 km² (0.2–0.7 sq. mi)
Nest: Deep, bulky bowl with a turned-in top, 14–16 cm (5.5–6.3 in) wide, of sticks, strips of cedar, birch and other bark, cocoons, lichens; lined with feathers and fur; usually built 2–7 m (6.6–23 ft) up on a level branch near the trunk of a spruce or other evergreen tree near north edge of an open bog or clearing
Average clutch: 2–4 peach-pit-sized, greyish- or greenish-white eggs cov-ered in tiny brownish spots
Incubation period: 18–19 days
Fledging age: 23 days
Average annual adult mor-tality: 17%
Average annual adult mor-tality of migrating song-birds: Often more than 50%
Lifespan: Up to 16 years in wild
Predators: Sharp-shinned hawks, goshawks, merlins; nests also raided by red squirrels, broad-winged hawks
Estimated Ontario popula-tion: 5 million

Nesting range: From Hudson Bay to the southern edge of the Canadian Shield, Manitoulin Island and the Kawarthas, though sparse south of Algonquin Park; also in all other provinces and territories

Also see: Blue Jay, Moose, Black Spruce

later with one dominant bird driving the others from home. The winner, two out of three times a male, stays with its parents, collecting and storing food through the summer and fall, then living off the stash with them through the following winter, unless it finds a newly widowed mate in a nearby territory before the snow flies. The ejected offspring are not so lucky: about 80 per cent perish before October. Those that survive usually manage by tagging along in the territory of a jay couple without a youngster of their own. Young birds may remain with older couples after a new nesting season begins and even help feed the new brood of jays once they've fledged.

In early autumn, gray jays redouble their food-gathering activities, venturing farther from their coniferous territories and often dipping and gliding into human company. Their buoyant flight is attributed to their long, wide wings and soft, broad feathers. Gray jays don't need the stiff, slim pinions that carry migratory birds through their arduous journeys north and south, because they remain on their territories year-round with the same mates for as long as they live.

Unfortunately, global warming appears to be pushing the bird's range north. Although there are still far more gray jays in Ontario than their better known blue cousins, a studied population near the southern limits of their range in Algonquin Park has dropped more than 60 per cent since the 1970s, possibly because higher temperatures cause more spoilage of winter food stores.

GREAT BLUE HERON
Motionless Giant in the Shallows

Nests per colony: Avg. 30–35, some more than 150
Height: Up to 1.2 m (4 ft)
Length: 1–1.4 m (3.3–4.5 ft)
Wingspan: 1.7–2 m (5.6–6.6 ft)
Weight: 2.1–2.5 kg (4.6–5.5 lb)
Beak length: 12–15 cm (4.7–6 in)
Flying speed: 30–50 km/h (19–31 mph)
Wingbeats per second: 2.3–3.2
Markings: Grey back (with bluish hue in the right light), white head and front of neck, long black head plume, bright yellow eyes
Alias: Blue heron, blue crane, grey crane, big cranky, *le grand héron, Ardea herodias*
Name for a group: A siege or sedge of herons
Calls: Loud shrieks, harsh squawks, deep crooks
Whereabouts: Shallow, weedy lakeshores and riversides, marshes, swamps, beaver ponds
Food: Fish mostly less than 7 cm (3 in) long; also frogs, crayfish, snails, snakes, mice, young muskrats, small birds, insects, carrion
Average daily food helping: 0.5 kg (1.1 lb)
Distance between nesting and feeding sites: Usually within 5 km (3 mi); up to 25 km (15.5 mi)
Average feeding territory: About 130 m (143 yd) of shore or 0.6 ha (1.5 acres) of marsh

Like a Flintstones air bus rising out of the primordial past, a great blue heron lifts high into the air with just a few slow, heavy flaps of its huge pinions. With long legs dangling and neck folded back in an S, herons in flight do evoke images of extinct pterodactyls. It is widely accepted, in fact, that birds evolved directly from dinosaurs, though pterodactyls were not dinosaurs and the first birds probably did not fly. Feathers are thought to be modified scales that evolved first for insulation rather than flight. In recent years, a number of dinosaur fossils have been found with primitive downy fluff,

Nest: Loose platform tangle of sticks, 0.5–1 m (1.6–3.3 ft) wide, usually 10–15 m (33–47 ft) up in deciduous trees

Average clutch: 3–5 light blue-green eggs, a little larger than chicken eggs

Incubation period: 25–30 days

Fledging age: 7–8 weeks

Age at first breeding: 3–4 years

Annual survival: About 30% in first year, 65% in second year, 80% afterwards

Lifespan: Avg. of 6–8 years for adults; up to 24 years in wild

Predators: Ravens, crows, gulls, hawks, owls, blue jays, raccoons and bears raid nests

Ontario population: More than 17,000 breeding pairs

Number of colonies in Ontario: More than 1,500

Average colony lifespan: 9 years

Oldest Ontario colony: More than 100 years

Bird species that live in colonies: About 12%

Spring migration in central Ontario: Early Apr. to early May

Fall migration in central Ontario: Mid-Sept. to mid-Nov.

Nesting range: Most of Ontario north to mid-boreal forest and James Bay; also in all other provinces except island of Newfoundland

suggesting to many paleontologists that the prehistoric beasts were, like birds, warm-blooded.

Herons are a tad more subtle than the dinosaurs of popular conception, but they are every bit as terrifying to just about anything that moves and will fit down their throats. Patience is everything to hunting herons. Starting early in the morning, they wade along the edges of marshes and streams and wait statue-still until a fish or frog comes within range of their lightning-quick bills. After spearing a fish, they may flip it into the air to catch and eat it head first. Given the chance, blue herons will also snap up small shorebirds, rodents and snakes, sometimes hunting on land or fishing at night if the light is good. Their powerful, muscle-bound neck must be doubled back in flight, unlike those of cranes, geese and swans, which employ their relatively lithe, long necks to leisurely gobble plants and insects.

Though they hunt alone and defend fishing holes from each other — sometimes in aerial combat — all is forgotten when herons congregate in colonies in their off hours. Heronries are generally densely packed, noisy, foul-smelling places in remote, hard-to-reach swamps, marshes and islands. White, acidic bird droppings cover the trunks and lower branches of nesting trees, often killing them after years of use. Huge stick nests teeter on flimsy branches, helping to keep raccoons away but making landings difficult. Sometimes eggs or chicks are even flung to the ground.

After eggs are laid in late April or May, at least one parent is always at the nest until the little ones are about a month old. Baby herons look like gawky little punk rockers with frizzy Mohawk hairdos. Life is not easy with all the commotion in the nest, and even after they fledge, the odds are stacked against them. Many do not learn the skill and patience needed for hunting and end up starving after they start fending for themselves when about 10 weeks old. Two-thirds of fledglings die in their first year and only about 10 per cent survive to mate. While some head south alone in autumn, flying night or day, the others may increase their chances of survival by joining migrant groups of herons, commonly numbering three to 12, though occasionally building up to a hundred birds.

Great blues have been hurt by development, water pollution, acid rain, wetland drainage, woodlot cutting and nest-site disturbance. The long, dark plume jutting from the back of the big bird's head was highly prized for ladies' hats in the late 1800s, spelling the demise of many a heron. Protection efforts in the 20th century restored their numbers in Ontario, though they apparently fell somewhat since the 1980s, possibly partly due to diminishing frog populations, an important heron food source. The greatest concentration of colonies is along the southern edge of the Canadian Shield, where rich wetlands and isolated woodlots are common, and from eastern Ontario to Algonquin Park.

Winter whereabouts: North shore of Lake Erie to Venezuela

Age of oldest bird fossils: 140 million years

Age when the long-necked ancestor of herons, storks and flamingos lived: 40–50 million years ago

Number of heron and bittern species nesting in Ontario: 6

Ontario's only threatened heron/bittern: Least bittern

Number of heron and bittern species worldwide: 60

Also see: Hummingbird, Osprey, Perch, Leopard Frog, Wetlands

HERMIT THRUSH
The Retiring Virtuoso

Calls: Resonant, ringing, melodious song sounds like a flute, with a clear, deep opening note followed by higher, rapid, fluttering couplets, fading at the end; often within a song, several phrases are repeated in a row, each 1–2 seconds long, varying in pitch and style; also low call notes of "tuk" or "chuk"

Number of pairs of muscles attached to a songbird voice box: 5–9

Number of pairs of muscles attached to a goose voice box: 1

Hermit thrush length: 16–18 cm (6–7 in)

Wingspan: 28–30 cm (11–12 in)

The ringing, fluted tunes of the hermit thrush make the speckle-bellied little bird one of the singing sensations of the northern woods. Performing most actively at dusk and dawn, the thrush achieves its far-reaching virtuosity by using its bronchial tubes, which branch off from the windpipe into the lungs, to sing two notes at the same time. Unlike a human, whose voice box is located at the top of the windpipe, or trachea, a bird produces sounds from the bottom of its trachea. The more muscles attached to the voice box, the greater the range of sounds it can produce.

In spring, lengthening sunlight stimulates the production of testosterone – the hormone that fuels machismo among humans – in male birds, putting them into breeding, serenading mode. But for all its echoing, mellifluous beauty, the hermit thrush, as its name suggests, is like a much-loved pop star that seeks anonymity. Unlike the treetop-singing robin, the most familiar of thrushes, the smaller hermit remains well hidden as it flutes, often on or near the forest floor, where it both nests and forages. It seems habitually nervous, cocking its tail and then slowly dropping it down. If spotted, the little bird usually plunges silently into dense shrubbery before the observer has a chance to identify its fleeting visage. Remaining unseen is vitally important for the male so that he can regularly steal away to the concealed nest, where he feeds his mate while she incubates their future family.

The instinct for reclusiveness is so strong among hermit thrushes that males at first chase away perspective mates that show up at their newly established territories in spring. It takes three or four days for the aggression to abate and a couple can finally settle down. Even afterwards, their relationship is rocky, the birds bickering if they come too close to one another except to mate or eat. After the breeding season, they keep to themselves, seldom joining in flocks as they turn from scratching for insects in the leaf litter to sampling the forest's ripening berry crops. Most migrate in October, mainly under the cover of night, stopping to rest and forage for about two to four days between each leg of their southward journey. The rugged individualists also winter much farther north than their tropical thrush brethren. While some may retreat to Mexico, many are content to take up quarters in the southern U.S.

Closely resembling the hermit in both looks and sound, the slightly larger **wood thrush**

Weight: 26–37 g (0.9–1.3 oz)
Markings: Black-spotted white breast, brown back, rusty brown tail and distinct white eye ring
Alias: Swamp angel, *la grive solitaire, Catharus guttatus*
Names for a group: A flute or mutation of thrushes
Whereabouts: Coniferous, mixed and aspen woods, black spruce bogs; often near forest edge
Food: Mostly beetles, grubs, caterpillars, ants and spiders in spring and summer; some worms, snails, salamanders, blueberries, blackberries; in fall and winter, elder, dogwood, pokeweed and poison ivy berries, wild cherries, seeds, buds, smaller amounts of insects
Breeding territory: 0.1–3.3 ha (0.25–8 acres), usually less than 1 ha (2.5 acres)
Nest: Neat cup, 10–15 cm (4–6 in) wide, of twigs, leaves, bark strips and an outer layer of moss and ferns; lined inside with rootlets, pine needles, grass and willow catkins; usually in a dip in the ground hidden beneath branches of a small evergreen, low shrubs or ferns; sometimes up to 3 m (10 ft) above ground in a small tree or shrub
Average clutch: 3–6 olive-sized light blue or pale turquoise eggs
Incubation period: 11–13 days

Fledging age: 10–15 days

Nest success rate: Avg. about 63%

Nests parasitized by cowbirds: 5–22%

Lifespan: Up to 9 years in wild

Predators: Sharp-shinned hawks; nests also raided by red squirrels, weasels

Estimated Ontario population: 2.5 million

Nesting range: From the tree line to just north of Lake Ontario and all of the Bruce Peninsula; sparsely scattered farther south to central Lake Erie; also in all other provinces and territories except Nunavut

Spring migration in central Ontario: Late Apr. to mid-May

Fall migration in central Ontario: Mid-Sept. to late Oct.

Winter whereabouts: U.S. Midwest, as far north as New York State in mild years, south to Guatemala

Number of thrush species nesting in Ontario: 7

Number of thrush species worldwide: About 175

Also see: Red-eyed Vireo, Veery, Yellow-rumped Warbler

haunts the deep interior of mature deciduous and mixed forests in central and southern Ontario. It lacks any red tint in its tail, and the first note of its song is more twittered than clear and low. Woodies also forage mainly on the ground, but usually nest two to five metres (6.5 to 16 feet) up in dense stands of understorey saplings. For winter, North America's entire wood thrush population funnels into the confined space of Central America. Habitat destruction both there and on their breeding grounds has reduced their continental numbers by 30 to 40 per cent since the 1960s. At the northern edge of their range, in the southern Shield, they seem to have declined by about 15 per cent since the 1980s, though they increased in eastern Ontario, where dense, low layers of tree regeneration – ideal habitat for woodies – have sprung up in vast stretches of forest thinned and damaged by the great ice storm of 1998.

HERRING GULL
Sublime Flight over Northern Lakes

Herring gulls and human beings have similar relationships with the Canadian Shield: while there are fewer opportunities for individuals to support themselves, those that are fortunate enough to live there enjoy the serenity away from the rat race to the south. Life in large gull colonies around the Great Lakes and urban areas can be brutal and vicious from start to finish, with constant fighting over food and territory, violation of spouses, and cannibalistic neighbours eating unattended nestlings.

In contrast, the less abundant food sources to the north usually support only small colonies or single nesting pairs. Though they're the same species as many of the gulls in the crowded south, northern herring gulls seem a different breed, beautiful and serene as they fly above wilderness lakes. Less alluring, spotty young gulls

Lifespan: Adults often live 15–20 years; up to 32 years in wild, 49 years in captivity
Flying speed: 25–67 km/h (16–49 mph)
Wingbeats per second: 2.8
Length: Females 56–62 cm (1.8–2 ft); males 60–66 cm (2–2.2 ft)
Wingspan: 1.3–1.5 m (4.3–5 ft)
Weight: Females 0.8–1 kg (1.8–2.2 lb); males 1–1.2 kg (2.2–2.6 lb)
Markings: White head, tail and undersides; grey back, black-tipped grey wings, pink legs, red spot on lower yellow bill; younger birds are mottled brown
Alias: Seagull, common gull, lake gull, winter gull, harbour

gull, *le goéland argenté,*
Larus argentatus
Name origin: *Gullan,* Cornish
for "wailer"
Call: Wide variety of loud
wails, squeals and clucks
Whereabouts: Lakes, rivers,
wetlands
Food: Omnivorous, preferring
small fish, mollusks, crayfish;
also mice, insects, bird eggs,
turtle hatchlings, wild berries,
carrion and Kentucky Fried
Chicken bones
Home range: 15–25 km² (9–
15.5 sq. mi)
Nesting territory: 5–50 m
(16.4–164 ft) around nest
Nest: Grass or moss often
laid in bare rock depres-
sions, 35–90 cm (14 in–
3 ft) wide, usually on small,
rocky islands or inaccessible
points
Average clutch: 3 spotted,
olive-coloured eggs, a little
larger than chicken eggs
Incubation period: 30–32
days
Fledging age: 45–50 days
Age at first breeding: Males
4 years, females 5 years
Annual survival: Eggs 70–
80%, chicks 50–70%, 1st-
years 50%, adults 60–90%
Predators: Mink, foxes, hawks,
falcons, eagles, great horned
owls and coyotes; nests also
raided by mink, raccoons,
skunks, snakes, ravens,
herons and other gulls
Ontario population: More
than 36,000 pairs on
Canadian side of Great
Lakes

also tend not to return to inland lakes until they are four or five years old and attired in smart breeding plumage.

Herring gulls frequent many different habitats because they are generalists – not specially adapted for any one thing, but taking advantage of opportunities wherever they find them. Despite their seemingly effortless wide-winged glides, they are not the strongest fliers, depending instead on updrafts and thermals. But few other birds are as well rounded. Gulls walk, swim and glide with equal ability. They can eat just about anything, but are mainly scavengers of dead fish, preferring to scoop them from the surface in their bills rather than dive. When the eating's good, herring gulls can wolf down equal to one-third their own weight in a single gorging. They will also eat the eggs and young of other birds, making them unpopular with both their feathered peers and some humans.

When they return in early spring, herring gulls embark on one of the most prolonged courtships in the bird world. Over a period of two months or more, males strut, call out, stretch their necks and offer gifts to passive debutantes to prove they'll be good providers. Among couples going steady, there is prolonged rubbing of bills, contorting of bodies and mutual preening. Finally, if the female decides she's found Mr. Right, she initiates copulation by pecking at his breast and then bending over to allow his cloaca – an all-purpose digestive, urinary and sexual opening for both sexes – to rub against hers. They mate up to 12 times a day for about six days before she lays her first egg, usually in May.

Both females and males make and aggressively defend the nests. Males also feed their mates and help incubate the eggs. For the first few crucial days after they hatch, the downy young live mainly off their egg yolk, while their parents concentrate on guarding them. The young birds begin venturing outside the nest two or three days after hatching. Mortality among them is high, but with each passing year, survival becomes easier.

Gull numbers have increased greatly since the beginning of the 20th century, when egg collecting as well as feather plucking for women's hats brought them close to extinction. They became protected by law in 1916, but pesticides and PCBs in the aquatic food chain in the 1960s and '70s caused thin eggshells, deformities and hormone imbalances among gulls around the Great Lakes. The banning of DDT and other controls led to a drop of most egg contaminants, some by as much as 90 per cent, by 1995.

Largest Ontario colony: About 2,500 pairs, on Lake Huron
Population density in central Ontario: Usually 2–10 pairs per 100 km^2 (39 sq. mi)
Nesting range: All of Ontario; also in all other provinces and territories
Spring migration in central Ontario: Early Mar. to late May
Fall migration in central Ontario: Early Sept. to Dec.
Winter whereabouts: Great Lakes to Atlantic coast and Gulf of Mexico; younger birds fly farther south than breeders
Estimated winter population on Atlantic coast: 1 million
Famous gulls: Jonathan Livingston Seagull; the slain gull of Chekhov's *The Seagull,* symbol of the destructive force of human whims
Age of oldest gull-like ichthyornis fossils: 85 million years
Gull capital of Ontario: Niagara Falls, where up to 14 gull species gather in winter
Number of gull species nesting in Ontario: 5
Number of gull species worldwide: 45
Also see: Canada Goose, Cormorant, Beetles, Minnows, Canadian Shield, Lakes

HUMMINGBIRD
Tiny Wonder Fuelled on Nectar

Wingbeats per second: Avg. 40–80; up to 200 in courtship dives

Flying speed: 43 km/h (27 mph)

Hummingbird wing loading: 0.24 g/cm² (0.05 oz/sq. in)

Great blue heron wing loading: 0.43 g/cm² (0.1 oz/sq. in)

Heartbeats per minute: 500–600 at rest, 50–180 in torpor, up to 1,260 in flight (fastest heart rate of all birds and mammals)

Respiratory rate: 250 breaths a minute at rest

Weight: 3–4 g (0.1–0.14 oz)

Weight of a nickel: 4 g

Length: 7–9 cm (2.8–3.5 in)

Wingspan: 10–13 cm (4–5.2 in)

Though ruby-throated hummingbirds are usually seen at sugar-water feeders throughout cottage country, they are a lot more common in the wilderness than most people imagine. In the wild, they're usually heard before they're seen, their whirring hum too deep a sound for a bee or other insect to produce. Ever on the lookout for nectar meals in colourful flowers, hummingbirds are often attracted by bright nylon tents or orange and red plastic tarps. Zipping through on wings moving too quickly to be seen, they may at first appear to be large dragonflies, but when hovering, they hold their tiny bodies vertical in flight. Their wings actually move in curving figure eights, allowing hummingbirds to fly straight up, down, backwards and even upside down. They can veer sideways on a dime or stop instantly, to hover while feeding.

One thing hummingbirds can't do is soar. To stay aloft, these smallest of all birds must keep their wings in perpetual hyperflap. The feat takes incredible strength and energy. A hummingbird's Herculean chest muscles – making up 30 per cent of its body – and its atomic-speed heart are both proportionally larger than those of any other bird. Nectar provides sugar that can be burned immediately as energy in the hummingbird's high-octane engine. Insects lapped up with the nectar or caught separately offer protein for building body tissue. Still, to keep going, hummers refill their bellies about every seven to 12 minutes. They may consume and burn food equal to half their weight every day. To sustain their metabolic rate, an 80-kilogram (176-pound) man would have to pack away 45 kilograms (100 pounds) of Smarties a day and drink five cases of beer to keep his skin from catching fire.

The buzzing birds are especially active just before dusk and after dawn, storing up or replenishing vital fuel. On most nights, they conserve energy by slowing down their heart and breathing rates by 90 per cent, dropping their body temperature to half the daytime average. In the cold highlands of their wintering grounds in Mexico and points farther south, hummingbirds go into a prolonged torpor. Their ability to revive from this deathlike state made them sacred to the Aztecs, who considered hummingbirds to be the spirits of dead warriors. Inca women roused the tiny hummers from their deep sleep by warming them between their breasts. In British Columbia, hummingbirds were depicted on totem poles as messengers of the dead.

Markings: Iridescent green back, grey-white belly; males have iridescent bright red throat and a forked tail

Average number of feathers: 940 (the least of any bird in the world)

Daytime body temperature: 41–43°C (105–109°F)

Alias: Ruby-throated hummingbird, common hummingbird, *le colibri à gorge rubis, Archilochus colubris*

Name for a group: A charm of hummingbirds

Name of a hummingbird aviary: Jewel room

Calls: High-pitched, twittering squeaks

Whereabouts: Mixed and deciduous forest edges, clearings, river- and lakeshores, islands, swamps, beaver-pond fringes

Food: Nectar, pollen, sap; up to 60% of diet is insects, including mosquitoes, flies, bees, aphids, caterpillars, insect eggs; spiders

Hummingbird-pollinated flowers: Jewelweed, columbine, cardinal flower, honeysuckle, fireweed, pink wintergreen, purple asters, thistles, willow catkins and some 20 other known wildflowers

Number of licks per second: 11–12

Time to digest a meal: 20–30 min

Time for a human to digest a meal: 1½–3½ days

Number of calories expended per minute of hovering: 11

Territory: Average about
0.1 ha (0.25 acres)

Nest: Neat, deep, thick-walled
cup about 4–5 cm (1.5–
2 in) wide, of moss, lichens,
grass, bud scales and plant
down, bound tightly and
achored with spiders' silk;
usually 3–6 m (10–20 ft) up
on top of a thin outer branch
of a small deciduous tree or
shrub, often in alders near
stream edges or in
meadows

Average clutch: 2 pea-sized,
oblong white eggs

Incubation period: 12–14
days

Fledging age: 18–22 days

Average annual survival:
Males 31%, females 42%

Lifespan: Up to 9 years in
wild, 12 years in captivity

Predators: Sharp-shinned
hawks, kestrels, bullfrogs,
large fish; nests also raided
by weasels, chipmunks,
crows, jays, snakes, preying
mantises, yellow jackets

**Number of hummingbirds
killed annually in the
tropics for fashion
accessories in late 1800s:**
About 5 million

**Estimated Ontario popula-
tion:** 500,000

Nesting range: Southern
Ontario to the mid-boreal
forest; also in Quebec and
prairie and Maritime
provinces

**Spring migration in central
Ontario:** Mid-May to early
June

One quite erroneous belief people once held was that hummers and other small birds migrated by hitching rides on the backs of larger birds such as geese. In truth, ruby-throats, the one hummingbird species to summer in eastern North America, can fly 800 kilometres (500 miles) nonstop across the Gulf of Mexico in 26 hours, fuelled on two grams (0.07 ounces) of fat, which makes up about half their body weight before starting out. Ruby-throats spend a couple of days rebuilding their fat supplies between each 170- to 340-kilometre (105- to 210-mile) leg of their journey overland. They migrate during the day, close to the ground.

When hummingbirds arrive in central Ontario in mid-May, most of the flowers they depend on are not yet open, while rain and bad weather limit access to others. For about a month they turn instead to the plentiful sweet sap oozing from rows of holes drilled into tree trunks by yellow-bellied sapsuckers, which return north a few weeks earlier than their tiny associates. One study has found that mother hummers always build their nests within a quick dash of regularly tapped sapsucker trees and rely solely on them during incubation. It is unlikely that humming-birds could breed on the Shield without the presence of their tree-boring benefactors.

Towards summer, more of the tubular flowers favoured by ruby-throats come into bloom. Hummers are especially attracted to red flowers, which often have no scent but big nectar payloads. While probing each deep blossom with its needlelike bill and lapping nectar from the bottom of the flower cup with a long, brushy tongue, a hummingbird picks up pollen on its head which may fertilize the next flower it visits. It may hit more than a thousand a day.

Ontario's abundance of summer flowers provides a rich breeding ground for hummers, but the birds don't stick around for long. Males arrive first, establish feeding territories and defend them against each other, calling out in high squeaks. Females stake out their own ground. These territorial half-pints aggressively fend off much larger brutes, from chickadees to turkey vultures, using their darting speed to advantage.

Female hummingbirds spend six to 10 days building tiny, well-camouflaged nests before seeking out the briefest of romantic liaisons. Courtship – involving males flying in wide, exact arcs, about four metres (4.4 yards) in diameter, as if suspended on a string – is followed by four or five seconds of sex. Then the female goes off to lay her eggs and raise her family while the red-cravated swinging bachelor looks for new partners. A pair of honeybee-sized, blind, naked chicks usually hatch in the early summer. They're fed nectar and insects from their mother's crop. When they fledge, they are good fliers right off the mark, their wings buzzing away like wind-up toys. In another four to seven days, they're independent. By then, some hummingbirds are already setting off for their tropical retreats. Most leave by late August, though a few may stick around until the first light frosts of early autumn pulverize the succulent stems of late-blooming jewelweed flowers.

Fall migration in central Ontario: Early Aug. to mid-Sept.

Winter whereabouts: South Florida and Texas to Costa Rica

Closest Ontario relative: Chimney swift

Number of hummingbird species in the Americas: About 320–340

Number of hummers elsewhere in the world: 0

World's smallest bird: Bee hummingbird, 5.7 cm (2.2 in) long, weighing 1.6 g (0.06 oz)

Lookalikes: 3 species of large clear-wing sphinx moths hover at flowers in daytime like hummingbirds

Also see: Yellow-bellied Sapsucker, Jewelweed, Speckled Alder

KINGFISHER
Author of the Riverside Rattle

Calls: Loud, harsh rattle, like the sound of changing bicycle gears; also screams and squeaks

Deepest dives: 60 cm (2 ft)

Flying speed: Up to 60 km/h (36 mph)

Wingbeats per second: 2.4

Length: 28–35 cm (11–14 in)

Wingspan: 56–58 cm (22–23 in)

Weight: 140–170 g (5–6 oz)

Beak length: 4.5–6 cm (1.8–2.4 in)

Markings: Grey-blue bushy crest, breast band and back; white undersides; red side and stomach band on females; young have darker breast band

Alias: Belted kingfisher, lazy bird, alcyon, *le martin pêcheur, Ceryle alcyon*

Sporting an improbably huge beak attached to its pigeon-sized, tiny-footed body, the cartoon-like belted kingfisher is a breed apart, announcing its presence with a distinctive rattling call as it patrols riversides and lakeshores. The high-crested, blue-mantled bird may hover briefly before dropping six to 12 metres (20 to 40 feet) straight down, its wings fixed like a little fighter jet, to catch a fish just below the surface. Its over-sized headgear is designed to take the impact of hitting the drink beak first.

Kingfishers hunt from favourite perches, commonly on dead branches overlooking open, clear, shallow water, often at riffles in streams. Captured fish are brought back to a tree perch, tenderized with a thorough whapping against the branch and swallowed head first. The tail end of a really big catch may stick out of a kingfisher's mouth while the bird's digestive juices go to work on the rest of the fish. A pile of regurgitated bones and scales on the ground below usually marks a regular kingfisher hunting perch.

In Greek mythology, the gods turned the sea-tossed queen Alcyone and her husband into kingfishers and afterwards stilled the winds for two weeks around the winter solstice each year – a time still known as the halcyon days – so that they could build a floating nest of fishbones. Though the belted kingfisher's scientific name, *alcyon,* pays tribute to the story, the crested bird actually nests, amazingly enough, in burrows dug into high banks on or near shorelines. The availability of shoreline territory and nest sites limits its numbers. Waterfront development, excessive nutrient loading in lakes and other habitat disturbances seem to have caused a steady continent-wide decline over the past four decades, with sightings of the birds dropping by more than 10 per cent in central Ontario since the 1980s

A select few kingfishers, usually males, stay year-round in the province wherever they can find open water in winter. Most males, however, begin arriving in April, about a month before their mates, to secure prime real estate and keep out rivals. Later, the fairer sex assesses the waterfront properties by alighting near their owners and eliciting a meal of fresh fish from them. Since they nest underground, female kingfishers have no need to defensively blend with their surroundings and, unlike most birds, are more colourful than their partners, bearing their red namesake belt across their belly and sides. Once paired, both mates take part in constant shoreline

Whereabouts: Clear streams, calm bays, small lakes, ponds, marshes
Food: Minnows, sculpins, sticklebacks, perch and fingerlings of larger fish, usually less than 10 cm (4 in) long; also frogs, tadpoles, crayfish, salamanders, dragonfly nymphs, grasshoppers, mice
Breeding territory: Avg. 800–1,200 m (880–1,320 yd) of shoreline; up to 5,000 m (5,468 yd)
Average non-breeding territory: 300–500 m (330–550 yd) of shoreline
Nest: Burrow 1–2 m (3.3–6.6 ft) long, 7.5–12.5 cm (3–5 in) wide, sloping up to nest chamber 20–30 cm (8–12 in) wide, 15–20 cm (6–8 in) high; usually near the top of a high sand, clay or gravel waterside bank; occasionally in a ditch, road cut or quarry up to 8 km (5 mi) from feeding grounds
Average clutch: 5–7 glossy white eggs, about the size of large chestnuts
Incubation period: 22–24 days
Fledging age: 27–29 days
Age at first breeding: 1 year
Predators: Sharp-shinned, Cooper's and red-tailed hawks; harriers, great horned owls, peregrine falcons, foxes; nests also raided by skunks, mink, raccoons and snakes
Estimated Ontario population: 200,000

Accolades: Featured on City of Halifax flag and on Canadian $5 bill, 1986–2002; namesake of a popular Indian beer

Nesting range: All of Ontario; also in all other provinces and territories except Nunavut

Spring migration in central Ontario: Early Apr. to early May

Fall migration in central Ontario: Early Sept. to mid-Nov.

Winter whereabouts: Rare in southern Ontario north to Manitoulin Island, Haliburton and Arnprior; south to Panama and West Indies

First appearance of kingfishers: 40–50 million years ago

Other burrow-nesting Ontario birds: Bank swallow, roughed-winged swallow, flicker (rarely)

Number of kingfisher species nesting in Ontario: 1

Number of kingfisher species worldwide: 87

Also see: Crayfish, Minnows, Perch, Lakes

patrols. They can distinguish each other's rattle from those of intruders, whom they vigorously drive away. They even sometimes escort canoes along the length of their territories.

Given good weather, a kingfisher duo can pickaxe their subterranean nursery chambers out of an embankment with their sturdy beaks in three to seven days, kicking plumes of sand out behind them with their feet. Males usually do about two-thirds of the digging. Mothers in turn undertake most of the incubating after laying their eggs in May or early June. The young hatch featherless and about a week later sprout tiny pinfeathers in sheaths, making them look more like porcupines than birds. Full feathers explode from the sheaths all at once about about a week later. When almost a month old, the youngsters emerge from their burrows ready to fly. Parents teach them to hunt by dropping fish into the water when they are hungry. Families break up within about three weeks of the young coming out, even the parents becoming estranged and staking out separate fishing holes.

LOON
Spirit of the North Woods

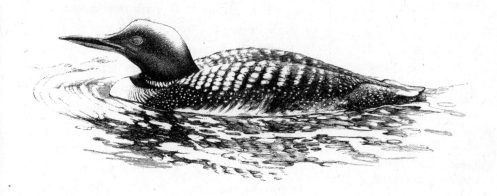

Minted in nickel, plated in bronze and indelibly embossed on the imaginations of generations of wilderness seekers, the loon is a quintessentially Canadian symbol. Human reverence for the bird is documented by the 5,000-year-old loon pictographs on cliffs scattered around the Great Lakes region. Loons, in fact, are sacred birds, bridging the material and spiritual worlds in a continuum of ancient lore from eastern North America all the way to central Siberia. In many remarkably similar versions of the creation story on both continents, it is the loon that retrieves mud from the bottom of primordial seas to form the Earth.

In addition to the diving bird's ability to journey both in the sky and in the watery depths, the almost human quality of its long, soulful call probably earned the awe of northern

Dive duration: Avg. 40–45 sec, up to 15 min
Average depth of hunting grounds: 2–5 m (6.6–16 ft)
Deepest dives: 600 m (1,968 ft)
Flying speed: Avg. 120 km/h (75 mph); up to almost 190 km/h (118 mph) in a swoop
Flying time from Lake Ontario to Algonquin Park: About 2½ hours
Wingbeats per second: 3.8–4.4
Loon wing loading: 2.5 g/cm² (0.6 oz/sq. in)
Barn swallow wing loading: 0.14 g/cm² (0.03 oz/sq. in)
Migrating altitude: 1,500–2,700 m (5,000–9,000 ft)
Length: 66–90 cm (2.2–3 ft)

Wingspan: 1.3–1.5 m (4.3–5 ft)
Weight: Females avg. 2.7–
4.6 kg (6–10 lb), males 4.4–
6.3 kg (9.7–14 lb)
Beak length: 7–9 cm (2.8–
3.5 in)
Markings: Iridescent black
head and neck, white necklace around neck, checkered
black and white back, white
breast and belly, long, pointy
black bill, red eyes; juveniles
younger than 3 years old
and adults in fall and winter
have dark grey backs and
white bellies
Alias: Common loon, great
northern diver, *le huart à
collier, Gavia immer*
Whereabouts: Deep, clear,
undisturbed lakes and large
rivers
Food: Perch, young bass, sunfish, minnows and other fish
weighing 10–70 g (0.35–
2.5 oz); also crayfish, frogs,
mollusks, leeches, aquatic
insects, water-lily roots and
other aquatic plants
Average daily food helping:
1 kg (2.2 lb), or about 30
small fish
Breeding territory: 5–200 ha
(12–494 acres), averaging
about 70 ha (173 acres)
**Portion of population that
switches mates annually:**
About 20%
Nest: Simple low pile of vegetation, about 60 cm (2 ft)
wide, just above the waterline, often on the lee side of
a small island or point, in a
cove or on an old muskrat
lodge

peoples. The familiar, modulating wail, sometimes heard in choruses on still nights or after a
rain, is actually just one of four distinct types of
loon calls, each rising in pitch according to the
intensity of emotion. The wail is used to summon
mates and offspring, or as territorial declaration
to neighbours.

Each male also has his own distinctive yodel
for territorial defence, most often heard early in
the season. Neighbouring loons can recognize
each other's yodels from those of interlopers.
Males sometimes yodel at low-flying planes.
When they sense danger, loons blurt out a
tremolo phrase like the laugh of a mad scientist,
probably the inspiration for the saying "crazy as
a loon." A fourth type of call consists of hoots
made by pairs, families or groups of loons as a
kind of random small talk.

Most of the communication between loons,
however, is by body language. American biologist William Barklow studied loons up close for
15 years, infiltrating their ranks by snorkelling
among them with a goose decoy painted to look
like a loon on top of his head. He noted more
than 25 regular communication body postures.
Among them, loons greet each other by gracefully stretching out their wings, show submission
by hunching low and indicate peaceful or
amorous intentions by pointing their beaks
downwards.

Normally, a breeding pair of loons maintains
an entire lake, or a bay in a large lake, as their
exclusive territory. In the rush to secure the best
waters, loons return to their breeding grounds
within days, sometimes even hours, of ice
breakup in April or early May. They often take

scouting missions from ice-free staging areas on the Great Lakes to check the progress of the thaw on inland lakes. Though mates overwinter separately, a happily nesting pair usually renews its bond with an elegant, quiet, diving courtship waltz when they return to their original honeymoon lake each spring. Competition from a rival, however, sometimes forces one of the former mates to hit the road and look for a new partner. Couples having little reproductive success may also break up and move on to other lakes.

Loons mate and nest on land, within a metre of the shore. That's about as far as they ever venture on dry ground, because their legs are placed so far back under their bodies that they can walk only by using their wings as crutches, though flapping enables them to run. The word *loon* itself comes from the Scandinavian *lom,* which in English means "lame." Loons' torpedo-like bodies are built more for swimming and diving than flying. Many of their bones are solid, rather than honeycombed with air spaces like those of most birds. Depending on the wind, they need takeoffs 20 to 400 metres (21 to 437 yards) long on the water to gain enough lift from their relatively small thrashing wings to fly. Takeoffs are impossible from land. Beneath the water, though, they pivot like otters and outswim many fish.

Even baby loons are in the water swimming within hours of hatching, usually in late June or early July. They paddle very close behind their parents, often riding on their backs during the first two or three weeks of their lives when they are tired, cold or in potential danger from underwater predators. Both parents take turns attending the sooty loonlings and start teaching them to fish

Average clutch: 2 olive-coloured eggs with dark spots, about as big as a mid-sized potato

Incubation period: 28–29 days

Fledging age: 11–12 weeks

Nesting success: 20–50%

Annual loonling survival: 70–85%

Age at first breeding: 4–7 years old

Lifespan: Adults avg. 7–10 years; up to 19 years in wild

Predators: Chicks or eggs eaten by ravens, gulls, crows, eagles, raccoons, skunks, snapping turtles, pike and other large fish

Greatest pests: Black flies

Portion of Ontario lakes with fish containing mercury levels that affect loon reproduction: 30%

Estimated Ontario population: 90,000 breeding pairs

Accolades: Official bird of Ontario, Minnesota and numerous outdoors organizations; bird on the $1 "loonie" coin

Number of lakes named "Loon" in Ontario: 33

Nesting range: Almost all of Ontario south to Lake Simcoe, the north shore of Lake Ontario, Lake Huron near Kincardine and a few scattered sites to around Guelph; also in all other provinces and territories

Spring migration in Central Ontario: Mid-Apr. to mid-May

Fall migration in central Ontario: Late Sept. to late Nov.

Winter whereabouts: Atlantic coast, especially from the Carolinas to northern Florida; smaller numbers along Gulf of Mexico and in the Great Lakes

Age of oldest loon fossils: At least 50 million years

Closest loon relatives: Penguins, albatrosses, petrels

Number of loon species nesting in Ontario: 3

Number of loon species worldwide: 5

Also see: Common Merganser, Black Flies, Perch, Painted Turtle, Lakes

when they're about four weeks old. In August, parents begin spending a few hours each day with growing groups of younger, non-mating loons for ritualized social gatherings on larger lakes, leaving their unfledged young at home. The visits grow longer until the young are fledged and can totally feed themselves, by September or early October. Then parents leave them for good, heading south in loose flocks forming long lines of up to hundreds of well-spaced birds, migrating by day. Fledglings form their own flocks and follow their elders south one to three weeks later. The last leave shortly before freeze-up. Young loons remain by the sea in their second summer because their flightless moulting period, lasting several weeks, occurs too late for them to join the return spring migration.

Their heavy dependence on fish, and their need for clear, undisturbed water to find their prey, has imperilled loons in areas under pressure from development. Sudden water-level fluctuations from dams and motorboat wakes can flood out nests. In lakes with heavy recreational angling, the biggest killer is lead poisoning from swallowed sinkers and jigs, which can finish a loon in as little as two days. Acid rain also decreases their fish supply in some lakes, while prey contaminated with mercury and other pollutants cause reproductive failure and nervous-system dysfunctions in loons. Thousands of the wintering birds wash up on Florida beaches some years, starved because they can no longer coordinate their muscles while trying to catch fish. So far, loon numbers in Ontario, which hosts about one-fifth of the summer North American population, appear to be stable. It is illegal to hunt them.

OSPREY
Crooked-winged Fishing Ace

Back in the 20th century, the banning of DDT may have come just in time for the osprey. At the top of the aquatic food chain, ospreys are the ultimate recipients of pesticides flushed by rain from farm fields, lawns and roadsides into rivers and lakes and collected in the fish they eat. DDT interferes with estrogen, the hormone that regulates calcium, leading to thin eggshells and nesting failure. Breeding ospreys nearly disappeared from the lower Great Lakes in the 1960s. The Canadian Wildlife Federation listed them as endangered in 1973. After DDT was banned, offspring survival rates slowly increased in the late 1970s and 1980s. Assisted by the erection of hundreds of artificial nesting platforms, ospreys are again prospering in Ontario, especially around Georgian Bay and the southern edge of the Canadian Shield, with several

Highest hunting dives: 40 m (130 ft)

Flying speed: 35–120 km/h (22–75 mph)

Length: 53–66 cm (1.7–2.2 ft)

Wingspan: 1.5–1.8 m (5–6 ft)

Weight: Males 1.4–1.6 kg (3–3.5 lb), females 1.6–2 kg (3.5–4.4 lb)

Markings: Black mask, white head and undersides, dark brown back, brown patches at front crook of white underwings, short fan-shaped tail with light and dark bars; females usually have a dark, streaky necklace

Alias: Fish hawk, sea hawk, *le balbuzard, Pandion haliaetus*

Call: Short, sharp, repeated whistle

Whereabouts: Lake shallows, rivers, beaver ponds, swamps

Average depth of fishing grounds: 1–2 m (3.3–6.6 ft)

Food: 99% catfish, sunfish, bass, perch, suckers, pike and other fish, usually 25–35 cm long; occasionally frogs, crayfish, snakes, rodents

Average fishing success rate: 20–25% of all dives

Average hunting time per catch: 12 min

Breeding territory: 50–100 m (55–110 yd) around nest

Nest: 0.7–2.5 m (2.3–8.2 ft) wide, of woven sticks, cattails and other aquatic plants, 9–19 m (30–66 ft) above shore or wetlands in the crown of a broken-topped, dead tree; about 40% of Ontario nests in artificial nesting platforms, utility poles and towers

Mating frequency until eggs laid: Up to 30 times a day, 10–20 seconds per bout

Average clutch: 3 creamy white to cinnamon pink eggs mottled reddish brown, the size of large chicken eggs

Incubation period: 5–6 weeks

Fledging age: 7–9 weeks

Age at first breeding: 3–5 years

Annual survival: 40–60% in first year, 80–90% for adults

Lifespan: Avg. 6–10 years for adults; up to 26 years in wild

score known nests occupied in the Kawarthas.

Ospreys are the most widespread birds of prey in both Ontario and the world. They fly over every continent except Antarctica. They're also one of Ontario's largest raptors, and the only one, save for the bald eagle, that catches fish. The black-masked birds usually hover 10 to 30 metres (33 to 98 feet) above shallow water, heads hanging as they angle for dinner. When they spot their mark, they tuck in their wings and drop straight down, braking as they snatch their hapless prey just beneath the surface. Their talons have sharp spines and a reversible toe to hold onto the slippery purchase. There are many accounts of bald eagles, which are bigger scavengers than hunters, accosting ospreys in the air and forcing them to drop their catch, which the eagle retrieves. Ospreys themselves are sometimes mistaken for eagles because of their large size and white heads. But crooked wings, looking like elbows, are the mark of the fish hawk.

Unlike many raptors, ospreys can cross over large bodies of water in migration. Though they often conserve energy by joining hawks soaring up on and gliding between columns of warm air rising above sun-baked patches of land, if they have to ospreys can flap long and hard because they have bigger wings relative to their bodies than do most other birds of prey. Sometimes they migrate carrying a fish; hawk watchers call this "packing a lunch." Most Ontario ospreys head south in early to mid-September, following the Mississippi Valley en route to the tropics. They return in April, usually travelling alone but following the same routes till they fan out on their breeding territories.

For about two weeks after they return, males swoop and dive in courtship flights, calling out loudly. Mates return to the same nest, or aerie, every year, repairing and adding to it, sometimes for generations. Nests can sometimes weigh up to hundreds of kilograms, with their fringes sub-letted by smaller nesters such as tree swallows or grackles. Occasionally, ospreys nest in the middle of heron colonies, which may prompt the herons to abandon the site. If they stay or return, however, the osprey presence ultimately benefits herons by keeping away many nest raiders.

Females lay their eggs in late April or in May and are fed by their mates while they tend the nest. Even after the clutch hatches, mothers remain constantly with their charges for a month. Males provide a kilogram (2.2 pounds) or more of fish a day, doubling the weight of the nestlings each week or so. While fathers continue feeding their young for up to several weeks after they fledge around mid-August, their mates usually head south about three weeks ahead of them. Migrating last, the young embark upon a tropical adolescence, hanging out along jungle rivers and not returning to Ontario until they are two or three years old.

Predators: Great horned owls, bald eagles; nests also raided by raccoons, ravens, crows

Estimated Ontario Great Lakes basin population: More than 900 pairs

Population density: Usually 1 pair per 100 km² (39 sq. mi), though more numerous in good fishing areas; a small osprey colony near Lindsay has nests only 250 m (273 yd) apart

Accolades: Official bird of Nova Scotia; featured on Canadian $10 bill, 1989–2001

Nesting range: All of Ontario, but sparsely scattered in far south; also in all forest regions throughout Canada

Spring migration in central Ontario: Mid-Apr. to late May

Fall migration in central Ontario: Mid-Aug. to early Oct.

Average migration altitude: 200–1,120 m (655–3,675 ft)

Winter whereabouts: Southern Mexico and Caribbean to central Argentina and Chile; most in northern South America

Ontario day-flying raptors at risk: Bald and golden eagles (both endangered), peregrine falcon (threatened)

Also see: Broad-winged Hawk, Great Blue Heron, Smallmouth Bass

PILEATED WOODPECKER
Monarch of the Tree Whackers

Bill length: 5.5 cm (2.2 in)

Territorial drumming: 14–17 beats/sec, lasting 1–3 sec, often repeated every 40–60 sec for an hour or more by males; females also drum occasionally

Ontario's fastest drummer: Ladder-backed woodpecker, 26–30 beats/sec

Length: 40–49 cm (16–19 in)

Wingspan: 69–76 cm (27–30 in)

Weight: 240–350 g (8.5–12 oz)

Markings: Mostly black, with a large, red triangular head crest, long beak, wide black and white stripes on face and neck, white underwings bordered with black flight feathers; males sport a red "forehead" and moustache; on females these are black

Alias: Log-cock, cock-of-the-woods, black woodpecker, carpenter bird, black log, king-of-the-woods, stump breaker, laughing woodpecker, johnny-cock, Indian hen, wood kate, cluck-cock, *le grand pic, Dryocopus pileatus*

Word origin of *pileated*: "Crested" or "capped," from Latin *pileus,* meaning "felt cap"

Name for a group: A descent of woodpeckers

The crow-sized pileated woodpecker bears a dagger bill longer than an eagle's beak and a bold red crest sticking straight up in the air. Surely the model for Woody the Woodpecker, the striking bird is the monarch of its kind. Indeed, it is sometimes attended by much smaller downy and hairy woodpeckers picking insect leftovers from the havoc wreaked by the pileated's jackhammer beak. Pileated woodpeckers actually listen for the hustle and bustle of a carpenter ant colony deep inside a tree, then tear through the hard outer layers of wood to reach the rotting, ant-infested heart. Once found, the colony is ravaged by the woodpecker's barbed, sticky and ultimately deadly tongue, which extends many centimetres beyond the bill.

Unfortunately, the square-shouldered, thin-necked regal woodpecker is rather retiring and seldom grants an audience. But it often leaves signs of its whereabouts. Piles of crayon-sized splinters and wood chips as big as a hand accumulate below pileated dinner trees. The deep holes themselves may be 30 centimetres (one foot) long and 10 centimetres (four inches) wide. A row of holes is sometimes joined together, forming a gash more than a metre (three feet) long. The birds also rip away and discard large sheets of bark from dead trees while searching for beetles and grubs, and tear apart rotten stumps and logs on the ground.

Loud, hollow-sounding, resonant "drum" rolls, heard as much as a kilometre (half a mile) away, also announce the pileated woodpecker's presence. Although they may perform year-round to mark their territories and keep in touch, they're especially active before breeding. In late winter and early spring, single males drum as often as twice a minute and fly above the trees, flashing their white underwings and calling loudly for female company. Like the rest of the spring birdsong orchestra, this percussion section performs most often in early morning and late in the day.

Once paired off, most pileateds stay close together for life, staying year-round on the same territory. Though quite often they use the same dead tree in which they nested the previous year, they usually excavate a new cavity, wary of parasites left over in the old hole. Both mates spend up to a month chiselling out their nesting

Calls: Loud, startling, repeated cackle, rising, then falling in pitch, variously rendered as "kyuk-kyuk-kyuk" or "wic-ka-wicka" or "wok-wok-wok," often lasting for many seconds; also several other "waaa" and "wuk" calls

Whereabouts: Dense, mature forests covering at least 40 ha (100 acres), with large, dead standing trees and water close by

Food: Carpenter ants, ground ants, beetles, cluster flies, moths, mosquitoes, caterpillars and other larvae; berries, nuts, acorns and cherries about 25% of diet

Number of ants counted in one stomach: 2,600

Breeding territory: 40–80 ha (100–200 acres)

Nest: In tree cavity 25–76 cm (10–30 in) deep, about 18–20 cm (7–8 in) wide, with vertical oval opening 9–12.5 cm (3.5–5 in) wide; usually 3.5–27.5 m (12–90 ft) up on south or east side of a dead deciduous tree trunk, sometimes in a large branch or in living trees

Average clutch: 4 chestnut-sized, white eggs

Incubation period: 15–18 days

Fledging age: 26–28 days

Lifespan: Up to 13 years in wild

Predators: Sharp-shinned hawks, Cooper's hawks, goshawks, great horned owls, martens; nests also raided by squirrels and weasels

Estimated Ontario population: 150,000

Species that use old pileated woodpecker holes: Flying squirrels, red squirrels, martens, fishers, owls, wood ducks, hooded mergansers, common mergansers, bluebirds, kestrels, starlings, mice

Nesting range: Southern Ontario, except extreme southwest, to southern James Bay and western mid-boreal forest; also in all other provinces except island of Newfoundland

Also see: Flicker, Yellow-bellied Sapsucker

chamber, starting in late March or April. Pileated woodpeckers are one of the few bird species known to actually pick up and carry their eggs to an alternate nest site if their chosen tree ever becomes unstable.

In May and June, the birds take turns through the day incubating the eggs and brooding the noisy hatchlings, with the devouted dads taking sole nest-sitting duties at night. Mothers sleep in roosting cavities nearby. Young woodpeckers begin sticking their heads out of the nest hole when about two weeks old, and continue to be fed by regurgitation for a while after fledging, usually around late June. They then start following their parents, and after watching Mom or Dad rip open a tree full of ants, they take over. Families stay together till September, when the young disperse, flying up to 30 kilometres (19 miles) before finding dead trees in which to carve winter roosting chambers.

RAVEN
Commanding Ancient Respect

From the time spear-bearing humans fanned out from Africa some 100,000 years ago, they have undoubtedly been intimates of the raven. The bold black bird commonly forms close associations with northern big-game hunters, scavenging at wolf kills and following polar bears out onto Arctic pack ice to clean up seal carcasses. The largest of all songbirds, the raven has a wide vocabulary and a complex social hierarchy, based on size and age. Pairs or groups of ravens often use teamwork to flush and ambush prey or steal food. The bird's size, smarts, grace and longevity, as well as its close association with death, must have made a profound impression on our forbears and sparked their imaginations. European cave paintings apparently investing birds with mystical significance date back as far as 32,000 years, and many

Brain as a percentage of body mass: Raven 1.3%, human 1.5%, chicken 0.1%

Calls: Scores of known utterances, including loud, resonant, croaking "oook, oook, oook," a deep "caw," a deep, bell-like "crong," a metallic "tok" and a buzzing burble like an electrical current; males have deeper voices

Mimicry: Able to imitate many sounds, including human words, machinery and explosions

Length: 55–68 cm (22–27 in)

Wingspan: 1.2–1.4 m (4–4.7 ft)

Weight: 1–1.5 kg (2.2–3.3 lb)

Beak length: 6–9 cm (2.4–3.5 in)

Markings: Adults are glossy black all over; juveniles are duller, with some brown in wings and tail

Colour origin: In Greek mythology, Apollo turned his snow-white raven messenger black in a fit of rage when it told him his girlfriend was unfaithful; British Columbia Native peoples said higher spirits changed Raven black because of his mischief; the Siberian Voguls said the raven was turned from white to black as punishment for eating corpses

Alias: Northern raven, common raven, corby, *le grand corbeau, Corvus corax*

Name origin: Both the scientific name *corax* and the ancient German *khraben,* from which derives "raven," are onomatopoeias of the bird's harsh calls

Name for a group: An unkindness of ravens

Whereabouts: Coniferous and mixed forests

Food: Carrion, birds as large as grouse, geese and gulls, eggs and nestlings, mice, squirrels and other small rodents, fish stolen from ospreys and eagles, crayfish, mussels, insects, berries, seeds; wolf droppings when all else fails

Home range: 30–200 km^2 (12–77 sq. mi) for resident nesters; non-breeders can wander over more than 1,800 km^2 (700 sq. mi)

Nest: Thick, bulky collection of sticks, twigs, clumps of grass and soil, 40–150 cm (1.3–5 ft) wide, 20–60 cm (0.7–2 ft) high, with a central depression lined with moss, lichens, bark shreds and fur; usually on a cliff ledge or on top of a tall pine or spruce; also in hydro and water towers

Telltale nesting signs: Piles of fallen sticks and streaks of white droppings on or below cliffs or trees

Average clutch: 3–5 plumsized, greenish eggs with dense brown and olive spotting or blotches

Incubation period: 20–25 days

Fledging age: 4–7 weeks

Nesting success: Avg. 70–80%

authorities believe the magical avian depictions are of ravens.

Northern cultures around the world had taboos against killing the brainy birds, which figure prominently in their cosmologies. Ravens play a role in most of the nearly universal flood stories. Among Ontario Native peoples, the bird is sometimes named as the first of several animals that after the deluge tried to gather mud to form a new world. In the Bible, the raven is the first creature sent by Noah to seek dry land. For the Native peoples of British Columbia and Alaska, the raven is not only the chief player in the flood tale, but the bringer of the sun, moon, stars and fresh water, as well as the creator of people. The Inuit said the raven, by flicking sparkling flakes of the mineral mica into the sky, created the Milky Way.

Early North Americans, Siberians, Chinese, Greeks and Scandinavians thought ravens controlled or at least influenced the weather. Norse and Celtic gods and semi-divine warriors often took the form of ravens or employed them as their messengers. Early Irish and Anglo-Saxon literature is also rife with references to ravens following armies to feast on the spoils of the battlefield. The Vikings embraced the gruesome association, hoisting the image of the black scavenger on their standards.

Christian lands pillaged by the hardy northmen came to associate the ravenous bird with pagan religions, death and ill omen. The raven was said to "shake contagion from her sable wing," and was blamed for the pestilence that came with war. Ravens seen scavenging on dead livestock and wild game were held responsible for their deaths. European settlers brought their persecution of the bird to North America. Guns, traps, poison and forest-clearing lumberjacks pushed ravens, with the wolf, from settled areas back into the fastness of the Canadian Shield.

In recent decades, ravens have prospered and pushed back into southern Ontario, especially along the Niagara Escarpment. In 1993, one male even nested with a crow in Toronto, the first-ever confirmed cross-breeding of the two species. Ravens and crows are almost identical, but ravens are about one-third larger than and twice as heavy as crows, with a stouter beak and shaggy throat feathers. The best way to tell them apart is to look for the raven's rounded, paddle-shaped tail in flight; the back of a crow's tail is straight-cut. Ravens also have a much deeper, hoarser voice than their smaller, adaptable cousins and are greater aeronautic enthusiasts, soaring, swooping, coasting and generally handling themselves more like hawks.

Ravens also don't migrate like crows. Mates remain together on the same territory for life. They spruce up their relationships early each year, performing breathtaking courtship flights in the bitterly cold, clear skies of February. Couples fly in sublime synchronized, circling manoeuvres, wing tips and talons occasionally touching, rising hundreds of metres before sometimes plunging in steep dives and somer-saulting just before pulling out of the descent. Upon landing, they often nuzzle beaks, preen and caress each other's breast and head feathers.

A choice cliffside or treetop nesting spot may be used off and on by successive genera-tions, some reportedly for up to 100 years.

First-year survival: About 50%

Age at first breeding: 3–8 years

Lifespan: Up to 17 years in wild, at least 44 years in captivity

Predators: Probably great horned owls, golden eagles and coyotes; nests also pos-sibly raided by hawks, martens, raccoons, bears

Estimated Ontario popula-tion: 600,000

Average population density: 2–10 pairs per 10 km^2 (4 sq. mi)

Raven takeoffs: Make 2 or 3 hops first, rather than lifting straight up like crows

Raven play: Sometimes seen sliding down snowbanks, fly-ing upside-down and frolick-ing in the sky, apparently playing tag and dropping sticks and other objects for each other to catch

Accolades: Official bird of the Yukon; battle standard of Danish Vikings and William the Conqueror; most fre-quently depicted figure on west-coast totem poles

Odin's ravens: Hugin and Mumin ("Thought" and "Memory") flew over the world every day and related all they saw and heard to the ruler of the Norse gods, giv-ing him universal knowledge

"Raven's knowledge": Irish term meaning to see and know everything

Ravenstone: An Old English name for the site of executions

Tower of London ravens:
After the Great Fire of
London, in 1666, ravens
were persecuted for scav-
enging, but King Charles II
was warned to keep them at
the Tower of London or dis-
aster would strike the
monarchy; six ravens have
been kept at the Tower cas-
tle ever since

Notable deeds: Ravens fed
Elijah in the Jordanian
desert, and a raven released
from a wayward Viking ship
flew west without returning,
leading the way to the settlement of Iceland

Nesting range: All Ontario
south to northeastern shore
of Lake Ontario, the Oak
Ridges Moraine above
Toronto, the Niagara
Escarpment to Burlington
and southern Grey and
Bruce counties; also in all
other provinces and territories north to Ellesmere
Island

**Age of oldest corvid (raven
family) fossils:** 25 million
years

**Number of corvid species
nesting in Ontario:** 2

**Number of corvid species
worldwide:** 47

Also see: Snowshoe Hare,
Wolf

Hawks and owls also often claim old raven nests.
A pair of ravens usually spends two or three
weeks building a new nest or renovating an old
one, breaking large, dead sticks off trees and
piling them up. They become quiet once egg-
laying begins, most commonly around mid- to
late March, the female tending the nest while
her mate brings home the bacon.

Things become noisy again when the nestlings hatch and start begging for food. As they
grow, the young cry out in a muffled crowlike
"caw." For about 18 days, fathers continue to be
the main providers while mothers shelter their
broods. Males sometimes even carry water in
their throats for the nestlings to drink.

Once fledged, the young hunt and scavenge
widely with their parents. After three or four
months, they drift off on their own, often forming
wandering winter flocks with other adolescents
up to several years old. Flocks often work coop-
eratively, with scouts leading others to new food
sources. Since mating pairs don't take kindly to
dinner guests in their territories, the younger
ravens use force of numbers to belly up at
carrion feasts. While a deer carcass might feed a
territorial pair for weeks in winter, a flock of
several dozen can strip it bare within a few days.
When the going's good, each bird takes portions
of a big feed to hide in the snow and returns to
them later.

RED-BREASTED NUTHATCH
Spike-nosed Conifer Hopper

Length: 11–12 cm (4.5–4.7 in)
Wingspan: 20–22 cm (8–
8.7 in)
Weight: 8–13 g (0.3–0.4 oz)
Markings: Blue-grey back
and wings; rusty-red undersides; black eye stripe and
crown; white cheeks, neck
and stripe above eyes
Alias: Canada nuthatch, red-
bellied nuthatch, topsy-turvy
bird, devil-down-head, *la sit-
telle à poitrine rousse, Sitta
canadensis*
Calls: Oft-repeated, high
nasal beeps, written "ank,
ank ank"; song is a weak
staccato trill, like a high-
pitched puttering of the lips,
given 12–50 times a minute,
heard mainly in March and
early spring
Flying speed: Estimated up
to 32 km/h (20 mph)
Whereabouts: Evergreen and
mixed woods with lots of fir
and spruce trees; often near
beaver ponds and other forest edges
Food: Conifer seeds, acorns,
beechnuts, cherry pits,
berries, sap, beetles, grubs,
caterpillars, moths, wasps,
crane flies, spiders, insect
and spider eggs
Breeding territory:
0.2–10 ha (0.5–25 acres)
Nest: Cavity 6–20 cm (2.3–
8 in) deep; entrance 2–9 cm

Nuthatches are munchkin-like birds with over-
sized beaks and feet, which they use to good
effect. Unlike most perching birds, which cling
to branches with three toes gripping forwards
and one back, a nuthatch's long, curving claws
are oppositely aligned. This enables them to
wind rapidly around branches and scoot down
tree trunks head first, finding hidden insect
larvae, spiders or their eggs missed by brown
creepers and downy woodpeckers searching
bark fissures and crevices from the opposite
direction. Nuthatches even follow woodpeckers
to snap up the rattled insects left in their wake.

(0.8–2.4 in) wide, with conifer resin smeared around it; twigs, bark strips and grass line cavity inside; usually 3–9 m (10–30 ft) up in a dead or dying tree, often aspen, balsam poplar or white birch

Average clutch: 5–6 raspberry-sized, reddish-brown-specked white eggs

Incubation period: 12–13 days

Fledging age: 18–21 days

Fledgling dependence on parents: At least 2 weeks

Age at first breeding: 1 year

Nesting success: About 70%

Lifespan: Up to 7 years in wild

Predators: Sharp-shinned and Cooper's hawks, merlins, red squirrels, weasels; nests also raided by house wrens, mice

Estimated Ontario population: 3 million

Nesting range: All Ontario except extreme southwest and western Hudson Bay lowlands; also in all other provinces and territories except Nunavut

Number of nuthatch species nesting in Ontario: 2

Number of nuthatch species worldwide: 31

Also see: Broad-winged Hawk, Balsam Fir, Red Pine, Trembling Aspen

Red-breasted nuthatches also habitually hang upside-down at flimsy branch tips, especially in winter, using their long, needlelike bills to pick seeds out of open fir and spruce cones. But because their vice-grip claws aren't adept at nimble tasks, they jam shelled seeds they collect from the ground into bark crevices so that they can extract the kernel. Similarly wedged nuts are "nut hacked" apart with their piercing beaks. They commonly stash such morsels away in nooks and crannies for later snacking, usually on the same day.

The pointy beaks come in handy as well for chiselling out nesting quarters in dead trees in March. Red-breasted nuthatches are the smallest of Ontario's cavity-carving birds, with the home handy-hen taking the lead while her partner stands guard and provides the meals. They only rarely choose to occupy an old woodpecker hole or natural cavity instead of doing the work themselves. After finishing the excavation in five to 16 days, they collect wads of thick, gooey sap oozing from wounds in nearby spruce, fir or pine trees. The pitch is smeared liberally around the rim of the entrance. The stubby-tailed birds must afterwards nimbly fly straight in and out of the hole to avoid touching and getting stuck in the goo. Some authorities speculate that the sticky resin may discourage nest robbers such as such as red squirrels and mice, as well as cavity-nesting competitors, from entering the chambers. Others believe it is aimed primarily at keeping out pests and parasites, such as ants, mites and ticks. Whichever the case, it seems to work, since nuthatches enjoy high nesting success for small songbirds.

After the nesting season, red-breast mates often remain on the same territory, though roosting in separate tree holes, through the winter. But when conifer-cone crops are poor, especially in northern Ontario, many pick up and leave for bird feeders and natural food sources to the south. Sizable irruptions occur roughly every two or three years, beginning as early as mid-summer but usually peaking in October. Most birds move to southern Ontario, Michigan, Wisconsin and Minnesota, though some fly as far as Florida and Texas. They often mix with foraging flocks of chickadees, kinglets, thrushes and other songbirds. Smaller numbers return in April, apparently because some find southern living to their liking and end up nesting in their new domain.

In deciduous and mixed forests, **white-breasted nuthatches** are more sedentary. They focus on pecking apart acorns and nuts in fall and winter and have a lower, less nasal call than their smaller red-breasted cousins. They also smear the portals of their nest cavities, but with the squashed bodies of insects, rather than resin. The bug bodies contain defence chemicals which may work in the same way as sap from evergreens. It's also been found that many hawks and some songbirds continually supply their nests with cedar bark and green leaves that contain natural pesticides.

RED-EYED VIREO
Seldom Seen, Always Heard

Calls: Song usually couplets of short, up-and-down whistled phrases of 2–5 notes each, similar to robin's but slower, repeated 25–85 times a minute; also sharp, high single notes and a catbird-like mew

Number of different phrases in a male's repertoire: 19–117, used in thousands of different combinations

Record for most songs sung by a male in 1 day: 22,197

Length: 12–13 cm (4.7–5.1 in)

Wingspan: 23–25 cm (9–10 in)

Weight: 16–20 g (0.6–0.7 oz)

Markings: Greenish-brown back, grey cap, white streak

Like a TV evangelist – "Do you believe? Do you repent?" – the red-eyed vireo, or preacher bird, seems to sermonize with an endless stream of rhetorical questions, its voice rising up and down in couplets all day long. Though the greenish birds are difficult to see, male red-eyes make their presence known by belting out up to 3,000 songs an hour from the treetops, from May till midsummer, including on hot days when most other birds are taking a siesta. They're known to sing even with their mouths full of insects, which they mostly pluck from leaves. Forests saturated with vireo song throughout much of Ontario testify to their status as one of the most abundant of woodland birds.

While males call attention to themselves high in the canopy, female red-eyed vireos nest silently in the understorey below. The retiring females build their nests in four or five days in late May or June and do all the egg-sitting. They also serve up three-quarters of the food after the nestlings hatch, with each offered several juicy caterpillars, beetles or spiders every hour. The nest usually hangs between thin, forked, outer branches of a sapling, which will not support raccoons, skunks and other predators. Dangers increase, though, if forest fragmentation brings edge habitat closer. The sleek, sparrow-sized birds need at least half a hectare (1.2 acres) of unbroken forest with an understorey shroud of shrubs and saplings to nest successfully. In vulnerable forests, up to 75 per cent of their nests fall victim to brown-headed cowbirds, parasitic denizens of open areas and forest fringes. Cowbirds lay single eggs in the nests of other species for them to raise, usually to the detriment of the hosts' real offspring.

Despite the perils faced by vireos on their nesting grounds, they and other tropical migrants find many compelling advantages to their northern nurseries. Warmer regions support a greater abundance and variety of life-forms than do northern temperate areas, which means there are also more predators, including a plethora of nest-robbing snakes, and more competition for space among resident nesters. An average of only about a quarter of all nesting attempts in the rainforest succeed, much less than in the north. Migrant songbirds probably evolved from tropical species that gradually extended their ranges northward into less crowded environs. They retreated with each renewal of winter but kept returning to the vast nesting opportunities and superabundance of insects available in a

over red eyes, white undersides

Alias: Preacher bird, greenlet, teacher, le viréo aux yeux rouges, Vireo olivaceus

Name for a group: A cheer of vireos

Whereabouts: Deciduous and mixed forests with aspens, birch, maples or beech and a continuous understorey of saplings and shrubs

Food: Caterpillars, beetles, wasps, bees, ants, flies, spiders; berries if insects are scarce

Breeding territory: 0.7–2.4 ha (1.7–6 acres)

Nest: Neatly woven, deep, thin-walled, like a pencil cup, 6–9 cm (2.4–3.5 in) wide, of fine bark strips, moss, grass and wasp-nest paper, bound with spider webs, camouflaged with lichens; slung between fork of a slender branch, usually 2.5–4.3 m (8–14 ft) up in a deciduous sapling

Average clutch: 3–4 olive-sized white eggs with dark brown marks; sometimes 2 broods a year

Incubation period: 12–14 days

Hatchling weight: 1.5–1.8 g (0.05–0.06 oz)

Fledging age: 10–12 days

Nesting success: Average 60–75%

Age at first breeding: 1 year

Annual survival: About 50% for adults

Lifespan: Up to 10 years in wild

Predators: Sharp-shinned
hawks; nests also raided by
blue jays, crows, grackles,
raccoons, skunks, red squir-
rels, chipmunks
**Estimated Ontario popula-
tion:** 9 million
Density in prime habitat:
1 pair/ha (2.5 acres)
Nesting range: All Ontario
except extreme northwest;
also in all other provinces
and territories except
Nunavut
**Spring migration in central
Ontario:** Mid-May to mid-
June
**Fall migration in central
Ontario:** Late Aug. to late
Sept.
Winter whereabouts:
Amazon rainforest
Other night-flying migrants:
Warblers, sparrows, thrush-
es, flycatchers, kinglets,
woodpeckers
**Portion of Ontario's bird
population that leaves the
province in fall:** More than
75%
**Number of vireo species
nesting in Ontario:** 6
**Number of vireo species
worldwide:** 43
Also see: Common
Yellowthroat, Veery, Yellow-
rumped Warbler

northern spring. Longer northern days also afford more hunting time and faster nestling growth.

Red-eyed vireo chicks start to fly when as little as 10 days old, though their parents keep feeding them for up to a couple more weeks. Their brown eyes don't take on their species-defining ruby hue until the birds' first winter. Vireos join large mixed flocks of warblers and other long-distance migrants heading south on August and September nights, many of them flying straight across the Gulf of Mexico. Like almost one-quarter of the billions of migrant songbirds reaching South and Central America, once in their Amazonian wintering grounds red-eyed vireos drop their almost exclusively insectivorous diet and become vegetarians, dining on tropical fruits until the Northern Hemisphere tilts back towards the sun in March and beckons them north to Ontario.

RED-WINGED BLACKBIRD
Bellicose Master of the Marsh

He'll be there beside the river,
When Winter finally breaks its bones,
He'll be king among the rushes,
He'll be master of his home.
— David Francey, "Red-winged Blackbird"

A dominant male red-winged blackbird in his prime is an iron-fisted patriarch commanding the best and biggest stretch of marsh, a harem of several mates and the fear and respect of his community. He is a warrior troubadour who, many bird experts believe, has learned more songs than any of his rivals, warding them off with his virtuosity. While he sings, he flashes his

Length: 17–25 cm (7–10 in)
Wingspan: 30–36 cm (1–1.2 ft)
Weight: Females 37–47 g (1.3–1.7 oz), males 62–70 g (2.2–2.5 oz)
Markings: Males black with scarlet and yellow wing epaulets; females streaked brown and beige, with yellowish orange head stripe and chin; juveniles similar to females, but year-old males develop reddish shoulder patches
Alias: Red-wing, marsh blackbird, red-winged starling,

red-winged oriole, *le carouge à épaulettes, Agelaius phoeniceus*

Calls: Song a gurgling "conk-a-ree," rolling at the end like a referee's whistle; also loud clicks, clacks, high whistles, chirps and chatters

Flying speed: 27–45 km/h (17–28 mph)

Whereabouts: Marshes, swamps, slow rivers, meadows, scrubby fields

Food: Caterpillars, dragonflies, damselflies and other invertebrates during breeding season; mostly seeds and small fruits from late summer to early spring

Breeding territory: 0.02–0.5 ha (0.06–1.2 acres) in marshes, avg. 0.16 ha (0.4 acres); 0.2–3 ha (0.5-7.5 acres) in thickets and grassland, avg. 0.3 ha (0.75 acres)

Portion of red-wings that are polygamous: Females 50–99%, males up to 90%

Nest: Deep, tightly woven basket, about 9 cm (3.5 in) wide, of strips of cattail leaves, sedges and grass, built on cattails, reeds, small trees or shrubs, usually less than 2 m (6.6 ft) above the water or ground

Average clutch: 3–5 black and purple speckled or light blue-green streaked eggs, about the size of grapes

Incubation period: 10–12 days

Hatchling weight: 2.75 g (0.1 oz)

bright scarlet epaulets, badges of age and experience that similarly convince others not to challenge him.

The flickering of red wing patches in flight, like technicolour strobe lights, is one of the earliest signs of spring. Flocks of male red-wings come first, often arriving when marshes are still frozen. They snap up weed seeds and tear into fluffy cattail seed heads for the tiny, overwintering caterpillars of the cattail worm moth nestled inside. Though they forage and roost together at first, they spend gradually more time each day staking out their turf in the marsh, singing boldly from prominent perches, chasing and tussling in a never-ending game of border encroachment. Less successful homesteaders are crowded out of prime marsh real estate and forced to establish territories in scrubby meadows or thickets.

Females, who arrive two to four weeks after the males, do not marry for love. They look for the safest, buggiest patch of marsh for raising a family, and mate with whoever happens to occupy it. Males will breed with and defend as many females as are interested in settling in their domain. Each female maintains her own nesting zone within her mate's territory, and tries to keep out potential new concubines. Two or three wives is common for a well-situated male, though harems of up to 15 have been noted. With these red-patched sultans monopolizing virtually all available females, there are many luckless bachelors, mostly one- and two-year-olds, forced to be non-territory-holding floaters, always on the lookout to usurp the holdings of older birds and constantly being chased off or thrashed by them.

Female red-wings are certainly not stand-by-your-man types. Although they may return to the same territory to mate every year, they show no qualms about having flings with trespassing scoundrels when the lord of the manor is away feeding or defending some other part of his realm. Studies suggest between one-quarter and half of hatchlings are fathered through extramarital affairs, usually involving next-door neighbours.

Resembling big brown-streaked sparrows, females effectively blend with their nests, which they build by themselves in late April or May. If predators are close by, their warrior mates try to distract or drive them away, exploding from the cattails with a loud burst and splash of colour. Male red-wings have even been known to strike humans that come too close to a nest. Blackbirds also commonly band together to mob owls, crows, hawks, foxes and weasels. Despite all the vigilance, predators often make suppers of the contents of about half of all red-wing nests in some areas.

Busy with all of their bellicose duties, fathers have almost no part in domestic duties, even leaving all or most of the feeding of their multiple broods to the opposite sex. As their offspring fledge, however, the distant dads contribute more substantially for up to a couple of weeks to help set them off in the world. Mothers shepherd and feed them for as much as three weeks more, in flocks that venture from the marsh on summers days to forage for seeds and berries in fields and clearings. Adult males form their own large, roving late-season flocks. Females usually migrate south first, after all the birds gravitate to

Feedings at nest: Avg. 11/hour

Fledging age: 10–13 days

Age at first breeding: Females 1 year, males 2–3 years

Nestlings that survive to fledge: 30–60%

Annual survival: Adults avg. 40–60%

Lifespan: Adults avg. 2–2.5 years; up to 15 years in wild

Predators: Sharp-shinned hawks, owls, herring gulls, foxes; nests also raided by mink, raccoons, skunks, weasels, crows, blue jays, grackles, marsh wrens, water snakes

Density in prime habitat: Commonly 10–100 pairs per km^2 (0.4 sq. mi), up to 1,000 pairs per km^2

Estimated Ontario population: 4 million

Nesting range: Most of Ontario except far northwest; also in all provinces and territories except Nunavut

Spring migration in central Ontario: Late Mar. to early May

Fall migration in central Ontario: Early Sept. to late Oct.

Average migration distance: 1,000–1,400 km (620–870 mi); females avg. 230 km (140 mi) farther than males; juveniles avg. 230 km farther than adults

Winter whereabouts: Southern Ontario to northern Florida, with most

traditional staging areas, such as Holland Marsh and the marshes of Long Point, where many thousands may roost together between late August and September while they moult and build up their fat reserves. Some winter roosts in the U.S. swell to several million. Indeed, red-wings are believed to be the most numerous single species of land bird in North America, with an estimated winter population of about 190 million. Their giant flocks are considered a plague in some agricultural areas. Hundreds of thousands of blackbirds a year are poisoned by pesticides or detergents that cause their feathers to lose their insulating abilities. But their numbers persist. Red-wings are a tough bunch.

Winter and migrant flocks of red-wings are mixed with smaller numbers of their blackbird relatives, primarily common grackles and brown-headed cowbirds. Piercing golden eyes set **grackles** apart in a sea of blackbirds. In flight, they're distinguished by their long, wedge-shaped tails. The black, iridescently feathered birds often settle into loose colonies of 10 or so nests, spaced as close as five metres (16.5 feet) from each other, in evergreens along watersides, forest edges and in swamps. They are decidedly omnivorous, eating everything from insects, berries, nuts and seeds to mice, frogs, snakes, crayfish, small birds, nestlings and eggs. They often show up around campgrounds and cottage decks, boldly vying with chipmunks and red squirrels for any peanut or piece of scrambled eggs falling on the ground or left unattended.

ROBIN
Perennial Springtime Favourite

The sight of a robin bob-bob-bobbing along on freshly thawed ground is one of the most fabled first signs of spring. But in southern and even parts of central Ontario, some hardy, resourceful robins never actually leave during winter. Instead they band together in small flocks and retire to sheltered areas, such as cedar swamps and dense, brushy ravines. Their numbers vary with the severity of the season and the abundance of mountain ash berries, hawthorn apples and other durable fruits. If the snow cover in their sanctuaries persists above about five centimetres (two inches), they often flee farther south, only to return as the snow pack diminishes.

Most forest-dwelling robins of the Canadian Shield, though, migrate out of the province. Unlike their outgoing, settled cousins to the south, forest robins are shy and reclusive, keeping

Calls: Long, loud, bursts of repeated, rising and falling whistled musical phrases, each with several syllables, often varying, but commonly described as "cheer up; cheerily, cherry"; also a stuttered, laughing call, chirps, squeals and tweets

Length: 23–28 cm (9–11 in)

Wingspan: 38–42 cm (15–16.3 in)

Weight: 70–95 g (2.5–3.35 oz)

Markings: Males have a brick red breast, dark, sooty grey back; females have duller orange-red breast, grey-brown back; spotted breast on juveniles

Flying speed: 27–51 km/h (17–32 mph)

Alias: American robin, Canada robin, northern robin, common robin, redbreast, *le merle d'américain, Turdus migratorius*

Name for a group: A nest of robins

Whereabouts: Forest edges and clearings, open woods, fens, bogs

Food: In spring and summer, mostly beetle grubs and adults, caterpillars, earthworms, ants, grasshoppers and other insects, snails, spiders; through summer, increasing quantities of raspberries, serviceberries, wild cherries, dogwood berries and other fruits; in fall and winter, 90% mountain ash, poison ivy and juniper berries, sumac seeds, the fruits of hawthorn and other trees and shrubs

Breeding territory: Avg. 0.1–0.25 ha (0.25–0.6 acres)

Nest: Deep, tidy cup, 8–20 cm (3–8 in) wide, of mud, grass and twigs, usually 2–6 m (6.6–19.7 ft) high in understorey trees and shrubs, with branches above for concealment and shelter

Average clutch: 3–4 light blue-green eggs, about the size of peach pits

Incubation period: 12–14 days

Fledgling age: 9–16 days

Age at first breeding: 1 year

Annual survival: About 50% for adults

Lifespan: Rarely more than 4 years; up to 14 years in the wild, 17 years in captivity

well away from humans. Migrant males usually start singing as soon as they come back in spring – up to a week ahead of their less brightly attired better halves – when the overwintering robins are still largely silent. To human ears, their melodic carolling is a simple joyful ode to spring, one of the most widely recognized of all birdsongs. An Ojibway legend says robins sing to cheer people because they are descended from a boy who became a bird to escape the suffering of a too-difficult vision quest – an initiation rite involving fasting and dreaming – set by his father.

Singing robins are most prolific early in the breeding season, leading off with revelry well before daybreak. The hours around dawn are generally the busiest for breeding birds, the time when they most vigorously define their territories through song and confrontation. Male robins are very territorial, chasing each other away as they carve out their turf. Their songs, by serving as proprietary proclamations and warnings, help to minimize dangerous and exhausting combat. Early morning is also often when mates first pair up. A second peak of activity comes before sunset.

Experienced nesters usually reoccupy their old stomping grounds. Female robins spend three to 10 days putting down layers of mud and grass on their emerging nests. Sitting inside, they mould them into shape by pushing with their wings and stamping their feet for up to 10 seconds before turning several degrees and repeating the process, sometimes until they have completed several full rotations. They do virtually all of the incubating and brooding, leaving the nest only for about 10 minutes an hour during the day. But males feed both them and, later, their rapidly growing little ones. Juicy beetle grubs, caterpillars and other morsels are brought to the nest six or seven times an hour. Within about two weeks, the young are 10 times their hatching weight and are making their first flights. Fathers take the fledglings under their wings around June, tutoring them in the ways of finding food while their tireless spouses lay another batch of eggs, often after building a new nest, free of parasites that may have built up in the first one.

Though males diligently guard their territories from each other throughout the nesting period, at night they commonly leave their nesting spouses and bunk down together in dense tree cover. The roosts swell when fathers start admitting their fledgling charges to the formerly all-male evening clubs. They're joined by mothers with the second broods after they fledge. Gradually building by the score, or even hundreds, flocks become very noticeable by September, prior to and during migration.

Predators: Sharp-shinned and Cooper's hawks, goshawks, great horned owls, kestrels; nests also raided by blue jays, grackles, ravens, house wrens, martens, red squirrels, chipmunks, flying squirrels, raccoons, garter snakes

Average forest population density: 1–10 pairs per 10 km² (4 sq. mi)

Estimated Ontario population: 10 million

Accolades: Featured on extinct Canadian $2 bill; state bird of Michigan, Wisconsin and Connecticut

Famous robins: Rockin' Robin; the Red Red Robin; Robin Hood, Batman's sidekick

Nesting range: All Ontario; also all Canada to the tree line

Spring migration in central Ontario: Mid- Mar. to late Apr.

Fall migration in central Ontario: Sept. to early Nov.

Winter whereabouts: From about North Bay to Mexico; most Ontario birds go to Gulf of Mexico states

Also see: Hermit Thrush, Red-eyed Vireo, Yellow-rumped Warbler, Big Dipper

RUFFED GROUSE
Drummer of the Forest

The abundance of ruffed grouse made them vitally important to the Ojibway and Cree, especially in winter. One Ojibway creation story tells of the grouse being the first-born of the world's primal mother, Spirit Woman. The grouse stayed behind with her after all her other bird children flew off. Similarly, the hare and the whitefish remained when the rest of her animal and fish offspring ran, swam and waddled away. Like the grouse, the other two faithful children were staple foods for Woodland hunters, and so became totem animals of large Ojibway clans.

With only limited powers of flight, ruffed grouse, commonly called partridges in many places, are secretive chickens of the forest. When flushed from their hiding places, they overwhelm observers, exploding out of nowhere so suddenly that they are out of view before the shock of their thunderous flapping wears off. Flushed grouse usually fly straight up with their tails fanned out and then arc swiftly to another well-concealed spot. In the winter they might burst out from beneath powdery snow, where they take shelter during extreme cold spells. Grouse can actually fly quite silently if they wish, but by stirring up a commotion, they throw potential predators off guard and warn others of their kind to flee.

Grouse on the Canadian Shield are subject to cyclical population crashes every two to ten years

Ruffed grouse are intrinsically associated with aspens, on which they depend for much of their food and shelter. Starting as early as late March, males hoping to attract mates climb onto carefully chosen fallen logs, usually in dense stands of young aspen where branch cover will obscure them from the view of raptors. They then "drum" by flapping their wings, starting slowly and accelerating into a high-speed whir for about 10 seconds, like a motor being started. The low, deep thumping, almost felt more as a vibration in the listener's stomach, is inaudible to menacing owls. It is caused by the sound of air popping back into the vacuum created beneath the grouse's wings with each rapid, blurred beat he takes. Duelling drummers signal back and forth to each other from up to a kilometre (0.6 miles) away, marking off their breeding territories. Like songbirds, their sessions are especially persistent at dusk and dawn, though they sometimes jam through the night.

Weight: Females 450–600 g (1–1.3 lb), males 500–750 g (1.1–1.65 lb)

Markings: Mottled brown back and crested head, grey breast, black band at end of square-edged tail; black, iridescent neck ruffs; bare skin over eyes usually orangish on males

Brain size: 2 cm³ (0.1 cu. in)

Human brain size: 1,300 cm³ (79 cu. in)

Calls: Clucks, alarm whistles, hisses

Alias: Partridge, woods pheasant, birch partridge, pine hen, drumming grouse, drummer, tippet, long-tailed grouse, white flesher, wood grouse, *la gelinotte huppée*, *Bonasa umbellus*

Name origin of *grouse*: From Old English *gris*, meaning "grey"

Name for a group: A covey of grouse

Whereabouts: Forests with dense aspen sapling stands mixed with stands of larger aspens and other deciduous and evergreen trees as well as alder and willow thickets and clearings

Food: In winter, prefer male flower buds of trembling aspen, but also buds and twigs of white birch, largetooth aspen, willow, alder and hazel; in early spring, aspen, birch and willow catkins; in late spring and summer, leaves of aspen and other trees and plants, insects, occasionally snakes and frogs; in late summer and fall, seeds, berries, acorns, nuts, mushrooms; young eat 70% insects and worms in their first 2 weeks, 5% by late summer

Home range: 2–15 ha (5–37 acres) for individuals, about 20 ha (50 acres) for families

Drumming territory: Avg. 2 ha (5 acres)

Number of drumming logs per territory: Up to 6

Nest: Ground depression, about 15 cm (6 in) wide, lined with leaves and feathers, usually at the base of a tree or stump, in an area with little ground cover

Average clutch: 10–12 buff-coloured, walnut-sized eggs

Incubation period: 23–24 days

Hatchling weight: 11–13 g (0.4–0.45 oz)

Fledging age: 5–7 days

Age at first breeding: Females 1 year, males 1–2 years (about 1/3 of males are non-territorial)

Nest predation rate: 25–40%

Chick mortality in the first 6 weeks: About 60%

Annual survival: 35–50% for adults

Lifespan: Few live more than 2 years; up to 8 years in the wild

Predators: Goshawks, harriers, broad-winged and other hawks, great horned owls, barred owls, ravens, wolves, coyotes, foxes, lynx, bobcats, fishers; nests also raided by

When a female shows up, her drummer boy goes into a song-and-dance routine as well, strutting in front of her with tail spread, comb erect, wings hung low and fanning his long neck feathers so they look like an Elizabethan ruff. All the while he chortles softly. The attraction, at least for the female, ends soon after mating, which lasts two to three seconds. She steals off to lay her eggs and raise the young on her own, while the father resumes his drumming, soliciting all available females well into May. In September, when the angle of the sun is the same as in spring, some males may resume drumming briefly, just as songbirds sing a fleeting reprise.

Three to seven days after mating, expectant mother grouse scratch out nests in the duff at the base of trees or under logs. They choose spots with little ground cover, affording an open view of their surroundings. The sitting hens themselves are almost imperceptible against the leaf litter. A female takes two weeks or more to lay all her eggs, waiting for the last to drop before she starts incubating so that they'll hatch simultaneously. Unlike most naked newborn passerines, the wide-eyed, downy grouse hatchlings leave the nest and follow their mother as soon as they are dry, within a few hours of emerging from their shells, usually in June. They come into the world alert and instinctively knowing how to obey their mother's command calls to freeze, hide, come out or run.

In Ernest Thompson Seton's story "Redruff," from *Wild Animals I Have Known* — perhaps the best-selling Canadian book ever — he tells of how a mother grouse, taking the newly hatched chicks on their first trip, resorts to the classic broken-wing distraction display when a fox shows up to spoil the parade. With a quick, clucked signal from the mother, her hatchlings immediately hide in the ground litter while she lures the fox away, keeping just out of his jaws, for half a kilometre. Then she flies up and circles back to the exact spot where the chicks remain in silent hiding until she gives the "all-clear."

Chicks stay close to their mother, always on the move, in a circuit of sites they visit through the spring and summer. After the young fledge, families roost and often feed together in trees. Those that survive to September are gripped with a crazed wanderlust that sends them off on their own, serving to disperse the population and avoid inbreeding. They may journey anywhere from less than a hundred metres (109 yards) to more than 10 kilometres (six miles) over two or three weeks. Seton described the movement, known as the fall shuffle, as a strange kind of madness that makes them frantic and clumsy, travelling at night and flying into things.

As far back as 1721, closed hunting seasons were imposed in Canada for ruffed grouse because of sudden scarcity. Like snowshoe hares, grouse on the Canadian Shield are subject to cyclical population crashes, especially in northern areas, about every two to 10 years. The reasons are still not known for sure, though hunting apparently has little to do with it. Some authorities tie the phenomenon to invasions of hungry goshawks – serious grouse connoisseurs – great horned owls and other avian predators flying from the north after snowshoe hare populations crash there. Others speculate that heavy-seed crop years may drain much of

red squirrels, skunks, raccoons, mink, weasels, crows

Normal grouse density in prime habitat: 7–22/km² (17–57 per sq. mi)

Fall density at peak of population cycle: 47–137/km² (123–355 per sq. mi)

Scat: Curved, grey-white droppings, 2–4 cm (0.8–1.8 in) long

Scat production: Avg. of 4 droppings per hour

Nesting range: Most of Ontario, except extreme southwest and far northwest; also in all other provinces and territories except Nunavut

First appearance of grouse: 55–67 million years ago

Number of grouse species nesting in Ontario: 3

Other upland fowl species native to Ontario: Wild turkey, northern bobwhite, willow ptarmigan

Upland fowl extirpated from Ontario: Greater prairie-chicken

Ontario upland fowl most at risk: Northern bobwhite

Upland fowl species introduced in southern Ontario: Ring-necked pheasant, gray partridge

Number of upland fowl species worldwide: More than 210

Also see: Snowshoe Hare, Hemlock, Trembling Aspen

the nutrients from trees, leaving too little in buds and twigs to support high grouse populations in winter. Over-browsed vegetation, such as aspen, birch and jack pine, may also produce less tasty, less nutritious foliage as a defence measure. Overcrowded grouse themselves probably become stressed. Parasites and disease spread easily in close company. The population then suddenly plummets to a tiny fraction of what it was. Though grouse are largely sedentary, such catastrophes can sometimes lead to mass movements on broad fronts.

SHARP-SHINNED HAWK
Diminutive Songbird Nabber

A sudden, deadly swoop has ended many a song-bird lover's moment of finch- or warbler-viewing bliss. The "tragedy" of a small bird suddenly snatched in the talons of a sharp-shinned hawk, bolting in from nowhere, has likewise befuddled outdoor instructors introducing the beauty of nature to schoolchildren at nature-trail bird feeders. Yet for many, even children, it's an exhil-arating rush to witness this pure force of nature.

A diminutive hawk about as small as a blue jay, the sharp-shin is a secretive, exquisitely designed small-bird nabber. It cruises silently at treetop level, scanning for feathered meals, and then darts down upon them. It also sometimes ambushes its prey, or stealthily stalks them. Relatively short, rounded wings and a long, rud-derlike tail make the sharpie very agile for ducking through tangled branches to capture

Number of visual cells in a hawk's retina: Up to 1 million/mm²

Number of visual cells in a human's retina: Up to 200,000/mm²

Flying speed: 26–96 km/h (16–60 mph)

Length: Males 24–27 cm (9.5–10.5 in), females 29–34 cm (11.5–13.5 in)

Weight: Males 85–115 g (3–4 oz), females 150–220 g (5–8 oz)

Wingspan: Males 53–56 cm (21–22 in), females 58–65 cm (23–25.5 in)

Markings: Both sexes have grey back and upper wings, rust-coloured horizontal bars on breast and belly, grey-and-white-barred outer underwings, long, narrow tail (fanned when gliding) banded black and grey on top, and grey and white on underside; immature birds have a brown back and streaked white breast

Eye colour: Young have yellow eyes, turning orange when 1 year old and blood red at age 4

Alias: Sparrow hawk, sharp-shin, bird hawk, little blue darter, bullet hawk, slate-coloured hawk, pigeon hawk, *l'épervier brun, Accipiter striatus*

Calls: Rapid, high, shrill "kik, kik, kik," something like a flicker's call; also a long, thin squeal; males notably higher pitched than females

Whereabouts: Large stands of moist, dense coniferous and mixed forests and bogs

Food: 75–90% birds; males take prey weighing up to about 30 g (1 oz), such as warblers, sparrows, vireos, kinglets, flycatchers and chickadees; females take larger birds such as robins, woodpeckers, jays and blackbirds; also small rodents, frogs, insects

Home range: 1–3 km² (0.4–1.2 sq. mi)

Nest: Dense mass of twigs, lined with flakes of bark, 50–65 cm (20–26 in) wide, usually built across sturdy branches close to trunk high in an evergreen tree; sometimes in an old crow's nest

tiny birds. It's long legs and specially protracted, dagger-pointed middle toes are adept at reaching deep into narrow spaces for tiny victims. As its catches are most often inexperienced young, sick or injured birds, the sharp-shin plays the same role as the wolf and other predators in permitting only the fittest prey to survive and reproduce.

With large waves of migrant sparrows and other songbird suppers arriving in Ontario in April under cover of night, sharp-shinned hawks soon follow, coming in on day flights from points south. Adult sharpies, at least two years old, arrive first, intent on securing good breeding territories. Veterans usually return to the same area they occupied before, performing courtship flights and wooing with shrill squeals. They normally build a new nest every year, usually towards the margins of dense evergreen stands. They're largely silent and seldom seen around the nest site, going farther afield to hunt.

About two weeks after returning, females begin laying their eggs. The incredible size difference between the mates – among the greatest of all birds – reflects their duties. Females are almost twice as heavy as their partners in May, when they fatten up to produce a batch of four or five eggs. They settle their warming, protective bulk onto their clutches for the duration of the incubation and are fed by their little, high-voiced husbands. Using their sleek build to their advantage, males can get in at the more plentiful smaller birds. Once their downy white offspring hatch, fathers must nail six to 10 hapless warblers, sparrows or vireos a day to keep the brood fed. They present the catches to their hefty spouses, who then feed the young. After about two weeks, as the bounty of small songbird nestlings and fledglings begins to diminish, females start hunting as well, catching larger, meatier fare such as woodpeckers and jays.

Parents continue feeding their young for four or five weeks after they fledge in July, eventually reducing their rations. As the family wanders away from the nest area, it gradually breaks up. Though adolescents still aren't skilled hunters, they become independent just as the first southbound songbirds are passing through in August and are relatively easy to catch on unfamiliar ground. Young female sharp-shins soon follow these migrant meals south, while their smaller brothers are able to hold out on less food in the north for a little longer.

Tens of thousands of sharp-shinned hawks pour from forests in eastern Canada and the northeast United States every year. Being smaller and lighter than other Ontario hawks, sharp-shins flap their wings more in migration, rather than simply gliding from one thermal to another. They don't migrate over large bodies of water, but join other raptors along the seasonal hawk highways following the shores of the Great Lakes and the Atlantic, as well as along the Appalachians. The traffic seems to bring out the worst in sharp-shins, who are known for diving at each other and even at larger hawks. Immature female sharp-shin numbers peak along the north side of Lake Erie a little past mid-September, while the largest movements of juvenile males come about a week later. The same pattern holds for adults, with female migration hitting full stride in late September and males trailing them in early October.

Average clutch: 4–5 apricot-sized, white or blue-tinted eggs with brown blotching

Incubation period: 30–35 days

Fledging age: 21–27 days

Age at first breeding: 2 years

Lifespan: About 20% live more than 3 years; up to 19 years in wild

Predators: Harriers, goshawks, Cooper's and other larger hawks, possibly also great horned owls; raccoons raid nests

Density in prime habitat: 1–2 pairs per 10 km^2 (4 sq. mi)

Nesting range: Most of Ontario, though sparse in the north; also in all other provinces and territories except Nunavut

Spring migration in central Ontario: Early Apr. to early May

Fall migration in central Ontario: Early Sept. to mid-Oct.

Average number of migrating sharp-shins counted in autumn over Holiday Beach, Lake Erie: About 14,000

Distance travelled per day in migration: Up to 180 km (111 mi)

Winter whereabouts: From Ottawa Valley and southern edge of Canadian Shield to Panama; most Ontario birds go to the southeastern U.S.

Average number of goshawk matings per clutch: More than 500,

among the highest known
rates of avian sexual activity

**Hawk of central Ontario's
forested river bottom-
lands:** Red-shouldered
hawk

Bog and marshland hawk:
Northern harrier

Open-area raptors: Red-
tailed hawk, northern harrier,
kestrel, merlin, peregrine
falcon

Also see: Broad-winged
Hawk, Snowshoe Hare

Cooper's hawks are also expert songbird snatchers, though they also pick off a fair number of chipmunks and squirrels. They look very like sharp-shins but are about twice as big, though a small male may be close to the size of a large female sharpie. Cooper's also have a round-tipped tail, rather than straight-cut or slightly notched like a sharp-shin's. They are far less common in central Ontario, concentrated mostly in the hardwood forests of Shield-edge areas such as Muskoka and the Rideau Lakes.

The sharp-shinned hawk's other close relative, the powerful, reclusive **northern goshawk**, is bigger than a crow, with a dark blue-grey mantle, whitish belly and a boldly flared white stripe above its piercing red eye. Goshawks inhabit scattered stands of mature maple, beech, birch and hemlock across the region, where they scan the forest floor from numerous concealed hunting perches. Like those of their smaller accipiter cousins, their long tails enable the hawks to manoeuvre through dense branches and understorey shrubs with great speed and dexterity, sometimes in prolonged, determined chases. They are central Ontario's only really non-migratory hawks, though they sometimes move farther south when their main prey — hares and ruffed grouse — are at lows in their population cycles.

SONG SPARROW
Virtuoso with a Wide Repertoire

Fair little scout, that when the iron year
Changes, and the first fleecy clouds deploy,
Comest with such a sudden burst of joy.
– Archibald Lampman,
"The Song Sparrow"

Song sparrows, in Latin *Melospiza melodia,* are fully deserving of their name. In very early spring, peals of exuberant song sparrow melodies signal the turning of the year. Males pour it out for hours on end, each bird drawing from a repertoire of eight to 10 songs – sometimes as many as 20 – to create kaleidoscopic stylings. Even female song sparrows sing short, soft tunes

Calls: Songs are highly variable, but mostly in pattern of the first whistled note or phrase repeated 2 or 3 times, followed by a complex string of buzzy trills, twitters and whistles, often in the rhythm of "maids, maids, maids, put on your tea kettle-ettle-ettle," lasting 2 or 3 seconds; also a nasal "tchep" call note

Songbird species that sing 2 or more songs: About 75%

Length: 13–17 cm (5–7 in)

Wingspan: 20–23 cm (8–9 in)

Weight: 17–25 g (0.6–0.9 oz)

Markings: Streaky brown back and streaked white breast with a telltale dark spot in the middle; tan eye stripe with reddish-brown band above

Alias: Ground sparrow, bush sparrow, hedge sparrow, silver tongue, everybody's darling, marsh sparrow, *le bruant chanteur, Melospiza melodia*

Name for a group: A host of sparrows

Flying speed: 26–48 km/h (16–30 mph)

Heartbeats per minute: Avg. 450

Body temperature: Avg. 43°C (109°F)

Whereabouts: Lakeshores, riversides and other shrubby forest edges and clearings; small islands, thickets, brushy fields, marshes, swamps

Food: Seeds of grasses, smartweed and other plants; 40–45% insects during breeding season, especially caterpillars May–Jun. and grasshoppers and crickets in Aug.; also berries and other fruits in summer and fall

Average full passage of food through digestive tract: 2 hr, 15 min

Breeding territory: 0.2–0.6 ha (0.5–1.5 acres)

Nest: Neat cup, 11–20 cm (4–8 in) wide, 5–10 cm (2–4 in) high, of grass, stems, bark strips, leaves and rootlets

Average clutch: 4–5 olive-sized light green or pale blue eggs covered in brown spots

Incubation period: 10–14 days

Fledging age: 16–17 days

Age at first breeding: Females 1 year, males 1–2 years

Nests parasitized by cowbirds: About 23%

Annual survival: About 20% in first year, 40–60% for adults

Lifespan: Adults avg. 2.5 years; very few more than 4 years; up to 11 years in wild

Predators: Sharp-shinned and Cooper's hawks, foxes; nests also raided by blue jays, crows, squirrels, mink, garter snakes

Estimated Ontario population: 3 million

Nesting range: Throughout Canada to the tree line

early in the year. The most vocally versatile males get the greatest attention from the opposite sex and deference from rivals. They must also be good listeners, learning to recognize dozens of different songs performed by next-door neighbours in order to distinguish them from rabble-rousing drifters.

As the cacophony of red-winged blackbirds drops off in early summer and warbler choruses begin to thin, song sparrow refrains rise to the fore and continue through the hot days ahead. Song sparrows stay in top form because many hold on to nesting territories long enough to raise two broods of future songsters. Females usually spend four to 10 days in April or early May building their first nests on the ground, hidden amid shrubs and the previous year's long, dry plant stems. Later, after the leaves open and their spouses take charge of their newly fledged young, mothers who successfully nested early enough turn to the cover higher up in bushes to locate their second nests. They usually begin laying a new clutch six to 19 days after their first broods take wing. Despite the equal amount of care given to the second brood, sparrows from the first clutch have better chances for survival because they have more time to gain experience in their first summer.

Youngsters become independent when about four weeks old. Males spend the following weeks learning the craft of their species, listening intently to the songs of surrounding adults. Adding their own improvisations, they begin singing original ditties by autumn. By the time they begin their first breeding season the following spring, they've developed a full songbook that they'll follow for the rest of their lives.

Song sparrows return each spring to the same general locale where they hatched. Since they learn to sing in that milieu, generations of birds perpetuate each area's distinctive musical styles. Song sparrow enthusiasts estimate the birds may have up to 900 local "dialects" across the continent. The sparrows are abundant through-out North America, their range stretching from the Aleutian Islands to Newfoundland and south to Florida. In cottage country, they're especially fond of lakesides. Gifted soloists fre-quently provide the musical accompaniment for morning or afternoon coffee down by the dock or by a campsite rockface.

In less shrubby, more open areas such as meadows and fields, song sparrows seem to often have a markedly different, high-pitched buzzing call. These are, in fact, **savannah sparrows**, which also have streaky undersides but lack the distinct, central breast spot of the famous songster. Savannahs also usually sport yellowish "eye-brows" and a white strip along the top of their heads. Arriving in spring about a month later than song sparrows, they build their nests in small ground depressions obscured by tall grass.

Spring migration in central Ontario: Late Mar. to early May

Fall migration in central Ontario: Late Aug. to late Oct.

Winter whereabouts: From around Ottawa and Midland to Mexico; most go to the U.S.

Number of native sparrow species nesting in Ontario: 18

Ontario sparrow most at risk: Henslow's sparrow, designated endangered

Number of New World sparrow species in the Americas: 156

Also see: Goldfinch, Red-eyed Vireo, White-throated Sparrow

SPOTTED SANDPIPER
Teeter-tail of the Shoreline

Length: 18–20 cm (7–8 in)
Wingspan: 37–40 cm (15–16 in)
Weight: Males 34–41 g (1.2–1.4 oz), females 43–50 g (1.5–1.8 oz)
Markings: Greyish-brown back, dark round spots on white breast and belly; females most heavily spotted
Alias: Gutter snipe, teeter-tail, sand lark, peep, spottie, peet-weet, *le chevalier branle-queue, Actitis macularia*
Calls: Sharp, ringing whistle, commonly described as "peet" or "peet-weet"
Flying speed: 30–50 km/h (18–30 mph)
Whereabouts: Shores of lakes, beaver ponds and rivers; wetlands, mud flats

Among spotted sandpipers, it is the females that love 'em and leave 'em. A spotted lass may breed with up to four males in a season, though two is more common. After an amorous liaison, she drops her eggs and moves on as soon as the next available fella comes along, leaving hubby number one to incubate and raise the motherless offspring.

Female sandpipers begin the role reversal by arriving first on the breeding grounds in late April and early May, establishing and defending territories from each other. Within minutes of the males' return, the larger, more aggressive females woo them with aerial displays, singing, strutting and ruffling their neck feathers. Pairs stay together for about 10 days, until all the eggs are laid, though a female usually helps out a little longer with her last clutch of the year. Multiple

clutches may have evolved to offset the high predation of sandpiper eggs, laid on the ground in
relatively open areas. Usually only about 20 to
40 per cent hatch successfully. If their clutch is
lost, males may also mate again.

Sandpiper eggs are large and take longer to
hatch than those of many-other species. But in
June and July, the young emerge fully feathered
and able to walk within four hours, and catch
their own food when only a day or two old.
Fathers brood them for about 10 days and tend
them for at least a month. Meanwhile, footloose
mothers head south first, starting in July.

Sandpipers spend most of their time probing
shorelines with their long beaks for insects, especially at dawn and dusk, their tails constantly
bobbing or teetering up and down.

Although there are hundreds of thousands
of spotted sandpipers in the province, their
numbers, like those of many other shore birds,
have been declining in recent decades. In the
southern Shield, their total population appears to
be down by about 30 per cent from the 1980s.

Food: Midge, fly and mayfly larvae; worms, beetles, grubs, grasshoppers, crickets, snails, fish fry

Nest: Grass- or moss-lined ground depression hidden by long grass, rocks or rotting logs on or near shoreline

Average clutch: 4 brown-spotted, walnut-sized eggs

Incubation period: 19–22 days

Fledging age: 11–15 days

Lifespan: About 3 years; maximum 12 years in wild

Predators: Harriers, weasels, merlins; eggs or chicks also eaten by gulls, crows, grackles, mink, mice

Nesting range: All Ontario; also in all other provinces and territories

Winter whereabouts: From coastal South Carolina to Argentina

Number of shore bird species nesting in Ontario: 23

Also see: Mink

TREE SWALLOW
Swirling Above the Waterside

Length: 13–16 cm (5–7.3 in)
Wingspan: 30–35 cm (12–14 in)
Weight: 18–24 g (0.6–0.8 oz)
Markings: Like a uniform, with metallic, iridescent dark blue back and head, contrasting strongly with bright, clean white chin and undersides; very pointy wings; immatures and first-year females greyish brown on top
Alias: White-bellied swallow, *l'hirondelle bicolore*, *Tachycineta bicolor*
Name for a group: A flight of swallows
Calls: Thin, liquid twitter; single little notes; a "weet, trit, weet" song ending in a liquid warble

Spring, blessings and fertility were long believed, from ancient Greece to China, to arrive on the wings of swallows. So high was their repute that killing a swallow or destroying its nest was considered ill luck, even a sin, in some cultures. Folk stories even told of benevolent swallows comforting Jesus at the Crucifixion, from which their name *svalow,* Old Scandinavian for "console," comes. Because they return so suddenly in early spring, swirling down from high in the air to skim the surface of the water for emerging insects, people also once believed swallows hibernated in the mud beneath lakes or the sea. Others suggested that they wintered on the moon or in the heavens.

Modern bird-banding projects have established that tree swallows come from winter homes spread around the Gulf of Mexico and the Caribbean Sea. They migrate during the day, flying too swiftly for most raptor predators to catch them, feeding on tiny flies transformed from larvae by early warm spells. They are thought to use the sun as a compass, gauging it by an internal clock that compensates for its changing place in the sky. Tree swallows start to arrive in mid-April, earlier than any other swallow species, in a race for unoccupied nesting cavities in Ontario. They are the only swallows that have the ability to switch to berries when insects disappear during early season cold snaps.

Often returning to the same sites every year, tree swallows nest in early May, using tree cavities as close as 15 metres (50 feet) from each other. Unable, with their tiny beaks, to dig their own homes, they rely on old woodpecker holes or natural cavities. Dead, flooded trees in beaver ponds provide ideal sites, but the high demand by many species for such prime, sheltered housing limits the tree-swallow population. Some even resort to nesting in floating hollow logs and stumps. A high percentage of tree swallows don't get to nest, creating a Wild West atmosphere of fighting among both females and males as birds try to wrest the best loft apartments from each other.

But tree swallows do have their fun side. They are often seen collecting feathers, mostly white ones, to line their nest cavities, playfully bobbing them in air. They've even been observed swooping and plucking feathers off the backs of farm ducks. Though males arrive on the breeding grounds first and secure the nest sites, females do the renovations inside their quarters. Both take turns incubating the eggs.

Flying speed: 8–36 km/h (5–22 mph), faster in short bursts
Whereabouts: Lakes, rivers, wetlands, beaver ponds, meadows
Food: 90% midges, black flies, beetles, ants, stoneflies, aphids, mayflies, gnats; also moths, bees, other flying insects, bayberries, seeds
Nest: Usually in cavities of dead deciduous trees, especially birch, 1.5–6 m (5–20 ft) above ground, lined with feathers, pine needles and grass
Average clutch: 4–7 white, jellybean-sized eggs
Incubation period: 13–16 days
Fledging age: 18–22 days
Nest success: 60–95%
Annual survival: About 20% in first year, 40–60% for adults
Lifespan: Avg. 2.7 years; up to 12 years in wild
Predators: Sharp-shinned hawks, kestrels, merlins, owls; nests also raided by crows, grackles, raccoons, martens, weasels, chipmunks, deer mice, snakes
Estimated Ontario population: 400,000
Nesting range: All Ontario; also in all other provinces and territories
Spring migration in central Ontario: Mid-Apr. to early May
Fall migration in central Ontario: Mid-July to early Sept.

Winter whereabouts: Mostly
Florida and Gulf of Mexico;
some south to Venezuela
and sometimes north on
Atlantic coast to
Massachusetts
**Number of swallow species
nesting in Ontario:** 6
**Number of swallow species
worldwide:** 89–100
Also see: Osprey, Yellow-
bellied Sapsucker, Beaver,
White Birch, Rain

After the young hatch, they are fed every two or three minutes. Spending more time aloft than any other songbirds, swallows are in almost constant flight, swooping gracefully to snap insects from the air. They glide in circles, then flap quickly three or four times to gain altitude. Sometimes they dart close to a canoeist's or boater's head, veering off at the last second in their dogged pursuit of bugs. Because they fly just above water or ground, chasing insects that keep low when the pressure drops and rain is on the way, swallows are traditional weather portents.

When nesting's finished and the young have fledged, around midsummer, swallows seem to acquire a festive spirit that brings them together in huge numbers at traditional roosts, such as downtown Pembroke's riverside, Kingston's Cataraqui Marsh, and Long Point and Holiday Beach on Lake Erie. Up to 175,000 swallows of every species may gather at a single site in late July and early August, darkening the sky in spectacular swirlings as they disperse in the morning to forage and return again at dusk. The birds migrate en masse in late August, forming even larger flocks when they land in the Florida Everglades. These can number into the millions.

TURKEY VULTURE
Graceful, Soaring Scavenger

Turkey vultures are usually seen drifting or circling on wind currents high over lakeshores, fields, roads or cliffs, their two-metre- (6.6-feet-) wide wings held in a shallow V, slowly tilting from side to side, almost never flapping. Though sometimes mistaken for hawks, vultures are actually much larger, second only to eagles in Ontario's pantheon of soaring birds. The two-tone underside of their wings is their chief distinguishing feature.

While turkey vultures long resided in extreme southwestern Ontario, they gradually expanded north in the 20th century. They began breeding on the Canadian Shield in the east in the 1950s and now venture deep into the boreal forest. Ontario's vulture population has more than doubled since the 1980s. The spread of roads and resulting roadkill, greatly increased

Average glide ratio: 18 m (59 ft) forward to 1 m (3.3 ft) of drop

Highest migration altitude: 6,400 m (21,000 ft)

Length: 65–80 cm (26–31.5 in)

Wingspan: 1.7–2 m (5.8–6.6 ft)

Weight: 2–2.4 kg (4.4–5.3 lb)

Markings: Underside of wings distinctively black near front and grey at back; very dark brown body; red, featherless head, black on young birds until fall

Alias: Turkey buzzard, red-headed buzzard, TV, *l'urubu à tête rouge, Cathartes aura*

Name for a group: A coven of vultures

Whereabouts: Over open areas, large lakes, islands, swamps, ridges, cliffs
Food: Carrion, though may kill defenceless animals such as newborn rabbits
Home range: 130–470 km² (50–180 sq. mi)
Nest: None made; eggs laid on cliffs, in caves, hollow broken tops of large, dead trees, holes in logs and stumps, rock piles; often in swamps or thickets
Average clutch: 2 brown-splotched nectarine-sized eggs
Incubation period: 38–41 days
Fledging age: 60–70 days
Annual survival: 75–80% for adults
Lifespan: Up to 17 years in wild, 20 years in captivity
Predators: Foxes, possibly raccoons; nests also raided by raptors, skunks
Estimated Ontario population: 20,000
Nesting range: Southern Ontario to mid-boreal forest; also in all western provinces and Quebec
Spring migration in central Ontario: Early Apr. to late May
Fall migration in central Ontario: Early Sep. to late Oct.
Average daily migration distance: 30–70 km (19–43 mi)
Number counted migrating along lower Great Lakes in fall: Up to 9,000

deer numbers and climate warming may have all possibly contributed to the scavenging birds' advance.

Because vultures evoke images of slow, parched death in the desert, there's a perception that they are the lowlifes of the bird world. They live on rotting carcasses, don't take time to make real nests and even pee on their own legs to keep cool. When cornered, they vomit foul-smelling, half-decayed flesh and then hide their heads, ostrichlike, rather than fight. Turkey vultures don't sing, just hiss or growl on occasion. And their featherless, gnarled red heads do nothing for their standing in avian beauty contests.

But it's captivating to watch turkey vultures soar almost effortlessly overhead. Vultures are also notable as highly skilled specialists, with an acute sense of smell not possessed by other birds. They may forage all day over many kilometres before detecting the sweet scent of something dead. Then they home in with their keen eyes. In the U.S., one resourceful maintenance crew checking for gas-pipeline leaks turned to turkey vultures for help. The crew pumped a gas that reeks of rotten egg through the 70-kilometre (43-mile) line, then, to find the leaks, simply looked for circling vultures.

From their isolated communal roosts and nurseries in swamps and on cliffs and small islands, turkey vultures set off when the morning mists have cleared and the sun has warmed the land enough to create thermals – the columns of warm, rising air that the birds ride upwards in circles. Their wings are too cumbersome to flap for very long. Though they typically forage alone, the sight of one vulture circling a find usually brings more. They'll eat anything from large mammals to fish and grasshoppers, as long as it isn't moving. Starting with the eyeballs, they'll strip the carcass to the bone. Vultures were respected by people of past cultures as mythic figures connected with the mysteries of death. Tibetans and Zoroastrians still leave their dead at sacred sites to be eaten by the soaring scavengers. The vulture's scientific name, *Cathartes,* of Greek origin, means "purifier." Ornithologists speculate that the bird's bald head allows it to dig deep into a corpse without soiling its feathers.

As March warms, turkey vultures arrive in southern Ontario from their winter haunts in the southeastern U.S. Up to 700 have been counted in a single day above Grimsby on their Niagara Escarpment migration route, usually flying at 300 to 750 metres (1,000 to 2,500 feet) on high-pressure fronts. Once settled, they keep comings and goings to a minimum at the dark, hidden retreats where they lay their eggs around late May and early June. Parents take turns at incubating 24 hours straight and, after hatching, limit their offspring's meals to two or three a day. Vulture chicks are kind of cute, covered in a cottony white down. They spend much of their first two months stretching out their wings to bask in the sun. This classic vulture stance can often be seen among perching adults as well. It enables nature's purifiers to conserve energy for their long flights in search of the deceased.

Number passing through Panama in fall: Up to 300,000

Winter whereabouts: Connecticut and Illinois to Paraguay; most along Gulf Coast states

Age of oldest New World vulture fossils: 60–70 million years

Number of vulture species worldwide: 7 in the Americas; 13 elsewhere, unrelated

Convergent evolution: Vultures of the Americas are most closely related to storks but resemble Old World vultures because they are adapted to similar scavenging lifestyles

Also see: Broad-winged Hawk, White-tailed Deer, Wind and Weather Systems

VEERY
Rippling-voiced Thrush

Calls: Song a flutelike tremulous spiral of descending notes; also a call that seems to say "view"

Length: 16–19 cm (6.5–7.5 in)

Wingspan: 29–32 cm (11–12.5 in)

Weight: 25–42 g (0.9–1.5 oz)

Markings: Russet brown on top and white below, with faded brown spots on breast

Alias: Willow thrush, *la grive fauve, Catharus fuscescens*

Whereabouts: Young, damp, low-lying deciduous and mixed forests, swamps with dense understoreys, willow-choked streamsides

Food: Adult beetles and grubs, wasps, ants, caterpillars, grasshoppers and other insects, spiders, slugs, worms, berries

Nest: Bulky cup of grass, bark shreds, twigs, stems, moss and rootlets, lined with leaves; usually on ground at base of a bush or other vegetation, sometimes on a stump or low in a shrub

Average clutch: 4 olive-sized, light-blue eggs

Incubation period: 10–14 days

Fledging age: 10–12 days

Nest success: Avg. 38%

Lifespan: Up to 10 years

Predators: Sharp-shinned hawks, foxes, raccoons;

There are things that render an Ontario forest magical in the dwindling daylight hours, such as the rich, golden light that paints the woods in a warm, glowing chiaroscuro. Another is the ethereal song of the veery, rippling through the trees in a gentle, fluted nocturne. The veery's voice seems unreal partly because it sounds like two birds harmonizing, repeating their own names in a descending "vee-ur, vee-ur, veer, veer." The truth is that a veery can sing two notes simultaneously. Like most other mellifluous thrushes, it sings most often in early evening and morning, but sometimes lets loose at other times of day as well.

Veery serenades usually don't begin until early June, about two weeks after the birds start arriving at their breeding grounds in thickety woods. As with most songbirds, rival males who ignore the melodic warnings and trespass into foreign territory are confronted violently by the owner. Females, meanwhile, build the nest and incubate the eggs, generally at a well-hidden address amid dense ferns and shrubs on the forest floor. Young veeries are introduced quickly into the world. The passage from new egg to fledged youngster takes about three weeks.

In some areas, veeries are only one-fifth as common as they once were

Seldom venturing out of their thick, moist, understorey haunts, the plainly attired, slender thrushes are among those elusive "dickey birds" that can drive birders nuts. It's often difficult to get a fix on them as they scamper through the underbrush. The first sighting is usually out of the corner of the eye. In the split second it takes to turn for a better view, the veery disappears like a forest sprite. Then peripheral vision picks up the bird's trail again . . . and then it vanishes once more. Other than by their song, veeries reveal their whereabouts mostly by their habit of kicking up fallen leaves, looking for tasty insect morsels. They also hunt from low perches, pouncing on both passing crawlies and fliers. Later in summer, with their offspring fully grown, they turn more to the woods' ripening berries. By mid-August they seem to have had their fill of Ontario and begin taking off for the faraway tropical tangles of the Amazon jungle.

Like many other tropical migrants, veeries have suffered from forest-clearing, both in their

nests also raided blue jays, crows, skunks, red squirrels, chipmunks, snakes
Estimated Ontario population: 2 million
Nesting range: Southern Ontario to Lake Abitibi, Hearst and Red Lake; also in all other provinces
Spring migration in central Ontario: Mid- to late May
Fall migration in central Ontario: Mid-Aug. to early Sept.
Average songbird migrating speed: About 50 km/h (31 mph)
Average songbird migration altitude: 150–300 m (490–985 ft)
Time it takes tropical songbirds to reach Ontario: 4–5 weeks
Winter whereabouts: Brazil
Chiaroscuro: The technique of using light and shade in paintings, practised most famously by Caravaggio (1573–1610, Italian) and Rembrandt (1606–1669, Dutch)
Also see: Hermit Thrush, Red-eyed Vireo, Yellow-rumped Warbler, Beaked Hazel

southern homes and here in the north. Although the veery is still the most common forest thrush in much of central Ontario, its numbers have declined steeply in recent decades. In some areas, veeries are only one-fifth as common as they once were. And those remaining may sing less often, because lower population densities put less pressure on territorial boundaries, causing fewer encounters. One can only imagine the volume of the divine chorus in better times.

In damp, low-lying fir and spruce woods, the fluted dawn and evening songs ripple in reverse, rising upwards in volume, performed by the grey-olive-backed **Swainson's thrush**. The reclusive bird's breast is more heavily spotted than a veery's, but it is best distinguished from other thrushes by its wide tan eye ring and its tendency to twitch its wings. The Swainson forages on the forest floor like its kin, but also often snatches insects from the air, like a flycatcher. Females usually hide their nests in shrubs or dense young evergreens up to two metres above the ground, while their mates often sing from the pinnacles of tall spruce trees.

WHITE-THROATED SPARROW
Lingering Whistle Defines Wilderness

Call: Song a clear, lingering whistle, lasting 2–5 seconds, usually in 5 or 6 notes, changing in pitch, often ending in subtly wavering triplets; single "tseet" call notes, loud clicks when frightened

Length: 15–18 cm (6–7 in)

Wingspan: 23–25 cm (9–10 in)

Weight: 22–32 g (0.8–1.1 oz)

Markings: White throat, white or tan head stripes, tiny yellow patch between eye and bill, reddish-brown back, grey undersides

Alias: Canada bird, Canadian song sparrow, whistlebird, nightingale, poor Sam Peabody, *le pinson à gorge blanche, Zonotrichia albicollis*

Name origin: Old English *spearwa,* "a flutterer"

Whereabouts: Shrubby coniferous and mixed forest edges; low, dense understorey of partly open woods, usually with lots of spruce, fir, white birch and aspen; areas of early regeneration after forest fires, thickets, bushy clearings, shrubby swamps, open bogs, beaver meadows

Food: In early spring, buds of maple, beech and oak, catkins of birch and hazel; in late spring and early

Patriotic Canadian birders swear that the white-throated sparrow sings, "O, sweet Canada, Canada, Canada," while Americans contend the song goes, "Old Sam Peabody, Peabody, Peabody" or "oh, sweet poverty, poverty, poverty." The tune, in fact, is known to come in 15 different versions, or song patterns, but birds do not actually pronounce letters of the alphabet. Fanciful phrases attributed to them are merely human lyrics to their music, memory aids that fit the rhythms of their songs.

Whatever the interpretation, the song is one virtually everyone hears up north in spring and early summer, hanging in the air and carrying over other sounds like a navy whistle calling order to the deck. White-throated sparrows sing especially at sunrise and into evening, sometimes even peeling off a few bars in the dead of night.

summer, 90% caterpillars,
grubs and adult beetles,
dragonflies, bees, flies and
other insects, spiders, snails,
millipedes; in late summer
and fall, mostly blueberries,
raspberries, dogwood,
mountain ash and other
berries, seeds of grasses,
smartweed and other plants

Breeding territory: 0.2–
3.2 ha (0.5–8 acres)

Nest: Cup of grass, twigs,
roots, pine needles and
lichens, 8–13 cm (3–5 in)
wide, usually beneath blueberry shrubs, dead ferns or
other low vegetation; occasionally off ground in a
brush pile, bush or low in an
evergreen

Average clutch: 4–5 olive-
sized light green, grey or
bluish eggs with numerous
brown spots

Incubation period: 11–14
days

Fledging age: About 12–14
days

Nesting success: Avg. 55–
60%

Lifespan: Adults avg. 2–3
years; up to 9 years in wild

Predators: Sharp-shinned
hawks, owls, kestrels, merlins, foxes, martens, weasels;
nests also raided by red
squirrels, chipmunks, garter
snakes

**Estimated Ontario popula-
tion:** 12 million

Density in prime habitat: Up
to 14 pairs/10 ha (25 acres)

Nesting range: All Ontario,
but sparsely scattered in far

Like other songbirds, they call to proclaim their turf and keep out intruders of their own kind. They usually whistle from an elevated branch where they can be easily seen by their rivals. Each recognizes the others by their individual calls. Once the lazy whistlers establish borders and neighbours get used to each other, squabbles diminish. They respond much more strongly if they detect a strange voice in the neighbourhood.

Less dominant males, usually one-year-olds, cannot establish their own territories and do not breed. Instead they become "floaters," silently stealing through the bush, ready to take over a piece of real estate if something should happen to the proprietor. They often fill the vacancy within hours of the other bird's disappearance.

In contrast to the floaters, some female white-throats actually join in the mating chorus, normally an exclusively male rite among song-birds. It's a phenomenon of colour-coded per-sonalities. Singing females have white head stripes and are more aggressive than their tan-striped sisters. They join their mates in chasing away intruders from their territories until they begin incubating. White-striped males, however, don't appreciate any birds, even females, singing their tune and look upon them as competition. So they take the more demure tan-striped females as partners, while the less aggressive tan-striped males, who sing only about one-fifth as much, find harmony with the feisty white-striped divas. This mating pattern is thought to be unique in the bird world.

White-throats often build their nests in the same spot every year, well hidden on or near the ground in mats of blueberries, bunchberries or other shrubs in clearings or forest edges. The expectant mother remains on the nest almost constantly. While largely vegetarian most of the year, both parents switch to insects when nesting. Tan-striped mothers tend to be better providers for their young, but their husbands lend less of a helping hand than tan-striped males. Insect outbreaks make for easy hunting and many more hatchlings survive.

After the young fledge, white-throats roost in evergreens and join roaming mixed flocks during the day. They scour the leaf litter, scratching and kicking with both feet at the same time, while other species in the flock specialize in trunks and the outer or inner branches of trees at various levels. Thousands of white-throats may migrate together at night, often mixed with yellow-rumped warblers en route to the same latitudes. Studies show sparrows may have the best night vision of all small night migrants.

south; also in all other provinces and territories except Nunavut

Spring migration in central Ontario: Mid-Apr. to late May

Fall migration in central Ontario: Late Aug. to late Oct.

Winter whereabouts: Most go to the southeastern U.S.; some as far north as extreme southern Ontario

Also see: Cedar Waxwing, Song Sparrow, Yellow-rumped Warbler, Blueberry

YELLOW-BELLIED SAPSUCKER
Making a Mark on the Forest

Drum roll: 4–6 beats/sec, highly variable but usually starts with several fast knocks, followed by a pause and more irregular knocks, often in pairs

Length of sapsucker: 18–22 cm (7–9 in)

Wingspan: 34–40 cm (13–16 in)

Weight: 43–55 g (1.5–2 oz)

Markings: Black-and-white-lined back, faint yellowish belly, white wing patch, red forehead; red throat on male, white throat on female; juvenile birds brownish

The red head-patches sported by yellow-bellied sapsuckers and most male woodpeckers in Ontario were symbols of bravery to the Ojibway, who hung them from their tobacco pipes. They said the patches were a gift from the trickster deity Nanabush, who had tried to copy the tree-knocking skill of his friend the giant woodpecker by placing two wooden pins in his nostrils and hammering away at a trunk. Instead, Nanabush knocked himself out and received a nasty wound. The giant woodpecker rescued him, stopped the bleeding and in return was dabbed with the blood of Nanabush to wear as a symbol of honour.

Woodpeckers were similarly venerated in Europe and Asia, where they were closely associated with rain, thunder gods and agriculture. The name for woodpeckers in many languages was "rain bird." They received their reputation both because they produced thundering sounds when knocking and because they frequented oaks, the sacred tree of Zeus, Mars, Thor and other thunder and agriculture deities of various cultures.

A family of woodpeckers usually patronizes one or two favourite trunks for most of their meals

The much ballyhooed yellow-bellied sapsucker is one of the most common and fascinating woodpeckers in central Ontario. With its long, brushy tongue, the bird laps up wasps, flies, moths and other insects attracted to the sweet sap oozing from the rows of evenly spaced holes it drills into trees. As with all woodpeckers, their strong head bones and neck muscles act as shock absorbers. White birch and aspen are favourite trees for the job. Early in the season, before those species leaf out and yield a strong sap flow, yellow-bellies prefer hemlocks. Hummingbirds, yellow-rumped warblers, nuthatches, red squirrels, flying squirrels and other creatures also frequent the sap wells. Sometimes, when the sap ferments, the whole party can get a little woozy. At night, bats come to snatch sap-supping moths.

Sapsuckers also invest in their future housing needs, or at least that of future generations, when they drill holes in trees. A family of woodpeckers usually patronizes one or two favourite

Alias: Yellow-belly, yellow-bellied woodpecker, common sapsucker, red-throated sapsucker, sap-sipper, supsap, *le pic maculé, Sphyrapicus varius*

Calls: Piercing, harsh, nasal whine, descending, slurred squeal, squeaks; generally silent

Whereabouts: Young, open mixed and deciduous forests with lots of white birch and aspen, especially near streams; hemlock, yellow birch, basswood, maple, red oak, young white pine and spruce all also tapped for sap

Food: Sap about 20% of overall diet; also lots of inner bark, aspen buds and inchworm caterpillars in early spring; carpenter ants, mayflies, beetles and budworms in late spring and early summer; moths, dragonflies, wasps and berries later in summer

Number of sap-well holes drilled a day: 2–20

Number of days sap flows from a hole: About 3

Tapping sequence: First horizontal line of sap wells usually drilled on trunk at or above the lowest set of live branches; new wells usually drilled 0.5 cm (0.2 in) above old ones, continuing upwards about 20 cm (8 in) over about 3 weeks

Number of sap-well holes drilled by a nesting pair annually: Avg. 3,000

**Number of bird species
known to feed at sapsuck-
er holes:** 35
Breeding territory: 0.6–3 ha
(1.5–7.5 acres)
Nest: Tree cavity with opening
4–5 cm (1.5–2 in) wide,
usually 3–15 m (10–50 ft)
up in an aspen, or some-
times a birch, beech, maple
or hemlock
**Nest excavation chiselling
rate:** 100–300 strikes/min
Mating bout duration: Up to
10 sec
Clutch: 4–5 shiny white,
olive-sized eggs
Incubation period: 10–13
days
Fledging age: 25–29 days
Age at first breeding: 1 year
Lifespan: Up to 7 years in
wild
Predators: Sharp-shinned
and Cooper's hawks; nests
also raided by raccoons, red
squirrels, weasels and bears
**Estimated Ontario
population:** 1.2 million
Nesting range: Most of
Ontario to southern James
Bay and the southern por-
tion of the Hudson Bay low-
lands; also in all other
provinces and territories ex-
cept Nunavut
**Spring migration in central
Ontario:** Mid-Apr. to mid-
May
**Fall migration in central
Ontario:** Mid-Sept. to mid-
Oct.
Sapsucker red-letter day:
Apr. 17, 1909, a northerly
gale grounded more than

trunks for most of their meals, riddling them with sap wells. The holes usually girdle the tree – cutting off the life-sustaining sap flow – or allow in wood-rotting fungi. It's estimated that the drilling of a pair of nesting sapsuckers leads to the eventual death of about one tree a year, making the birds agents of forest change. At the same time, the dead or dying trees provide them, and many other animals, with ideal shelter.

Aspens infected by thick, hoof-shaped, dark grey bracket polypores called false tinder fungus are most commonly used by sapsuckers for their nest holes. The fungus rots the centre of the trunk but leaves the outer sapwood alive, pro-viding the birds with a carvable core surrounded by strong walls. The availability of such trees is the biggest limiting factor on sapsucker and other cavity-nesting populations. Yellow-bellies usually spend two to four weeks chiselling out new holes in late April and May, often in trees used before, resulting in what's been described as something resembling a multistoried tenement. Indeed, flying squirrels often take up residence in old holes while sapsuckers are living on another floor. Many other species depend on old woodpecker holes for nesting or shelter as well.

After they return to Ontario in April, a week or so ahead of their mates, male sapsuckers seek out dead, dry trees that will reverberate resound-ingly for courtship drumming. They usually use one or two main drumming posts. Their love code, much louder than their regular tapping, has an uneven cadence, with quick drum rolls often preceded by or ending in a few slow, ten-tative knocks. Females also drum in territorial defence, though less often and more quietly, while their spouses are busy doing all of the nest-hole digging. After the work is done, sapsuckers are gripped in the throes of passion for one to two weeks before the first egg is laid. Males take the incubating night shift. After the young hatch, both parents feed them a sweet porridge of sap and insects. Fledglings are soon cut off but continue to visit their parents' sap wells for six to eight weeks. By then, their mothers have started to leave on night flights, sometimes in large numbers, to southern wintering grounds. Adult males are the last to depart, between late September and mid-October.

5,000 migrating yellow-bellied sapsuckers in Kingston after they crossed Lake Ontario

Winter whereabouts: Long Island, southern Ohio and Illinois south to Costa Rica and West Indies, with far more females flying to the tropics and more males to the southern U.S.

Also see: Flicker, Ruby-throated Hummingbird, Tree Swallow, Red Squirrel, Mushrooms, Red Oak, Trembling Aspen

YELLOW-RUMPED WARBLER
Outgoing Bundle of Energy

Length: 12–15 cm (5.3–6 in)
Wingspan: 20–23 cm (8–9 in)
Weight: 12–14 g (0.4–0.5 oz)
Additional bulking up before migration: 4–5 g (0.14–0.18 oz)
Markings: Yellow patches on top of head, in front of wings and above base of tail; males have black-streaked bluish-grey back, black mask and chest and white throat and belly; females, grey-brown back, streaked breast and white belly; male colours fade to resemble female in fall
Alias: Myrtle warbler, butter butt, *la fauvette à croupion jaune, Dendroica coronata*
Calls: Loud, sharp "chip"; song an indistinct, flat, slow, gentle trill, usually 1–3 sec long

There are more brightly coloured summer wood warblers in the forest than any other group of birds. Legendary ornithologist Roger Tory Peterson called them the butterflies of the bird world. Unfortunately for people who delight in seeing them, many of these tiny, hyperactive insect-eaters are "skulkers" of the thick, tangled undergrowth. Or they frequent high, dense foliage, avoiding the gaze of all but the most dogged birders. Yellow-rumped warblers, one of the most common of all, break the mould, being exceedingly outgoing as they forage in small groups among lower branches, affording the oft-heard, if somewhat embarrassing, cry "I've got a great view of a yellow-rump!"

Yellow-rumped warblers also spend more time in Ontario and winter farther north than any other warbler. Unlike most of the rest, they're generalists and can live on berries, seeds and even sap before the really good eating starts, when insect numbers pick up. They're also known as myrtle warbles because of their winter subsistence on wax myrtle and bayberry, the fruits of which most other birds can only stomach in small quantities because of their waxy coatings. The berries were once boiled in water to collect their wax for making candles.

Stirred by lengthening daylight on their wintering grounds in the southeastern U.S., yellow-rumps begin arriving in Ontario on warm fronts in late April, initiating a parade of migrant warblers that continues for two months. Most other species, though, come from the tropics and take four to five weeks to reach Canada. They migrate at night, when there's less turbulence and the air cools feverishly working muscles. In ideal conditions, on clear nights with a good southerly tailwind, advancing waves of millions of migrating songbirds have been detected by radar. Most fly 150 to 600 metres (500 to 2,000 feet) high. They rest and catch insects to rebuild their fat supplies for several days between flights.

Night migrants follow the stars. Heavy cloud or rain at night grounds them. In studies conducted inside planetariums in spring, white-throated sparrows, indigo buntings and other species flutter and orient themselves towards the North Star in night-sky projections. Other studies reveal most learn the skill rather than genetically inheriting it. Some species also may navigate using the Earth's magnetic field, the pressure shifts of weather fronts, or low-frequency background sounds, such as ocean waves or winds thousands of kilometres away.

Whereabouts: Mature fir and spruce forest edges; also pine, cedar, hemlock and mixed forests; bogs

Food: Caterpillars, grubs, leaf beetles, ants, grasshoppers, mosquitoes, flies, insect eggs, spiders, poison ivy, dogwood, mountain ash and other berries, seeds, willow buds, sap

Time taken to digest and pass a spruce budworm: 2½ hours

Breeding territory: Avg. 0.5–0.8 ha (1.2–2 acres)

Average area of a football field: 0.8 ha (2 acres)

Nest: Deep cup, 7–15 cm (3–6 in) wide, of twigs and grass, lined with feathers and hairs, usually 1.5–6 m (5–20 ft) up in an evergreen

Average clutch: 3–5 grey-and-brown-speckled and -blotched white eggs, the size of small marbles

Incubation period: 11–13 days

Fledging age: 10–14 days

Lifespan: Up to 8 years in wild

Predators: Sharp-shinned hawks, kestrels, shrikes, gulls, blue jays, raccoons, skunks, snakes; nests also raided by ravens, crows, red squirrels

Estimated Ontario population: 12 million

Density in prime habitat: 60–100 pairs/km² (0.4 sq. mi)

Yellow-rumped warbler nests parasitized by cowbirds: About 30%

Nesting range: From tree line near Hudson Bay south to Sarnia and Long Point areas; also in all other provinces and territories except Nunavut

Spring migration in central Ontario: Late Apr. to late May

Fall migration in central Ontario: Early Sept. to late Oct.

Average nightly migrating distance: 312 km (193 mi) in spring, 88 km (55 mi) in fall

Winter whereabouts: Most along U.S. Atlantic and Gulf coasts; some south to Panama and West Indies and sometimes as far north as the north shore of Lake Erie

Also see: Common Yellowthroat, Red-eyed Vireo, Yellow-bellied Sapsucker, Moths, Poison Ivy, White Spruce, Wind and Weather Systems, North Star

Spring warbler migration peaks in mid- to late May, when insect populations are exploding in Ontario. It's often an all-you-can-eat bonanza — the reason they fly so far north to raise families. Populations of many warbler species go up dramatically with outbreaks of spruce budworm and other insects. Warbler chicks, fed by their parents about every 10 minutes, are stuffed with their own weight in insects each day. The highly nutritious diet turns hatchlings into fledglings within two weeks.

After a fairly quiet nesting period, with both parents attending, yellow-rumped warblers return to their noisy ways when the young fledge in July. They forage in small flocks in the lower branches and up the trunks of evergreen trees, sometimes launching from their perches to catch flying insects in the air. In the fall, they turn up at shorelines, open areas and thickets. Switching to seeds and berries as insects become scarce in cooler weather, most put off their return migration till late September. Some stay on to mid-October.

CREEPY CRAWLIES

More than one million insect species are known to science, and at least several times that number are undoubtedly yet to be identified. It's reckoned that they account for some 73 per cent of all animal species on Earth. Other tiny invertebrates, such as spiders, mites, worms, snails and springtails, make up the most of the balance. Mammals represent just 0.04 per cent of the total. Among the insects themselves, one-third are beetle species, of whom fireflies are Ontario's flashiest representatives.

As anyone acquainted with the outdoors in spring and summer knows, Ontario has its share of creepy crawlies, with some 50,000 known invertebrates. The Canadian Shield is legendary for its profusions of black flies, mosquitoes and other irrepressible flying insects. The same insects are also one of the main reasons the wilderness has so many beautiful insectivorous birds. There are plenty of striking dragonflies and spiders keeping bug numbers in check as well. Indeed, invertebrates are a vital link in the food chain, feeding fish, amphibians, many reptiles, bats, shrews, even bears.

The very process of decomposition, from which all new plant life springs, depends heavily on countless armies of springtails, termites, beetles, mites, ants, worms, centipedes and many others living above and beneath the ground. And without beautiful butterflies, moths and above all bees to pollinate flowers, many species of plants and trees would perish. A world without insects would be virtually unrecognizable.

BEES, WASPS AND HORNETS
Societies of Heavily Armed Females

It's true that only female bees, wasps and hornets have stingers. They're actually modified ovipositors, or abdominal egg-laying tubes, used by most insects to deposit eggs with accuracy. Stingers instead inject venom while sawing through the skin with tiny barbs. Honeybee stingers are so barbed that they often break off while being pulled out, leading to the death of the bee. Bumblebees, wasps and hornets, on the other hand, can live to sting again. Hornets are reputed to be particularly painful, though yellow jackets are more aggressive and more likely to administer multiple stings. With only the females bearing such awesome weapons, there's little wonder that social bees and wasps form solidly matriarchal societies.

Bees form a unique superfamily within a very large group, or order, of insects that also includes wasps and ants. Unlike most of the others in the group, bees are strictly vegetarians, living on flowers. Over millions of years, they evolved in tandem with flowering plants, forming one of the most vital links in nature. Flowers produce nectar solely for the purpose of attracting bees and like-minded creatures. Their sweet fragrance and bright colours are designed to advertise their wares to pollinators, which pick up and spread pollen as they buzz from one flower to the next. Plants help ensure their own survival by taking turns – blooming in succession, one species after another through the year – which allows bees and others to stay fed and get around to them all.

Among the first hardy pollinators to appear in early spring are husky, densely furred bumblebee queens (illustrated). Their insulation allows them to be active in temperatures too cool for other species, though they often avoid the midday heat. After hibernating alone beneath the ground all winter, a bumblebee queen searches out early flowers and willow catkins for high-protein pollen needed to produce eggs. Having mated and obtained a year's worth of sperm the previous fall, she builds a small wax-chambered nest in the ground, often in an abandoned mouse burrow or under a tree stump, and lays eight to 10 eggs. Some 20 to 30 days later, the larvae have hatched, grown, pupated and become working adults. These infertile female bumblebee workers take over the tasks of collecting nectar and pollen, enlarging the nest and serving as nannies for another generation of young. The queen concentrates on laying more eggs.

Towards the end of summer, when the colony's population reaches up to several hundred

Bumblebee length: 1.3–2.5 cm (0.5–1 in)

Bumblebee markings: Hairy yellow and black, with smoky wings

Bumblebee colony population: 100–400 by late summer

Bee food: Nectar, pollen

Average amount of honey in a bumblebee nest: About a teaspoon (used as a food store for rainy periods)

Distance of a bumblebee foraging trip: Up to 10 km (6 mi)

Number of calories burned by a flying bumblebee per minute: 0.5

Bumblebee worker lifespan (from hatching as a larva): Avg. about 4 weeks

Honeybee length: 1–1.6 cm (0.4–0.6 in)

Honeybee markings: Striped black or brown and yellow abdomen, mostly black head and thorax

Honeybee worker lifespan: Avg. 6–8 weeks

Lifespan of honeybee queen: Usually 2–3 years, up to 5 years

Maximum lifetime distance a honeybee worker travels: 800 km (500 mi)

Foraging trips required to make 1 g (0.03 oz) of honey: About 60

Number of honeybee lifetimes to produce a teaspoon of honey: 12

Honeybee colony population: 40,000–80,000 in

summer, 5,000–20,000 in
winter

**Amount of honey needed
by an average honeybee
colony to get through the
winter:** 25 kg (55 lb)

**Annual honey production of
a commercial beehive:**
More than 50 kg (110 lb)

**Temperature at which hon-
eybees become active:**
15°C (59°F)

Suicidal liaisons: With thousands of male honeybees
for every queen, very few get
a chance to mate, and those
that do die instantly, their reproductive organs exploding
upon contact

Royal treachery: If an old
honeybee queen fails to
leave the nest to start a new
colony, a new princess may
sting her to death, along
with her royal siblings still in
their pupal shrouds

Yellow-jacket length: 1.2–
1.8 cm (0.5–0.7 in)

Yellow-jacket markings:
Smooth, bright yellow and
black bodies

**Length of yellow-jacket
stingers:** About 4 mm
(0.016 in)

**Yellow-jacket worker life-
span:** Avg. 3 weeks

**Yellow-jacket colony popu-
lation:** Avg. 2,000–4,000 by
late summer

Wasp food: Insects, spiders,
insect eggs, carrion, nectar,
plant and fruit tissues and
juices, honeydew

Bald-faced hornet length:
1.2–2 cm (0.5–0.8 in)

bumblebees, the queen lays a batch of unfertil-
ized eggs that hatch into male drones. Other late
eggs, which are given large chambers, extra food
and special care, become new queens. The sole
job of the drones is to leave the nest, establish
territories and mate with young queens that
come their way. They die soon afterwards. The
workers in the colony, along with the old queen,
also perish with the killing frosts of fall. Only
young, fertilized queens, after loading up on
nectar from goldenrods, asters and other late-
blooming flowers, survive by crawling beneath
the ground for the winter, with the future of
new colonies resting with each of them.

Ontario's other major colonial nesting bee is
the honeybee. Its large colonies in tree cavities
and crevices are like permanent cities, persisting
through the winter, sometimes lasting for years
or even decades. Honeybees survive the cold
months on large stores of honey, made by them
from nectar. Huddling together for warmth,
they conserve their energy and live longer than
quickly burnt-out summer honeybee workers.

Until sugar became widely available in the
past few centuries, honey was Europe's main
sweetener. Indo-European peoples learned the art
of domestic beekeeping, or apiculture, more than
4,000 years ago, and brought the first honeybee
colonies with them to North America in the early
1600s. Native peoples called honeybees the white
man's flies. The bees spread quickly into the wild,
since queens frequently lead swarms from
crowded nests to start new colonies in late spring
or early summer, leaving pupal heirs behind to
assume their old thrones. Since the mid-1980s,
however, North American honeybees have been

devastated by parasitic mites from Europe and other poorly understood pathogens.

More than a dozen wasp species in Ontario are also colonial. Bald-faced hornets and yellow jackets, both members of the same family of wasps, have life cycles very similar to bumblebees. Hornets – which specialize in killing flies – and aerial yellow jackets build the familiar grey, oblong aerodromes, up to the size of basketballs, that become noticeable among bare tree branches in late autumn and winter. They are the original paper producers, chewing wood fibre into sheets of saliva-soaked pulp that dries into the fine, grey paper walls of their nests. Starting out small, the nest expands in progressive layers as the colony grows through the summer. Paper wasps use the same material, but their umbrella-shaped nests consist of an unwalled, single-layer comb of paper cells suspended by a central stalk from a tree branch or beneath a ledge.

Other kinds of yellow jackets usually construct large, spherical nests in excavated underground cavities, hollow logs and stumps, or inside cracks and nooks in cottage walls. Several of these species are primarily scavengers of dead insects and carrion, which provide protein for their larval siblings. For themselves, adult yellow jackets sup on nectar, ripening fruits, aphid honeydew and any other sweet food sources. These are the wasps that often become pests at picnics and deck barbecues in August and September when their numbers are peaking and the workers scour far and wide to feed the final generation of young queens and mating drones.

Entomologists – bug experts – liken each selfless member of an insect colony to a single

Bald-faced hornet markings: Black body with white markings on abdomen and head

Bald-faced hornet colony population: 100–600 by late summer

Only true hornet species in Ontario: European hornet, 3 cm (1.2 in) long

Paper-wasp length: 1.5–2 cm (0.6–0.8 in)

Paper-wasp markings: Black, brown or amber body with 2 large reddish spots on sides of abdomen, very thin waist and long legs

Paper-wasp colony population: 30–50

Mud dauber length: 3–3.5 cm (1.2–1.5 in)

Stump stabber wasp length: 2.5–7.5 cm (1–3 in)

Sweat bees: Black or metallic green, 3–12 mm (0.1–0.5 in) long; some species attracted to human sweat; may sting if touched, but not as painfully as better-known stingers; some solitary, others build underground nests with up to a dozen workers

Carpenter bees: Resemble bumblebees but chew holes 0.6–1.2 cm (0.25–0.5 in) in wood to lay eggs provisioned with pollen

Smallest wasps: Fairyflies, which parasitize insect eggs, are as small as 0.2 mm (0.01 in) long

Materials used by various solitary bee species to line their nest chambers: Wax, paste made of chewed plant fibres, cut pieces of leaves and petals, plant down, flower oil

Predators: Spiders, bee flies, robber flies, flycatchers and many other birds, skunks, mice, raccoons, bears; many wasps specialize in eating the larvae of other wasps

Portion of world's crops pollinated by bees: About 75%

Portion of world's crops pollinated by wasps: About 5%

Other common pollinators: Hoverflies (a.k.a. flower flies), bee flies; many members of the longhorn, soldier and checkered beetle families; moths and butterflies

Range of bees and wasps: All of Ontario and rest of Canada to the Arctic Circle

Number of Ontario bee species: About 200

Portion of Ontario bee species that are solitary: 90%

Number of Ontario yellow-jacket species: 15

Number of bee species worldwide: About 30,000

Number of known wasp species worldwide: About 108,000

Also see: Moths, Moccasin Flower, White Trillium, Red Oak

cell of an organism. The vast majority of bees and wasps, however, are solo fliers, hunting or foraging and nesting alone and very rarely ever stinging humans.

Most wasps are parasitoids, using non-stinging ovipositors to inject their eggs into or on live insect prey. Stump stabbers, a group of very large black and yellow ichneumon wasps, tap tree trunks with their long antennae until they detect a wood-boring horntail larva (another relative of wasps and bees) deep inside. The wasp then unfurls its threadlike ovipositor, which can be up to 11 centimetres (4.3 inches) long, and somehow drives it through bark and wood directly into the larva or its tunnel, and then injects its egg. Alternatively, spider wasps and sand wasps dig holes in the ground for their eggs and stock them with flies, spiders or caterpillars they have paralyzed with their stings. When the larvae hatch, their food is laid out in front of them, fresh, alive and immobile. Mud dauber wasps work the same way, building numerous mud tubes, often stuck on cottage walls, and leaving several spiders and one egg in each.

Many species aren't readily recognizable as wasps. A large number are extremely small. Others are coloured black and white, or completely black. Spider wasps spend most of their time running along the ground rather than flying. At the same time, hoverflies, bee flies and clear-winged moths look like bees or wasps, having evolved to imitate the bright colours that warn birds and animals to stay away from many stinging insects. Flies, however, have shorter antennae and just one pair of wings, rather than the four wings sported by wasps and bees.

BEETLES
Greatest of the Animal Orders

Insects account for three-quarters of all known animal species on Earth. The bulk of this planet-dominating army is an armoured corps of beetles, the greatest order in the animal kingdom. With hundreds of thousands of varieties to choose from, it's little wonder Charles Darwin began his career in natural history as a beetle collector. Amid the intellectual tumult sparked by Darwin's theories of evolution, one scientist commented that the one thing that can be known about the Creator, if one exists, is that God had a particular interest in beetles.

Employing a design patented more than a quarter-billion years ago, virtually all beetles are

Number of known beetle species worldwide: 300,000– 370,000

Number of known Ontario beetle species: 3,843

World's biggest insect: Goliath beetle of central Africa, up to 15 cm (6 in) long, 10 cm (4 in) wide, weighing 100 g (3.5 oz)

World's smallest beetles: Hairy-winged beetles, 0.25 mm (0.009 in) long

Alias: *Les scarabées*, order Coleoptera

Meaning of *Coleoptera*: From classical Greek *koleos*,

meaning "sheath," and *pteron,*
meaning "wing," in reference
to hard wing shields

Word origin of *beetle:* From
Old English *bitula,* meaning
"biter"

Biggest biters: Though mainly sap drinkers, male stag
beetles have huge, hornlike
mandibles capable of painful
bites; gamblers in the tropics
pit stags with mandibles
several cm (more than 1 in)
long against one another

**Biggest Ontario stag bee-
tle:** Elephant stag beetle, a
rare species, has mandibles
extending up to 2 cm
(0.8 cm) beyond its 4-cm-
(1.6-in-) long body

Most impressive antennae:
Northern sawyer, a mottled
grey beetle up to 3.5 cm
(1.4 in) long, bears curved
antennae even longer than
its body; it often flies to
lanterns and cottage lights
at night

Top beetle running speed:
2 km/h (1.2 mph)

Calls: Large numbers of bess
beetles, shiny black and
about 3 cm (1.2 cm) long,
sometimes chirp from inside
rotting logs or trees

Food: Various species eat
vegetation, nectar, plant
juices, rotting wood, fungi,
other beetles and insects,
spiders, small fish and amphibians, carrion, animal
droppings

**Number of aphids eaten
daily by a ladybug:** Up to
100

shielded by hardened wing covers, called elytra, resembling shiny coats of armour. The elytra lift forward to free the wings for flight. Whether hunters, scavengers, vegetarians, fungus eaters, parasites or pollinators, beetles and their seg-mented, wormlike larvae, known as grubs, also sport sharp, biting mandibles for munching their meals.

Perhaps the most popular of all beetles, lady-bugs are themselves divided into more than 3,000 species around the world, 83 of them in Ontario. Named for deities in some 50 languages, they've been honoured since ancient times for their services in eating aphids and other crop-damaging insects. In medieval England, they were associated with the blessings of the Virgin Mary – "Our Lady" – and are still greeted with delight upon landing on a human hand. As with many brightly coloured beetles, their pretty black-spotted orange or red attire is thought to serve as a warning to predators of their bitter taste. Most huddle together in dormitories beneath fallen leaves or bark for the winter and may be seen well into autumn and soon after the snow melts in spring. Several native ladybugs, however, have been threatened or displaced in recent decades by the alien seven-spotted ladybug and the mul-ticoloured Asian ladybug (illustrated), both ini-tially introduced in the U.S. to rid farm fields and orchards of pests and now the most common species in much of the province.

Among other widely recognized beetles, June bugs make their presence known on hot summer nights when they're drawn to lights, often whacking into lanterns and cottage screen doors. The hefty, reddish-brown bombers spend their first two or three years of life initially as white, subterranean, root-gnawing grubs, then as resting pupae on their way to becoming adults. In agricultural areas, they're among the choicest morsels snatched up by gulls and blackbirds following farmers' ploughs. Emerging as adults in late spring, June bugs sleep beneath the ground by day and fly up to snack on tree leaves after dark.

In ancient Egypt, the scarab was a sacred symbol of resurrection and the sun

June bugs are part of the scarab beetle family, whose members include a vast assortment of shiny, round sanitation workers known as the dung beetles. From rabbit pellets to moose muffins, dung beetles set to whatever falls their way. They not only feed on the waste but roll small balls of it into little burrows then lay their eggs in it so that upon hatching, their offspring find a ready food supply. It may not be a pretty way to make a living, but it was well appreciated by early agricultural societies, which recognized the vital job the beetles did in cleaning up and in fertilizing the soil. In ancient Egypt, the scarab was a sacred and much-reproduced symbol of resurrection and the sun. Its practice of rolling balls of dung was a reminder of the way the sun was rolled across the sky. After dying, the scarab apparently rose again from the mud in great numbers every year. Its dung-nursery constructions may even have been the inspiration for Egyptian tomb-building and mummification in preparation for rebirth.

Eggs laid per female: 1–10,000; most species lay eggs singly

Lifespan: 3 days to 15 years; most species 1 year

Predators: Skunks, raccoons, foxes, shrews, moles, snakes, woodpeckers and many other birds; also spiders, fish and other insects

Beetle defences: Some predatory, nocturnal ground beetles produce foul odours when threatened; bombardier beetles make a popping sound as they release toxic liquids that can irritate human skin or create diversionary puffs of vapour; dogbane beetles secrete distasteful droplets

Love potions: The Mediterranean blister beetle is the fabled "Spanish fly," whose body secretions are used to make the aphrodisiac of the same name (there's no scientific proof it works). The beetles were collected since Roman times to extract the substance, called cantharidin, which is toxic and causes skin blisters and was used in medicine. It also promotes hair growth.

Clickers: Flat-bodied click beetles are unable to roll over when on their backs and instead snap their bodies, producing an audible "click," which flips them right side up

Ant impostors: Some rove beetles look and smell so

much like ants that they can live in and sponge off of ant colonies

Largest beetle family:
Weevils, long-snouted vegetarians, make up about 1/6 of all beetles

Number of ladybugs sold annually to gardeners in North America: About 2 million

Winter whereabouts: Most species hibernate as adults beneath ground cover, on or in trees and shrubs or under the water; some overwinter as eggs, larvae or pupae

Range: Throughout Ontario and rest of Canada to above the Arctic Circle

Age of oldest known beetle fossils: More than 250 million years

Age of oldest known *Homo* fossil: About 4 million years

First appearance of Beatles: AD 1960

Number of known insect species worldwide: More than 1 million

Probable total number of insect species worldwide: 3–10 million

Also see: Bees, Wasps and Hornets; Fireflies, Spring Peeper, Goldenrod, Water Lily

Carrion beetles are similarly intriguing insects working in a grim milieu. Members of the family known as sexton beetles actually bury deceased beasts as large as mice or chipmunks, though they themselves are only one to 2.3 centimetres (0.4 to one inch) long. Working in mating pairs and driving others off, the usually black and red or orange undertakers either dig beneath the corpse where it lies or drag it up to a metre (three feet) away to a prepared shallow grave. Females of some species, after laying eggs in the burial chamber, stay to tend and feed their young.

Black or dark brown water scavenger beetles provide their own cleanup services in ponds and still inlets. The big swimmers, up to four centimetres (1.6 inches) long, dine on decomposing organic material in the murky depths.

Similar in size and look, but far more ferocious, are diving beetles, which swiftly tackle live prey as large as tadpoles, minnows and spring peepers in the weedy margins of calm bays and streams. By trapping air beneath their wing covers, they are able to remain under water for minutes at a time. At night, they may fly from pond to pond looking for mates. Wormy diving-beetle larvae, called water tigers, are up to seven centimetres (3.8 inches) long and every bit as carnivorous as their parents, their mouths brandishing a pair of predatory sickles.

The surface of still waters is the domain of whirligig beetles. Resembling steely oval beads, they often appear in large groups soon after the ice melts, rising from muddy winter quarters. By swimming in high-speed circles, shiny black whirligigs create radiating waves that they use like radar signals to detect food, usually dead or struggling flying insects that have fallen onto the water. Where currents run faster, water penny beetles find their niche by clinging to plants and debris. The beetle is named for its flat, round, copper-coloured larvae, which stick to submerged rocks like suction cups and feed on algae.

Just as picking rocks from swift streams may turn up water pennies, so woodpile logs and large dead branches strewn over the forest floor often display the work of an arboreal group of beetles. Called engraver or bark beetles, most are only about three to five millimetres (0.1 to 0.2 inches) long. They burrow unseen between a tree's inner bark and sapwood, eating as they go and leaving squiggly tunnels in their wake. After females lay their eggs in a long central chamber, larvae hatch and tunnel away from it in all directions, leaving intricate designs, revealed on the surface of debarked limbs. Each of Ontario's 90 bark beetle species creates its own unique pattern, further evidence of the immense diversity within beetledom.

BLACK FLIES
"The Worst Martyrdom I Suffered"

Estimated late-spring densities: Up to billions per ha (or acre)

Number of emerging adults per m² (1.2 sq. yd) of prime stream habitat: Avg. 36,000; up to more than 100,000

Alias: Buffalo gnats, boxers, humpback gnats, turkey gnats, family Simuliidea

Black fly public enemy number 1: *Simulium venustum*, the "white-stockinged black fly"

Markings: Most species black or dark brown, some dark grey, reddish brown or yellowish; *Simulium venustum* has white markings on legs

Length: 1–5.5 mm (0.04–0.2 in)

And the black flies, the little black flies
Always the black fly no matter where you go,
I'll die with the black flies a-picken' my bones
In North Ontario, i-o
In North Ontario
    —Wade Hemsworth, song about a survey crew on the White River

Just as the first fine days of May come along, the sun and warmth give rise to swarms of biting black flies. Though they mass around the face, they are like commandos, landing silently behind ears or on necks, or burrowing under clothes. Black flies are especially attracted to dark colours. Their bite is quite unlike the precise pinprick of a mosquito. Instead, they rip into the flesh with jagged, scissorlike jaws and slurp from a blood-filled bowl in the open wound. A set of long, barbed "stylets" also push into and hook under the severed skin, the reason the well-anchored little hunchbacks are so hard to brush off. The swollen, blood-encrusted ring of purple skin they leave behind is generally bigger and more itchy than the work of mosquitoes. A French Recollet brother travelling up the Ottawa River in the early 1620s wrote of his black fly tormentors, "I confess that this is the worst martyrdom I suffered in this country."

Only female black flies bite. It takes them up to three minutes of feeding to get enough blood to nourish a full batch of developing eggs. Fully tanked up, they are double their original size and must stagger away and lie low for one or two hours while they filter the blood's protein and drain its water content.

The Canadian Shield is prime black fly country, perhaps the world's most notorious, because it courses with the fast, clear waterways needed by their young. Females stick eggs to rocks, plants and other debris in or beside rivers and streams. Groups of black fly larvae are easy to see, forming dense, greenish masses that look like moss on rocks. The larvae anchor themselves by secreting a silky goo onto surfaces and sinking tiny hooks at the end of their abdomens into it. As they sway in the current, they filter plankton – microscopic plants and animals – from the water with the bristles of two long brushes projecting from their mouths. If one loses its grip and is swept into the current, it releases a silk safety line, attached to the gooey base on the rock, from its abdomen. If it reaches a calm spot in the water, the larva uses its head and hooks to slowly winch itself back to its original spot.

Whereabouts: Areas with clear running water; some species in forests, others in open areas

Lowest temperature at which adults active: 10°C (50°F)

Flying speed: 1.7 km/h (1 mph)

Food: Algae, plant particles, plankton and bacteria in larval stage; blood, nectar and honeydew when adults

One full blood meal: 2 mg (0.0001 of a tsp)

Number of days eggs laid after a full blood meal: 4–7

Eggs per blood meal: 200–700; female produces up to 6 batches

Dispersal after mating: Up to 36 km (20 mi)

Egg development period: 4–30 days, depending on temperature

Larvae: Greenish grey or beige, up to 1.5 cm (0.6 in) long

Lifespan (from hatching as a larvae): Up to 1 year; females live 3–6 weeks as adults, males much less

Number of generations per year: Most species have 1, a few have 2 or 3

Predators: Dragonflies, damselflies, spiders, brook trout and other fish, bats, flycatchers, swallows and other birds

Winter whereabouts: In streams as eggs or active larvae

Range: All Ontario and throughout Canada

Portion of world's crops pollinated by fly species: About 19%

Number of Egypt's biblical plagues that were insect-based: 6

First appearance of black flies: About 175 million years ago

Number of Ontario black fly species: 65

Number of Ontario black fly species that feed on humans: 5

Number of black fly species worldwide: 1,660

Also see: Black Duck, Yellow-rumped Warbler, Dragonflies, Mosquitoes, Brook Trout

The species that attack in early May are black flies that hatch in the fall and grow slowly as larvae beneath the ice through the winter, moulting six to eight times. As rivers warm in spring, they spin cocoons and take several days to metamorphose into adults. When the cocoon opens, the black fly floats up to the surface inside an air bubble and flies away. Building to peaks in mid-May and June, depending on the weather, they die off quickly after five or six straight hot days, their tiny bodies drying out.

Most species of black flies hatch from eggs in spring and do not become biting adults until June, July or later. Their numbers are not as great as the early-spring hordes. Most specialize in blood from birds, amphibians or mammals other than man. One preys solely on loons. Parasites spread by some are a major cause of duckling mortality. Many other species don't drink blood at all, though their swarms can be bothersome. Luckily for nocturnal animals, most varieties restrict their feeding frenzies to daylight, though they become meaner and more numerous in the hours before sunset and on overcast, humid days. They're docile indoors, even inside tents or cars.

Though universally reviled, black flies play a vital role in the ecosystem. Their swarms draw tropical birds from as far away as South America to feast and raise their young on black-fly protein. Their young, as well, are an important food for brook trout and other stream fish, while the larvae themselves cleanse the water of vast amounts of bacteria and other detritus. Black fly adults live primarily off plant nectar and pollinate flowers. Even purveyors of pain have a hand in creating sweetness and beauty.

DEER FLIES AND HORSE FLIES
Big, Persistent, Serious Biters

Deer flies and horse flies are the brutes of the biting-insect crowd, lacking the daintiness of mosquitoes or the stealth of black flies. Instead, they zoom in and quickly seem to take a good-sized chunk of you. The sensation is akin to having a burning ember alight on your skin.

Although more painful than the bites of black flies or mosquitoes, those of the bigger flies usually do not swell or itch so much afterward, probably because the larger flies' quick work does not require a heavy injection of saliva, used by the smaller biters to keep blood from clotting while they suck. Their spongelike lower lips swiftly take up the blood that spills from incisions made by their mouth blades.

Like most other biting insects, only female deer flies and horse flies strike, using blood to produce eggs. As their name implies, deer flies –

Top speed of world's fastest insect: 145 km/h (90 mph), by horse fly *Hybomitra hinei,* native to Ontario

Wind speed at which deer flies and horse flies become inactive: 10 km/h (6 mph)

Species illustrated: Deer fly, *Chrysops callidus*

Deer fly length: 8–15 mm (0.3–0.6 in)

Horse fly length: 10–25 mm (0.4–1 in)

Horse fly weight: Avg. 0.2 g (0.007 oz)

Deer fly markings: Dark bodies of some species marked with black, brown, grey, orangish or yellow stripes or spots; most have a large black dot or black patterns on each wing; colourful eyes often have iridescent green, copper, gold or purple patterns

Horse fly markings: Most are dark grey or black, less colourful than deer flies, with clear wings

Number of lenses per eye: Up to 1,000

Horse fly alias: Gadflies, green-headed monsters, breeze flies, ear flies, tabanids, *les taons,* family Tabanidae

Deer fly alias: *Les chrysops,* genus *Chrysops*

Whereabouts: Shorelines, wetlands, clearings and paths

Food: Larvae eat aquatic and soil insects, worms, snails and other invertebrates; adults feed on nectar, pollen, plant juices and honeydew

Eggs per female: Clumps of 100–1,000 long, flat, black, overlapping eggs

Egg development period: Usually 4–12 days

Number of larval stages: 5–11

Eggs destroyed by other insects: About 50%

Lifespan (from hatching as a larva): 4 months to 3 years, but about a year for most species; adults survive for 3–4 weeks

Predators: Birds, dragonflies, wasps, robber flies, spiders

Winter whereabouts: Most as larvae in mud near or be-

members of a single genus within the horse fly family – probably evolved to prey mainly on medium-sized animals such as deer. Most deer flies are a little larger and fatter than house flies. They attack both deer and humans high up on the body, circling around the head as they scout for a good place to land. They often follow a moving target with dogged tenacity and constant buzzing, less deterred by insect repellent than are mosquitoes and black flies.

Both horse flies and deer flies have very good long-distance vision

Horse flies, the fastest insects on the wing, are gargantuan moose-feeders, many usually hitting low on the legs. A moose can lose up to a cup of blood a day to the six-legged vampires. Humans are usually too puny for horse flies' liking and are less often attacked by them than by the smaller deer flies.

Both horse flies and deer flies have very good long-distance vision. Horse flies are especially attracted to swimmers by the shimmer of wet skin in the sunlight. It may take many long dives underwater to get one off your trail. Along with deer flies, they are extremely partial to hot, sunny days and usually disappear quickly when the sun goes behind the clouds. Both keep out of sight in temperatures below 13°C (55°F).

Four to eight days after getting their blood meal, horse flies and deer flies lay their eggs in various wet habitats, often on stems or beneath leaves just above the water surface. When they

DEER FLIES AND HORSEFLIES 145

hatch, the maggots drop into the water or wet soil and become predators of aquatic insects and other invertebrates, sticking their heads completely inside their victims to suck out their innards. They're capable of a painful bite if handled. Most spend eight to nine months, through the winter, in their larval state. In mid-spring, they begin crawling onto dry ground and spend about one to three weeks pupating into adults, commonly half buried in the soil. The first newly transformed adults take wing in late May or early June. Each species has its own emergence period through the summer. Males come out first, forming groups in clearings, on hills or along paths and waiting for the females to follow. Once mated, it's curtains for the males within a few days. Females live on for another couple of weeks, searching for blood to nourish their eggs and tormenting their victims in the process.

neath streams, ponds and wetlands

Range: Throughout Ontario and Canada south of the tree line

Deer fly patches: Commercially sold double-sided sticky patches put on back of hats snag deer flies because they commonly attack around the back of the head

Age of oldest fly fossil: 225 million years, of a crane fly

Number of Ontario horse fly species: 48

Number of Ontario deer fly species: 50

Number of deer fly and horse fly species world-wide: 3,750

Number of fly species worldwide: 120,000

Also see: Black Flies, Mosquitoes, Pegasus and Andromeda

DRAGONFLIES
A Mosquito's Worst Nightmare

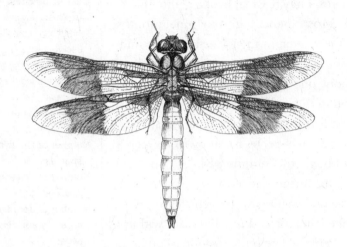

Flying speed: Up to 60 km/h (37 mph)

Wingbeats per second: 30–50

Biggest Ontario dragonfly: Swamp darner, 8–9.4 cm (3–3.7 in) long

Smallest Ontario dragonfly: Elfin skimmer, 2 cm (0.8 in) long, found in bogs and fens

Common whitetail (illustrated) length: 3.8–4.4 cm (1.5–1.7 in)

Green darner length: 7–8.5 cm (2.8–3.3 in)

Green darner wingspan: 10–11 cm (4–4.4 in)

Wingspans of ancient proto-dragonflies: Up to 1 m (3.3 ft)

First appearance of proto-dragonflies on Earth: About 325 million years ago

Dragonflies are among the deadliest friends a human can have. They may look scary, but they do not harm people. Rather, they're like helicopter gunships coming to the rescue, striking fear into the hearts of marauding mosquitoes and black flies. A single dragonfly in a clearing or meadow on a sunny day can quickly clear swarms of biting insects away from a suffering human.

Little wonder the dragonfly was admired by in Japan as *katsumushi,* "the invincible insect," and once adorned the swords and helmets of samurai warriors to ensure victory. The earliest Japanese poetry tells of an irreverent horse fly that bit an emperor and was swiftly dispatched by a loyal dragonfly, prompting the grateful monarch to proclaim his realm the Dragonfly Islands. Ancient Japanese entomological understanding seems considerably more advanced

than notions once held in the West, where dragonflies were sometimes called horse stingers
because they were often seen around skittish
horses (no doubt attracted by the real biting
marauders causing the distress).

From the moment they hatch in the water,
dragonflies are fearsome predators. Their larvae,
called nymphs, are stocky, crablike aquatic creatures that inhabit the muddy bottoms or weedy
tangles of ponds, lake shallows and streams. Like
a living nightmare from the movie *Alien,* they
have hooked projectile mouthparts that spring
out in a fraction of a second to snatch their prey.

In late spring and summer, most often after
sunset, fully grown nymphs crawl just above the
surface on emergent plants or at the water's edge
to slowly wiggle out of their juvenile skin. They
keep the tip of their tail, containing internal gills,
in the water until their air-breathing equipment
kicks in. The newly emerged dragonfly spends
up to six more hours drying off and pumping
fluid into the veins of its two pairs of wings
before lifting off on its maiden flight. Alfred,
Lord Tennyson eloquently recounts the drama in
his poem "The Two Voices":

> An inner impulse rent the veil
> Of his old husk: from head to tail
> Came out clear plates of sapphire mail.
>
> He dried his wings: like gauze they grew;
> Thro' crofts and pastures wet with dew
> A living flash of light he flew.

Newly minted dragonflies may rove widely
away from the water into forests and meadows.

Age of oldest known insect fossils: 400 million years old

Dragonfly weight: 0.1–1 g (0.004–0.04 oz)

Flight muscles' portion of total weight: 30–40%

Alias: Mosquito hawks, darning needles, horse singers, snake charmers, snake doctors, *les libellules,* order Odonata; larvae called nymphs, naiads or bass bugs

Whereabouts: Various species specialize in beaver ponds and meadows, wetlands, lakeshores, slow or fast-flowing rivers and streams

Food: Adults eat mosquitoes, black flies, deer flies, horse flies, midges, butterflies and other insects; nymphs eat other insect larvae, worms, snails, crayfish young, tadpoles, tiny fish

Number of mosquito larvae eaten during nymph stage: Avg. 3,000

Eggs laid per female: About 500 to more than 3,300

Egg development period: A few days to 9 months, depending on species; 1–4 weeks for most

Nymphs: 0.2–6 cm (0.08–2.4 in) long, various shades of plain to heavily patterned brown, green or yellow

Period spent as a nymph: A few months to a year for most species; nymphs in the Arctic may live up to a decade before transforming

Period spent as an adult:
Avg. 4–6 weeks for most species; up to 6 months for some

Predators: Red-winged blackbirds, swallows, kingbirds, hawks, kestrels, ducks, frogs, fish, robber flies, wasps, spiders; nymphs also eaten by giant water bugs and turtles

Parasites: Aquatic mites, tiny wasps

Best sense: Sight; huge eyes contain some 30,000 separate lenses, providing a 360-degree field of view and ability to see objects up to 15 m (49 ft) away; estimated 80% of brain is devoted to vision

Sunbathing: Bask in morning and shutter wings to warm flight muscles enough to fly

Peak activity times: Midday, warm, sunny weather

Shady characters: A few species, such as shadow darners and fawn darners, fly in shade, on overcast days or at dusk

Winter whereabouts: Most species overwinter as inactive nymphs at the bottom of ponds, lakes and streams; at least 8 species migrate south to parts unknown

Range: Throughout Canada to the Arctic

Species that often land on humans: Chalk-fronted skimmer, black-shouldered spinyleg

Earliest dragonfly depictions in art: Seal-stone

Within one to three weeks, however, males return to establish and defend mating territories over prime egg-laying waterside sites. The large darner dragonflies tirelessly patrol their bailiwicks for prey, mates and interlopers, many cruising high along the edges of slow streams and ponds. In contrast, the skimmer species, among the most territorial and aggressive of dragonflies, keep an eye on their realms from shoreside perches, from which they launch low, erratic sorties over the water. One male skimmer's domain may cover an entire small pond, or many may occupy a calm bay. A common whitetail (illustrated) commands from 17 to 150 square metres (20 to 180 square yards) of shallow stream or marsh by frequently scrambling for brief aerial dogfights with rivals, often with a loud thrashing of opposing wings.

Dragonfly mating equipment is so varied and specialized, entomologists make no qualms about magnified examination of their private parts to make a positive ID of difficult species. Before mating, a male doubles over to deposit sperm from the tip of his tail into a special storage space beneath the base of his abdomen. When a receptive female comes his way, they form an acrobatic circle with their two bodies, the male holding her head by the tip of his tail while the female's tail swings forward to take the sperm from his cargo hold. A female can store the sperm and mate with other dragonflies. Since the last to mate usually has the biggest share of offspring, males often jealously guard their partners, remaining attached to them or flying just above, driving off competitors until the eggs are laid. Ambitious males may try guarding two mates at once.

Varying egg-laying methods are responsible for the naming some of major groups of dragonflies. Female skimmers "skim" low over the water for four or five minutes as they drop their eggs, two dozen or more at a time, each egg sinking to the bottom of the pond. Darners use the sharp tip of their abdomens to slice open stems just beneath the surface of the water and deposit their eggs inside. Spiketail dragonflies swiftly dunk into the shallows to inject one egg at a time into the bottom, while in weedy waters, baskettails drop just one big payload of eggs, which are strung together and become strewn over submerged vegetation.

The first dragonfly to appear in spring, and one of the last around in autumn, is usually the green darner, among the largest and fastest species in Ontario. While most dragonflies overwinter as nymphs beneath the ice, many green darner populations migrate, hitching rides on north winds behind cold fronts to fly south between late August to October, often in large squadrons. Hundreds of thousands sometimes congregate at Point Pelee and other spots along Lake Erie. No one knows for sure where they go, though their range reaches Central America. Like monarch butterflies, only their descendants return, as early as April. The migrants mate, lay eggs and generally die off by mid-June. Though less common in central and northern Ontario, there are also non-migratory green darners that begin emerging in late May or June and fly through the summer. As they dwindle away, the nymphs of the southbound population emerge to transform in late summer and early fall.

engravings on Crete from 1500 BCE

Damselflies: Also members of the Odonata order; more slender than dragonflies, have more widely spaced eyes and a slower, more fluttering flight; dragonflies hold their wings horizontally when resting, while damselflies fold them upwards or half spread over their backs

Number of Ontario dragonfly and damselfly species: About 165

Number of dragonfly and damselfly species worldwide: 5,500–6,000

Also see: Monarch Butterfly, Mosquitoes

FIREFLIES
Sex Flashers of the Wilderness

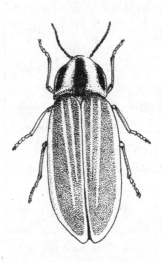

Species illustrated: Angled candle firefly, one of first species to signal in June, emitting a rapid orange flicker every 2–4 sec at dusk

Number of fireflies needed to equal the illumination of a 13-watt compact fluorescent light bulb: 25,000

Flashing activity duration: From about 30 minutes for some early-evening species in June to up to 6 hours for late-night, treetop species later in summer

Length: 0.5–2 cm (0.2-0.8 in)

Markings: Most species black or brown, with yellow, orange or red trim, lines or dabs

Alias: Lightning bugs, lampyrid beetles,

Compared to our own crude attempts at illumination, fireflies are far more efficient. Only 2 per cent of their bioluminescent energy is lost as heat, compared with 23 per cent for compact fluorescent lights and 92 to 95 per cent for incandescent bulbs. These high-tech beetles with the power of light confounded ancient philosophers, and even modern scientists have been unable to copy the wonder of "cold light" economically. We do know that the chemical luciferin and the enzyme luciferase react with oxygen in fireflies' abdomens to make them appear, as they did to the ancients, like sparks from a fire coming to life. Researchers believe the reaction is triggered by nitric oxide, the same neural gas that Viagra stimulates in humans to promote blood-vessel constriction and sexual arousal.

On clear, early summer nights, choruses of bellowing bullfrogs and brilliant flashes of countless fireflies, seeming to multiply the stars, perform a mystical sound-and-light show over still lakes. An Ojibway story traces firefly origins to a ferocious celestial lacrosse game between young Thunderbirds, the supernatural raptors responsible for rain, thunder and lightning. The ball, made from the lightning of a great storm, was thrown far past the goal towards the earth below. Its impact created Hudson Bay and caused stars to fall from the sky, breaking into thousands of blinking pieces that became fireflies.

Though greenish, yellow or orange firefly flashes seem most noticeable in June and early July, there are different species occupying various habitats, from wetlands to treetops, each flashing at a different time of the summer and of the night. Each variety has its own signal, a sexual Morse code ensuring the rendezvous of two bugs made for each other. Males on the make usually flash and fly, while females stay put on or near the ground waiting for the right signal before responding. This also makes it possible to flirt with fireflies by mimicking their blinking patterns with a flashlight, to which they respond. Females of the common Pennsylvania firefly are able to fake the flash of smaller species. Once seduced, the duped male fireflies are eaten.

To top off their powers of alchemy, fireflies contain steroids called lucibufagins that make birds and mammals puke. Most predators learn quickly to pass up meals that blink. Toads, though, are undeterred by the chemical defence and occasionally sport glowing tummies after tucking in to luminous helpings of the glowing

glowworms, *les lucioles,* family Lampyridae

Whereabouts: Moist meadows, wetlands, open woods, forest edges; stream, pond and lake margins

Food: Larvae eat slugs, snails, worms, insect larvae and mites; adults of some species eat nectar, pollen, other fireflies

Mating duration: 1 hour to all night, depending on species

Egg development period: 2–4 weeks

Larvae: Flat, segmented, spindle-shaped, with six legs; hatch 1–2 mm (0.04–0.08 in) long, grow up to 1–1.5 cm (0.4–0.6 in)

Pupal stage: About 2 weeks

Lifespan: 1–2 years; adults survive 1–3 weeks

Predators: Frogs, toads, spiders, birds, mice, bats

Winter whereabouts: Larvae hibernate in the ground

Range: Throughout Ontario and Canada south of the Arctic

Other bioluminescent life forms: Certain species of glowworms (family Phengodidae), ground and click beetles, fungus gnats, midges, fly maggots, springtails, crayfish, deep-sea fish, shrimp, jellyfish, mullusks, annelid worms, sponges, corals, fungi, marine protozoa, algae, bacteria

Arts homage: 1912 opera *The Firefly,* by American composer Rudolf Friml; 1928 novel *Fireflies,* by

Indian author Rabindranath Tagore

Medical research: Firefly luciferin and luciferase are used to measure differences in cells in studies into heart disease, cancer, multiple sclerosis and many other conditions because they light up when exposed to adenosine triphosphate (ATP), the chemical that metabolizes energy in human cells

Number of Ontario firefly species: 19

Number of firefly species worldwide: More than 2,000

Also see: Beetles, American Toad, Falling Stars

beetles. Pennsylvania fireflies, however, do not produce such steroids, which is why they prey on other firefly species, to siphon off the protective substance from them and pass it on to their eggs.

Already glimmering in their eggs, spindle-shaped firefly grubs hatch beneath moist leaf litter and other debris in midsummer and spend most of their lives as killer glowworms, using their poisonous mouth parts to paralyze, liquify and slurp the insides from slugs, snails, worms and other insect larvae. They overwinter in marble-sized soil chambers and emerge metamorphosed as adults late spring or summer, though the females of one Ontario species remain plump and wingless. The tanklike armoured adults live only one to three weeks, and most don't eat at all. They have but one purpose left in the love-lit climax of their lives.

MAYFLIES
Swarming Fabled Fated Fliers

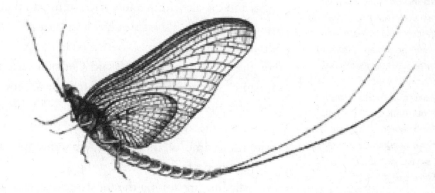

The sudden appearance of countless millions of bizarre, fairylike creatures filling the sky is a spectacular event at lakesides across the province. Seeming to materialize from nowhere, thick swarms of big-eyed, long-tailed mayflies flutter across open spaces and gravitate towards lights at evening, sometimes covering the sides of cottages, triangular wings held upright together over their backs. Yet within 24 hours they may be gone again, or lying lifeless in thick heaps beneath outdoor lights, along lakeshores and upon the water.

The largest and thickest-swarming mayflies are also called shadflies and generally show up in June, though not as numerously some years as others. Smaller numbers of other species appear from mid-April to August, making learned entomologists of the fly-fishing enthusiasts who

Water-bottom nymph densities: Up to 10,000/m² (1.2 sq. yd)

Length: 0.3–3 cm (0.1–1.2 in)

Markings: Most species various shades of brown or dusky yellow, some black, olive or reddish

Alias: Shadflies, fishflies, dayflies, duns, spinners, lakeflies, drakes, trout flies, quills, cocktails, sailors, dotterels, mackerels, willow flies, cisco flies, river flies, cob flies, salmon flies, June bugs, *les éphémères,* order Ephemeroptera

Name origin: In Greek mythology, the Ephemerides were beings that lived for only a day

Feather fishing lures imitating mayflies: Blue wing olive, quill Gordon, March brown, royal coachman, dark Cahill, white-gloved howdy, Hendrickson

Whereabouts: Various species found in and around wide range of waters, from mud-bottomed lakes and weedy wetlands to fast, rocky streams

Maximum depth nymphs found at: 60 m (197 ft)

Food: Nymphs mostly eat algae, plankton and bits of decaying vegetation

Eggs per female: 50 to several thousand, depending on species

Egg development period: From a few minutes to 11 months, depending on the species

Lifespan (from hatching as a nymph): 3–12 months for most species; as short as 6 weeks or up to 2 years for others

Predators: Trout, pickerel, bass, suckers, frogs, salamanders, swallows, flycatchers and other birds, bats, crayfish, dragonflies, diving beetles, stoneflies, water striders, spiders; snails and caddisfly larvae eat eggs

Winter whereabouts: Water bottoms, as nymphs or eggs

Range: Throughout Ontario and Canada to arctic tundra

First appearance: 350 million years ago

Bioindicators: Mayfly numbers and diversity widely

have modelled their artificial lures on a vast variety of mayflies for hundreds of years. Each species has a brief moment of glory. Most spend virtually all their lives beneath the water as aquatic "nymphs," transforming to fly, mate, lay eggs and die all within a few days. Some do it all in 90 minutes. "Nature holds a couple of draughts from the cup of love to be fair payment for the pains of a lifetime," said German writer Johann Goethe of the fabled fated fliers. Since the time of Aristotle, their evanescence has been taken as a metaphor for human life. Fittingly, the scientific name of their order, Ephemeroptera, means "living for a day with wings."

Mayflies are among the most ancient insects. With little time for wide dispersal, each species tends to be geographically limited, which has made comparison of mayfly types an important aid in piecing together the history of continental drift.

Offspring of many varieties of the large, delicate insects hatch in lakes, streams and wetlands within a few weeks of their parents' passing. The eggs of others may lie dormant for months. The nymphs have sets of gills along the sides of their distinctly segmented abdomens. They scuttle along the bottom with sharply bent, pointy legs, hiding beneath rocks and amid weeds, or burrow into the mud, depending on the species, to avoid fish and other predators. Nymphs that survive may moult up to 50 times as they grow larger.

The year's first mayflies are smaller species, emerging from snowmelt-swollen rivers, usually on sunny spring days. Later in the year, much of the action is at dusk or dawn. Congregating near shorelines and shallows just above deep water, transforming nymphs rise up en masse as their old skin splits. They burst from the top of their larval shells as they hit the surface and in as little as 10 seconds their wings unfold, dry and lift them up in clumsy maiden flights to the nearest landfall, usually waterside trees and shrubs. Before liftoff, they drift helplessly like tiny sailboats, but mass emergences ensure that feasting trout, bass, pickerel and other fish won't get them all. The dull brown, cloudy-winged survivors, called duns, moult again within a day or two, the only insects known to do so after they've received their wings. In their final form, they are shiny, soft-bodied adults with clear, intricately veined wings.

Adult mayflies don't eat. Instead, swarms of eligible bachelors fly synchronized courtship manoeuvres over the water, repeatedly rising and floating back down. With extra-long front legs, a male grabs any lass drawn to the dance and mates with her in midair for up to 30 seconds. The female lays her gooey eggs in small batches on the water within an hour or so of mating, and then, spent, lays herself down on the waves. Her lifeless mate soon joins her. They leave behind their unhatched offspring and inspiration for poets and philosophers. As Benjamin Franklin wrote in a whimsical satire, quoting a mayfly, "Alas! Art is long and life is short."

used to measure environmental health because of the order's great range of habitat preferences and low tolerance for polluted water
Number of Ontario mayfly species: 166
Number of mayfly species worldwide: 2,100
Also see: Brook Trout, Lakes

MONARCH BUTTERFLY
Destiny Bound by Mexican Siesta

Migration distance to Mexico: Up to 4,800 km (3,000 mi)

Duration of trip from Ontario to Mexico: 6–12 weeks

Average distance covered by one generation migrating north: 1,700 km (1,000 mi)

Daily migration distance: Avg. 70 km (43.5 mi), up to 425 km (264 mi)

Flying speed: 8–18 km/h (5–11 mph) in still air; up to 50 km/h (31 mph) with strong tailwinds

Wingbeats per second: 5–12

Minimum temperature needed to fly: 13°C (55°F)

Wingspan: 9–10.5 cm (3.5–4 in)

Of all butterflies that flutter and glide, the monarch, for its beauty, familiarity and extraordinary migrational feats, flies supreme in the imagination. Faced with the prospect of winter, most other butterflies and moths spin cocoons beneath bark and leaf litter or lay eggs before they die. Monarchs, instead, fill up on nectar, convert it into fat, gather on hilltops, fields and the north shores of the Great Lakes in August and September and head south. They employ the same strategy as migrating hawks, spiralling upwards on warm columns of rising air, called thermals, climbing up to 1,500 metres (5,000 feet), then gliding in the wind until they hook onto another thermal. They rest en masse in trees at night and on days when the wind is against them.

By early November, hundreds of millions of monarchs from all over eastern North America converge on about a dozen volcanic mountains in central Mexico's Sierra Madres. Yet none has ever made the trip before. They settle into a handful of colonies 3,000 metres (10,000 feet) above sea level, in stands of fir trees, each colony covering one to three hectares (2.5 to 7.4 acres). Turning the sky and scenery orange, they crowd onto tree limbs and go into intermittent semi-dormancy for several months, the cool mountain air, which hovers around the freezing point, enabling them to conserve energy. Mexicans living near the wintering sites traditionally said that monarchs were the souls of children, their arrival coming around the time of All Souls' Day, November 2, an important festival in Latin America known as the Day of the Dead.

The generation of northern-bred monarchs that spends the winter in Mexico is very long-lived by butterfly standards. The key to their longevity is remaining chaste until longer late-winter days and rising temperatures stir them from their siesta. Then their delayed hormones kick in and the butterfly fiesta begins. Females, however, once mated, take off around late March in a race to be the first to lay eggs on milkweeds emerging from the soil in the northward advance of spring. Most burn out after leaving eggs in Texas and other Gulf states, though a tough, tattered few may reach Ontario in late May. The bigger waves that arrive around the start of July are a second generation, hatched from eggs laid in northern Mexico and the southern United States.

Though adult monarchs feed from and pollinate many different kinds of flowers, only the leaves of milkweed can nourish their young.

Weight: 0.3–0.75 g (0.01–0.03 oz)

Markings: Black-veined, bright orange wings with white-spotted black borders; black body also marked with white; males have a black spot on hind wings and thinner black veins than females

Alias: Milkweed butterfly, King Billy, *le papillon monarque*, *Danaus plexippus*

Whereabouts: Meadows, forest edges, marshes, shorelines

Food: Caterpillars eat milkweed leaves; adults sip nectar

Mating duration: 16 or more hours, during which the male forms and transfers a sperm capsule equalling 5–10% of his weight and includes protein to help female produce substantially more eggs; both sexes mate with up to a dozen different partners

Number of eggs per female: Avg. 700 pinhead-sized green eggs, with 20–80 laid a day, attached singly to the underside of milkweed leaves

Egg development period: Usually 3–4 days; up to 12 days

Caterpillar: Up to 4 cm (0.8 in) long; yellowish green after hatching, turning to bands of bright yellow, black and white

Time from hatching to emergence as an adult: 3–4 weeks

Adult survival in spring and early summer: 2–6 weeks
Survival of adults emerging in late summer: 7–8 months
Predators: Birds, mice, shrews, wasps, spiders
Range: Southern Ontario to James Bay and southern boreal forest in northwestern Ontario; also in all other provinces
Estimated number of monarchs that passed through Point Pelee, on Lake Erie, in 90 minutes on Sept. 17, 1996: 350,000
Winter whereabouts: Concentrated in colonies covering 3–21 ha (7.5–52 acres) in mountains of central Mexico
Portion of original Mexican hibernation grounds lost to logging: Up to 90%
Number of overwintering monarchs in Mexico: 200 million to 1 billion
Lookalikes: Viceroy butterfly, smaller, with a black band running across the veins of the hind wings
Number of other Ontario butterflies that migrate south: At least 22
Also see: Broad-winged Hawk, Dragonflies, Moths

Growing in meadows, fields and watersides, most milkweed species produce, in their milky sap, toxins that protect them from many browsers. Monarchs find milkweeds a safe haven for their caterpillars, which have themselves evolved a tolerance for the poisonous tissues. In fact, milkweed toxins stored in the insect's body make both the caterpillars and adults unpalatable to vertebrate predators. Once most birds have a bitter taste of one of the flamboyant caterpillars or butterflies, they steer clear of others in the future.

Starting off less than two millimetres (a tenth of an inch) long, monarch caterpillars eat constantly for nine to 15 days, go through five skin sheddings and grow to 2,700 to 3,000 times their hatching weight. In human terms, it would be like a three-kilogram (6.6-pound) infant putting on eight or nine tonnes. The caterpillar then suspends itself from a silk pad stuck to a branch or leaf and transforms into a beautiful gold-speckled green pupa. The pupal covering gradually becomes transparent and, after about 10 to 15 days, a butterfly emerges. It spends about an hour inflating its wings with fluid, then flies away. Two or three generations of monarchs hatch through the summer in Ontario, the last returning again to Mexico.

MOSQUITOES
Straw-nosed Marauders

Mosquitoes owe their survival to warmhearted individuals – mammals and birds whose bodies course with warm blood. Aside from the species that feed on amphibians and reptiles, female mosquitoes are straw-nosed marauders that produce their eggs from the protein of a warm-blood soda. Their antennae tracking systems lock on to the carbon dioxide exhaled by humans and animals and follow increasing concentrations to the source. As they get closer, body heat, odour, moisture and sight also guide them. They're especially attracted by dark colours, such as brown, grey and navy blue. Mosquitoes and black flies also seem partial to certain chemical compositions or levels in sweat and skin vapours, such as lactic acid, that vary from one person to another. They generally find women more appealing than men.

Upon landing, a mosquito drills into the flesh with several razor-thin stylets held within its long proboscis. As it sinks its sucking tube into a tiny blood vessel, it injects saliva containing anaesthetic and an anticoagulant into the wound to keep the blood coming. The body responds to foreign compounds from insect bites or stings by surrounding the wound with histamine, a

Distance humans can be detected by mosquitoes: Up to 30 m (100 ft)

Wingbeats per second: 300–600

Fastest wingbeats on Earth: Up to 1,046/sec, by midges

Flying speed: 5 km/h (3 mph) in calm air

Wind speed at which mosquitoes take cover: 15 km/h (9 mph)

Length: Most species 3–9 mm (0.1–0.4 in)

Largest Ontario species: Gallinipper (*Psorophora ciliata*), about 2.5 cm (1 in) long

Monster "mosquitoes": Crane flies, up to 5.5 cm (2.2 in) long, with very long legs; attracted to lights but don't bite

Alias: Scitters, flies, *les moustiques,* family Culicidae

Name origin: Spanish *mosca,* meaning "fly"

Most troublesome late-spring biters in central Ontario: *Aedes punctor* and *Ochlerotatus communis*

(illustrated), a.k.a. snow mosquito, formerly *Aedes communis*

Most troublesome summer biter: *Aedes vexans,* a.k.a. floodwater mosquito, most common at dusk

Food: Nectar, honeydew, plant juices, blood; larvae filter algae, bits of decaying vegetation, pollen, protozoa and bacteria from the water; gallinipper larvae eat smaller mosquito larvae

Blood taken per bite: Avg. 2–3 mg (0.001 of a tsp)

Breeding grounds: About half of Ontario species in temporary pools; more than a dozen in tree holes or water cupped in leaves; 11 mainly in wetlands; 11 others mainly in weedy ponds, lake shallows and slow rivers

Sex identification: Males have much bushier antennae

Number of eggs produced per blood meal: 60–400

Maximum number of lifetime full blood meals taken by *Aedes vexans:* 8

Egg development period: 1–5 days in summer; eggs of some species can lay dormant up to 5 years

Larvae: Beige, wormlike, bristly, 1–2 mm (0.04–0.08 in) long after hatching, growing to 7–15 mm (0.3–0.6 in)

Larvae per ha (2.5 acres) of prime habitat: Up to 80 million

Larval development period: 7–10 days in summer, up to 4 weeks in spring

chemical that marshals natural defences such as white blood cells to sweep away and destroy toxins. Swelling, itching and redness around the bite are all part of the allergic defence reaction. Reactions are worst with the first bites of early spring. Outdoor types, though, often build up a resistance to the saliva of biting insects and are liberated from much scratching.

A mosquito needs a few minutes of uninterrupted siphoning to get a full tank. If brushed away before finishing, it tries again until it has the blood it needs. A good feeding can double or quadruple its weight, the little vampire's abdomen ballooning red with blood. If the weather is warm, the acquired protein yields a batch of eggs a few days afterwards. Both mosquitoes and black flies may lay several batches in their lifetimes, returning for blood for each. They need mate only once, storing the sperm internally for all future needs.

About half of all Ontario species are known as snowmelt mosquitoes, which lay eggs in shallow forest puddles or depressions likely to flood in spring. They go through just one generation in a year because their eggs must first freeze in winter before hatching. Their frigid vernal nursery pools come alive with mass hatchings in April and early May. Wormlike mosquito larvae are called wrigglers because they squirm rapidly from the surface to the bottom of the water to feed then float vertically back up again to get air through a long tube at the end of their abdomens. They filter algae and nibbles of decaying vegetation from the water with long hairlike fans near their mouths. After moulting four times over one to four weeks, depending on water temperatures, they metamorphose inside curved, brown pupal casings. The pupa, called a tumbler, can't eat but can shoot to the bottom of the water if threatened. After a few days, the shell opens and becomes a floating launch pad for the winged adult.

A rainy April and warm May are ideal for nurturing the greatest multitudes of wrigglers into adulthood. Large numbers of mosquitoes usually appear within days of the blooming of chokecherry trees, one of their favourite food sources. They feed primarily on nectar from flowering trees and shrubs, as well as honeydew – sweet drops excreted by insects that suck plant juices. Once satiated on sweets, a day or so after emerging, females go looking for the boys, who form thick, harmless evening swarms. Each species tends to swarm over a particular kind of landmark, such as spruce trees or watersides. Males, which don't bite, use their brushy antennae to detect the distinct whine of female wingbeats. Both sexes may mate several times. A few days later, females are out for blood.

The mosquito hordes usually build to a peak in June then trail off all too slowly through the summer. While most adults live only a few weeks, at least two dozen Ontario species go through several pestering generations. One species breeds only in pitcher plants but does not suck blood. Some in the *Culex* genus hibernate as adults, using a blood meal in the fall to sustain them through winter.

Though each type of mosquito may have its own niche, most are stirred by rising and falling light levels, making them most annoying at dusk and dawn. During the heat of the day, they rest in the shade on plants and trees. Being slow

Pupae: Brown, comma-shaped, up to 6 mm (0.25 in) long

Lifespan (from hatching as larvae): 1–12 months, depending on species

Adult survival: Avg. 2 weeks for most; up to 3 months for species with just one generation a year; 6–8 months for overwintering adults

Predators: Swallows, flycatchers, nighthawks and other birds; bats, frogs, toads, dragonflies, wasps, spiders; larvae also eaten diving beetles and other aquatic insects

Moon effect: Studies show up to a fivefold increase in mosquito numbers on full-moon nights

Temperature restraints: Become sluggish below 16°C (60°F) and inactive at 10°C (50°F)

Winter whereabouts: Most as eggs in water or leaf litter; about 8 species hibernate as larvae in mud or tree holes and 8 as adults in animal burrows, hollow logs and tree cavities

Range: All Ontario and Canada

Reputed mosquito capital of Canada: Winnipeg

Protection provided by repellents with 30% Deet: 5–6½ hours

Protection provided by citronella, lavender and soybean oil repellents: 30 min to 3 hours

Discredited bug defences:
Eating garlic, not washing,
taking vitamin B (though
many swear by it)

High-tech flops: Studies
show fewer than 1% of
insects killed by electric bug
zappers are biters, which are
not attracted to lights, while
many of those zapped are
mosquito predators

Biggest 19th-century anti-bug advance: Steel mesh
window screens, invented in
1862

First appearance of mosquitoes: 70 million years
ago

Name for mosquito experts:
Culicidologists

Number of mosquito species native to Ontario:
57

Number of mosquito species worldwide: About
3,400

Also see: Tree Swallow, Black
Flies, Dragonflies, Little
Brown Bat, Chokecherry

fliers, they also take cover even in light wind. Camping in breezy locations, such as the east side of lakes, where prevailing winds have room to sweep in, is one of best ways to avoid bugs.

Humans have probably experimented with ways of ridding themselves of biting pests since the dawn of time. Even wedge-capped capuchins – the famous organ-grinder monkeys – spread the caustic secretions of huge millipedes over their fur to protect themselves from mosquitoes in Venezuela's rainy season. Native North Americans smeared themselves with animal grease and red ochre for protection, prompting John Cabot to speak of seeing "red Indians" in the new land. The main ingredient of most modern repellents – Deet, or Diethyl-m-toluamide – was developed in the 1940s, financed by the U.S. military, which is still the biggest funder of insect-repellent research in the world. No one is sure how exactly it works, though it seems to block sensors in the mosquito's antennae, mouth and legs.

Two mosquitoes found south of the Canadian Shield are known to spread diseases such as malaria, encephalitis and dengue fever in warmer parts of the world. Malaria, brought in by workers from the tropics, spread in several southern and eastern Ontario epidemics in the 19th century, including one that temporarily stopped construction of the Rideau Canal in the late 1820s, slaying hundreds of Irish labourers. Though West Nile virus has spread to the province in recent years, the mosquitoes that carry it are also uncommon on the Shield and the disease has had little impact beyond the urban south. Luckily, the AIDS virus is too fragile to survive in the harsh biochemical environment inside a mosquito.

MOTHS
Pollinators of the Night

When darkness descends on summer nights, the air around campfires, lanterns and cottage windows becomes filled with swirling moths seemingly intent on self-destruction. Moths were once said to be the souls of the dead flying out of the darkness in search of the light. These days, the suicide fliers are thought to be drawn to the flames and light because they normally navigate a straight course by keeping constant the angle of moonlight or sunbeams falling on their eyes. Night lights created by humans disorient moths, causing them to flutter round and round the source without being able to get their bearings.

Moths take over from butterflies at night in pollinating a wide array of flowers as they suck up nectar with their long, coiled tongues. Nocturnally blooming flowers, such as evening

scent of female; each species has a unique scent, except those that use no scent at all

Distance a male cecropia moth can smell a female: Up to 11 km (7 mi)

Wingless moths: Wormlike females of species such as bagworms, cankerworms and white-marked tussock moths depend wholly on their scent to attract winged males

Egg development period: From less than 10 days up to 10 months, depending on species

Inchworms: Very slender caterpillars of the Geometrid moth family that loop their bodies into the air as they pull their back ends up towards their front to move forward

Hornworms: Plump, smooth sphinx moth caterpillars that bear a pointy horn on their tail, which they raise and wave when threatened

Caterpillar defences: Bristles on many species provide protection, and those of woolly bears can irritate human skin; spines of lomoth caterpillars have a painful sting

Cocoon metamorphoses period: As little as 10 days for tent caterpillars; up to 10 months for silkworm moth family

Lifespan: About 1 year for most species; 3 weeks to 10 months as caterpillars, a few

primrose and jimsonweed, are usually white or light toned, making them easier to see in the darkness than the deeply coloured flowers butterflies visit by day. Still, if some flowers are fragrant enough, they can attract pollinators around the clock.

Some moths are also active by day, though many can be easily mistaken for other insects. Clearwing moths look like wasps, benefiting from bold colour patterns that predators associate with painful stings. Hummingbird moths, with a wingspan of up to nine centimetres (3.5 in), resemble hummingbirds but produce a softer buzz as they hover at flowers. Eight-spotted foresters, arrayed with bright white and yellow spots on velvety black wings, look strikingly like butterflies, lacking only the large knobs found at the ends of all butterfly antennae.

Far more moths, however, have dull wings, which most keep outspread while resting to blend with tree bark and other surfaces. In contrast, butterflies – which account for only about 10 per cent of the vast, moth-dominated order Lepidoptera – usually perch with their wings folded together, except when basking in the sun to increase their metabolic rate.

When they lift off to fly, the large luna (illustrated), cecropia and polyphemus moths, together with some sphinx moths, flash pairs of large spots on their wings that look like eyes, which may startle an attacking predator. The otherwise concealed colours on the hind flappers of midsized underwing moths serve the same purpose. Underwings, as well as other owlet and geometrid moths, also have thin membranes stretched over tiny air cavities on their abdomens or thoraxes for picking up ultrasonic sound waves screeched by bats for their sonar tracking of flying prey. On tiger moths, these special sets of "ears" also emit ultrasonic clicks to warn bats of their extremely distasteful flavour. The youngsters of the Isabella tiger moth are the well-known fuzzy, reddish-brown woolly bear caterpillars commonly seen along paths and roadsides in autumn and early spring.

Though generally most noticeable as adults, moths have the greatest impact on the ecosystem when they're caterpillars. Some species, including early-summer flying cecropia and luna moths, do not even eat as adults, living only long enough to mate and lay eggs. Their offspring, though, are food factories, devouring incredible quantities of leaves and concentrating nutrients into their plump, juicy, bite-sized bodies for birds and other animals. Studies on caterpillars in mixed forests have found that they collectively outweigh all birds, moose, bears and chipmunks put together. Even seed- and fruit-eating birds depend heavily on the high-protein caterpillar meals that allow their nestlings to reach adult size in a matter of weeks. Outbreaks of spruce budworm – a moth caterpillar – cause population explosions of many bird species, such as Cape May and bay-breasted warblers, as well as the defoliation of large tracts of evergreens, leading to more forest diversity.

To avoid their many predators, caterpillars employ a wide range of dining styles directed towards eating in anonymity. Some string out silk from spinnerets near the mouth to pull the edges of leaves up around them, or to tie bundles of evergreen needles together into snack shacks.

days to several months as adults

Predators: Bats, birds, mice, shrews, skunks, raccoons, beetles, wasps, tachinid flies, flesh flies, ants, spiders

Common beauties attracted to lights: Luna, polyphemus, cecropia, one-eyed sphinx, pine looper, underwing and rosy maple moths

Other insects attracted to lights: Night-flying mayflies, lacewings, caddisflies, dobsonflies, beetles, midges, flies and true bugs

Portion of Ontario moths that fly by day: 2–5%

Cold-weather moths: Small, grey-brown cankerworm and Bruce spanworm moths mate and lay eggs in late autumn; other pale Geometrid family moths overwinter as adults and emerge early in spring

Common autumn caterpillars: Woolly bears and other tiger moth larvae, fall webworms

Winter whereabouts: Beneath bark, soil or leaf litter, in galls, wrapped in pine needles or amid other debris; most as eggs or in cocoons, some as caterpillars or adults

Natural antifreeze glycerol content in blood of hibernating woolly bear caterpillars: Up to 26%

Moth range: All Ontario and Canada to the Arctic

Only fully domesticated insect: Silkworm moth, which,

unlike honeybees, cannot survive in the wild; domesticated in China at least 2,500 years ago

Number of cocoons needed to make a silk handkerchief: Hundreds

Gypsy moth origins: Imported from France to Massachusetts in 1869 in failed attempt to cross them with native moths to produce commercial silk; escaped gypsies ravaged North American forests, reaching Ontario in 1970

Average period between forest tent caterpillar outbreaks: 11 years

Mexican jumping beans: Caused by movement of moth caterpillars eating into beans

Age of oldest moth fossils: 190 million years

Number of known Ontario moth species: About 1,500

Number of known moth and butterfly species worldwide: 150,000–165,000

Also see: Evening Grosbeak, Red-winged Blackbird, Yellow-rumped Warbler, Monarch Butterfly, Little Brown Bat, Goldenrod, Red Oak, White Spruce

Bagworm caterpillars live and munch within small hanging sacks of silk, twigs and other plant bits. Tiny leaf miners create splotches or trails in leaves that start out small, where an egg hatches, and grow wider as the caterpillar winds through the leaf, ending at the point where it pupates and emerges as a moth. Other moth larvae hatch from eggs laid in plant tissues and cause some of the bulging galls common in goldenrod stems and oaks. As the caterpillars eat away at a stem or acorn from the inside, the plant or tree surrounds the area with hard, tumourlike gall tissue. The hidden munchers eat a hole out of the gall before transforming into adults.

Others, such as fall webworms, eastern tent caterpillars and chokecherry tentmakers, live communally, spinning large silk nests for refuge. Forest tent caterpillars, which congregate on silken pads rather than in tents, can number up to 20,000 per tree during outbreaks, defoliating vast swaths of aspen, sugar maple and red oak. Most moth caterpillars also use silk safety lines if they fall or get blown off their perch and encase themselves in silk cocoons before transforming into adults. Butterflies, in contrast, metamorphose inside a skin covering as a chrysalis.

MOURNING CLOAK BUTTERFLY
First Flutter of Spring

On a bright, beautiful March day, when the mercury rises above freezing and everything radiates with the glow of the strengthening sun, thoughts of spring can materialize on the dark wings of a mourning cloak butterfly. Cold winds and more snow invariably drive this protospring away and send the yellow-fringed butterfly back to bed for several weeks more. But the mourning cloak, with its first foray, will have claimed the forest for the coming season of rebirth.

Named for their sombre, dark wings, likened to a funeral cape, mourning cloaks are one of only a small number of butterflies that hibernate as adults. They're usually the first kind to appear in spring. In preparation for the climax of their lives, rousing mourning cloaks fortify themselves for the first plunge into spring air by revving up their flight muscles, causing their wings to shiver

Wingspan: 8–10 cm (3–4 in)

Markings: Dark brown wings with yellow trim and a black band with light blue spots; dull underwings look like a dead leaf or bark when closed; fuzzy brown body and white-tipped antennae

Alias: Camberwell beauty, yellow edge, antiopa butterfly, willow butterfly, yellow-bordered butterfly, grand surprise, antiope vaness, white border, spiny elm caterpillar, *le morio, Nymphalis antiopa*

Name origin of *butterfly*: From the butter-yellow colour of European brimstone butterflies; alternatively, possibly from Old Dutch *boterschijte,* meaning "butter pooper," referring to appearance of droppings

Whereabouts: Deciduous and mixed forests and meadows

Food: Caterpillars eat leaves of willows, birch, aspens and elm; butterflies sip sap, nectar, fruit juice and moisture from mud

Clutch: Up to 250 ridged, whitish eggs in a long, neat cluster around twigs near tips; eggs turn tan before hatching

Caterpillar: Up to 5 cm (2 in) long, spiny, black with white specks and a row of orange-red spots along back; red feet

Chrysalis: About 2 cm (0.8 in) long, dark grey or light tan with pink-tipped points, hanging from twigs, often many close together; develops for 10–15 days

Lifespan: Up to 1 year; several weeks as caterpillars, usually 10 months as adults

Predators: Birds, dragonflies, beetles, wasps, assassin bugs, parasitic flies, spiders

Minimum butterfly body temperature needed to fly: 27°C (81°F), usually over 33°C (91°F)

Best senses: Sight and smell; chemoreceptors on antennae and leg tips detect preferred nectar sources and pheromone emissions of opposite sex; butterflies cannot hear

Winter whereabouts: Narrow tree cavities, rock crevices,

and their internal temperature to rise 60 to 80 per cent. Then, stepping from winter dens in narrow tree and rock fissures, they press their furry bodies against sun-warmed surfaces to absorb radiant heat. At the same time, they spread their dark, heat-absorbing wings to bask in the direct sunlight. Evolutionary theorists speculate that insect wings may have evolved from what were initially solar panels.

While most of their brethren are too chilled even to fly on overcast summer days, hardy mourning cloaks, through all their efforts, can raise their body temperatures to up to 25°C (77°F) above the air around them. That ability, combined with a wandering tendency, has made them one of the most widespread butterflies in the world. They fly in the enduring summer sun of the Mackenzie River delta, Siberia and to the northern reaches of Europe, and occasionally Britain, where they're highly prized by collectors and called Camberwell beauties. Mourning cloaks may journey up to 70 kilometres (43 miles).

The butterflies come out of hibernation for good around late April or early May. Their prime directive during their one or two remaining months of life is to seek each other out and mate. Eggs are commonly laid around the twig tips of willows, where the butterflies gather to sip catkin nectar, and on aspens and birch, where they lap up sap from holes bored by yellow-bellied sapsuckers.

Mourning cloak caterpillars hatch in June, just in time to munch upon fully unfolded new leaves, around which, working together, they build protective webs. They're so gregarious that when threatened the spiny-backed grazers rise together on their hind prolegs.and do a menacing Watusi. Even after they enter the pupal stage, if a metamorphosing mourning cloak perceives danger outside its chrysalis, it begins swaying inside, setting off its siblings encased nearby until they are all rattling their shells against the branches and the neighbourhood is rocking with the sound and furry of the shaking pupae.

The band breaks up when the butterflies burst free in July. Many butterfly species live just a matter of days or weeks once they spread their wings, but most northern mourning cloaks must fly through a whole summer and sleep through winter before they're ready to breed. If summer is hot and dry, they go dormant, but resume fluttering through September and into October, building up fat for the winter. Their unique yellow wing trim, bright when freshly transformed, fades with time to white, becoming worn down to almost nothing by the end of their long lives.

beneath loose bark, under logs

Range: Throughout Ontario; also in all other provinces and territories

First appearance of butterflies: Probably 80–100 million years ago

Biggest Ontario butterfly: Giant swallowtail, wingspan 10–15 cm

Other Ontario butterflies that hibernate as adults: Milbert's tortoiseshells, Compton tortoiseshells, question marks, gray commas, green commas, hop merchants, satyr commas, occasionally black swallowtails and red admirals

Number of resident or regular migrant butterfly species in Ontario: About 140

Number of butterfly species extirpated from Ontario: 5

Number of butterfly species worldwide: About 17,500

Also see: Yellow-bellied Sapsucker

SPIDERS
Spinners of Insect Fate

Largest Ontario spider:
Dock spider, *Dolomedes tenebrosus* (illustrated), with a legspan of up to 13 cm (5 in)

World's largest spider:
Goliath bird-eating spider of South America, with a legspan of up to 28 cm (11 in)

Dock spider running speed:
Up to 75 cm/sec (30 in/sec) on top of water

Dock spider dive duration:
Commonly 5–10 min; maximum at least 45 min

Spider density in Ontario forests: Up to 20,000/ha (50,000 per acre)

Estimated weight of insects eaten annually by spiders in Canada: Equal to the

Spiders are the very essence of "creepy" in the popular mind, the mere sight of one giving countless Miss Muffets the willies. Freud contended that spider phobias arise from a primal fear of a cannibal witch or ogre with long, pointy, bending fingers, subconsciously identified with the arachnid's legs. Despite the immense importance they have in controlling insect populations, spiders have long been associated with witches and Halloween. Both Greek and Hindu goddesses were represented as spiders, spinners of fate, while flies were often regarded as the souls in transition from one life to the next. The image of a fly caught in a spider's web represented, to the ancients, the helplessness of humanity in the web of fate.

Some 40 to 50 per cent of spider species don't actually spin webs, but all of them have spinneret glands, at the rear underside of their abdomens, that produce silk. Jumping spiders, which stalk and leap upon their prey, remain anchored to a silk safety line in case they fall. Crab spiders too tie themselves off while lying in wait inside flowers to ambush pollinating insects. Nocturnal wolf spiders run down their quarry but use silk to lash together shelters.

Silk is made of protein strands. The strands are coated in fungicides and bactericides to protect them from other hungry organisms. The antibiotic qualities of spider webs have made them, in many cultures, a common folk remedy for wounds. Layers of webs from large spiders have also been used for fishing nets by the people of Papua New Guinea. Though a silk strand may be 1/100 the diameter of a human hair, it is twice as strong, for its size, as steel. Web strands are also incredibly elastic, stretching up to four times their original length. In the industrialized world, spider silk is used mostly for the crosshairs of optical equipment, but researchers are reproducing the genes of spider webs with the aim of creating building materials with the same diverse qualities.

Spiders can spin different types of silk from different glands for their varying needs. There are eight kinds of silk in all, though no one species has all eight brands. The spider adjusts its spinneret valves to control the thickness, elasticity and strength of the silk as it spins. Orb-web spiders join strong strands, like girders, to a central point across a vertical space, then thread concentric rings through them with a special sticky silk that catches flying insects. A thick zigzag strand is woven through the webs of some

weight of the country's entire human population

Alias: Arachnids, *les araignées,* order Araneae

Name origins: Spider comes from Old English *spinthron,* meaning "spinner"; *arachnid* derives from Greek mythology's Arachne, a maiden changed into a spider by Athena after defeating the goddess in a weaving contest

***Cobweb* word origin:** Another Old English name for spider was *attorcoppe,* later shortened to *coppe* or *cob*

Name of a group: A smother of spiders

Number of eyes: 8 for most species; orb-weavers and most other web-makers have very poor eyesight; jumping spiders, wolf spiders, dock spiders and other roving hunters see well

Food: Insects, other spiders, mites, daddy longlegs, tadpoles, tiny fish

Eggs per female: 2 to several thousand, depending on species

Web-making frequency: Many orb-weavers rebuild webs nightly, first gobbling up and recycling most of old tattered strands, then re-stringing remaining frame in as little as half an hour

Lifespan: Most Ontario species less than a year and a few up to 3 years; tarantulas up to 30 years

Predators: Birds, toads, frogs, salamanders, shrews,

snakes, wasps, tiger beetles, centipedes, other spiders; eggs eaten by many insects and birds

Winter whereabouts: Most species hibernate beneath loose bark, in logs or under dead leaves, grass and stones; eggs or hatchlings of others in egg cases in similar locations

Range: All Ontario and Canada to high Arctic

Number of people bitten annually in Ontario by black widows: Avg. 2, usually involving spiders in fruit crates from the southern U.S. and Mexico

Famous spiders: Inky Dinky, Charlotte, Boris, Shelob, The Spiders from Mars

First appearance of spiders: Probably at least 180 million years ago

Birds that use spider silk in nests: Hummingbirds, vireos, flycatchers, kinglets, goldfinches, tree-nesting warblers

Spider relatives: Daddy long-legs, mites, ticks, scorpions, pseudo-scorpions, horseshoe crabs

Number of known Ontario spider species: About 1,500

Number of known spider species worldwide: About 36,000

Also see: Bees, Wasps and Hornets; Moose

species to make it visible to birds and mammals, which can see the big picture better than insects can. The works of many other eight-legged trappers contain no sticky silk at all. Funnel-web and sheet-web weavers – both large families whose flat, silken mats glisten in the grass or leaf litter with early morning dew – lie hidden beneath their webs until an insect alights above them.

All spiders also have venom, which they inject into their prey through small, fanglike appendages. The paralyzing serum gives them the option of consuming their catch right away or wrapping it up and keeping it fresh and alive for later imbibing. Spiders actually drink, rather than eat, liquifying their victim's insides with their venom and sucking out the slurry through a pump in their digestive system.

The minority of spiders that have big-enough chompers to break human skin bite only in self-defence, though the fangs of a dock spider can be as painful as a bee sting. In Ontario, only the very rare, retiring black widow spider, found as far north as Gravenhurst and the Bruce Peninsula, presents more of a threat to humans. The venom of the dark little arachnid with the red hourglass icon on its belly usually causes fever, breathing trouble and paralysis for one or two days, though it can be fatal to very small children or sick people.

Female black widows are also synonymous with the femme fatale because they sometimes devour their mates after males have served their purpose. In fact, the practice occurs among many spiders. To avoid being eaten even before mating, the generally much smaller male may strum love notes on a strand of a potential mate's web, signal to her with his legs in a kind of sexual semaphore or send a chemical message. If she appears receptive, he rushes in and fertilizes her. But fleet-footed males usually manage to hit the road before giving their hungry partners a chance to heartlessly devour them for a quick protein fix to nourish their eggs. In the heat of passion, males sometimes tie their mates down to help ensure their escape afterwards.

Most species mate in early summer and then wrap their eggs in yellowish cocoons, which mothers closely guard. Some, such as dock spiders, tote their egg sacs with them for a couple of weeks. Wolf spiders even carry their hatchlings on their backs for up to 10 days. Soon after hatching, though, most tiny spiderlings swarm to the tops of plants and shrubs and spin a thin strand of silk, which catches in the breeze and lifts them up into the air, sometimes thousands of metres. This "ballooning" spreads them out over wide distances, keeping their populations from becoming too concentrated in one area. As night falls, the silk becomes moisture-laden and the little paratroopers drop back down to Earth. They can sometimes enshroud bushes or shrubs with silk.

The ranks of eight-legged arachnids are swelled by many other species that, like true true spiders, lack the antennae of insects. **Daddy longlegs**, or harvestmen, have only two simple eyes on a single "turret" and can neither spin silk nor inject venom. Instead, they mostly scavenge dead insects and forage for spider and insect eggs. If they are themselves seized, their easily detachable limbs continue to quiver after being severed, distracting the predator and giving daddy longlegs a chance to escape. Unlike spiders and mites, however, they cannot regrow lost legs.

The most abundant of the eight-leggers – more numerous even than any group of insects – are **mites**, spherical, often brightly coloured beasts ranging from a quarter of a millimetre to half a centimetre (0.2 inches) in diameter. They are a diverse group, found in every type of soil and aquatic environment, and have been around for more than 400 million years. Some are predators of tiny invertebrates and micro-organisms or parasites of dragonflies and other insects. Many eat vegetation, while still others play vital roles in breaking down decaying plant matter and spreading fungal spores.

TIGER SWALLOWTAIL BUTTERFLY
Yellow Beauties of June

Wingspan: 6.5–8 cm (2.5–3 in)

Wingspan of Ontario's largest butterfly: 10–15.5 cm (4–6 in), giant swallowtail

Wingspan of world's largest butterfly: Up to 30 cm (12 in), New Guinea's Queen Alexandra's birdwing, member of swallowtail family

Wingspan of world's smallest butterfly: 1–2 cm (0.4–0.8 in), pygmy blue butterfly

Tiger swallowtail markings: Yellow wings with partial black stripes and borders, blue and orange spots along border near tail; body dark brown or black on top, yellow with black stripe on sides

In cultures around the world, the ethereal beauty of butterflies has stirred the imagination. The ancient Greeks used the same word, *psyche,* for both the soul and butterflies. The fluttering insect represented immortality because it was transformed and resurrected from a deathlike state in its chrysalis. An Ojibway story says butterflies were created after the first humans were born – a pair of twins. The children showed no interest in learning to walk, so the Great Spirit told their benefactor, Nanabush, to collect a pile of colourful stones in the western mountains and throw them in the air. The stones became butterflies, followed Nanabush back to the twins and, by staying just beyond their grasp, enticed them to sit up, walk and run for the first time.

Among North America's most familiar butterflies, the tiger swallowtail has always cheered observers with its black-striped yellow wings and double-pointed rear fins. It was one of the first creatures recorded by the English in the New World, painted during a 1587 expedition to the ill-fated Roanoke Island colony off North Carolina. In Ontario woodlands, the tigers appear from late May through early July, everywhere there are open spaces and forest edges. Like their largely tropical swallowtail kin, they characteristically flutter their wings while drinking nectar from flowers, which they sample first with taste buds on their feet.

Groups of swallowtails are often seen sipping water from muddy puddles and wet ground, especially near roadsides, to obtain salt. They also visit animal droppings and corpses to suck up amino acids. Most of the imbibers are males, who concentrate salt and proteins into their sperm capsules, or spermatophores. Upon fluttering behind a butterfly maid and convincing her to land and join abdomens, the yellow charmers provide, with their sperm, a rich nutrient loading for her fertilized eggs. Females then look for suitable nursery sites, usually leaves up to 2.5 metres (eight feet) high on the south side of yellow birch, aspen or black cherry trees.

Producing only one generation a year, the butterflies unfortunately die after early summer, leaving only their crawling or dormant young behind. Hatching soon after the eggs are laid, swallowtail caterpillars are at first disguised as tiny black and white bird droppings. As they grow, feeding mainly at night, they turn green, blending with the leaves, save for two black-dotted orange or yellow spots on the high hunch behind their tiny heads, giving the impression of

Alias: Canadian tiger swallowtail, northern tiger swallowtail, *le papillon tigre du Canada*, *Papilio canadensis*

Whereabouts: Meadows and edges of mixed and deciduous forest

Food: Caterpillars eat leaves of yellow birch, aspen, black cherry, willow, ash; butterflies sip nectar of milkweed, dogbane, Labrador tea and other flowers, and fluids from carrion and animal droppings

Eggs per female: Several hundred, laid scattered apart, green at first, turning greenish yellow with reddish-brown specks

Caterpillar: Up to 5 cm (2 in) long, lime green with a pair of large yellow or orange "eyespots" with black "pupils"

Chrysalis: Up to 3 cm (1.2 in) long, light brown with blotches of green and black, resembling stub of a broken twig; attached to branches

Lifespan: Up to 13 months; several weeks as a caterpillar, 10–11 months in chrysalis, up to 1 month as an adult

Predators: Birds, mice, shrews, spiders, ants, parasitic wasps and flies

Range: All Ontario except far south; also in all other provinces and territories

Eastern tiger swallowtail: Virtually identical to Canadian tiger swallowtail, but tends to be a little larger, has 2 generations a year and mainly feeds on tulip trees and other southern species as a caterpillar; occurs as far north as the southern edge of the Shield and hybridizes with its northern cousin where their ranges overlap

Number of Ontario swallowtail species: 6

Number of swallowtail species worldwide: 534, mostly in the tropics

Also see: Snowshoe Hare, Chokecherry, Yellow Birch

the face of a green snake. If that doesn't fool predators, the future tigers pull out their secret weapon: a forked appendage, called the osmeterium, that pops out from behind the head and emits a smell that ants, spiders and parasitic wasps find most disagreeable.

In their later youth, the caterpillars keep mostly out of sight, often spinning silk pads over the upper sides of leaves to make them curl up, creating solar-heated homes up to 3.5°C (5.4°F) warmer than the surrounding air. The warmth speeds their development, and sometime between mid-June and early July, they turn brown and become inactive as they begin to pupate. They remain entombed inside their chrysalis for 10 or 11 months, until emerging as butterflies in the latter half of May.

WATER STRIDERS
Staying Afloat on Tippytoes

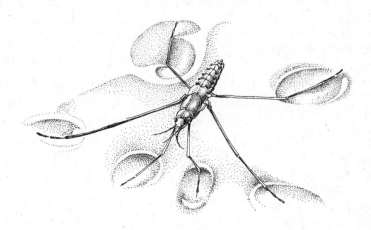

The water strider is a miracle bug, walking on water with seemingly the greatest of ease. It accomplishes the feat by spreading its weight out in a sprawled stance. Each leg is tipped with many tiny waterproof hairs. Each hair in turn is tipped with a microscopic air-filled groove, so that the insect never breaks the water's surface tension, which forms a film of closely packed molecules. If a solid object punctures the water's thin film, the bug falls through into the water.

Lying still, water striders are almost invisible. When they move, with their long, jointed legs acting like oars, their shadows glide across the shallow bottom of their pools. They often congregate in large groups in calm channels, the water surface coming alive with their activity. They move quickly towards any small surface disturbance, looking for a meal that has dropped

Length: 2–15 mm (0.1–0.6 in)

Markings: Various species may be black, dark grey or yellow on top, with brown or grey markings, and white beneath

Wings: Some species, especially in temporary ponds, have a winged stage, most often flying at night, sometimes attracted to lights

Alias: Pond skaters, Jesus bugs, gerrids, *les patineurs,* family Gerridae

Whereabouts: Calm water in streams, ponds, lake margins, swamps

Food: Insects, spiders, springtails, mites

Mating ripple frequencies: 2-5/sec attracts females;

35-45/sec warns other males to stay away

Egg development period: About 2 weeks

Lifespan: About 6 months; most species have 2 generations a year

Predators: Fish, frogs, salamanders, other aquatic insects

First appearance: At least 55 million years ago

Range: All Ontario; also in all other provinces and territories

True bugs: Scientifically speaking, only insects with beaklike, sucking mouth parts, belonging to the order Hemiptera, which includes water striders, can properly be called "bugs"; other members include cicadas, stink bugs, aphids, leafhoppers, assassin bugs

Ontario's largest aquatic insect: Giant water bug, up to 5 cm (2 in) long

Number of Ontario water-strider species: 11

Number of water-strider species worldwide: About 500

See also: Beetles, Spiders

in – often another insect that has fallen into the water. Using their two short forelegs to grab their victims, water striders then pierce their prey with their needlelike mouth parts and suck out their life juices.

After hibernating since October beneath rocks or other debris on dry ground, water striders appear as soon as the ice melts and mate through spring and early summer. Potential mates go to egg-laying sites and signal their intentions by creating special-frequency mating waves. Couples may cling together in a love embrace for more than an hour. Females lay creamy white, waterproof eggs on floating objects. Young water striders look like small versions of their parents. They grow and moult five times within 40 to 60 days and are then ready to mate themselves.

FISH (AND AQUATIC COMPANIONS)

O *ntario has long been considered an angler's paradise. Pickerel, pike and trout are veritable cultural institutions in cottage country. But rod and reel are not prerequisites for experiencing the inhabitants of the deep. Fish can be viewed jumping out of the water at low-flying insects at dusk, flitting amid the weeds of a small stream, or spawning near shore and along creek beds in spring, summer or fall. Average weights and sizes of species featured here are given for Ontario's inland waters rather than for the Great Lakes and farther south, where many fish tend to be larger.*

We also feature other easily viewed non-fishy inhabitants of the drink. Crayfish abound in lakes and streams, hiding beneath rocks by day and lurking in the shallows at night. Mussels, too, can often be found in the shallows, while leeches invariably find us. Most fun of all are Ontario's apparently numerous lake monsters, which offer anyone the opportunity of joining in the biggest fish stories of all.

BROOK TROUT
Speckled Beauty of Pristine Waters

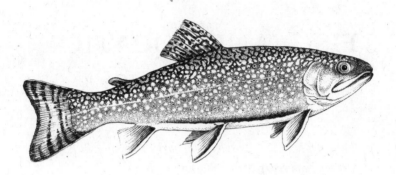

Length: Avg. 15–25 cm (6–10 in) in small streams, 30–40 cm (12–16 in) in larger rivers and lakes

Average weight: 200–900 g (0.4–2 lb)

World record brook trout: 6.6 kg (14.5 lb), 80 cm (31.5 in) long, caught in the Nipigon River, Ontario, 1915

Markings: Dark olive-green back with lighter green swirls, sides splattered with white spots and red dots bordered by light blue, white belly, reddish fins

Alias: Speckled trout, eastern brook trout, brookie, native trout, *l'omble de fontaine, Salvelinus fontinalis*

Name of a group: A hover of trout

Anglers have a saying that God made trout last after practising on the other fish. Brook trout, in particular, are fondly admired for their speckled beauty, their challenging eccentricities and the untrammelled wilderness settings in which they're usually found. Thriving in rushing water like few other large fish, they hold sway in cold, clear headwater streams. They're also common in the headwater lakes of highland areas, especially in Algonquin Park.

The best time to see brook trout is after the ice breaks up in spring or when they're spawning in late autumn. During those periods they're near the shore, often jumping completely out of the water when flying insects are near. Brookies can't live in water warmer than 20°C (68°F), so they either keep to small, deeply shaded streams or, as the top layer on lakes and rivers warms up in June, head for deep, cooler water. They also need ample oxygen, which keeps them out of the lowest depths in summer and concentrated into a transition zone between the top and bottom layers of lakes, three to 12 metres (10 to 40 feet) beneath the surface.

As the surface cools again in autumn, brook trout move into the shallows to feed. When the water temperature falls to 4.5 to 9.5°C (40 to 49°F), they spawn in the riffles of creeks and brooks or on gravel or sandy lake beds, commonly one to two metres (three to seven feet) deep, returning to the same sites every year. The beds must have springwater percolating up through them, which keeps the buried eggs clean and aerated and may protect them from acidic meltwater in the spring. Amid congregations of up to hundreds of trout, a female spends long hours plowing through the gravel to create a small nest, or redd, often with an eager male or two – which develop deep red lower sides during spawning season – standing guard over her. After she shakes and releases her eggs into the nest, the male fertilizes them with his milt. She may fill three or four nests with eggs over several days of mating with various partners, spending up to an hour after each episode covering the clutch with gravel.

The transparent orange or reddish eggs hatch from February to April, depending on how cold the water is. The fry stay put beneath the gravel for about a month, living off large yolk sacks attached to their undersides. Later, some keep to log-strewn stretches of lakeshore, while others swim upstream for the summer to forest creeks as shallow as 15 centimetres (six

Whereabouts: Shallow, clear, cold headwater lakes and streams with sand and gravel bottoms, lots of rocks, logs and some vegetation; often beneath overhanging trees and bushes in fall, winter and spring; 3–12 m (10–39 ft) below surface in summer

Preferred water temperature: 12–15°C (54–59°F)

Peak activity times: Early morning and late evening

Food: Minnows, perch, sculpins, frogs, crayfish, stoneflies, mayflies, midges, dragonfly nymphs, caddisfly and black fly larvae, snails, clams, worms

Dietary source of carotenoid pigments that turn males' lower flanks deep scarlet during spawning: Crayfish

Eggs per female: Avg. 200–1,000; very large females produce up to 5,000

Egg development period: 2–5 months

Survival rate of eggs: Avg. 15–65%

Length at end of first growing season: Avg. 7.5 cm (3 in)

Age of first-time breeders: Most 2–3 years

Lifespan: Few live longer than 3–4 years; maximum more than 20 years

Predators: Mink, otters, osprey, pike, sea lampreys; young also taken by herons, kingfishers, water snakes, snapping turtles, bass,

pickerel; eggs eaten by crayfish, perch, whitefish, brown
bullheads

Range: Most of Ontario except far south and far west;
also in all other provinces

**Number of brook-trout
lakes in Ontario:** About
2,100

**World's greatest concentra-
tion of brook-trout lakes
and streams:** Algonquin
Park, with 230

**Number of brook-trout
lakes with acid levels that
can affect trout reproduction:** About 40

**Number of lake-trout lakes
in Ontario:** About 2,300

**World record lake trout (net-
ted):** 46 kg (102 lb), 3.2 m
(10.5 ft) long, caught in
Lake Athabasca, 1961

**Number of salmon family
species in Ontario:**
13 native, 5 introduced

**Number of salmon family
species worldwide:** 70

Also see: Mayflies, Minnows,
Smallmouth Bass, Lakes

inches), where insect food is probably more
plentiful.

Because trout are less active in frigid water
beneath the ice, those in larger water bodies do
most of their growing in spring and fall, feeding
in the rich shallows. This is especially true of the
brookie's much larger, greenish-grey cousin, the
lake trout, which retreats down to about 20
metres (66 feet) or so in the coldest lower layer
of lakes during summer. Because of their deep-
water needs, lake trout are restricted to clear
lakes usually 20 hectares (50 acres) or bigger. In
the smaller lakes, they grow very slowly because
they have only algae, plankton and insect larvae
to eat during the summer. In larger lakes they
can pick off prey such as perch and whitefish that
enter into their summer zone. Adults average
about 1.3 kilograms (three pounds).

While near rocky shores and above boulder-
strewn shoals in the fall, lake trout mate at night
– unlike day-spawning brook trout – usually in
1.5 to 4.5 metres (five to 15 feet) of water. The
Ojibway and other Native groups took advantage of these rare near-shore visits of the big
lakers to net them. They also speared brook trout
and whitefish as the fish were preoccupied with
autumn spawning, and smoked them for valuable winter stores.

CLAMS AND MUSSELS
Sedentary Filter-feeders

While clams and mussels evoke images of briny seashores, Ontario's lakes, rivers, creeks and wetlands have their own smattering of the hard-shelled filter-feeders. Mussels are the more conspicuous, with the largest of central Ontario's half-dozen common species reaching up to 16 centimetres (6.4 inches) long. Most live at depths between 30 centimetres (one foot) and two metres (6.6 feet), though the high-domed shells of fat mucket mussels (illustrated) are common in finger-deep water just off riverbanks.

The region's more than two dozen clams, on the other hand, are much smaller, most just a centimetre (0.4 inches) long or less. They dwell anywhere from a few centimetres to many metres beneath the water. One group, called fingernail clams – which actually look more like toenails – live amid the submerged vegetation or

Largest Ontario freshwater mussel: White healsplitter, up to 19 cm (7.5 in) long

Smallest Ontario freshwater clam: Perforated pea clam, maximum length 1.7 mm (0.07 in)

Mussel markings: Outer shells of most usually a shade of off-brown, but may be yellowish or greenish to almost black; inner shells can be white, pink, purple, bluish or yellow

Best buttons: Smooth, colourful, often iridescent inner lining of freshwater mussel shells, called "mother-of-pearl," once commonly used to make shiny buttons

Clam markings: Outer shells off-white, yellowish or brown

Mussel name origin: From Latin *musculus*, "little mouse," because the dark, hunched shells beneath the water reminded early observers of crouching mice

Food: Planktonic algae, protozoa, bacteria, organic waste

Bivalve sex: Males release sperm into the water to be filtered out by any female nearby; some species produce both eggs and sperm

Growth rings: The thickest, peaked portion is the oldest part of a shell; periodic secretions of liquid calcium carbonate harden along the edges, forming new layers that show up as distinct ridges on the exteriors of many species

Mussel lifespan: Avg. 15–20 years and up to 30 for some common Ontario species; seashore quahogs can live more than 200 years

Pea clam lifespan: Most just up to 1 year

Fingernail clam lifespan: Up to 8 years

Predators: Otters, raccoons, mink, muskrats, sunfish, trout, whitefish and other fish, ducks, ravens, gulls

Edibility: Freshwater mussels are edible but accumulate any pesticides and other pollutants in the water

Mussel density in sandy or muddy shallows: 1–100/m² (1.2 sq. yd)

Zebra mussels: Native to Caspian and Black Sea area; discovered in Lake St. Clair

sediments of rivers, lakes or ponds, while the even smaller pea clams generally keep to the mud and fine sand of lake bottoms.

Lying half-buried underwater, mussels and clams set up shop by simply opening their shells slightly and flushing water through their systems, siphoning oxygen to breathe and bits of plankton for food. Two strong muscles attached to each shell near the rear hinge contract to snap the protective covers shut whenever needed. The molluscs dig themselves down or, rarely, move short distances by extending a central muscular lobe, called a "foot," forward into the mud and then contracting the rest of their body so that it's pulled towards the foot. Mussel trails are sometimes visible in calm, shallow waters as grooves usually about a metre (3.3 feet) long in the sand or sediment, though sometimes reaching up to three metres (10 feet).

Mussels and clams do most of their real travelling when they are very young. Developing for up to nearly a year inside a special brood pouch within their mother's gills, microscopic mussel young are called glochidia, from the Greek for "arrow point," because of their shape when their tiny shells are agape. The mussels leave home in the stream of their mother's waste water when still about half a millimetre long and within a few days must clamp onto the fins or gills of a passing fish or die. The lucky few take up residence as parasites in the fish's gills. Usually after several weeks of steady blood-nutrient meals and travelling far and wide with their hosts, the mini-mussels bail out and settle down to adult life in the muck.

Fingernail and pea clams also hitch rides, but as accidental tourists rather than parasites.

They're so small after leaving their mother's brood pouch that they're picked up on the feathers or muddy feet of water fowl or even the legs of large insects, such as dragonflies. Fresh-water clams are so easily spread that many Ontario species are found as far away as Australia and Hawaii. Ontario's most common, the aptly named ubiquitous pea clam, is the world's most widespread mollusc, found on every continent. One species, Harrington's fingernail, is so used to air transport that it specializes in small bodies of water that dry up for part of the year.

The white shell of another tiny clam, the megis, was the symbol and source of power of the Ojibway's sacred Midewiwin Society. The megis is said to have appeared on a number of occasions as a brilliant light in the water. Though a marine clam of the east coast, its shells were brought inland through trade, as were quahog shells, used to make the cylindrical beads of widely prized wampum belts. Clam shells are, in fact, one of the world's oldest items of trade and have been used for human ornamentation for at least 30,000 years. The abundance of shell piles excavated at sites of human activity up to 120,000 years old also attests to the importance of molluscs as a staple for early bands of people living along coasts and rivers.

in 1988; probably released from foreign freighter bilge water; has spread to the Muskoka, Kawartha, and Rideau lakes; free-swimming microscopic hatchlings become tiny clams, sticking en masse to hard surfaces

Clam and mussel range: Throughout most of Ontario; also in all other provinces and territories

Appearance of first clams: More than 400 million years ago

Number of Ontario freshwater mussel species: 40 native, 2 introduced

Number of Ontario freshwater mussel species at risk: 11 endangered, 1 threatened

Number of Ontario freshwater clam species: 31 native, 3 introduced

CRAYFISH
Ontario's Biggest Footloose Invertebrates

Density per m² (1.2 sq. yd) in prime shoreline habitat: 3–24

Largest Ontario species: Robust crayfish, up to 20 cm (8 in) long

Smallest Ontario crayfish: Northern clearwater crayfish, avg. 4.5–7 cm (1.8–2.8 in) long

Markings: Various species range from darkly mottled olive to grey-brown back or rusty orange

Alias: Crawfish, crawdads, *les écrevisses,* family Astacidae

Whereabouts: Shallow water of lakes, streams, marshes, swamps, ponds

Homes: Most common species beneath rocks or logs, marked by a semicircle of pushed-out gravel and mud

Food: Decomposing organic material, aquatic plants, algae, snails, insect larvae, fish eggs, other recently moulted crayfish

Average clutch: 60–300 eggs, depending on species

Lifespan: Most species 1–3 years, some up to 5 years

Predators: Bass and other fish, turtles, frogs, mud puppies, snakes, gulls, herons, kingfishers, raccoons, mink, otters, dragonfly nymphs, giant water bugs

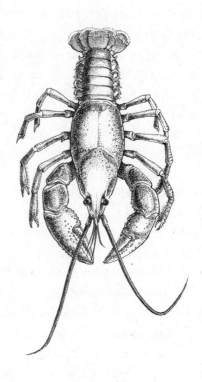

The shorelines of many lakes are teeming with crayfish. Their total biomass is commonly 10 times as great as all fish present. Often only a few rocks need to be removed near shore to reveal the miniature lobsterlike creatures hiding from the light of day. Crayfish are nocturnal crustaceans, preying and scavenging on smaller invertebrate animals. They are themselves the largest footloose invertebrates in Ontario (the fattest mussels can weigh more). Their exoskeletons are made out of chitin, a fingernail-like armour that covers all insects. But unlike insects, crayfish have two sets of antennae, which they use to feel around and detect chemical scents in the water.

Crayfish are devoted mothers
to their clinging offspring

Despite their mini-monster appearance, crayfish are devoted mothers to their clinging offspring. Most species mate from April to May or August to October. The following May, June or July, females lie on their backs and bend their tails forwards to stick eggs to their undersides. Even after they hatch, the young hang on beneath their mother's tail for two or three weeks. As they grow, young crayfish, like insects, shed their old exoskeletons up to 10 times, tripling in size by their first winter. Their new, softer skin is inflated before it hardens to give them space to grow inside the new shell. In this soft stage, which lasts several days, crayfish are delectable morsels for fish, birds, mammals and Cajun restaurant goers. To escape quickly, they flip their tails beneath them and catapult backwards at high speed.

Range: All Ontario, except far northwest
Number of crayfish species in Ontario: 7 native, 2 introduced
Number of crayfish species worldwide: About 500
Also see: Brook Trout, Smallmouth Bass

LAKE MONSTERS
Relics from Past Ages?

Locations of sightings:
Lakes Huron, Ontario, Erie, Simcoe, Mazinaw, Muskrat, Georgian Bay, Lake of Bays and the Niagara River

Number of lakes in Canada with reported monster sightings: 94

Length: Estimates range from 3–23 m (10–75 ft)

Markings: Various monsters are dark grey, silver, green, mahogany, orange, brown or black; head may be shaped like a horse or a dog, with fiery eyes and wide, gaping mouth; pointed, fishlike tail and dorsal fins, sometimes with 2 legs

Whereabouts: Deep, cold lakes, especially with rocky shores offering possible underwater cave lairs

Given the number of deep lakes in Ontario, the province's abundance of lake monsters is not surprising at all. Lake Simcoe even has two, Kempenfelt Kelly and Igopogo. Generally, the lake leviathans are described as long, winding, serpentlike creatures, which, although fearsome-looking, do not appear to be particularly nasty. The odd, no-doubt-accidental capsizing of a small motorboat in calm water usually seems to be the worst they can manage. Tobey, a horned, black-eyed serpent up to 18 metres (60 feet) long sited as recently as 1972 off of Tobermory, though, is credited with causing the sinking of the *Intrepid* in 1877, after the schooner hit the beast, which reportedly just raised its head and swam away. Nowadays, sport fishers have added high-tech detection to Ontario monster lore by picking up very large creatures on their sonar fish finders.

Lake-monster sightings are certainly no recent phenomenon created by wayward Scots nostalgic for Nessie. Native peoples told of both good and bad beings inhabiting the waters they paddled. The May-may-gway-siwuk were shy creatures resembling humans but with strange faces and fishlike tails. Offerings of tobacco moved them to calm the waters and protect Ojibway travellers. When Champlain came up the Ottawa River in the early 1600s, the Algonquins told him of a large creature that dwelt in Muskrat Lake, near Petawawa. Great snaky beasts were first spotted in eastern Lake Erie in 1817 and in Lake Ontario in 1829. More sightings followed throughout the 19th century.

As with all great mysteries, there is no hard and fast evidence supporting the existence of lake monsters. But cryptozoologists – those who study reports of unknown animal species – are hot on the trail. Some believe the largest of these unknown creatures, or "cryptids," could be rare, secretive descendants of giant long-necked reptiles called plesiosaurs, which lived in the dinosaur era more than 65 million years ago. They cite the discovery of a living coelacanth, an ancient fish previously known only from fossils 70 to 320 million years old, off the coast of South Africa in 1938. Gorillas were similarly dismissed as primitive fantasies until white men encountered and, inevitably, started shooting them in the mid-19th century.

Other theories propose that various lake monsters may be remnant populations of marine mammals, such as snakelike zeuglodon whales, stranded after the ancient Champlain Sea receded from the interior 9,500 years ago. Whale

Food: If related to plesiosaurs, whales or other marine mammals, probably fish or plankton

Famous lake monsters and sea serpents: Nessie, Puff, Kempenfelt Kelly, the Mazinaw Monster, Tobey, Mussie, Ogopogo, Champ, Nogle, Leviathan, Behemoth, Cetus, Hydra, Grendel, Cecil

Largest fish ever caught in Ontario: 140 kg (308 lb) lake sturgeon 2.4 m (8 ft) long, in Lake Superior in 1922

Length of Fraser River sturgeon in British Columbia: Up to 3.6 m (12 ft)

Plesiosaurs: Were up to 12 m (43 ft) long, with flippers and a long neck and tail

Zeuglodons: Snakelike whales that flourished up to 20 million years ago

Giant squids: Genus *Architeuthis,* up to 15 m (50 ft) long, the largest living invertebrates

Also see: Lakes, Pegasus and Andromeda

bones from that period have been found in the Ottawa Valley. Dolphins have been found in China's Lake Tung Ting and seals in Siberia's Lake Baikal, both deep in the interior of Asia.

The Muskrat Lake monster, christened Mussie, has been reported several times since 1968 and is described as being three to four metres (9.8 to 13 feet) long, with a large tusk. Ichthyologists, or fish experts, have also suggested that especially large sturgeon, known to live more than 150 years and exceed two metres (6.5 feet) in length, may be behind all the mysterious sightings. The Chamber of Commerce of Cobden, on Muskrat Lake, hasn't waited for scientific confirmation, putting up large billboards with cartoon images of their friendly monster welcoming tourists to the town. Two UFO landings have also been reported around Muskrat Lake.

There have also been repeated sightings of Ontario's own Sasquatch-type creature. Members of the Weenusk First Nation, near Hudson Bay, have known of it for hundreds of years and reported finding huge footprints with a 1.8-metre (six-foot) stride in 2001. Similar sightings of a dark apelike creature with a long, light-coloured mane, dubbed Old Yellowtop or Precambrian Shield Man, have been made in the Cobalt area since 1906, most recently by a busload of miners in 1970.

LEECHES
Stealthy Silent Suckers

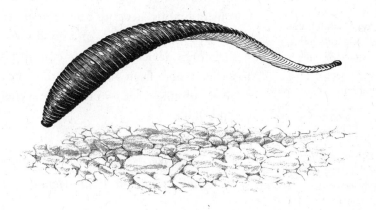

Leeches figure prominently in the annals of camp and swimming infamy, even if more out of revulsion than for any real pain they inflict. The soft, slimy bloodsuckers can be abundant but are mainly nocturnal, hiding under submerged rocks, logs and stumps by the day, coming out only if they smell food.

Of the 20 common leech species in Ontario, only four are true bloodsuckers, only three bite humans. Most are predators of insect larvae, snails, worms and other bottom-dwelling invertebrates. Others are parasites of fish, turtles and ducks, feeding through a proboscis rather than possessing the jaws of true bloodsuckers. The dark, thin bait leech commonly used by anglers is a scavenger. Mercifully, the largest sucker, the giant horse leech, measuring up to 36 centimetres (14 inches), is toothless and indifferent to *Homo sapiens*.

Number of ornate leeches found on a single snapping turtle: Up to 1,000

Length: Most species 2–6 cm (0.8–2.4 in); American horse leech and American medicinal leech are 2.5–15 cm (1–6 in)

Biggest Ontario species: Giant horse leech, up to 36 cm (14 in) long

Mouth: True bloodsuckers have 3 serrated jaws, forking like a clover; ornate leech and many others have a needlelike proboscis

Number of eyes: Most common bloodsuckers have 5 pairs; some species have none

Best senses: Smell, through chemical receptors in skin, and touch

Number of leech body segments: 34

Alias: Bloodsuckers, *les sangsues,* class Hirudinea

Name origin: From Old English *laece,* meaning "physician"

Meaning of giant horse leech scientific name *Mollibdella grandis:* "Big sucker"

Whereabouts: Shallow water with lots of rocks, stumps and weeds

Food: Various species consume mammalian, waterfowl, turtle, frog, fish, snail and clam blood or fluids, insect larvae, worms, tiny crustaceans, tadpoles, carrion, eggs of fish and amphibians, plankton

Number of full feedings needed by most bloodsuckers to reach maturity: 3

Lifespan: 1–3 years

Predators: Fish, waterfowl, garter snakes, salamanders, dragonfly nymphs, diving beetles

Winter whereabouts: Buried in mud

Range: All Canada to Arctic

Adjective for a creature that feeds on blood: Sanguivorous

Bioindicators: Leeches are used to measure water quality because they are highly sensitive to acidification and accumulate higher concentrations of contaminants than other aquatic invertebrates

Those leeches that do latch onto people, however, hold on tenaciously by a sucker mouth and a suction cup at end of the tail. They inject an anticoagulant to keep their liquid lunch flowing and an anaesthetic to keep their victims oblivious. Leeches can be easily removed, though, with salt, burns or a good yank. Left to their own devices, they may continue slurping for anywhere from an minute to more than an hour, swelling from two to 10 times their original weight.

All leeches are hermaphrodites, having both male and female parts

The number-one offender in Ontario is the American horse leech, a finger-sized bloodsucker that usually looks black but is actually dark grey with black spots. It preys mostly on other invertebrates. But if alerted by wave motions and the smell of dinner, it will rouse from daytime slumbers at the prospect of a juicy feast of human blood, which can keep its belly full for one to seven months. The other common adversary of swimmers is the similarly large American medicinal leech, which has a bright orange belly and rows of red and black spots on its dark back. It normally feeds on turtles, frogs and fish. The smaller, aptly named ornate leech, sporting fancy white markings on its dark green or grey back, often attaches itself to canoers at beaver dam liftovers. It usually contents itself on turtles and fish.

For more than 2,000 years, well into the mid-1800s, doctors commonly attached leeches to their patients as a remedy for just about anything. As barbaric as it sounds, "bleeding" may have had at least some beneficial effects. Many surgeons today apply leeches after operations for skin grafts and for reattaching severed body parts. The leeches drain off congested blood, giving capillaries time to grow back together without becoming deluged. Medical studies have also shown that a synthesized version of leech anticoagulant, hirudin, is a more effective drug for heart patients than traditional blood thinners. Researchers are studying leech chemicals for possible treatments for arthritis, glaucoma and cancer as well.

All leeches, like earthworms, are hermaphrodites, having both male and female parts, with partners exchanging sperm when they meet. They leave their spongy egg-bearing cocoons at the water's edge over the winter. Horse leeches and some other species sometimes crawl onto land to migrate to other bodies of water or to prey on terrestrial invertebrates at night.

Far-distant relations:
Though appearing similar, leeches and earthworms form separate classes of the same phylum, making them about as close to each other as humans are to frogs
Number of Ontario leech species: 32
Number of leech species worldwide: 650
Also see: Snapping Turtle, Lakes

MINNOWS
Huge Family of Little Fish

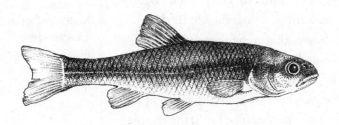

Length: Most species 5–8 cm (2–3 in)

Biggest native minnow: Fallfish, up to 60 cm (2 ft) long and 0.8 kg (1.8 lb)

World record carp: 26 kg (58 lb), caught in Lake Erie, 1957

Alias: Cyprinids, *les vairons,* family Cyprinidea

Name origin: Old English *myne,* meaning "small fish"

Food: Plankton, algae, aquatic plants, insect larvae, fish fry and eggs, crayfish young

Eggs per female: Up to 3,000

Egg development period: 4–10 days

Lifespan: 2–5 years for many species, up to 8 years

While seemingly inconsequential little fry, minnows constitute the largest and perhaps most important single family of freshwater fish in the world. They form a vital link in the aquatic food chain, eating vast quantities of algae, plankton and aquatic insects and passing on their energy and nutrients to most of the other larger fish as well as to fishing birds and other animals.

Ontario's three dozen minnow species occupy virtually every aquatic habitat, each finding its own niche. Creek chub (illustrated), which may grow up to nearly 30 centimetres (one foot) long and have iridescent silvery-purple sides, are one of the most common stream minnows. Northern redbelly dace, which average five centimetres (1.9 inches) long, live in the tea-coloured, acidic waters of boggy lakes and beaver ponds. Other minnows, such as fatheads –

Minnows form a vital link in the aquatic food chain, eating vast quantities of algae, plankton and aquatic insects

often the most abundant fish in small lakes, bogs and slow brooks – are less tolerant of acid rain than any other Ontario fish. Lake chub live in larger lakes but move into rocky streams to spawn. Large schools of golden shiners and emerald shiners, inhabiting river mouths and shallow, weedy lakeshores, are probably the most popular bait used by anglers.

Though most tiny fish, including the fry of many large species, are commonly called minnows, true members of the family are set apart by possessing just a single soft-rayed fin on their backs. They're also a lippy lot, with teeth located at the back of their throats rather than on their jaws. Oddly enough, two Eurasian imports few would take for minnows are included in their ranks: goldfish and carp. Some carp in the Great Lakes can weigh in at 14 kilograms (31 pounds).

Predators: Trout, bass, pike, many other large fish, kingfishers, mergansers, loons, gulls, cormorants, wading birds

Defences: Many minnows produce "alarm" pheromones if they are injured or eaten by predators, prompting others to form in tight schools and swim away

Range: All Ontario; also in all provinces and territories except island of Newfoundland

Number of Ontario minnow species: 34 native, 3 introduced, 1 recent natural immigrant

Number of minnow species worldwide: About 2,100

PERCH
Schools Seeking Warm Currents

Number in a school: Avg. 50–200

Length: Avg. 10–25 cm (4–10 in), up to 36 cm (14 in)

Weight: Avg. 100–300 g (4–11 oz), up to 1.8 kg (4 lb)

Markings: Green or yellow back and sides, with 6–8 dark vertical stripes; white or grey underside, 2 dark dorsal fins, orange lower fins, yellow or green eyes

Alias: Yellow perch, lake perch, American perch, panfish, *la perche, Perca flavescens*

Whereabouts: Usually less than 9 m (30 ft) deep in lakes and rivers with clear, open water

Food: Zooplankton, dragonfly and mayfly nymphs,

Perch find safety in numbers, but chance encounters with their schools provide sudden bonanzas for anglers, who catch more perch than any other fish in Ontario. From the time they hatch, perch fry form schools, often mixing with minnows, near the shore. They find no protection from their parents, who remain in adult groups and could very well be disposed to devour their own children. Transparent at first, the five-millimetre- (quarter-inch-) long hatchlings grow more slowly in colder water but live longer. In lakes with high population densities, adults may never exceed 15 centimetres (six inches), while perch in the Great Lakes can be twice that size.

Like herds of bison or caribou, perch schools travel in definite migration patterns. After spawning, they move farther offshore as waters warm towards the centre of lakes in summer. Preferring temperatures of between 20 and 24°C (68 to 75°F), perch generally stay in the warm, upper layer. They move into shallows to feed at dusk and dawn, and rest at the bottom at night. In winter, the schools become more dispersed but continue to actively feed beneath the ice, keeping legions of ice-fishing enthusiasts happy through the season. Many esteem the small, spiny fish to be the tastiest freshwater has to offer.

Male perch begin mating when they are three years old and females when they are four. Some swim up the tributary streams of their resident lakes to spawn. They usually spawn at night and in early morning in weedy or log-strewn, shallow water near shore soon after ice-out, when the water is 7 to 12°C (45 to 54°F). Depending on her size, a female releases between 10,000 and 90,000 eggs in sticky strands up to two metres (6.6 feet) long and 10 centimetres (four inches) wide. They hatch in eight to 20 days. Being such prolific breeders, they often become overcrowded in smaller water bodies, resulting in whole populations of stunted perch.

bloodworms, caddisfly larvae and other aquatic insects, snails, leeches, crayfish, minnows, fish fry and eggs

Hatchlings: 4–7 mm (0.2–0.3 in) long

Lifespan: Few live more than 7 years

Predators: Pike, pickerel, trout, bass, loons, osprey, cormorants, kingfishers, herons, otters

Common parasites: Blackspot flatworm larvae form cysts in perch, emerge as adults when perch are eaten by kingfishers and lay eggs that return to the water with the birds' droppings; yellow grub worms have a similar life cycle involving perch and great blue herons

Range: Southern Ontario to James Bay in northern boreal forest; in all other provinces except island of Newfoundland and Prince Edward Island; also in Northwest Territories

Tiny relations: Most of Ontario's 12 species of darters are less than 5 cm (2 in) long and easily mistaken for minnows, but are members of the perch family, bearing 2 spiny dorsal fins, like the yellow perch

Also see: Pickerel

PICKEREL
Ontario's Favourite Game Fish

Length: Avg. 35–50 cm (14–20 in)

Weight: Avg. 0.5–1.4 kg (1.1–3 lb); often 2.5–4 kg (6–9 lb) in large, prime lakes

Ontario record: 93 cm (36.5 in) long, 10 kg (22 lb), caught in Niagara River at Fort Erie in 1943

Markings: Variable, most often back and sides olive to dark brown flecked with yellow, with dark vertical bands on smaller fish; white underside, sometimes tinted yellow; lower tail fin tipped white, black spot on spiny dorsal fin; cloudy silver eyes

Alias: Walleye, wall-eyed pickerel, yellow walleye, yellow pickerel, pike-perch, yellow pike, walleye pike, dory,

At innumerable shindigs across most of central and northern Ontario, usually on the first exuberant night of the Victoria Day weekend, angling celebrants cast off at midnight to inaugurate the much-anticipated pickerel fishing season. It is the most commonly caught game fish and, therefore, the most loved. Pickerel thrive on deep Canadian Shield lakes like nowhere else and are eager biters. Best of all, for those of the rod and reel, the golden-hued whoppers are as tasty as perch but considerably larger, and put up a spirited fight before surrendering to fate as a fillet.

Pickerel are, in fact, really gargantuan perch, the biggest members of the family, though they're sometimes confused with a couple of similarly named pike species. Indeed, the word *pickerel* means "little pike." The name was probably bestowed on the predatory fish because of their fair size, ample jaws and big canines, which they love to sink into their smaller relatives.

When the sun sets, loose schools of pickerel go on roving picnics, searching out yellow perch and other fish slumbering amid underwater debris and weeds. In cloudy-watered lakes, they also hunt during the day. They scan the darkness with large, light-sensitive eyes that shine orange-red in the beam of a flashlight, like those of a deer or a cat. Up close, the eyes have a smoky look, responsible for the pickerel's other common name, walleye. In traditional rural parlance, a blind animal was called wall-eyed because both of its cloudy eyes stare outward in different directions – the opposite of cross-eyed.

Pickerel are usually caught at dusk and dawn, or on an overcast day or in murky waters. Sunlight drives them to the shade near vegetation or beneath sunken logs and rocks, where they themselves may be vulnerable to predation by their chief nemesis and competitor, the northern pike.

Throughout the winter, pickerel continue to prowl through near-blackness beneath the ice. Once the frozen mantle breaks apart on rivers in April, males cruise upstream to boulder-strewn riffles, rapids, waterfalls and dams. The opposite sex gradually joins them, and night spawning begins when water temperatures reach 7° to 9°C (45° to 48°F). Pickerel runs on tributaries of large lakes may last three weeks, peaking with hundreds of thrashing, spawning fish visible along a single stretch of frothy white water. Females, noticeably larger than their partners, usually release all their eggs in frequent spurts

glass eye, marble eye, *le doré jaune, Stizostedion vitreum*

Whereabouts: Usually around 15 m (49 ft) deep in lakes and rivers with rock, sand or gravel bottoms; often on shoals, venturing to both shallower and deeper waters to feed at night

Maximum depth found at: 21 m (69 ft)

Peak activity periods: Sunset to 11p.m. and 3a.m. to sunrise

Home range: Usually wander over 5–10 km (3–6 mi) in schools, but migrate much farther to spawn

Food: Perch, minnows, darters, sunfish, suckers, ciscoes, whitefish, burbot, bass, catfish, sticklebacks, alewife, smelt, crayfish, frogs, mudpuppies, snails, mayflies and other insects, rarely small rodents; eat each other when other fish wanting

Eggs per female: Avg. 25,000–100,000; up to 600,000

Egg development period: 12–18 days

Hatchlings: 6–9 mm (0.02–0.04 in) long

Fry survival: As low as 1%

Age at first spawning: Males 2–4 years, females 3–6 years

Lifespan: Usually about 7 years for adults; up to 29 years

Predators: Pike, muskies, osprey, otters; young eaten by perch, older pickerel and other fish

Range: Throughout Ontario, but mostly absent from high-land areas, such as Algonquin Park; also in the Prairie provinces, Quebec, New Brunswick and the Northwest Territories

Number of Ontario perch-family species: 15

Recent extinctions: Blue pickerel, once one of the most widely caught fish on Lake Erie, unseen since the 1960s

Number of perch-family species worldwide: 150–160

Number of Ontario fish species: 128 native, 31 non-native

Also see: Perch, Pike, White Sucker

over one night and leave, while males stick around to mate again, lying low during the day just downstream from spawning grounds.

The sticky fertilized eggs settle downstream on rocky beds or sand, kept clear of vegetation by the fast current. Some eggs also develop on shallow lake shoals, where pickerel also spawn. In some years, cold weather, wind-whipped waves or heavy currents can doom virtually a whole generation of pickerel before or after they hatch. In good years, five to 20 per cent of the eggs produce fry.

Tiny hatchlings emerge a couple of weeks after the eggs are laid, but stay put to absorb their yolk sacs for another 10 to 15 days before swimming towards the surface to dine on plankton. Perch take the opportunity to pick off as many of the potential menaces as possible while they're still small and vulnerable. By autumn the survivors are about 10 centimetres (four inches) long and are back near the bottom towards shore, eating aquatic insect larvae and other invertebrates.

PIKE
Stuff of Fishy Stories

Commanding fear and respect in the aquatic world, the mighty pike is the big game icon of clear, weedy waters across most of Canada to the Arctic Circle. With treacherous teeth set in a huge pair of jaws, the long, stout, lunging beast takes the last bite in the proverbial chain of bigger fish eating littler fish. Ducklings, snakes and young muskrats are also snapped up. Though the fearsome fish commonly weighs in at a couple of kilograms, wily old prize codgers can reach eight kilograms (18 pounds).

Monster-pike-versus-angler duels are the stuff of fishy stories stretching back into the reaches of time. Native peoples of the Yukon and Alaska told tales of remote demon lakes where giant pike could swallow a man whole, along with his canoe. Pike are also native to Asia and Europe, which were rife with stories of 45-kilogram

Length: Avg. 45–75 cm (18–30 in)

Weight: Avg. 1–2 kg (2.2–4.4 lb)

Ontario record: 19 kg (42 lb), caught in Delaney Lake, near Kenora, in 1946

World record: 23.8 kg (53 lb), 129.5 cm (4 ft 3 in), caught in Ireland

Markings: Green, olive or almost brown on top, shading to lighter green on sides, lined with yellowish spots and flecked with gold; white or creamy belly; gold, squiggly lines on cheeks; bright yellow eyes; green or yellow fins with dark splotches; young have wavy white or yellow vertical bars

Alias: Northern pike, great northern pike, Canadian

pike, jackfish, jack, great
northern pickerel, *le grand
brochet, Esox lucius* and
some 40 other local names
Name origin: Originally pike-
fish, from Old English *pic,*
meaning "pointed thing," also
the origin of *peak* and the
tool *pick*
Whereabouts: Weedy, warm,
clear waters, from shallows
to 4.5 m (15 ft) deep, in
quiet bays, small lakes and
slow rivers
Greatest depth found at:
More than 30 m (100 ft)
Food: 90% fish, including
perch, suckers, catfish, shiners, bass, pickerel; also frogs
and crayfish, occasionally
ducklings, snakes, mice and
young muskrats
Eggs per female: Avg.
10,000–100,000 sticky,
clear, amber eggs; up to
595,000; each about
2.5 mm (0.1 in) wide; about
half are infertile
Egg development period:
Usually 12–14 days
**Portion of eggs yielding fry
that survive more than a
few weeks:** 0.2% in one
study
Hatchling length: 6–8 mm
(0.2–0.3 in)
**Length by end of 1st sum-
mer:** Most about 15–20 cm
(6–8 in)
Age at first spawning: Males
2–3 years, females 2–4
years
Lifespan: Often 6–9 years;
up to 13 years in southern
Canada, 26 years in far

(100-pound) alligator-like pike pulling mules and maidens into watery graves. Fishing guides of a few centuries ago claimed that pike lived up to 200 years and were spontaneously formed from aquatic vegetation and ooze heated by the sun.

For much of the time, pike do seem to be one with their weedy surroundings. Largely sedentary creatures, they hide in lairs within shallow beds of submerged plants, pickerelweed or sedges, where they wait in ambush. When something comes within reach, they thrust out with lightning speed, just as the similarly built and sharp-toothed barracuda hunts in the sea. With a fish clamped in its jaws, a pike returns to its private quarters to swallow the meal head-first. Fish approximately one-third of a pike's own length are preferred, though pike can be found with more than two dozen perch in their stomachs.

Pike move a little deeper during the peak of summer heat and also for the winter, when they stay active but eat a little less. As soon as the ice starts melting from shorelines, they begin jour-neys to spawning grounds, usually just a couple of kilometres (about a mile) upstream. Hundreds of pike may make a single run, which lasts about a week. Mating takes place during the day in 10 to 45 centimetres (four to 18 inches) of water, often over spring-flooded banks of grass and shrubs or on marshy lake margins. Females may spend several days periodically releasing batches of five to 60 eggs as they vibrate alongside one or two milt-spewing partners, all thrashing their tails after each episode to scatter the roe.

Sticking to submerged branches and stalks of grass, eggs and immobile hatchlings are at the mercy of receding waters, late cold spells and caviar-loving predators. Surviving fry leave spawning areas several weeks after hatching, quickly switching from a diet of waterfleas and insect larvae to attacking baby fish hatched around the same time as they, such as white suckers. A three-centimetre (1.2-inch) pikelet will even fratricidally dine on one of its own just a half-centimetre smaller.

Because pike fry hatch about two weeks earlier, they also tend to eat and out-compete **muskellunge** young. Grownup muskies, however, average about half as long again and are at least twice as heavy as northern pike. The two fish occasionally interbreed, producing offspring called tiger muskies.

Sporting dark vertical bars along their sides, muskellunge are most abundant in the Kawarthas, and are found along the rest of the Trent-Severn Waterway, the Rideau Lakes, Lake Nipissing, and the Ottawa, French and Mattawa rivers. They mostly lurk towards the edge of the weeds or along rocky shoals. The water wolves are almost revered for presenting the greatest of freshwater fishing challenges. In waters where both fish are common, experienced rod handlers catch an average of three pike every two hours. The average muskie comes with a hundred hours of quasi-religious perseverance. One storied metre-long muskie, nicknamed Moby Dick, eluded anglers on the Trent River throughout the 1950s and 60s, winning epic battles that lasted up to seven hours.

north; 75 years in captivity; females live longest

Predators: Osprey, eagles and bears take small adults, usually while spawning; young or eggs eaten by herons, kingfishers, loons, mergansers, otters, mink, snapping turtles, perch, minnows, dragonfly nymphs, water tigers, older pike; silver lamprey parasitize but rarely kill adults

Privy etiquette: Because minnows produce alarm pheromones to alert each other to danger, which show up in the waste of pike that have eaten one of them, evolution has favoured fastidious pike that dump their loads off territory, thereby not giving their lairs away

Age of oldest pike-family fossil: 62 million years

Range: All Ontario, but rare in headwater regions such as the Haliburton and Algonquin highlands and in the Kawarthas; also in all other provinces and territories except the Atlantic provinces

Ontario muskie record: 29.5 kg (65 lb), 147 cm (4 ft 10 in), caught in Blackstone Harbour on Lake Huron in 1988

World muskie record: 31.5 kg (70 lb), 1.6 m (5 ft 4 in) long, caught in the St. Lawrence River

Also see: Minnows, Perch, White Sucker, Pickerelweed

PUMPKINSEED SUNFISH
Glimmering from the Shallows

Length: Avg. 10–15 cm (4–6 in) in brooks and ponds, 18–23 cm (7–9 in) in lakes
Weight: 28–340 g (1–12 oz)
Maximum size in Ontario: 25 cm (10 in), 480 g (17 oz)
Markings: Gold sides in alternating shades forming vertical bars, most noticeable on females, and covered with oval spots of olive, orange and red; golden-brown to olive top, bright yellow, bronze to reddish-orange bottom; wavy blue-green lines on orange cheeks, distinct bright red spot on gills; spiny fins, big golden eyes, small mouth; colours intensify in spawning territorial males

Never was there a better-named fish than the flat, yellow-bellied dazzler of warm, weedy waters. Probably the most vibrantly hued swimmer in the province, the almost two-dimensional pumpkinseed sunfish glistens iridescent like "a brilliant coin fresh from the mint," in the words of famed naturalist and philosopher Henry David Thoreau. Indeed, it's only when the sun shines that its namesake fish ventures forth into the shallows to feed. The brief shadow of a passing cloud is enough to send schools of sunfish back into deeper water. "Pumpkinseed" alludes to the fish's oval shape, though its numerous oval spots are also reminiscent of the seeds.

Like other sunfishes and bass, many pumpkinseed males are hardworking homebodies, while females are absentee moms. When shoreside waters warm to near room temperature around late June or early July, robust male stalwarts, usually six or seven years old, begin sweeping away debris with their tails and pulling out roots from weed beds to form circular nests about twice their own length. Nurseries of 10 to 15 nests, about a metre (three feet) or more apart, are often established by groups of the maternally inclined bruisers.

Many male sunfish, however, are young turks with no taste for the settled life. At least a third smaller than the established pumpkinseeds, they are fast-living, cheating scoundrels. They stand back and observe as members of the opposite sex come to inspect nest colonies. The females are chased about by the eager residents until convinced by one to come back to his place. As a couple slowly circle around the nest, her body inclined towards his in the act of spawning, a young sneaker will dash in close and squirt a stream of his own milt into the mix and then try to make off before being detected.

The sneak-and-squirt strategy is a successful one. Nest-tending fathers often unknowingly raise more offspring of other fish than their own. Most of their real sons remain celibate until later in life, when they're big enough to hold down a good nesting spot and drive others away. Foster sons, however, mainly grow up to be shiftless, promiscuous cheaters like their biological daddies, sexually active by the time they are two. Putting more of their internal resources into sperm production, they never grow as big as the territorial males. All the fast living and being chased from one nest to another also burns them out more quickly – few live more than five years. Many die from fungal infections

Alias: Common sunfish, yellow sunfish, sunny, punky, sun bass, pond perch, ruff, kivry, *le crapet-soleil*, *Lepomis gibbosus*

Whereabouts: Shallow, warm, waters of pickerelweed-choked or water-lily-covered rivers, ponds, bays, small lakes, marshes, muddy brooks

Food: Dragonfly and mayfly nymphs, bloodworms and other insect larvae, snails, small crustaceans, salamander tadpoles, fish eggs and fry, clams, leeches, worms, algae

Nest: Shallow, saucer-shaped clearing in weeds and debris, 10–40 cm (4–16 in) wide, in less than 75 cm (2.5 ft) of water

Eggs per female: 600–5,000, light amber, each 1 mm (0.04 in) wide

Egg development period: 3–10 days

Age at first spawning: 2 years for "sneaker" males, 5–6 years for territorial males, 4–5 years for females

Lifespan: Up to 10 years

Predators: Pike, pickerel, sauger, muskies, otters, osprey and kingfishers; young or eggs eaten by bass, perch, catfish, other sunfish and older pumpkinseeds

Winter whereabouts: Largely inactive at bottom of deep water early Sept. to early May

of fin wounds inflicted by jealous homesteaders.

Often mating with several partners, territorial males can accumulate piles of more than 15,000 eggs. They fan them constantly, to keep them aerated in the warm water, and fiercely attack any other fish that intrudes, even biting human fingers. After the minuscule, transparent fry hatch, fathers watch over them in the nest for up to another 11 days, until the young swim off on their own. Many males then mate again and raise a second batch.

Bluegill sunfish are almost as common in central Ontario. Pumpkinseeds sometimes either mate with bluegills or take over their nests. The two fishes are similar in most ways, with the bluegill having blue-green or olive colouring reflecting a purple iridescence. It differs from the pumpkinseed mainly in having a more vegetarian diet.

Another widespread sunfish of shallow, weedy waters, the **black crappie**, is a dedicated minnow hunter that grows up to 35 centimetres (14 inches) and commonly weighs twice as much as most pumpkinseeds. Its bulk makes the crappie more worthwhile for anglers to catch than other sunfish, and it's reputed, despite its name, to be delicious.

SMALLMOUTH BASS
Crayfish-loving Twilight Feeder

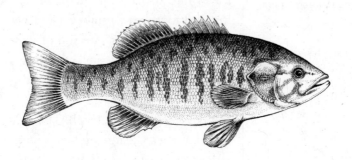

The sudden appearance of saucer-shaped impressions in near-shore sand and gravel shallows in late May and early June can look like the tracks of extraterrestrials lured by intergalactic rumours of good fishing. The circles, however, are entirely aquatic in origin. They are the love nests of male smallmouth bass, which have an impressively maternal bent.

Despite their reputation among anglers as feisty fighters, male smallmouths are truly sensitive, dedicated family fish. They spend up to two days sweeping away sand and debris with their tails to form their distinct, shallow, pebble-bottomed nests, usually a metre or two (3.3 to 6.6 feet) deep offshore. The nest-builders defend their sites against all interlopers but steer fertile members of the opposite sex – whose background colours fade to contrast with their dark

Length: Avg. 25–50 cm (10–20 in)

Weight: Avg. 225–1,350 g (0.5–3 lb)

World record: 5.4 kg (12 lb), caught in Kentucky, 1955

Markings: Usually green, sometimes brown or yellowish, with dark hash marks along sides and dark spots on back; white belly; sunlight causes colours to temporarily lighten

Alias: Bronzeback, northern smallmouth, black bass, green bass, *l'achigan à petite bouche*, *Micropterus dolomieu*

Name of a group: A shoal of bass

Whereabouts: From steep shorelines to 6 m (20 ft)

deep in clear, rocky lakes,
bays, river mouths and slower stretches of streams

Food: Crayfish, minnows,
perch, darters, fish fry, small
frogs, tadpoles, mayfly
nymphs and other insect larvae, leeches, snails

**Water temperature needed
for spawning:** Above 15°C
(60°F)

Nest: Circular, rock- and grav-
el-bottomed depression,
30–75 cm (1–2.5 ft) wide,
usually sheltered by a large
rock or log, 1–6 m (3.3–
19.7 ft) deep near calm
shores; same sites often
used for years

Clutch: Up to 10,000 tiny, yellowish eggs, often laid by
several females

Egg development period:
3–10 days

**Number of hatchlings per
nest:** Avg. about 2,000

Nest failure rate: Often
about 40%

Age at first breeding: Males
3–5 years, females 4–6
years

Lifespan: Often 5–7 years;
up to 20 years

Predators: Pike, pickerel,
muskies, osprey, cormorants;
young also taken by perch,
catfish, rock bass, loons

**Water temperature at which
bass become inactive:**
13°C (55°F)

Winter whereabouts: Lying
dormant in rubble and
crevices at bottom of water

Range: Southern Ontario to
Kapuskasing, Lake Nipigon

markings – to the nest. After some fishy foreplay, with the eager male rubbing and nipping, the female releases eggs in numerous four- to 10-second spurts over about two hours, interspersed with promenades around the nest. The male releases his milt to fertilize the eggs. She then leaves him to care for them. Male and female may both spawn with several other partners, usually at night, over a period of six to 18 days.

The eggs, which stick to the gravel at the bottom of the nest, are fanned and guarded by their fathers from caviar-gulping predators in the days before they hatch. The feisty fish are even known to charge human swimmers and, in rare instances, to bite them. All the while they eat only prey that come within their nesting area. Black hatchlings, about the size of rice grains, emerge in three to 10 days and are protected by their devoted dads for one or two more weeks in the nest and another two to four weeks in open water, until the schools of tiny siblings begin to break up.

Young bass must eat well in their first months if they are to survive the winter, during which they fast. If spring and summer are cool, delaying their hatching and development, most are goners. Heavy storms also destroy nests, and bass fry are more susceptible to acid rain than just about any other major sport fish. Adverse weather often results in a bass-fishing drought three years later, when the lost generation would have reached the age when most smallmouths are caught.

Smallmouth bass spend hot summer days in shadows beneath steep banks, overhanging shoreline branches or in deeper water. They lie motionless most of the time around rocks, logs, submerged tree roots and other debris, waiting to ambush a swimming snack or two. Mealtime really arrives at dusk and dawn, when bass move into shallow rocky areas as crayfish, their favourite food, come out of their lairs to forage. After twilight fades, it's too dark for smallmouths to hunt.

Largemouth bass are nearly identical, but prefer calmer, weedier, more shallow waters, often farther upstream. Tending to be a little bigger than smallmouths, they're prized by anglers more for their heft than their fight, as well as for the challenge of finding them. They too, like all members of the sunfish family, feature nest-building, fry-rearing males.

The **rock bass**, another relative, is more squat, bony and homely, with blood red eyes. Being smaller than other bass, it's not highly valued as a sport fish and is often castigated for devastating local fish populations in lakes where it's spread. In fact, all three bass species, which are warm-water fish, have had negative impacts in many areas of central Ontario where they've been introduced either intentionally or through bait-bucket dumping. They upset the ecological balance in lakes where they haven't co-evolved with the local population, generally outcompeting larger species such as brook trout and eating much of their young.

and Sioux Lookout; also in all other provinces except island of Newfoundland, Prince Edward Island and Alberta

Number of lakes with smallmouth bass in Ontario: 2,400

Natural pH of most Canadian Shield lakes: 6.2–7

Lake pH level at which smallmouth bass disappear: 5.5

Lake pH level at which pike disappear: 4.7

Fish that often lay eggs in bass nests: Common shiners, golden shiners, long-nosed gar

Other nest-tending fish: Largemouth and rock bass, sunfish, catfish, fathead minnows, bluntnose minnows, creek chub

Also see: Brook Trout, Crayfish, Pumpkinseed Sunfish, Lakes

WHITE SUCKER
Big, Lumbering Bottom-dweller

Length: Avg. 30–50 cm
(12–20 in)
Weight: Avg. 450–900 g
(1–2 lb)
Ontario record: 58 cm
(23 in) long, 2.4 kg (5.4 lb),
caught in Lake Joseph in
1996
World record: 3.3 kg (7.2 lb),
caught in Wisconsin in 1978
Markings: Olive-brown,
bronze or black backs, silver-
grey sides, white or creamy
belly, smoky fins
Alias: Sucker, common sucker, mullet, coarse-scaled
sucker, fine-scaled sucker,
black mullet, carp, *le meu-
nier noir, Catostomus com-
mersoni*
Whereabouts: Usually 6–9 m
(20–30 ft) deep in lakes,

"Look at the snout on that sucker!" The expression is apropos for the big, lumbering fish that
scours lake and river bottoms, vacuuming up its
meals. Fleshy, overhanging lips and a jowly face
give the white sucker the look of a portly, be-
wigged aristocrat at the court of King George III.
With its toothless mouth placed at the bottom
of its ample snout, the fish simply drops its lips
and sucks in minute bloodworms and micro-
crustaceans by the tens of thousands. Comblike
teeth in its throat shred the food with each gulp.

Bottom-feeding being a little-respected pro-
fession, suckers are generally looked down on by
anglers, sometimes even wrongly accused of
depleting trout populations by eating their eggs.
In truth, the broad-bodied suckers are good
eating fish, if a little bony. They're easy to catch
and seldom show up with trout eggs in their

stomachs. And if it weren't for suckers feeding off the dense concentrations of life on the water bottom, over much wider areas than shallows-loving catfish, there would likely be far fewer game fish around; as it is, white suckers are often the most abundant species in many lakes and streams, feeding many pike and pickerel.

Most active at dusk and dawn, suckers are nearly invisible from above, even in low water, because of their darkly shaded backs. On spring spawning runs, though, when their silvery sides break the surface in shallow, gravelly streams, creeks and lake margins, they're hard to miss. Some runs involve thousands, with as many as a hundred passing by every minute in a writhing mass. In May, the thronging, spawning fish were so easy to catch that the Ojibway called it the month of the Sucker Moon. Stumbling upon a sucker run can also mean a hearty breakfast for bears recently roused from hibernation or for ospreys just in from South America.

Breeding males take on a golden tint and sport a temporary red, black or cream racing stripe down their sides. For 10 to 14 days, especially at dusk and dawn, the male contestants occupy spots where the currents are fast, and intercept fertile females venturing from their own gatherings just downstream. Two to four males, usually, close in alongside a streaming feminine bomber, the whole group thrashing and vibrating as they release eggs and milt in spurts of a few seconds, anywhere from half a dozen to 40 times an hour. Eventually, the sated female returns downstream until she's ready to spawn again.

When the party's over, the fish migrate back to their regular haunts in lakes and deeper water.

bays, rivers and small streams flowing into large lakes

Adaptability: Happy in clear or cloudy waters; populations fall in acidified lakes

Greatest depth found at: 46 m (151 ft)

Greatest depth longnose sucker found at: 183 m (600 ft)

Food: Usually about 50% bloodworms (midge larvae), but 60–90% bottom-living waterfleas in summer; also snails, caddisfly larvae, worms and vegetation

Most important senses: Taste and touch

Eggs per female: 20,000–50,000 yellow eggs

Egg development period: About 2 weeks

Fry survival in first 2 weeks: As low as 3%

Age at first spawning: Males 2–3 years, females 3–4 years

Lifespan: Most 2–6 years; up to 17 years; females live longest

Predators: Pike, muskies, pickerel, burbot, osprey; taken during spawning by otters, bears and other mammals; young also eaten by bass, trout, mink, kingfishers

Slang: A "sucker" is someone who's as naive and easy to fool as an unweaned toddler

Range: All Ontario; also in all other provinces and territories except Prince Edward Island and island of Newfoundland

**Number of Ontario sucker
species:** 12

**Number of sucker species
worldwide:** About 65, mostly in North America

Ontario's only venous fish:
Stonecat and tadpole mad-
tom catfish, both up to 9 cm
(3.5 in) long, have glands at
the base of fin spines behind gills that can cause a
prick as painful as a bee
sting

Also see: Pickerel, Pike,
Black Bear, Lakes

The hundreds of thousands of eggs left behind on the gravel bottom begin hatching within two weeks, with a sucker born every minute. Upon digesting their egg sacs, fry join adults downstream but initially feed on plankton near the surface close to lake edges. When the young are almost two centimetres (0.8 inches) long, their mouths move from the front to the bottom of their faces, and they start feasting in weedy shallows. Suckers reaching 20 centimetres (eight inches) become too hefty for most predatory fish and commonly mingle with schools of pickerel.

The bottom-feeding way of life is shared by a wide variety of fish in Ontario, from a number of types of minnows, seven kinds of catfish and 11 other sucker species to the biggest fish in the province, the **lake sturgeon**. Sometimes more than one and a half metres (five feet) long, sturgeon are armoured with rows of fearsome, jagged ridges but scour the depths with a fleshy, toothless protractile mouth located far back on the underside of their snout. Females don't mate until 14 to 23 years old and may live up to 150 years.

Central Ontario's most abundant catfish, the **brown bullhead**, keeps mostly to warm, weedy, mud-bottomed shallows, hiding under rocks, logs or overhanging banks during the day and coming out at night to forage. It feels its way around in the dark and probes the silty sediments for food with highly sensitive, soft barbels that sprout from its face like the long whiskers of a wise old cat. Several hundred thousand taste buds line its entire body, especially concentrated along the barbels, making the bullhead's very existence a continuous taste sensation.

MAMMALS

*P*erhaps the most exciting wilderness experience of all is to encounter wild, free-roaming mammals. Partly it is because mammals are probably the most seldom-seen beasts, aside from ever-present and audible red squirrels and chipmunks. Not that other mammals are not around. Flying squirrels are as common as red squirrels but swoop about like bats in the night. There are often more mammals than birds in a forest, but most of them are tiny and hidden during the day. Ontario's nine native species of mice and voles, eight varieties of bats, nine weasel relatives, four bunnies, raccoons, porcupines, beavers, foxes, coyotes, wolves, bobcats, lynx and others are all solely or primarily denizens of the dark. Others, such as the seven shrew species and several moles in the province, seldom emerge above the ground or leaf litter. In all, there are 69 different native terrestrial mammal species in Ontario, more than 50 of them in the central region of the province.

Although mammals are elusive, their signatures are all around us: beaver lodges and dams, muskrat homes, bear-clawed trees, the rustling of mice scurrying in the night, paw- and hoofprints in the mud and a galaxy of droppings, or scat. At the right time and place, a moose may be watched in the flesh, neck deep in a quiet bay, feasting on water lilies. In fact, central Ontario is one of the best places in the world to view moose, bears and many other wild animals, or to hear the spine-tingling howls of a wolf pack at night.

As with other aspects of nature, the world of mammals has not been static in recent years. Central Ontario's wolf has been identified as a *distinct, separate species from its northern brethren, while the woodland caribou has been designated a threatened species. Controversy rages over the end of the spring bear hunt. Southern flying squirrels have moved north and deer numbers have swelled with frequent mild winters.*

BEAVER
Builder that Laid Foundation of Nation

European explorers came to Canada looking for the Northwest Passage. Instead, they found the beaver, and for 200 years Canadian history revolved around the quest for its cherished pelt. The fur trade was Canada's biggest industry until logging overtook it in the 1800s, earning the beleaguered beaver acclamation as national mascot. Both the Canadian beaver's abundant numbers and the denseness of its soft inner fur, needed for warmth in frigid waters, made it more important to humans than any other fur bearer. In the days before umbrellas, upper-class heads were kept fashionably dry with broad hats of beaver felt. Mercury, used to separate the fur from longer guard hairs and break it down into felt, frequently caused mental deterioration among the ranks of ungloved hatmakers, giving rise to the term "mad as a hatter."

Dive duration: Up to 15 minutes

Time it takes a beaver to cut an aspen 12 cm (5 in) thick: 3 min; it takes about 3 times as long to cut harder birch wood

Thickest tree ever recorded cut by a beaver: 1.2 m (4 ft)

Annual number of trees cut by an adult: Avg. more than 200, mostly saplings

Dam length: Avg. 30–60 m (98.5–197 ft)

Biggest beaver dam ever recorded: 1,500 m (5,000 ft) long, 3 m (10 ft) high, in Saskatchewan

Longest measured beaver canal: 230 m (150 ft), in Colorado

**Heart rate while under-
water:** As low as 20% of
normal rate

Body length: Avg. 60–90 cm
(2–3 ft)

Tail: 23–33 cm (9–13 in)
long, 11–15 cm (4.3–6 in)
wide

Weight: Avg. 16–27 kg (35–
59.5 lb)

Heaviest beaver ever found:
50 kg (110 lb)

Markings: Glossy chestnut
brown to black body, scaly
black tail

Alias: Canadian beaver,
American beaver, buckie, *le
castor, Castor canadensis*

Name origin: From Old
English *beofor,* "brown"

Calls: Mumble, hiss or nasal
blowing when angry; cries
when frightened

Best senses: Smell and
hearing

Whereabouts: Small, muddy
lakes, ponds, meandering
streams and marshes
flanked by aspen and birch
stands and willow thickets

Beaver pond size: Avg. 4 ha
(10 acres)

**Area of aspen forest need-
ed to support a colony annually:** 0.4–0.8 ha (1–2
acres)

Colony territory: 0.6–2.2 km
(0.3–1.8 mi) along a stream
or shoreline

Home: Domed lodge of
branches and mud, about
2 m (6.6 ft) high and 4–8 m
(13.3–14.6 ft) wide above
waterline, hollowed out from
an underwater entrance;

Before the coming of the white traders, Native bands followed sustainable economies, fine-tuned through millennia, with each family's traditional hunting and trapping territory defined by a watershed. Families rotated their activities from one river branch to another within the larger basin, ensuring that beavers and other animals they hunted could rebuild their population in each area. They maintained intimate knowledge of the land rather than seeing it as a vast, unfathomable expanse.

The Native system was disrupted by the steel-age goods and technology of Europeans. Metal pots, axes, guns and other trade items offered huge time-saving advantages and luxuries but hooked Native people into the European market system, while they lost their own complex survival technologies. Traditional family trapping grounds were quickly exhausted to satisfy the new demands for fur. Both Native people and traders pushed farther west. The Iroquois, seeking control of the trade routes, nearly wiped out the Huron nation in Ontario as well as several other peoples in the Beaver Wars of the mid-1600s. A chain reaction of disruption spread across the continent until, by the turn of the twentieth century, there were few beavers, but much dependency.

In the 1930s, Grey Owl captivated the world with the image of a Native trapper from the forests of Canada turned wildlife crusader. Though after he died Grey Owl turned out to be a wayward Englishman named Archibald Belaney, he helped reinforce conservation efforts to save the beaver. In 1937, the animal was put on the back of the Canadian nickel. Going full circle, the government began assigning trapping territories on the basis of watersheds. In Ontario, the Ministry of Natural Resources restocked areas where beavers had been wiped out, with animals taken from the protected population in Algonquin Park. The beavers took quickly to prime, unused habitats and became so abundant that they're now often considered pests in some agricultural, cottage and even urban-fringe areas.

Both beavers and people are driven by the urge and ability to change and control their environment. A Native tradition holds that the Creator took the power of speech away from beavers to keep them from becoming superior to humans. The Ojibway said that beavers could change form, into birds or other animals. The animals were highly respected and an important food source, especially their rich, fleshy tail. It was taboo to throw a beaver's bones to the dogs, for fear of insulting its spirit.

Beavers form essentially matriarchal societies. According to some experts, when the young leave home for good, swimming downstream in search of new horizons, females choose their mate for life and determine where they will live. If her partner dies, the female recruits a replacement and life goes on. If a matriarch dies, the colony usually breaks up. After mating in the water, beneath the ice, in January or February, mothers give birth sometime between late April and early June. Newborns are fully furred, and their eyes are open. They are able to swim within hours. Unlike most mammals, they continue growing until late in life, when they are five or six years old.

built at the centre of ponds or side of deep lakes; occasionally a bank burrow with a hidden, underwater entrance

Average number of beavers per lodge: 5–9

Food: Water lily, arrowhead, duckweed, watercress, cattail, grasses, sedges, leaves, berries and ferns in summer; bark and twigs of aspen, willow, birch, poplar, mountain ash, red maple and aquatic plant roots in winter

Average daily food helping: 0.5–2.5 kg (1–5.5 lb) of bark and twigs in winter; about 330 g (12 oz) of green plants in summer

Size of submerged winter larder of tree stems and branches: Up to 7 m (23 ft) long, 2.5 m (8 ft) wide and more than 1 m (3.3 ft) high

Foraging distance from water: Usually less than 45 m (150 ft); rarely up to 90 m in wolf-inhabited areas, up to 200 m (650 ft) elsewhere

Mating duration: 30 seconds to 4 minutes, underwater in winter; repeated several times a day between 20–60 minute breaks

Gestation period: 3½ months

Average litter: 2–4

Birth weight: 230–680 g (0.5–1.5 lb)

Age at which young beavers leave home: Usually 1 year; some stay for 2 years

Age at first breeding: Usually 2–3 years

Lifespan: Avg. 4–5 years; up to 20 years in wild, 23 years in captivity

Tracks: Front feet 6–10 cm (2.5–4 in) long, handlike, with 5 fingers; back feet webbed, 13–16 cm (5–6.3 in) long

Scat: Usually in water and very rarely found; oval, dark brown, sawdustlike pellets at least 2 cm (0.8 in) long; nutrient-rich initial droppings are eaten again for full digestion

Swimming speed: Usually about 4 km/h (2.4 mph), up to 10 km/h (6 mph)

Predators: Wolves; occasionally coyotes, foxes, fishers, lynx and mink; rarely otters

Number of lodges per km² (0.4 sq. mi) in Algonquin Park: Avg. 0.4–1

Number of beaver pelts traded for a musket from the Hudson's Bay Company in 1700s: 10–12

Number of hats made from one large beaver pelt in 1700s: About 18

Famous beaver hot spots: Montreal (Hochelaga, Iroquoian for "where the beaver dams meet"); Albany, New York (formerly Beaverwyck, centre of the Dutch fur trade)

Debut of first Canadian beaver stamp: 1851

Age of oldest beaver fossils: 35 million years

Common beaver pond inhabitants or visitors: Muskrats, mink, otters,

Unlike the bear-sized sabre-toothed beaver that became extinct with the close of the Ice Age 10,000 years ago, the modern beaver survived climate change because it was an engineer. Beavers – still the largest rodents in North America – can go to work wherever there is a stream and an ample supply of deciduous trees, especially aspen. If the water is shallow or intermittent, they build a dam, creating a reservoir deep enough to swim and dive in safety, one that will not freeze to the bottom in winter. The inundated area, often covering several hectares, is like a farm, growing the succulent water plants beavers eat in the summer. As well, it's a conduit for reaching and transporting felled hardwoods. Wherever the ground is soft, beavers may dig thin, shallow canals and tunnels into the woods and across peninsulas.

By controlling the water level, beavers ensure their lodge will not be flooded out or left high and dry by seasonal watershed fluctuations. A pair of beavers can build an incredibly solid dam in three or four days, with branches stuck diagonally into the mud so that the wall slopes downstream, fully braced against the force of the constrained water. Beavers scoop up mud with their paws to fill in the structure once all the branches are woven in place. They often build a series of dams along a stream, sometimes reaching up to three metres (10 feet) high and 500 metres (1,640 feet) long.

Beavers in a well-established colony may not be busy at all during the relatively carefree days of spring and early summer. They are active mostly from dusk to dawn, occasionally warning each other to dive for safety with a loud tail slap on the water when danger approaches. From September until freeze-up, though, they live up to their reputation, attacking shorelines like crazed lumberjacks, often extending their nocturnal toilings into the day, to build up a winter food supply of branches. Old hands say the timing and severity of winter can be predicted by how hard beavers work and how early they start. (Biologists are not so sure.) When cutting down trees, beavers stand on their hind feet, propped up by their tails. They can't control where a tree falls, but heavy growth on the tree's sunny side usually topples it towards the water. A larder of tasty trunks and branches, piled and submerged beside the lodge, may equal more than 30 cubic metres (1,000 cubic feet) by November, allowing beavers to remain holed up for most of the winter.

Flooded areas behind beaver dams become swampy, often creating rich habitat for a succession of plants and animals, in the water and in the dead and dying trees. As beavers cut down alder, birch and aspen near shore, they accelerate forest succession by eliminating shade over young evergreens. After perhaps several generations of beavers have used up all the young broad-leaved trees they can safely reach, they desert the area for greener pastures. The caretakers gone, their dams slowly deteriorate and the ponds drain, leaving behind rich, silty soil that becomes a meadow. Eventually, the forest reclaims the spot. If aspen and birch take root again – which is especially common if a fire sweeps through the area – they're usually large enough within five to 10 years to support another pair of beavers searching for a new homestead.

moose, great blue herons, black ducks, wood ducks, hooded mergansers, osprey, harriers, woodpeckers, geese, tree swallows, frogs, brook trout, sunfish, minnows

Estimated Ontario beaver population: 1.5–2 million

Range: All of Ontario, except part of southwest; also in all other provinces and territories except Nunavut

Number of Ontario rodent species: 23 native, 2 introduced

Number of rodent species worldwide: About 1,690

Also see: Snowshoe Hare, Wolf, Trembling Aspen, Canadian Shield

BLACK BEAR
Big Sleeper with Special Powers

Top running speed: About 56 km/h (35 mph)

Hibernation breathing rate: As low as once every 45 seconds

Heartbeats per minute: About 40 when active, as low as 8 during hibernation

Length: Females avg. 1.2–1.5 m (4–5 ft), males 1.5–1.8 m (5–6 ft)

Height at shoulder: 60–90 cm (2–3 ft)

Weight: Females avg. 45–80 kg (100–176 lb), males 90–160 kg (198–353 lb)

Biggest Ontario bear ever recorded: 330 kg (726 lb)

Biggest black bear ever recorded: 399 kg (880 lb), shot in North Carolina in 1998

Does a bear defecate in the woods? Well, not during hibernation. Neither does one urinate, eat or drink, though females do give birth in late January or early February, nursing and tending their young between intermittent deep slumbers.

Bears are considered true hibernators, although their body temperature drops only a few degrees Celsius in winter and they can wake easily. Denning bears have a unique chemistry that achieves wonders beyond the ability of other true hibernators. If most animals went without peeing for more than a few days, backed-up waste would result in fatal urea poisoning. Even hibernating groundhogs must relieve themselves once in a while. Bears, however, recycle urine from their bladder into new proteins. Water from the recycled urine and from fat reserves prevents dehydration. Unlike other animals denied food or room to move for long periods, a bear lives off its fat without losing muscle or bone mass. The fat fuel causes winter cholesterol levels to double, without resultant cardiovascular problems.

The system works so well that while most other species are going through their most difficult and dangerous season, 99 per cent of all bears survive comfortably through winter. Scientists are working diligently to isolate the bear chemicals that could help humans suffering from kidney and bone diseases to recycle urea and calcium.

Mother bruins carry recycling to the point of ingesting their babies' waste, recapturing the fluids lost through nursing. It also keeps the den clean. Although bears mate in June or early July, embryos don't start developing until 10 weeks before birth, when sows have stored enough nutrients needed to get them through winter. Newborns are little bigger than chipmunks, very lightly furred, deaf, toothless and blind. They are not, however, formless bits of mush sculpted by their mother's tongue, a folk belief responsible for the expression "licked into shape." Following only their sense of touch, they find their mother's nipples by moving towards the heat that can be felt from them.

Each year of a bear's life is like a big Viking feast. Although the black bear is central Ontario's largest carnivore, it concentrates on a changing smorgasbord of easily obtained food sources through the warm months. From 75 to 90 per cent of its diet is vegetarian.

After sleeping off the previous year's banquet, bears emerge between mid–April and early May,

Markings: Completely black, except for tan or brown snout and sometimes a white patch on chest; rarely, reddish, brown or blond

Alias: American black bear, *l'ours noir, Ursus americanus*

Name origin: From proto–Indo-European *bheros*, meaning "brown"; probably a euphemism for the bear's true name, which was too sacred to utter, a common practice regarding bears among northern peoples around the world

Name of a group: A sloth of bears

Calls: Grunts, growls, loud blowing, teeth clacking

Best senses: Can smell carrion more than a mile away; hearing range wider and probably twice as sensitive as humans'

Eyesight: Colour vision, about equal to humans'

Whereabouts: Mixed-age forests with dense understories, large patches of trees less than 90 years old, berry-rich clearings, abundant oak or beech trees, wetlands and rivers

Core home range: Avg. 5–25 km² (2–10 sq. mi) for females, 20–65 km² (8–25 sq. mi) for males

Distance travelled to fall foraging grounds: Up to 100 km (60 mi) or more

Food: Berries, currants, cherries, acorns, nuts, grass, roots, leaves, buds, inner bark of evergreen trees, ants, beetle grubs, caterpillars, fish, frogs, birds, eggs, small mammals, fawns, moose calves, carrion

Daily calorie intake in late summer: 20,000

Calories burned daily during hibernation: Avg. 4,000

Recommended daily human calorie intake: 1,800–3,200

Gestation period: 7 months, including 3–4 months delayed implantation

Average litter: 2–3

Birth weight: 200–400 g (7–14 oz)

Fat content of bear milk: 20–40%

Fat content of human milk: 4%

Period cubs stay with mothers: 16–17 months

Safety trees: Sleeping or temporarily unattended cubs kept near big, branchy trees with deeply furrow bark, usually white pines or hemlocks, that they can easily climb in case of danger, mainly from other bears

Age at first breeding: Females 3–5 years, males 4–6 years

Annual survival: Cubs avg. 80%, yearlings less than 65%, adults about 90%

Lifespan: Avg. 3–5 years in some hunted populations, 10–15 years in protected areas; up to 33 years

Predators: Small cubs sometimes taken by adult male bears, wolves, lynx, eagles

groggy, 15 to 40 per cent lighter but not yet peckish. It takes about two weeks to clear the head and shake off the hibernative state before eating resumes. They start off light, with a green salad of grasses, sedges, horsetails, and aspen and willow catkins, most in abundance before other vegetation sprouts in early spring. Roots, rotting logs filled with ants and grubs and the occasional animal or spawning fish are important supplements. Late spring serves up fresh aspen leaves. Bears continue losing weight until they plunge into the main course with the ripening of berries in early July. Then they start steadily gaining a kilogram (2.2 pounds) or more a day. From August to October, eating goes into overdrive, as the bear spends up to 20 hours a day devouring high-fat and -protein acorns, beechnuts and hazelnuts, mountain ash berries, cherries and other berries, sometimes venturing more than 60 kilometres (100 miles) from its home range to where the eating is good.

If the nut and berry crops are plentiful, bears may not bed down until early November and there's plenty of snow on the ground. As early as September, though, they may begin preparing their winter sleeping chambers, spending up to 10 days digging out a den, sometimes up to a metre and a half (five feet) deep. Before blissfully retiring, the stuffed bruins fast for about a week and then eat dry leaves, grass, pine needles and hair that together form into a wad, sealing their other end for the next six months or so.

Throughout its days of foraging, the black bear lumbers through forest and meadow with impunity, having few if any enemies to challenge it. Bears, though, are generally shy of humans and move away from their presence. Before the advent of the gun, the only way Native hunters could readily kill a bear was to find one in its winter den or to set a pit or falling-log trap for it. Hunters asked permission from the spirits that presided over bears to kill it (as they did with other animals), and offered apologies afterwards. Bears were supremely respected as symbols of strength and courage, the primary Earth and healing spirits. Veneration of the bear, with remarkably similar lore, was also practised by hunting cultures from eastern North America through Siberia to Scandinavia. The earliest evidence of religious thought on Earth is found in bear-cult cave shrines left by Neanderthals in central Europe at least 75,000 years ago.

In more recent times, bears have engendered widespread affection as cuddly, inanimate childhood companions and good-natured cartoon buffoons. The most famous bear of all, in fact, was a Canadian, from Ontario. Winnie-the-Pooh was actually a female cub named Winnipeg, bought on the railroad platform in White River, north of Lake Superior, by an army horse veterinarian on his way to the front in 1914. The vet gave Winnipeg to the London Zoo, where she captivated a boy named Christopher and inspired his father, A. A. Milne, to write the immortal tales of the bear of very little brain. South of the border, big-game-hunting U.S. president Theodore Roosevelt's refusal in 1902 to shoot a bear that had been carefully leashed to a tree for his convenience captured the public's – and a toy manufacturer's – imagination and spawned the "teddy" bear.

Tracks: Hind foot 15–18 cm (6–7 in) long, resembling a wide human foot; front foot 10–15 cm (4–6 in) long

Scat: Generally blunt and cylindrical, up to 5 cm (2 in) wide, varying in size, shape and colour with food eaten, distinctly bearing loose masses of berries or nut-shells, seeds, matted grass, ants, roots and wood fibres

Winter whereabouts: Den dug beneath roots of trees, logs, brush piles, rock ledges, or in rock crevices and hollow trunks of very large trees, lined with grass, moss, lichens, evergreen boughs, rotted wood

Population density in Algonquin Park: 1 per 3–4 km² (1–1.5 sq. mi)

Ontario bear population: 75,000–100,000

Number of bears shot annually in Ontario: About 4,900

Range: All of Ontario south to edge of Canadian Shield, Manitoulin Island, Grey, Bruce and Simcoe counties; also in all other provinces and territories except Prince Edward Island and Nunavut

Famous bears: Yogi, Smokey, Winnie-the-Pooh, Fozzie, Gentle Ben, Baloo, Paddington, The Three Bears, Artio, Brer Bear, Misha, Bruin

Origin of a "bear market": From British proverb, "to sell the bearskin before catching the bear"

Number of Ontario bear species: 2
Number of bear species worldwide: 7
Also see: White Sucker, Groundhog, Blueberry, Chokecherry, Beech, Red Oak, Trembling Aspen, White Pine, Big Dipper

Roosevelt's noble sentiments have not necessarily carried over to all modern hunters. The preferred bear-hunting method of many – especially a large overflow of big-game enthusiasts from American states where hunts are much more restricted – is to sit in trees and blast bears attracted to large quantities of rotting meat left below. One reason Ontario's spring bear hunt was ended in 1999 was out of concern over the shooting of females, some of them mothers, which have a lower reproductive rate than those in warmer, more biologically diverse areas. As much as one-third of the population was being taken in some areas. The issue remains controversial, with claims of increased nuisance bears in many areas since the spring hunt was cancelled, though provincial government biologists say the overall black bear population has stayed the same. Fall hunting continues in Ontario. An unknown number of bears are also shot by poachers seeking parts to export to Asia. Bear gall bladders, considered a panacea in traditional Asian medicine, can sell for as much as $30,000 in Taiwan or Korea. Bear-paw soup, said to bestow power and fertility, is served up at more than $1,000 a bowl.

CHIPMUNK
Hoarding Hermit Warrior

Cute, cuddly, tame, adorable by popular acclaim, chipmunks are, in fact, highly secretive, independent and aggressive animals. They usually don't enter the holes to their underground burrows while being watched. Though many will take food from your hand, chipmunks never become dependent on humans. They spend most of their days, from the time they emerge from hibernation in early spring, filling their cheeks to bulging with food and carrying it back to their burrows, often storing away a lifetime's supply in a single season. Lawrence Wishner, the American dean of chipmunkology, who spent six years living among the tiny beasts, says they are driven by an "obsessive genetic fear of starvation."

Their paranoid hoarding has helped establish one of the longest-standing niches of any mammal in the forest. Primordial chipmunks

Cheek holding capacity: Up to 32 beechnuts or 48 wild cherry pits

Body temperature: 35–41°C (95–106°F) when active, 5–7°C (41–45°F) in hibernation

Breaths per minute: More than 60 when active, less than 20 in hibernation

Body length: Avg. 14–16 cm (5.6–6.4 in)

Tail length: 6.5–11.5 cm (2.6–4.6 in)

Weight: 70–125 g (2.5–4.4 oz)

Markings: Tawny brown back and sides with 9 black and whitish stripes; 2 stripes on face; white undersides and chin

Alias: Eastern chipmunk, chipping squirrel, *le suisse*, *Tamias striatus*

Name origin: *Chipmunk* is Algonkian for "head first," after the manner in which it descends trees

Calls: "Chip," "chuck," trills, whistles, squeals, chatter

Whereabouts: Mature, open upland hardwood forests and woodland edges with lots of logs, stumps and rocks

Home range: Avg. 0.1–0.2 ha (0.25–0.5 acre); up to 1.3 ha (3.2 acre)

Food: Acorns, beech and hazel nuts, maple keys and other seeds, berries, cherries, mushrooms, buds, root bulbs, snails, slugs, insects; occasionally frogs, bird eggs and nestlings, young mice, snakes

Winter food stores: Up to 7 L (6 quarts)

Home: Burrow, about 45–85 cm (1.5–2.8 ft) underground, football- to watermelon-sized; entrance hole neat, round, 4–5 cm (1.6–2 in) wide

Gestation period: 31 days

Average litter: 4–6

Birth weight: 3 g (0.1 oz)

Weaning age: 5–6 weeks

Age upon reaching adult size: 2–3 months

Age at first breeding: Females as young as 10 weeks, males 1 year

Annual adult survival: Up to 50%

Lifespan: Adults avg. 1–2 years, with few living more than 3 years; up to 12 years in captivity

roamed the Earth 25 million years ago, their ancestors having split from proto-squirrels 15 million years earlier.

With hefty larders, chipmunks can finally take it easy through winter. Unlike squirrels, they sleep most of the season away, stirring every few days to grab an ample bedtime snack. With so much riding on their stash, chippies are exceedingly testy about any of their own kind getting near it. They live alone and harbour a keen dislike for each other, like warrior hermits. When they meet, there are almost always strong words, scraps or chases. Chip and Dale could never have been pals.

Accordingly, woods abounding with chipmunks ring with chattering discord. Yet, in a moment of common peril, they pull together. Whenever a fox, raccoon or other mammal predator is spotted, they spread the alarm by joining in a chorus of sharp, repeated warning "chips." For hawks and other big birds, the alarm call is a distinctly different, lower series of "chucks." When hordes of nervous, inexperienced six- to eight-week-old youngsters set off on their own in June, the pickings are prime for carnivores and the chips and chucks can reach fever pitch. The waifs that survive their troubled youth usually find sanctuary within a few weeks in old, empty burrows anywhere from five to more than 700 metres (5.5 to 765 yards) from their natal homes.

When excavating new quarters, chipmunks finish them off by ingeniously digging a second entrance tunnel and transferring the dirt from it to seal the opening of their original three- to 15-metre- (10- to 50-foot-) long working shaft.

The pile of excavations at the end of the first passage then no longer marks a hole for predators. The new entrance is often hidden beneath a log, rock or brush pile. If used for several generations, a burrow may acquire up to 30 tunnels, with all but the main entrance sealed from beneath.

After a comfortable winter of intermittent sleep in leaf-lined chambers, male chipmunks resurface in a lustful state in late March or April, as patches of bare ground emerge in the melting snow. They go calling on still-slumbering neighbourhood females, only to be thrashed and rejected until the fairer sex is ready. If two or more suitors are present when sleeping beauty rises, a chase ensues that can last all day. The female accedes to the pursuer who can stick with it the longest. Then love briefly conquers chipmunk belligerence and a couple will nuzzle, play, lounge and squeak together for hours before and after mating. Beyond that, the relationship's over. Mothers give birth between mid-April and late May.

Predators: Hawks, foxes, wolves, coyotes, raccoons, martens, weasels, snakes
Top running speed: 12 km/h (7.5 mph)
Swimming speed: 11 km/h (7 mph)
Best sense: Hearing
Density in prime habitat: 1,000-5,000/km^2 (0.4 sq. mi)
Winter whereabouts: In light hibernation beneath ground
Famous chipmunks: Chip and Dale; Simon, Alvin and Theodore
Range: Southern Ontario to tip of James Bay, Lake Nipigon and just north of Kenora; also in Manitoba, Quebec and Atlantic provinces
Number of Ontario chipmunk species: 2
Number of chipmunk species worldwide: 21 in North America, 1 in China
Also see: Broad-winged Hawk, Mink, Red Squirrel, Red Pine

DEER MOUSE
Legions of the Night

Population density in prime habitat: 230–10,000/km² (0.4 sq. mi), generally tripling from winter to summer and fluctuating up to tenfold between years of high and low seed crops

Heartbeats per minute: 320–860

Average human heartbeats per minute: 60–200

Top running speed: 13 km/h (8 mph)

High-jumping ability: Up to 30 cm (1 ft)

Number of naps per day: Up to 20

Body length: 7–10 cm (2.4–4 in)

Tail length: 5–11 cm (2–4.4 in)

Weight: 12–32 g (0.4–1.2 oz)

When the sun goes down, the meek inherit the earth, emerging from every crack, crevice and hole in the ground to skitter across their dark domains. Mice are among the most numerous mammals in the forest, and have some of the most profound influences on the ecosystem. Forests teem with hundreds or even thousands per square kilometre, rivalling the total number of birds. Mice are far less conspicuous because they stick with the oldest of mammalian survival tactics, being tiny, nocturnal and partly subterranean. It was only after a giant meteorite, comet or some other shattering catastrophe struck the Earth 66 million years ago and ended the reign of the dinosaurs that furry animals began coming out into the light of day and putting on weight. Even today, rodents, which have sharp front gnawing teeth that grow throughout their lives, account for 40 per cent of all mammal species worldwide.

Mice have long had a dubious reputation in Western civilization, defamed as the creation of witches or the devil, and as omens of all four riders of the apocalypse. The very word *mouse* is evolved from a Sanskrit word meaning "thief."

But in Native North American legends, the mouse is usually a good and trusted friend. Such respect may have been born out of an intrinsic understanding and reverence among hunting cultures of their food chain. A host of larger predators are directly dependent on the droves of mice that sprout from the earth. The abundance of prey, contrary to popular myth, has far more control over the numbers of predators than vice versa.

Forest-mice populations rise and fall with the tree-seed cycles, which vary greatly from year to year to keep seedeaters in check. Mice, in turn, form one of the largest corps of seed distributors in the forest, unwittingly planting trees in forgotten caches and spreading minute herb pits and mushroom spores in their droppings. Those droppings fertilize the soil, while mouse tunnels help air, water and roots spread through the ground. Together with shrews, mice eat up to 80 per cent of the cocoons of the European sawfly, an insect that can do much damage to trees.

Deer mice are the most common mice in most Ontario forests. Their rustling in the leaves and even singing, described in the writings of Ontario naturalist R. D. Lawrence as "an incredibly high, yet soft, crooning," can be heard throughout much of the night. More laid-back than most of their relatives, deer mice rarely put

Markings: Grey to reddish-brown back and sides, white belly, feet and chin
Alias: Woodland deer mouse, vesper mouse, singing mouse, *la souris sylvestre, Peromyscus maniculatus*
Calls: Shrill, buzzing trill lasting up to 10 sec a burst; squeaks, chitters
Whereabouts: Prefers mature forests with rich soils, but found in woodlands of almost any type and age
Home range: About 400–1,300 m² (478–1,555 sq. yd)
Home: Ground burrows, tree cavities, hollow logs, inside stumps and brush piles; usually 10–15 cm (4–6 in) wide, lined with shredded materials; usually several per mouse
Food: Mostly seeds, especially conifer and maple; also berries, nuts, buds, flowers, beetles, caterpillars, centipedes, grasshoppers, snails, spiders, moths, birds' eggs, carrion of birds and small animals
Food cache volume: Up to 4.5 L (4 quarts)
Gestation period: 22–23 days; 24–30 days if nursing a previous litter
Average litter: 3–6
Litters a year: Usually 2; up to 5
Birth weight: 1.5 g (0.05 oz)
Inbred individuals: Up to 10%
Weaning age: 3–4 weeks
Distance young disperse from birthplace: Up to 500 m (547 yd)

**Age upon reaching adult
size:** About 6 weeks
Age at first breeding:
Females about 7 weeks,
males 9 weeks
Nestling survival: About 50%
Winter survival: As low as
10%
Lifespan: As few as 5% live
more than a year; probably
up to 2–3 years in wild; up
to 8 years in captivity
Predators: Owls, foxes,
martens, weasels, raccoons,
skunks, coyotes, shrews,
snakes, almost all other full
or partial meateaters
**Average number of mice
eaten by a long-tailed
weasel in one year:** 1,300
Winter state: Reduced activity in tunnels beneath snow
and ground, living off caches
of seeds and nuts, torpid for
days at a time
Range: All Ontario; also in all
provinces and territories except Nunavut and island of
Newfoundland
Famous mice: Mickey,
Minnie, Mighty, Jerry,
Speedy Gonzalez, Topo
Gigio, Algernon
**Greatest mouse achieve-
ment in space:** In 1960, 3
lab mice, Sally, Amy and
Moe, travelled 1,100 km
(660 mi) above Cape
Canaveral, higher than any
other animal had gone, and
returned alive
Past medicinal uses:
Ingested for a wide range of
ailments, especially for

up a fight against intruders into their territory unless population densities get high. In winter, while occasionally scurrying beneath or above the snow, they mostly snuggle together for warmth in dens of up to 12 mice, living on stored seeds. They breed from April through August, with females inviting suitors into their love nests for several minutes of romance before kicking them out again and raising babies on their own. The young are weaned and scattered, or drift away, about three weeks after birth, allowing Mom to meet a batch of new fellows and raise another family.

Around campsites and cottages, deer mice can be quite tame, standing up on their hind feet, their large, beady black eyes searching hopefully for a discarded crumb or raisin. They'll crawl into or industriously gnaw through food bags left on the ground. Unlike the "city mouse" image of the rather distantly related house mouse from Europe, the deer mouse is fastidi-ous, carefully grooming and preening itself for up to 20 minutes at a time with its dexterous little paws.

A menagerie of other tiny creatures crosses paths with deer mice throughout the wilderness. The almost identical **white-footed mouse** is more territorial than its amiable cousin but becomes scarce towards the northern limits of its range in the deciduous forests of central Ontario. It spends much of its time in trees. The **woodland jumping mouse**, which unlike most other mice hibernates seven to nine months of the year, frequents tangled debris near streams. Sporting huge feet and tails nearly twice as long as the mice themselves, they bound in zigzaging leaps of one to two metres when in a hurry.

Voles, which have shorter tails and ears than mice, making them look more beaverlike, skitter day and night through a variety of habitats. **Red-backed voles** abound in boggy or mossy spruce and fir forests, hemlock stands and dense, log-strewn areas where there's plentiful regeneration after fires, blowdowns or budworm outbreaks. Around beaver meadows and other open areas, the grass-eating **meadow vole**, or meadow mouse, at the peak of its two- to four-year population cycle, lives in densities up to 10 times as high as its forest relatives. In captivity, these voles can produce up to 17 litters a year, more than any other mammal on Earth. They eat and tramp down a labyrinth of regular paths beneath the tall grass of a meadow.

Barrelling along the same runways are also the smallest and among the most ferocious of all mammals. Ontario's various species of shrews, weighing between 2.5 and 29 grams (0.1 to one ounce), are almost constantly on the move, their meteoric metabolism demanding they eat every two hours, consuming up to three times their weight in food a day, or starve. Insects, slugs and other invertebrates are their mainstay, but shrews also kill and eat animals much larger than themselves, such as mice, voles, frogs, snakes, even baby rabbits.

Venom released from glands at the base of the hooked lower teeth of the **short-tailed shrew** allows it to take down prey as big as baby hares and snakes. One of only three known venomous mammals on Earth, the short-tail's bite

children, from bad breath to bedwetting

Hantavirus: Very rare disease, potentially fatal to humans, spread by inhaling dust contaminated with infected deer mouse droppings or urine; mouse-contaminated surfaces should be aired out and mopped, not swept, with disinfectant

Respiration rate (air breathed per gram of body weight per hour): Humans 0.2 cm^3, mice 3.5 cm^3, short-tailed shrews 5 cm^3

Short-tailed shrew population density in prime habitat: 160-20,000/km^2 (0.4 sq. mi)

Number of Ontario shrew species: 7

Number of Ontario mouse, vole and lemming species: 12 native, 2 introduced

Also see: Barred Owl, Goldfinch, Muskrat, Red Fox, Red Pine, Little Brown Bat, Falling Stars

can cause burning pain and week-long swelling in human flesh. The venom enables the shrew to paralyze its victims and store them, still alive, for up to five days. The little body snatcher has pinpricks for eyes that probably perceive only light. It navigates instead by echolocation, like a bat, uttering ultrasonic clicks and listening for the sound bouncing back along tunnel walls. Though as many as 90 per cent of all short-tailed shrews may perish in winter, the survivors produce up to four litters a year, making them the most abundant mammal in the province.

With their long torpedo snouts and coats of dense, grey, velvety fur, shrews are rarely seen, spending most of their lives beneath the leaf litter or in other hidden locations.

FISHER
Prickly Prey a Forte

Each member of the weasel family has a slightly different specialty. Confusingly, the fisher's is not to catch fish, though it often forages along streams for muskrats and other prey. The stocky mustelid was probably named for its resemblance to the European *fichet*, also called a polecat. Sometimes as big as a fox, with shorter, more powerful legs, fishers commonly clamber up dead trees and rip into nest holes to reach flying squirrels or other occupants. Hunting day or night, they also take larger prey – especially snowshoe hares – far more often than does their closest relative, the diminutive marten. On occasion, they'll even go after raccoons, which are generally too ornery for larger predators.

But what fishers do better than anything else in the world, save for speeding cars, is dispatch porcupines. With a swiftness and agility second

Body length: 48–67 cm (19–26 in)

Tail length: 25–38 cm (10–15 in)

Weight: Females avg. 1.3–3.2 kg (3–7 lb), males 2.2–5.4 kg (5–12 lb); maximum more than 9 kg (20 lb)

Height: Males avg. 23–26 cm (9–10 in) at shoulder, the hunched back a little higher

Markings: In winter, mostly dark brown, sometimes almost black; in summer, grey-brown; black legs, rump and tail; often small white patches on throat and between legs; black eyes shine bright, light green in lights at night

Alias: Fisher marten, black cat, fisher cat, wejack, black fox, Pennant's cat, *le pekan, Martes pennanti*

Calls: Growls, hisses, chuckles, soft trills

Whereabouts: Dense mixed forests, often in coniferous woods and swamps in winter

Home range: Females avg. 7–20 km² (3–8 sq. mi), males 25–40 km² (10–16 sq. mi)

Homes: Tree cavities, hollow logs, ground burrows, rock and brush piles, old muskrat and beaver lodges

Food: Hares, porcupines, mice, voles, red squirrels, flying squirrels, chipmunks, shrews, ruffed grouse, carrion, occasionally smaller birds and their eggs, frogs, fish, ermine, martens, young beavers, insects, berries and nuts

Average daily food helping: About 675 g (1.4 lb)

Gestation: 11–13 months, including delayed implantation of more than 6 months

Average litter: 2–3

Birth weight: 40 g (1.4 oz)

Age at first breeding: Most females 1 year, males 2 years

Lifespan: Commonly 7 years; up to about 10 years in wild, 18 years in captivity

Predators: Possibly great horned owls, lynx, bears, coyotes; young under 2 years old most commonly killed by older fishers

Tracks: Pawprints 5–10 cm (2–4 in) long and 5–7.5 cm (2–3 in) wide, bigger when fishers run and back feet land in prints made by front

to none, they run circles around the big pincushions, dodging the swishing tail while repeatedly biting their victim's face until, after a half-hour or more, the porcupine succumbs. Then it's merely a matter of flipping the porcupine on its back to feast on the soft, unquilled underside. By stashing a good-sized porky beneath leaves or snow, a fisher has enough meat to keep it going for a couple of weeks.

> *Fishers have always been*
> *far less numerous than mink,*
> *martens and other smaller weasels*

Fishers also stick close to winter-killed deer or wolf leftovers whenever they find them. They generally hunt along regular circuits that take four to six days to complete, but deep snow limits their movements considerably, and extreme cold or storms can keep them denned up for days. Come late March and April, however, males venture far and wide off their usual territories in search of the opposite sex. Females, often just a week after they've given birth, strike up liaisons with visiting suitors that may last several days, during which they may mate for one to five hours in a single stretch.

Though often just half the size of adult males, mothers keep their callers well away from the lofty tree-cavity dens where they keep their young. When the kits are eight to 10 weeks old, the mothers bring them down to a ground borrow. By midsummer, when the young stop nursing and are learning to hunt for themselves, tempers start running short among siblings and their parent. A month or so of family squabbles finally sends the nearly full-grown young off on their separate ways in August or September.

Fanning out to establish large individual territories, fishers have always been far less numerous than mink, martens and other smaller weasels. In areas where they eat a lot of snow-shoe hares, their numbers often rise and fall a year or two behind the hares' well-known 10-year population cycle. Logging, poison wolf baits and a particularly high demand after the First World War for lustrous fisher pelts brought the animals close to extinction by the 1930s. Only strict regulations, such as assigning trapping licences based on watersheds rather than townships, turned things around for both fishers and martens in the early 1950s. Draftees from a strong remnant population in Algonquin Park have since been used to reintroduce the fisher in the Ottawa Valley, the Georgian Bay hinterlands, Manitoulin Island and the Bruce Peninsula. As a result, dense populations of tree-destroying porcupines have declined, going some way to restoring the natural balance.

Scat: Usually 2.5–5 cm (1–2 in) long, thin, black or dark brown, containing hair, sometimes quills or berries

Peak activity periods: Around dusk and dawn

Population density in untrapped areas: 1 per 6.5 km^2 (2.5 sq. mi)

Number of fishers trapped annually in Ontario: Usually fewer than 5,000

Range: Northern Ontario to the southern edge of the Canadian Shield, Manitoulin Island and the Bruce Peninsula; also in all other provinces and territories except Prince Edward Island, island of Newfoundland and Nunavut

Also see: Marten, Porcupine, Snowshoe Hare, Big Dipper

FLYING SQUIRREL
Gliding Through the Nightshift

Rate of gliding descent: Avg. 1 m (3.3 ft) down for every 3 m (10 ft) forward

Density in prime habitat: Up to 1,000/km² (2,600 per sq. mi)

Body length: 14–19 cm (5.5–7.5 in)

Tail: Almost as long as its body, resembling a flattened bottle-brush; serves to stabilize glides and acts as an air break when flipped upward

Weight: Avg. 70–140 g (2.5–5 oz)

Markings: Light greyish-tan to reddish-brown back, light grey undersides; large black eyes shine red in lights at night

Alias: Northern flying squirrel, *le grand polatouche*, *Glaucomys sabrinus*

A soft wisp of wind, faint scratching in the night, a peripheral glimpse of something scurrying through the trees – all could lead to a keen pair of eyes shining orange-red in the beam of a well-aimed flashlight. Gliding and scampering largely undetected under the cover of darkness, northern flying squirrels occasionally swoop down upon branches behind an evening wilderness campfire or turn up after hours at cottage bird feeders. They're said to be partial to peanut butter.

Like inhabitants of a fairy realm, flying squirrels are mysterious nocturnal creatures that sail through the air and visit hidden places where mushrooms flourish. Though the fur-caped aerialists are little known, they're as plentiful as the bigger red squirrels that chatter vociferously through the day. Night-gliders sleep through the sunlit hours in tree holes or in spherical bark nests, and rise for the nightshift soon after the cantankerous reds and chipmunks call it a day.

Just as regular squirrels use well-worn routes that allow them to flash through the branches with hardly a thought, flying squirrels navigate along regular flight corridors, with takeoff spots marked by their urine and other body scents. Tossing themselves into the air, they spread their legs to unfold a continuous furred flap of skin reaching to each of their four feet, turning themselves into flying carpets. They can remain airborne for several seconds, swiftly gliding down to the lower trunk of their target tree, up to 50 metres (164 feet) away. Most glides, though, are closer to 20 metres (66 feet). Upon landing, they climb up the tree until attaining a sufficient height to launch off again. The mouse-eyed sprites can seamlessly dodge around trunks and branches, turn sudden right angles or drop straight down by spinning in a tight spiral.

Like so much that rarely meets the eye in the wild, flying squirrels may play an important role in the forest ecosystem, one that's only starting to be studied. The nocturnal nymphs are true mushroom fanatics, sniffing out and digging up even gumball-sized subterranean fruiting fungi. Such mushrooms, called false truffles, may be spread largely through the droppings of their animal foragers. A great variety of trees and plants in turn form close symbiotic relationships with these types of organisms, known as mycorrhizal fungi. Tree roots entwine with the fungal threads and provide them with sugars created through photosynthesis in return for nutrients and water collected from the ground by the extensive fungal networks.

Calls: Chucks, squeaks, sharp squeals, birdlike chirping and calls beyond human hearing range

Whereabouts: Mature coniferous and mixed forests

Home range: Avg. 3–12 ha (7–30 acre)

Homes: Old woodpecker holes or natural cavities lined with shredded leaves, moss, lichens, grass, bark strips, fur or feathers; in summer, also build spherical nests of sticks, bark, moss, leaves and lichens in forked branches, usually of an evergreen, and in witch's broom tangles at tops of black spruce, occasionally in a covered-over bird nest; each squirrel usually has several nests

Food: Mushrooms, nuts, acorns, raspberries and serviceberries in summer and fall; lichens, cached mushrooms and conifer seeds in winter; maple sap and buds of aspen, alder and willow in spring; also flowers, bird eggs and nestlings, beetles, moths, mayflies, insect larvae, carrion; said to be the most carnivorous of squirrels

Gestation period: 37–42 days

Average litter: 2–4

Birth weight: 4–6 g (0.14–0.2 oz)

Weight of a nickel: 4 g (0.14 oz)

Age at first breeding: 9 months for females, later for males

Lifespan: Most less than 4
years, up to 13 years in
captivity

Predators: Owls, hawks,
ravens, martens, fishers, raccoons, weasels, foxes, lynx,
wolves and coyotes

Peak activity periods: For 2
hours after sunset and 1
hour before sunrise

Top running speed: 13 km/h
(8 mph)

Range: All of Ontario except
extreme south and above
tree line; also in all other
provinces and territories except Nunavut and island of
Newfoundland

**Number of Ontario flying
squirrel species:** 2

**Number of flying squirrel
species worldwide:** 38

Also see: Yellow-bellied
Sapsucker, Fisher, Red
Squirrel, Lichens,
Mushrooms, Black Spruce

In winter, northern flying squirrels also eat lots of hanging tree lichens, a low-nutrition food on which few other animals, save caribou, can get by. The night-gliders also become quite social during winter, in contrast to the fierce individualism of daytime squirrels. On cold days, as many as nine flying squirrels will curl close together in tree cavities for warmth. As the sun rises higher in the sky and mild days fore-shadow spring in mid- to late March, the velvet-furred rodents develop a keen romantic interest in one another. New litters result in May. Little Rockies leave the nest to learn to glide in early summer, but continue to be fiercely defended by their mothers until August or September.

In mature hardwood forests as far north as Algonquin Park, **southern flying squirrels** can also be found. They're a little smaller than their northern brethren and have white, rather than grey, undersides. The southern fliers' diet is centred on more traditional squirrel fare, such as acorns and beechnuts, which nevertheless are col-lected unseen after nightfall. In recent decades, they've been gradually spreading north, possibly beckoned by the effects of climate change.

GROUNDHOG

Sleeping Through Its Greatest Moment

Away from the bright lights and fanfare, almost all Ontario groundhogs are fast asleep on their one day of celebrity. Only in Wiarton, Ontario, does one rotund, grumpy, albino star bask in the limelight on Groundhog Day, coaxed in front of the cameras by formally attired civic officials. A lot rides on Wiarton Willie. If he sees his shadow, it is supposed to mean six more weeks of winter – probably because February 2 is often a typically crisp, sunny, midwinter day that produces a good shadow. If he fails to find a shadow, spring is said to be imminent. The tradition is based on the old European folk belief that badgers and hedgehogs could predict the weather. February 2 used to be a holiday, called Candlemas in Christian times, though originally it was the pagan festival of Brigid, celebrating the first stirrings of spring. It was one of many days

Heartbeats per minute: 80–400; in hibernation 4–15

Body temperature: 34–42°C (93–108°F) when active; 2–14°C (36–57°F) in hibernation

Time between breaths during hibernation: As long as 6 minutes

Body length: Avg. 40–50 cm (16–20 in)

Tail length: 10–15 cm (4–6 in)

Weight: Avg. 2–3 kg (4.4–6.6 lb) in April, 3–5 kg (6.6–11 lb) in autumn

Weight loss during hibernation: Adults avg. 25–30%, juveniles 50%

Markings: Varying shades of coarse brown fur, darkest on feet, face and tail

Alias: Woodchuck, chuck, whistle pig, bulldozer, marmot, *la marmotte, Marmota monax*

Origin of name *woodchuck*: Derived from Algonkian language name for "groundhog," called *wejack* by Ojibway

Calls: Loud, shrill warning whistle, like a sonic squeak, heard up to 300 m (328 yd) away; low churring when threatened; barks and growls when fighting

Whereabouts: Open woods, rocky hillsides, meadows and forest edges with lots of grass or leafy ground cover and thick loam or sandy soil

Home range: Up to 100 m (330 ft) wide

Home: Ground burrows, often on a south-facing hillside or gully; usually about 4–7 m (13–23 ft) long, 1–2 m (3.3–6.6 ft) deep, with 2 entrances, plus plunge holes that drop straight down, bathrooms and a bedchamber, 30–45 cm (12–18 in) wide and 30 cm (12 in) high, lined with grass and leaves

Number of burrows occupied in summer: Avg. of 2–3 per groundhog

Soil excavated for a burrow: up to 320 kg (700 lb)

Food: Grass, leaves and stems of many plants, flowers, seeds, berries, occasionally insects, snails, rarely bird eggs or nestlings; bark, buds and twigs in early spring

farmers gathered to, among other things, guess the weather for the coming growing season.

In a sense, groundhogs do forecast the weather, since they know Ontario winters rarely end even six weeks after February 2. The big rodents – oversized members of the squirrel family – keep sleeping right on through. Groundhogs are true hibernators and remain curled tightly in a largely uninterrupted, deep sleep for four to seven months. Their body temperature can drop to just above freezing, bringing their metabolism almost to a standstill, so they use just a trickle of their stored fat. When males emerge in late March or April, with snow still on the ground, they must have enough fat to live off for several weeks longer, subsisting on a starvation diet of buds, bark and twigs until fresh grass and leaves sprout. This period of early-spring groundhog activity, coming at the leanest point in the year for both wildlife and humans, often provided a much-needed meal for Native people in past times.

Groundhogs rouse themselves from deep torpor by metabolizing deposits of special blood-rich brown fat, stored between the shoulders, which quickly heat up and accelerate the heart, jolting their sluggish circulation into a rushing torrent. Males awake with romance rather than breakfast on their minds. Venturing above ground for one to five hours at midday, they establish their territories and reputations while searching out the boudoirs of the opposite sex by rubbing scent from their muzzles on burrow entrances, tree trunks and other objects and fighting or chasing away other males. A successful warrior woodchuck carves out a fiefdom containing the dens of several females.

Though a courting male enters the winter den of a bachelorette wagging his tail like a puppy, more often than not the randy marmot is chased right back out by the wakened, grouchy occupant. When he finally finds an agreeable mate, he may be permitted to shack up with her for a while, though the honeymoon usually lasts just a few days. Then he's on his way again to knock on other doors, while a month later she gives birth and raises the family alone.

Plump, inquisitive groundhog pups begin viewing the surface world when four to six weeks old. By the latter half of June, they weigh about half a kilo (1.1 pounds) each and crowd the natal burrow. Mothers often set some up in old dens nearby or dig new burrows for them, which they continue to visit. A month later, however, the young strike out on their own, journeying anywhere from a few hundred metres (or yards) to much farther away before either finding an abandoned burrow or quickly digging their own. Older animals usually have summer burrows in open areas and winter homes in or at the edge of a forest.

Around early June, a groundhog's metabolism begins to slow, permitting considerably faster weight gain. Stuffed and sleepy by the time most of their remaining food withers with killing frosts in early autumn, the whistle pigs block off their hibernating chambers before turning in, allowing other animals to use the rest of the burrow through the winter. The young of the year – eating longer to catch up with larger, older groundhogs – like true teenagers, both go into hibernation and wake up later than their elders.

Daily food helping: About 700 g (1.5 lb)
Gestation period: 30–32 days
Average litter: 3–5
Birth weight: About 30 g (1 oz)
Weaning age: 5–6 weeks
Age at first breeding: 2 years for most
Annual survival: Avg. about 25% in first year; adults 70%
Lifespan: Commonly 2–3 years for adults; up to 6 years in wild, 10 years in captivity
Predators: Foxes, wolves, coyotes, mink, bears, lynx, hawks, great horned owls
Top running speed: 16 km/h (10 mph)
Famous forcasters: Wiarton Willie, Punxsutawney Phil, Shubenacadie Sam, Dunkirk Dave, Pennichuck Chuck, General Beauregard Lee
Range: All Ontario; also in all other provinces and territories except Nunavut, island of Newfoundland and Prince Edward Island
Closest Ontario relatives: Squirrels, chipmunks
Animals that use old groundhog burrows: Foxes, skunks, raccoons, rabbits, hares, porcupines, mink, otters, weasels, squirrels, mice, shrews, snakes
Also see: Black bear, Red Fox, Clouds

LITTLE BROWN BAT
Symbol of Fortune and Fertility

Frequency of sonar calls: 40–100 kilohertz

Upper limit of human hearing: 20 kilohertz

Average frequency of human conversation: Less than 5 kilohertz

Flying speed: 20–35 km/h (12–22 mph)

Wingbeats per second: 6–8

Body length: 8–10 cm (3–4 in)

Wingspan: 22–27 cm (8.5–10.5 in)

Weight: 7–14 g (0.25–0.5 oz)

Weight of a loonie: 7 g (0.25 oz)

Body temperature: 37–40°C (99–104°F) when active; up to 64°C (147°F) in nursery colonies; 2–8°C (36–47°F) in hibernation

The crusading efforts of Batman aside, bats remain enshrouded in myth and misconception, most of it bad. The only mammals to really fly have been looked on since the Middle Ages of Western culture as unnatural, the associates of witches and vampires or the incarnation of the devil himself. In other cultures, bats represent fertility, because they have exceptionally long penises, spanning two centimetres (0.8 inches) in the case of the little brown bat, nearly a quarter of its body length. The length is needed to get around the skin membrane that joins the female's legs together.

In one Ojibway tale, the bat was originally a squirrel that was burned, deformed and blinded while heroically freeing the sun from the tangled branches of a tall tree. The sun rewarded its seriously singed rescuer with the power of flight and the ability to see in the dark. In the mystic East, the Chinese greeted bats as omens of good luck. The Wu-fu charm, traditionally hung above the doors of Chinese homes, depicts five bats circling the tree of life, representing the five top human blessings – virtue, wealth, children, longevity and a contented death.

Without doubt, bats do descend like a blessing on warm summer nights to devour the hordes of flying insects that torment larger mammals such as humans. The little brown bat, Ontario's most common, can catch and is believed to eat more than 10 mosquitoes a minute on the wing, scooping them up in its wide tail membrane and flipping them into its mouth. In a single night, the little brown can eat enough insects to equal half its weight. For nursing females, it might be more than their entire weight. Extensive studies in the U.S. turn up fewer mosquito bites in areas with lots of bats. Little browns prefer hunting three to six metres (10 to 20 feet) above water, especially in the first two or three hours after sunset, and before dawn.

While it is not true that bats are blind, hearing is certainly their most important sense for capturing large quantities of bugs. Using sonar, or echolocation, little brown bats emit a steady stream of high-pitched squeaks that bounce off objects and insects within a range of two metres (6.6 feet). Their large ears and brain interpret the distance more accurately than human sonar devices. The sonar calls are too high for human hearing, though bats can make audible squeaks of fright if threatened.

Before engaging their sonar systems, bats depend on highly tuned internal temperature

Heartbeats per minute: More than 1,300 in flight, 100–200 when stationary, as low as 10–15 in hibernation

Markings: Mostly medium brown, darker on shoulders, ears, face; lighter on underside; dark brown wings and tail membrane almost hairless

Alias: Flittermouse, reremouse, *la petite chauve-souris brune, Myotis lucifugus*

Name origin: From Old Norse *bakke,* meaning "flutter"

Whereabouts: Forage over lakes, streams, wetlands, ponds, meadows and open forests

Roosts: Usually in sunny spots near forest edges beneath loose bark, in tree cavities, under rocks, cottage attics, in crevices as narrow as 1 cm (0.4 in); often used for decades

Hanging ability: Able to sleep hanging upside down because of a special catch in toe tendons that closes tight with the suspended pull of a batnapper

Food: Moths, mosquitoes, mayflies, midges, beetles, caddisflies and other flying insects

Number of times bats chew per second: 7

Average time food takes to go through a bat's system: 20 min

Gestation period: About 60 days after delayed implantation

Litter: 1
Fledging age: 18–21 days
Age at first breeding:
Females 1 year, males 2
years
Lifespan: Avg. probably 10
years, up to 35 years in the
wild
Predators: Owls, hawks,
martens, skunks, raccoons
Winter whereabouts: Large
groups hibernate in caves
and old mines
**Weight loss during hiberna-
tion:** 20–40%
**Nighttime temperature
bringing bats out of hibernation:** 10°C (50°F)
Range: All of Ontario, except
far northwest; also in all other provinces and territories
except Nunavut
Age of oldest bat fossils: 60
million years
**Other animals that use
echolocation:** Shrews, dolphins, whales, cave-dwelling
birds
Migratory Ontario species:
Red bat, hoary bat, silver-
haired bat
**Number of Ontario bat
species:** 8
**Number of bat species
worldwide:** About 925
**Portion of world's mammal
species that are bats:**
About 25%
Also see: Barred Owl, Yellow-
bellied Sapsucker,
Mosquitoes, Moths

readings to tell them if it is worth going out to look for insects. Without temperatures high enough to guarantee plentiful insects, it is too dangerous for bats to gear up to full metabolism. Instead they go into semihibernation, even on cool nights in the summer, with their body temperature, heart and respiratory rates dropping to put their systems on slow burn until warm air rouses them.

Although three of Ontario's bat species migrate to the southern U.S. for winter, flying as high as 3,000 metres (10,000 feet), little brown bats hibernate in colonies in caves or abandoned mine shafts. Some 300,000 to 400,000 little browns winter in a score of protected old mine sites in the Great Lakes states and Ontario, including at Detour Lake, 300 kilometres (186 miles) northeast of Timmins. One old mine in New York State houses little browns 1,160 metres (3,800 feet) below the surface, deeper than any other mammals have been found in the world. The bats travel up to 800 kilometres (480 miles) to return to traditional hibernaculas – group hibernating sites – starting to swarm around them in mid-July or August. They mate in late summer, with both males and females having more than one partner and forming no pair bonds in what York University bat specialist Brock Fenton refers to as the "disco-mating system." By late September or October, they settle in for the winter, the males in tight clusters, the females hanging alone or in small groups. The biggest cause of death among little brown bats is usually lack of fat reserves among first-year young too inexperienced to catch enough insects before going into hibernation.

Since 2006, however, a mysterious condition called white-nose fungus has killed hundreds of thousands of wintering bats in the northeastern U.S. and threatens to spread to Canada. The fungus infects the wings and face, causing the bats to rouse frequently from torpor and burn their fat stores, leading to starvation.

Normally, females come out of hibernation first, in mid-April or May, and fly to nursery colonies, often in a hollow tree that can house up to hundreds of bats. Males and non-breeding females, lacking the food needs of expectant mothers, slumber until warmer temperatures arrive in mid-May, then spread out to smaller summer roosting sites. Newborns, delivered in June, cling to their mothers' undersides during nightly hunting flights. When the babies get too big, they are left in the nursery but can fly and hunt themselves when they are little more than three weeks old.

In flight, little brown bats are jerky and undulating as they outmanoeuvre insects in the air. Such a sight should not inspire fear. Contrary to myth, they do not become entangled in people's hair and have a very low incidence of rabies. Little browns die soon after contracting the virus and their teeth are reportedly too small even to break human skin. A small number of people, however, have been infected by silver-haired and pipistrelle bats, usually after handling the animals directly. Neither is common in central Ontario.

Bats carry no other human disease, very few parasites and, in fact, are quite clean, spending a half hour at a time grooming and cleaning their all-important ears with twists of their tiny thumbs. To admirers, they are charming, intelligent, even cute, like downy little mice with wings. Biologists believe bats may be closely related to monkeys. Like primates, they have just two nipples for nursing their young. Though Ontario's species are insectivorous, fruit- and nectar-eating bats in the tropics are among the principal agents for propagating rainforests by pollinating plants and spreading seeds. Their numbers are rapidly decreasing because of habitat destruction and hunting.

MARTEN
Taking to the Big Trees

Body length: Females 35–38 cm (14–15 in), males 41–43 cm (16–17 in)

Tail length: 15–23 cm (6–9 in)

Weight: Females avg. 0.4–0.7 kg (0.9–1.5 lb), males 0.6–1 kg (1.3–2.2 lb)

Markings: Most often golden to yellowish brown, sometimes reddish, light or dark brown; darker on legs and tail; greyish face, ears trimmed grey or white, throat and chest orange or yellow

Alias: Pine marten, American marten, Canadian sable, pussy marten, Hudson Bay sable, *la martre, Martes americana*

Calls: Growls, snarls, hisses, clucks

Whereabouts: Mature coniferous and mixed forests with lots of deadfall; cedar swamps

Home range: Avg. about 1 km² (0.4 sq. mi) for females, 2–3 km² (0.8–1.2 sq. mi) for males

Homes: Tree cavities, hollow logs, ground burrows or rock crevices, lined with grass, moss and leaves

Food: Red-backed voles, mice, hares and ruffed grouse most important; also red squirrels, chipmunks, flying squirrels, smaller birds and their eggs, frogs, snakes, weasels, mink, fish,

The most arboreal members of the weasel clan, martens are probably better suited to mature forests than any other predator. The cat-sized prowlers can sail through the trees with the speed and dexterity of squirrels. They spend most of their time, however, on damp, mossy ground, pouncing on voles and mice. During winter, they frequently tunnel beneath the snow while hunting bunnies, as suggested by their Cree name, *wabachis,* meaning "hare chaser."

Though martens are widely reputed to be squirrel catchers, the rodents make up only a very small portion of their diet in Ontario. Up in the trees, most healthy resident red squirrels are usually too sure of their territories and regular escape routes through the tangle of branches to be captured by even the fastest assailants. But ailing or injured squirrels, or dispersing young on unfamiliar turf, are occasionally captured.

Martens work fairly small territories and can be quite abundant in mature stands with plenty of deadfall, especially when their prey populations are at the peak of their cycles. Still, the slightly foxy-faced predators are so stealthful, they're almost never seen. They move swiftly and silently, preferring to bound from one fallen log to another, frequently marking them with droppings and scent from their musk glands.

Martens were once trapped nearly to the point of extinction in central Ontario

Seeking each other out during the warm days of summer plentitude, marten mates may stay together for a few days before going their separate ways. Both sexes may have more than one tryst during the breeding season. Like most of their weasel relatives, though, pregnant martens hold their fertilized eggs in a state of suspended animation until late winter, so that the young, born the following April, have a full warm season to grow. Mothers often keep their charges high up in tree cavities until after their eyes open and they become active, usually in June. Families then relocate to ground nests, where they stay together for a couple more months before the full-grown offspring venture up to 80 kilometres (50 miles) away in search of good hunting territories.

insects, carrion, berries, nuts, conifer seeds

Daily food helping: At least 3 mice, or their equivalent

Gestation period: About 7–9 months, including delayed implantation

Average litter: 3–4

Birth weight: Avg. 28 g (1 oz)

Weaning age: About 6 weeks

Age at first breeding: 1 year

Annual survival in untrapped, unlogged areas: Avg. 80–90% for adults

Lifespan: Commonly 5–6 years; up to 14 years in wild, 18 years in captivity

Predators: Fishers, lynx, foxes, wolves, coyotes, great horned owls

Tracks: Usually in 7.5- to 12-cm-wide (3- to 4.8-in-wide) pairs, each print about 5–7.5 cm (2–3 in) long and 3–7 cm (1.2–2.8 in) wide, with back feet landing in marks made by front; strides averaging 38–84 cm (15–33 in); occasionally walks more slowly, with each foot sometimes leaving a separate print

Scat: Usually several cm (1 or 2 in) long, less than 1 cm (0.4 in) wide, black or dark brown with fur, bits of bone and sometimes seeds

Density in prime habitat: 0.5–2 per km² (0.4 sq. mi)

Estimated Ontario marten population: 100,000–300,000

Number of martens trapped annually in Ontario: Up to 63,000

Range: Northern Ontario to the southern edge of the Canadian Shield and Manitoulin Island; also in all other provinces and territories except Nova Scotia, Prince Edward Island and Nunavut

Also see: Deer Mouse, Fisher, Red Squirrel

Never able to resist bait, martens were once trapped nearly to the point of extinction in central Ontario, but have made a considerable comeback since the 1930s. Farther north, however, the species is drawing increasing concern. There, numbers are decreasing over wide areas where clearcutting and logging roads have destroyed old-growth boreal habitat and provided easy access to trappers in the remaining fragmented forest.

MINK
Among the Smallest of Carnivores

A mink's rich, luxurious coat, underlain by an inner layer of supersoft, dense fur, is ideally suited for its semiaquatic lifestyle in sometimes frigid waters. Body oils spread during grooming keep it glossy and waterproof. Together with its streamlined lay, the fur's qualities have long attracted humans and made mink one of the most highly prized pelts to grace the backs of the genteel. It takes about 70 to 80 minks to make a full-length coat. Fortunately for those in the wild, about 90 per cent of the market today is supplied by commercially raised animals.

Mink are probably the most commonly seen species of Ontario's weasel family, other than skunks, because they frequent shorelines and other open areas. For savage killers, they are deceptively cute, with little pointy faces, small round ears and long, thin bodies on short legs.

Dive duration: Usually 5–20 sec, up to 2 min

Body length: 33–52 cm (13–20.5 in)

Tail length: 16–20 cm (6–8 in)

Weight: Females avg. 0.7–1.1 kg (1.5–2.4 lb), males 0.9–1.6 kg (2–3.5 lb)

Markings: Light to dark brown or black, darkest on the back, with white chin patch, often a white chest spot, bushy tail

Alias: American mink, *le vison d'Amérique, Mustela vison*

Calls: Snarl, squeak, bark, hiss, purr

Whereabouts: Along forest streams, lakes and marshes

Territory: Avg. 0.5–3 km (0.3–1.8 mi) of shoreline for

females, 2.5–5.5 km (1.5–
3.3 mi) of shoreline for males
Homes: Maintains a number
of dens in bank burrows
about 10 cm (4 in) wide, log
cavities, under roots and
rocks, sometimes in old
groundhog holes or muskrat
lodges
Food: Muskrats, fish, frogs,
crayfish, mice, voles, hares,
rabbits, squirrels, waterfowl,
small birds, eggs, garter
snakes, salamanders, clams,
worms, snails, slugs, insects,
grasses
Average daily food helping:
About 100 g (4 oz)
Gestation period: 40–79
days, depending on delayed
implantation
Average litter: 4–6, born
April to mid-May
Birth weight: 6–10 g (0.2–
0.35 oz)
Weaning age: About 5 weeks
Age at first breeding:
Females 1 year, males
almost 2 years
Lifespan: Few live more than
3 years; up to 8 years in
wild, 14 years in captivity
Predators: Lynx, bobcats,
foxes, wolves, bears, coyotes, great horned owls,
snowy owls
Top running speed: 10–
12 km/h (6–8 mph)
Swimming speed: 3–4 km/h
(1.8–2.4 mph)
Tracks: Rounded, 2.5–3.5 cm
(1–1.4 in) wide, with 4 toes
Scat: Dark, 1 cm (0.4 in) long,
in piles, with bone chips and
scales

Mink usually walk or run with their backs gracefully arched. Chancing upon a non-threatening
human, one may stop close by, stand up on its
hind feet and curiously check out the scene.
Although they are mainly nocturnal, relentless
hunting often keeps them going through the day.

Weasels – mink included – are the smallest
but among the fiercest and most agile of all carnivores. Mink often attack and eat animals larger
than themselves, killing with a bite to the neck.
Even muskrats – themselves ferocious – are
attacked in their lodges and literally eaten out of
house and home, the mink gaining both a meal
and a new den. When the tables are turned,
larger predators have great difficulty catching
and outfighting a mink. Adding insult to injury,
mink produce a stench from their anal musk
glands more rank than that of any member of
the weasel family save the skunk. A mink cannot
direct its spray like a skunk, but it lets fly with its
musky defence far more readily, at the slightest
threat. *Mink* is, in fact, a Swedish word meaning
"stinky animal."

Besides defence, musk glands are used by
mink to communicate with each other and in
seeking carnal company between late February
and early May. Indeed, the world of odours is
everything to mink and other weasels. When
hunting, even during a chase, mink use their
nose more than their eyes, becoming so absorbed
that they're known to run right over the feet of
human spectators without seeming to notice
them. Males hunt on long circuit routes that
may take a week to complete, finding prey both
at the bottom of deep, watery dives and on the
forest floor. Overnight dens along the route are

often stocked with carcasses for the mink's next trip through, especially in winter. Up to a month's supply of food has been found in some mink storehouses.

Though the mink on the Canadian Shield suffer much less than their southern brethren from contamination by water pollution, they do become scarce in areas of intensive cottage development. Shorelines cleared of the shrubs, deadfall, rocks and debris that are ceaselessly searched by the foraging serpentine mustelids have little left to offer them.

Short-tailed weasels, which hunt mostly on the upland forest floor or in the tunnels of rodents, look very much like mink, but are less than a quarter the size. They are intense, twitchy, ferocious little mousers that are usually too fast to be seen as they lope in a blur from bush to tree and underground burrow. Short-tails have white undersides, and in winter, like long-tailed and least weasels, turn completely white, except for a black-tipped tail. In their white coat they are known as ermines. Their silky fur has been used since the Middle Ages to trim the sumptuous vestments of royalty. With the physique of an elongated mouse, the regal weasels are built for chasing rodents down into their tunnels beneath the snow and right into burrows as narrow as two or three centimetres (about an inch). Because their build exposes so much surface area to the cold in winter, they burn two to three times as much energy to stay warm as a stouter creature of the same size and must devour a great deal every day.

Density in prime habitat:
Avg. 3 per km² (0.4 sq. mi)
Range: All Ontario; also in all other provinces and territories except Nunavut
Mink raised on farms worldwide: 20–60 million annually
Short-tailed weasel density in prime habitat:
40–110/km² (0.4 sq. mi)
Number of mustelid species native to Ontario: 10
Ontario mustelids at risk: Wolverine, threatened, restricted largely to far northwest; badger, endangered, found along Lake Erie
Number of mustelid species worldwide: About 63
Also see: Fisher, Marten, Muskrat, Skunk, Otter

MOOSE
A Gentle Giant Until the Rut

Height at shoulders: 1.5–2.3 m (5–7.5 ft)

Antler spread: Up to 1.7 m (5.6 ft)

Body length: Females avg. 2–2.6 m (6.6–8.6 ft), males 2.4–3 m (7.9–10 ft)

Weight: Females avg. 375–530 kg (825–1,170 lb), males 400–540 kg (880–1,190 lb)

Biggest moose ever recorded: 816 kg (1,800 lb), 2.3 m (7.7 ft) at shoulder, in Alaska, 1897

Surface area of scent cells in a moose's nose: Avg. 830 cm² (129 sq. in)

Scent-cell coverage in a human nose: 4–5 cm² (0.6–0.8 sq. in)

Average daily food helping: Up to 25–30 kg (55–66 lb)

Huge, strong, silent and a little funny-looking, the moose is another quintessential Canadian symbol. It is by far the biggest animal in central Ontario. Even tubby black bears going into hibernation weigh much less than the lanky, stilted herbivore. Yet, for most of the year, the moose is like a towering, gentle farmhand. It is usually calm and benevolent even when awestruck canoeists drift close by as it feeds on succulent water lilies in the early morning or late afternoon.

In one age-old story, the moose is one of the few large beasts not downsized by Glooscap, a deity of the Mi'kmaq, before he set humans upon Earth. The great ungulate kept his size because of his humility and stated goodwill towards the newcomers. Moose were highly valued by northern forest peoples. A single animal could feed a family through much of the winter, in addition to yielding the favoured leather for moccasins and wool from its mane for mittens and socks.

But Shakespeare was right when he wrote, "Hell hath no fury like a lovesick moose" (the unpublished Stratford, Ontario, Folio). During the fall rut, which peaks in late September and early October, males become aggressive and unpredictable, even crazed. Their mood starts to change in late August when, after growing antlers for five months, they begin rubbing off the nourishing velvet lining on bushes and trees, colouring their huge racks orange-brown with dried blood and plant juices. Males challenge each other to establish their status for the breeding ahead. Antlers are the measure of a moose, and the less impressive of two contesting bulls usually backs down before a fight develops, left only with the psychological wounds of antler envy. Occasionally, they do drop the gloves, pushing head to head until one loses ground and retreats. Most younger males, lacking the rack dimensions and strength of their elders, don't get to mate.

The biggest antlers also have the deepest, most impressive resonance for females listening to distant bulls thrashing them against branches. Females moan longingly for up to 40 hours straight to attract bulls through the dense forest to their breeding arenas in meadows and boggy lake edges. Biologists in the role of female impersonators imitate the sound by squeezing their noses, cupping their hands and calling. The mooses' great, long donkey ears and acute sense of smell serve them well in locating each other

in summer and 15–20 kg (33–45 lb) in winter

Markings: Dark brown body, in shades from almost black to rust; greyish-white lower legs and nostrils; calves reddish brown

Alias: Elk (European name), swamp donkey, *l'orignal*, *Alces alces*

Calls: Usually silent, but during rut, males make long, hoarse, guttural, 2-syllable grunt or loud roar; females make a drawn out, moaning bleat or moo, up to 5 sec long, audible for up to 3 km (2 mi)

Whereabouts: Forests with abundant patches of broadleaf trees up to 15 years old, diversely mixed with mature conifer stands, meadows, beaver ponds, lakes and wetlands

Home range: 10–15 km^2 (4–6 sq. mi) for females, 20–40 km^2 (8–16 sq. mi) for males

Food: In summer, water lilies, pondweed, deciduous leaves, ferns, horsetail, asters, jewelweed, grass, sedges; in winter, buds, twigs and bark of fir, beaked hazel, red and mountain maple, birch, mountain ash, aspen, poplar, willow, dogwood, juneberry and cherry

Frostbitten bells: A bull's beardlike "bell," or dewlap, is much larger than a female's and, drenched with saliva and urine, is used to slap his scent onto a mate during courtship; it diminishes with

age, probably due to recur-
ring frostbite
Gestation period: 8 months
Average litter: Usually 1; 2
common in large tracks of
abundant browse after fires
or logging
Birth weight: 12–17 kg
(25–35 lb)
Weaning age: About 3 months
First-year survival: Less than
50%
Age at first breeding: Most
females 2.5 years; most
males don't mate regularly
until about 5 years old
Lifespan: Avg. 7–8 years; up
to 18 years in wild, 27 years
in captivity
Predators: Wolves; bears may
attack young
Top running speed: 56 km/h
(35 mph)
Swimming speed: Avg.
10 km/h (6 mph)
Dive duration: Avg. 30 sec,
up to 50 sec
Deepest dives: 6 m (20 ft)
Tracks: Cloven hoofprints
15 cm (6 in) long, pointed in
direction of travel
Scat: Piles of greenish-
tinged, dark brown, pecan-
to olive-sized, fibrous pellets
in winter; less distinct,
greenish black or brown
plops, like cow pies, in summer; dried pellets can be
burned as spruce-scented
incense and have been var-
nished and sold as
Christmas tree decorations,
earrings, key chains and, in
Sweden, used to make
fancy grey paper

during the rut. Males also kick up the ground, pee and then wallow in the depressions to perfume themselves, especially their antlers and beardlike bell. A courtship may last a week. With all the searching and challenging and waiting, bulls can drop up to 20 per cent of their weight during the mating season.

Rutting moose seem to have trouble distinguishing their competitors from other things that are large and loud. In addition to chasing humans up trees, bulls have been known to demolish trucks in head-on collisions and even to challenge trains. On the other hand, males have also mistaken cattle for potential mates. In one celebrated Vermont love affair, a moose in 1986 wooed and occasionally nuzzled a brown and white Hereford named Jessica for 76 days. As with all moose, both his antlers and his interest finally dropped off in late December and he slunk back into the woods.

Baby moose are similarly apt to follow humans or other species, mistaking them for their mothers. Mothers can be as dangerous as rutting males when guarding against such possibilities and generally seclude their offspring for as long as possible.

Females repair to islands, swamps or waterside alder thickets safe from wolves, in May or early June, to give birth. Newborn calves are about a metre (one yard) long. Moose milk – not to be confused with the Yukon rum-and-canned-milk drink of the same name – allows moose babies to grow faster than any other mammal in North America, gaining a kilogram (2.2 pounds) a day in their first month and up to three kilograms (6.6 pounds) daily afterwards.

Yearlings may weigh more than 200 kilograms (440 pounds), over 15 times their birth weight, before their mothers shoo them off to make way for new babies.

During the summer, calves sometimes rest their heads or front legs over their mother's neck when they get tired of swimming. Moose spend much of the season immersed in calm bodies of water feasting on water lilies and other sodium-rich aquatic plants. In late summer they move to dense forests to browse the understory, and continue eating leaves in autumn even after they fall to the ground. After the snow comes, they switch to twigs, and occasionally bark when the sap starts to run. The name *moose* is derived from the Algonkian word *moosee,* meaning "bark or twig eater."

With their long legs, moose are much better suited to deep snow than are white-tailed deer. Where winter conditions are mild enough to allow high densities of deer, moose often become scarce because of a parasitic nematode commonly called brainworm. The parasite evolved over millions of years to live off white-tailed deer without harming them. Moose, however, are recent immigrants from Eurasia, arriving within the past 11,000 years. In them, the brainworm causes disorientation, blindness and eventually death. Snails feeding on deer droppings spread the parasite when moose suck them up while browsing. However, maturing forests and severe winters from the late 1950s to early 1970s caused a crash in Algonquin Park's deer population, leading to a tenfold increase in moose.

Daily scat productivity: Roughly about 13 piles of more than 100 pellets

Domestication: Some Eurasian moose, which are the same species as in North America, were once tamed and ridden like horses by Siberians and the Swedish cavalry

Rambling youth: After shooed away by their mothers, some adolescent moose wander far; a yearling named Alice, tagged in the Adirondacks in 1998, turned up in Algonquin Park, 320 km (200 mi) away, 3 years later

Estimated Ontario moose population: About 110,000 in midwinter

Average population increase in spring: 20–25%

Estimated moose-carrying capacity of Ontario range: 150,000–200,000

Number of moose shot by hunters each fall in Ontario: 9,500

Number of moose hit annually on the Trans-Canada Highway: Hundreds

Range: Most of province, from the tree line to southern edge of Canadian Shield; also in all other provinces and territories

Self-proclaimed moose capital of Canada: Hearst, Ontario

Famous moose: Bullwinkle

Also see: Gray Jay, Deer Flies and Horse Flies, Porcupine, White-tailed Deer, Wolf, Water Lily, Hemlock

MUSKRAT
Giant Mouse That Saved the World

Dive duration: Up to 15 minutes
Body length: 23–36 cm (9–14 in)
Tail: 18–27 cm (7–11 in) long, dark, scaly, vertically flattened like an eel
Weight: 0.7–1.8 kg (1.5–4 lb)
Markings: Dark to reddish brown back and sides, greyish undersides
Alias: Marsh rat, marsh hare, rat, *le rat musqué, Ondatra zibethica*
Calls: Squeaks, squeals, hisses
Whereabouts: Marshes, swamps, lakes, ponds and streams with emergent aquatic vegetation
Female's territory: 20–40 m (65.5–131 ft) wide in dense

Muskrat is the hero of many Native creation stories. In an Ojibway version, after menacing water spirits flooded the world, the magical protagonist Nanabush sent diving animals to the bottom to fetch mud. Loon, Beaver and Otter all tried and failed before Muskrat finally emerged with wet muck in his paws. Nanabush used the material to create the new world. The Iroquois said the muskrat spread mud over the back of a turtle to form the Earth.

The muskrat was a natural for its role in the creation stories, since it spends most of its time in the water. If it needs to stay underwater a long time, it can, like beavers, drop its heart rate by half and reduce body temperature to burn less oxygen. The rodent's stiff eel-like tail is both a rudder and, underwater, a propeller. Dense fur traps air during dives, providing buoyancy and insulation. Even in winter, muskrats remain active, foraging for water-plant roots beneath the ice. They expand their area of operations from their lodges by gnawing holes in the ice and pushing up mounds of mud and vegetation to keep the spots ice-free. These "push-ups" become sheltered stopoffs where the water rats can catch their breath, eat and rest.

The name *muskrat* is actually derived from the Algonkian word *musquosh,* though the English approximation fits well. A muskrat is essentially a giant mouse that produces musk, emitted by males in hope of attracting partners for fleeting muskrat love. Musk is used as a base for perfumes, keeping them from evaporating quickly on skin, but muskrat musk is rarely used for this purpose.

In more southern realms, muskrats are renowned for multiplying rapidly, producing several litters a year, until viral epidemics cause the local populations to crash. However, vast expanses of cattails – the nocturnal rodents' favourite food and habitat – are uncommon on the Canadian Shield, and the growing season is shorter, keeping most muskrats to one litter a year. They mate in the water around late April and the young are born a month later. Fathers provide little help in their upbringing, while mothers can be extremely territorial.

Late summer or fall is the busy season for muskrat home-building and reno. They erect lodges by piling mud, plant stalks and sticks in shallow water and then hollowing out the insides. Some are built as duplexes on the sides of beaver lodges. Many Shield muskrats, though, dig burrows in stream banks and lakesides. Up to a dozen animals may huddle together for warmth in their grass-lined chambers during the winter.

populations, up to hundreds of metres wide elsewhere

Home: Domed pile of cattails, reeds, grass, sticks and mud, up to 3 m (10 ft) wide and rising up to 1 m (3.3 ft) above the surface in water 40–100 cm (16–40 in) deep; or a bank burrow with underwater entrance

Food: Cattails, pondweed, horsetail, sedges and other aquatic plants, grasses; some mussels, snails, crayfish, fish, frogs and carrion if vegetation scarce

Gestation period: 28–29 days

Average litter: 4–7, born in spring

Weaning age: About 4 weeks

Age at first breeding: 1 year

First year survival: Commonly around 13%

Lifespan: Very seldom more than 2 years; up to 4 years in wild, 10 years in captivity

Predators: Mink, red foxes, coyotes, red-tailed hawks, great horned owls, occasionally raccoons, bobcats and harriers; young sometimes eaten by snapping turtles and pike

Range: All Ontario; also in all other provinces and territories

Also see: Mink, Painted Turtle, Cattail, Wetlands

OTTER
Playful Master Fish Catcher

Dive duration: Up to 4 minutes

Deepest dives: 17 m (55 ft)

Swimming speed: Usually 5–10 km/h (3–6 mph)

Running and sliding speed over snow: Up to 30 km/h (18 mph)

Daily activity spent in play: About 6%

Body length: 53–82 cm (21–32 in)

Tail length: 27–51 cm (11–20 in)

Weight: 5–15 kg (11–33 lb)

Markings: Dark brown to light chestnut back, lighter brown with some grey on sides; appear black when wet; young born black

Alias: River otter, northern river otter, land otter,

Quiet wilderness lakes and rivers are animated by the arrival in August of otter families from backwater natal retreats up small streams and remote beaver ponds. Moving through the water in an undulating train of sleek dipping and rising bodies, appearing like one long, snaking lake monster, they often venture within clear reconnoitring distance of passing canoes. Looking beaverlike when just breaking the surface, their heads rise on long, weaselly necks as they stop, snort and turn to get a good look at their paddle-flapping companions on the water.

Otters are creatures of boundless enthusiasm and famed curiosity. They're said by some to be one of the few animals besides humans known to engage in play even as adults. Dispassionate biologists caution that many otter antics, such as playing tag and diving for pebbles, serve as practice for hunting, and that instances of groups repeatedly using mud or snow slides are fairly rare in the wild. Still, the aquatic animal's intelligence, hyperactivity and keen interest in all things are universally acknowledged. The otter is sacred to many Native groups throughout North America. It was one of the Ojibway Midewiwin Society's most important spirit guides and protectors. Otter pelts, the most durable of all furs, were used for medicine bags, quivers, bow casings, hats and robes.

For their part, otters have every reason to be upbeat creatures. They're largely impervious to the weather, have few if any predators and enjoy a food supply so plentiful and easily caught that they have lots of time to lounge and amuse themselves. Insulated by a layer of fat and by air bubbles trapped within their fur, otters glide stealthily underwater, taking fish unawares with lightning strikes. Though streamlined like seals, they're actually one of the largest members of the weasel family. Special flaps close tight within their ears and nostrils while submerged. Long, prominent, highly sensitive whiskers help otters probe darkened waters at night and beneath the ice of winter, picking up waves fanned by their prey. Their eyes, too, are so specialized for scanning the submerged nocturnal world that in the surface realm otters seem actually near-sighted.

Even in winter, otters have little trouble going about their business. They use the snow to their advantage, alternately running and sliding while journeying overland several kilometres from one body of water to another. To get into the water, they break through the ice at weak points around rocks, logs and stumps, keeping

common otter, Canadian otter, *la loutre de rivière*, *Lontra canadensis*
Calls: Coughing snorts, sniffs, grunts, chirps, growls, hisses, humming and high whistles
Whereabouts: Quiet wilderness lakes, rivers, creeks and beaver ponds, interspersed with marshes and swamps, and in water with lots of submerged fallen trees and logjams
Home range: 30–250 km (19–155 mi) of shoreline; 2–3 times bigger in winter than in summer
Home: Old bank burrows or lodges of muskrats and beavers, uprooted trees, eroded root tangles, hollow logs and stumps, rock crevices, dense thickets of willow and alder, old groundhog burrows; lined with grass, leaves and sticks
Food: Mostly slower-moving fish 7–13 cm (3–5 in) long, including minnows, sunfish, catfish, suckers, perch and sculpins; less often bass or trout; also crayfish, frogs, salamanders, mussels, water beetles, stonefly nymphs, worms and snails, occasionally ducklings, muskrats, mice, water snakes, ground-nesting birds and their eggs; some grass, blueberries, algae and aquatic vegetation
Average daily food helping: 1.3 kg (3 lb)
Gestation: 11–13 months depending on delayed implantation

Average litter: 2–3
Weaning age: 4–5 months
Dispersal: Mothers leave
young when they are 8–11
months old; siblings together
till 12–13 months old
Age at first breeding:
Females 2–3 years; males
2–7 years
Annual survival in trapped
populations: 50–60% in
first year; 55–70% for
adults
Lifespan: Up to 15 years in
wild, 25 years in captivity
Predators: May be taken on
land by wolves, coyotes, lynx
Peak activity periods:
Predawn to midmorning, late
afternoon to midnight
Scat: Called spraints; small,
slimy lumps, most often
black, quickly washing away
in rain to leave behind scattered fish scales, reddish
bits of crayfish shells and
small bones
Best senses: Touch, smell
Range: Northern Ontario to
the north shore of Lake
Ontario; also in all other
provinces and territories
Number of "Otter Lakes" in
Ontario: 46 officially
named, 34 unofficially
named
Number of otter species
worldwide: 13
Also see: Beaver, Mink

several openings clear in a given area. Otters can also catch a breath at air pockets left beneath the ice by changing water levels. They also frequently slip through open spots at the spillways of beaver dams, sometimes tearing holes into the dams themselves. With beavers creating ideal habitat for otters, peaceful coexistence between the two species is generally the rule.

In late April and May, male otters often join females who have given birth a month or so before at dens on or near beaver ponds or quiet streams. Taking time out from maternal duties, mothers join their visitors to mate in the water for 15 to 25 minutes at a time. After repeated performances, males usually depart, looking for more mating opportunities.

The pups first leave the den and are taught to swim, when about two months old. Several weeks later, when the young are adept, families troop out to larger bodies of water where food is more plentiful. Small groups of adult males also form and move into larger lakes around the same time. There, otters may wander along many kilometres of shoreline, and become a common sight of late summer.

PORCUPINE
Cute, but Not Quite Cuddly

Sometime within the past 15 million years, porcupines calmly waddled their way from South to North America after the two continents collided at the isthmus of Panama. Armed with a dense coat of formidable quills, they met with little resistance. Though porcupines will attempt to escape up a tree when threatened, they resort to their prickly defence if their slow-moving legs don't carry them away in time. The quills are modified hairs with hundreds of tiny, overlapping barbs. Porcupines don't actually shoot their quills but cause them to stand on end, like bristling fur, when they are in danger. A swat from their tails can release hundreds on contact. Once embedded, the hollow quills swell, burn and work their way into the flesh every time a victim's muscles contract, digging a millimetre (.04 inches) deeper each hour. Eventually they

Number of quills: About 30,000

Quill length: Up to 13 cm (4 in)

Body length: 50–85 cm (1.6–2.8 ft)

Tail length: 15–20 cm (6–8 in)

Weight: Avg. 3–9 kg (6.6–20 lb); large males up to 18 kg (40 lb)

Height at shoulder: Avg. 30 cm (12 in); large males up to 46 cm (18 in)

Markings: Black- or brown-tipped yellowish or grey-white quills, mixed with dark, dense underfur; black face

Alias: American porcupine, Canada porcupine, porky, quill pig, hedgehog (really another species), *le porc-épic, Erithizon dorsatum*

Name origin: Latin *porcus*, meaning "pig," and *spina*, "thorns"

Calls: Mumbling, grunts, hisses, whines, wails, teeth chattering

Whereabouts: Evergreen and mixed forests; hemlock stands with rock ledges favoured in winter

Average territory: Females 12–80 ha (30–200 acres), males 30–150 ha (75–315 acres); average 7 ha (17.5 acres) in winter

Homes: Deep crevices beneath rock ledges and outcrops, caves, tree cavities, hollow logs, brush piles, ground burrows; smell of porcupine pee, sometimes with large piles of scat at entrance; used mainly in the winter

Food: Buds and catkins, especially sugar maple, basswood, willow, alder and aspen in spring; leaves of aspen, basswood, beech, ash and yellow birch, water lilies, raspberries, grass and other plants in summer; acorns, beechnuts, mushrooms and leaves in fall; buds, twigs, inner bark and needles of hemlock, pine, fir, spruce and tamarack in winter, along with some aspen, birch, beech and sugar maple bark

Gestation period: 7 months

Average litter: 1

Birth weight: About 490 g (1.1 lb)

Weaning age: 7–10 days

emerge through the skin again, though sometimes they spear right through the body. An animal with a mouthful of needles may starve.

A predator needs to learn only once to leave a porcupine alone. Lynx, when extremely hungry and unable to catch anything else, may give it a try anyway. The fisher, however, is a skilled porcupine killer. It uses its speed and agility to snake around a porcupine's rearguard defence and viciously bite its face until it dies.

A porcupine's quills were also of little help against Native hunters. Because they are slow and about the only animal that can be killed simply with a large rock, porcupines were a godsend in times of scarce game. They were accordingly honoured, and like the beaver's, their bones were kept away from dogs out of respect. Native people also wove elaborate dyed quillwork decorations into clothing, moccasins, belts, mats, necklaces, bracelets and bags. Because the work was so time-consuming and highly valued, quill embroideries were used as a medium of exchange before the coming of Europeans.

Of course, pincushion bodies seem a little impractical when it comes to sex. Porkies have it all figured out, however, when males go courting females on their territories in autumn. Couples dance in circles when they meet, admiring each other's cute brushcuts, rubbing noses and eliciting loud, high wails and low murmurings of lust. At the moment of truth, the female flips her tail up over her back so that the male can rest with his similarly unarmed belly on its quill-less underside. Later they return to their solitary lives, remaining active through the winter, eating buds and starch-rich inner tree bark, only the coldest nights keeping them den-bound.

Baby porcupines are born in May or early June, about 25 centimetres (10 inches) long, with open eyes and soft quills that harden as they dry. They can climb trees when only a day old. Their ready defence makes juvenile mortality extremely low among porcupines, allowing the species to get by comfortably with just one baby a year. Four-month-old females leave home to establish their own territories. Males stay closer to Mom. Being slow, with a low-energy diet but with plenty to eat, porcupines usually don't travel too far. They spend most of their time in trees, as high as 20 metres (65 feet) up, sleeping during the day and eating at night. Because they often feast on and sometimes kill the most common tree species in an area, they are an important agent of forest diversity.

Though porcupines are consummate vegetarians, mineral imperatives in their diet also govern their behaviour. All animals must balance potassium inside their cells with sodium outside to conduct the electrical charges that make muscles move. Most plant tissues have much more potassium than sodium, except water lilies and some other aquatic plants, which porcupines swim out to, buoyed in the water by their hollow quills. They also get salt from mineral licks, such as high-sodium pockets of clay, or by gnawing discarded antlers or bones. The salt of human sweat is another big attraction, the reason porcupines chew unattended canoe paddles, axe handles and outhouses in the night. Road salt is largely responsible for the strong showing of porcupines in roadkill stats. Porkies even gnaw aluminum, probably to help wear down their teeth.

Age at first breeding: Females 18 months, males 2 years

Lifespan: Often 7–8 years; up to 15 years in wild, 18 years in captivity

Predators: Fishers, great horned owls, rarely bobcats, lynx, foxes, bears, wolves

Best senses: Smell, touch

Tracks: Tail often leaves a trough up to 23 cm (9 in) wide in snow, often obscuring pigeon-toed, oval footprints 6–10 cm (2.3–4 in) long, with long claws

Dining signs: "Nip twigs" cut at 45° angle, with buds, nuts or needles removed, littered beneath feeding trees; bark gnawed in distinct patches on conifer trunks and in crosshatch patterns on deciduous trees

Scat: Brown, fibrous, jelly-bean-sized, capsule-shaped pellets

Daily pellet production: 75–200

Density in prime habitat: Up to 30 per km² (0.4 sq. mi) in areas where fishers are scarce; as low as less than 1 per km² areas with fishers

Range: All Ontario to about Brantford and Kincardine; also in all other provinces and territories except Nunavut, Prince Edward Island and island of Newfoundland

Also see: Fisher, White-tailed Deer, Water Lily, Basswood, Hemlock, Trembling Aspen

RACCOON

Thriving in City and Wilderness

Body length: 40–75 cm (1.3–2.5 ft)

Tail length: 20–33 cm (8–13 in)

Shoulder height: 23–26 cm (9–10 in)

Weight: Females avg. 5–8 kg (11–17.6 lb), males 8–10 kg (17.6–22 lb)

Markings: Two-tone brown and tan fur, with black mask over eyes, black and tan striped tail

Calls: Chattering trills; low growls, snarls, hisses, whines; a hoarse, staccato whimpering when afraid; cubs purr when content

Whereabouts: Near lakes, streams and swamps in mixed and deciduous forests

Home range: Avg. 40–100 ha (100–247 acres)

An omnivore par excellence, the raccoon is so adaptable that it is more likely to be spotted at night in the city than in the wild. Metro Toronto's raccoon population is estimated at 6,000 to 16,000, with Rosedale boasting some of the biggest, best-fed bandits found anywhere. Even in the wild they often show up brazenly at campsites in the night, drawn by the irresistible aroma of food scraps and garbage.

Raccoons are extremely bright. They reportedly beat dogs, cats and foxes in animal IQ tests. And, like humans, raccoons have a very sensitive sense of touch. Their front paws, in fact, have many thousands more nerve endings than do human hands. With dexterous fingers, raccoons reach under crevices in shallow water, feeling their way to crayfish and frogs without actually seeing them or even seeming to pay attention.

Cubs can climb even before they can see or hear. Driven by a keen curiosity, raccoons explore the nocturnal world with their paws, constantly picking up objects and thoroughly feeling their food before eating. Biologists believe their sense of touch is actually enhanced by water. Raccoons are not really washing food when they wet it in a stream. Their scientific name, *lotor,* is Latin for "washer." The word *raccoon* itself is derived from the animal's Algonkian-language name, *arough-con,* meaning "hand scratcher."

Like bears, raccoons are religiously omnivorous and grow most corpulent in fall, gorging on acorns and other bounties of the season to build up enough heft to nourish them in their winter dens. A thick layer of fat may account for half their weight by the time the snow flies. They are not adapted, however, to survive long without eating, and hard winters cause many to starve. On mild days, they come out to search for torpid frogs and crayfish beneath cracks in the ice. In February and early March, weather permitting, black-masked male Casanovas are also on the make. They shack up for a week or more with a willing female before moving on to the next address in their little black books. Females, however, indulge in just one fling per year.

Most raccoon cubs are born around early May, but don't emerge from the den until they're six or seven weeks old. In the summer, they follow their mother on her nighttime rounds. Though not fully grown, some move out into their own digs in autumn. Others stick with Mom through their first winter and until she's ready to give birth again in spring.

Home: In cavities 6–12 m (20–40 ft) high in trees, often facing south, or old burrows, large abandoned nests and beneath large rocks

Food: Crayfish, frogs, clams, turtle and bird eggs, fish, birds, small rodents, snakes, snails, insect larvae, berries, nuts, seeds, carrion

Gestation period: 63 days

Average litter: 4

Weaning age: 2–3 months

Age at first breeding: 40–60% of females mate at 10 months, most others and males at 22 months

Lifespan: Adults avg. 3–5 years; up to 10 years in wild, 16 years in captivity

Predators: Wolves, fishers, lynx, bobcats, coyotes, great horned owls and eagles sometimes prey on cubs

Top running speed: 25 km/h (15 mph)

Swimming speed: 5 km/h (3 mph)

Tracks: Handlike, 5–9.5 cm (2–3.7 in) long

Scat: Small piles or single, shotgun shell-sized droppings, brown, grey, black or yellow

Estimated Ontario raccoon population: About 1 million

Number of raccoons per km² (0.4 sq. mi) in Toronto: 12–15, up to 100

Range: Southern Ontario to about Lake Abitibi and far north of Lake Nipigon and Kenora

Number of raccoon family species worldwide: 18, all in New World

Also see: Crayfish, Black Bear, Porcupine

RED FOX
Crafty Catlike Canine

Maximum jumping distance: 4.6 m (15 ft)

Body length: 60–70 cm (2–2.3 ft)

Tail length: 30–46 cm (1–1.5 ft)

Weight: 3–7 kg (6.6–15.4 lb)

Markings: Orange or yellow-red back and sides, white chin, chest and tail tip, black legs; all-black "silver foxes" or greyish brown "cross foxes" are less common colour forms of same species

Alias: *Le renard roux, Vulpes vulpes*

Name for a group: A skulk or den of foxes

Calls: A shrill, barking yelp, high-pitched howls, whines

Food: Voles, mice, hares, rabbits, groundhogs, chipmunks,

From Aesop's fables to Native North American legends, from Chaucer and Dante to Kafka, the fox is cited for its beguiling cunning and intelligence. Not all the press is good – Machiavelli said rulers must have the deceit of a fox. At the heart of such tales is an animal that employs a broader range of strategies to fill its plate with a much greater variety of pickings than does its canine cousin, the wolf.

Foxes have a vegetarian bent and will go to great lengths to get what they want. But their staple is meadow voles, which they capture by first listening with sensitive ears for scurrying in the long grass, or beneath as much as 12 centimetres (4.8 inches) of snow. Then they make a precision pounce, like a cat, upon their unseen prey. The master mousers can hear a squeak up to 45 metres (150 feet) away. Similar feline-style stealth − including the silent footing of semi-retractable claws − is used to get as close as possible to larger prey before making a fast, deadly dash. Foxes, in fact, are the only canids whose pupils turn into catlike vertical slits during the day, protecting their light-sensitive eyes. A special reflective layer behind the retina doubles the light available to photoreceptors, causing a greenish eye-shine in the dark.

The search for a mate in late January and early February also often brings foxes into the light of day. The larger male may follow a vixen around for a couple of weeks before she finally lets him nuzzle up to her. If there are competing suitors, they may go nose to nose in screaming matches until one backs down. Their celebrated bushy tails are also brandished with effect, with the owner of the biggest plume often intimidating his rivals. Fights are rare, though contestants may jump up and push each other with their forepaws.

The winner of a vixen's heart helps her raise the young, whose arrival in late March or April coincides with shrinking blankets of snow, creating excellent vole-hunting conditions in the long, matted grass beneath. Cubs remain in the den for about a month, nourished by a puppy chow of regurgitated meat. In the fall, the family breaks up, with the young males travelling an average of 30 kilometres (19 miles) away from their mother's home range. Vixens stay closer to home. Foxes often survive the winter by feeding on the remains of animals killed by wolf packs. At night, they wrap their bushy tails over their noses and feet to keep from freezing as they sleep.

squirrels, grouse, ducks, gulls, small birds, eggs, snakes, grasshoppers, beetles, crickets, berries, nuts, grass, carrion

Average daily food helping: About 5–40 mice or voles

Whereabouts: Forest edges, shorelines, meadows, open woods

Home range: 5–20 km² (2–8 sq. mi)

Home: Dens in ground burrows up to 25 m (62 ft) long, often in dry, sandy, south-facing hillsides; also under dense tree roots or in old groundhog burrows; with several entrances 25 cm (10 in) wide; often stocked with food stores

Average litter: 4–7

Gestation period: 51–53 days

Weaning age: About 2 months

Age at first breeding: 10 months

Lifespan: Rarely more than 4 years, up to 12 years in wild, 19 years in captivity

Predators: Wolves, coyotes, bobcats, lynx, bears; cubs killed by fishers and great horned owls

Top running speed: About 45 km/h (29 mph)

Swimming speed: 4–5 km/h (2.4–3 mph)

Best senses: Hearing, smell

Tracks: Front foot 4.5 cm (1.8 in) wide and 5–6 cm (2–2.4 in) long, with 4 toes

Scat: Like small dog droppings, about 5–8 cm (2–3 in)

long, with bits of hair and
bone chips

Famous individuals:
  Reynard, Brer Fox, Seminole
  Sam, Russel, Mr. Todd

**Average number of foxes
  per km² (0.4 sq. mi) in
  southern Ontario:** 1

**Average number of foxes
  per km² (0.4 sq. mi) in the
  boreal forest:** 0.1

Range: All of Ontario and
  throughout Canada north to
  Baffin Island

**Number of Ontario pelts
  sold a year:** About 6,000

**Number of Ontario fox
  species:** 3

**Number of fox species
  worldwide:** 13

Also see: Deer Mouse,
  Groundhog, Wolf

Powers of adaptability have made the red fox the most widespread carnivore on Earth, with the same species bounding across North America, Eurasia, and North Africa and introduced into Australia. Because they thrive around forest edges, foxes became more common with the opening of the countryside by European settlement. The British, in the interest of their much-loved equestrian hunts, bolstered numbers with red foxes from Europe, essentially the same species as in North America. In the 20th century, coyotes from the prairies spread over the same rural countryside. Occupying roughly the same niche as foxes, a coyote usually drives off the smaller canines from its territory.

Still, overcrowding in many areas spurs diseases such as distemper and encephalitis, which send fox populations falling in roughly eight- to 10-year cycles. Foxes are also very susceptible to rabies, once averaging 1,500 reported cases in Ontario a year, about 40% of the provincial total. The rabies virus, which attacks nerve cells, first spread to Ontario from the Arctic in 1954, and the province soon had the highest incidence in North America. Since 1989, however, the provincial government has reduced the number of rabid foxes found annually to single digits by air-dropping bait laced with vaccine over vast areas.

RED SQUIRREL
Loud, Hot-blooded Cone Hoarder

The red squirrel lives in the fast lane. It's a high-strung, cantankerous bundle of energy, racing at hyperspeed along branches and around tree trunks during the day. Its specialized vision allows it to make instant trigonometric computations using vertical objects, mainly trees, to judge leaping distances between limbs. Sensing hairs guide the squirrel to twist and contort its body around obstacles as it navigates through the forest canopy. Potential competitors, such as gray jays, flying squirrels and even the larger grey squirrel, are chased off or soundly thrashed. Roosting owls are harangued until they fly off to find peace. Even trespassing humans may be berated with loud, angry chirping, the protester stamping its feet and jerking its tail violently with each syllable.

Behind all the ill temper is the red squirrel's driving need to guard jealously from pilferers any

Maximum jumping distance: 2.4 m (8 ft)

Top running speed: 25 km/h (15 mph)

Body length: 18–23 cm (7–9 in)

Tail length: 10–15 cm (4–6 in)

Weight: 140–300 g (5–11 oz)

Markings: Reddish brown back and tail, brighter in winter; white underside and eye ring; flattened, bushy tail

Alias: American red squirrel, pine squirrel, chickaree, red robber, boomer, bummer, chatterbox, rusty squirrel, barking squirrel, *l'écureuil roux, Tamiasciurus hudsonicus*

Name origin: From the Greek *skiouros,* meaning "shadow

tail"; the Ojibway name, *adji-daumo,* means "tail in the air"

Calls: Loud, ratcheting cherr, sharp squeak, bark, squeal

Whereabouts: Coniferous and mixed forests, bogs, cedar swamps

Territory: 0.2–2 ha (0.5–5 acres)

Home: Nest, or "dray," made in tree cavities, often old pileated-woodpecker holes, twig, leaf and bark bundles in branches, or ground burrows, lined with shredded vegetation

Food: Mostly pine, hemlock, spruce and fir cones; also beechnuts, cherry pits, hazelnuts, acorns, maple keys, berries, mushrooms, cedar, birch and aspen buds, bark, roots, maple sap, insects; occasionally carrion, baby hares, bird eggs or nestlings

Total winter food stores: Up to 350 L (10 bushels)

Average litter: 3–6

Gestation period: 31–35 days

Birth weight: About 7 g (0.25 oz)

Age at first breeding: 10–12 months

Annual survival: 20–40% in first year, 80% in second year

Lifespan: Few more than 3 years; up to 8 years in wild, more than 12 years in captivity

Predators: Hawks, owls, fishers, martens, mink, weasels, foxes, coyotes, bobcats, lynx

of a number of well-stocked food stores in its territory. A single cache may contain more than 50 litres (1.4 bushels) of cones and nuts. Altogether, thousands of cones may be stashed in tree cavities, hollow stumps, under logs or hidden at the base of trees, where they stay moist, keeping them from opening and losing their seeds.

In late summer and fall, red squirrels tirelessly cut green cones from branches with their razor-sharp teeth and drop them to the ground for later collection. They also spread and dry mushrooms on sun-soaked branches before storing them. These nonperishable supplies allow them to stay active throughout all but the coldest days of winter. A red may polish off more than 100 spruce cones a day, each with an average of 80 seeds. Middens of discarded cone scales beneath a prime feeding spot used by generations of squirrels sometimes rise more than a metre (3.3 feet) high.

In an average year, red squirrels often collect up to two-thirds of the available cones of some conifer species. Though each type of evergreen tree produces a cone bumper crop every two to seven years, a good stockpile can get a rusty rodent through a succeeding year of food scarcity. Two bad years in a row, however, can lower the red squirrel population by as much as 80 per cent from peak levels.

The strong resins and tannins of raw nuts and seeds, even the poisons of many mushrooms, have no ill effects on squirrels. According to folk belief, squirrel meat may have psychedelic fallout. Woodlore traces the expression "squirrelly" to trappers and others who went a little funny eating too many squirrels, suggesting active ingredients remain potent within their flesh.

Sometimes it seems as if the squirrels are a little crazy themselves, chasing each other round and round tree trunks in a dizzying whirl. While usually this is a part of their territorial squabbling, in late winter, and sometimes again in early summer, the chase involves males trying to outlast each other in pursuit of a receptive "cow" female. Each female is usually in heat for only one day in a season and ends the bond with her mate shortly after consummating it.

Around the time their own little ones are born, usually in late April or May, red squirrels commonly lapse from strict vegetarianism to sample the season's assortment of birds' eggs, nestlings and, especially, baby snowshoe hares up to two weeks old. The extra protein probably provides a valuable boost for mothers, who nurse their litters for five to seven weeks. Young reds set off on their own later in the summer.

Without the security of home and family, many juveniles don't make it far in a world of hungry squirrel eaters. Those that manage to survive establish their own territories, where they learn every branch, perch and hideout along their regular foraging routes and become very difficult for any predator to catch.

In hardwood forests, **grey squirrels** are a little less tense, possibly because they don't carry all their nuts in a few baskets, like the hot-blooded reds do. Instead, greys bury their food a nut or two at a time, relying on a wide dispersal to stay fed. In central Ontario, most grey squirrels are actually black – a colour that absorbs more heat in winter – and don't range much farther north than Parry Sound and Algonquin Park.

Tracks: Back feet, 2–3 cm (3–4 in) long, spaced 8–10 cm (3–4 in) apart; land in front of smaller hind feet
Density in prime habitat: 30–400 per km^2 (0.4 sq. mi)
Best senses: Sight and smell
Range: All Ontario; also in all other provinces and territories except Nunavut
Famous squirrels: Rocky, Nutkin, Goody & Timmy Tiptoes, Slappy, Skippy, Twiggy the water-skiing squirrel
Number of Ontario squirrel species: 5
Also see: Blue Jay, Chipmunk, Pileated Woodpecker, Flying Squirrel, Mink, Snowshoe Hare, Red Pine

SKUNK
The Sweet-faced Stinker

Maximum spraying range:
6 m (20 ft)
Amount of spray in each fully loaded scent gland:
About 15 ml (0.5 fl oz)
Body length: 35–51 cm (1.1–1.7 ft)
Tail length: 17–30 cm (7–12 in)
Weight: 1.8–4.5 kg (4–10 lb); may lose up to half their weight during winter
Markings: Black body with two wide white bands running down the back, joining at the bushy tail and top of the head; also thin white vertical line between the eyes
Alias: Striped skunk, Canada skunk, wood pussy, big skunk, line-backed skunk, polecat (really a European

When the French first caught wind of the skunk in Canada, they dubbed it *l'enfant du diable,* "child of the devil." At first, the folks back in the old country couldn't believe the fantastical stories of the sweet-faced forest pussycat striking terror in the hearts of man and moose. The English adopted the Algonkian name *seganku,* simplified to *skunk,* and quickly learned to steer clear of the animal. Early twentieth-century naturalist Ernest Thompson Seton described the skunk's smell as "a mixture of strong ammonia, essence of garlic, burning of sulphur, a volume of sewer gas, a vitriol of spray, a dash of perfume musk," all mixed together and intensified a thousand times.

A skunk has a double-barrelled spray that squirts from two little nozzlelike projections on its anus. To fire, the skunk tightens its sphincter, popping the nozzles out, and lets fly an oily, yellow-green fluid. About 30 centimetres (one foot) out, the two streams merge and turn into a fine misty spray. A skunk can shoot three to four metres (10 to 13.3 feet) with accuracy. The stream is usually directed at an enemy's eyes, where it causes blinding pain for 15 to 20 minutes unless washed out. The active ingredient, butyl mercaptan contains sulfuric acid, bearing a stench that can wreak, or reek, havoc on noses over more than six square kilometres (two square miles). A skunk, however, stores only enough musk for four or five sprayings and takes several weeks to fully replenish an empty tank. The spray is used only as a defence of last resort. If threatened, a skunk first lifts its tail, stamps its feet, arches its back and growls. Finally, it forms a horseshoe, face and bum towards the assailant, flips up the tip of its tail and squirts.

All members of the Mustelidae, or weasel, family have musk glands, used for marking territory and attracting mates. Skunk musk is so odious that it evolved as a perfect defence mechanism, allowing skunks to forgo the sleek, swift body of their weasel brethren (though some zoologists contend skunks should be placed in a separate family). Instead, with their malodorous reputation preceding them, they waddle casually about, seldom running from anything. The white stripes are a warning so that none can mistake them in their nocturnal wanderings. In more recent times, the skunk's fearlessness — and its penchant for road-killed carrion — has made it one of the most common victims of the automobile.

Skunks are more generalists than other weasels, adapting to a wide range of habitats and

animal), *la mouffette rayée, Mephitis mephitis*

Calls: Grows, screeches, hisses, but usually silent

Whereabouts: Forest edges, shorelines, thick brush, open areas

Home range: 1–3 km² (0.4–1.2 sq. mi)

Homes: May have 2–20 dens in hollow logs, under rock piles, ground burrows about 60 cm (2 ft) deep; sometimes old groundhog or fox holes; lined and plugged with leaves and grass

Food: In summer, mostly grasshoppers, crickets, beetle grubs, bees, wasps, caterpillars and other insect larvae; also spiders, worms, snails, bird and turtle eggs, nestlings; in colder months more mice, rats, chipmunks, squirrels, frogs, salamanders, snakes, berries, nuts, roots, fungi, carrion

Portion of diet made up of species considered pests to humans: 70%

Gestation period: 62–64 days

Average litter: 5–7

Weaning age: 6–8 weeks

Age at first breeding: Females as young as 9 months, males about 1 year

First-year survival rate: 30–50%

Lifespan: Few live longer than 3 years in wild; up to 13 years in captivity

Predators: Great horned owls, rarely foxes, coyotes, wolves, bobcats

Running speed:
 10–16 km/h (6–10 mph)
Limit of vision: 6–7 m (20–
 23 ft)
**Number of rabid skunks
 found annually in Ontario
 in recent years:** 7–30 (17–
 32% of total wildlife cases)
Density per km² (0.4 mi):
 0.5–26 in wild, up to 36 in
 urban areas
Range: All Ontario except for
 northwest; also in all other
 provinces and territories except Nunavut, Yukon,
 Newfoundland and Labrador
Famous skunks: Pépé Le
 Pew, Flower, Miss Ma'm'selle
 Hepzibah, Jimmy Skunk
Famous skunk hot spots:
 Chicago, meaning "Place of
 the Skunk"; Skunk's Misery,
 in southwestern Ontario
Skunk spray remedies:
 Mixture of 1 L (1 qt) of 3%
 hydrogen peroxide, 50 ml
 (0.25 cup) of baking soda,
 5 ml (1 tsp) of dish soap;
 vinegar and detergent;
 tomato juice
**Number of skunk species
 worldwide:** 13
Also see: Mink, Raccoon

food sources, including plants. They're more common in open areas than deep forest and are probably more often seen around human habitations than in the wild. When temperatures drop to freezing, rather than slogging it out with lean winter hunting like other weasels, females and young nestle together for long periods in their dens and live off their fat. Adult males may brave the cold down to −10°C (14°F). But torpid skunks are not true hibernators, and their body temperatures, heart and breathing rates are little altered. On mild days, they often wake and dig for sleeping snails, snakes, jumping mice or chipmunks.

Between late February and mid-March, skunks come out of their winter sleeps to mate. A male may have more than one partner, sometimes overwintering with harems of 10 or more. He doesn't assist any of his mates, however, after the young, called kits or skunklets, are born in May. After about two months they follow their mother, single file, on nightly food-gathering journeys, their own musk glands fully functional. Many wander off on their own in late summer or fall, when they are about half grown. For all their negative reputation, skunks are said to make playful, affectionate pets and great mousers, although keeping them domestically is illegal in Ontario.

SNOWSHOE HARE
Humour, Mystery and Procreation

Silent, inscrutable, yet somehow intrinsically funny, hares have always been subjects of fable and magic. Among the 500-year-old engravings in the marble rock face of Petroglyphs Provincial Park, near Peterborough, appears a hare-headed supernatural teacher common to most northern Algonkian-speaking peoples. The Ojibway called the spirit Nanabush. He is credited with remaking the world after a great flood, stocking it with game animals and giving humans fire, the canoe, hunting weapons and the sacred pipe for communicating with the spirits. In innumerable humorous and moral tales, and in both male and female manifestations, Nanabush, in the role of trickster, shows the pitfalls of improper social behaviour through the trouble he/she makes for him/herself.

American anthropologist Daniel Moerman theorizes that the hare's practice of eating its

Maximum jumping distance: 4 m (13 ft)

Highest jumps: 2 m (6.7 ft)

Top running speed: 50 km/h (30 mph)

Number of hare or rabbit taste buds: 17,000

Number of human taste buds: 9,000

Number of taste buds of average bird: 200

Length: 38–50 cm (15–20 in)

Weight: Avg. 1.2–1.6 kg (2.6–3.5 lb)

Ear length: 6–7 cm (2.4–2.8 in)

Markings: Buff, greyish or dark brown, with white undersides, in summer; white in winter, except for black-tipped ears

Alias: Varying hare, snowshoe rabbit, bush rabbit, *le lièvre d'Amérique, Lepus americanus*

Name of a group: A husk of hares

Calls: Rarely, snorts, grunts, low chips; deep groan when fighting, loud bleat or scream when frightened

Whereabouts: In summer, dense aspen, birch and jack pine sapling stands; alder and willow thickets; in winter, forests of low-limbed spruce and cedar, and frozen swamps and shrubby swales

Home range: 1.5–4 ha (4–10 acres)

Homes: Several lairs in depressions of leaves and litter under bushes, low-hanging evergreen boughs, and logs or in old ground-hog holes

Food: Herbs, grass, leaves, ferns, fungi, almost any green vegetation in summer; conifer needles, twigs, bark, buds, especially birch, aspen and jack pine in winter

Hare browse signature: Twigs cut at clean, 45-degree angle

Gestation period: About 36 days

Average litter: 2–4, with 2 or more litters a year

Birth weight: 70–80 g (2.5–2.9 oz)

Weaning age: 3–4 weeks

Age at first breeding: About 1 year

Annual survival: 3–40% in first year; adults 12–50%

own droppings is at the root of its mystical status. After partial digestion and storage in its long appendix, a hare's food is excreted at night as soft, vitamin-rich, greenish pellets and is eaten again for full digestion. (Waste from food on its second time through is left as the familiar, berrylike rabbit pellets.) Like the carrion eaten by ravens and coyotes – culture heroes in other regions – the hare's food is a transitional substance, somewhere between living matter and dust.

Camouflage, stillness and silence are a hare's first line of defence against predators

The abundance of snowshoe hares was of vital importance for Native people, especially where bigger game was scarce in the winter. Leaving large tracks with their oversized "snowshoe" feet, specially adapted for staying aloft in deep snow, hares were readily trapped along their regularly travelled paths. In peak years there might be more than 2,000 hares per square kilometre (0.4 square miles) in some areas. High densities quickly lead to stress, disease, depletion of food and cover and concentration of predators, bringing populations crashing down. Densities may drop to one or two hares per square kilometre. The disappearance of hares at the bottom end of these nine- to 10-year population cycles caused extreme privation for northern hunters. Fear of cannibalism in times of famine helped give rise to stories of windigos, demons that ate humans who neglected their responsibilities or behaved badly.

With their famed procreative exuberance – undoubtedly at the heart of the Easter Bunny's pre-Christian fertility-symbol origins – hares can spring back from their cyclical lows. One promiscuous buck, may mate with two dozen females. To do so, he may have to out-race and outfight a number of other bucks chasing the does, jumping up and administering boots to the head with his great furry hind feet in bouts of bunny jousting. Before she pairs off, a female may perform a mating dance, thumping her own feet on the ground. From the start of mating in March, does may have two to four litters a year.

Most hares are very short-lived. On top of high baby-bunny mortality, more than half of the adult population dies each year. Fewer than two per cent see their fifth birthday. The hare's high reproductive rate provides a conveyer belt of little bunnies for a cafeteria full of predators. The rarely seen lynx, hunting at night in dense thickets and swamps, depends on snowshoe hares for 70 to 97 per cent of its diet.

Camouflage, stillness and silence are a hare's first line of defence against predators. It stays put beneath ground cover, dropping its heart and breathing rate, and runs only when it's sure it's been spotted. Much of a hare's time is spent sleeping or grooming in one of several ground or litter depressions, called forms, beneath thick bushes, low coniferous branches or piles of snow. It comes out to forage in the evening.

The snowshoe hare was once Ontario's only bunny, but European settlement brought new breeds of long-ears. The **eastern cottontail rabbit** hopped north across the U.S. border in the mid-19th century, occupying forest edges to

Lifespan: Very few live longer than 2 years; up to 6 years in wild, 8 years in captivity

Predators: Lynx, bobcats, weasels, martens, mink, fishers, wolves, coyotes, foxes, hawks, barred and great horned owls; red squirrels often take biggest portion of newborns

Scat: Called marbles, vary with diet and season, often about the size of plump Smarties

Tracks: 10–15 cm (4–6 in) hind feet land ahead of much smaller, circular front feet; toes of hind feet may spread up to 12.5 cm (5 in) wide

Famous bunnies: Bugs Bunny, Peter Cottontail, Thumper, Roger Rabbit, Harvey, Flopsy and Mopsy, Fiver, Bigwig, Brer Rabbit, The White Rabbit, Fletcher Rabbit, Raggylug, Cuwart

Range: All Ontario south to about Hamilton and Sarnia, though rare south of the Shield and Bruce Peninsula; also in all other provinces and territories

Number of Ontario hare or rabbit species: 1 native, 1 introduced, 2 natural immigrants

Number of hare and rabbit species worldwide: About 50

Also see: Raven, Red Squirrel, Ruffed Grouse, White-tailed Deer, Painted Turtle, Trembling Aspen

a little past Algonquin Park. Unlike hares, which are born fully furred and able to hop within hours, rabbits are slow starters, born helpless, naked and blind in hidden nests. Cottontails have greyish to reddish brown backs and white undersides and are about the same size as snowshoe hares, though not as hefty. **European hares**, introduced from Germany in 1912, are much larger, weighing three to six kilograms (6.6 to 13.2 pounds) and sporting big donkey ears. They live mainly in agricultural areas. Unlike the snowshoe hare, the newcomers do not have the ability – vital to many northern mammals – to put on a white winter coat. The new growth, like many seasonal wildlife alterations, is triggered by the decreasing amount of daylight in fall.

WHITE-TAILED DEER
Speed, Grace and Tension

White-tailed deer are all grace, beauty, tension and bounce. They are wound like a tightly coiled spring, their hooves kicking into the air after barely touching the ground. Watching deer leap over obstacles in the flash of an eye, covering up to six metres (20 feet) in a single bound, their white tails waving goodbye, you might find it impossible to imagine any predator ever catching one.

A deer's life, however, is one of almost constant stress, with its survival dependent on its powers of flight. Its chronic nervousness would send blood-pressure levels skyrocketing in humans. White-tails, in a sense, eat on the run, not fully digesting their food during early morning and evening grazings in clearings. Later, retreating to safe, sheltered spots in deep woods, they ruminate like cows, summoning the

Top running speed: About 70 km/h (42 mph)

Maximum jumping distance: 8.8 m (29 ft)

Highest jumps: At least 2.1 m (7 ft)

Swimming speed: About 7 km/h (4 mph)

Height at shoulder: Avg. 0.7–1.1 m (2.3–3.5 ft)

Length: Females 1.6–2 m (5.25–6.6 ft), males 1.8–2.2 m (6–7.2 ft)

Weight: Females avg. 55–80 kg (120–175 lb), males 90–135 kg (200–300 lb)

Markings: Reddish-brown back in summer, dull grey brown in winter, white undersides; fawns have white-spotted backs in first summer

Alias: Long-tailed deer, ban-
nertail, American fallow deer,
*le cerf de Virginie,
Odocoileus virginianus*
Calls: Squawks, snorts,
grunts; fawns bleat
Whereabouts: Broadleaf and
mixed forests mixed with
abundant clearings and scrub
Food: Grasses, sedges, flowers, wintergreen, fresh tree
shoots and seedlings, especially on aspen, yellow birch,
mountain maple and
chokecherry in spring; leaves
of aspens and other trees,
berries, water lilies and other
plants in summer; acorns,
beechnuts, hazelnuts, large-
leaved aster, evergreen
plants, mushrooms, berries in
fall; buds, twigs and bark,
especially of yellow birch,
hazel, red maple, aspen and
dogwood and foliage of
hemlock, cedar and white
pine in winter
Daily food helping: 2.5–4 kg
(5.5–8.8 lb)
Summer home range: 0.8–
8 km² (0.3–3 sq. mi)
Gestation period: 6½
months
Average litter: 1–2
Birth weight: 1.5–3 kg (3.3–
6.6 lb)
Weaning age: About 6 weeks
Age of first-time breeders:
Does mate at six months in
low-density populations, 2.5
years in high densities
**Fawn survival in first 5
months:** 60–80%
Fat reserves in late fall: 10–
25% of body weight

cud back up into their mouths to chew before swallowing it again for further processing in their four-chambered stomachs. All the while, their huge ears and sensitive nostrils scan far beyond the field of vision for every rustling or whiff of danger. When a threat is detected, a raised, waving tail of one deer is a flag to all the others, signalling them to flee. They're sneaky, and often circle around to get upwind of a pred-ator. Normally only the young, sick or injured are caught. Rarely, a lynx or bobcat will ambush deer from a tree. As a last resort, a deer's sharp hooves can disembowel a predator.

In Ontario, the cold grip of winter is prob-ably the greatest reaper of white-tailed deer. Some 15 to 20 per cent commonly perish in an average season. Alternatively, mild winters since the 1970s have allowed southern Ontario's deer population to quadruple.

When snow piles up 40 or 50 centimetres (16 to 20 inches) deep, foraging over wide areas becomes too exhausting for deer. Small family groups and lone males migrate, sometimes as much as 90 kilometres (54 miles), to traditional deer yards. Near the tip of the Bruce Peninsula, up to 4,000 deer congregate in a yard covering less than 10 square kilometres (3.8 square miles). A series of yards in the Loring Valley south of Lake Nipissing attracts up to 15,000. The refuges are in lowland hemlock, spruce and fir stands or cedar swamps, providing dense shelter from the wind and snow. Loose herds of 50 or so deer tramp down the snow and find some safety in numbers against predators. Food is limited, with the ungulates relying on their fat reserves for up to a third of their energy needs through the season. When the best food is all eaten, deer turn to less nutritious, harder-to-digest species, such as spruce and balsam fir, to stay alive.

The often haggard and hungry deer that survive winter may increase their numbers by 30 or 40 per cent when fawns are born in May and June. More than half of newborns, however, may not survive their first month after a severe winter. Does find hidden, secluded spots in deep forests or grassy thickets to have their babies. The fawns, with almost no odour and with their white-spotted backs blending in with their sun-dappled surroundings, remain well concealed for several weeks, until they can run fast enough to keep up with the herd.

While groups of a few does and their young travel together along regular deer trails through-out spring and summer, bucks lead more reclu-sive, solitary lives. Males start to grow antlers in April – budding, horny manifestations of their rising testosterone levels. The largest, strongest deer in their prime, between four and six years old, grow the biggest antlers, signifying their status to both potential mates and rivals. Native shamans often wore antlers in recognition of the power they represented. The Iroquois crowned their chiefs with antlers, saying they were like antennae, making them supersensi-tive to their surroundings. Male deer shorn of their antlers, in fact, quickly lose their aggres-sion and sexual drive.

Testosterone continues to build in bucks even after their antlers stop growing in September and they've rubbed off the once-soft velvety linings. As the November rut approaches, their necks swell to twice their normal size and they

Winter mortality: 10–50%

Lifespan: Usually 2–8 years for adults; up to 16 years in wild, 20 years in captivity

Predators: Wolves, coyotes, bears, red foxes

Pests: Deer flies, black flies, mosquitoes

Best senses: Smell, hearing

Tracks: About 7 cm (2.8 in) long, double, curved, wedge-shaped hoof marks

Scat: Brown pellets, called fewmets, peanut- to jelly-bean-sized, in piles of 20–30, in winter, lasting up to a year; less-often-seen soft clumps of irregular black pellets stuck together in summer dissolve more quickly

Daily scat productivity: Average of 13–15 piles of 30–40 pellets each in winter

The study of animal drop-pings: Microhistological analysis

Browse signs: Roughly chewed or broken twig ends; lakeside cedars often have distinct winter browse lines where deer, standing on their hind legs, reach up to 1.8 m (6 ft) above the snow

Range: Southern Ontario to around Timmins, Lake Nipigon and a little north of Kenora; also in all other provinces except island of Newfoundland

Famous deer: Bambi, Rudolph

First appearance of deer: 45 million years ago

Estimated fall Ontario deer population: 450,000–500,000

Number of deer shot in Ontario each fall: More than 50,000

Number of people hunting deer in Ontario each fall: 173,000

Number of wild animal car collisions (mainly deer and moose) reported annually in Ontario: About 9,000

Number of Ontario deer species: 4

Number of deer species worldwide: 40

Also see: Deer Flies, Horse Flies; Moose, Wolf, Hemlock, Trembling Aspen

become gripped with a mixture of lust and rage, marking out territories and seeking mates, but eating little. After out-pushing their rivals in head-to-head matches, victorious bucks may strike up mating relationships, each lasting a day or two, with a number of does, coupling with them frequently and passionately during their brief time together. Their antlers form a separation layer and break off in January or February, providing a source of vital calcium and salt for mice, rabbits, porcupines and other gnawing vegetarians.

In areas of deep, extensive forest that have few open patches with shrubs for browsing, deer are relatively rare. The earliest French explorers reported no white-tailed deer in their travels through the dense forests of central Ontario. But Europeans denuded the wilds to the south of hundreds of thousands of deer a year for food and buckskins in subsequent centuries. Then farming and logging gradually opened up vast new areas for white-tails. The North American white-tail population stood at a low point of fewer than 500,000 around the turn of the 20th century, before strict game laws brought protection. Today, there are probably more than 30 million. In areas where no hunting is permitted, such as most provincial parks, deer often become somewhat tame and, driven by their own mammalian curiosity, can linger around and even be drawn near to patient observers.

Of Ontario's other deer family species, besides moose, the **woodland caribou**, the grey ghost of the north woods, once roamed as far south as Algonquin Park. Each small, loose herd of caribou, however, needs an average of 12,000 square kilometres (7,460 square miles) of undisturbed habitat, migrating to old-growth stands to subsist on lichens for the winter. These caribou are now a threatened species, their range receding north by an average of 34 kilometres (21 miles) every year as clear-cut logging pushes into the northern reaches of the boreal forest.

Another large deer, the **elk**, was extirpated from the province by forest clearing and hunting in southern and central Ontario in the 1800s. After a number of largely unsuccessful earlier attempts to reintroduce elk to the province, several hundred were released in recent years in the Bancroft, Burwash and Lake-of-the-Woods areas and seem to be prospering.

WOLF
Respected, Feared and Slandered

Body length: Avg. 1–1.3 m (3.3–4.3 ft)

Tail length: 33–48 cm (13–19 in)

Weight: Females avg. 20–30 kg (44–66 lb), males 25–35 kg (55–77 lb)

Shoulder height: 60–68 cm (2–2.2 ft)

German shepherd shoulder height: 70–79 cm (2.3–2.6 ft)

Biggest wolf ever found in Ontario: 54 kg (119 lb)

Biggest wolf found anywhere: 89 kg (196 lb), in Alaska

Probably no other animal has a more complex psychological relationship with humans than the wolf. Despite an ancient, deep-rooted fear of the great canine among humans, "man's best friend" is a wolf, domesticated as a dog. All dogs descended from wolves at least 12,000 years ago, possibly much earlier, and the two can still interbreed. Like all domesticated animals, dogs have proportionally smaller brains than their ancestor. Originally, they were probably lone wolves who learned to follow human bands, living off their scraps. Gradually, the stragglers were accepted into a human social and behavioural structure not unlike their own.

Given the respect hunter-gatherer peoples in North America had for the wolf, which was regarded as wise and trustworthy, it is probable that modern animosity towards wolves evolved along with pastoralism. Reviled by shepherds, ranchers and farmers for preying on their stock, big bad wolves became the nemeses of the Little Red Riding Hoods and Three Little Pigs of folklore. The most cursed of individuals assumed the form of the hated beast, becoming were-wolves. At the end of the world, in Norse mythology, the ravenous Fenris-wolf would be let loose to wreak death and destruction.

There has never been an authenticated case of wild wolves killing humans in North America

On the arctic tundra, a sometimes-naked Farley Mowat studied wolves in the early 1960s and concluded in *Never Cry Wolf* that their fearsome reputation was "a palpable lie." In truth, documented true-wolf attacks on humans are extremely rare throughout history. There has never been an authenticated case of wild wolves killing humans in North America. Even rabies is extremely uncommon among them. Yet the tenth act passed by the first legislature of Upper Canada, in 1793, put a bounty on wolves, which remained in place for 180 years. Park rangers routinely killed wolves in Algonquin until 1958, and it is still legal to shoot or trap wolves throughout most of the province. A bag limit of two per year was set in 2005.

Crushing power of a wolf's jaws: About 100 kg/cm^2 (1,400 lb/sq. in)

Crushing power of a German shepherd's jaws: About 50 kg/cm^2 (700 lb/sq. in)

Markings: Usually salt-and-pepper grey, brown or fawn, with reddish brown on lower legs, muzzle and behind ears; amber or brown eyes

Alias: Eastern wolf, eastern Canadian wolf, Algonquin wolf, eastern timber wolf, *le loup de l'est, Canis lycaon;* formerly designated *Canis lupus lycaon*, a subspecies of grey wolf

Running speed: Can trot at 10 km/h (6 mph) for hours and sprint up to 70 km/h (42 mph)

Daily distance travelled: Avg. 15–30 km (9–18 mi)

Distance wolves are able to smell a moose: Up to 2 km (1.2 mi)

Calls: Deep howls, growls, barks, whines

Audible range of wolf howls for human ears: About 3 km (2 mi)

Whereabouts: Extensive un-broken forests; beaver meadows, open bogs and marshes used as ren-dezvous sites for young in summer

Pack territory: Avg. 120–240 km^2 (46–93 sq. mi); up to 500 km^2 (193 sq. mi)

Number of wolves per pack: Avg. 4–7 in winter, 8–11 after pups born

Food: In spring, summer and fall mostly deer fawns, moose calves and beavers, as well as hares, groundhogs, mice, voles, muskrats, squirrels, grouse, insects; in winter and early spring mostly young, weak, old or scavenged deer and moose, some hares and beavers

Daily food helping: 1–6 kg (2.2–13 lb); can go without food for at least 17 days

Time it takes a pack to eat a deer: 18–32 hours

Attacks on deer or moose successfully completed: 8–10% or less

Number of deer taken by a pack annually: Avg. 60–180

Den for cubs: In ground burrow, 1.5–9 m (5–30 ft) long, sometimes an enlarged fox burrow, hollow log or rock outcrop; near water

Gestation period: 63 days

Average litter: 4–6

Weaning age: 6–8 weeks

Dispersal: Most leave in late winter and early spring when almost 2 years old

Age at first breeding: Females 2 years, males 2–3 years

Annual survival: Avg. 20–50% in first year, 80–94% for adults in protected populations

Estimated portion of wolf population killed annually by humans in parts of Ontario: Up to 20%

Lifespan: Avg. 4–8 years; up to 13 years in wild, 15 years in captivity

The campaign of extermination and rampant habitat destruction drove wolves out of southern Ontario. Agitation for their demise continues from recreational hunters competing with wolves for moose and deer. While wolf predation does impose a natural equalibrium on prey populaitons, the availability of browse and the severity of winters have a far greater influence on them. Studies show wolves usually taking no more than 2 to 7 per cent of deer in their winter yarding areas.

With longer legs, wider feet and a leaner build than dogs of comparable size, wolves are built for long-endurance running in snow. If they can stay within 100 metres (109 yards) of a fleeing deer or moose, they stick with it for up to 40 kilometres (25 miles), running it down in deep snow, often on frozen lakes. Where there are no winter concentrations of deer, they switch to hunting moose over larger territorites. A healthy adult moose standing its own ground can normally keep a pack at bay with its hooves. Most victims are young, old or weakened animals. By eliminating them, wolves help isolate disease, ease pressure on limited browse from older non-breeders and keep the weaker young from passing on their genes.

Wolves carefully regulate their own numbers through their social structure to ensure overhunting doesn't threaten their food supply. Packs usually consist of a dominant mating pair, one or more generations of offspring and sometimes aunts, uncles or lone wolves accepted into the pack. Only the dominant female breeds, between February and mid-March. She may sometimes be the pack leader. When the pups are born in spring, they may double the size of the pack. All members help in raising them, but the cubs are at the bottom of the totem pole. They are the last to eat, and during hard winters all may perish. If some adults leave the pack or die, there's room for more pups to survive and the pack's number remains relatively constant.

Packs also maintain very large, exclusive territories for their long-distance hunts, keeping population densities low. They mark their domain with urine and droppings and declare proprietorship over all the land within earshot of their howling, which on still nights can be heard up to five kilometers (three miles) away by their own kind. Wolves also howl to locate each other when individuals are hunting separately, as they often do in the summer. Each wolf has unique harmonic overtones that can be recognized by others in the pack. Often, before or after a nightly foray, all join in a group howl in excited anticipation of a feast. Next to actually eating, it is probably when wolves are happiest, tails wagging, joyously bonding like humans in the warm glow – or drunken revelry – of a singalong. The pack leader starts off with a deep, long howl, joined by the others at different pitches and the cubs with yips and whines. They're especially vocal in August and September, when cubs are honing their singing abilities and howl at the drop of a hat.

Central Ontario's wolves are much smaller and generally more reddish than northern grey wolves and were long considered a distinct subspecies. Mounting genetic evidence since the late 1990s, however, identifies southern Shield canines as northern versions of the nearly extinct

Predators: Bears and possibly large hawks kill cubs

Tracks: Front feet 11–13 cm (4.4–5 in) long, back feet 8–9.5 cm (3–3.8 in) long, proportionally wider than a dog's foot

Scat: Like dog droppings, but usually greyish, with fur, bone fragments and pointed ends, usually 8–13 cm (3–5 in) long

Largest protected refuge of eastern wolves: Algonquin Park

Estimated number of wolves in Algonquin Park: About 150 in winter, avg. 2–3/100 km² (39 sq. mi)

Estimated number of eastern and grey wolves in Ontario: 7,000–9,000

Range: From near southern edge of Canadian Shield to southern boreal forest, overlapping and hybridizing with northern Ontario's grey wolf (which average 50% larger) at least as far south as Temegami and Sault Ste. Marie; also in Quebec and Manitoba; grey wolf in all provinces and the territories except the Maritimes and island of Newfoundland

Tweed wolves: Animals along southern edge of Shield resulting from the crossbreeding of eastern wolves and coyotes, which expanded into Ontario from the west over past century

Portion of Algonquin Park wolves bearing some coyote genes: 50–60%

Accolades: Featured on provincial flags of the Yukon and Northwest Territories

Famous wolves: The Big Bad Wolf, Akala, Lobo, Fenris-wolf

First appearance of canines: At least 25 million years ago

Number of red wolves surviving in the U.S.: About 300, most in captivity

Animals that depend on wolf leftovers during the winter: Foxes, martens, fishers, coyotes, ravens, eagles

Number of native Ontario canine species: 6

Number of canine species worldwide: 37

Also see: Raven, Moose, Red Fox, White-tailed Deer

red wolf of the southeastern U.S., more closely related to coyotes than to grey wolves. Though wolves first evolved in North America, the ancestors of the grey wolf migrated to Eurasia one to two million years ago and developed separately, before returning home on an Ice Age land bridge some 150,000 to 300,000 years ago. Around the same time the Eurasian wolves began coming back, the canids that remained in North America split off into two species, coyotes in the southwest and what are now commonly called eastern wolves. Acknowleging their unique status and relatively small numbers, Canada designated them as a species of special concern in 2001.

REPTILES AND
AMPHIBIANS

F or many, our earliest experiences with wildlife involve catching frogs at local ponds or creeks. Through our lives, the spring and summer night choruses of many and varied froggy voices speak of tranquility and refuge from busy urban lives. From thumbnail-sized spring peepers to fat, bellowing bullfrogs, they clamour for attention in the business of propagating their species each year.

By contrast, salamanders and newts scurry in the leaf litter, or glide through aquatic habitats, in a silence that masks their immense numbers. Rarely seen, they are the modern representatives of the first vertebrates to crawl onto dry land hundreds of millions of years ago.

Reptiles, too, are largely inaudible. Like amphibians, they are cold-blooded and cannot produce their own body heat to keep from freezing when the temperature drops below zero. Consequently, Ontario, with its relatively cold winters, is not the most hospitable place for reptiles. Only one lizard, the five-lined skink, dares to inhabit the province, eking out an existence in a few southern fringe areas. Similarly, just a handful of turtles make their portable homes in Ontario, and only painted and snapping turtles can be said to be common.

Among the 15 native snake species, the ubiquitous garter snake is the one seen by most people nine out of 10 times. Only one, the massasauga rattlesnake, is poisonous.

Many of Ontario's turtles, and particularly its snakes, are rare because of human persecution. Too often, fear and ignorance have won over the natural fascination and curiosity we have as children for these often colourful, limbless or shelled wonders. Most are now protected by law, though their futures remain far from certain.

Similarly, in a world increasingly under threat, it is the amphibians that are among the first to suffer. Creatures of both water and land, literally breathing through their permeable, moist skins, they are especially susceptible to environmental adversities of all kinds. As night choruses fall silent in many areas, awareness of them as early-warning signals for all creatures on Earth has grown.

AMERICAN TOAD
Land-loving Warty Wonder

Toad, that under cold stone
Days and nights has thirty-one
Sweltered venom sleeping got,
Boil thou first i' the charmed pot.

Shakespeare's witches in *Macbeth* were not the first to employ toad poison for dark deeds. England's King John was rumoured to have been poisoned in 1216 via a cup of ale spiked with toad venom by a monk who had overheard the unpopular monarch's plans to raise the price of bread. The poison in question is a bitter white liquid that toads, when molested, exude from their "warts" and the paratoid glands behind their heads. The secretion irritates the mucous membranes in the mouth, eyes and nose of predators. The substance does not cause warts, however. Toads can also puff up their bodies with

Adult length: Males avg. 5–7.5 cm (2–3 in), females 6–10.5 cm (2.5–4 in); up to 20 cm (8 in)

Markings: Mottled brown, tan, rust or green on back and sides, with "warts," grey-white underside, large eardrums; males' throats darker than females

Alias: Eastern American toad, *le crapaud d'Amérique, Bufo americanus*

Name for a group: A knot of toads

Call: High, musical trill in 15- to 30-sec bursts

Whereabouts: Moist forests, meadows; shallow ponds and marshes in spring

Food: Beetles, moths, grasshoppers, flies, ants,

insect larvae, worms, slugs, spiders, millipedes; tadpoles eat algae, plankton and bacteria

Nightly serving: Up to 100 insects

Eggs per female: Avg. 4,000–7,000; up to 12,000; released like a double-stranded, gooey string of beads around submerged vegetation, rocks or sticks

Egg development period: 3–12 days

Tadpoles: Fat, black, with short wiggling tails

Newly transformed toadlet length: About 1 cm (0.4 in)

Age at first breeding: Males 2 years, females 3–4 years

Lifespan: Few live past 3–4 years; up to 10 years in wild, 36 years in captivity

Predators: Skunks, raccoons, hognose snakes, garter snakes, water snakes, broad-winged hawks, crows, herons, owls; tadpoles also eaten by dragonfly nymphs, diving beetles, turtles, fish

Winter whereabouts: Up to 1.3 m (4.3 ft) deep in sandy soil on land

Range: All of Ontario except extreme northwest; also in Nova Scotia, New Brunswick, Prince Edward Island, Quebec, Labrador and Manitoba

Ontario's only other toad: Fowler's toad, listed as threatened, scattered along Lake Erie

Number of toad species worldwide: More than 300

air to nearly twice their normal size, a defence especially handy for convincing snakes that they are too big to be swallowed.

With their relatively thick, dry skin and terrestrial lifestyle, toads appear to be closer to reptiles than any other amphibian. Their hind legs are smaller than frogs' legs, limiting them to shorter hops or outright walking. Their colouring blends with the leaves and needles on the forest floor and can change slightly with their surroundings, becoming darker when they are in moist, brown earth. Moisture requirements keep toads mainly in soft dirt depressions or under debris during the day. They can dig with their back feet quite quickly.

Sun-warmed waters allow toad hatchlings to develop faster than most other amphibians in Ontario

After more than six months of winter dormancy below the frost line, toads reemerge and retrace their steps of May to almost the exact spot where they first emerged from the ponds of their youth. Once there, the males call out in slow trills at first, speeding up with their metabolism as the weather grows warmer. Though the breeding season may continue through June, toad socials can be very brief in any one pond, with females leaving as soon as they lay their eggs.

Hatching just days later, tiny black toad tadpoles soon school in dark, darting clouds. Sun-warmed waters in their shallow nursery pools allow them to develop faster than most other amphibians in Ontario, sprouting legs in six to nine weeks, just in time to escape the mid-summer disappearance of many ponds. The toadlets fan out over the land and on rainy nights they move farther, some travelling more than a kilometre (0.6 miles) as they become acclimatized to dry land.

Most of the toads people notice are the small, two- to three-centimetre (0.8- to 1.2-inch) variety, in their troubled-youth stage, through which few survive. Those that do, continue to grow throughout their lives and may reach the size of bullfrogs.

Also see: Fireflies, Raccoon, Gray Treefrog, Wood Frog, Wetlands

BLANDING'S TURTLE
Yellow-necked Bottom-walker

Shell length: Avg. 15–25 cm (6–10 in), up to 27 cm (10.8 in)

Weight: Up to 1.2 kg (2.6 lb)

Markings: Highly domed black or dark brown shell with faint yellow or tan specks, more noticeable on younger turtles; very dark brown or blue-grey head and limbs with deep yellow chin and throat; yellow plastron with dark splotches; males have a longer tail, females have a yellow upper jaw

Alias: Semi-box turtle, *la tortue mouchetée, Emydoidea blandingi*

Named for: Dr. William Blanding, early-19th-century Philadelphia herpetologist

A very long, deep yellow neck sets the Blanding's turtle apart from all other northern terrapins. With just its head breaking the water surface, the shelled reptile can look like a thick yellow-bellied water snake. Blanding's turtles spend most of their time walking the bottoms of shallow, weedy bays and marshes. They use their long necks to reach between and beneath rocks and driftwood to get at crayfish and snails, which they vacuum into their mouths. Though designated a threatened species, they are regularly spotted across Muskoka, Haliburton, eastern Algonquin Park and east along the southern edge of the Canadian Shield.

A good time to see Blanding's turtles is after they rise from hibernation in late April or early May, around the same time as painted turtles. On sunny days for about the next month, when the air warms above 15°C (60°F), they spend long stretches basking either at the water's surface or on logs or low alder branches, attempting to get their metabolism up and running at full throttle. They are, however, quite shy, and plunk into the water at the slightest disturbance.

Blanding's turtles have
a special hinge across
their bottom plastron

The early days of sun-seeking are also a time of turtle romance. Though Blanding's, like other turtles, may mate at any time in the summer and fall, the most intensive breeding is in the first weeks out of torpor. Males search out and chase domed damsels to the bottom of the water. Wooing then begins, with the pursuer climbing onto the female's back, clasping the edge of her carapace with his four clawed feet and imploringly caressing her head with his chin, nibbling her neck and swinging his head from side to side. If, after up to 70 minutes, she decides he's the one she's been waiting for, she lets her tail slip from her shell to entwine with his, and they consummate their brief union. Their reptilian rapture lasts 15 to 30 minutes before they depart from one another for good. They are quite promiscuous, however, and the eggs in most clutches are suspected to have been fertilized by more than one father.

From mid-June to early July, both sexes may boldly venture onto land. Males sometimes travel more than a kilometre (half a mile) from one body of water to another over a two-day

Herpetology: Study of reptiles and amphibians, from the Greek *herpein,* "to creep"

Calls: Sometimes hisses when threatened

Whereabouts: Marshes and shallow, quiet lakes and bays with lots of vegetation and mucky, silty bottoms

Food: Crayfish, mayfly larvae, dragonfly nymphs, beetle grubs and other aquatic insects, snails, slugs, leeches, tadpoles, frogs, fish, carrion and some berries and plants

Home range: Avg. 0.4–2.3 ha (1–5.7 acres)

Portion of adult females mating each year: About 50%

Nest hole: About 18 cm (7 in) deep, 18 cm (7 in) wide at bottom, in exposed, sandy ground

Average clutch: 6–11 dull white, plum-sized eggs

Incubation period: 73–104 days

Consistent temperature at which eggs produce all males: 22.5–26.5°C (73–80°F)

Consistent temperature at which eggs produce all females: 30–31°C (86–88°F)

Hatchling shell length: Avg. 3 cm (1.2 in)

Age at first breeding: males 12–20 years, females 20–25 years

Lifespan: May exceed 77 years

Clutches found by predators: 43–93%

Predators: Raccoons, foxes, skunks, herons, large fish and snapping turtles eat eggs or soft-shelled young

Winter whereabouts: Submerged in weeds, partially buried by mud, occasionally waking to move to different sleeping spots

Range: Scattered pockets in southern Ontario to Manitoulin Island, Sudbury and northern Algonquin Park; also in southwestern Quebec and southern Nova Scotia

Number of turtle species native to Ontario: 8

Number of Ontario turtle species at risk: 2 endangered, 3 threatened, 2 species of special concern (making turtles the most imperiled order of animals in the province)

Number of turtle species worldwide: 257

Also see: Crayfish, Painted Turtle, Speckled Alder

period, resting under cover along the way. Most female forays are egg-laying missions, often taking them 100 to 200 metres (110 to 220 yards) away from the water. Setting out under the falling veil of dusk, pregnant turtles head to open, sandy sites, where they spend up to three and a half hours digging a hole with their back feet and laying and burying their clutch. Most return to the drink by 11 p.m.

Blanding's turtles have a special hinge across their bottom plastron that allows them to close the front of their shell tighter than any other native Ontario species. The added protection equips them for both their long journeys and short foraging around shorelines for berries, leaves, worms and grubs. They're also the only pond turtles that don't need to submerge their heads in water in order to swallow food.

Hatchlings burrow out from the ground in September. Their shells are yet to harden, so they keep low in the mud, sedge and alders to avoid being eaten by all manner of beasts, including their own kind. For their part, adult Blanding's turtles begin slowing down in late summer, eating little, and finally lapsing into hibernation around mid- to late October.

While Blanding's turtles are most active in the morning, the ignobly named **stinkpot turtle** wanders over the same marshy lake shallows and on edges of slow streams after dark. The diminutive stinker, just eight to 13 centimetres (three to five inches) long, is named for its habit of releasing a musky odour when picked up. Despite being fairly common in some areas, the dark, beak-snouted turtle is very rarely seen, sleeping beneath logs or lily pads by day. Even when laying eggs, it usually goes no farther than a muskrat lodge or pile of rotting vegetation along the water's edge to dump its load. It nibbles mostly on aquatic plant seeds, insects and soft, young crayfish.

The stinkpot's distinction of being Ontario's smallest hard-shelled reptile is shared with the endangered **spotted turtle**. Protected by a yellow-dotted black carapace, spotties breed in shallow bogs, marshes and fens along Georgian Bay's hinterland, but are often on land in summer. **Map turtles**, living along the same zone in the deep water of large, slow rivers and lakes, have flattened black shells with yellow swirls and may grow up to 25 centimetres (10 inches) long.

BULLFROG
Big, Hungry and Loud

Maximum jumping distance: 2.5–3 m (8–10 ft)

World's record frog jump: 6.2 m (20.3 ft)

U.S. professional-jumping-frog school: Croaker's College, Sacramento, California

Adult length: Avg. 10–15 cm (4–6 in); up to 23 cm (9 in)

Weight: Avg. 100–350 g (4–13 oz); up to 900g (2 lb)

Markings: Green or greenish-brown back, with black blotches on younger frogs; grey-white or pale yellow undersides; yellow throat and chin, brightest on mature males; large brown or grey eardrum circles, on mature males bigger than the eye

In the amphibian world, the bullfrog is king. Larger than any other green hopper in Ontario, and a big eater, a bullfrog will devour just about anything it can subdue, including, on occasion, bats and small birds flying too close to the water, other frogs and even its own kind. But mostly it nibbles on insect finger food.

Bullfrogs were named for their deep calls, so like the distant bellowing of a bull. The French name, *oua-oua-ron,* imitates the repeated drone of amorous males. The bigger the frog, the deeper its voice and brighter yellow its chin. If not dissuaded by the sight and sound of each other, males will fight for territory, wrestling until one is dunked and sent packing.

Bullfrogs are more aquatic than most other frogs, and are seldom seen on land. They emerge from hibernation in the muddy sediments of lake bottoms in May. The ancient Greeks believed frogs were spontaneously formed from mud and could dissolve back into it, making them symbols of both fertility and resurrection. Their sudden appearance with life-giving rain also gave them status as rainmakers the world over. The multitudes of frogs that came with the annual flooding of the Nile inspired the depiction of a frog as the hieroglyph representing the number 100,000 and the symbol of the midwife goddess Heqit. The Egyptian water goddess, Heket, also had the head of a frog. The Hurons said all the world's water was held inside a giant frog until the creation hero Iosheha stabbed it.

Water temperatures have to rise a fair bit to rouse bullfrogs from their winter sluggishness and get them in the mood for breeding. Males establish territories several metres wide by June, calling loudly to keep rivals away and to advertise for mates. Females usually choose the best mating territory – cool, deep water with abundant underwater vegetation for hatching eggs – rather than the best male. When they've found it, they check in with the proprietor, who obligingly hops on the back of all comers. Up to six females may use the same nursery site, if it's a good one. They come already bloated with eggs, which are chemically attracted to the male's sperm as both are released simultaneously into the water. The process can take hours, yielding gooey rafts of up to one metre square (10.75 square feet) containing as many as 20,000 floating eggs. Each egg is a tiny incubator, with a clear, porous membrane that swells like a balloon on contact with the water.

Alias: Giant bullfrog, jumbo, mammoth jumbo, jug-o'-rum, *l'oua-oua-ron, Rana catesbeiana*

Call: Male mating call a deep hoarse drone, usually lasting about a second and repeated in contagious choruses; loud, deep croak when startled

Whereabouts: Marshy bays with lily pads; fens and large ponds

Food: Insects, crayfish, minnows, other frogs and tadpoles; occasionally baby turtles and snakes, small birds, mice

Average breeding territory: 1–6 m (3–20 ft) wide

Egg development period: 4–20 days, depending on temperature

Tadpole: Black-spotted green back, white belly, up to 12 cm (5 in) long

Age at first breeding: 4–6 years old

Annual survival of newly emerged frogs: Less than 20%

Eggs resulting in sexually mature adults: 0.01%

Lifespan: Few more than 5 years; up to 16 years in captivity

Predators: Fish, dragonfly nymphs, giant water bugs, leeches eat tadpoles; mink, raccoons, skunks, great blue herons, water snakes, pike, bass, snapping turtles eat adults

Average number of bullfrogs per ha (2.5 acres) on suitable lakes: About 30 in

June, 200 in July, 100 in
August
Range: Southern Ontario
north to about Temagami
and the southeast shore of
Lake Superior; also found in
Quebec, New Brunswick,
Nova Scotia and southwest
British Columbia
Look-alikes: Green frogs, in-
habiting slow streams and
ponds, resemble small bull-
frogs but are distinguished
by 2 fine ridges running
down the back
**Number of frogs used for
science or entrées in
North America:** More than
15 million annually
**Number of frog species na-
tive to Ontario:** 11
**Number of frog species
worldwide:** More than
5,000
Also see: Leopard Frog,
Lakes

In warm weather the eggs hatch quickly. The bullfrog's breeding season extends well into July because, unlike most smaller species, its tadpoles do not need to transform into adults before winter. Bullfrog pollywogs hibernate beneath the ice as their parents do, and take two years, sometimes even three, to sprout legs and begin to hop. After emerging in frog form in July, they take another two or three years to reach breeding age.

Perhaps more than other frog species, the king is in trouble in Ontario. Its big, meaty legs have long been prized in fancy restaurants, though bulls can no longer be collected without a fishing licence, and not at all in most of eastern Ontario to the Kawarthas. Poaching, habitat destruction, pesticide poisoning, acid rain, global warming and the thinning ozone layer are also cited as possible causes of their decline in many areas. Because they breathe through their permeable skin, which is protected only by gland secretions, amphibians easily absorb impurities. High acidity in lakes and ponds in spring kills eggs and tadpoles. Because they are so sensitive both on land and in water, amphibians are increasingly regarded as vital indicators of ecosystem health. A world without them would mean lean times for many predators, and would leave lakes and ponds choked with algae and skies darkened with swarming insects.

GARTER SNAKE
Ontario's Most Successful Reptile

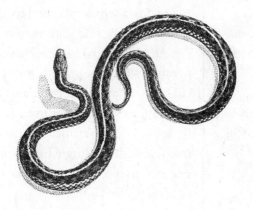

Garter snakes are common and familiar just about everywhere, primarily because they are more adaptable than most other snake species, which are in retreat across the province. Garters are generalists, hunting anywhere and eating almost any prey they can get their expandable jaws around. Their horizontal black and yellow colour pattern – resembling the old-fashioned garters used to hold up socks – blends well with the grass, leaves and litter in many habitats, giving garter snakes the advantage of stealth when stalking or when hiding from larger predators.

A foolproof reproductive system also allows garters to be quite fruitful. In April, at group-hibernating spots, called hibernacula, "mating balls" of many randy, writhing, tongue-flicking serpents form for up to several hours at a time. As each cold, bleary female emerges from her winter

Length: Males avg. 30–50 cm (12–19 in), females 40–75 cm (16–30 in)

Maximum length: 124 cm (4 ft)

Markings: Usually 3 yellow stripes on a black, brown or dark green background, sometimes with a reddish tint; undersides greenish-white or yellow; populations of completely black garters occur in some locations

Number of times adults shed skin annually: 2–4

Alias: Common garter snake, *la couleuvre rayée*, *Thamnophis sirtalis*

Whereabouts: On ground almost anywhere, especially near water

Home range: Up to 0.8 ha (2 acres)

Home: Rests under rocks, logs

Food: Frogs, toads, earthworms, insects, salamanders, mice, voles, small birds, fish, tadpoles

Saliva: May contain toxins and enzymes that help immobilise amphibians and other small creatures; not venomous to humans, but may cause swelling or burning rash for some

Digestion: Large meals may take days, during which garters remain inactive, hiding beneath rocks or debris. Slow metabolism allows them to go weeks without food if necessary

Average litter: 10–20

Length at birth: 12–20 cm (5–8 in)

Age at first breeding: 2 years

Annual survival: 20–40% in first year; 35–50% for adults

Lifespan: Up to at least 9 years in wild, 14 years in captivity

Predators: Raccoons, mink, skunks, foxes, coyotes, broad-winged hawks, owls, herons, ravens, crows, larger snakes

Peak activity period: Midday in spring and fall; early morning and late afternoon in summer

Winter whereabouts: Hibernate in large groups, often with other species, in rock piles, crevices, stumps and decayed root passages

sleep, she's joined by numerous waiting males, whose collective body temperature swiftly raises her own from about 4°C (39°F) to about 20°C (68°F), leaving her no longer sluggish and vulnerable to predators. Some emerging males also derive the thermal benefits of this group hug by producing a female pheromone that dupes other fellows to their side until they've warmed up.

As with all snakes, males have a choice of two penises, which pop up from the base of their tails. As well as producing many young at a time, females can store sperm from a single mating in their bodies to fertilize future eggs for up to five years. Thus a single snake can slither far and wide to start a whole new population without needing to find a male.

Like some other snake species in Ontario, garters give birth to live young, usually around the end of August. Live birth allows them to range much farther north than egg-laying species, whose eggs don't have enough time to hatch before winter. Mother garters may stay near their babies for several days afterwards, and siblings often stick together for a few weeks, growing by frequently shedding their skin, including the clear scales that protect their unblinking eyes. Even as adults, snakes continue to grow, though much more slowly.

All snakes lack apparent noses or ears, are near-sighted and probably do not have a sense of taste. Yet their senses are finely honed for survival. They smell by constantly darting their tongues out to pick up odours from particles in the air or whatever they touch. When they withdraw their tongues, the forked tips touch a set of twin sensory sacs at the roof of the mouth, called Jacobson's glands, which transmit the odours to the brain for identification. Snakes are also extremely sensitive to vibrations, which are relayed via the jawbone to their inner ear. They can judge from an animal's vibration whether it's small enough to be eaten.

Anything more than about a metre away is a blur to a snake. To focus close up, it must move its head back and forth like a magnifying glass, because the lens of its eye cannot change shape. All of the retina, however, is sensitive to movement, which can be detected in a very wide field of view because the eyes sit on the sides of the head.

Snakes themselves betray almost no body scent, and their heads appear tiny and harmless when poking through the grass. They strike like lightning, lunging up to half the length of their bodies, and usually eat prey headfirst and whole, the easiest way to both restrain and swallow still-struggling food. A snake's loosely hinged jaws can open almost 180 degrees. A garter has six rows of tiny, sharp, backwards-curving teeth for drawing its mouth over prey rather than for chewing. To keep themselves from being eaten by mammals, garters when caught release a bad-tasting, pale greenish-brown liquid from a gland at the base of their tails. The defence is not as effective against birds, which usually have a poor sense of taste.

The less common **ribbon snake** is related to and closely resembles the garter, with bright black and yellow stripes. But it's usually much smaller and slender, with a more distinct "neck" between its head and body. Found as far north as Parry Sound and Pembroke, it specializes in catching amphibians and usually frequents the edges of lakes, ponds, streams or wetlands.

a metre (3.3 ft) or more beneath the ground

Largest known garter colony: Estimated 75,000 snakes in several limestone-crevice hibernacula in Manitoba, site of the famous snake-pit scene in Indiana Jones movie *Raiders of the Lost Ark*

Migration range to hibernacula: Up to 10 km (6 mi)

Hibernation cue: Migrates to hibernacula in early autumn, but waits before retiring until ground surface forms frozen crust or daytime temperatures remain below 12–15°C (53.5–59°F), the threshold for digesting food

Average weight loss during hibernation: About 25%

Mortality during hibernation: Often 30–50%

Range: All Ontario to mid-boreal forest and almost James Bay; also in all other provinces except island of Newfoundland

Age of oldest known snake fossil: 135 million years

Also see: American Toad, Water Snake

GRAY TREEFROG
Ontario's Arboreal Chameleon

Length: Avg. 3–5 cm (1.2–2 in); up to 6 cm (2.4 in)

Markings: Variable grey, bright green, brown or almost black back and sides, with irregular black-bordered darker blotches; bars across hind legs; yellowish-white belly; square white spot below each eye; yellow-orange beneath hind thighs; wide toe-disks; males have grey or black throats

Alias: Eastern gray treefrog, tree toad, greater gray treefrog, slow call gray treefrog, tetraploid gray treefrog, *la rainette versicolore*, *Hyla versicolor*

Scientific name meaning: *Hyla* is classical Greek for "wood"; *versicolor* is "changing colour" in Latin

Calls: Trills lasting 1–3 seconds each, cricketlike but much deeper, repeated up to 700 times an hour

Whereabouts: Forests most of year; shrubby wetlands, ponds, bogs, and pools in June

Swale: A wide, shrubby area in standing water, often with a creek or stream running through

Food: Beetles, caterpillars, flies, moths, ants, spiders, leafhoppers

Breeding territory: At least 1.5 m (5 ft) across

There's little wonder why treefrogs are seldom spotted yet so abundant. They are the orangutans of the frog world, living most of their lives high in the canopy of the tallest trees. In addition to being nocturnal and little, the long-toed, wide-mouthed amphibians are chameleons. In the space of an hour, by expanding or contracting three different layers of pigment cells beneath their transparent skin, they can change from bright green to brown to varying shades of grey, keyed by temperature and humidity. On cool days, and when breeding in the water, they often turn almost black to absorb as much heat from the sun as possible. Pressed into the service of science, treefrogs have even changed their colouring to approximate checkered black and white backgrounds.

Like countless other amazing creatures in the wild, treefrogs alert other, more terrestrial, beings to their existence only when caught up in the drama of reproduction. For several weeks around late May and June, males call out in the evening in loud, deep trills, inflating their throats like balloons. The sound might be mistaken for crickets, except it's far too early in the year for the chirping insects to take their cue. Hopping down onto the ground and to nearby shrubby pools, swamps and swales, the singers perform on prominent overhanging alder and willow branches. They guard the territory around their perches closely, rumbling with any competitor that ignores their musical warnings to back off.

Trilling becomes faster as the air warms, reaching a frequency that finally draws females to the pond, usually a night or two after males arrive. The meeting of the sexes cranks up the music a couple of notches as the feminine frog makes her choice and invites a partner to cling to her before she drops to the water. The embrace usually lasts six to eight hours, while she ovulates, before they finally release eggs and sperm together. While they're gone, the singing perch may be occupied by a previously silent male waiting in the wings less than a metre (three feet) away, who tries to beckon a mate before the star returns.

Upon sticking the last batch of fertilized eggs to a submerged branch or stem, a mother treefrog departs the water for the rest of the year. The masculine singers hang around for the

Eggs per female: Up to 2,000 grey and white eggs, in batches of 10–40

Egg development period: 7–10 days

Tadpoles: 2.5 cm (1 in) long and yellow after hatching, turning bright olive-green, with white bellies and long, wide reddish tails; growing up to 5 cm (2 in) long

Reason for tadpole's red tail: Possible warning to predators of protective tadpole skin toxins

Age at first breeding: 2 years

Lifespan: Usually less than 4 years; up to 9 years in captivity

Predators: Garter snakes, bullfrogs, birds, shrews; tadpoles also eaten by fish, salamander tadpoles, giant waterbugs

Winter whereabouts: Beneath fallen leaves, rocks, logs and in old burrows of mice and other small animals

Range: Southern Ontario to Lake Nipissing and Sault Ste. Marie; also in Manitoba, Quebec and New Brunswick

First appearance of treefrogs in evolution: 26 million years ago

Number of treefrog species native to Ontario: 5

Number of treefrog species worldwide: 630

Also see: American Toad, Spring Peeper, Wood Frog, Speckled Alder, Wetlands

whole breeding period in hopes of another coupling with later-arriving females. Only about a quarter of all males, however, successfully mate each season, and very few get a second crack at it. When it's over, they return to the trees, occasionally breaking into song later in the summer on humid or warm, rainy evenings.

After hatching quickly in June and spending six to nine weeks of life as vegetarians, the tadpoles develop legs, lungs and an appetite for insect flesh. The newly transformed, cricket-sized froglets hunt near the water among shrubs and cattails in late August or September, waiting for a rainy night for their amphibious invasion of the trees beyond. They have smooth, brilliantly bright green skin at first, which becomes rougher and bumpy, more like that of a toad, as they grow older and moult.

Blending perfectly with the grey bark, green leaves or lichens on which they rest, treefrogs can remain perfectly still for hours then suddenly leap more than a metre into the air, catch a passing bug and land on another branch. When they jump, bright yellow and orange markings on their inner legs suddenly flash into view, possibly serving to startle pursuing predators. On occasion, they may also use their sticky, bubbly toe-disks to walk up cottage walls and windows, hunting moths attracted by night lights. During the day, they generally sleep beneath leaves or bark or inside small tree cavities.

Around October, gray treefrogs come down to the earth and snuggle into the leaf litter, under rocks or in the abandoned burrows of small animals. Winter's deep layer of snow provides considerable insulation. Even so, during cold weather with little snow, up to 65 per cent of their body fluids may actually freeze without causing the frosty frogs internal damage. High levels of glycerol and glucose usually keep them from freezing solid until they rouse from their slumbers again around mid-May.

LEOPARD FROG
Denizen of Pond and Meadow

Leopard frogs are probably the most-often-seen frogs because they are common both on land and in water. (In the latter they lie stretched out, their eyes just breaking the surface.) They are, in fact, the most widespread frog species in North America. With their attractive, spotted markings, they blend well with the green grass and shadows of summer meadows or with algae beneath the water. Their main defence is in sitting still, hopping only a short distance to a new hiding spot when chased. But since frogs are better at perceiving movement than focusing on objects, a slow-moving heron may easily sneak up on one. Leopard frogs especially are set upon by all manner of predators, from bullfrogs and cruel little boys to fishermen and companies supplying high school biology classes.

First appearance of frogs on Earth: 190–150 million years ago

Adult length: Avg. 5–9 cm (2–3.5 in), up to 11 cm (4.3 in)

Markings: Black, irregular, raisin-shaped spots on bright green or sometimes light brown or grey back; white undersides

Average time between skin sheddings for amphibians: 1 month

Alias: Northern leopard frog, meadow frog, grass frog, *la grenouille léopard, Rana pipiens*

Food: Algae and decaying vegetation when a tadpole; grasshoppers, crickets, beetles, flies, spiders, snails, smaller frogs when an adult

Call: Deep staccato snore or chuckle about 1–3 sec long (often described as the sound made by rubbing a balloon), usually followed by grunts; a piercing scream when attacked

Haydn's impression of a croaking frog: 2 violins, 1 viola and 1 cello in Quartet No. 49 in D Major, Op. 5, No. 6

Whereabouts: Ponds, slow rivers, lakes, swamps, marshes, and moist meadows near water with grasses 6–12 cm (2–5 in) high

Summer home range: 15–600 m² (18–700 sq. yd)

Egg batch: Avg. 3,500–4,500 eggs, in spherical globs of jelly, about 15 cm (6 in) long and 5 cm (2 in) wide, often stuck to stems or twigs in shallow water

Tadpole: Up to 9 cm (5.5 in) long, speckled olive back, white belly

Age at first breeding: 2–4 years

Tadpole survival in first 6 weeks: 1–5%

Annual adult survival: Fluctuates greatly, averaging 40%

Lifespan: Up to 4 years in wild, 9 years in captivity

Predators: Dragonfly larvae, fish, aquatic insects, leeches eat tadpoles; raccoons, mink, weasels, otters, garter snakes, water snakes, bullfrogs, great blue herons, kingfishers, bitterns, hawks, turtles, trout, pike, bass, and

In late April or early May, rising water temperatures stir leopard frogs from their muddy winter beds deep beneath the water, where they draw oxygen through their skins. Air temperatures rising to about 10°C (50°F) warm the cold-blooded creatures enough to give them the jump they need for overland migrations to breeding sites in flooded wetlands and shallow ponds, where there are few or no fish to eat their eggs and offspring. Most of their nuptial treks cover a few hundred metres (or yards), though some can be up to three kilometres (two miles).

Once in breeding pools, leopard frogs soon join the choir of spring peepers, wood and chorus frogs already singing. Males, calling from under the water as well as above, make a snoring or chuckling noise to attract females, followed by grunts to warn other suitors to back off. By late May, most have mated and spread out to summer hunting grounds around moist, grassy streams, ponds and wetlands.

Their eggs hatch 10 to 20 days after being laid, yielding tadpoles that are like pieces of clay, constantly being remoulded by metamorphoses to become something completely different. The temperature of the water controls the speed of their changes. At first, tadpoles are tiny sluglike larvae, blind and with no mouth, hanging onto their egg jelly or to vegetation by sticky structures under their heads. They are nourished by absorbing their egg yolk. Gills filter oxygen from the water. Soon the pollywog's eyes clear, a mouth breaks open on its head and it grows a tail, enabling it to swim and scrape up algae and decaying plant material to eat. All frog or toad tadpoles are strict vegetarians.

Over time, tiny hind legs begin to sprout and flaps of skin grow over the gills as lungs form. Front legs develop inside the covered gill chambers, breaking through the skin about a week before the amphibian uses them to crawl onto land. During the last stages of rapid change, the pollywog is like an awkward adolescent and cannot eat. Instead, it lives off the reabsorbed tissue of its shrinking tail, losing about 25 per cent of its tadpole weight. Bones harden, true teeth form, eyes rise up from the head, a long tongue develops and the intestine shortens to that of a meat eater. Nine to 13 weeks after hatching, the once fishlike creature has become a tiny froglet. Before it goes into hibernation with the first cold days of fall, it may have doubled its weight again.

In late April or early May, rising water temperatures stir leopard frogs from their muddy winter beds

Long winters can be hard on leopard frogs, causing those resting beneath smaller ponds to use up all of their oxygen. Large local die-offs are also caused by viral epidemics and other diseases. Such epidemics, combined with over-harvesting for bass bait (and the dumping of diseased frogs in previously unaffected waters) and habitat destruction, are suspected of playing a big part in the decline and disappearance of leopards from large areas across the Canadian Shield in recent years. Their eggs are also more susceptible to destruction by acid rain runoff than most other common Ontario frogs.

many more species eat adults

Winter whereabouts: Half buried in silt, mud or gravel in shallows of lakes, streams, ponds and wetlands

Range: Southern Ontario to mid-boreal forest; also in all other provinces except island of Newfoundland

Pickerel frog range: Southern Ontario to southern Georgian Bay and Algonquin Park

Famous frogs: Kermit, Jeremy Fisher, Jeremiah, Dan'l Webster, Davey Croakett, Grandfather Frog

Also see: Great Blue Heron, Bullfrog, Spring Peeper, Wood Frog

Leopard frogs have a close cousin in the bog- and creek-dwelling **pickerel frog**, which has a similar speckled pattern. Pickerel frogs, however, have straight rows of squarer spots on a light brown background. Their skin secretions are poisonous to other frogs and snakes. The slightly smaller **mink frog** has splotchy, less distinct markings on its olive green back. It sports a yellow chin. Mink frogs are a more northern species, inhabiting still rivers and bays to just south of Algonquin Park. They are named for the musky smell they produce if captured, likened by some to that of a mink and by others to the whiff of rotting onions. Their hollow call, sounding like two large sticks being struck together, can be heard well into August.

PAINTED TURTLE
Basking by the Riverside

In Iroquoian cosmology, the Earth rests on the back of a great turtle. The turtle had rescued the goddess Antaentsic after she fell from the sky into a vast ocean below. Mud scooped from the bottom of the sea by a muskrat or toad was placed over the turtle's back, forming her new realm, the Earth, Turtle Island. In a similar Hindu story, the world was started on the back of Vishnu, transformed into a turtle after a great flood. Among some Algonkian-speaking peoples, who also had flood creation stories, the great turtle Makinak was the symbol of fertility.

Perhaps the best domed hero for the creation story would be the painted turtle, which spends much of its time sunning itself above the water, usually on rocks and logs. Basking is more than just California dreaming for turtles. Temperature is everything to these cold-blooded

Shell length: Avg. 11–18 cm (4–7 in)

Weight: Males avg. 200–300 g (7–10.5 oz), females 300–450 g (10.5–16 oz)

Markings: Olive, black or brown shell, with sections divided by pale yellow lines; bright red dabs around the edge of shell, red and yellow streaks on dark grey skin of head and neck, red streaks on front legs; yellow plastron (underside)

Calls: Squeak or sigh

Whereabouts: Marshes, shallow, muddy-bottomed bays, slow rivers and ponds with abundant lily pads, pickerel-weed or other aquatic plants, as well as logs or rocks for basking

Alias: Midland painted turtle, *la tortue peinte, Chrysemys picta*

Name for a group: A bale of turtles

Food: Lily pads, duckweed and other aquatic plants, algae, snails, leeches, mayfly and caddisfly nymphs, beetles, tadpoles, crayfish, fish, fish eggs, salamanders, carrion

Average clutch: 5–10 capsule-shaped white eggs, about size of cherry tomatoes; about 15% of females lay a second clutch 1–2 weeks after first

Incubation period: 60–100 days, depending on the temperature

Hatchling length: About 2.5 cm (1 in)

Age at first breeding: Males 7–12 years old, females 11–16 years old

Nests usually lost to predators: About 70%

Annual adult survival: Up to 99%

Lifespan: Many live more than 40 years; some possibly more than 100 years

Predators: Skunks, raccoons, foxes, mink, weasels, crows, bullfrogs, snakes, fish and other turtles eat eggs or hatchlings

Winter whereabouts: Up to 90 cm (3 ft) deep in mud beneath water or in bank burrows, old muskrat lodges

Number of algae species that grow on shells: 5

creatures, whose body temperature rises and falls with that of their surroundings. Most reptiles need temperatures of at least 10°C (50°F) to function. But because they don't need to stoke an internal furnace with food to heat their bodies, the way warm-blooded mammals and birds do, their food requirements are much less. Painted turtles can't eat if their body temperature falls below 15°C (59°F). With a sun-powered metabolism, the more they bask, the faster they digest and the more they can eat and store fat for the winter.

Temperature even determines turtle gender. After mating, usually early in spring, female painted turtles crawl onto land late on June afternoons in search of sandy stream bands or open hillsides, generally within 180 metres (197 yards) of water, in which to lay their eggs. They spend about 45 minutes digging out nests, about 10 centimetres (four inches) deep, with their back feet, dropping their eggs, covering them and patting down the dirt with their plastrons before leaving. The nest's location, whether it has a northern or southern exposure or is partially shaded, and the summer weather then dictate the sex of the developing embryos. Eggs that warm under fairly steady temperatures of 22 to 26°C (72 to 79°F) yield male turtles. At temperatures several degrees above or below that, Yertle becomes Myrtle. In central Ontario, about 85 per cent of painted turtles hatch as females.

Regardless of their gender, many painted turtle hatchlings in Ontario have to wait till spring to see the light of day. To survive the winter, the broods, which hatch in late August and September, usually remain in their subterranean birth nests, living off their egg yolk. During cold snaps they literally turn into turtcicles. Their heart and breathing stop, and ice crystals form in their blood. The babies' temperature can drop to −8°C (18°F), and up to 58 per cent of their body fluids freeze without harming them. Within shrunken blood and tissue cells a portion of unfrozen fluid remains. Though some frogs and insects have similar abilities, the painted turtle is the only reptile able to maintain this semi-freeze-dried state. Their little bodies, however, cannot remain so for long, and a prolonged deep-freeze is fatal.

Once spring does arrive, hatchlings head straight for the water and stay there for the rest of their lives, save for brief sojourns by egg-laying females or occasionally by turtles relocating between feeding ponds and deeper water bodies for winter. Painted turtles eat, sleep and hibernate underwater. Like all submerged turtles, they breathe by filtering water through special tissues in the cloaca, an all-purpose excretory and reproductive opening beneath the base of the tail. The water is held in two small sacs, like aquatic lungs, that draw oxygen from the water into the blood in exchange for the body's carbon dioxide waste. Even if all of a pond's oxygen is used up during their muddy winter slumbers, painted turtles can go without for up to 150 days, longer than any other known vertebrate species. Such abilities, together with their protective shells, help give adult painted turtles the highest annual survival rate of any animal species ever studied, offsetting the heavy predation on their nests and young.

Range: Southern Ontario to about Temagami and Wawa; also found in the southern portions of northwestern Ontario and in all other provinces except Prince Edward Island and island of Newfoundland

Famous turtles: Yertle, Michelangelo, Donatello, Churchy La Femme, Brer Tarrypin, Makinak, Kumaa

Also see: Snapping Turtle, Wood Frog, Water Lily, Milky Way

REDBACK SALAMANDER
Seldom Seen, but Everywhere

Density in prime habitat: Up to 1 salamander per m² (1.2 sq. yd)

Average adult length: 5–10 cm (2–4 in), including tail; up to 12.7 cm (5 in)

Markings: Reddish-brown back, dark grey sides, mottled with light grey near salt-and-pepper belly; less often solid dark back and sides

Alias: Northern redback salamander, eastern red-backed salamander, *la salamandre rayée, Plethodon cinereus*

Whereabouts: Mature deciduous, white pine or hemlock forests with thick, moist litter layer, strewn with logs and rocks

Home range: Usually stays within 0.2–0.3 m²

Salamanders are the oldest vertebrates on dry ground, closely resembling the first amphibians that evolved from fish and crawled out of the water almost 400 million years ago. Every summer, that moment in evolution is played out in the greatest historical re-enactment on Earth, as amphibians emerge from their youthful aquatic stage to actually breathe air. With one foot in the water and the other on land, amphibians have lived through four planetary cataclysms, each causing the extinction of between 50 and 95 per cent of all species on Earth.

Even today, amphibians are by far the most numerous of all land animals with backbones, constituting up to 75 per cent of the vertebrate biomass in temperate forests. In moist hardwood forests redback salamanders are more abundant than any other vertebrate, often outnumbering all the birds put together. But they are seldom seen and never heard, being completely mute. They spend almost their entire lives under the soil, rocks and debris of the forest floor. Only in damp earth can they maintain the coating of moisture essential to their survival. So mysterious were salamanders to the ancients that the Greeks gave them their name, which means "fire animal," because they believed their moist skin allowed them to crawl through flames unscathed.

Without moist skin, salamanders would, in fact, be unable to breathe. Redback salamanders do not even have lungs. They use their skin and the roof of their mouths to filter oxygen from the air and to release carbon dioxide. Biologists speculate that they evolved in fast-flowing, cold streams. Without lungs, they were less buoyant and sank to the rocky bottom rather than being carried away with the current.

Evolution, however, has taken redbacks out of the water entirely. They go through their aquatic stage, with gills, inside the fluid of their egg cases, which the mother salamander hangs in bunches from the ceiling of her nest cavity, usually in a rotting log, in June or early July. A mother stays with her eggs for two months. She wraps her body around the bunch, guarding it and keeping it moist but not mouldy with her skin secretions. The young look like miniature versions of adults when they hatch. They may stay with their mother for a few weeks before heading out on their own in early autumn.

Young salamanders are "floaters" at first, and can have a hard time of it, especially during dry summer weather, when larger, older salamanders occupy and fiercely defend territories in

(2–3.5 sq. ft), but may travel more than 90 cm (3 ft) on wet nights

Food: Beetles, flies, ants, worms, spiders, mites, snails, slugs, sow bugs, centipedes

Best sense: Smell; groves between mouth and nostrils detect scent of prey and other salamanders marking territories

Mating season: Sept. to early Oct.; females, breeding once every 2 years, release pheromones to attract mates on wet nights; males perform an intricate courtship dance before re-leasing a gelatinous sperm capsule, which females pick up with their cloaca muscles

Average clutch: 6–10 white eggs, hanging in bunches like grapes

Incubation period: 30–60 days

Hatchling length: 2–2.5 cm (0.8–1 in)

Age at first breeding: 2 years old

Lifespan: Up to 30 years

Predators: Snakes (especially ring-necked), owls, shrews, herons, thrushes and other birds

Winter whereabouts: Below the frost line, up to 1.1 m (3.5 ft) deep, in rock crevices or passages left by decayed roots, living off fat reserves stored in tail

Range: Southern Ontario to Chapleau, Temagami and around Lake Superior; also in Nova Scotia, Prince

Edward Island, New
Brunswick and Quebec

**Age of oldest amphibian
fossils:** 370 million years

Cloaca: All-purpose excretory
opening at base of tail in
most non-mammalian
animals

**Largest Ontario salaman-
der:** Mudpuppy 25–50 cm
(10–20 in)

**Number of salamander
species native to Ontario:**
10

**Number of Ontario sala-
mander species at risk:** 2
endangered, 1 threatened

**Number of salamander
species worldwide:** More
than 500

Also see: Red-spotted Newt

shrinking pockets of moisture within rotting logs and deep mineral soil. Up to 30 redbacks may stake out turf beneath or inside a large deadfall. Spring and early autumn, on the other hand, are times of plenty, when salamanders chance open-air adventures on moist nights or, much more rarely, rainy days. Such conditions serve up a bountiful buffet because the salamanders can cover more ground and imbibe in the vast selection of other little creatures beckoned to the wet surface.

RED-SPOTTED NEWT
Amphibians with Triple Lives

Masters of change, newts take metamorphosis one step further than other amphibians. After spending two to five years completely on land, newts change colour, regrow finned tails and return to breed and spend the rest of their active lives in ponds. Newts can also regenerate rough approximations of severed tails or legs. When threatened, they lift their tails high above their heads, ready to escape when a predator snatches their expendable appendage.

Normally, though, slow-moving newts – called "efts" during their terrestrial stage – are less harassed by predators than are other sala-manders. They possess nasty glands on their backs containing the same poison, albeit at lower concentrations, that makes the famous Japanese fugu, or puffer fish, potentially fatal. After being swallowed by snakes and toads, efts have been

Minimum dose of eft toxin to kill a mouse: 0.16 micrograms

Minimum dose of strychnine to kill a mouse: 10 micrograms

Average adult length: 10–12 cm (4–5 in), including tail

Eft length: 3–10 cm (1–4 in)

Hatchling length: About 1 cm (0.4 in)

Markings: Efts have rows of black-bordered vermilion spots on their orange-red backs and pale undersides with black spots; aquatic adults have red-spotted, olive-green, yellow or brown backs and yellow undersides

Alias: Eastern newt, red eft, pond newt, *le triton vert*, *Notophthalmus viridescens*

Whereabouts: Beaver ponds, swamps, slow, clear stretches of streams and shallow bays with abundant submerged vegetation or bottoms with lots of deadfall and few predatory fish; efts occupy moist, mature forests with lots of logs and thick leaf litter

Deepest depth found at: 13 m (40 ft) in larger lakes

Eft density in prime habitat: Up to 1 per 3 m² (3.6 sq. yd)

Food: Adults and tadpoles eat larvae of mayflies, caddisflies, midges and mosquitoes, as well as water fleas and frog eggs; efts eat springtails, mites, fly larvae, beetles, grubs, spiders, caterpillars, snails, slugs, worms

Eggs per female: Up to 375 eggs, laid singly on submerged stems and leaves, 6–10 per day, over several weeks of multiple breedings

Egg development period: 20–35 days

Larvae survival: 1–3%

Eft stage duration: Usually 2–5 years, up to 7 years

Lifespan: Adults avg. 7–10 years; up to 15 years

Predators: Insects, leeches eat eggs; dragonfly nymphs, diving beetles eat larvae; fish, herons and watersnakes eat adults

Winter whereabouts: Under rocks, logs, and in banks below the frost line, or beneath ice in ponds

known to survive for up to half an hour before being regurgitated and making their escape. Their bright orange-red colour serves to warn would-be assassins of the unpleasant taste in store for them if they bite, allowing efts to wander about in daylight, in rainy weather, far more often than most salamanders.

After spending the first two or three months of their lives in the water, feeding by night and hiding in bottom debris during the day, larval newts develop lungs and lose their feathery external gills and finned tail edges. Their moist brown skin turns red and becomes rough and dry as they crawl onto dry ground in August or September. These red efts are land-loving, carefree, prepubescent newts. They mostly live under logs or leaf litter during the day and roam about on moist nights, travelling up to 800 metres (870 yards) away from their natal ponds in their first year on land. Small groups of them sometimes gather to absorb radiant heat around the base of tree trunks in spring, or gravitate towards the moist beds of evaporated ponds in June. In August and September, they frequent large decaying mushrooms where they can feast on fly larvae.

When the time comes to grow up, efts migrate back towards the ponds of their origin. They often travel through the summer along stream beds and down slopes to get there, and are believed to navigate by magnetic fields actually visible to their eyes at night. They usually complete their journey in late summer. Some, perhaps still migrating in autumn or in spring, colonize temporary pools along the way and mate with waysided newts there from other ponds, allowing crossbreeding between populations. As they become sexually mature, their skin turns soft and moist again; thin, finlike keels reform on their tails; and they head back into the water. They also change colour to olive, but retain the striking set of black-bordered vermilion spots trailing down the back also sported by efts. In addition, they keep their lungs and have to come to the surface to breathe.

Though some breeding occurs in autumn, early spring is the most popular time for newt nuptials. If a female is ready and willing, mating can occur quickly, with little ceremony. If she needs convincing, a male resorts to the all-important mating dance, for which he retains very rough skin on his inner hind legs, used to clasp her behind the neck and hold on tightly for up to several hours. All the while he ritually waves his tail over her, fanning towards her nostrils a chemical aphrodisiac released from a gland at the base of his tail. Finally, he lets go, moves ahead of her and drops a capsule of sperm for her to pick up in her cloaca. Females can either fertilize and lay their eggs immediately or store the sperm sac, along with those of several other males, for future fertilization.

Adults remain in the water for the rest of the summer. Some may hibernate during winter on land, below the frost line, while others remain active beneath the ice. If their pond dries up, newts turn brown again and either go searching for a new pool or wait several days in hope that their old waterhole fills up once more. This makes them particularly well adapted to survive changing conditions where beaver ponds are started or left to drain.

Range: Southern Ontario to Kirkland Lake and Wawa; also found in Nova Scotia, Prince Edward Island, New Brunswick and Quebec; the central newt, a subspecies, is found from the northwestern shore of Lake Superior to around Sioux Lookout and Kenora

Number of newt species native to Ontario: 1

Number of newt species worldwide: 43

Also see: Beaver, Redback Salamander

SNAPPING TURTLE
Relic of the Dinosaur Past

Lifespan: Adults normally live for more than 30 years; maximum known to be more than 70 years and probably more than 100 years

Oldest definite recorded age of a turtle: 152 years, Marion's tortoise

First appearance of turtles on Earth: 200–250 million years ago

Shell length: Avg. 20–35 cm (8–14 in), up to 50 cm (20 in)

Length from beak to tail tip: Up to 1 m (3.3 ft)

Weight: Adults avg. 4.5–9 kg (10–20 lb), 60–70-year-olds 14–15 kg (31–33 lb); largest kept in captivity reached 39 kg (86 lb)

Record Canadian snapper: 22.5 kg (50 lb)

With their long, jagged-ridged dragon's tails, snapping turtles are living relics from the age of dinosaurs 70 million years ago. Effective, protective shells have given turtles little need to change through the ages. Snappers, though, are actually one of the few species of turtles that cannot fully retract their limbs into their dome when in danger. A small plastron, or underside shell, and very thick, meaty legs prevent the classic turtle defence. A razor-sharp beak and powerful jaws – some say capable of detaching a human finger – are instead the snapper's salvation.

Despite its fearsome reputation, the snapping turtle is mainly vegetarian. It is most carnivorous in the spring, before aquatic weeds are abundant, when it sniffs out water-bottom nooks and crannies for insect larvae and crayfish, and sucks up slow-moving fish and tadpoles. Larger prey is dragged down to the bottom to drown before being ripped apart by the turtle's huge claws. But a snapping turtle almost always retreats swiftly when a larger animal comes near in the water. Only when trapped on land will it lunge quickly and accurately, up to 20 centimetres (eight inches), with its long neck outstretched. Once they bite, snappers hang on tenaciously. Some have had to have their jaw muscles cut before they let go. They also ooze a foul-smelling, syrupy musk.

Normally, snapping turtles don't chance being trapped on land. They spend most of their time underwater, often partly buried in mud during the day, sometimes poking their hooked snouts and eyes just above the surface while resting in shallows. They become active mainly at night. Occasionally, usually in spring, they sun themselves on rocks, logs or water's edge, a quick dive away from safety.

From June to early July, however, females venture onto dry ground to dig out nests in sandy or gravelly waterside embankments or hillsides. Most excavations are within 10 metres (11 yards) of water, but expectant mothers may swim a dozen kilometres (7.5 miles) over a couple of days to return to favourite natal sites. Coming ashore in the evening or early morning, they spend 45 minutes to three hours finding the right spot, scooping out a 10- to 18-centimetre- (four to seven-inch-) deep hole with their powerful hind feet and depositing a few dozen eggs before covering them back up and returning to the drink. The site must be in the open, where the sun can incubate the eggs. Under such exposed conditions, 50 to 90 per cent of all nests

Markings: Dark shell, often covered with algae; dark grey or brown skin; underside plastron can be dull yellow

Alias: Common snapping turtle, snapper, *chelydre serpentine*, *Chelydra serpentina*

Calls: Sometimes hisses when threatened

Food: Mostly algae, water-lily roots, other aquatic plants, and insects; occasionally fish, crayfish, frogs, ducklings, baby muskrats, snakes, snails, leeches, carrion

Whereabouts: Muddy lake shallows, slow rivers, creeks, ponds and marshes, with abundant submerged vegetation

Territory: Avg. about 3 ha (7.5 acres)

Water temperature needed for snappers to efficiently digest food: 15°C (59°F)

Mating season: Soon after emerging from winter torpor, when water temperature reaches 16°C (61°F), in late Apr. and May

Clutch: Avg. 20–40 round, rubbery white eggs, like mini ping-pong balls, each laid 1–2 minutes apart; up to 70 eggs

Incubation period: 55–125 days

Hatchlings: 2.5–3.8 cm (1–1.5 in) long, 7–14 g (0.25–0.5 oz)

Age at first breeding: 16–18 years old

Survival of hatchlings in their first 5 years: Probably less than 1%

Annual adult survival in roadless wilderness areas: Usually more than 99%

Predators: Skunks, foxes, mink, muskrats, raccoons and otters eat eggs; blue herons, crows, hawks, bull-frogs, snakes and fish eat hatchlings; adults killed by otters and, rarely, bears and coyotes

Pests: Leeches

Best sense: Smell

Winter whereabouts: Inactive beneath mud, vegetation or logs at bottom of water, or dug into banks, often in groups

Density in shallow lakes and rivers: 1 per hectare (2.5 acres)

Range: Southern Ontario to around Lake Timiskaming, the north shore of Lake Superior and Red Lake; also in Saskatchewan, Manitoba, Quebec, New Brunswick and Nova Scotia

Also see: Leeches, Painted Turtle

are cleaned out by predators. In addition, many summers in central Ontario are too short and cool for any surviving snapping turtle eggs to hatch. Most of the tiny turtles that do hatch in September and early October have fairly soft shells and are soon eaten by birds and fish. To survive, they probably have to bury themselves in the mud quickly and go into hibernation before even having their first meal.

The fine balance between low reproductive success and long-lived fecund adults is easily upset by excessive roadkill, especially where open, gravelly roadsides offer tempting nest sites. An additional annual loss of even one to two per cent of adult females above natural mortality rates can have catastrophic consequences for a whole population. Such consequences, though, may not become fully apparent until decades too late. Some communities have responded by marking notorious stretches of roads with turtle crossing signs.

The snapping turtle was finally designated as a species of special concern in Canada in 2008. Yet snappers are still hunted by humans in Ontario. Some 5,000 to 8,000 a year were taken until 1990, when commercial hunting was outlawed, but fishing-licence holders may still catch them. Near settled and agricultural areas, they've been found with PCB and pesticide levels up to five times the safety limit, resulting in deformed hatchlings and lower reproductive rates.

SPRING PEEPER
The Loudest Animal on Earth

Gram for gram, the spring peeper is probably the loudest animal on earth. Small enough to fit easily on a loonie and rarely actually seen, peepers make themselves very conspicuous on late April and May nights, when their high, musical calls join together in a resonating din. Choruses of untold numbers sound to some ears like distant sleigh bells. To sing, males squeeze air over their vocal chords and amplify the sound by inflating their throats into balloonlike bubbles, producing a springy note that can carry for at least half a kilometre (a third of a mile).

Together with the larger wood frog, which sports a black mask and quacks like a duck, spring peepers are the first frogs to sing in spring. Awakened by the thawing of the earth around their winter beds beneath the leaf litter, they rise en masse on the first rainy nights of the season,

Sound level of spring peeper call at 10–20 cm (4–8 in): 110–120 decibels

Sound level of a jet engine at 64 m (70 yd): 120 decibels

Sound level of average conversation: 60 decibels

Conspiratorial, subdued conversation: 40 decibels

Maximum jumping distance: More than 50 cm (20 in)

Adult length: 2–3 cm (0.8–1.2 in)

Markings: Tan, greenish-brown or grey back with a dark X; black bands on legs; white throat and belly

Alias: *La rainette crucifer, Pseudacris crucifer*

Call: Shrill, piercing "peeeep" with a rising pitch, lasting about a second, constantly repeated

Food: Algae when a tadpole; mosquitoes, gnats, ants, beetles and other small insects, sometimes worms and snails, when an adult

Whereabouts: Wetlands, small, temporary ponds in spring; damp forests and bushes near marshes in summer and fall

Home range: 1.2–5.5 m (4–18 ft) wide

Breeding territory: 10–45 cm (4–18 in) wide

Eggs per female: About 200 eggs laid singly or in small clusters

Egg development period: 5–15 days

Tadpoles: Up to 2.5 cm (1 in) long; green back speckled with gold; white belly

Age at first breeding: 3–4 years old

Predators: Fish, other frogs, turtles, snakes, birds; salamanders, dragonfly nymphs, diving beetles, giant water bugs eat tadpoles and eggs

Winter whereabouts: Hibernate beneath ground or leaf litter

Range: Most of Ontario to James Bay; also found in Nova Scotia, New Brunswick, Prince Edward Island, Quebec and Manitoba

Also see: Gray Treefrog

when temperatures hit around 9°C (48°F). In rare cases when conditions are ideal, the ground crawls with thousands of peepers, wood frogs and blue- or yellow-spotted salamanders, drawn to their ancestral ponds like zombies, entranced by the urge to breed. Often migrating with patches of snow still on the ground, they slip in under the ice at the edge of ponds.

Though they are treefrogs, spring peepers rarely climb higher than low bushes and shrubs

Males immediately take up positions around the pond, several days before the opposite sex will be drawn by their serenades. The singers usually sit on floating twigs, tufts of grass or low branches, allowing each shrill peep to resonate freely over the water. Along the southern fringe of the Shield, tiny chorus frogs, also members of the treefrog family, sometimes join in, with a call that sounds like the teeth of a comb being flicked. During cold snaps they quieten down. But as the nights warm, they pick up the tempo, with each member of the peeping choir calling out in counterpoint to others around them, as often as once every second. Some researchers speculate that those with the fastest, loudest peeps attract the most females. If a balladeer can attract an admirer plump with eggs, he jumps on her back and swims with her for hours, often all night, fertilizing her eggs as she releases them onto submerged vegetation and debris.

Peeper choruses fall silent by the end of May, though a few individualists sometimes call before retiring for the season in October. While risking fatal late freezes, the spring peepers' early breeding gives tadpoles a chance to mature into tiny, bee-sized frogs by the end of July, as their small ponds are drying up in the summer heat. More than half of the ponds in one study usually evaporated before or during peeper transformation.

With remnants of their youthful tails still trailing behind their new legs, rookie peepers spread out over wide areas and spend the rest of the year on land, hunting for insects at night, resting during the day under logs, rocks and leaves. Though they are treefrogs, clinging to vertical surfaces with sticky, bubbly pads at the end of each toe, spring peepers rarely climb higher than low bushes and shrubs. In addition to projecting their voices great distances, they can leap more than 17 times their own body length when moving from branch to branch.

WATER SNAKE
Graceful Swimmer Demands Respect

Length: Avg. 60–100 cm
(2–3.3 ft), up to 135 cm
(4.5 ft)
Diameter: Up to 5 cm (2 in)
Markings: Alternating bands
or blotches of dark brown or
black with lighter brown, tan
or grey, though less distinct
on older snakes; rusty-
speckled whitish to yellow
undersides; often appears
uniformly black when wet
Maximum dive duration:
More than 1 hour
Alias: Common water snake,
*la couleuvre d'eau, Natrix
sipedon*
Whereabouts: Lakes, bays,
slow-moving rivers, wetlands
and rocky shorelines
Food: Minnows, perch and
other fish, frogs, tadpoles,

Though all Ontario snakes can swim, the northern water snake is an aquatic specialist. It glides
quickly and smoothly through the water, swimming just below the surface, a huge, dark, waving
serpent. When water snakes catch prey, however,
they bring them out of the water to eat, then hide
on shore for up to a week while they digest. On
sunny days they bask on rocks, logs and old beaver
lodges, or in tree branches overhanging the water.
They also come out of water in May or early
June to mate, entwining around each other for
hours on reeds or other vegetation sometimes in
groups. In late August or September, they give
birth to live young.

Unless cornered near shore, water snakes
seldom attack large mammals or people in the
water. If captured or threatened, however, they
can be very aggressive. They attempt to strike

repeatedly and can inflict a painful bite. Water snakes have four rows of 30 to 40 very sharp teeth, curving inwards to hold their slippery aquatic prey. Unlike most other snakes, when they bite, they rip their victim's flesh as they remove their teeth. The bite injects an anticoagulant that makes bleeding hard to stop. Like many species, they also flatten themselves to appear bigger when threatened, and release a stinky fluid from their cloacal gland if caught.

The water snake's aggressive defence has brought much persecution by humans. Fortunately, it is now protected in Ontario, illegal to kill or capture. When swimming, it's often thought to be a water moccasin, a poisonous species found only in the southeastern U.S. On land, its blotchy appearance is often mistaken for the similarly patterned **massasauga rattlesnake**, Ontario's only venomous serpent. Though once common, massasaugas are now rare in Ontario. Rattlers prey mainly on frogs and rodents and do not bite people unless cornered or startled. Their poison causes severe pain, swelling and discolouration within 15 minutes, but rarely death. Nonetheless, fearful humans almost invariably killed them whenever they were found. As a threatened species, rattlers were finally granted protected status in 1991.

Snakes have long inspired fear and loathing in Western cultures, from the appearance of the serpent, as evil incarnate, in the Garden of Eden. The Genesis story, however, is just one version of a very old tale involving an earth goddess and a fertilizing phallic snake, told by the earliest agricultural societies in Asia, Africa and Europe. The ancients viewed the wonder of a snake

salamanders, toads, crayfish, occasionally mice or shrews

Average litter: 20–25

Hatchling length: 16–25 cm (6.3–10 in)

Age at first breeding: 2–3 years

Lifespan: Up to at least 7 years

Predators: Great blue herons, mink, raccoons, skunks, foxes, red-shouldered hawks, herring gulls, pike, bass and other large fish, turtles

Winter whereabouts: Hibernates in rock crevices or beneath water

Mortality rate during hibernation: Up to 40%

Range: Southern Ontario to about North Bay and Sault Ste. Marie; also in southwestern Quebec

Massasauga rattlesnake length: Avg. 45–70 cm (1.5–2.3 ft)

Rattler markings: Dark brown blotches on a light grey or tan background; more uniformly dark with age

Rattler whereabouts: Scattered in marshes and coniferous forests in Bruce Peninsula, Muskoka and a couple of spots in southern Ontario

Average number of people bitten by massasauga rattlesnakes per year in Ontario: 3

Number of people who have died of massasauga rattlesnake bites in Ontario: 2

Biggest Ontario snake: Grey rat snake, 1–2 m (3.3–6.6 ft) long

Number of snake species native to Ontario: 15 or 16, depending on red-sided garter snake's classification as a species or subspecies

Number of Ontario snake species at risk: 2 endangered (plus 1 subspecies), 4 threatened, 2 species of special concern

Extirpated from Ontario: Timber rattlesnake, not found since 1941

Number of snake species worldwide: More than 2,700

Number of venomous snake species worldwide: About 45

Also see: Minnows, Garter Snake, Lakes

shedding its skin as a symbol of rebirth. The power of snake venom must also have engendered a strong reverence. Hindu, Norse and Egyptian cosmology all featured a great snake supporting or enfolding the world. The polar star, upon which the Earth's axis seems to spin, was said to be the eye of the serpent that fertilized the Earth. In China, snakelike dragons were powerful but beneficial beings that brought summer rains with their thunder. Zombie was a West African snake god.

In the Americas, snakes were everywhere regarded as important spirits. Quetzalcoatl, the great deity of the Aztecs and other Central American peoples, was a feathered snake. A vanished agricultural people that lived in large towns left a giant serpent-shaped earthen mound in Ohio. A much smaller version, probably made by the same people, overlooks Rice Lake at Serpent Mounds Provincial Park. Ojibway lore features both benevolent and dangerous snakes. Nanabush's enemies were the serpent people that lived beneath the water. But the creator, Kitche Manitou, gave snakes the job of protecting plants from overindulgent browsers.

WOOD FROG
The Deep-freeze Forest Bandit

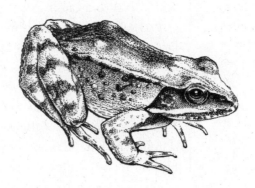

Wood frogs should be added to the pantheon of great Canadian wildlife symbols, alongside the beaver, loon and moose. The black-masked forest bandits inhabit the land from sea to sea to sea, hopping within sight of the Arctic Ocean in the Mackenzie River delta ("A river so Canadian it turns its back on America," said the poet F. R. Scott), farther north than any other amphibian on the continent.

Woodies are tough frogs, settling into dry forest litter in the autumn, pulling its cover over them and waiting for the snow to fall. They can slumber on a bed of frosted leaves as cold as −8°C (21°F) and withstand up to 65 per cent of their body fluids turning to ice. In the late 1700s, Hudson's Bay Company explorer Samuel Hearne wrote of digging up wood frogs from the frozen moss that were as cold and hard as ice.

Length: Avg. 3–6 cm (1.2–2.4 in), up to 8 cm (3 in)
Weight: Avg. 7–9 g (0.25–3 oz)
Markings: Distinct yellow-lined black "mask" running behind each eye; brown, tan, grey or reddish-brown back and sides; white undersides, sometimes darkly mottled; dark bars across legs; males darker brown during breeding season
Vocal sacs: Gleaming white when inflated at the sides of males' heads
Alias: Robber frog, *la grenouille des bois*, *Rana sylvatica*
Scientific name meaning: *Sylvatica*, from Latin *sylva*, meaning "wood"

Calls: Mating song sounds like high-pitched duck quacks; males also chirp when grabbed by other lusty fellows to tell them they've made a mistake; sometimes purrs when picked up

Whereabouts: Damp portions of the forest floor; shrubby, temporary woodland ponds, swamps and marshes in early spring

Home range: 3–370 m² (3.5–440 sq. yd)

Food: Beetles, flies, mosquitoes, ants, caterpillars, spiders, snails, slugs; tadpoles eat algae and bacteria

Portion of males that get to mate each year: About 20%

Portion of males that mate twice in a season: About 1%

Clutch: 400–2,500 black-centred eggs in a round clump, 2–10 cm (0.8–4 in) across, around a submerged stem or twig, turning green with algae after about a week

Egg development period: About 2–3 weeks

Tadpoles: Hatch 7–10 mm (0.25–0.4 in) long, grow to 3–5 cm (1.2–2 in), yellow-spotted olive backs with iridescent, pink-tinted bellies

Portion of eggs that yield tadpoles surviving to frogdom: About 4%

Age at first breeding: 2–3 years

Lifespan: Up to at least 4 years

Predators: Raccoons, mink, garter, ringneck and ribbon

To keep from completely freezing, wood frogs flood their bodies with glucose from carbohydrates stored in their livers. By thus elevating their blood-sugar levels to some 60 times the summertime norm, they create a sweet natural antifreeze that prevents crystals from forming within cells and causing damage.

As soon as the snow is mostly gone and the litter layer thawed, in mid-April to early May, male wood frogs stir. The world's most posthumously famous idler, Henry David Thoreau, wrote of the early-rising frog in the spring of 1859, "He is wholly of the earth, sensitive as its skin in which he lives and of which he is a part. His life relaxes with the thawing ground." The newly roused bachelors make straight for the leaf-filled meltwater pools, ponds and wetlands where they first hatched. There, floating largely unseen in the water, they begin quacking like phantom ducks as the mercury rises towards 10°C (50°F). They may fall silent again if a cold front or late snowstorm rolls in. The larger females join them a few days later, each drawing half a dozen or more males around her in a quacking frenzy. He who holds on the tightest remains fastened to the object of his desire anywhere from an hour to three days, until they finally spawn.

Parents have no time to lose if their young are to develop legs before natal swimming holes dry up. The mating prom may be over in as little as a few days at a given pond. With gatherings starting earlier on open marshes than in dark forest ravine pools, wood frog calls may be heard for two or three weeks before finally fading out, leaving a background chorus of spring peepers.

In a choice spot, where a submerged branch lies exposed to the sun, many wood frog mothers mass gooey globs of dark-centred eggs. The globs absorb and hold heat, protecting the eggs – especially those near the centre – from cold spells and re-forming ice. After a couple weeks, the tadpoles hatch and develop faster than the larvae of any other North American frog, with aquatic childhoods as brief as 40 days. By early summer, the few that have survived the cold, predators and competition for food take to land around their shrinking ponds as air-breathing, thumbnail-sized froglets. After growing up together with wriggling mosquito larvae, the newly carnivorous hoppers avidly pick off their insect pool-mates who are transforming around the same time.

Throughout the summer, wood frogs stalk insects in the forest. They are the most terrestrial of Ontario's frogs, often rustling in the leaves and ferns along trails, and are easily mistaken for tiny toads, save for their signature black masks. Though they assume the same earth-brown colour as the land-loving toad, wood frogs have smooth skin and, like other frogs, must remain moist, always dwelling in damp, shadowy haunts. If found and picked up, they also have the uncanny ability to purr like a cat.

snakes, herons, bitterns and other large birds; tadpoles eaten by turtles, red-spotted newts, yellow-spotted salamanders, diving beetles, leeches, caddisfly larvae

Winter whereabouts: In the forest litter layer and under rocks, logs and stumps

Range: Throughout Ontario; also in all other provinces and territories

Medical service: The wood frog and its deep-freeze abilities have been studied extensively by researchers developing ways to freeze and store human organs for transplants without damaging them

Also see: Mosquitoes, American Toad, Spring Peeper

PLANT
KINGDOM

PLANTS

*I*t is said that the Native peoples had no word for "wilderness." The bush was their home, their provider, a vast pharmacopoeia and treasure trove of life-giving substances, with each plant having its place and purpose, its secrets and mysteries. Many Native peoples saw plant spirits as benevolent healers aiding them against diseases sent by offended animal spirits when hunters did not show them proper veneration. Recognition of the curative powers of plants and appreciation of their beauty stretch far back into humanity's prehistory. Soil studies of 60,000-year-old Neanderthal grave sites have revealed that the dead were laid to rest on beds of spring flowers, all known in more recent times as traditional folk remedies.

Native or folk medicines, such as those mentioned in this book, are not recommended for those unschooled in their preparation. The same active ingredients that give plants their curative powers can also be toxic in high concentrations or if not prepared properly.

In addition to Ontario's many hundreds of species of flowering plants, including trees and grasses, there are many other kinds of vegetation in the province, such as spore-producing ferns and horsetails. Strictly speaking, mushrooms and lichens, which are included in this section, are not part of the plant kingdom at all, though they are popularly perceived as such. They predate the evolution of modern plants and reach back towards the origins of life.

BLUE BEAD LILY
Lush Leaves and Forbidden Fruits

Berries: Navy blue, shiny, 8–10 mm (0.3–0.4 in) wide, each on a long stalk and usually containing 10–15 seeds; ripening around mid-July

Alias: Clintonia, yellow clintonia, corn lily, northern lily, dogberry, wild corn, *la clintonie jaune, Clintonia borealis*

Genus name origin: Bestowed in honour of DeWitt Clinton, an early-19th-century naturalist and governor of New York who organized the building of the Erie Canal

Whereabouts: Moist coniferous and mixed forests

Height: 15–40 cm (6–16 in)

Flowers: Pale to greenish yellow, loosely bell-shaped, 3–8 per plant at top of stem, each 2 cm (0.8 in) wide, with 3 petals and 3 petal-like sepals, 6 golden stamens and a long green pistil; most pollinated by bumblebee queens or self-pollinated; each plant blooms for about 8–11 days

Portion of plants blooming in a large patch: Usually less than 10%

Leaves: Up to 30 cm (1 ft) long, 4–9 cm (1.6–3.6 in) wide, thick, glossy, bright green above, downy on bottom, with bluntly pointed tip

The blue bead lily stands out in the heart of the summer forest with lush, tuliplike leaves and tall green stems bearing large, shiny round berries, like navy-blue beads, giving the plant its name. The lily's other common name, yellow clintonia, is more applicable between late May and mid-June, when its greenish-yellow flowers nod from the stem tops. Each flower, which turns more purely yellow as it matures, produces a single berry.

Happily gobbled by birds, deer and chipmunks, the attractive berries are nonetheless bitter and mildly poisonous to humans. The leaves, however, contain diosgenin – the same anti-inflammatory chemical that is synthesized to make progesterone – and were used by the Ojibway as a poultice for burns, bruises and infections. Forest-food enthusiasts praise the cucumber taste of the newly sprouted, still curled leaves.

Blue bead lilies develop very slowly in the deep forest shade, producing only a singe leaf for many growing seasons, not blooming until at least 10 years old. In summer, each plant sends a thin rhizome – a horizontal underground stem – up to nine centimetres (3.5 inches) through the soil, forming a bud at its tip in autumn. Large plants in optimal conditions produce two budding rhizomes. An interconnected colony of mutually supporting plants gradually fans out and is particularly robust because each connecting rhizome lasts from six to 15 years, significantly longer than those of most other colonial forest wildflowers.

and parallel veins; usually 3 arch from base of flowering stem, occasionally 2, 4 or 5

Roots: A thin, knotted, branching rhizome, 15–80 cm (6–31.5 in) long, near surface, producing colonies of clones

Lifespan: Colonies of a few plants more than 20 years old; colonies with more than 100 plants can be as old as the forest itself

Range: All Ontario except far northwest; also in Manitoba, Quebec and Atlantic provinces

Also see: Doll's-eyes, Trout Lily

BLUEBERRY
Best Loved of Wild Fruits

Berries: Green at first, turning pink, reddish purple and finally dark blue-purple when ripe in late July in southern Shield areas and in Aug. towards Temagami

Average number of seeds per berry: More than 100

Flavour cells: Most sweetness is in the skin, making wild berries more tasty than large, pulpy commercial varieties

Alias: Lowbush blueberry, low sweet blueberry, whortleberry, bilberry (really European varieties of blueberry), *le*

It must be on charcoal they fatten their fruit.
I taste in them sometimes the flavor of soot.
And after all, really they're ebony skinned:
The blue's but a mist from the breath of the
    wind,
   – Robert Frost, "Blueberries"

Thick networks of buried root runners ensure that blueberry patches survive ground fires and rebound to flourish like never before. Native peoples such as the Ojibway knew this well and regularly burned choice areas to encourage bountiful harvests. Blueberries were an important food source for groups who were primarily hunter-gatherers. Dried or charred berries, added to wild rice, meat or bread, provided vital nutrients during the long winter. Crushed berries were also used to make a blue-grey dye.

Blueberry takes root and thrives best in dry, rocky habitats, helping to hold down the thin layer of soil painstakingly built up by lichens, moss and grass. Once established, it spreads out in dense, tangled colonies, sending forth underground stems that sprout new plants. As with many other heath or open-area shrubs, discarded blueberry leaves are slightly toxic to tree seedlings in the surrounding litter, keeping them from growing up and shading out the shrubs.

In May and June, blueberries produce tiny white flowers that hang downwards and are pollinated by small bees. The insects dig deeply into the flowers to reach the nectar, at the same time inadvertently shaking sticky pollen onto themselves. They cross-pollinate by brushing their pollen-laden bodies against the female pistil near the opening of the next flower they visit. Widely varying amounts of nectar in each flower increase cross-pollination by keeping insects flitting from one to another until they finally hit a jackpot. Though black flies were also long thought to be major blueberry pollinators, recent research in Ontario suggests they are rather "nectar thieves," supping from the flowers without transferring any pollen.

Blueberry flowers can also be pollinated by their own male parts, but that option usually yields smaller berries that ripen later than the others. Cold, wet springs result in low pollination and berry-set rates, which can have a major effect on wildlife populations.

bleuet, Vaccinium angustifolium

Whereabouts: Dry, acidic soil in rocky or sandy clearings, along shorelines, islands, open hillsides and ridges, bog edges, open spruce-fir forest, jack pine barrens and recently burned areas

Height: Usually 30–35 cm (12–14 in); up to 60 cm (2 ft)

Flowers: White, like tiny bells, up to 6 mm (0.2 in) long, in clusters

Leaves: 1–3 cm (0.4–1.2 in) long, rounded, leathery, turning reddish purple in exposed areas, crimson in fall

Frequent diners: Bears, deer, coyotes, foxes, raccoons, martens, hares, chipmunks, mice, voles, ruffed grouse, cedar waxwings, robins and other thrushes, white-throated sparrows, blue jays, scarlet tanagers, catbirds, orioles, chickadees, brown thrashers

Native remedies: Ojibway used leaf tea as a blood purifier and inhaled fumes of dried, heated flowers for mental illness; leaves contain the chemical myrtillin, which acts like insulin to reduce blood sugar, as well as other minerals that serve as blood purifiers and are used to treat kidney problems, though it can be toxic in high concentrations

Range: All of Ontario; also in all eastern provinces, Manitoba and Saskatchewan

The fruits' conspicuous colour advertises their presence to birds, while their sweet smell attracts many mammals, from mice to bears. By enticing wildlife with juicy flesh, blueberries and other fruit-producing plants have their seeds spread and fertilized by way of bird and mammal droppings. Their ripening is perfectly timed, through millions of years of natural selection, for just after the late-spring/early-summer bug-population peak, when birds are searching for new sources of food. Even most fruit- and seed-eating birds nest when insect numbers are highest, because bug meals, with up to 70 per cent protein, are needed for their hatchlings to reach adult size in the space of a couple of weeks. After the young have flown the coop, many birds are happy to switch back to fruits and berries, which are three to 13 per cent protein. Like most other summer berries, blueberries are high in carbohydrates, or sugars, and low in fats. Fruits and berries ripening later in the year are higher in the easily stored, longer-burning fats needed by birds in migration.

CANADA MAYFLOWER
Unsung Floral Emblem

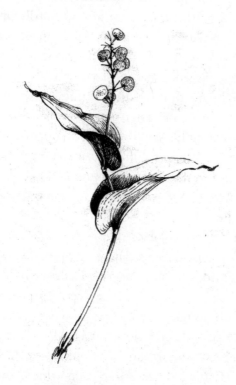

Canada mayflower is often not given its due, being passed off with names such as "false lily-of-the-valley," implying secondary significance to a refined garden import. In fact, Canada mayflower was considered a true lily until a recent breaking up of the family by busybody botanists. But it remains perhaps the most common plant found in the mixed and ever-green forests that cover most of central Ontario. The sheer ubiquity of its lacy white spires of blossoms, in multitudes throughout the country, could easily make it Canada's national flower.

But Canada mayflowers are tiny and bloom early. The vast majority produce no flowers at all,

Flowers: 10–40 minute white blossoms, each 4–6 mm (0.15–0.2 in) wide, with 4 fine "petals" (2 are really sepals) and 4 jutting stamens; on an erect spike, 1.5–5.5 cm (0.6–2.2 in) long, above the leaves

Berries: About 4 mm (0.2 in) wide, initially hard, green, turning whitish and translu-cent, speckled with purple and finally deep red when ripe in autumn; each con-tains 1–4 seeds

Flower success rate of pro-ducing berries: 5–30%

Alias: Canada maianthemum, wild lily-of-the-valley, false lily-of-the-valley, May lily, beadruby, *le muguet, ma-iantheme du Canada, Maianthemum canadense*

Scientific name meaning: From the Latin *Maius,* meaning "May," the month the Romans named after Maia, the goddess of growth and spring; *anthemum* means "flower"

Anglo-Saxon name for May: *Thrimilcmonath,* "three-milk-month," referring to cows' ability to produce enough to be milked three times a day in mid-spring

Whereabouts: Mature upland mixed, deciduous and ever-green forests

Height: Avg. 5–15 cm (2–6 in), up to 25 cm (10 in)

Leaves: 2–10 cm (1–4 in) long, 1.5–5 cm (0.6–2 in) wide, shiny, pointed, smooth-edged, with notched base that hugs around stem; 2 or rarely 3 on flowering plants, just 1 on sterile plants; turn brown and wither back from tips in autumn

Stem: Usually changes angle where it joins with leaves on flowering plants

Roots: Shallow, stringy, creeping white rhizomes, up to 91 cm (4 ft) long, with many fine tan-coloured rootlets ending in rounded swellings in fall

Frequent diners: Solitary bees, bee flies and hover flies pollinate flowers; chipmunks, mice, hares, grouse and grey jays eat berries; slugs, leaf miner caterpillars nibble leaves

Traditional uses: Ojibway and Potawatomi used root in medicine for sore throats and headaches

Range: Throughout Ontario; also in all other provinces and territories except Nunavut

Companion plants: Bunchberry, moccasin flowers, violets, wintergreen, wood sorrel, twinflower, goldthread, red baneberry, Solomon's seal, starflower, blue bead lily

Lost lily status: Formerly considered a member of the lily family, recently reclassified, together with Solomon's seal and false Solomon's seal, into the new, separate "butcher's-broom" family, Ruscaceae

just a single leaf that rises a few centimetres above the ground. Though the lush little leaves carpet wide stretches of forest, they're so commonplace that they seem to go virtually unnoticed. Having been pre-formed in underground shoots during the previous growing season, tightly curled, pointed mayflower leaves burst straight up through the rotting leaves of the forest duff soon after the snow is gone. But unlike trout lilies in hardwood stands, which disappear from view in June, mayflower plants persist until the frosts of autumn.

Most mayflower shoots are clones, sprouting from networks of connected underground stems. Some colonies of loosely spaced, genetically identical plants can be up to six metres (20 feet) wide and 60 years old. Each single-leaved sterile plant is part of a team, sending energy to a select number of confrères growing in the best light and soil conditions. These lucky few are the breeders, sending up two or, less often, three leaves along a flowering stalk, which usually blooms in late May and June. Up close, the flowers resemble little globes with white antennae and give off a strong, sweet perfume. Now that Canada mayflower is no longer considered a lily, bending down to sample the fragrance need not evoke worries over the old English superstition that smelling lilies causes freckles.

About a month after starting to bloom, the flowers give way to hard, little, speckled green berries that ripen through the summer, becoming soft and deep red by fall. They're feasted upon by an assortment of birds and animals. The Ojibway called the plant *gunkisaehminuk*, "chipmunk berry." The bittersweet berries are edible to humans, but have been known to cause frequent trips to the privy.

A closely related plant that can be mistaken for the Canada mayflower at first glance is three-leaved **false Solomon's seal**. With longer, more upwardly pointing leaves and a sparser spike of flowers or berries, it most commonly grows amid the sphagnum of open or partially forested bogs and cedar swamps. A very close look also reveals the plant in flower has six tiny petals, while the Canada mayflower has four.

Number of *Maianthemum* **species native to Ontario:** 4

Number of *Maianthemum* **species worldwide:** 30

Also see: Chipmunk, Solomon's Seal, Trout Lily

CATTAIL
Nature's High-yield Stocks

Height: 1–3 m (3.3–10 ft)

Alias: Broad-leaved cattail, common cattail, swamp bulrush, reed mace, *la massette quenouille, Typha latifolia*

Whereabouts: Wet soil or water up to 80 cm (2.6 ft) deep in marshes, swamps, wet meadows, open ponds, calm bays and watersides

Flowers: Cylindrical, velvety female seed head, 10–15 cm (4–6 in) long, lime green in early summer, turns dark brown after pollination; spiky male pollen head above, 10–20 cm (4–8 in) long, dark green at first, turns yellow

Number of seeds per cattail: 117,000–268,000

Leaves: 1–2.5 cm (0.4–1 in) wide, up to 3 m (10 ft) long, pointed, like swords

Root content: 30% starch and sugars, 8% crude protein

Number of cattail-nesting Ontario bird species: More than 20

Cattail foods: Iroquois and Ojibway dried and pounded autumn roots into a sweet flour for bread and puddings, or cooked them like potatoes

Range: Southern Ontario to mid-boreal forest and southern James Bay; also in all other provinces and Northwest Territories

Cattails rise up in the richest habitats in the wilderness. Like other marsh plants, they are extremely efficient at filtering nutrients and even impurities from the water. Cattail root stocks have a nutrient content similar to rice and corn, but have a much higher yield. A Syracuse University project in the 1950s estimated cattails could provide up to 70 tonnes (77 tons) of dry flour per hectare (2.5 acres), far more than wheat, rye, oats or corn.

As winter nears, the plants suck all their nutrients back into the roots. They breathe air through dry, hollow stalks sticking up through the ice and water. In spring, the root stores are used to send up fresh green stalks, which rapidly overtake the previous year's pale, dead relics.

In June and July, the wind blows clouds of yellow pollen from the spikes that form above the familiar dense, velvety female seed heads, which look like big hotdogs on roasting sticks. Seeds emerge in fall and winter on fluffy fibres that travel far on wind, water or an animal's fur. Though tiny, they remain viable for up to five years if the marsh temporarily dries up. Once established, cattails spread like vines by sending out underground stems that establish circular colonies of clones around a parent plant. In ideal conditions, a single seed can produce a colony of almost 100 stalks within a year.

Number of native Ontario cattail species: 2

Number of cattail species worldwide: 10

Also see: Red-winged Blackbird, Muskrat, Wetlands

DOLL'S-EYES
Alluring Poison Berries

Berries: Large, oval, greenish at first, turning bright white, with a single black dot at tips, borne in a cluster on stout stalks that turn purple as berries ripen; several seeds tightly packed inside berries; very bitter and poisonous

Alias: White baneberry, necklace weed, white beads, white cohosh, whiteberry, whiteheads, snake root, grapewort, herb Christopher, *l'actee blanche, Actaea pachypoda*

Whereabouts: Deciduous and mixed forests

Scattered through hardwood forests of maple, beech and yellow birch, bunches of doll's-eyes stare boldly out from deep red stalks in August and September. The large, white, black-eyed berries command attention wherever they ripen. Yet, for all their allure, doll's-eyes are reputed to be deadly poisonous. They're also known as white baneberries, from the Old English word *bona,* meaning "killer."

Authorities don't agree on just how poisonous doll's-eyes are to humans. Few want to take the test themselves. A single berry is said to be so bitter it would discourage anyone to try another. Other reports put fatal dosages at two berries for a child and something above six for a previously hale and healthy adult. Mice, ruffed grouse and other animals seem to snap up the white fruits happily.

Ojibway women drank a tea made from doll's-eyes roots, also considered poisonous, to reduce heavy menstrual bleeding and cramps, while the men ate the root for stomach problems. They called the plant *weekizgum*, meaning "that which extracts." It may be that, as with other plants and fungi known to be deadly, Native practitioners using careful preparations distilled just enough toxin and turned it to beneficial use.

A close relative of doll's-eyes, **red baneberry** has large, bright red berries and is also said to be poisonous. It grows in small colonies, rather than singly, in mixed as well as deciduous forests. Both varieties of baneberry are perennial herbs, with purplish shoots rising from overwintering roots each spring.

Height: 30–90 cm (1–3 ft)

Flowers: A spike of small white flowers, composed mainly of stamens and stigmas, with petal-like sepals that fall off soon after opening in late May or June

Leaves: Compound, composed of 3 groups of 3–5 sharply pointed leaflets with large-toothed edges

Roots: Thick rootstock

Range: Southern Ontario to about Wawa and North Bay; also in Quebec and the Maritimes

FERNS
Descendants of Giant Tropical Trees

Lifespan: Up to 100 years for a colony, possibly up to thousands of years

Tallest Ontario fern: Ostrich fern (illustrated), up to 2 m (6.7 ft)

Smallest Ontario fern: Wall rue, usually about 6 cm (3 in)

Alias: Fiddleheads, *les fougères,* order Filicales

Name origin of *fern*: From proto–Indo-European *porno,* meaning "feather"

Spore casings: Many species have "fruitdots" containing spores on the undersides of fronds, others have separate sterile and markedly different fertile fronds or spikes bearing dense clusters of spore casings; spores travel on air currents

Number of spores produced by a single frond: Millions

Common wetland species: Sensitive, ostrich, royal, lady, New York, marsh, cinnamon, oak and crested shield ferns

Species of mainly deciduous forests: Maidenhair, bulblet, spinulose wood, intermediate wood, New York, Christmas, rattlesnake and silvery glade ferns

Ferns of rocky limestone areas: Maidenhair, speenwort, smooth cliffbreak, polypody, fragile, bulblet, marginal

One person's fiddlehead could be another's black gold – that is, if they live hundreds of millions of years apart. Today's ferns are the diminutive remnants of the Carboniferous period 300 million years ago, when giant, tree-sized ferns and horsetails dominated the Earth's first steamy jungles. The buried, fossilized material of those jungles – preserved from rotting by the acidic conditions of vast bogs and swamps – forms today's coal deposits.

Ferns appeared long before plants had developed flowers or seeds, reproducing instead by spores, like mushrooms. Ferns, however, are more advanced than algae, lichens, mosses and fungi, which depend on the slow diffusion of water and nutrients through their tissues to grow. Vascular canals, like veins, transport a fern's supply of water and nutrients much more quickly, allowing it to grow both higher and faster.

As the Earth's climate cooled, giant ferns perished in temperate zones, leaving behind only species that buried their woody trunks underground as horizontal stems, called rhizomes. The visible ferns that appear above the ground are the plant's leaves, called fronds. There are still some tree ferns in the tropics that reach heights of 25 metres (80 feet) and are easily mistaken for palm trees.

Collecting succulent ostrich fern fiddleheads is considered a rite of spring in many parts

Old European beliefs held that fern "seeds" were produced only on Midsummer's Eve and had the power to make people invisible and to open locked doors. No one has ever found a fern seed to test the theory. Fern spores are dustlike particles. Unlike a seed, which contains a minute, inflatable, rolled-up plant and a supply of protein to nourish it, a spore is a single cell. It grows by dividing after it has landed in a suitable site. After several weeks, it produces a tiny, heart-shaped plant called a prothallium, usually less than a centimetre (0.4 inches) wide, lying flat and close to the ground.

The prothallium is short-lived and, unlike its parent, reproduces sexually. As with primitive water plants, the underside of the leaf releases

shield, hart's tongue, walking and Clinton's ferns

Traditional remedies: The Ojibway boiled lady fern and sensitive fern into a tea for relieving pain and to help nursing mothers to produce more milk; fresh, moistened lady fern was also slapped onto scrapes and bruises to ease pain; Native people wore bracken ferns on their heads to ward off black flies, used rattlesnake fern in a poultice for snakebites and brewed maidenhair fern tea for respiratory ailments

Name for fern enthusiasts: Ferners or pteridologists

Self-proclaimed fern capital of Ontario: Owen Sound

Range: All Ontario; also in all other provinces and territories

Other spore-producing plants: Horsetails, club mosses, mosses, liverworts, quillworts, spike mosses

First appearance of vascular spore-producing plants: 360–400 million years ago

Number of Ontario fern species: 75

Number of fern species worldwide: 8,000–12,000

Also see: Mushrooms, Limestone, Wetlands

sperm, which travels through a film of rain or moisture to fertilize an egg cell on the same or another leaf nearby, which develops into a new tiny fern, drawing nutrients from the prothallium until it sinks its own roots. The rhizome that spreads underground sends up more fronds.

Ferns have evolved to occupy a wide range of habitats, though most prefer shady, moist conditions. Graceful, circular clusters, or "crowns" of various wood fern species are very common in most Ontario forests, from the diminutive, lacy bulblet ferns growing in rich, damp humus to the lofty, arching ostrich ferns (illustrated) in wet bottomlands. A few species, such as the thigh-high-canopy-forming bracken – the world's most widespread fern – settle both in forests and in dry, open expanses.

Many, including bracken, sensitive, bulblet and lady ferns, are browned and withered by the first frosts of autumn. Some wood ferns, though, as well as rock-loving polypody, remain green through the winter. But most produce new curled fiddlehead sprouts in spring. Collecting succulent ostrich fern fiddleheads is considered a rite of spring in many parts. Defence toxins, however, begin building up in all ferns as they sprout and authorities warn against eating large amounts of even the youngest fiddleheads.

GOLDENROD
Multi-tiered Insect Cities

And she's bound his wounds with the
    goldenrod, full fast in her arms he lay
And he has risen hale and sound with the
    sun high in the day.
  – Archie Fisher, "The Witch of the
    West-Mer-Lands"

Alien plants often dominate Ontario fields and
meadows, having arrived as part of the package
with European settlers, agriculture and the
clearing of forests. But come August, in the same
open spaces, native goldenrods steal the scene.
Though they are composites – sporting tiny
flowers on each flowerhead, like many aliens

Height: 20–200 cm
(8–80 in)
Tallest foreign goldenrod:
Subtropical species in
Florida reach 5.5 m (18 ft)
Alias: Woundwort, Aaron's
rod, blue mountain tea, *la
verge d'or, bouquets
jaunes,* genus *Solidago*
Flowers: Up to 2,000 tiny yellow flowerheads per stem,
each with numerous female
ray flowers around its edge
and at least 20 disk flowers
at its centre with both male
and female organs; numer-
ous flowerheads form a
plume, with those on top
blooming first
Blooming period: Late July
to late Sept.
Seeds: Minute, with fluffy fibres that carry them on the
wind; emerge from split,
dried flowerheads through
fall and winter; eaten by
many birds and mammals
Leaves and stem: Many different forms, depending on
species; both die back in autumn, though remain standing through winter
Roots: Some of the deepest
taproots of any native herb,
the Canada goldenrod
reaching 3.3 m (11 ft) below
ground in prairies; also
spreading horizontal
rhizomes
Development: Usually no
flowers produced in first
year. In second autumn, 4 or
5 rhizomes spread beneath
ground from stem base,
each sending up a new stalk

the following spring; colonies of clones may grow to several metres wide

Lifespan: More than 100 years for some colonies in the prairies

Dry meadow species: Canada (illustrated), grey, early and tall goldenrods

Forest edge species: Blue-stemmed, early, late and Canada goldenrods

Open forest species: Zigzag goldenrod

Shoreline species: Tall, Canada, grass-leaved and early goldenrod

Wetland and wet meadow species: Grass-leaved, bog, rough-stemmed and Canada goldenrod

Non-yellow goldenrod: Silverrod and upland white aster (actually a goldenrod), both with white flowers

Non-medical uses: Leaves brewed as tea substitute; flowers long used for home-made yellow dyes; rich, golden honey produced by goldenrod-addicted honey-bees; diviners once used stems to find water

Common residents: Ambush bugs, goldenrod beetles, goldenrod spiders, and the larvae of flies, moths, midges and tree-hoppers

Common visitors: Honeybees, bumblebees, monarch butterflies, paper wasps, hover flies, long-horned beetles, soldier beetles, praying mantises, *Formica* ants, downy

such as dandelions and daisies – goldenrods are as Canadian as Beaver McGee at centre ice. They spread rapidly by both roots and seeds, forming large colonies that hold their ground against foreign upstarts.

Yet, as with many wholesome native species, goldenrod has been denunciated, persecuted and uprooted. It is widely, and erroneously, reviled as a hay-fever-causing weed. In truth, goldenrod produces large, sticky grains of pollen that are picked up by insects rather than the wind. The real great hay-fever culprit is ragweed, a small, inconspicuous plant that also blooms in late summer and sends out vast clouds of dry, tiny, windborne pollen that finds its way to many an unhappy nose.

The castigation of goldenrod as a noxious weed is especially misguided given that its scientific name, *Solidago*, means "make whole" or "solid" in Latin, a tribute to its ancient use in healing wounds. The Ojibway called it *geezisomuskiki*, meaning "sun medicine." They, as well as many other Native nations and settlers after them, brewed the flowers into a tea for a wide assortment of ailments, from fevers and chest pains to ulcers, kidney problems, even excessive flatulence. The Ojibway also added the flowers to a pipe blend that was smoked to bring success in hunting, and applied the boiled roots as a poultice for burns and sprains. Many modern herbalists still consider goldenrod a panacea.

In recent years, goldenrod has even been used to heal the earth. It is planted, along with species such as poplar, cattail and duckweed, in polluted habitats because it has enzymes that break down organic toxins contaminating the soil and water.

Wherever they grow, goldenrods are of vital importance to an incredible assortment of tiny inhabitants, forming veritable multi-tiered cities. Offering vast quantities of nectar and pollen, the flowers dominate the attentions of bees, butterflies, wasps, moths, hoverflies and other pollinating insects during late summer. Meanwhile, goldenrod beetles and their larvae eat the plant's leaves, and tree-hoppers siphon off sap. Amid all the activity, predators such as ambush bugs, crab spiders and even praying mantises select from the bounty of inhabitants, like lions on the Serengeti. The offspring of at least one species of tree-hopper, however, enjoy the protection of organized bands of *Formica* ants, who in return sup on the waste sap exuded by the larvae.

Even in winter, when goldenrod stalks stand dry and lifeless, the young of many insects lie sleeping within the plant's derelict tissues. These winter quarters are created when small flies use their pointy ovipositors to inject eggs into goldenrod stems during the growing season. When a maggot hatches and begins nibbling at its natal chamber, the plant responds by rapidly constructing new tissue around the irritant, resulting in the characteristic spherical bulges, called "galls," found on many goldenrod stems. More oval-shaped galls are caused by minute moth caterpillars, while midge larvae create black blister-galls on leaves and bunchy, flowerlike galls at branch tips. Ambush bugs, midges and tree-hoppers, as well, leave their eggs in the overwintering leaves and stems.

To top it all off, gall-causing larvae often have company. Many other insect species specialize in taking advantage of the little gall forts created by

woodpeckers, juncos, sparrows and finches

Number of known gall-causing insects: About 2,000, 75% wasps or gnats

Other gall causers: Mites, nematodes, fungi, bacteria and viruses

Portion of plant galls that appear on leaves: 95%

Oldest fossil galls: More than 100 million years old

Gall ink: Aleppo galls from the Middle East have been used to make high-quality ink and dyes for more than 1,000 years, still used both for printing paper money and for tattoos

Common alien meadow species: Ox-eye daisy, dandelion, common buttercup, bird's-foot trefoil, silvery cinquefoil, toadflax, common St. John's wort, orange hawkweed, chicory, viper's bugloss, purple vetch, heal-all, mullein, knapweed, tansy

Common native composite meadow flowers: Asters, Joe-pye weed, yarrow, fleabane, pearly everlasting, black-eyed Susans, pussytoes, beggar's ticks, boneset, wild lettuce

Other common native meadow flowers: Milkweed, fireweed, evening primrose

Goldenrod range: All Ontario; also in all other provinces and territories

Number of goldenrod species native to Ontario: 30

Number of goldenrod species threatened or endangered in Ontario: 6
Number of goldenrod species worldwide: About 150, most in North America
Also see: Bees, Wasps and Hornets; Beetles, Moths

others. These insects are called inquilines, meaning, literally, "lodgers" in Latin. But before both homeowner and freeloader are ready to chew their way out of the gall and transform into adults, they may be joined by the worst lodgers of all, the parasitic larvae of ichneumon wasps and beetles, which feed upon the occupants themselves. Their world can also be shattered by the gall-probing beaks of downy woodpeckers in search of fresh grubs in the dead of winter. Ice fishers in need of bait sometimes resort to galls as well.

INDIAN PIPE
Ghostly Plant Without Chlorophyll

Deep in the darkest forest shade, where nary a green plant dares to venture, one may encounter a bowed, stunted ghoul. Appearing in small groups of what look like bizarre, emaciated fungi, Indian pipe is the custodian of the forest's inhospitable nether regions. Amazingly, it's actually a flower, though one that seems to have defected to the ranks of mushrooms. It survives by subversive means, getting the sunlight denied other forest-floor plants by stealing its energy from the roots of the light-hogging trees. Accordingly, it has no need for leaves and chlorophyll, the green cells that allow plants to capture sunlight and use its energy.

Flowers: White, waxy-looking, bell-shaped, 1.5–2 cm (0.6–0.8 in) long, formed by 5 overlapping petals, with 10 yellow stamens surrounding round white pistil inside; scentless; blooms June to Sept.

Alias: Ghost flower, ice plant, corpse plant, fairy-smoke, convulsion root, fitroot, eye-bright, Dutchman's pipe, convulsion weed, *le monotrope uniflore*, *Monotropa uniflora*

Whereabouts: Rich, acidic humus or mossy soil in deep

forest shade, especially beneath pines, spruce, fir, oaks;
black spruce bogs

Height: 10–20 cm (4–8 in),
rarely up to 30 cm (1 ft)

Seeds: Brown, dustlike, released from large, upright
capsules at top of stem

Stem: White or pale pink,
translucent; turning brown
and woody in autumn

Roots: Small, dense ball of
brittle brown rootlets matted
in fungal fibres

Companion plants:
Wintergreen, bunchberry

Range: Southern Ontario to
northern boreal forest; also
in all other provinces

**Only other monotrope
species:** Pinesap, also
found in Ontario

Also see: Moccasin Flower,
Mushrooms, Beech

Indian pipe, however, is no welcome convert in a collegial world of mushrooms. Rather than obtaining nourishment directly, its dense rootlets cluster around and parasitize fungal fibres of many common red and white mushrooms that acquire nutrients from tree roots.

The roots of other closely related plants in the heath family, such as shinleaf, pyrola and prince's pipe, maintain close, symbiotic bonds with certain kinds of fungi, fusing with their subterranean fibres and sending them photosynthesized energy in sugar compounds in return for moisture and soil nutrients collected by the fungi. Indian pipe somehow acquired the ability to tap into tree-root fungi as well, probably with "attracting" hormones that fool the fungi into fussing with it. Finding life easier as a parasite than as a symbiont, it discarded its green attire, today bearing only tiny, gauzy vestiges along its stem of what were once real leaves. Seeming to enter a realm of shades between plant and mushroom, Indian pipe acquired its strange, not-quite-mortal aspect.

As if its pallid, waxy appearance weren't enough, the plant bruises black when handled. If picked, it bleeds a thick, gooey liquid. The whole business seriously creeped out many 19th-century botanical writers, who denounced Indian pipe as "weird," "ghostly" and "degenerate."

Others saw dignity in the ghost flower. They found that once fertilized, it slowly, solemnly raises its head to stand straight up. The motion is noted in the plant's scientific name *Monotropa*, which means "one turn." Once out of its "pipe" posture, the plant becomes hard, tough and woody as it darkens to dusty brown or smoky black. From late summer through to spring, it remains standing, though now lifeless, gradually releasing dustlike seeds from slits in the pipehead capsule. But even as the plant lets its stem dry out, its roots form new flower buds, which push up as translucent, silvery sprouts early the following summer.

Native healers embraced the plant. They mixed its thick juice with water to use as an eye lotion and for colds and fevers. The dried root was also enlisted by 19th-century doctors to help cure fainting, epileptic fits and nervous disorders.

Indian pipe's sister plant, **pinesap**, is more rare, growing mainly in pine and evergreen woods, where it, too, parasitizes tree-root fungi. It is similar to Indian pipe but is pale yellow, orangish or sometimes tinted red and has several nodding flowers at the top of a stem, rather than just one.

Another, completely unrelated, plant that thrives without chlorophyll is, amazingly, an orchid, the spotted **coral-root**. Hoisting a spike of small and inconspicuous tubular flowers, coral-root's slender stem, up to 50 centimetres (1.6 feet) tall, is often a striking deep purple-red. Like Indian pipe and pinesap, it has densely clustered, coral-like roots, deriving all their energy and nutrients from fungi. However, the fungal victims get their food from decaying leaf mould rather than tree roots.

There are, as well, parasitic non-green plants that live off tree roots without the help of fungi. Calling little attention to themselves amid the crumpled fallen leaves at the foot of beech trees are slim, knobby, reddish-brown "twigs," growing about 30 centimetres (one foot) high. They're called **beechdrops**, and they attach themselves directly to the trees' roots. With a few, purplish-lined, ascending branches, they bloom fleetingly around late September with tiny, tubular brownish-purple-striped flowers.

JACK-IN-THE-PULPIT
The Transsexual Preacher

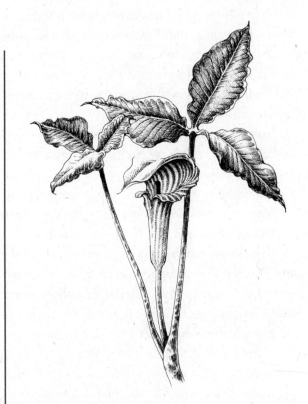

Flower: Green or purplish-brown hood, often striped, called a spathe, about 4–8 cm (1.5–3 in) long, surrounding a thick, club-shaped, green or purple spadix, 3–6 cm (1.2–2.4 in) long, which bears many tiny yellow male or green female flowers near its base; blooms mid-May to early June

Alias: Woodland jack-in-the-pulpit, Indian turnip, marsh turnip, pepper turnip, wild turnip, bog onion, brown dragon, starchwort, dragon root, devil's ear, cuckoo plant, priest's pintle, *le petit-prêcheur, Arisaema triphyllum*

Whereabouts: Rich, moist soil in broadleaf forests; swamp and bog edges

Height: Usually 30–40 cm (12–16 in), up to 90 cm (3 ft)

Berries: Scarlet, waxy, corn-kernel-shaped, about 1 cm (0.4 in) long, in a tight, oval cluster of up to more than 2 dozen; 1–3 seeds per berry

Leaves: 3 dark green, pointed compound leaflets, 1 set on male plants and usually 2 on females, on separate stems from flower; with wavy edges, pale green undersides

Roots: Bulbous, starchy rhizome up to 6 cm (2.4 in)

In the forest cathedral, jack-in-the-pulpit is a silent preacher, ministering to the more brightly coloured spring ephemerals. Wearing simple vestments of striped green, it may easily be overlooked at first. But the elegant, shade-loving flower holds secrets which, upon close inspection, prove to be as intriguing as its name.

The name comes from the plant's likeness to a figure, "Jack," standing in an antiquated church pulpit with a canopy (designed to project the preacher's voice). A modified leaf forms the hood-shaped canopy enclosing Jack, a thick column that pokes its head out from the top of the pulpit. The plant's name may actually mix the sacred and profane, since Jack was once a common nickname for the penis, while another name for the flower is priest's pintle – *pintel* being an Old English word for the male member.

Jack-in-the-pulpit's flowers are very tiny, growing in clusters hidden down in the pulpit around the base of the column. Overhead, the drooping canopy keeps rain from pooling in the pulpit and drowning the dwarfish flowers.

The pulpit's stately lines may guide flying insects to its centre. Thrips are common visitors, as are small fungus gnats perhaps mesmerized by the preacher's perfumed homily into believing the plant is a mushroom on which they can lay their eggs. But once inside, the insects are trapped by slippery, narrowing walls, forcing them down onto the floor of the pulpit. If they're lucky, it is a male plant and they can escape, covered with sticky pollen, by crawling out through a passage at the bottom of the pulpit. If they make the same mistake twice, though, and the next stop is a female plant, there is no way out, and they must remain there to pollinate the flowers. The sexual strategy leads some evolutionary entomologists to speculate that the plant may eventually evolve into a meat-eater, like pitcher plants or sundew.

Jack-in-the-pulpit begins life as a sterile plant with just a single three-parted compound leaf or as a male, with pollen-bearing flowers. But as soon as it stores up enough nutrients and energy, often when about three years old, the preacher has a sex change. Jack becomes Jill, a larger plant with female flowers. While the jack and pulpit of a male plant withers with its flowers, the female pulpit remains, protecting the

thick, with root filaments trailing from it; new rhizomes often form at the ends of roots, sending up clones of parent plant, forming colonies

First sign in spring: A green or purplish pointed shoot pushes up from the ground, unfolding its leaves when 20–30 cm (8–12 in) high

Lifespan: Maximum at least 25 years

Range: Southern Ontario to the southern boreal forest; also in Manitoba, Quebec, New Brunswick and Nova Scotia

Close Ontario relatives: Water arum, sweet flag, skunk cabbage, green dragon, arrow arum

World's largest arum: *Amorphophallus titanum*, with a spathe and spadix up to 3 m (10 ft) long

Number of arum species worldwide: Probably more than 3,500, mostly in tropics

Number of *Arisaema* species worldwide: More than 100

Also see: Doll's-eyes, Pickerelweed

fruits developing on the column, or "spadix," until late summer. Then the hood falls away to reveal a cluster of bright green berries. Later turning scarlet, the berries bag hungry birds, such as thrushes and wood ducks, who serve as flying seed-dispensers. But if a jack-in-the-pulpit is damaged or conditions change somehow to diminish the nutrients needed to produce berries, the plant may become male again. To complicate things further, the spadix of a large plant sometimes bears both male and female flowers.

While its flowers, leaves and stems wither and die with autumn's frosts, the plant survives winter by storing supplies in its rhizome, a small, bulbous underground stem just beneath the surface. This bulb also contains another of the jack-in-the-pulpit's secrets: minute, needle-shaped calcium oxalate crystals that if eaten immediately burn and blister the mouth severely. Jack-in-the-pulpit is, in fact, a member of the arum plant family, whose name derives from the Arabic word for fire. All other parts of the plant are also toxic, despite birds eating the berries. Even sap from handling jack-in-the-pulpit can cause skin irritation. Antihistamines and topical ointments or creams help relieve the irritation, while milk, cold liquids or ice in the mouth provide some soothing if the root or leaves are eaten.

JEWELWEED
Custom-made for Hummingbirds

Dangling like delicate orange earrings, sparkling in the dew, jewelweed flowers are the highlight of an exceptional plant. To start with, their colour, orange, is one of the rarest in the wild, outside of autumn. The plant's succulent stems and its leaves also seep a watery, orange-tinted juice when crushed. Native peoples and others have long rubbed the liquid on the skin for quick relief from insect bites, poison ivy, nettle stings, athlete's foot and general itching. Jewelweed juice has also been used to make yellow dye.

Unlike most forest plants, jewelweed lives only one year. Growing in dense patches on mucky ground, the plants' water-filled stems shoot up more than a metre (3.3 feet) in the space of a few weeks. They begin to bloom around mid-July and continue until frosts in September create expanding ice crystals that destroy the

Flowers: Intricate hanging, horn-shaped structures, 2.5–3 cm (1–1.2 in) long, orange, sometimes yellowish, speckled with rust red; top of flower cavity shows white pollen during male stage and pointed green pistil during female stage; cleistogamous buds 1–2 mm (0.04 in) long

Alias: Spotted jewelweed, spotted touch-me-not, orange jewelweed, snapweed, silver leaf, *l'impatiente du cap, le chou sauvage, Impatiens capensis*

Ojibway name: *Muklkeebug,* meaning "frog petal"

Whereabouts: Along creeks, ravine bottoms, shorelines, beaver meadows, hardwood and cedar swamps, marshes, low-lying soggy clearings

Height: 50–150 cm (1.6–5 ft)

Seeds: Pop out from green pods that are 1.5–2 cm (0.6–0.8 in) long

Leaves: 3–9 cm (1.2–3.6 in) long, thin, light green, with pointed ends and large-toothed edges, appearing particularly silvery when glistening with dew; temporarily wilting in hot weather

Stem: Shiny light green, sometimes mauve; succulent, translucent

Roots: Short, thin, pink, claw-like

Companion plants: Ostrich ferns, sensitive ferns, turtlehead, blue marsh violets, goldthread, marsh marigolds, jack-in-the-pulpit, raspberry, black currant, sweet flag, grasses

Frequent diners: Hummingbirds, bees, wasps, sphinx moths sip nectar; mice and ruffed grouse eat seeds; hares browse stems and leaves

Range: Most of Ontario, almost to the tree line; also in all other provinces

Number of *Impatiens* species native to Ontario: 2

Number of *Impatiens* species worldwide: 500–600, mostly in tropical Asia and Africa

Also see: Hummingbird, Violets

tender stems from within. While they flourish, their flowers' uncommon colour is perhaps key in flagging jewelweed's principal partner in survival, the ruby-throated hummingbird. Storing nectar deep inside conical spurs, the flowers are ideal vessels for the hummingbirds' needlelike bills and long, probing tongues. With its nose in the flower, a tiny hummer picks up pollen on its forehead and then cross-fertilizes the next receptive plant it visits. Bees and wasps also seek out jewelweed nectar, though they usually cheat the flowers by biting holes through the back of the spur and bypassing the sexual organs.

Jewelweed flowers' small seed pods feature the best known of all the plant's tricks

But plants robbed of all their nectar, without receiving another's pollen, can still produce seeds. Jewelweed, like a number of other Ontario species, has a backup system. Later in the summer, on its lower branches, it grows many very tiny flower buds that never open. Instead, they pollinate themselves internally. Called cleistogamous – "hidden marriage" – flowers, they have no nectar and require less energy for their production. The seeds they produce are genetic clones of a single parent, without the variation that makes cross-pollinated seeds more adaptable. But they ensure that another generation will get a chance at life. It's an important contingency given that jewelweed is only an annual. Where conditions are drier or otherwise more difficult, the plants produce greater numbers of closed flowers.

Regardless of how they are pollinated, fertilized jewelweed flowers develop small seed pods that feature the best known of all the plant's tricks. About a month after fertilization, a mere touch or even a strong wind will burst the ripened pods open, their seeds flying as far as two metres (seven feet). Seeds landing in water can be transported long distances to spread the plant. Mice and grouse eat any seeds they find on the ground. The pods' hair-trigger propensity to explode is the source both for jewelweed's other common name, touch-me-not, and of the scientific designation for its genus, *Impatiens*.

LICHENS
Two Organisms in One

Hard, brittle and dormant when dry, with a little rainfall lichens transform into a soft, spongy, glowing carpet, a delight to bare feet. A rocky open area can sport a riot of different lichen species, a veritable world unto itself. Deriving their sustenance from thin air, lichens are the hardiest of all "plants," though they are not really plants at all. They form the dominant ground cover in dense boreal forests, arctic tundra and sometimes even rocky deserts. Some survive more than a year without water. Others thrive around hot springs at temperatures above 200°C (392°F), while in Antarctica, 400 species flourish. Crustose lichens form a wafer-thin living layer over bare rock on the Canadian Shield, continuing a process of colonization that began hundreds of millions of years ago when plant life first edged its way from the sea onto sterile, barren land.

Lichens gained a foothold on dry ground through a unique symbiosis of two organisms in one. All lichens are combinations of fungal threads entwined around cells of algae. Both life-forms make up their own kingdoms of species, separate from plants or animals. The fungi provide shelter, shade and water-absorbent tissues for algae. The algae capture the sun's energy with their chlorophyll to make carbohydrates for both organisms from rainwater and carbon dioxide in the air. Although lichens have no roots, they stick to bare rock and produce acids that slowly break down stone, creating depressions to anchor themselves more securely. Mineral grains of broken rock gradually mix with past generations of decayed lichens, a process that created the world's first organic soil on land. As mosses and larger plants evolved, they took root in these pockets, expanding the soil base to eventually clothe the Earth in an ever-thickening mantle that sustains all terrestrial life.

Crustose lichens are the pioneers, clinging flat on rock, bark and soil and growing outwards in crusty rings. About half of Ontario's lichen species are in the crustose group. They grow very slowly. Colonies of light green map lichens on some Canadian Shield rockfaces date from the last retreat of the glaciers. Another type of crustose lichen grows along rocky waterlines, leaving even black tracings that mark the high-water point of lakes and streams.

Foliose lichens are also flat but are attached to rock, tree trunks or humus by small filaments only at their centre. Common species such as dog's tooth and waxpaper lichen often have

Portion of woodland caribou diet provided by lichens: Up to 70%

Other Ontario lichen-feeders: Eaten primarily in winter by moose, deer, northern flying squirrels, red-backed voles and spruce grouse; eaten in summer by bagworm and lichen moth caterpillars, springtails, barklice, snails, slugs and mites

Number of North American birds that use lichens for nesting material: 46

Lichen hammocks: Northern parulas build their nests hidden within clumps of old man's beard lichen hanging from tree branches

Lichen line: Because many tree lichens cannot live if buried in snow, the height of the snowpack in a forest is often distinctly marked, and observable in summer, by the point at which the lichens appear on trunks and branches

Lichenometry: The use of lichen colonies growing on rocks to date landslides, earthquakes and the retreat of glaciers from a given area, with the oldest colonies present often originating from shortly after the event; lichenologist Trevor Goward refers to lichens as the "minute hand of the geological clock of the north"

Date lichens were discovered to be a symbiosis of fungi and algae: 1867, by

Swiss botanist Simon
Schwendener

Doctrine of signatures:
Ancient belief that certain
plants are shaped like parts
of the body they can heal;
thus wispy old man's beard
lichen was used to treat
baldness, leafy lungwort
lichen for respiratory problems and dog's tooth lichen
for rabies

Range: All of Canada to the
high Arctic

**Earth's land surface on
which lichens are the
dominant vegetation:** 8%

**Date first land plants
emerged:** 400–430 million
years ago

**Portion of world's known
fungi species that form
lichens:** 20%

**Number of lichen species in
Ontario:** 700–800

**Number of lichen species
worldwide:** 15,000–20,000

Also see: Flying Squirrel,
White-tailed Deer,
Mushrooms

curled edges and leaflike lobes. Rock tripe grows abundantly in circular black or dark brown clusters on granite lakeshores and boulders. Crispy when dry, it becomes rubbery in the rain, with its underside like velvet.

A third group, fruticose lichens, is made up of three-dimensional, often intricately shaped, species. False pixie cups (illustrated) look like tiny trumpets. British soldiers (also illustrated) are little light green spouts topped with bold scarlet. Both are very common but less than a couple of centimetres (0.8 inches) tall. They often grow in rocky clearings or light shade, together with finely branched, silver-green rein-deer and shrubby coral lichens, which are both used as miniature bushes in dioramas and model railroad sets. Pale yellow-green old man's beard dangles in wispy strands from trees, especially old spruce, fir and jack pines. Old-growth forests in general have the greatest diversity of lichen species. Canadian naturalist-artist Aleta Karstad reports identifying 20 types of lichens on one climb up a white spruce, each occupying a different zone.

A lichen is named for the fungus rather than the alga in the pairing, because the fungal portion makes up about 95 per cent of the structure. More than one type of alga may also be present. Algae reproduce asexually, by cell division, within the lichen, while some fungi grow tube- or flask-shaped fruiting bodies that spread spores in the wind. The spores must land where the right kind of alga is already present in order for a new lichen to develop. But lichens reproduce mostly by fragmentation, with new colonies starting from broken-off pieces of old ones or from special powdery sheddings of fungal threads rolled with a few algae cells, like minute balls of lint.

Instead of dying when there is no water, lichens simply go dormant, often appearing dead. When it does rain, some species can hold up to 30 times their dry weight in water, which in turn can be absorbed by other plants, along with the nutrients it contains. But because they are designed to maximize water retention and do not lose any tissue during the cold months, lichens can't filter out air pollutants. Accumulated toxins in their tissues soon kill them, which is the reason there are few species in urban areas and why lichens are used by biologists as biomonitors. Lichens, however, are highly resistant to radiation. Rapid accumulation of radioactive fallout by Scandinavian lichens after the Chernobyl nuclear accident in 1986 led to the cull of thousands of reindeer, which feed primarily on lichens in winter.

Lichens' own natural, bitter acids make them unpalatable to humans. When food was scarce, however, Native people and northern explorers sometimes resorted to eating rock tripe and various other species in soups and stews, neutralizing the acids by boiling. Native people also found partially digested lichens from the stomachs of slain caribou much easier to eat. Many historians even believe that the manna that nourished the biblical Israelites in the Sinai may have been greyish-white lichens that are sometimes blown from rocky areas into the desert lowlands. There are historical accounts of these lichens piling up to 15 centimetres (six inches) deep over wide areas and feeding large numbers of people and livestock. Two species are still eaten by local Bedouins.

Lichens were also used in antiquity to produce soft-coloured dyes and medicine. The word *lichen* is taken from the Greek term for "leprous," both for its scaly appearance and because it was used to treat the disease. In North America, Native people used reindeer lichen to treat fevers, coughing, convulsions and jaundice. Natural antibiotics produced by lichens for protection against microscopic grazing organisms have been extracted and used by humans in modern times. Lichens also provide fibres used in clothing, unique chemicals for cosmetics and stabilizing perfumes and the dye used in litmus paper.

MOCCASIN FLOWER
June's Pre-eminent Forest Orchid

Flower: Pink, with 2 narrow, inconspicuous upper petals and 1 large, specialized lower petal curling inward to form a hollow sack, about 5 cm (2 in) long

Alias: Pink lady's slipper, stemless lady's slipper, squirrel's shoes, nerve root, old goose, two-lips, Indian moccasin, *le sabot de la vierge, Cypripedium acaule*

Orchid name origin: From *orkhis*, Greek for "testicle," referring to the shape of roots of some species

Rising from carpets of fallen pine needles, moss and lichen, moccasin flowers are the standout beauties of June, the pre-eminent orchids of the Canadian Shield. Though coming in many varieties, most orchids are like precious gems, transfixing but all too rare to behold. Moccasin flower is the bountiful exception, blooming generously in small patches throughout mixed and evergreen forests.

Like other orchids, moccasin flower is highly specialized, near the summit of high-tech wildflower development. When it blooms from late May through June, the flower's beautiful lower petal curves inward to form a large hollow chamber, like a slipper. This is called an insect-ambush design. Most often, it's a bumblebee queen – before her first batch of offspring pupate and take over her foraging duties – that's attracted to the flower's splash of pink and fragrance. Pushing through the long slit where the two curled lips meet at the front of the flower, the bee is sadly surprised when she gets inside. There is little or no nectar to reward her efforts, and the front doors do not bend backwards to let her out. There is light, however, coming from a pair of openings at the top of the flower, which the bee follows to escape. Precisely placed stamens deposit a glob of pollen on the queen's back on her way out through the narrow passage.

Though the ungratified bee is unlikely to be drawn into a nearby moccasin flower in the same colony, she may eventually bumble into a distant unrelated one, with the pollen still stuck on her back, and cross-fertilize it.

The whole process is still a long shot, dependent on limited encounters with forgetful bees. Studies show that in some areas, only about two to 10 per cent of moccasin flowers are fertilized each year. They play the odds, by being very long-lived and by producing tens of thousands of seeds that spread like dust in the wind when their lucky number comes up. They often take a well-deserved break the following year by failing to bloom or even remaining dormant beneath the ground. Moccasin flowers also propagate themselves by spreading runners that send up more flowers, creating small colonies.

Orchid seeds are much smaller than those of all other flowering plants, lacking a well-formed embryonic seedling or the significant store of

Meaning of *Cypripedium*: Roughly, "Aphrodite's slippers," from one of the Greek goddess of love's titles, Kypria, owing to her reputed birthplace in Cyprus, and *perido,* a general reference to footwear

Moccasin flower designation in Iroquois lore: The whip-poor-will's shoes

Whereabouts: Acidic, sandy soil in coniferous and mixed forests, especially beneath pines, and around bog edges; sometimes on oak ridges or in birch-aspen stands

Height: 30–40 cm (12–16 in)

Leaves: 2 large, pointed leaves, 10–20 cm (4–8 in) long, attached near the base of flower stem; shiny, dark green with parallel veins

Seeds: 50,000–60,000 produced by a single plant in a green capsule, 4–5 cm (1.6–2 in) long, with 3 ribs, which splits in autumn to release seeds to wind

Roots: Dense, numerous strands radiating from base of plant

Lifespan: Avg. 24 years for mature plants

Companion plants: Bunchberry, wintergreen, blueberry, trailing arbutus, fringed polygala, violets, bearberry, leatherleaf, bog orchid

Pollinators: Bumblebees, leafcutting bees, mining bees

Folk medicines: Roots used as a sedative, to calm nerves, to relieve headaches and to treat tremors, epilepsy, fever and hysteria

Range: Southern Ontario to mid-boreal forest; also in all other provinces except British Columbia

Accolades: Official flower of Prince Edward Island and New Hampshire

Edible orchids: Seedpods of several closely related tropical species are the source of vanilla

Number of orchid species native to Ontario: 60

Number of orchid species worldwide: 17,500–35,000 (much debate between species "lumpers" and "splitters" among taxonomists)

Portion of the world's flowering plants that are orchids: 7–10%

Portion of orchid species at risk or threatened with extinction worldwide: 25–33%

Also see: Bees, Wasps and Hornets; Indian Pipe, Mushrooms, White Trillium

food that constitutes the largest portion of most seeds. Instead, upon germination, they must link with the minute threads of a symbiotic fungus that provides them with the nutrients and water they need to survive. In return, the plant sends the fungus sugars produced through photosynthesis after it sprouts leaves. Growth is slow at first. The moccasin flower often remains unseen as a minuscule root bulb for its first three or four years before sending up its first leaf, and takes nine to 16 years to produce its first blossom. Once established, however, a colony may live as long as the forest.

All orchids are highly specialized for their own niche, forming partnerships with specific pollinators and fungi. In regularly sprayed forest plantations, few moccasin flowers survive the disappearance of bumblebees. Charles Darwin, recognizing in orchid diversity an ideal model for explaining how natural selection works, wrote an entire book on them as the sequel to his earth-shaking *Origin of Species.* The multitude of ways orchids are pollinated by insects, he concluded, "transcend in an incomparable manner the contrivances and adaptions which the most fertile imagination of man could invent." Or as Shakespeare before him wrote, "There are more things in heaven and earth . . ."

MUSHROOMS
Tying the Forest Together

Late-season rains summon the hidden kingdom of fungi to the surface of the forest in a profusion of form and colour. Mushrooms, with their intricate inner structures, develop in a matter of days. Just as yeast, one type of fungus, makes bread rise, so minute, rain-saturated fungal filaments grow at a phenomenal rate, intertwining and merging like animated strands of Plasticine. Most mushrooms flourish only long enough to produce and disperse their spores, perhaps a week or so, before decomposing into pulp. Some of the smaller species last just a few hours.

Bracket fungi, or polypores, on the other hand, persist for weeks, months or years. Rows of flaky-thin turkey tail on fallen logs are usually hard and dry through the seasons but become rubbery after rainfalls, the moisture sharpening their sand-and-rust concentric rings to resemble

Ontario's biggest mushroom: Giant puffball, up to 50 cm (20 in) wide and 22 kg (48.5 lb)

Number of spores or microscopic fungal colonies in 1 g (0.03 oz) of soil: 300,000–3 million

Number of spores in a single mushroom: Millions to billions

Average spore diameter: 0.015 mm (0.0006 in)

Length of time spores can remain dormant: Up to 20 years

Rate of growth: Under ideal warm, moist conditions, a new fungus can sprout several kilometres of filaments in a few days

Mushroom sex: Strands of two fungi grow and fuse together, uniting nuclei of the opposite sex to create a reproductive, spore-producing organism

Fairy rings: Rings of mushrooms or dead grass left in fields by mushrooms produced by a spreading central underground fungus; usually less than 10 m (33 ft) wide, one 700-year-old fairy circle in France is more than 1 km (0.6 mi) across; a large ring near Ottawa once garnered international attention as the possible site of a UFO landing

Fairy steps: Long-lasting, woody bracket fungi on trees

Mushroom responsible for most Ontario poisonings: Fly agaric (illustrated)

Other common poisonous mushrooms: Poison pie, destroying angel, red-tinged parasol, death cap; most have gills on the undersides of their caps

Number of poisonous mushroom species in Ontario: More than 40

Origin of "toadstool": Folklore held that the whitish flakes on the caps of fly agaric mushrooms were poisonous warts left by toads after sitting on the mushroom

Fly agaric name origin: In Europe, bowls of milk with pieces of the mushroom were left out to poison house flies

Lifespan of underground portion of fly agaric organism: Maximum more than 100 years

Portion of Ontario mushrooms that are mycorrhizal, symbiotic with trees and plants: About 15%

Mycorrhizal name origin: From Latin *myco*, "fungus," and Greek *rhiza*, "root"

Common Ontario mycorrhizal mushrooms: Fly agaric, destroying angel, boletes, *Tricholoma*, *Hebeloma*, *Inocybe* and *Laccaria* species

Most expensive mycorrhizal fungi: Edible truffles from France and Italy, sold for up to $4,000/kg (2.2 lb)

Number of edible Ontario mushroom species: More than 130

the fanned tail feathers of their namesake gobbler. Artist's conk, a thick woody polypore that grows on live trees, can grow to more than 50 centimetres (1.6 feet) wide. Banded grey and brown on top, its smooth white underside stains dark brown where scratched and has long been used for handicraft etchings.

Mushrooms and tree-clinging polypores are only the external, spore-producing, fruiting bodies of extensive fungal organisms. Aside from tree roots, networks of microscopic fungal fibres comprise an estimated 90 per cent of the subterranean biomass in forests. Fungal threads, called hyphae, weave through every nook and cranny of the upper soil of most habitats, forming a mesh on the undersides of decaying leaves, intertwining with roots and entering rotting logs, live trees, dead animals and droppings – an immense living web literally tying everything together. A thimbleful of soil can have two kilometres (1.2 miles) of microscopic fungal strands running through it.

The world's biggest known fungus, a single honey mushroom organism in Washington state, has a network of fibres covering about six square kilometres (2.3 square miles), sprouting mushrooms throughout. In a Michigan hardwood forest, the network of another honey mushroom – a golden-brown edible species that also grows in Ontario – is estimated to weigh more than 100 tonnes (110 tons) and be at least 1,500 years old. Fungal networks are like veins and capillaries in the soil, keeping ecosystems alive. Mushrooms and other fungi cannot produce chlorophyll, so they have to get their energy from plants. The great majority are decomposers.

Latching onto dead vegetation to reclaim nutrients back into the life cycle, fungal strands secrete enzymes that dissolve the organic material into food molecules they can absorb. A succession of different fungus species is usually involved in breaking down the sugars, cellulose, lignins and hemicellulose that form leaves, wood and other organic material, like the processes of a pulp mill breaking down wood fibre.

About 90 per cent of all dry vegetable material is consumed by decomposers rather than by herbivores, and 80 to 90 per cent of the energy from decaying organic matter goes to fungi and bacteria. Mushrooms are especially abundant in Ontario's coniferous forests, where the acidic soil and thick litter layer are inhospitable to many bacteria. Without fungi and bacteria, all the carbon required for life would become locked up in a growing layer of dead material that would never break down. Life would peter out within a few decades.

Some mushrooms and other fungi are parasites, rather than decomposers, responsible for most plant and many insect diseases. Many others, however, engage in an interspecies chemical trading network with 95 per cent of all plants and trees. By entwining their filaments around rootlets, these mycorrhizal fungi transfer water and nutrients, most notably nitrogen and phosphorus, to trees and plants. In return, trees and plants pass about 10 per cent of their high-energy sugars, created through photosynthesis, on to the fungi. Fossil evidence of the relationship dates back 400 million years. A single spruce or fir tree can have 30 or 40 different mycorrihizal species attached to its roots. In effect, the

Edible-mushroom nutrients: Folic acid, vitamins D and B7

Puffball scientific name origin: *Lycoperdon* is Latin for "wolf flatulence," after the clouds of dustlike spores sent up by bursting puffballs

Spore dispersal: By wind, rain, insects and mushroom-eating animals

Most important animal dispersers of spores: Mites, both on their bodies and in their droppings

Pungent-fungi spore spreaders: Northern flying squirrels sniff out and eat the underground fruiting bodies of some mycorrhizal fungi; flies are attracted to the rancid-meat smell of slimy stinkhorn fungi

Mushrooms that glow in the dark: Jack o'lantern, luminescent panellus, honey mushroom (only its fibre network)

Meat-eating fungi: Some species, such as the large, edible oyster mushroom, a wood-rooting fungus, use looped strands to snare roundworms or paralyze them with toxic drops, afterwards secreting enzymes to digest them

Amount of carbon returned to the air by microorganisms accounted for by fungi: 13%

People who study mushrooms: Mycologists

People who fear mushrooms: Mycophobes

People who are addicted to mushrooms: Mycophagists
Other forms of fungi: Yeasts, moulds, mildew
First appearance of fungi in ancient oceans: Probably about 2.5 billion years ago
Number of known Ontario mushroom species: More than 1,100
Number of other Ontario fungi species with fruiting bodies visible to the naked eye: Probably more than 4,000
Estimated number of fungi species worldwide: At least 1.5 million, more than 100,000 named
Also see: Yellow-bellied Sapsucker, Flying Squirrel, Indian Pipe, Lichens, Moccasin Flower, Beech, Tamarack, White Birch

fungi are middlemen that connect all living things beneath the ground, even transporting important materials from one plant to another and producing chemicals that protect trees from microbial diseases and parasitic fungi species.

Fungi also manufacture a stew of other chemicals for their own protection and competition. Some produce antibiotics to make it difficult for bacteria and other fungi to grow near them. In 1928 in Britain, Alexander Fleming isolated one of these substances from the *Penicillium* mould and produced the first modern medical antibiotic, penicillin.

Defence chemicals are probably the active ingredients in most poisonous mushrooms, known as toadstools. Ancient shamans and oracles learned ways of taking small doses of toxic mushrooms to achieve a state of ecstasy and enter the spirit world. The Roman writer Seneca called such mushrooms "voluptuous poison." Fly agaric (illustrated), the speckled mushroom depicted in *Alice in Wonderland* and many other children's storybooks, was used ritually throughout much of Asia and Europe and is also common in Ontario. Soma, the sacred elixir of Indo-European peoples more than 4,000 years ago, is believed to have been made from a deadly mushroom, possibly fly agaric, that grew on the steppes of central Asia. It induced a battle rage among warriors that made them fearless and heedless of pain. Many of the rites involving wine in Christian denominations come from the soma ceremony, via Zoroastrianism in ancient Iran.

PICKERELWEED
Watery Beds of Purple Beauty

Rising in dense swathes from quiet, shallow, muddy waters under full sun, pickerelweed is a joy for human and beast alike. The Ojibway called the aquatic beauty *kinozhaeguhnsh,* "the pike's plant," because the great-fanged fish often lurks amid the plant's submerged tangled stems, waiting to ambush its prey. The English version became the plant's common name, *pickerel* originally being another name for pike, as well as for walleye.

Though colonies of pickerelweed may cover hundreds of square metres, they are often populated by clones of the same plant, replicating

Flowers: Small, bluish-purple, vase-shaped, many densely clustered on a vertical spike up to 10 cm (4 in) long

Alias: *La pontederie condée, Pontederia cordata*

Whereabouts: Up to 1 m (3.3 ft) deep in clear water of muddy-bottomed streams and sheltered lakesides; often around outlets or inlets

Height: 30–120 cm (1–4 ft) high, usually reaching 30–60 cm (1–2 ft) above water

Leaves: Arrow-shaped, 5–25 cm (2–10 in) long, glossy, succulent, 1 per plant, on separate stalk attached at base of main stem underwater

Stem: Green, thick, erect, though often snaking, filled with air chambers

Seeds: 1 per flower, covered by a ridged jacket about 6 mm (0.25 in) long

Companion plants: Arrowhead, water lilies, cattail

Common visitors: Pike, ducks, kingbirds, turtles, bullfrogs, muskrats, deer

Range: Southern Ontario to about Temagami, and in Thunder Bay area; also in Quebec and Atlantic provinces

Number of *Pontederia* species native to Ontario: 1

Number of *Pontederia* species worldwide: 25

Also see: Pike, Cattail, Wetlands

itself by rapidly spreading rootstocks rather than by setting seed.

Each pickerelweed blossom remains open for a single day, with the multiple-flowered spire gradually blooming from bottom to top between July and early September. The finished flowerheads droop down to let their seeds fall to the water. Those not eaten by ducks or muskrats may find their way to another ideal spot where they can sink into the muck and generate a new colony. New leaves emerge on the surface around late May or early June, and many are munched upon by deer and muskrats.

POISON IVY
"Leaves of Three, Let It Be"

Three pointed leaves, or leaflets, are always cited as the warning identification of poison ivy, a rare northern member of the tropical cashew group, but there are many plants, such as raspberry, that feature leaflets growing in threes. Further complicating the issue, poison ivy is a shape shifter. It can grow as herblike ground cover, a low woody shrub or – in areas along Lake Ontario, Lake Erie and the lower Ottawa Valley – a vine running along the ground or up trees, with long rootlets clinging to bark crevices. The shiny, waxy green leaflets themselves may be wide or narrow, smooth-edged, toothed or sometimes

Leaves: Branching into 3 slightly asymmetrical, pointed leaflets, each 5–15 cm (2–6 in) long, with the two lower leaflets meeting close together, separated from the third by a small space; edges highly variable, often with a slight notch and/or a few irregular teeth or smooth; unfold reddish or purplish in May or early June, shiny green in summer, bright red in early fall, yellow in shaded areas

Amount of poison-ivy resin needed to cause a rash: As little as 1 nanogram (1 billionth of a gram), but usually about 100 nanograms

Remedies for relieving itching: Soap and water, calamine lotion, wet compresses of equal parts whole milk and ice water, baking soda in cold water, plain cold water, juice from crushed jewelweed stems

Alias: Poison creeper, markweed, three-leaved ivy, climbing sumac, picry, climath, poison vine, *l'herbe à la puce, Toxicodendron radicans*

Whereabouts: Forest gaps and edges, along paths, stream banks, open woods, meadows, islands, swamps, rocky ridges

Height: Shrub form usually 10–80 cm (4–31.5 in); vine form up to 15 m (49 ft)

Flowers: Tiny, waxy, greenish white, clustered along a stem 5 cm (2 in) long beneath leaves; blooming June to July; pollinated by bees

Berries: White or dull greenish yellow, about 5–6 mm (0.2 in) wide, dry, each containing 1 seed; in a cluster; appear in mid- or late July, some remaining on plant all winter; eating berries can cause severe irritation to digestive system and even death

Roots: Long, woody, spreading rhizomes, running just

slightly lobed. They tend to droop in spring but straighten up later in the summer. In the cluster of three, the two lower leaflets meet close together, while the middle one is separated from them by a little space. In its shrub form, poison ivy often grows in dense patches, in which it spreads quickly by underground runners.

All of a poison-ivy plant's tissues contain a pernicious oil, called urushiol, that can cause a painfully itchy rash, usually within a day or two of contact. Beadlike blisters often follow a couple of days later. The reaction usually lasts less than two weeks, disappearing as the affected skin is lost in the normal process of shedding.

Even in winter, when it has lost its leaves, the plant's blackened twigs and white berries are hazardous. Sweet-smelling smoke and vapour from burning poison-ivy branches can also cause the rash and inflame respiratory passages. The oil can remain active on pets' fur or on shoes and unwashed clothes for weeks or even years. One botanist got a rash after examining dried, 100-year-old leaf specimens. Little wonder urushiol was once used as the base to make indelible ink. The oil derives its name from the Japanese word for lacquer, *urushi,* made for more than 4,000 years from the Japanese lacquer tree, a sister species in the same genus as poison ivy.

Depending on the dose, it can take minutes or hours for the resin to bond with the skin. It can sometimes be washed off with soap and water before that happens. Rubbing the juice of crushed jewelweed leaves and flowers – which often grow near poison ivy – immediately after contact is an Ojibway and folk remedy that seems to work for some people.

Not everyone is affected to the same degree. Somewhere between 15 and 50 per cent of people have no reaction at all. Others may acquire only a mild itch. Lighter-skinned people are more prone to react than those with dark complexions. But any one person's susceptibility may change with time, depending on her or his body chemistry, diet and exposure to the sun. The chance of an allergic reaction generally increases with repeated contact.

There's actually nothing toxic about poison ivy. Humans bring the trouble on themselves with a defence reaction by their immune systems. Most animals don't seem to be bothered by it at all. Hares, deer and mice eat the leaves and stems with relish. Many species of birds and rodents gorge on the shrub's berries with no ill effects, spreading its seeds in their droppings. Poison-ivy leaves exposed to sunlight turn bright red in autumn, like their close sumac relatives, literally waving a red flag to migrating birds that berries are available below to fuel their flights.

below the ground, send up new plants, establishing clonal colonies

Frequent diners: Berries eaten by robins, crows, starlings, chickadees, woodpeckers, juncos, catbirds, yellow-rumped warblers, phoebes, white-throated sparrows, purple finches, ruffed grouse, wild turkeys

Closest Ontario relatives: Poison sumac and other sumacs that are not poisonous

Range: Southern Ontario to about Cochrane and Kenora; also found in all other provinces except island of Newfoundland

Also see: Cedar Waxwing, Jewelweed

SOLOMON'S SEAL
Mystically Marked Herbal Healer

Flowers: White or greenish white, bell-shaped, 1–1.5 cm (0.4–0.6 in) long, usually hanging in pairs, sometimes single or in threes, beneath arching stem

Berries: Bluish-black, containing several seeds

Alias: Hairy Solomon's seal, true Solomon's seal, conquer-John, *le sceau-de-Salomon à deux fleurs, Polygonatum pubescens*

Ojibway name: *Nauneebidaeodaekin,* meaning "those which grow together hanging"

Scientific name meaning: *Polygonatum* is Latin for "many kneed," in reference to the zigzag joints of the stem;

Early Greek writers named the Solomon's seal of the Old World after the mysterious circular scrawlings resembling Hebrew letters on its thick rootstock. Legend held that they were from the ring of King Solomon, marking the root for its medicinal powers. A long tradition esteemed the wise King Solomon as the first learned botanist because the Bible mentions his fascination with trees of all kinds. Judging from the fabled number of great cedars of Lebanon used to build his temple in Jerusalem, around 950 BCE, his interest in trees might well have stemmed more from an enthusiasm for construction.

In truth, the "Hebrew letters" are scars, marking where each year's stem has risen from the plant's perennial root. The rhizome, though, has indeed long been used for treating bruises, stomach aches, broken bones and troublesome complexions. Similarly, many Native groups on this continent employed roots of the closely related North American Solomon's seal as a poultice for bruises, sores, wounds and black eyes. The Ojibway brewed the roots into a tea to treat coughs and inhaled the steam from a preparation that was placed on hot stones. The Iroquois ate the root raw, cooked or pounded into flour.

False Solomon's seal is easily distinguished by its prominent plume of frothy, tiny white flowers

Solomon's seal's graceful, arching stems rise from the ground in May, their pointed leaves unfolding to reveal tiny pairs of bell-like flowers dangling in a long row below them. Many continue blooming into June and early July. After they are pollinated by bees, the flowers yield bluish-black berries later in the summer. The berries are eaten by birds, which spread the seeds in their droppings.

A distant relative – in the same family but a separate genus – **false Solomon's seal**, looks very similar, with the same zigzag, arching stem and alternating pointed leaves. The two plants sometimes grow side by side and bloom around the same time. False Solomon's seal is easily distinguished by its prominent plume of frothy, tiny white flowers at the end of its stem – hence its other name, Solomon's plume. The flowers have

pubescens means "hairy," after the fine hairs lining veins on the leaf bottoms
Whereabouts: Upland hardwood forests, often mixed with white pine; hardwood swamps
Height: 50–100 cm (1.6–3.3 ft)
Leaves: 5–15 cm (2–6 in) long, 1.5–7.5 cm (0.6–3 in) wide, with conspicuous veins, stalkless, pointed at both ends; pale bottoms; turning yellow in autumn
Roots: Deep, 1–2 cm (0.4–0.8 in) thick, knotted, white rhizome
Companion plants: Trout lilies, Canada mayflowers, blue bead lilies, violets, rose twisted-stalk, wild sarsaparilla, evergreen wood ferns, foamflowers
Range: Southern Ontario to Lake Temiskaming and Batchawana Bay, and in southern portion of northwestern Ontario; also in Quebec, New Brunswick and Nova Scotia
Number of true Solomon's seal (*Polygonatum*) species native to Ontario: 2
Number of true Solomon's seal species worldwide: About 20
Also see: Canada Mayflower, Wild Sarsaparilla

a disagreeable odour and produce pale, purple-dotted green berries, which weigh down the tips of the arching stems. By late summer, the berries soften, shrink somewhat and turn bright red.

Rose twisted-stalk also bears a strong resemblance to both true and false Solomon's seal but is a member of the lily family. Unlike the other two plants, its wavering stem actually divides into several arching branches. In late May and June, it blooms with small, flared, pink flowers hanging from beneath its leaves. Soft, translucent red berries ripen in summer and are said to have a mild cucumber flavour.

TROUT LILY
Early Spring's Green Mantle

The old year's cloaking of brown leaves, that
    bind
The forest floor-ways, plated close and true –
The last love's labour of the autumn wind –
Is broken with curled flower bud white
    and blue
In all the matted hallow, and speared through
With thousand serpent-spotted blades
    up-sprung,
Yet bloomless, of the adder-tongue.
    – Archibald Lampman, "April"

In early spring, the first signs of growth on the
hardwood forest floor are usually the pointed,

Number of trout lily plants per m² (11 sq. ft) in broadleaf forests: 400 common, up to 1,100

Flowers: 3–3.5 cm (1.2–1.4 in) wide, nodding, with 3 backward-curving yellow petals with a purple stripe on the back of each, and 3 petal-like, deeper yellow sepals curving back even more; 6 orange or yellow stamens and a green pistil at centre

Alias: Dogtooth violet, yellow adder's tongue, fawn lily, yellow lily, yellow bells, yellow snowdrop, rattlesnake

tooth, rattlesnake violet, yellow snake's tongue, lamb's
tongue, snake root, *l'ail
doux, Erythronium
americanum*

Ojibway name:
Numaegbugoneen, mean-
ing "sturgeon leaf"

Whereabouts: Rich, moist soil
in deciduous and sometimes
mixed forests

Height: 10–25 cm (4–10 in)

Leaves: Shiny, green, mottled
with purple-brown or grey,
10–20 cm (4–8 in) long, 2–
4 cm (0.8–1.6 in) wide, tapered at top and bottom,
with smooth edges and parallel veins; cool to the touch;
just 1 on non-flowering
plants, 2 growing from the
base of flowering stems

Stem: Light green, slightly
leaning, extending 10–
23 cm (4–9 in) straight
below ground to bulb

Roots: Older corms brown
and scaly, young ones white,
thin and pointed, like a dog's
canine tooth

Seeds: Contained within oval
green pod

**Plant biomass created by
trout lilies each spring:** Up
to 165 kg/ha (175 lb/acre)

Past medicinal uses:
Poultice from leaves used to
treat skin disease, ulcers and
tumours; parts of plant also
ingested to induce vomiting

Range: Southern Ontario to
about Wawa and Lake
Temiskaming; also found in
Quebec, New Brunswick
and Nova Scotia

tightly rolled, purple leaves of trout lily, also called adder's tongue, poking up en masse through the previous year's brown fallen leaves. With patches of snow still on the ground nearby, the scene resembles a rolling medieval battlefield with countless thousands of Lilliputian spears hoisted high. As they unfurl, the leaves – mottled like the skin of a brook trout – transform the ground into a transitory sea of green, speckled here and there with yellow clumps of trout lily flowers. The glory is short-lived. As soon as green spreads to the treetops, it drains from the ground, the lily leaves fading and dying as they're cut off from the sun.

In truth, many trout lily colonies are as old as the same sugar maples, beech and yellow birch trees that shade them out every June. After its leaves crumble, a trout lily plant resumes its life deep underground, May's captured sunlight fuelling it for the next 10 months. Its bulb, or corm, is the plant's powerhouse and factory. After taking a summer siesta, it kicks into operation in late August. The next spring's leaves and flowers are formed in tightly packed buds on shoots that push towards the surface through autumn and winter. Trout lilies also spread runners up to 25 centimetres (10 inches) through the soil to create new bulbs. These cloned corms send up their own leaves in spring. The process repeats itself year after year, decade after decade, forming extensive subterranean networks that help hold the soil together. Some are up to 300 years old.

More than 99 per cent of trout lily corms produce just one leaf. As the colony spreads ran-domly, eventually some bulbs grow in choice spots with enough light, moisture, nutrients and shelter to support flowers. Still, it takes a seed or new corm in a good location at least five years to flower. Most, in fact, take seven or more years, producing bigger leaves each growing season and pushing deeper in the soil until the bulb is 10 to 20 centimetres (four to eight inches) below the surface. Flowers often bloom in small patches, usually about two weeks after first sprouting enclosed within two curled leaves. The blossoms nod towards the ground, protecting their nectar and pollen from rain. The backward-curving petals also close at night and during showers.

Only a small percentage of the flowers are pollinated, probably by early flying solitary mining bees, dark, hairy, smokey-winged fliers that dig branching tunnels in the soil for their broods. Fertilized trout lilies develop green pods holding a few seeds. Like those of trilliums and most other spring flowers, the seeds have large, whitish oily appendages, called elaiosomes, that exude a chemical aroma that brings ants running in late spring. Dragging the seeds back to their underground community larders, up to 60 metres (200 feet) away, the diligent insects feed the nutritious attachments to their larvae and chuck the hard-shelled leftovers into refuse tunnels.

Trout lily also plays a vital role in the forest ecosystem that goes beyond its brief spring appearance. Because it dominates so thoroughly immediately after the snow melts, it draws up to almost half of all nutrients – such as nitrogen and potassium – accumulated from the breakdown of fallen leaves by bacteria working beneath winter's insulating snow. Without the trout lily's quick action, much of these nutrients would be washed away in spring runoff before the

Companion plants: Spring beauty, red and white trilliums, true and false Solomon's seal, wild sarsaparilla, jack-in-the-pulpit, starflowers, violets

Other common spring flowers with seeds spread by ants: Trilliums, violets, spring beauty, hepatica, fringed polygala, Dutchman's breeches, bloodroot, wild ginger

Portion of deciduous forest plants whose seeds are spread by ants: Up to 40%

Name for someone who studies ant-seed relationships: Myrmecochorigist, from Greek words *myrmex*, meaning "ant," and *chore*, meaning "farm"

Summer light levels in a mature broadleaf forest: 1–5% of full sunlight

First appearance of lily family: At least 35 million years ago

Number of lily species native to Ontario: More than 20

Number of lily species worldwide: About 500

Also see: Violets, White Trillium, Sugar Maple

dormant roots of trees and other plants begin to stir. This enormous nutrient load, combined with abundant snowmelt and unobstructed sunlight, creates the incredible burst of trout lily leaves. When opening tree buds shade out the ground in late May, whatever nutrients not drawn into the trout lily corms are released by the plants' rapidly decaying leaves into the soil and absorbed by the rest of the forest vegetation.

Blooming alongside of trout lilies in the year's first great surge of growth, though scattered more sparsely, are tiny bouquets of delicate **spring beauties**. The aptly named flower's five white or pinkish petals bear dark pink strips that steer ladybugs, roused from hibernation in the leaf litter below, and other pollinating insects to the nectar they seek. A true spring ephemeral, spring beauty already begins to loose its early sprouting leaves by the time it blooms and the entire plant disappears with the receding sea of trout lily leaves in June.

In sandier spots, pink, white or lavender-blue **hepatica** flowers are also among the very first ephemerals to bloom. Extremely fuzzy flowering stems help to steel them against the early spring chill. Emerging at the same time, though less common on the Shield, **bloodroot** initially huddles against the elements by closely cupping its flowering stem in a single, lobed, kidney-shaped leaf. During its brief blooming, its eight snowy white petals lie flat in the morning, point straight up in the afternoon and close in the evening. The deep red juice of its roots was once used by Native peoples as a dye.

VIOLETS

Sweet, Nutritious Flowers of Love

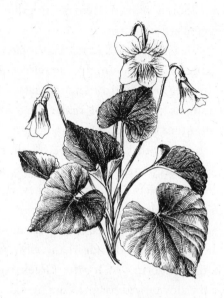

Cherished by lovers, prophets and generals, violets come not just in purple but in varying shades of white, blue, pink and yellow as well. The colour violet was actually named after one of the purple varieties. In central Ontario, there are at least 16 species, adapted to a wide assortment of habitats. Those of late April's leafless hardwood forests are the first to bloom, including the woolly blue violet (which, to add to the confusion, is really violet in colour). Wetland fringes, meadows and evergreen forests soon brighten with their own violets, with the greatest profusion of bloomings coming in June.

In their highly varied colours and sizes, violets everywhere share a very similar design and layout. All feature a specialized lower, central petal that forms an organ and nectar-bearing tube stretching towards the back of the

Number of parma violets needed to produce half a kg (1.1 lb) of essential oils for perfume industry: 2 million

Volume of violet leaves equal to vitamin C content of one orange: 30 ml (2 tbs.)

Flowers: 0.3–3 cm (0.1–1.2 in) wide, 5 petals, with nectar held in enclosure, called a spur, formed by the lowest petal

Alias: *Les violettes,* genus *Viola*

Height: 2.5–45 cm (1–18 in)

Seeds: Sprung by "ballistic ejection" from dividing, 3-chambered beige capsules 4–12 mm (0.2–0.5 in) long, flying up to 1 m from plant

Leaves: Usually heart-shaped (notable exceptions being lanced-leaved and kidney-leaved violets), pointed at tips and curled at base, with toothed edges, 1–10 cm (0.4–4 in) long, 1–12.5 cm (0.4–5 in) wide

Roots: Species with leaves and flowers on separate stalks have numerous thin roots and runners; species with leafy flower stalks have thick, branching woody roots

Deciduous forest species: Sweet white, Canada, downy yellow and woolly blue violets

Coniferous forest species: Northern blue (illustrated), northern white and sweet white violets

Wetland species: Marsh blue, sweet white, downy yellow,

woolly blue and northern
white violets

**Shoreline and forest edge
species:** Lance-leaved, blue
marsh, northern white, northern blue, dog, shore and
Canada violets

Wet meadow species:
Northern white and marsh
blue violets

Meadow species: Dog,
Canada and smooth yellow
violets

Frequent diners: Bees, butterflies, mice, grouse, juncos,
woodcocks, mourning doves

Nibblers: Cutworms, fritillary
butterfly caterpillars, slugs

**Official flower of New
Brunswick:** Blue marsh
violet

Napoleon's nickname:
Corporal Violette

Shakespeare's Viola:
Warmhearted heroine of
Twelfth Night, whose exem-
plification of love, while disguised as a man, wins over
all and snags her a husband
by play's end

Range: Throughout Ontario;
also in all other provinces
and territories

**Number of violet species
native to Ontario:** 31
(much hybridization and
much debate as to what to
label species or subspecies)

**Number of violet species
worldwide:** About 500

Birthplace of violet genus:
The Andes of South
America

Also see: Bees, Wasps and
Hornets; Trout Lily

flower. The front of this petal also serves as a landing platform for incoming flying insects, complete with runway markings in the form of brightly coloured veins. Drawn by the flower's delicate scent, flying insects follow the veins straight to the rich payload of nectar. Violets also display (appropriately enough) ultraviolet patterns, visible to bees and other pollinators but not to humans, which must make the veined petals even more striking in appearance.

The attributes that attract insects – alluring colours, structure and sweet scent – have also long endeared violets to humanity. They flourished in the gardens of ancient Greece and served as a symbol of Athens, the most cultured city of the classical world. Indeed, the word *viola* is the Latin rendering of Io, the Greek name both for the flower and for the daughter of the river god Inarchus. According to one story, the Olympian philanderer Zeus, after casting his affections on Io, turned her into a white cow to save her from his significantly ticked-off other, Hera, queen of heaven. As consolation, he created violets to provide sweet fodder for his beloved cow goddess.

Mortals also enjoy the sugary violet. The petals have been added to jams, syrups and liqueurs and used both as a dye and as flavouring in many candies. The flower decorations topping cakes today imitate the old practice of placing sugar-coated violets on desserts. Crystallized violets were also once commonly sold in drugstores as a sweet cough drop known as violet plate. And the sweet essential oils of Mediterranean violets are one of the oldest sources of perfumes.

Violet leaves are used in salads and added to

soups and omelettes, though they are somewhat more bitter than the flowers. What they lack in sweetness is, however, more than compensated for in nutrition. The leaves of some species have five times more vitamin C than oranges and more than twice the vitamin A content of spinach. Many violets also contain salicylic acid, the same active ingredient in willow bark that led to the development of Aspirin. Not surprisingly, violets have been used for centuries by both Europeans and North American Native people for ailments ranging from insomnia to epilepsy and sore throats to heart problems. The Romans considered violets excellent hangover remedies and covered their banquet tables with the flowers, both for decoration and as a prudent nibble.

Violets are probably more highly regarded, however, for their symbolic value than for any practical benefit. Equated with modesty, chastity, love and loyalty, they have been worn by brides or carried in their bouquets since the days of Helen of Troy. The garden pansy, developed from a small European violet, derives its name from the French *pensée,* meaning "thought" or "remembrance," after the custom of offering violets as a courting gift aimed at turning the admired one's thoughts towards love. Violets were also said to be the favourite flower of the prophet Muhammad and of Napoleon, who, when being sent into his first exile, said, "I shall return with the violets in spring." Unfortunately, he returned to Waterloo.

For all the fame and glory of their blossoms, most violet species actually reproduce mainly without them. These species are colonial, spreading thin underground runners that send up many clones of the original seed-propagated plant. In addition, while cold weather or other mishaps often prevent insects from pollinating many violets, the plants still produce seeds with a second set of smaller flowers that never actually bloom. These cleistogamous buds are usually formed near or below the ground in summer and pollinate themselves without opening, eventually producing even more seeds than the conventional flowers.

Seeds developed in both conventional and aboveground cleistogamous flowers are shot a metre (three feet) or more into the air with the pressure released by the splitting of their pods, which gradually contract as they dry. Those not eaten right away by mice and birds are picked up by ants, which also collect seeds from the subterranean buds.

WATER LILY
Bloom of the Gods

Flowers: Up to 15 cm (6 in) wide, with many white petals around yellow centre; strong fragrance similar to licorice; blooming late June to Aug.

Alias: Fragrant water lily, white water lily, water nymph, sweet-scented water lily, water cabbage, toad-lily, lotus, *le nénuphar blanc, Nymphaea odorata*

Ojibway name: *Anung pikobeesae,* "star fallen in the water," from the story of a star maiden who became embodied as a water lily so that she could live on Earth close to people

Whereabouts: 15 cm–5.5 m (6 in–15 ft) deep in calm bays, ponds and slow

The lotus flowers sacred to Buddhists, Hindus, ancient Egyptians and Mayans are tropical relatives of Ontario's water lily. Some water lilies are eaten in parts of Africa because of their hallucinogenic effects, which ethnobotanists speculate may have been at the root of the lotus's universal status as a sacred plant. The Buddha, Brahma and Ra are often portrayed seated on lotus flowers. In these cultures, the lotus represents the primal womb of Mother Earth. Because it floats, radiant and serene, in stagnant ponds, the flower symbolizes the powers of light and beauty emerging from darkness. Similarly, the floating leaves, which remain dry on top, represent the inner self unsullied by the temptations of the senses.

Lily pads are designed to remain dry on top because, unlike land plants, their upper surface rather than their underside has air-breathing pores. If a lily pad is blown over, the waxy, water-proof top does not stick to the water as the slimy underside does. The red pigment of the leaf's bottom also increases its temperature slightly above that of water. The extra heat helps the leaf get rid of the excess water through transpiration from pores on the upper surface, keeping the plant buoyant. Skipping-rope-like water-lily stems have air tubes that keep them afloat as well. As soon as the ice is gone in spring, overwintering rootstocks send up new floating stems with leaf and flower buds ready to sprout, enabling the buds to reach the surface for light and air.

Root-eating *Donacia* beetle grubs siphon the water lily's air supply by tapping into the plant with special spines. Lily pads, meanwhile, are etched and pockmarked by tiny, dark nibbling waterlily leaf beetles and their grubby offspring, while midge larvae leave conspicuous snaking trails through the leaves. Among a plethora of other animals frequenting the plant are China-mark moth caterpillars, which eat through the pad from portable airtight homes of woven leaf strips anchored beneath.

The resplendent flowers themselves provide sustenance to metallic adult *Donacia* beetles, bees and flies. The flowers ensure cross-pollination by having their male, pollen-producing parts mature later than the female pistil on the same plant. Laden with pollen picked up on older flowers, the insects stumble into the fluid-filled enclosure of stamens on younger ones, washing off the pollen and fertilizing the plant. The flowers open early in the morning but close by midafternoon, possibly conserving the pollen to ensure overlap between young and old flowers.

streams with deep organic silt bottoms

Leaves: 7–30 cm (2.5–12 in) wide, dark green, waxy on top, purple-red on undersides, round or heart-shaped, with a V-shaped cut to the centre; floating separately from flowers

Seeds: 600–700 per flower, mature in late summer or early fall

Roots: Up to 1 m (3.3 ft) long and 6 cm (2.5 in) thick, lying horizontally

Average water-lily sodium content: 9,375 parts per million

Average sodium content of terrestrial plants: 9 parts per million

Browsers: Moose, deer, beavers, porcupines and muskrats eat leaves, stems and roots; ducks and geese eat seeds

Pollinators: Bees, flies, beetles

Other common nibblers and occupants: Waterlily leaf beetles, Donacia beetles, China-mark moth caterpillars, dock spiders, bloodworms (midge larvae), dragonflies, caddisflies, aphids, leeches, frogs, painted turtles

Native remedies: Root tea widely brewed for coughs, sore throats and tuberculosis; roots pounded into poultice for sores and swellings

Range: Southern Ontario to mid-boreal forest; also in all eastern provinces and Manitoba

A flower blooms for three to five days, unless fertilized earlier, and then closes for good. At the same time, its stem begins to coil, gradually pulling the flower beneath the surface, where seeds develop for three to four weeks. Eventually, one to three dozen large, air-filled capsules containing many seeds break off from the shrivelled stems in late summer and autumn and float away. As the slimy pod membrane dissolves, seeds sink to the bottom. They germinate in the spring and take about three years to produce a flower. New plants are also started by spreading rhizomes and by root fragments that break off and float away.

Water lilies survive winter by withdrawing all their nutrients into their deep, thick rootstocks, which are a mainstay of beavers, moose, muskrats and even fish-eating loons. The plant's high sodium levels make it an important salt source for many vegetarian animals, such as porcupines. The rhizomes of yellow bullhead lilies, which tend to prefer slightly more shallow water, were once collected from muskrat lodges or pulled up by Native women in spring and late fall, when their nutrients are most concentrated. High in sugar and starch, they can be eaten like potatoes after soaking and boiling to get rid of bitter tannins. Seeds can also be eaten raw or ground into flour, while leaf and flower buds are eaten in salads.

WHITE TRILLIUM
Monarch of Spring Woods

During the First World War, when the public longed for an official flower to mark the graves of soldiers, federal bureaucrat James Burns Spencer proposed the white trillium as a national emblem for Canada. He said the white petals bespoke purity while their number represented the Holy Trinity and the foundations of the British Empire – England, Scotland and Ireland. Though a national flower was never named, Spencer's arguments, and the votes of thousands of high-school students, led Queen's Park in 1937 to name the trillium Ontario's floral emblem.

White trillium is the monarch of the spring ephemerals. But its reign is brief, taking over from trout lilies, hepaticas and spring beauties in May, and lasting for two to four weeks, until deciduous tree leaves unfold and cut off the light overhead. Spring forest flowers take advantage of

Flower: 3 white, pointed petals, 2.5–8 cm (1–3 in) long, fading to pink before they die; yellow organs at centre; 3 narrow, sharply pointed, green sepals beneath petals; each blooms for about 2–3 weeks

Alias: Great white trillium, snow trillium, large-flowered trillium, white wake-robin, trinity lily, bath flower, white lily, *le trille blanc, Trillium grandiflorum*

Name origin: From Latin *tres,* meaning "three," in reference to number of petals, leaves and sepals on each plant

Whereabouts: Rich soil in mature broadleaf forests

Height: 20–45 cm (8–18 in)

Leaves: Wide, pointed, smooth-edged, 3.5–15 cm (1.5–6 in) long; 3 per plant, meeting together at stem below flower; wither by mid- to late summer

Seeds: 9–10 contained in a single, dark red, hexagonal capsule, about 1.3–2.5 cm (0.5–1 in) wide, ripening around late July; go through 2 winters before germinating

Roots: Short, thick, tuberlike rootstock; rootlets reach at least 13 cm (5 in) below surface

Pollinators: Bees, especially bumblebees; also beetles, flies

Companion plants: Trout lily, spring beauty, red trillium, jack-in-the-pulpit, violets, Dutchman's breeches, bloodroot, toothwort

Green-striped trilliums: A mutation caused by a micro-organism spread by sap-sucking insects

Native remedies: Ojibway spread the juice of ground, boiled trillium roots on rheumatic joints and then punctured the skin with thorns or bone needles; though the root is considered poisonous, many Native peoples also brewed tea from it for menstrual cramps or made it into a poultice for sore eyes

Range: Southern Ontario to about North Bay and Sault Ste. Marie; also in Quebec

Portion of forest flowers that bloom before mid-summer: About 70%

the time between the thawing of the soil and leafing out, when the sheltered woods are actually warmer than open fields, to grow very rapidly. Naturalists say dead leaves may be heard rustling on still nights as the flowers push their way up from the ground – the sound of plants growing. Meadow flowers, on the other hand, with the benefit of the sun all the time, bloom throughout summer to early autumn.

Reproduction requires great amounts of energy from plants. With the limited sunlight they receive in spring, trilliums usually take about six years from the time their seeds sprout until they produce their first flowers, all the while storing energy captured by their leaves in thick roots. If the leaves are picked, the plant usually dies. When it's ready, a trillium takes about one month to produce a flower. Because its sunlight window of opportunity is much shorter than that, the plant, like other spring ephemerals, pre-forms the flower in a tightly packed bundle at the tip of its root the year before it blooms, allowing it to sprout and inflate soon after the soil thaws enough to water its roots the following spring.

Being sheltered by trees, forest flowers depend on insects rather than the wind for pollination. Trilliums are considered unspecialized flowers because, like the world's first flowers, which appeared at least 140 million years ago, their simple petals are on a horizontal plane, offering a broad landing pad for incoming insects. Furry foragers tend to leave most flowers alone because many contain bitter-tasting psychoactive chemicals. Deer and groundhogs, though, delight in trillium leaves. Birds, chipmunks and other small animals also eat the plant's mealy, berrylike red capsule, probably spreading its seeds with their droppings. Many more of the sticky brown seeds are dispersed as the capsules rot by ants attracted by their special nutritious handles, enticements which they feed to their young before throwing the rest of the still-viable seeds away.

Many Native peoples brewed tea from trillium root for menstrual cramps or made it into a poultice to be placed on sore eyes. The Ojibway innovated an early form of inoculation by spreading the juice of ground, boiled trillium roots on rheumatic joints and then puncturing the skin with thorns or bone needles.

Native people also ate **red trillium** roots to help stop bleeding after childbirth and for many other ailments. Red trillium, which also blooms in May, is more tolerant of acidic soil than its snowy cousin and is actually more common on the Canadian Shield, especially in highland areas. It is dark purple-red with straight-edged, sharply triangular petals, though it is also sometimes light yellow. Red trillium has no nectar, but is pollinated by carrion flies, attracted by its faint rotting-flesh smell. A similar strategy is used by jack-in-the-pulpit and skunk cabbage.

Red trillium range: Southern Ontario to the southern boreal forest
Number of trillium species native to Ontario: 5
Number of trillium species worldwide: About 43–48
Also see: Bees, Wasps and Hornets; Jack-in-the-pulpit, Trout Lily, Sugar Maple

WILD IRIS
Flower of Myth and Majesty

Flower: 2 or more per plant, each 6–8 cm (2.4–3.2 in) wide, with 3 violet true petals standing erect and 3 larger, down-curving sepals, which are violet with white and yellow bases veined with deep purple

Alias: Blue flag, purple iris, wild blue flag, larger blue flag, wild blue iris, American fleur-de-lis, liver lily, poison flag, water flag, snake lily, flag lily, dagger flower, dragon flower, flower de luce, *la fleur-de-lys*, *Iris versicolor*

Whereabouts: Moist ground and shallow water of shorelines, marshy sites, bog fringes, swamps, fens

Height: 20–90 cm (8–35 in)

Leaves: Bright green and shiny, grasslike, 20–80 cm (8–31 in) long, 0.5–3 cm (0.2–1.2 in) wide, standing upright; maximizes energy intake in dense colonies by absorbing light on both sides of leaf, rather than on just one like most other plants

Stem: Bright green, glossy

Seeds: Light brown, triangular, many held in 3-chambered, ridged pod 4–5 cm (1.5–2 in) long, maturing by late summer

Roots: Thick, soft, spreading rhizomes with many fibrous rootlets

Displaying one of the largest and most opulent flowers in the wild, iris commands attention and captures the imagination wherever it blooms. Irises carry a long tradition in both myth and majesty. Egyptian pharaohs topped their sceptres with an iris design, its three petals representing wisdom, faith and courage. In ancient Greece, Iris was the name of both the female messenger of the gods and her bridge to Earth, a rainbow. Because she was usually the bearer of ill tidings (Hermes got to carry all the good mail), rainbows were a sign of foreboding. According to one story, Iris was yet another of Zeus's illicit girlfriends, and to save her from the wrath of his wife, Hera, he changed her into a flower. Other accounts hold that irises got their name because the various species come in most colours of the rainbow. The pigmented part of the eye is called an iris for the same reason.

A white iris was adopted as the symbol of French royalty by the 12th-century king Louis VII and became known as the *fleur-de-Louis,* later shortened to *fleur-de-lys.* An old legend relates that an earlier king, Clovis, won a great victory in 496 after irises on a section of the Rhine river pointed the way to a ford where his army could cross and outflank an invading German horde. The *fleur-de-lys* continues to fly on Quebec's flag. The Québécois call wild purple iris *fleur-de-lys,* and after long agitation it was recently finally declared the province's official flower, replacing the madonna lily, a non-native plant whose white petals resemble the stylized flower on the flag.

Humans are far from the only devotees of wild iris. Bumblebees, butterflies, flies and other insects actively seek out its ample pools of nectar, guided there by the prominent veins lining the flower's large, purple sepals. As an insect scurries inwards, bearing pollen from the last flower it visited, its back brushes against and fertilizes the petal-like purple stigma arching above the sepal. Farther inside, another set of stamens replenish the pollen on the bug's back. After drinking, the insect leaves by way of the open space between the arch of the stigma and the sepal.

Fed by the abundant nutrients of its marshy habitat – the richest of Ontario's natural settings – wild iris serves up steady meals for its pollinating helpers all summer long. Each plant

Common visitors: Bumblebees, skipper butterflies, moths, flies

Native uses of leaves: All parts of the plant are poisonous, but leaves were used for making green dyes, baskets and mats

Range: All of Ontario except far north; also in Manitoba, Quebec and Atlantic provinces

Number of iris species native to Ontario: 2

Number of iris species worldwide: 150–200, mostly in Asia

Also see: Bees, Wasps and Hornets; Rainbows, Wetlands

produces many large, nectar-brimming flowers, with several blooming at any given instant. After pollination, the flowers wilt, giving way to fruiting pods that in time slowly split to let seeds fall one by one to the water below. In spring, the seeds germinate and send up leaves. It takes at least another year, more often two, before the roots have stored enough energy for the plant to produce flowers.

Though highly poisonous, even deadly, iris roots are valued for a variety of uses. They were used in small doses by both Native people and settlers to induce vomiting, relieve constipation and increase urine flow, perhaps giving rise to its Ojibway name, *weekaehn,* meaning "that which extracts." In later times, diuretic drugs called irodin and blue flag were made from the rhizomes. The roots of various kinds of irises are also a source of black dyes, ink and a substance called orris root, which is extremely good at drawing in and then gradually giving off the scents of other things, making it an important fixative for perfumes, soaps and cosmetics.

WILD SARSAPARILLA
The Original Backwoods Root Beer

"Sarsaparilla" conjures up images of 19th-century soda fountains and old country doctors dispensing tried and true natural tonics. The aromatic, nutritious root bark of the wild plant was the prime ingredient of homemade root beer and medicinal pioneer teas. The tea was adopted from Native peoples, who also dug up the root as an emergency food when travelling. The Ojibway, Hurons and other Native peoples also pounded, crushed or chewed the root into a poultice for wounds, burns and sores.

Perhaps not surprisingly, wild sarsaparilla is in the same family as ginseng, the priceless wonder root of Chinese herbal medicine. Ginseng's

Flowers: Tiny, white, spiky, usually in 3 spherical clusters branching from a stem rising from the base of the plant, separate from leaf stem; sometimes 2 or up to 7 clusters

Alias: American sarsaparilla, false sarsaparilla, wild licorice, rabbit root, small spikenard, *l'aralie à tige nue, la salsepareille, Aralia nudicaulis*

Name origin: Named after the unrelated Central American sarsaparilla plant, long exported as a medicine and later as a root extract used to flavour soft drinks; the Spanish *sarza* means "bramble," and *parilla* is "little vine"

Whereabouts: Mature broadleaf and mixed forests

Height: 30–60 cm (1–2 ft)

Leaves: Compound, with 3 groupings of 3–5 broadly pointed leaflets, each 5–12.5 cm (2–5 in) long, with finely serrated edges, purplish brown at first, deep green in summer, yellow or bronze in fall

Berries: Purple-black, each usually containing 5 seeds, edible but disagreeable

Roots: Tough, woody horizontal rhizomes up to more than 2 ft (61 cm) long

Companion plants: Trilliums, true and false Solomon's seal, jack-in-the-pulpit, trout lily, spring beauty, violets, rose twisted-stalk, twinflowers, foamflowers

Reputed medicinal uses of root: Skin diseases, rheumatism, syphilis, general aches and pains; once a tonic for purifying blood; also used as a stimulant and diuretic

Range: Throughout Ontario; also in all other provinces

Number of ginseng family species native to Ontario: 6

Number of ginseng family species worldwide: About 700, mostly tropical trees and shrubs

discovery in 1718 by a Jesuit in Quebec set off a North American ginseng-hunting frenzy that nearly wiped it out. Dwarf ginseng, which looks vaguely like wild sarsaparilla, grows in hardwood forests in central Ontario, though it is not very common.

Certainly, there's no scarcity of wild sarsaparilla in Ontario forests. Its outstretched leaves are legion, forming a second storey of growth and shading woodland ground-cover plants. Sarsaparilla's own tiny white flowers are also hidden beneath those leaves. Blooming in small spherical clusters in June, they have no trouble attracting a wide assortment of flies and other pollinating insects with their heavily perfumed scent. By August the clusters of flowers are transformed into globes of purple-black berries that are eaten by foxes, skunks, bears, chipmunks, thrushes and white-throated sparrows.

Few sarsaparilla plants, however, actually flower and produce berries. Like most forest herbs, sarsaparilla puts relatively little of its resources into sexual reproduction, which demands a great deal of energy to produce the necessary nectar, pollen and seeds. Instead, with sun-supplied energy in relatively short supply on the tree-shaded forest floor, sarsaparilla spreads mostly by underground rhizomes that establish colonies of self-supporting clones.

In more dry, sandy, open places, such as rocky shorelines and forest edges, the closely related **bristly sarsaparilla** is also common. Its somewhat larger spheres of flowers and berries are considerably more striking because they are borne on prickly, reddish, woody stems well above the plant's leaves.

WINTERGREEN
Little Leaf with Bubblegum Flavour

The taste that flavours chewing gums, toothpaste and cough drops is not hard to find in the woods. Simply plucking a stiff, shiny little wintergreen leaf and giving it a quick chew yields instant essence du bubblegum. Growing on mossy or sandy ground in mixed and coniferous forests, wintergreen was long used – from northern Cree country to the tilled lands of the Iroquois – to flavour food, drink and tobacco. The Ojibway tied up bundles of the leaves, which remain green through the winter, with stringy strands of basswood bark to brew as an aromatic tea. Adopted by early settlers, wintergreen tea later became quite popular in rebel cups after the Boston Tea Party.

A chemical substance known as oil of wintergreen is also present in some other plants and extracted from them commercially for food

Flowers: White, waxy-looking, barrel-shaped, 5–10 mm (0.2–0.4 in) long, hanging beneath leaves, blooming in summer

Berries: Scarlet, about 1 cm (0.4 in) wide, containing capsule with seeds inside

Alias: Checkerberry, teaberry, spring wintergreen, Canada tea, partridgeberry, grouse berry, creeping wintergreen, spicy wintergreen, chinks, ground-berry, one-berry, spice-berry, red pollom, box-berry, deer-berry, mountain tea, *le thé des bois, Gaultheria procumbens*

Whereabouts: Acidic, mossy or sandy soil in mixed and coniferous forests and clearings

Height: 10–15 cm (4–6 in),
rarely up to 20 cm (8 in)

Leaves: 1–5 cm (0.4–2 in)
long, oval, fragrant, shiny;
evergreen, flexible in first
season, becoming dark
green, stiff and leathery,
turning reddish with age,
always pale on undersides;
3–4 per stem

Stem: Short, bare, woody,
topped by several leaves; is
actually one of many stalks,
or branches, rising along
length of rhizome

Roots: A thin, woody rhizome
running on or just below
the ground, with many
rootlets along its length,
hence the scientific name
procumbens, Latin for
"prostrate"

Companion plants:
Goldthread, blue bead lilies,
moccasin flowers, Canada
mayflowers, bunchberry,
wood sorrel, twinflowers,
trailing arbutus

Common diners: Mice, chipmunks, deer, bears, ruffed
grouse, bumblebees

Medicinal uses: Preventing
tooth decay; soothing aching
muscles; treating colds,
stomach aches, toothaches

Namer of species: 18th-
century Swedish botanical
explorer Pehr Kalm first described wintergreen for science after chumming around
on field trips with Quebec
naturalist Jean-François
Gaultier

Range: All of Ontario except
extreme southwest; also in

flavourings and perfume. Early manufacturers found it easiest to obtain large quantities from the bark of "sweet" or cherry birch, a southern tree found only near St. Catharines in Ontario. Today the flavour is widely synthesized. Because it soothes irritations, the oil was also used in medicine. It yields methyl salicylate, similar to the active ingredient in Aspirin, also found in willow bark. One of its greatest uses, however, was as an ingredient to cover the taste of "miracle formulas" – made up largely of alcohol – peddled by 19th-century snake-oil salesmen.

Still, wintergreen's real powers as a mild stimulant and astringent seem to have been well known to Ojibway and Algonquin paddlers, who said they chewed the plant's leaves during portages and other exhausting activities to increase their endurance. They also credited the plant's red berries, which they ate fresh or preserved, with aiding digestion. Herbalists warn, however, that too much wintergreen oil can cause allergic reactions in some, especially children, who should be discouraged from eating the leaves and berries. The pitted berries are, reportedly, most palatable after they have spent a winter mellowing on the vine, hanging beneath the plant's evergreen leaves deep in the snow. Perhaps that's why, though they're eaten by mouse and bear alike, they're not snapped up as soon as they ripen in autumn.

Wintergreen is sometimes called **partridge-berry**, which is more properly the name of a small, mat-forming forest ground vine, also a member of the heath family, which produces pairs of similar, winter-persistent red berries. Both provide a ready food source for early

migrant birds returning to their breeding territories in spring before insects become abundant.

Snowberry, wintergreen's closest relative in
Ontario, also sounds the wintery theme, though
its name actually alludes to the plant's white
berries. Like wintergreen, it has tiny, waxy white
bell flowers, but they're borne on vinelike, hairy
branchlets forming mats over the ground in
coniferous forests and sphagnum bogs. Its leaves
are also very tiny, just two to 10 millimetres
(0.08 to 0.4 inches) long, lining the length of
the branchlets.

Both wintergreen and snowberry have the
scientific surname *Gaultheria,* a genus named
after Jean-François Gaultier, who served as the
king's physician to New France from 1742 to
1756. The position was that of a surgeon-
general and chief scientist for the colony rolled
into one. It was Gaultier's job to catalogue and
investigate the great stream of newly discovered
Canadian plants, which outpost commanders
were ordered to collect for him. Canadians, often
described as a weather-obsessed people, can also
look to him as the founder of the country's first
meteorological station.

Manitoba, Quebec and
Atlantic provinces
**Number of *Gaultheria*
species native to
Ontario:** 2
**Number of *Gaultheria*
species worldwide:** About
200, most in the Andes of
South America
Also see: Basswood, Yellow
Birch

WOOD SORREL
Far-flung Shamrocks of Mossy Realms

Flowers: 1.5–2 cm (0.6–0.8 in) wide, 5 small white, sometimes light-pink, petals with thin, dark-pink stripes and a tiny yellow dot at the base of each petal; 1 per plant, on a separate stem from leaves

Alias: Common wood sorrel, upright wood sorrel, white wood sorrel, true wood sorrel, shamrock, sleeping beauty, cuckoo flower, sour trefoil, hearts, *l'oxalide de montagne, Oxalis acetosella*

Scientific name meaning: *Oxalis* comes from the Greek word for a sour, sharp or acid taste

Name origin of shamrock: From Irish *seamróg,* meaning "little clover"

Even when not in bloom, wood sorrel is very distinctive, its three glossy, smooth-edged leaflets forming three perfect hearts joined together at their pointed tips. The plant, which also grows in Europe and Asia, is sometimes hailed as the original shamrock, a sacred symbol of the ancient Celtic druids used by St. Patrick to explain the concept of the Holy Trinity to the pagan Irish. There are, however, several other leading shamrock candidates, including common clovers.

Growing happily in some of the deepest shade of Canada's northern evergreen forests, wood sorrel is a lonely adventurer, boldly striking out like a coureur de bois, far from its own ken and kind. Most of the little plant's large family warm their leaves in Africa and South America, and only one other close relative is native to Ontario. The family must have emerged before the two southern continents separated, about 80 million years ago, with only a handful of its offspring fortifying themselves to survive the northern climes.

Indeed, the dainty wood sorrel of the Canadian Shield is tougher than it looks. Like many other plants growing under coniferous trees, it is itself an evergreen, bolstered by sugary antifreeze compounds that allow its leaves to persist, dormant but alive, beneath the snow. The leaves also contain salts that make them taste quite sour, hence the name *sorrel,* which comes, via French, from the ancient Germanic word *suraz,* meaning "sour." The taste probably discourages browsing insects and snails. The leaves were used in rural areas to curdle milk and to add a nice tartness to salads, soups, pies and apple sauce. The Ojibway, who called the plant *zeewunubugushk,* or "sour leaf," made a bittersweet dessert of the leaves cooked with maple sugar.

Still, eating too many wood sorrel leaves can cause kidney damage and internal bleeding. Cows and sheep have reportedly died from overgrazing the plant. Oxalic acid from wood sorrel is caustic enough to have been used in Europe as a stain remover, called "salts of lemon." A similar, synthesized chemical is used in industry to bleach clothes and wood and for cleaning automobile radiators.

Wood sorrel employs a few other strategies for success in the northern forests. Like many woodland herbs, it stays close to the ground, where carbon dioxide levels are 25 per cent higher than in open areas. The extra supply of carbon – the primary building material of living cells – helps compensate for the poor supply of

Whereabouts: Mossy, acidic ground in coniferous and mixed forests, often beneath hemlocks and yellow birch, or in bogs

Height: 5–10 cm (2–4 in), rarely up to 15 cm (6 in)

Seeds: Have white ridges, shot out from small pod when ripe

Leaves: Like tiny, distinct, smooth-edged, glossy clovers, 1–3 cm (0.4–1.2 in) wide

Stems: Light green or pink, several joined together at ground

Roots: Slim, scaly vertical rhizome with slender connecting runners

Companion plants: Canada mayflowers, goldthread, bunchberry, gay-wings, moccasin flowers, northern blue violets, twinflowers, wintergreen, blue bead lilies

Frequent diners: Hares and deer graze leaves; chipmunks, ruffed grouse, juncos and sparrows eat seeds; pollinated by beetles, flies and moths

Folk remedies: Once used by Europeans for heart problems because leaves are heart-shaped; also a popular spring tonic and medicine for heartburn, liver ailments, fevers and mouth ulcers; Algonquins considered it an aphrodisiac

Age of oldest known flowering plant fossils: 120 million years

Range: Southern Ontario to about Kapuskasing and the

northeast shore of Lake
Superior; also in Quebec
and Atlantic provinces
**Number of *Oxalis* species
native to Ontario:** 2
**Number of *Oxalis* species
worldwide:** 800
Also see: Violets, Yellow Birch

sunlight. The leaves also forecast bad weather, folding together before rain or cold temperatures, as well as at night. As a contingency in case of unsuccessful pollination, common when frosts encroach upon its early-summer blossoms, wood sorrel has both a backup flowering system and a colonial rooting network. After its regular flowers bloom in June and July, the plant produces low green buds, usually unseen beneath the leaf litter, containing self-fertilizing flowers that never actually open. Like the plants sprouting from spreading colonial roots, the abundant seeds yield genetic clones of the mother plant.

TREES

L *ooking out from a hilltop over the seemingly endless expanse of forest in Ontario's interior, one may find it hard to imagine how loggers could ever have cleared such vast tracts of green. Yet much of the province, and almost all of central Ontario, has been visited by the axe and saw. Most of today's red and white pines have grown up since lumberjacks began felling the province's ancient towering forests 100 to more than 200 years ago.*

Luckily, central Ontario is blessed not only with the great pines, but also with many trees characteristic of two quite different forest zones to the north and south. Dominating hills in much of the region, sugar maples transform the countryside with rich hues of red, orange and yellow in autumn. At the same time, the boreal zone's wealth of birch, aspen and Christmas-tree forests of fragrant fir and spruce spill over into much of the central region. Together these trees clothe the land and give it its character.

Tree sizes listed in the sidebars are based on Ontario averages. Some species may get a little bigger farther south, where the growing season is longer. Beaked hazel, which is really more of a tall shrub than a tree, is included in this section because it is an important element of the understorey in many forests. Chokecherry and speckled alder, for their part, are usually small, shrubby trees.

BALSAM FIR
The Fragrance of the Forest

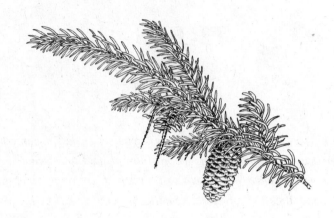

Mature height: Avg. 12–
18 m (40–60 ft)

Trunk width: Avg. 30–45 cm
(1–1.5 ft)

Ontario giant: 30.5 m
(100 ft) tall, 47 cm (1.5 ft)
thick, at Mignet Lake,
Nipigon District

Lifespan: Avg. 60–70 years;
up to about 200 years

Alias: Blister fir, Canada balsam, white fir, balm of
Gilead, church steeple, silver
pine, *le sapin baumier*,
Abies balsamea

**Number of Christmas trees
grown and sold in Ontario
annually:** 750,000–1 million

Whereabouts: Moist lowlands
of silt loam soil or dry, sandy
uplands, often on north-
facing slopes

Balsam is derived from an ancient Hebrew word for aromatic tree resins used for balms – soothing ointments or salves. In Ontario, it is the rich, sweet essence of the forest. The balsam fir's thick, sticky resin literally bubbles up beneath its bark, oozing from old knots and wounds and caking its buds and cones, making them difficult for squirrels and birds to eat. When fungus attacks, a fir increases sap produc-tion, laying it on thick where invading fungal strands seek to penetrate the tree's soft wood. Native people and lumberjacks took their cue from the trees and squeezed fir "gum" from the bark blisters to use as an effective antiseptic seal for cuts and wounds. The clear resin has also long been used for Canada balsam, a glue for mounting specimens on microscope slides and securing the lenses of optical equipment.

The gooey sap common to all northern conifers is, in fact, the key to their survival through winters too harsh for the watery sap of most deciduous trees. It acts as a sugar-rich natural antifreeze in the roots and branches, allowing the tree to hang on to its dormant waxy needles through the winter. As soon as temperatures rise above freezing, the needles can start photosynthesizing, allowing them to be productive through the entire short growing season. From spring thaw till June, the energy they capture goes to the season's new sprouting growth. Afterwards, as in other trees, most of the energy is used in forming new buds containing all the tissue for the following spring's shoots.

In pagan times, Germans celebrated the winter solstice Yule festival by bringing evergreen boughs – holding the promise of spring and providing shelter for visiting elves – into their homes. Hundreds of years later, they brought the *Tannenbaum* tradition with them to North America. It really caught on in Canada in the late 1800s after Queen Victoria, herself of not-distant German lineage, was pictured with her family gathered around a tabletop Christmas tree in the *Illustrated London News*. Balsam fir, along with white spruce and Scotch pine, continues to be among the most popular choice for Christmas trees everywhere today.

In a forest of Christmas trees, firs can be distinguished from spruce at a distance by the way they taper more narrowly to a perfect point. Up close, fir can be seen to have flat needles, unlike four-sided spruce needles, which are easily rolled between the thumb and forefinger.

Bark: Grey, smooth, with horizontal specks and raised blisters filled with resin when young; brownish scales form on older trees

Needles: 2–3 cm (0.8–1.2 in) long, blunt, dark green on top, 2 white lines on underside; curving upward in flat, horizontal rows on lower branches; shed after 3–4 years

Sex: Purple-red male flower conelets, 6 mm (0.2 in) long, clustered at base of needles along twigs; much larger, dark female cones stand erect higher up on tree; wind pollinated in late May and June; puberty usually after 20 years

Cones: 5–10 cm (2–4 in) long, dark purplish, erect, near top of tree; mature in several months, then disintegrate on branch in autumn, leaving behind pointy spindles; big crops every 2–4 years

Seeds: Tiny, attached to wing 1–1.5 cm (0.4–0.6 in) long, about 135 per cone, most falling late Aug. to Oct.

Wood: White, soft, knotty, weak, brittle, with straight, coarse grain, 385 kg/m³ (24 lb/cu. ft)

Heat equivalent of 1 m³ (35 cu. ft) of wood: 93.5 L (20.5 gal) of oil

Companion trees and shrubs: Spruce, jack pine, aspen, white birch, red maple, white pine, hemlock, cedar, chokecherry, beaked

hazel, mountain maple,
juneberry

Associated plants: Canada
mayflower, bunchberry, wintergreen, blue bead lily,
goldthread, large-leaved
aster

Common nesters: Gray jays,
evening grosbeaks, yellow-
rumped warblers, black-
throated blue warblers,
purple finches

Frequent diners: Red squirrels, mice, voles, bears,
moose, ruffed grouse and
spruce grouse eat seeds,
buds, inner bark or needles,
though not a preferred food
for most

Tiny nibblers: Spruce budworm, hemlock loopers, balsam woolly adelgids,
ambrosia beetles, longhorn
beetles

**Number of fir saplings in a
healthy fir-spruce forest:**
Avg. 4,000/ha (1,600/acre)

**Number of spruce saplings
in a healthy fir-spruce forest:** Avg. 500/ha
(200/acre)

Accolades: Provincial tree of
New Brunswick

Range: All Ontario except extreme southwest and far
northern boreal forest; also
in all other provinces except
British Columbia

**Number of fir species na-
tive to Ontario:** 1

**Number of fir species
worldwide:** About 40

Also see: White Cedar, White
Spruce

Because balsam is more tolerant of moist soil and shade than white spruce, its seedlings often dominate the forest floor even where spruce tower above. Fir, however, is shorter-lived and more prone to many stresses. With a lower cellulose content, its wood is not as dense as spruce, allowing rot to set in when some trees are as young as 40 years old. Weakened firs, anchored by shallow roots, are easily toppled by the wind.

Fir forests can also be especially volatile tinderboxes. Spruce budworms love balsam fir above all other trees, creating huge tracts of soft, dry, dead and dying wood during outbreaks. The thick layer of needle litter on the ground also makes coniferous forests more prone to fires than deciduous trees. When humidity levels drop below 30 per cent – as they often do in May and June in boreal forests – the fire hazard becomes extreme. Trees dry out, trying to keep their needles moist, and lose billions of gallons of water to the air through transpiration. Such conditions led to one of the worst infernos in Canadian history, the Chapleau-Mississagi fire of 1948. Though no one was killed, it burned for a month, covering 2,660 square kilometres (1,000 square miles) and blackening the skies with smoke clouds that necessitated street lights as far away as Texas to be turned on during the day.

BASSWOOD
Rope, Honey and Porcupine Fodder

Though never a dominant tree in the mixed and hardwood forest, basswood has been highly important to both beast and *Homo sapiens*. To the Ojibway, Algonquins, Ottawa, Hurons and Iroquois, it was the tree that binds. Basswood's inner bark holds some of the longest, strongest, toughest natural fibres on the continent. It was used for rope, thread, twine, thongs, nets and woven bags. In spring, Native people easily stripped bark from the trees and either soaked it for several weeks – the softer material rotting away to leave only the strongest fibres – or boiled and pounded it until stringy and malleable. They then twisted the strands together to

Mature height:
  Avg. 18–21 m (60–70 ft)
Width: Avg. 60–75 cm
  (2–2.5 ft)
Ontario giant: 23 m (76 ft)
  tall, 1.9 m (6.2 ft) thick, in
  Dungannon Township,
  Hastings Co.
Lifespan: Commonly about
  140 years; up to 200 years
Alias: Linden, lime, American
  basswood, whitewood, bass,
  beetree, spoonwood, *le
  tilleul d'Amérique, Tilia
  americana*
Name origin: From *bast,* the
  fibrous inner bark, or

phloem, of trees, used to make rope

Whereabouts: Deciduous forests with deep, rich soils, often on hillsides, less often in mixed forests

Leaves: 13–20 cm (5–8 in) long, about 7.5–15 cm (3–6 in) wide, slightly lopsided, with a pointed tip and large-toothed edges; long stems; turn crispy brown from edges towards centre in fall

Bark: Dark grey, with long, thin, flat ridges

Sex: Clusters of 10–20 small, fragrant, yellow flowers joined by a single stalk to the midpoint of a narrow leaflike blade 7.5–12.5 cm (3–5 in) long; each flower has 5 petals and both male and female parts

Seeds: Bunches of several hard, pea-sized, green nutlets covered by soft, rust-brown hairs, holding 1–2 seeds; hang on branches into winter; then fall, still attached to leaflike blades, which act as parachutes; take 2 years to germinate; big crops every 2–4 years

Buds: Shiny, reddish, squat, slightly lopsided, about 6 mm (0.25 in) long

Roots: Deep, widespread, well anchored

Wood: Creamy white to light brown, smooth, soft, fine-grained, even-textured, weak, 465 kg/m³ (29 lb/cu. ft)

Heat equivalent of 1 m³ (35 cu. ft) of wood: 113 L (25 gal) of oil

make flexible white rope and string esteemed by its makers for being softer on the hands and less likely to kink and tangle than the white traders' hemp. Birchbark containers, clothes, lodge poles, reed mats, even wounds were all held together by the wonder fibre.

The settlers also took to basswood in a big way, though not so much for its rope. They worked the wood, taking the lead of the Iroquois, who carved False Face masks right on the trunks of live trees, then cut them off and hollowed them out. Softest and lightest of all the hardwoods, with a fine, smooth, straight grain that is easily worked, basswood has long been highly valued by carvers. It was lathed to make bowls and platters and carved into wooden spoons and toys. Today it is still crafted into duck decoys, wood sculptures and models. Because the light wood could be worked thin and bent without cracking, it was also used for canoes and musical instruments, as well as picture frames, window sashes and yardsticks.

In the forest, basswood never forms pure stands. In the dark understorey, shade-tolerant basswood saplings have the virtue of patience. With huge, lopsided leaves, often bigger than a fully spread hand, they grow slowly. When a spot opens up in the canopy they shoot up and join the big trees. When an old basswood falls, rather than give up a hard-won place in the sun, the still-living base sprouts new shoots, creating a clump of trunks where there had been just one. Standing dead basswood trunks are also very important for cavity-nesting or roosting woodpeckers, owls, mammals and bee colonies.

Even when basswood leaves are only high

above on mature trees, porcupines make the effort to reach them. In many areas, basswoods are one of the most important foods of the moving pincushions. The mild-tasting, high-nitrogen leaves are about 13 per cent protein. When the leaves fall in autumn, they replenish the earth with higher levels of concentrated calcium, nitrogen and potassium than most other decomposing leaves. The trees' buds are also eaten by deer, chipmunks and ruffed grouse.

The strong, sweet scent of basswood flowers, sometimes noticeable for more than a kilometre (half a mile), attracts droves of bees that cross-pollinate the widely scattered trees. For the three weeks or so that basswood blooms in late June and July, its nectar is the focus for local hives, where it is made into a high-quality, strong-tasting white honey. Heavy cutting of basswoods around the start of the 20th century brought lean times for Ontario's beekeepers. Perhaps the flowers and honey are what prompted the ancient Greeks to associate the closely related European linden tree with sweetness, modesty, gentleness and conjugal love. The trees were said to be the husbands of the dryads, the wood nymphs.

Companion trees: Sugar maple, yellow birch, beech, black cherry, ironwood

Frequent diners: Porcupines, deer, chipmunks, squirrels, mice and ruffed grouse eat seeds, leaves or buds

Tiny nibblers: Linden loopers, basswood leaf rollers, forest tent caterpillars

Average leaf decomposition time: 2.5 years

False Face masks: Fierce images of the spirits that protected against disease and crop blights, worn during Iroquois False Face ceremonies before the start of each growing season; carved from living basswoods so that the mask would hold life, after rituals seeking the trees' permission

Range: Southern Ontario to around Lake Nipissing and Sault Ste. Marie; also in Manitoba, Quebec and New Brunswick

Number of *Tilia* species native to Ontario: 1

Number of *Tilia* species worldwide: About 30

Also see: Bees, Wasps and Hornets; Porcupine

BEAKED HAZEL
Understorey Nut Shrub

Mature height: Avg. 1–3 m (3.3–10 ft), up to 4 m (13 ft)

Stems: Usually 2–3 cm (0.8–1.2 in) wide

Alias: Hazel, filbert, *le noisetier à long bec, Corylus cornuta*

Whereabouts: Mixed forests, woodland edges and clearings, streambanks, often in thickets

Nuts: Round, hard shells about 12 mm (0.5 in) long, within light-green, densely bristled sheath that forms a 3–4 cm (1.2–1.6 in) long, open-ended "beak," appearing in pairs, less often singly or in groups of 3–6; 13% protein, 62% fat; bristles irritating to skin

Leaves: Oval; 5–12 cm (2–5 in) long, 2.5–7 cm

The commonplace beaked hazel seems to blend undistinguished with the saplings and bushes that often crowd the hardwood and mixed-forest understorey. It stands out, though, in April and early May, as one of the first shrubs to bloom. Winter's upright columns of closed male catkins suddenly unfurl and dangle from hazel branches as the year's last snow melts away on the ground below. Still more striking are the tiny, wind-pollinated female flowers, with their bold, bright red stiles. Only after the shrub blooms do its leaves, and those of other understorey inhabitants, open to grab the sun and turn the forest interior green.

For the rest of spring and summer, hazelnuts slowly develop. Covered by a densely bristled, Velcro-like husk narrowing to a long, beak-shaped end, the nuts are both edible and nutritious, with high levels of thiamine, which builds muscle tissue, as well as compounds that lower blood cholesterol and remove liver fats. They're relished by a wide array of forest critters and often seem to disappear from the branch just as they ripen in late August. The Algonquins, Ojibway and Cree made a point of collecting the nuts, often peeling and then burying them for a few days to leach away any bitterness. They were eaten raw or boiled in soups. Many were also dried for winter. The Iroquois ground hazelnuts and mixed them into breads and puddings and boiled them to remove their oil for use with other foods.

On the other side of the Atlantic, the European hazel, also known as the domestic filbert, was important to traditional cultures as well. Forked hazel branches were the choice of diviners in searching for water. The shrub was once said to be sacred to Thor, the Norse thunder god, both embodying lightning and preventing it from striking. Hazel-twig charms protected sailors from shipwreck and riders from horse-spooking fairies. The colour hazel is named after the yellow-brown shell of the filbert nut, as Shakespeare notes in *Romeo and Juliet:*

Native peoples found a number of other uses for beaked hazel. The Ojibway used the shrub's thin, pliable twigs as the ribs for baskets, and the thicker branches were ideally suited for drumsticks, because they are often crooked and provide just the right enlarged base.

Thou wilt quarrel with a man for cracking
    nuts,
Having no other reason, but thou hast hazel
    eyes.

(1–3 in) wide, tapering to pointed tip, with unevenly toothed edges, bright green above, lighter below; high in calcium and manganese

Bark: Smooth, grey

Sex: Upright male flower catkins 2–3 cm (0.2–1.2 in) long after forming in autumn, open out up to 5 cm (2 in) long and dangle in spring; tiny female flowers have hairlike, bright red styles protruding from closed buds.

Roots: Extensive, shallow, mat-forming roots and rootlets with underground stems

Companion trees and shrubs: Sugar and red maples, beech, aspens, yellow and white birch, hobble-bush, white pine

Associated plants: Canada mayflower, wild sarsaparilla, bunchberry, large-leaved aster

Common nesters: Red-eyed vireos, indigo buntings, chestnut-sided warblers, black-throated blue warblers

Frequent diners: Chipmunks, squirrels, bears, raccoons, mice, blue jays, wild turkeys, hairy woodpeckers eat nuts in late summer; moose, deer, hares, ruffed grouse and woodcocks browse buds, catkins or leaves; beavers eat bark

Range: Southern Ontario to the southern edge of the Hudson Bay lowlands; also in all other provinces

Many species of viburnum shrubs also join beaked hazel in the understorey and at forest edges. One of the most common in central Ontario, **hobblebush**, has a distinctive look that sets it apart. Its large, rounded leaves grow in regimented pairs, on upright stalks, along the shrub's arching or horizontal branches. Sometimes the long, graceful limbs arch so low that they touch the ground and put down roots from their tips. The resulting snare formed by the grounded branch can trip up hikers cutting through the thick underbrush, which is how the species got its name. In late May and early June it sprouts wide bouquets of large-petalled white flowers which in turn yield small green berries that turn red, purple and finally blackish in September.

Taller **pagoda dogwoods**, usually two to four metres (6.6 to 12.2 feet) high, also produce dark blue to black berries, borne on short, bright red stalks, which ripen as early as late July. In sandy or rocky open forests and ravines, **round-leaved dogwoods** have light-blue or greenish-white berries. The dogwood fruits are extremely important to a wide variety of songbirds and other wildlife.

BEECH
Signpost of the Ages

Or shall I rather the sad verse repeat
Which on the beech's bark I lately writ
—Virgil, ca. 1st century BCE

A stand of beech trees can have an almost surreal, storybook presence, the silvery smooth, curvaceous trunks like the gnarled limbs of sentient giants. The thin, seamless bark of beech trees is more like living skin than the bark of most other trees. On oaks, maples and conifers, dead bark cells gradually build up, crack open and form deep ridges or plates. Dead beech-bark cells are soon shed like powder from the tree's surface.

Mature height: Avg. 18–25 m (60–82 ft)

Trunk width: Avg. 60–100 cm (2–3.3 ft)

Ontario giant: 28.4 m (93 ft) tall, 92 cm (3 ft) thick, in Springwater Conservation Area, Elgin Co.

Lifespan: Commonly 200–300 years, maximum more than 400 years

Alias: American beech, beechnut tree, *le hêtre à grandes feuilles, Fagus grandifolia*

Whereabouts: Upland broadleaf forests with rich, sandy loam soil

Bark: Smooth, light bluish-grey, thin

Leaves: 5–13 cm (2–5 in) long, shiny green, pointy, serrated, with straight, prominent veins, papery texture

Sex: Clusters of greenish-yellow male flowers like round tassels, each 2 cm (0.8 in) wide, hanging on long stalks; tiny reddish females on short stalks near branch tips; open with leaves; wind-pollinated

Nuts: Three-sided nuts, 13 mm (0.5 in) long, usually 2 contained in round, bristled reddish brown husk that splits when ripe; 22% protein, 50% fat; fall for several weeks after first heavy frosts; big crops every 2–8 years

Buds: Spearlike, 1–2 cm (0.4–0.8 in) long, slender, very pointy

Roots: Dense, widespread mat of fine rootlets, usually shallow, but can reach 1.5 m (5 ft) down in deep soils; tree sends out suckering shoots

Wood: Pale to reddish-brown heartwood, thin whitish sapwood, hard, strong, stiff, 670 kg/m³ (42 lb/cu. ft), close-grained, long- and hot-burning

Heat equivalent of 1 m³ (35 cu. ft) of wood: 184 L (40.5 gal) of oil

Companion trees and shrubs: Sugar maple, yellow birch, hemlock, basswood,

Like skin, beech bark can scar permanently, forming wound cork that rises up like a bump along the scar. These qualities have made beech a favourite signpost for lovers' initials and other graffiti since before Shakespeare's day. In fact, the word *book* is believed to be derived from the old Germanic word for beech, *boko,* because ancient runic inscriptions were carved on beechwood tablets.

According to one story, the tree actually triggered the greatest revolution of the written word ever, after Johannes Gutenberg, one day in the 15th century, idly carved some letters in beech bark then wrapped the still-damp letter shavings up in paper and carried them home. When he later discovered that they left impressions on the paper, a light bulb went on and the printing press was born.

Their thin skin does not allow beech trees to survive winters much farther north than Algonquin Park, or to withstand fires. Wounds also allow wood-rotting fungi into the tree, a common cause of demise for many beeches. In recent years, the invasive European beech scale insect has spread through southern Ontario to the doorstep of Muskoka. The pernicious interloper taps into the tree's bark to suck sap, leaving holes that become infected by an accompanying alien canker fungus that gradually covers the trunk with ugly pockmarks, usually killing a beech in three to five years.

In good conditions, the tree can be long-lived. It is 40 to 60 years old before it even starts producing nuts, which are fed upon by hordes of deer, squirrels, foxes, raccoons, porcupines, mice, ducks, blue jays, grouse and wild turkeys. Black bears cause beech wounds, clawing their way up the trunks to get at nut-laden branches. More damaging still, they often leave "bear nests" in the crotches of trees, where they sit and pull in branches while gorging, breaking limbs and twigs as they munch.

The nutritious nuts are edible to humans as well, as noted by the tree's scientific name, *Fagus,* from the Greek word for "eat." The original Indo-European word for beech, *bhagos,* may have meant the same thing.

Beechnuts, like maple seeds, sprout fairly big, strong seedlings, whose roots can penetrate the forest's thick litter layer. Like maples, they are content in the shade, growing very slowly until a mature tree falls and brings the sun's light down on them. Eventually they come to dominate the canopy. In more open areas, older beech trees often propagate themselves by spreading out sucker roots, resulting in clumps of beeches around a mature tree.

In contrast to sugar maples, beech tend to turn a dull yellow or bronze in the autumn. On lower branches and saplings, these leaves often don't fall, because their stem bases do not fully form the corky abscission layer that on most trees separates autumn leaves from the twig. Instead, they remain on the branch, becoming bleached by the winter sun, until they are pushed off by new leaves in the spring. Early settlers often stuffed dry beech leaves into their mattresses because they are springier than straw.

white pine, red maple, black cherry, beaked hazel

Associated plants: White trillium, trout lily, spring beauty, Canada mayflower, violets, wood ferns

Common nesters: Great horned and barred owls, red-shouldered and Cooper's hawks, scarlet tanagers, rose-breasted grosbeaks, pileated woodpeckers, yellow-bellied sapsuckers

Common ailments: Thin bark susceptible to frost cracks, small ground fires and sucking insects such as beech scale and aphids; infected by more than 70 species of fungi, more than any other hardwood; roots siphoned by beechdrops, sticklike parasitic plants that grow near the trunk

Range: Southern Ontario to about North Bay and Sault Ste. Marie; also in Quebec and the Maritime provinces

Number of beech species native to Ontario: 1

Number of beech species worldwide: 10

Also see: Blue Jay, Black Bear, Indian Pipe, Trout Lily, Sugar Maple

BLACK ASH
Fabled Tree in Many Cultures

Mature height: 12–18 m (40–60 ft)

Trunk width: 20–60 cm (8 in–2 ft)

Ontario giant: 29.5 m (97 ft) tall, 76 cm (2.5 ft) thick, on Lake Opeongo, Algonquin Park

Alias: Swamp ash, basket ash, hoop ash, *le frêne noir, Fraxinus nigra*

Leaves: Composites of 7–11 opposite, narrowly pointed, dark green leaflets, each 10–13 cm (4–5 in) long, with fine teeth on edges; pale yellow turning rust early in autumn

Bark: Soft, grey, corky with flaky ridges

Sex: Clusters of tiny, shaggy, greenish yellow, petal-less

Ash trees occupied an important place in early mystical beliefs on both sides of the Atlantic. A common story among Algonkian-speaking peoples tells of the first humans emerging from a hole made in an ash by an arrow shot by the supernatural hero Glooscap. Similarly, the Romans, Greeks, Vikings and others all had legends of the first people coming from an ash or other tree. The Norse world tree, Yggdrasil, which held Heaven and Earth, was a European ash, similar to the black ash.

Though a member of the southern olive family, the slender, straight-trunked black ash is common in swampy areas in Ontario, often in pure stands. It moves into the edges of swamps as they begin to dry up, though it may stand in shallow water in spring and early summer. In its wet habitat, it usually grows slowly, not leafing out until June and starting to turn colour after the first frosts. Black ash is easy to pick out because it is one of central Ontario's only trees with oval leaflets spreading out in pairs opposite to each other.

The slender, straight-trunked black ash is common in swampy areas, often in pure stands

Black ash wood has a unique quality – when cut into short, peeled logs, soaked, and thoroughly beaten – of separating at the divisions between its annual growth rings. The Ojibway, Iroquois and many others used the resulting thin circular strips for weaving baskets. Pioneers used them for barrel hoops and woven chair seats.

male flowers; smaller ragged females usually on separate trees

Seeds: 2.5–4 cm (1–1.5 in) long, green, flat, paddle-shaped wings, ripening in dense, hanging clusters in September; eaten by evening grosbeaks, purple finches, wood ducks, wild turkeys, squirrels, mice

Wood: Dark greyish-brown heartwood, whitish sapwood, coarse grain, stiff, medium strength, 560 kg/m³ (35 lb/cu. ft)

Roots: Very shallow

Whereabouts: Rich loam or organic soil in swamp forests, floodplains, water-sides and other low, moist sites

Range: Southern Ontario into mid-boreal forest; also in Manitoba and all eastern provinces

BLACK SPRUCE
The Hardy Bog-dweller

Mature height: Avg. 3–9 m (10–30 ft) in wetlands, 9–18 m (30–60 ft) on dry sites

Trunk width: Avg. 15–25 cm (6–10 in)

Ontario giant: 23 m (69 ft) tall, 41 cm (16 in) thick, at Loon Lake, Kenora District

Lifespan: Avg. 180–220 years; up to 250 years

Alias: Bog spruce, swamp spruce, *l'épinette noire*, *Picea mariana*

Whereabouts: Bogs, swamps, watersides, thin-soiled uplands

Needles: 6–12 mm (0.2–0.5 in) long, shed after 10 or more years

Bark: Dark grey-brown, thin, very flaky

Sex: Small crimson male flower conelets and deep red female conelets in dense clusters in crown, appearing in May and early June

Cones: 2–3 cm (0.8–1.3 in) long, oval, brown to purplish, with thin, dense scales that open gradually to release very tiny winged seeds over several years

Roots: Very shallow, extensive, intricate; trees prone to windfall

Companion trees: Tamarack, white spruce, white birch, trembling aspen

Associated plants: Feather moss, sphagnum moss,

Dark, spindly stands of black spruce, with little lichen-draped branches hanging down like shrivelled, dropping arms of ghouls, give some people the heebie-jeebies as they drive through northern Ontario's boreal forest. Yet to others, the trees evoke a sombre, sublime solitude, hauntingly reproduced in the works of the Group of Seven. Black spruce is also the most important commercial tree in the province, feeding northern pulp and paper mills in untold numbers.

Though not as common in central Ontario, black spruce usually fringe remote bogs and swamps, where difficult growing conditions mimic the north. Bogs maintain a microclimate that is cooler than the surrounding forests. Black spruce, one of the first cold-resistant trees to follow the retreat of the glaciers back into Ontario, remained clustered around bogs in the south long after more temperate trees took over more fertile, hospitable ground.

Black spruce is the most important commercial tree in the province

Black spruce are the best bog-dwellers because they can make do with less better than all the trees that crowd them out elsewhere. Their stringy roots – which were split and used by Native peoples to sew the seams of birchbark canoes and containers – spread and intertwine through a bog's spongy moss mat. Spruce gets by on a minimum of nutrients in the acidic wetland, growing slowly, managing to sprout only tiny branches.

lichens, Labrador tea, leatherleaf, bog orchids, bog laurel

Common nesters: Gray jays, kinglets, olive-sided flycatchers, northern parulas, blackburnian warblers, red squirrels

Frequent visitors: Spruce grouse, pine grosbeaks, nuthatches, white-winged crossbills

Accolades: Provincial tree of Newfoundland and Labrador

Range: All Ontario, except far south, to tree line; also in all other provinces and territories

CHOKECHERRY
Harsh Fruits, Mellowing with Age

Mature height: Avg. 2–4 m (6.6–13.2 ft)

Width: Avg. 5–15 cm (2–6 in)

Ontario giant: 16.2 m (53 ft) tall, 26 cm (10 in) thick, at Point Abino on Lake Erie

Alias: Common chokecherry, chuckley-plum, red chokecherry, wild cherry, *le cerisier à sauvage, Prunus virginiana*

Whereabouts: Mixed with deciduous trees and shrubs along streams, forest and wetland fringes, open woods, rocky ridges and clearings

Cherries: Bright red to purple-black, pea-sized, with large stones; big crops every 2 years

Leaves: Dark green, 2–12 cm (0.8–4.8 in) long, 1–6 cm

They are like small rubies
For a young queen who is small and graceful.
– Irving Layton, "Red Chokecherries"

Since time immemorial, cherries have drawn hungry crowds seeking their sweet, juicy flesh. Cherry-eating creatures propagate the trees by swallowing the pits and spreading them in their droppings. Some, though, such as evening grosbeaks and chipmunks, cheat the trees by biting into the pits to eat the seeds inside. Bears tear branches off to get at the small red fruits, sometimes breaking or crushing most of the trees in a thicket during big crop years in August and September.

Chokecherries are not as dangerous as their name suggests, though they can taste harsh and astringent, causing the mouth to pucker and dry.

The riper they become, especially when tempered by a frost, the sweeter and more palatable they are. But eating large numbers with their pits, or eating those of any other cherries, can cause vomiting and even death. The pits, inner bark and leaves of all cherry species are laced with prussic acid, or hydrogen cyanide, from which cyanide can be produced. A kilo (2.2 pounds) of cherry leaves is said to contain enough poison to kill 30 humans. Chokecherry leaves wilted by drought or frost are particularly poisonous to browsing cattle.

When cooked and dried, however, pit-bearing chokecherries are safe. The Ojibway mashed and dried them to mix into cakes. Farther west, they were one of the main wild berries added to flavour and sweeten pemmican, the dried-meat staple that fuelled the fur trade. Cherries were also dried or powdered for winter, when they were added to soup. Today they're most often used in jams, pies, juice and wine. The Québécois, having long cultivated chokecherries, produce fairly sweet strains with fruits up to 2.5 centimetres (one inch) wide.

Pin cherry, with smooth, shiny, reddish-brown bark laced with hash marks, tends to grow in clumps and patches, as does chokecherry. But it's more limited to drier, open, rocky areas, most often where there's been fires or logging; hence its other common name, fire cherry. Pin cherry's blossoms and shiny, red, long-stemmed fruits appear a little earlier than those of chokecherry. Fast-growing and spreading by root suckers, pin cherry quickly colonizes open spaces, often dominating them in the early years after a disturbance. It is a nurse tree

(0.4–2.4 in) wide, egg-shaped, broader than other cherry species, with finely serrated edges; turn dull yellow or reddish in fall

Bark: Smooth or finely scaled, dark grey; almost black on older trees

Sex: White blossoms, 8–10 mm (0.4 in) wide, clustered tightly around an erect central stalk, 5–15 cm (2–6 in) long at branch tips, with male and female parts found together in each tiny, 5-petalled flower; blooming in late May and early June, a week or more after leaves open; cross-pollinated by mosquitoes, bees and other flying insects

Buds: Brown, 6–12 mm (0.2–0.4 in) long, sharply pointed

Roots: Deep, extensive, spreading by rhizomes

Wood: Light brown, hard, dense but weak and porous

Companion trees and shrubs: Elderberry, raspberry, pin cherry, dogwood

Common diners: Bears, foxes, moose, deer, chipmunks, red squirrels, flying squirrels, raccoons, hares, skunks, mice, evening grosbeaks, cedar waxwings, ruffed grouse, thrushes, woodpeckers, catbirds, brown thrashers, blue jays, grackles, white-throated sparrows, orioles, scarlet tanagers, rose-breasted grosbeaks

Common nester: Chestnut-sided warbler

Tiny nibblers: Eastern tent caterpillars, chokecherry tentmakers, fall webworms

Range: All Ontario except northern Hudson Bay lowlands; also in all other provinces and Northwest Territories

Mature black cherry height: Avg. 20–22 m (66–72 ft)

Homeland of the domestic cherry: Western Asia and southeastern Europe

Divine cherry tree: Buddha is said to have been born under a cherry tree called Sala

Other members of *Prunus* genus: Plums, peaches, apricots, almonds

Number of *Prunus* species native to Ontario: 6

Number of *Prunus* species: About 200

Also see: Evening Grosbeak, Mosquitoes, Black Bear, Yellow Birch

for spruce and other slower-growing, shade-tolerant evergreen seedlings inching their way up beneath it, providing them with shelter and building up a fertile layer of humus with its fallen, decomposing leaves.

Black cherry differs considerably from its shrubby relatives, becoming a tall flaky-barked tree maturing deep in the forest. It still needs open sunlight to get started, though, often getting its chance in the space opened up by an old, wind-fallen tree in maple and beech forests. Less tolerant of extreme cold than the smaller cherries, it doesn't grow much farther north than Parry Sound and the Algonquin highlands. In many areas, the axe and saw have made it much less plentiful than it once was. The tree's attractive, fine, smooth-grained wood was highly coveted for musket butts, carriages, cabinets, counters and bars, and is still considered by many to make the best canoe paddles. The characteristic mahogany-red colour is, in fact, the result of a stain applied to the naturally light pink wood. Its black cherries were also widely used to flavour rum and whisky, giving the tree the alternative name "rum cherry."

HEMLOCK
Providing Clear, Sheltered Havens

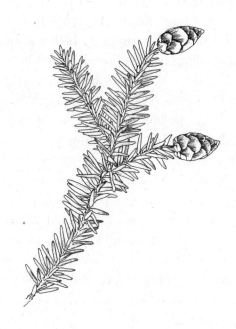

Lifespan: Commonly 300–600 years; up to 988 years

Mature height: Avg. 18–24 m (60–80 ft)

Trunk width: Avg. 60–90 cm (2–3 ft)

Ontario giant: 30 m (98 ft) tall, 1 m (3.3 ft) thick, on Big Trout Lake, Algonquin Park

Alias: Eastern hemlock, Canada hemlock, common hemlock, hemlock gum tree, hemlock spruce, white hemlock, weeping spruce, *la pruche de l'est, Tsuga canadensis*

Whereabouts: Cool, moist, rocky acidic ground in mature mixed forests, often near shorelines, on north-facing slopes, rocky shelves with deep-seeping water and in humid ravines

Needles: Flat, 1–2 cm (0.4–0.8 in) long, dark, shiny green on top, 2 white lines on underside; shed after 3 years

Bark: Scaly, orange-brown when young, becoming deeply furrowed with thick, purplish grey-brown ridges with age

Sex: Tiny yellow male flower conelets at base of needles; larger, pale green female conelets at twig tips; appearing in May; puberty at 15–30 years

Cones: 1–2 cm (0.4–0.8 in) long, pale green ripening to reddish brown, dropping seeds Oct. through winter; big crops generally every 2–3 years

Eastern hemlock is not the poisonous plant Socrates was obliged to sample by the leading citizens of Athens in 399 BCE. The Old World toxic shrub lent its name to our broad, graceful evergreen because European settlers fancied the scent of its burning needles was similar to that of poison hemlock. But they learned from Native people that the fine twigs and needles, far from being toxic, could be brewed into a nutritious tea.

Hemlocks have it made in the shade. They thrive in mature mixed forests along cool, rocky lakeshores, ridge tops and north-facing hillsides, usually on thinner, moister soil than is preferred by sugar maples. Where lower branches

Roots: Usually shallow, wide-spread, very fibrous, sometimes stilted; deeper in better drained soils

Wood: Light yellow-brown with reddish tinge, rough, harder than most softwoods, 465 kg/m³ (29 lb/cu. ft), very sparky when burned

Heat equivalent of 1 m³ (35 cu. ft) of wood: 108 L (24 gal) of oil

Companion trees and shrubs: Yellow birch, white cedar, white pine, white spruce, sugar maple, hobble-bush, mountain maple, striped maple

Associated plants: Canada mayflower, goldthread, wood sorrel, starflower, club moss

Common nesters: Blackburnian warblers, black-throated green warblers, northern parulas, golden crowned kinglets, juncos, pine siskins, saw-whet owls, sharp-shinned and red-shouldered hawks

Bear havens: Mothers and cubs often stay close to the safety of the hemlock's easily climbed branches in spring and sometimes hibernate at the hollow base of very large trees, which can be more than 1.2 m (4 feet) wide

Frequent diners: Red squirrels, red-backed voles, mice, ruffed grouse, red-breasted nuthatches, chickadees and white-winged crossbills eat seeds; deer, porcupines, moose and hares eat buds,

on other evergreens die and drop off as the shade above grows too great, densely needled hemlock limbs stretch out and flourish. Scant sunlight penetrates through to nourish undergrowth on the forest floor, making hemlock groves ideal clear, sheltered campsites. A thick mat of constantly falling needles provides a soft bed while making the ground too acidic for most plants, save for the tree's own seedlings or those of the occasional yellow birch or white cedar, all usually taking root on rotting logs, stumps or mossy mounds.

Young hemlocks grow very slowly in the deep shade. Apparent saplings only a few centimetres thick can be 200 years old. When a big tree falls and opens up a hole in the canopy above, such patient, stunted old-timers can suddenly shoot up with youthful vigour, rising dozens of centimetres in one growing season and potentially living on for centuries.

In the deep freeze of winter, mature hemlocks provide vital sanctuaries for a great host of birds and beasts. No other tree, in fact, shelters a greater variety of wildlife. The tree's flexible upsweeping boughs, intricately branched with flat splays of small-needled twigs, keep most snowfall from reaching the ground. Deer, which bog down in snow deeper than half a metre, often congregate in scattered clumps of 15 to 20 hemlocks connected by corridors of more singly spaced hemlocks. In addition to these "deer yards" providing easy movement and a microclimate several degrees warmer than the surrounding hardwoods, their lower twigs and seedlings, and those of accompanying yellow birch, are relished by the herbivores.

Near the northern limit of the deer's range, Algonquin Park's once-thriving population depended heavily on hemlock yards for its survival. Logging in the 19th century created vast areas of new browse for deer while largely sparing hemlock because the knots of its abundant branches render the lumber of little economic value. But vast numbers of park hemlock were cut in the 1950s and 1960s to provide shoring timbers for tunnels during the construction of Toronto's subway system. Already hard-pressed for food in a maturing forest, deer numbers plummeted with the loss of habitat. Several heavy winters in the late 1960s and early 1970s also contributed to their decline.

Moose and snowshoe hares also eagerly browse on hemlock. Higher up, ruffed grouse hop from branch to branch sampling buds, while porcupines may perch in a single tree for days at a time gnawing on the inner bark of the upper branches. Even the tree's interior can be occupied, with the base of a very large, old, hollow hemlock a favourite winter den site for bears. The snow beneath hemlocks is usually heavily sprinkled with tiny light-brown seed flakes, which rain down throughout the winter. The oil-rich seeds feed many mouths, from red squirrels and mice to chickadees, juncos, pine siskins and wild turkeys. Bumper crops bring white-winged crossbills, nomadic boreal birds which use their specialized beaks to pry seeds from the cones before they fall. Crossbills sometimes even nest in the middle of winter if there's plenty of food.

twigs or bark; yellow-bellied sapsuckers drink sap late Apr. to mid-May

Tiny nibblers: Hemlock loopers, grey spruce looper, and caterpillars of porcelain grey, hemlock angle and bi-coloured moths; hemlock borers, weevils, hemlock scale insects

Range: Southern Ontario to just north of Lake Nipissing and North Channel of Lake Huron and between Lake Superior and Lake of the Woods; also in Quebec, New Brunswick, Nova Scotia and Prince Edward Island

Number of hemlock species worldwide: 10

See also: Yellow-bellied Sapsucker, Black Bear, Porcupine, White-tailed Deer, Yellow Birch

JACK PINE
Fire Frees Seeds to Sprout

Most famous jack pine: Subject of Tom Thomson's 1916 *Jack Pine,* painted, some say, on the shore of Grand Lake in Algonquin Park

Mature height: Avg. 12–20 m (40–65 ft)

Trunk width: 20–30 cm (8–12 in)

Lifespan: Commonly 60–150 years; up to 240 years

Ontario giant: 25 m (82 ft) tall, 70 cm (27.5 in) thick, on Big Woman Lake, Kenora District

Alias: Scrub pine, grey pine, banksian pine, pine princess, princy, *le pin gris, Pinus banksiana*

Whereabouts: Usually on dry, sandy or rocky sites, open shorelines, outwash plains

Needles: 2–5 cm (0.8–2 in) long, thick, stiff, rough, pointy, curved, in bunches of 2; shed after 2–3 years

Bark: Reddish brown to grey when young, turning with age to dark brown or grey, in large furrowed flakes

Sex: Tiny, dark purplish female flowers near branch tips; light brown males in clusters at base of shoots in May; puberty at 5–10 years

Cones: 2.5–7.5 cm (1–3 in) long, curved, in pairs, green at first, turning grey with age, sometimes fused into branch

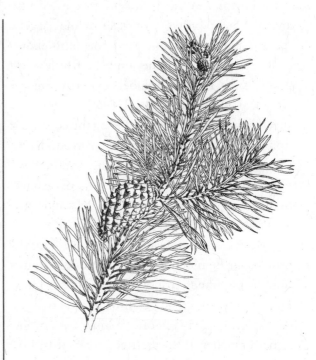

Though jack pine seems like the poor cousin of the majestic taller pines, it's a far hardier and much more widespread tree, covering vast tracts of boreal forest. Though usually straight when growing in big stands of its own kind, out in the open it's often twisted, knotty and scruffy-looking, with its small tufts of needles on downward-bending branches. Early settlers thought the tree poisoned the ground and futilely tried to clear them, only to find more sprouting up.

The truth is that jack pine is one of the few trees that will grow on very poor ground. It takes root in dry, sandy, rocky sites, often on steep, south-facing hillsides, where even hardy red pines have trouble. Its flexible, contorted limbs are wind resistant, and it clings tenaciously to exposed sites. Having evolved with the frequent-fire ecology of the boreal forest, it specializes in growing in burnt-over or logged areas, particularly if damage to the soil has been too severe for competing pioneer species such as aspen. Unable to live in the shade of other trees, jack pines mark the spot of such disturbance.

Jack pine is one of the few trees that will grow on very poor ground

Having little chance of success without their specific site requirements, jack pines do not even bother to release their seeds at regular intervals like other trees. Instead, most cones remain on the tree for up to 25 years, tightly closed, sealed in resin, until fire or very hot temperatures in direct sunlight open them. Fires also release minerals from burnt vegetation into the soil to nourish the new fast-growing seedlings.

Range: Southern edge of Canadian Shield to northern boreal forest, and in tree plantations in southern Ontario; also in all other provinces and territories except British Columbia, island of Newfoundland, Prince Edward Island and the Yukon

RED MAPLE
Flowering Early for a Head Start

Mature height: Avg. 12–27 m (65–90 ft)

Trunk width: Avg. 40–80 cm (16–32 in)

Ontario giant: 31 m (102 ft) tall, 1.3 m (4.2 ft) thick, on Squirrel Island, Lambton Co.

Lifespan: Commonly 100–150 years

Alias: Swamp maple, scarlet maple, soft maple, water maple, curled maple, *l'érable rouge, Acer rubrum*

Whereabouts: Edges of swamps, bogs and beaver ponds, on sandy loam bottomlands and dry, sandy sites

Bark: Smooth, silvery grey on young trees, darker and ridged when older

Leaves: 7–13 cm (3–5 in) long, toothed edges, V-shaped notches between lobes, pale undersides

Sex: Clusters of tiny bright red flowers, females on long stems, males in short bunches with yellow anthers; mainly wind pollinated, but honeybees and plasterer bees also collect pollen; open long before leaves

Seeds: 1.3–2.5 cm (0.5–1 in) long with wings, in pairs; travel up to 160 m (525 ft) in moderate winds

Wood: Light brown, moderately strong, hard, 610 kg/m³ (38 lb/cu. ft)

Red maple is named for its bright purple-red shoots, buds, flowers, seeds and unfolding leaves in spring. Early settlers made red ink and dye by boiling its bark. In fall, however, its leaves are not simply red. Unlike most other trees, red maples most often feature either all-male or all-female flowers on one tree. Come autumn, the female trees change various shades of yellow or orange, while males, which are much more numerous, range from orange-red to scarlet.

Because it is not as shade-tolerant as sugar maple, red maple is not as common. It's not as fussy as its cousin, however, about soil. In hardwood forests, it wins out mainly in areas that are wetter for longer periods of the year or on dry, sandy sites. In northern Ontario, where their sugary cousins dwindle, red maples persevere, springing up on disturbed sites that previously held conifers, or on the forest fringe. Red maple seeds are smaller and lighter than those of sugar maple, so they can travel farther to find those sites. They also get a head start because red maples flower early, often with snow still on the ground, and release seeds in late June.

The deeply notched **silver maple** – said to have inspired Toronto schoolteacher Alexander Muir to write "The Maple Leaf Forever" in 1867 – also grows in swamps and on floodplains, but rarely anywhere else. The **striped maple** is a common understorey shrub, with huge three-pointed leaves and distinctive vertical white stripes on its green bark. Another shrub, **mountain maple**, is abundant in Temagami's pine forests, where other maples are extremely rare.

Companion trees: Black ash, white elm, red oak, white pine
Range: Southern Ontario to about Lake Temiskaming and Wawa, and from Thunder Bay to Lake of the Woods; also in all other eastern provinces
Also see: Sugar Maple

RED OAK

"Beware of an oak,
It draws the stroke"

Mature height: Avg. 16–25 m (52.5–82 ft)

Trunk width: Avg. 30–90 cm (1–3 ft)

Ontario giant: 31.1 m (102 ft) tall, 1.9 m (6.4 ft) wide, in Harwich Township, Kent Co.

Lifespan: Commonly 150–300 years

Alias: Northern red oak, eastern red oak, grey oak, champion oak, *le chêne rouge, Quercus rubra*

Whereabouts: Most common on rocky ridge tops and dry, sandy uplands, though grows better in richer soils

Leaves: 10–23 cm (4–9 in) long, 7–15 cm (3–6 in) wide, with 7–11 pointed lobes between rounded notches; unfold later than

The tall, wide crown of oak trees makes them particularly susceptible to being struck by lightning. Even in predominantly beech forests, oak is estimated to be hit by lightning 10 to 20 times as often as beech. When hit, oak often bursts into flame. The ancient Europeans saw in this spectacular phenomenon a direct connection with the gods, and the thunder tree was venerated above all others.

The most ancient Greek traditions depicted Zeus, the thunder god, as an oak or at least living in one. Oaks were sacred to Thor and Jehovah, both thunder-and-lightning deities. Oak was similarly the supreme god of the Gauls, and the name of the Finnish thunder god was Ukko, meaning "oak." Sacred oak groves were the scenes of oracles by Greek priestesses, ceremonies by the Druids and Roman women beseeching oak nymphs for safe births. Roman poets wrote that acorns were the first food to sustain newborn humans. Even the oak tree's parasite, mistletoe, was deified and is still hung at Christmas. Unable to shake pagan reverence for sites of sacred oaks, where sacrifices were made to older deities, the Christian Church eventually took over the sanctuaries by blessing them and erecting crucifixes and images of Mary.

In central Ontario, red-oak groves are most often found on dry, rocky ridgetops and south-facing slopes, where deep roots and tough, waxy leaves give the trees an advantage in finding and retaining scarce groundwater. Elsewhere, red oak is usually crowded and shaded out by faster-growing, more shade-tolerant maples and beech. Oak also cannot withstand prolonged periods of extreme cold, and becomes increasingly rare north and west of Algonquin Park. Even where it is rare, red oak is very noticeable from a distance in the spring because its high levels of tannin – a bitter-tasting, acidic defence chemical against animal browsing – makes newly unfolding leaves bright red. Later, chlorophyll production kicks in to turn them green. When the green fades in October, the tannin pigment re-emerges to colour hilltop oaks rusty brown. The leaves remain long after maples and other trees drop theirs. Tannin is also the compound, released by slowly rotting vegetation, that turns swamp water brown.

Native people sometimes ate the seeds inside red oak acorns, but only after prolonged boiling, soaking for days in running water or burying them for the winter to leach out their bitter tannin. The acorns of white oak, on the other

maple and many other trees in spring, turn rusty red to brown in autumn

Bark: Smooth and dark grey when young; wide furrows between long, flat, light grey ridges on older trees; intersected higher up on trunk by slight horizontal bulges

Sex: Dangling, greenish-yellow male catkins 10–13 cm (4–5 in) long; tiny, reddish female flowers at base of leaf stalks on new shoots; wind-pollinated; blooming in mid-May; puberty at 20–25 years

Acorns: 1–3 cm (0.4–1.2 in) long, woody, holding 1 seed, green at first, turning reddish brown, with brown cap of scales; very bitter-tasting, contain 8% protein, 37% fat; take 2 summers to ripen; 100–4,000 per tree, with big crops usually every 2–5 years

Buds: About 6 mm (0.2 in) long, pointy, shiny reddish brown

Roots: Deep, widespread, often with taproot

Maximum daily water uptake by roots of a mature oak: More than 1,000 L (220 gal)

Wood: Reddish-brown to pink heartwood, whitish sapwood, coarse-grained, very strong, hard, porous, 690 kg/m³ (43 lb/cu. ft), very warm-burning

Heat equivalent of 1 m³ (35 cu. ft) of wood: 181 L (40 gal) of oil

Companion trees and shrubs: White pine, red pine, jack pine, red maple, aspen, beaked hazel, bush honeysuckle

Common nesters: Great horned owls, hawks, white-breasted nuthatches, pewees, scarlet tanagers

Frequent diners: Bears, raccoons, foxes, squirrels, chipmunks, mice, blue jays, nuthatches, ruffed grouse, wild turkeys, wood ducks, flickers, pileated woodpeckers and grackles eat acorns; moose, deer and hares browse leaves

Tiny nibblers: Forest tent caterpillars, oak-leaf shredders, oak-leaf rollers, filbert worms and many other moth caterpillars; gall wasps, acorn weevils, sap beetles, wood-boring beetles, aphids

Ontario forest infested by forest tent caterpillars 2007: 3,700 km^2

Ontario forest infested by forest tent caterpillars at peak in 2001: 130,000 km^2

Range: Southern Ontario to a little north of Lake Timiskaming, Sudbury and Sault Ste. Marie, and in a thin band from Thunder Bay to Quetico Provincial Park; also in Quebec, the Maritimes and planted in British Columbia

Accolades: Official tree of Prince Edward Island and New Jersey

Famous oaks: Niagara-on-the-Lake's Parliament Oak,

hand, are sweeter and edible even raw, though Native people usually dried and ground them to make into cakes and add to soups.

Most wildlife, however, aren't as fussy about eating raw red-oak acorns. In fact, as autumn draws near, red-oak stands become the centre of attraction for all manner of hungry birds and beasts. Deer, raccoons, chipmunks, ruffed grouse, wood ducks and nuthatches come from far and wide to munch on one of the most nutritious of woodland foods. Bears fatten up for hibernation by climbing up oaks and pulling limbs towards them to get at the acorns, often leaving conspicuous "bear nests" of broken branches behind. Squirrels, blue jays and white-footed mice help spread the seeds by storing acorns in various locations. Those they fail to retrieve have a high germination rate. Populations of diners in some areas may rise and fall from year to year with acorn-crop cycles. Millions of migrating passenger pigeons, which once blackened the skies over Ontario, were dependent on acorn and beechnut crops. Their extinction is believed to have greatly limited the oak's ability to spread.

Oaks are also a major attraction for many species of wasps, which lay eggs on leaves, twigs, acorns and roots. When the eggs hatch in spring, the wasp larvae eat into the vegetation. In response, the tree starts building up dense tissue that gradually hardens around the cavity, forming a tumourlike gall. Oak leaves can have up to 100 tiny galls each. Other galls on branches may be five centimetres (two inches) long. Although beetles, moths, butterflies, aphids and flies cause galls on a wide variety of trees, they most commonly use oaks. A key chemical called purpurogallin, produced in nutgalls on oak trees, was discovered, by researchers at the University of Toronto, to prevent cell damage in laboratory animals. It may eventually be used to treat arthritis, stroke and cancer.

The **bur oak**, with its large tapered leaves and burred acorns, also grows in central Ontario, but it is rare, restricted mainly to clay bottom-lands. The great **white oak**, sporting round-lobed leaves and more flaky-ridged bark, is common in southern Ontario but reaches only the fringes of the Canadian Shield and up the Ottawa Valley. Bearing the strongest, densest, best-quality wood of any oak, it was widely used for the strong, sturdy beams of wooden ships. England had already cut down most of its own once-great oak forests in order to rule the waves, with up to 3,500 trees going into the building of one warship. Vast white-oak stands in eastern Ontario were ranked next to white pine in importance to the loggers of the early 1800s. Because white-oak wood is so dense and heavy, early river drivers had to lash timbers of pine to it to keep it from sinking. Today, both red and white oak are used for floors, furniture trim and veneers. Because white-oak wood is not porous like red, it is also used for wine and whisky casks, contributing a singular flavour to their contents.

the Oak of Mamre, Sherwood Forest's Major Oak, Charleston's 1,500-year-old Angel Oak; Seven Oaks, Manitoba, scene of 1814 battle of same name; King Arthur's Round Table, made from the cross-section of a great oak trunk

Largest remnant oak savannah in North America: About 1,500 ha (3,700 acres) in Pinery Provincial Park, near Grand Bend, Ontario

Portion of North America's original 1.3 million ha (3.2 million acres) of oak savannah that remains: 0.02%

Number of oak species native to Ontario: 11

Number of oak species worldwide: 500–600

Also see: Blue Jay, Black Bear, Red Squirrel, Thunder and Lightning

RED PINE
Drawing Strength from Adversity

Mature height: Avg. 18–25 m (60–80 ft)

Trunk width: Avg. 30–60 cm (1–2 ft)

Ontario giant: 37.5 m (123 ft) tall, 113 cm (3.7 ft) thick, in Algonquin Park

Height at 50 years old: 14–23 m (45–75 ft)

Lifespan: Commonly 300 years; up to 400 years

Alias: Canadian red pine, hard pine, bull pine, Norway pine, *le pin rouge, Pinus resinosa*

Name origin of *pine*: From proto-Indo-European *pit,* meaning "resin"

Whereabouts: Usually sandy, dry, acidic soils, outwash plains, rocky, windswept lakeshores (most often on east sides), islands, ridges, steep, exposed slopes

Needles: 10–16 cm (4–6.5 in) long, dark green, coarse, thick, stiff, 2 to a stalk, sharp points and finely toothed edges; shed after 4–5 years

Bark: Flaky and reddish or pinkish brown, furrowing into long, flat ridges on older trees

Sex: Bunches of purplish male flower conelets 1–2 cm (0.4–0.9 in) long, appearing at base of shoots in late May or early June; purple or scarlet female flower conelets, 2–4 mm

Red pine is a tough, resilient, almost invincible giant of the forest, springing from underdog seeds that stand little chance of success in competition on fertile ground. The tree grows poorly in shade but thrives along exposed, rocky lakeshores, steep slopes and severely burnt-over areas, places where winter winds are too severe for many other species to prosper. With its strong roots set in these harsh niches, red pine can endure for hundreds of years, withstanding disasters that claim most trees.

More saturated with thick, protective resin than the other pines, red pine is resistant to most harmful insects and fungi, and can live through cold snaps of more than −50°C (−58°F). Large trees often survive forest fires because their thick bark scorches but doesn't readily burn and there are usually no branches for the flames to climb on the lower half to three-quarters of the trunk. Red pines also often grow well spaced apart from each other and have relatively narrow crowns, while their buds are protected within thick bunches of long, slow-burning needles, helping to protect the trees in all but the most intense forest fires.

Every three to seven years, red pines over a large area produce up to a fivefold increase in cones

Though most old-growth red pine was cut long ago, the qualities that make the tree so resistant have made it a highly favoured species for tree plantations. Large monoculture plantations, however, are far from the ideal of nature, with few understorey plants and shrubs and little wildlife diversity. Dense rows of planted trees are also more vulnerable to fire than sparser natural red pine stands.

Whether in natural settings or plantations, red pine cones are not immune from the attentions of squirrels and birds such as crossbills. To ensure some seeds survive, the species follows the strategy of most conifers and many other trees. In most years, only a small number of pine cones are produced, with few escaping the hungry jaws of seed-eaters. But every three to seven years, red pines over a large area produce up to a fivefold increase in cones, nurtured by

(0.1–0.2 in) long, higher up on tree, partly hidden by tufts of needles at branch tips; puberty at 15–60 years

Cones: 4–7 cm (1.5–2.7 in) long, squat, dark at first, fading to tan-brown; opening in their second Sept., dropping most seeds Oct.–Nov., some falling through to next summer; up to 725 per tree in good crop years

Seeds: Winged, about 1.3 cm (0.5 in) long, avg. 30–45 per cone; land up to 150 m (500 ft) from parent trees

Buds: 1–2 cm (0.4–0.8 in) long, pointy, resinous

Roots: Widespread, moderately deep, very strong

Wood: Light to reddish-brown heartwood, yellowish-white sapwood, straight-grained, harder than white pine, 450 kg/m³ (28 lb/cu. ft), very resinous

Heat equivalent of 1 m³ (35 cu. ft) of wood: 119 L (26 gal) of oil

Companion trees: White pine, jack pine, hemlock, aspen, red oak, cedar, fir

Frequent diners: Red squirrels and red crossbills eat seeds; porcupines, moose, deer and hares eat seedlings, twigs, bark or needles

Tiny nibblers: Pine false webworms, European pine-shoot moths, pine weevils

Fungal feeders: Scleroderris pine-canker fungus, blister rust

Range: North shore of Lake Ontario to the mid-boreal forest; also in all eastern provinces and Manitoba
Number of pine species native to Ontario: 4
Number of pine species worldwide: About 100
Also see: Red Squirrel, White Pine

particularly warm temperatures and plentiful rainfall in June and July almost two years before, when the buds that yield them begin forming. With up to 90,000 cones per hectare (2.5 acres) suddenly available, birds and squirrels cannot possibly eat or store all the seeds, allowing some to germinate the following year. Any population rise in seed-eaters that results from the bounty is reversed when only a few cones are forthcoming the following year.

With distinctive tufts of long needles on relatively short, snaking branches, red pine has a splotchy appearance in silhouette. The shape is quite different from the more sweeping, layered white pine. Though less common than its taller cousin the white pine, red pine, with much of its trunk often clear of knots and branches, was also prized for ships' masts in the early days of logging. It was loaded at the bottom of the holds of timber ships sailing to Britain because it's heavier than white pine.

SPECKLED ALDER
Little Tree with Special Powers

Being small shrubby trees, alders weren't given a second glance by the first lumberjacks hacking their way through Ontario's forests. Finnish loggers, though, seemed to have some intuition about these trees' special powers. When they introduced the Swede saw – which cut trees twice as fast as the old one-person crosscut saw – into Ontario's lumber camps in the 1920s, they used alder wood for their homemade saw frames, saying it had a spirit that kept lumberjacks from cutting themselves.

Before the saw-happy Finns came along, Native people boiled alder bark to make a poultice for wounds and to treat rheumatism. Like

Mature height: Avg. 2–6 m (6.6–20 ft)

Trunk width: Avg. 2.5–5 cm (1–2 in)

Ontario giant: 14.3 m (47 ft) tall, 27 cm (10.5 in) thick, at Hamilton's Royal Botanical Gardens

Alias: Tag alder, grey alder, black alder, hoary alder, *l'aune commun, Alnus rugosa*

Whereabouts: Shorelines, shrub swamp thickets on river and creek floodplains, wet meadows

Bark: Reddish brown, thin; smooth surface densely

TREES

speckled with small, horizontal, pale marks

Leaves: 5–10 cm (2–4 in) long, oval, pointed, dull green, with serrated edges and straight, distinct veins that feel like ribs on the underside; wrinkled above; fall while still green in autumn

Sex: Bunches of 3–5 dangling, cylindrical male catkins, 2 cm (0.8 in) long, appear in late summer and expand to 5–10 cm (2–4 in) in April and early May, before leaves unfold, along with clusters of 2 or 3 oval female flowers, 1.5–3 cm (0.6–1.2 in) long

Seeds: 1–1.5 cm (0.4–0.6 in) long, oval, woody cones open in fall to release winged seeds; cone may remain on tree for several more years

Buds: Dark red-brown, on a distinct stalk

Roots: Shallow, with small clusters of yellow, coral-like nodules

Wood: Light, soft, pale brown, not very strong

Companion trees and shrubs: White cedar, red maple, fir, black spruce, tamarack, black ash, balsam poplar, willow, red osier dogwood, elder, chokecherry

Associated plants: Sedges, grasses, cattails, wild iris, jewelweed, sweetflag, winterberry, cinnamon fern

Common nesters: Hummingbirds, chickadees, goldfinches, red-winged

willow and trembling aspen, the bark contains salicin, the active ingredient in Aspirin. The inner bark, combined with the roots, bark and berries of various other plants and trees, was also used to make red and yellowish-brown dyes for porcupine quillwork.

Perhaps more than anyone else, Canadian beavers know the value of alder. The little tree, thriving in fast-growing, dense curtains along shorelines, is their most common dam-building material. The water-tolerant trunks and branches are particularly durable in beaver constructions. They're also well designed for depredations caused by the bucktoothed builders, with multiple stems sprouting from the spiky stumps left behind. Alders send up clones from underground shoots, as well, and reroot at branches that bend to the ground.

In fact, speckled alder's unique qualities make it vitally important as a nourisher of all life in the forest – plant and animal, terrestrial and aquatic. Because its abundant cone clusters begin forming in late summer and don't release nutlets until autumn of the following year, alder feeds high-energy seeds, flowers and buds throughout the year to ruffed grouse, wood warblers and a large variety of other birds and animals. Its dangling catkin flowers, among the first to open in spring, attract hordes of bees. Thick, extensive lakefront or swampside alder tangles also provide shelter for both birds and mammals. Its dense, colonial rooting networks, which reach into streams and lakes to get oxygen from running water, help stabilize banks, while its crooked, overhanging stems and branches provide cover for fish and other creatures.

Unlike other trees, alder can also fix nitrogen from the air passages in the ground. Though it constitutes almost 80 per cent of the atmosphere, nitrogen is one nutrient most plants cannot absorb in its gaseous form. But it is needed to make proteins and enzymes in all lifeforms. Alder, along with legumes such as clover and beans, has clusters of knobby chambers, called nodules, on its rootlets, containing symbiotic bacteria that take nitrogen from the air and transform it into ammonia, a form plants can absorb. This ability promotes extremely rapid growth in alders. The trees nurture the bacteria with sugars.

Alder leaves contain three or four times as much nitrogen as the leaves and needles of most trees. When they are shed, they provide about 160 kilograms of nitrogen per hectare (140 pounds per acre). In the water, they feed aquatic insect larvae, injecting precious nitrogen into the entire aquatic food chain. On the ground, nitrogen compounds from fallen alder leaves are absorbed by other trees and plants. The high nitrogen content also causes the leaves to decay more quickly than most others, in about a year. Although it cannot grow in shade, alder has soil-enriching powers that make it an important pioneer species in burnt or cut-over areas. If logging companies, spraying to destroy "weed trees," kill too many alders, they may impoverish the soil and decrease the long-term chances of success for commercially grown trees.

blackbirds, woodcocks, catbirds, alder flycatchers, golden-winged warblers

Common visitors: Chickadees, redpolls and pine siskins eat seeds; ruffed grouse eat buds and catkins; muskrats, hares, deer and moose sometimes browse leaves and twigs; breeding treefrogs and spring peepers call from branches; also beavers, snipes, swamp sparrows

Tiny nibblers: Caterpillars of luna, large looper, rusty tussock, white-marked tussock and cutworm moths; soldier, flathead borer and alderleaf beetles

Range: All Ontario to tree line; also in all other provinces and territories except Nunavut

Number of alder species native to Ontario: 3

Number of alder species worldwide: About 30

Also see: Beaver, Gray Treefrog, Mushrooms

SUGAR MAPLE
Sweetness, Colour and Pride

Mature height: Avg. 18–27 m (60–90 ft)

Trunk width: Avg. 60–90 cm (2–3 ft)

Ontario giant: 39.6 m (130 ft) tall, 1.2 m (4 ft) wide, in Wellesley Township, Waterloo Region

Lifespan: Avg. 200–300 years

Oldest in Ontario: The Comfort Maple, said to be more than 500 years old, is 25 m (82 ft) tall, 1.9 m (6.2 ft) wide, on the Comfort farmstead near St. Catharines

Minimum width for tapping: 25 cm (10 in), usually when 25–30 years old

Rate at which sap rises: 30–120 cm (1–4 ft) per hour

Total spring sap collected per tree: 0.5–4 L (1–8 pt)

Average number of litres of sap to make one litre of maple syrup: 35–40

Sugar content of sap: Avg. 2.5–3%, up to 7%

Sugar content of sap of most other maples: Avg. 1–2%

Sugar content of maple syrup: Avg. 66%

Alias: Hard maple, rock maple, sweet maple, black maple, sugar tree, *l'érable à sucre, Acer saccharum*

Genus name origin: *Acer* derived from Latin for

A sugar-maple leaf graces the Canadian flag. In central Ontario's upland forests, sugar maple is the most common tree, though it becomes rare north of Algonquin Park. The tree's abundance is due to many qualities that might figuratively be attributed to the nation itself, among them strength, tenacity and the ability to grow in the shade of others.

The secret to the sugar maple's dominance is its tough, early-sprouting seedlings and their extreme shade-tolerance. They often cover the forest floor, up to 150,000 seedlings per hectare (2.5 acres). Though most die within a few years in the limited sunlight, some may last 15 to 30 years. If a space opens in the canopy above, the lucky sapling directly below wins the lottery and shoots upwards. Once there, it hogs all the sunshine. A maple branch, with its large, abundant leaves, captures or reflects 90 per cent of the sunlight hitting it. Beneath the eight to 12 leaf layers of the deep, solid canopy of a mature maple, few plants other than its own offspring can grow in the summer.

The wider and deeper the crown
of a sugar maple, the more
abundant and sweeter its sap

The amount of sunlight sugar maples receive is critical for both autumn colours and spring maple-syrup production. The sunnier the autumn, the brighter the colours, with the best oranges and scarlets appearing on the most exposed or southern side of trees. Sugar maples begin to change colour in September, when they've already withdrawn more than half of the nutrients from their leaves back into their branches in preparation for winter and they begin losing their ability to make green chlorophyll. At the same time, their leaves use accumulated sugars, most abundantly produced on warm, sunny days, to make red anthocyanin — the same pigment that colours cherries, grapes, beets, radishes and many other vegetables and flowers. The pigment may help protect the leaves from cold, or the combination of cold and sunlight, so they can salvage as many nutrients as possible before nights below 7°C (45°F) cause a waterproof abscission barrier to form at

"sharp," because sturdy maple saplings furnished spears for Roman legions

Whereabouts: Rich, deep, moist, well-drained sandy loam soil, especially on glacial-till hills

Average number of maples in a 15-year-old 1-ha (2.5-acre) stand: 50,000

Average number of mature sugar maples in a 1-ha (2.5-acre) stand: 38

Leaves: 8–13 cm (3–5 in), smooth edges, wide V- or U-shaped spaces between prominently pointed lobes; growing in opposite pairs on branch

Bark: Smooth and grey when young, becoming darker with age, with long, broad, chunky ridges, often curling outwards

Sex: Clusters of tiny greenish-yellow petal-less flowers, hanging like tassels from branch tips in early to mid-May; first blooms when about 35 years old

Seeds: Green, winged keys, 2–4 cm (0.8–1.6 in) long, joined in pairs with both wings pointing in same direction; only one key in each pair contains a seed; shed in autumn; big crops, up to 12.5 million seeds per ha (2.5 acre), every 3–5 years

Distance falling maple seeds travel: Up to 160 m (528 ft)

Buds: Reddish brown, pointed

Roots: Deep, widespread

Wood: Light yellow-brown, close-grained and often wavy,

hard, heavy, strong , durable, 705 kg/m³ (44 lb/cu. ft), very warm-burning

Heat equivalent of 1 m³ (35 cu ft) of wood: 192 L (42 gal) of oil

Canuck sluggers: Since 1997, dense sugar-maple baseball bats made by Ottawa carpenter Sam Holman have become a high-quality alternative in major leagues to less durable traditional white ash bats

Companion trees and shrubs: Beech, yellow birch, black cherry, white pine, hemlock, basswood, red oak, red maple, beaked hazel

Associated plants: White trillium, trout lily, spring beauty, jack-in-the-pulpit, Canada mayflower, wild sarsaparilla, violets, wood ferns

Common nesters: Red-eyed and warbling vireos, robins, broad-winged and other hawks, blue jays, scarlet tanagers and many other birds

Frequent diners: Squirrels, mice, evening grosbeaks, ruffed grouse, purple finches and many other birds eat seeds; deer, moose and porcupines browse leaves, twigs and bark

Common sap-sippers: Yellow-bellied sapsuckers, squirrels, chickadees, cedar waxwings, goldfinches, nuthatches

Tiny nibblers: Forest tent caterpillars, sugar-maple borers, maple trumpet skeletonizers, Bruce spanworms

the end of leaf stems. Then the green fades completely to reveal the brilliant red and orange hues. The acidic soils of the Canadian Shield make for the deepest reds.

Eventually, as anthocyanins that remain break down, red and orange leaves join those in shadier parts of the tree in fading to yellow. Jack Frost is not responsible for painting leaves. He shrivels and oxidizes them, turning them brown.

In Ojibway legend, a stand of bright autumn maples near a waterfall hid Nokomis, grandmother of the fabled magician Nanabush, from a band of evil windigo spirits chasing her. Through the mist of the waterfall, the windigos were convinced they were staring at a blazing fire in which Nokomis must have died. Nanabush rewarded the sugar maples by giving them sweet, strong-flowing sap.

Both the Ojibway and Iroquois tapped sugar maples by placing a flat stick, hollowed alder stem or reed in a gash in the bark and collecting the sap drips in birchbark containers or hollow logs. The first run of sap, during the time of greatest privation at the end of winter, was greeted with ceremonies of thanksgiving. A family group commonly spent the better part of a month tapping hundreds of trees and collecting up to several thousand gallons of sap in a hereditary sugar bush within their traditional hunting grounds. The sap was boiled, then strained or dried in the sun on birchbark. Much of the maple sugar produced was stored for use during the following winter. Until about the 1840s, this was the main source of sugar for pioneers as well.

March days, with temperatures up to 5°C

(41°F) and nights below freezing, increase pressure within the tree, which stores sugars during winter in its roots and sapwood. Sap flows only if there is a tap hole or natural wound in the tree, providing an outlet for the pressurized, melted sugar-water solution. The end comes when sap-swollen buds start producing amino acids, which get into the tree's circulation, giving any resulting syrup a bitter taste. It's sometimes called the "frog run" because it occurs around the same time that spring peepers start calling from newly thawed forest ponds.

The wider and deeper the crown of a sugar maple, the more light it captures and the more abundant and sweeter its sap. Over the past few decades, the crowns of many sugar maples in central Ontario have withered under the combined assault of acid rain, invading gypsy moths from Europe, lower snowfalls and higher temperatures. Because soil nutrients dissolve into acidic water solutions more readily than usual, they are washed away in acid-rain runoff more quickly than they can be replenished by decaying vegetation. At the same time, acid precipitation frees up 10 to 30 times as much aluminum into soil solutions as is normal. Aluminum is toxic to trees. To avoid absorbing it, roots diminish their uptake, further starving themselves of nutrients in the process. Once undernourished, trees fall easy prey to heart-rot or root fungi and other natural afflictions.

Parasites: Honey fungus, yellow cap fungus, stereum fungus, spongy rot fungus, mossy top fungus

Secrets of maple resilience: Glassy crystals in leaf tissues and hard veins wear down caterpillars' teeth; tannins in leaves taste raunchy to mammals

Range: Southern Ontario to southern edge of boreal forest; also in Quebec, New Brunswick, Nova Scotia and Prince Edward Island

First appearance of maples: More than 90 million years ago

Early uses of maple leaf as an emblem: By the St-Jean-Baptiste Society in 1834; *Maple Leaf* literary journal, in 1848; first Canadian penny in 1858; coat of arms of both Ontario and Quebec in 1868; Canadian Expeditionary Force in the First World War

One-cent botanical blunder: Canadian pennies since 1938 incorrectly depict two maple leaves with stems attached at alternating points along a twig, though maples are among the few native trees, along with ashes and dogwoods, with leaves arranged in opposite pairs

Number of maple species native to Ontario: 7

Number of maple species worldwide: About 150

Also see: Deer Mouse, Beech, Red Maple, Big Dipper, Lakes

TAMARACK
The Deciduous Conifer

Mature height: Avg. 10–20 m (33–66 ft)

Trunk width: Avg. 30–60 cm (1–2 ft)

Ontario giant: 29 m (95 ft) tall, 67 cm (26 in) thick, in Cardiff Township, Haliburton Co.

Lifespan: Avg. 150–200 years, up to 330 years

Growth rate: Up to 10 times faster on drier ground than in bogs, often reaching 15 m (49 ft) in 25 years

Alias: Eastern larch, American larch, takmahak, hackmatack, red larch, black larch, *le mélèze laricin, Larix laricina*

Whereabouts: Bogs, swamps, lakeshores, riversides or drier, rocky, open sites

Needles: 2–2.5 cm (0.8–1 in) long, soft, in tufts of 15–60 from round knobs, or singly near branch tips, sprouting bright green in early May, darkening to bluish green

Bark: Smooth and grey when young; flaky, pinkish brown on older trees

Sex: Tiny, round, brownish male conelets; slightly larger, bright purple female conelets; growing at round twig knobs in May

Cones: 1.3–2 cm (0.5–0.8 in) long, oval, light brown, with thin scales opening in late summer, releasing seeds through autumn; crops of up

The lacy, dangling limbs of tamaracks are unique among Ontario's coniferous trees in that they shed their soft needles every fall. Tamarack needles are soft because they do not need the waxy coating and strong cells that allow other conifer needles to survive winter. Before dropping, the needles turn stunning hues of gold in October, enlivening the dark environs of the bogs and swamps where they're often found.

Tamaracks can afford to shed their needles because they usually grow close to running water and draw new nutrients from it each spring. They are also fed by many species of mushrooms, which wrap their subterranean threads around tamarack rootlets and transfer nutrients. Many of these mushrooms, ranging in colour from bright wine-red to smokey brown, sprout from the moss beneath the trees in late summer and autumn.

Tamaracks can afford to shed their needles because they usually grow close to running water

Moving water also provides tamarack roots with the oxygen they must have to live in soggy, acidic soils. Its willowy branches allow lots of light through for other plants to grow beneath it. Its seedlings, however, must have full sunlight to grow. The more shade-tolerant black spruce usually dominates most of a densely treed bog, leaving tamarack mainly along the open edges.

to 20,000 cones per tree every 3–6 years
Roots: Shallow, widespread
Wood: Yellowish-brown to reddish-brown heartwood; thin, white sapwood, rough, often spiral-grained, fairly hard, flexible, oily, rot-resistant, 560 kg/m³ (35 lb/cu. ft)
Companion trees: Black spruce, balsam fir, white spruce, trembling aspen, white birch
Range: All Ontario, except extreme southwest; also in all other provinces and territories
Accolades: Official tree of Northwest Territories
Also see: Mushrooms, Black Spruce, Wetlands

TREMBLING ASPEN
Stirred in the Slightest Breeze

Portion of Ontario's forest made up of trembling aspen and other poplars: 21%

Mature height: Avg. 12–25 m (39–82 ft)

Trunk width: Avg. 18–40 cm (7–16 in)

Ontario giant: 38 m (125 ft) tall, 80 cm (2.6 ft) wide, in Limerick Township, Hastings Co.

Lifespan: Commonly 50–120 years, up to 225 years

Alias: Quaking aspen, golden aspen, quiver-leaf, mountain aspen, trembling poplar, popple, *le peuplier faux-tremble, Populus tremuloides*

Whereabouts: Well-drained sandy, loam or gravel soils, from bottomlands to upper slopes, where previous forest cleared by fire or other disturbances, and at edges of beaver ponds, streams and wetlands; more common on drier soils than white birch

Bark: Smooth, glossy, pale green when young, becoming silver-grey or whitish, lightest on south side, with rough black patches and horizontal marks; dark grey and furrowed with age; young bark can photosynthesize like leaves

Leaves: Squat and rounded, 3–7 cm (1.2–2.8 in) long,

Murmuring and shimmering in the slightest breeze, the trembling aspen has a name that fits. The trembling is due to long, flat leaf stems that are more easily swayed by the wind than if they were round. North American Native peoples called the tree "noisy leaf" or "noisy tree," while in several European languages it is referred to, at least by the men, as "woman's tongue."

Along with white birch – which it resembles, though aspen bark is not papery and peeling or as white – aspen was long considered a scrawny "weed tree" by the forest industry because it springs up so quickly after fires or clearcutting. Faced with dwindling supplies of more favoured species, however, the industry has turned to fast-growing aspens to produce chipboard, plywood and pulp, especially for magazine stock.

Aspen swiftly takes advantage of new forest openings because its tiny, light seeds, borne on tufts of fluff in June, travel for kilometres in the wind. Most aspens, though, are clones produced by numerous suckers sent up from the surviving roots of trees that have been burned, over-browsed or cut down. If a fire or logging occurs in April, the sprouts can emerge in the same season. A hectare or more may be covered by clones of just a few trees, creating extremely dense stands of up to 280,000 new shoots per hectare (2.5 acres). Those numbers drop quickly, down to a thousand or so survivors per hectare within a few decades.

Without a major disturbance, the short-lived trees begin to give way in 60 years or so to shade-tolerant spruce, firs and other species that are nurtured in aspen's nutrient-rich leaf litter. But if a forest is ravaged frequently enough, aspen root networks can survive indefinitely. In Utah, a stand of more than 47,000 genetically identical aspens is estimated to be one million years old and weighs six million kilograms (13.2 million pounds), making it, by some definitions, the world's largest and oldest organism.

The sun-fed vitality that raises an aspen clone up to two metres (6.6 feet) in its first year packs an abundant store of energy for other life forms. In winter, ruffed grouse and evening grosbeaks depend heavily on aspen buds. Moose, deer and porcupines feast on the tree's sprouting twigs and catkins in spring. The catkins contain about 20 per cent crude protein, more than

with small pointed tip, finely toothed edges, green above, silvery pale below, turning yellow in autumn; unfolding earlier in spring than on most other trees

Sex: 4–8 cm (1.5–3 in) long, hanging yellowish-green flowering strands, called catkins, usually either all male or all female on a tree; flowers open before leaves in mid-Apr. to May for efficient wind pollination; blooming as early as 2–3 years of age for clones, 15–20 years for trees starting from seed

Seeds: Tiny, light brown, attached to fluff; released after female catkins reach about 10 cm (4 in) long; germinate or die within a few days; big crops every 4–5 years

Roots: Mostly shallow, very widespread, producing numerous suckers; thin sinker roots can reach down 3 m (10 ft)

Wood: Greyish white, with a fine, straight grain, soft, brittle, weak, 450kg/m^3 (28 lb/cu. ft), much heavier when green

Heat equivalent of 1 m^3 (35 cu. feet) of wood: 117 L (26 gal) of oil

Common nesters: Woodpeckers, tree swallows, chickadees, nuthatches, saw-whet owls and wood ducks in trunk cavities; broad-winged hawks, yellow-rumped warblers, robins, juncos, warbling vireos in branches; ruffed grouse, hermit thrushes and ovenbirds often on the ground below

Tiny nibblers: Forest tent and large aspen tortrex caterpillars, as well as 300 other known species of caterpillars and insects

Fungal feeders: False tinder conk commonly infects 40–70% of mature aspens; also other bracket fungi, *Hypoxylon* canker, root rot

Range: All Ontario to tree line; also in all other provinces and territories except Nunavut

Number of poplar species native to Ontario: 4

Number of poplar species worldwide: 35–40

Also see: Ruffed Grouse, Tree Swallow, Yellow-bellied Sapsucker, Beaver, Black Bear, Mushrooms, Red Pine

cereal crops. The fresh new leaves are usually the main course for bears in late May and June, while aspen bark is the beaver's favourite winter food. Hares and mice also prize the bark, which is a living layer that photosynthesizes like leaves.

Young trees and fresh spring shoots, which have not yet built up natural chemical phenol defences, are preferred as food. Older leaves can double their phenolic concentration – which can reach up to 17 per cent of their dry weight – within three days after an insect attack on nearby branches. Such chemicals may have caused the extremely bitter taste of the medicine pioneers and lumberjacks brewed from boiling the inner bark of aspen in water.

Among the nutrients packed into aspen leaves are beta-carotenes, molecules that trap and transfer the sun's energy for photosynthesis in chlorophyll. They're a vital link for all animal life. When leaves are eaten, each beta-carotene breaks into two vitamin A molecules. They give carrots, oranges, squash and egg yolks their colours. A related molecule, xanthophyll, which protects chlorophyll from burning up in sunlight, gives trembling aspen its pale yellow colour in autumn. **Largetooth aspen**, usually growing on drier sites, with its bigger leaves and fuller crown, turns a more brilliant gold about a week earlier. Yellow pigments are uncovered after trees withdraw nutrients from leaves, stopping chlorophyll production, which normally reflects green light while absorbing the other colours of the spectrum in the sun's rays.

WHITE BIRCH
Water-resistant, Born to Burn

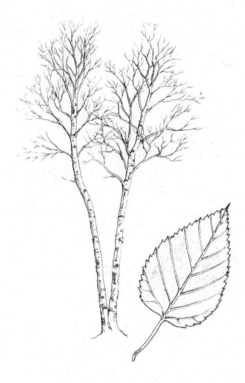

Birchbark has a special quality that makes it famous: it resists water and decomposition. A natural wax base makes the bark impermeable, allowing it to last for years on the moist forest floor and still burn long after the wood it surrounds turns to mush. Fossilized birch has been found in Siberia with bark still in its original state, while birchbark manuscripts in central Asia are up to 2,000 years old. This characteristic was of inestimable importance to northern woodland peoples, such as the Ojibway, who depended on the bark for their wigwams, canoes, containers, moose-calling cones, as a quick fire starter even when wet and to wrap their dead for burial.

Mature height: Avg. 12–21 m (39–69 ft), up to 25 m (82 ft)

Trunk width: Avg. 25–40 cm (10–16 in)

Ontario giant: 1.2 m (4 ft) thick, 13.6 m (45 ft) tall, in Sundridge

Lifespan: 60–80 years for most; up to 225 years

Time it takes a white birch log to go soft: 1–2 years

Time it takes a spruce log to go soft: 5–10 years

Alias: Paper birch, canoe birch, silver birch, *le bouleau à papier, Betula papyrifera*

Whereabouts: Cool, moist silt loam or sandy bottomlands to upper slopes and ridges of disturbed sites, forest openings or lakeshores

Bark: Shiny dark reddish brown for about 10 years until peeling back to reveal mature, papery white bark with prominent black hatch marks, called lenticels, which allow air through the bark; stripping bark off trees leaves black scars, weakens and sometimes kills them

Leaves: Light green, about 5–10 cm (2–4 in) long, spade-shaped, serrated, amber or yellow in fall

Sex: 7–10 cm (3–4 in) long, hanging greenish-tan, tassel-like male catkins at twig tips; upright green female flower catkins 3–5 cm (1.2–2 in) long, farther back on branch; open before leaves in May; first blooms when about 15 years old

Seeds: Winged, 4 mm (0.15 in) long; take 2 summers to mature; most released in fall and early winter from brown, hanging cones, 4–5 cm (1.6–2 in) long

Buds: Greenish-brown, gummy, 5–7 mm (0.2 in) long

Roots: Generally shallow, less than 60 cm (2 ft) deep

Wood: Thick, creamy white sapwood, pale brown heartwood, with fine, straight grain, smooth, hard, strong, 640 kg/m³ (40 lb/cu. ft), very warm-burning

Heat equivalent of 1 m³ (35 cu. ft) of wood: 155 L (34 gal) of oil

Companion trees and shrubs: Trembling aspen, red maple, white spruce, balsam fir, balsam poplar, beaked hazel, red osier dogwood, chokecherry, pin cherry, willow

Associated plants: Bunchberry, wintergreen, blue bead lily, wild sarsaparilla, starflower, blueberry, strawberry, bracken fern

Common nesters: Woodpeckers, nuthatches, tree swallows, chickadees, red-eyed vireos

Frequent visitors: Hummingbirds, nuthatches, ruffed grouse, black-and-white warblers, common redpolls, pine siskins, hares, porcupines, beavers, deer, moose

Common nibblers: Bronze birch borer, birch leaf miners, forest tent caterpillars, birch

Birchbark was an ideal material for the perfect design that is the canoe. It took two people about two weeks to make one, with men usually supervising and women doing most of the work. Bark was most easily stripped in early summer, whole tree lengths being used. Seams were stitched together with pliable spruce, cedar or tamarack roots and sealed with spruce gum. Ribs were made from strong, flexible spruce or cedar boughs. The canoes were swift, light to portage and easy to fix, their materials abundant everywhere without recourse to Canadian Tire. European explorers and fur traders quickly adopted birchbark canoes as the best means of travelling in the water-laced northern interior. Birch was also used to make boats in the boreal forests of Russia, but the true canoe – *canoe* was one of the first Native words Columbus learned – is a New World perfection.

Perhaps because of its beauty, the birch was considered a magical tree in northern Europe. Brooms were made out of its twigs to sweep away evil, and the maypole of pagan spring rites was a birch. In Ontario, Ojibway stories tell of birchbark acquiring its black marks from the magician–deity Nanabush variously thrashing the drowsy tree with a pine branch for allowing some meat it was supposed to be guarding to be stolen by birds, or from a collision with pursuing thunderbirds whom he craftily deked out.

Though its thin, flammable bark makes white birch an unlikely forest-fire survivor, flames are actually its salvation. Having evolved around a cycle of renewal brought by frequent lightning strikes in tinder-dry, resin-soaked boreal woods, birch was born to burn. The tree cannot grow in shade, but by flaming faster than almost any other natural material, birchbark fosters the best conditions for regeneration. Newly burnt-over areas provide sunlight and exposed mineral soil for birch to take root and prosper, often in pure stands. Winged, confetti-sized birch seeds, released from August into winter, can travel great distances to find such sites, especially when blown across the crusty surface of the snow. Birch also resprouts from the base of stumps, producing clumps of two to six trunks, nurtured by surviving root systems that give them a leg up on the seeds of the competition. Like other pioneer species, white birch in general grows more rapidly than the progeny of most other trees, reaching up to three metres (10 feet) in its first five years.

Because birch trees grow so quickly, however, their trunks are composed of mostly porous sapwood and contain considerable moisture and sugars, relished by wood-rotting fungi (the reason it's so hard to find a fallen birch log worth burning). The wood is also low in the rot-resistant chemicals common in conifers. When little more than 60 years old, white birch tends to become susceptible to heart-rot, wood-boring insects and the woodpeckers that seek them, causing the tree to gradually die from the top down. Such trees provide ideal sites for cavity-nesting birds and animals. The upper branches are often already in advanced decay before the trunk finally topples.

skeletonizers, birch case-bearers, gypsy moth caterpillars, beetle grubs, sawflies

Portion of Ontario's forest made up of white birch: 7%

Range: Almost all Ontario, from about London and Sarnia to tree line; also in all other provinces and territories

Accolades: Official tree of Saskatchewan and New Hampshire

Number of birch species native to Ontario: 6

Number of birch species worldwide: About 50

Also see: Black-capped Chickadee, Yellow-bellied Sapsucker, Beaver, Black Spruce, Trembling Aspen, Yellow Birch, Canadian Shield, Lakes

WHITE CEDAR
The Tree of Life

Lifespan: Commonly 200–300 years, maximum more than 1,000 years on cliffsides

Mature height: Avg. 10–18 m (30–59 ft)

Trunk width: Avg. 30–45 cm (1–1.5 ft), often divided into 2 or more stems

Ontario giant: 22.6 m (74 ft) tall, 1.1 m (3.6 ft) wide, in Acton

Alias: Northern white cedar, arbor vitae, swamp cedar, eastern thuja, *le thuya de l'est, Thuja occidentalis*

Whereabouts: Wet, organic soil or boulder-strewn areas along lakeshores and streams and in swamps with flowing water, or thin, moist, sandy loam soils around limestone cliffs and rocky slopes

Foliage: Light yellow-green, flat, waxy, scalelike splays, lasting up to 5 years before turning bronze in winter and shedding

Bark: Light grey to reddish brown, soft, in stringy, shredding vertical strips, spiralling slightly up trunk

Sex: Yellowish male conelets, 1–2 mm (0.08 in) long, on tips of splays in late Apr. and May; pinkish female conelets, 7–12 mm (0.3–0.5 in) long, usually on separate branches

Cedar was revered by Native peoples. To many, it represented the east, one of the four sacred directional elements (north, west and south were sweetgrass, tobacco and sage, respectively). The sweet scent and smoke of its crackling, burning foliage was used to purify a person, place or thing, or to make offerings of thanks to the Creator. Even today, cedar-leaf oil is used in perfumes and medicines and as a deodorizer and insect repellent.

The tree has also been used as medicine for a vast array of ailments. Among cedar's many medicinal uses, an effective poultice was made from its fibres and placed on the eyes to cure snow blindness. Tea was also brewed from its foliage for headaches, congestion and scurvy. Like the needles of many other evergreens, cedar contains more vitamin C than oranges. Native people saved Jacques Cartier and his crew from the ravages of scurvy during their first winter in Canada, in 1536, with cedar tea. Cartier brought seedlings of the wonder tree back to France, where the king promptly named it *arbor vitae,* the "tree of life." Cedar is believed to have been the first North American tree planted in Europe.

The tree of life is an apt name given cedar's amazing tenacity, as well as its ability to lean, bend, twist and turn to find the sunlight. Roots, similarly, snake through rocks and cliffs, wedging into the narrowest crevices and tiniest pockets of soil. Branches of uprooted cedars can shoot up to become the trunks of new trees or can burrow into moist soil and form roots. Fallen, mossy logs are also the most common seedbeds for cedars.

Dendrochronologists – people who study tree rings – have discovered scraggly cedars growing in extremely harsh conditions, on the cliff faces of Mazinaw Rock in Bon Echo Provincial Park and along the Niagara Escarpment, that are 400 to 1,000 years old. Many are little more than a metre (3.3 feet) tall and 5 centimetres (two inches) thick. Some, with annual growth rings only one cell thick, are considered the slowest-growing trees in the world. Protected in their inaccessible locations from wildfire and lumberjacks, communities of the cliffside dwarfs probably form the most ancient old-growth forests in Ontario.

Cedar lives long on steep cliffs and wetlands because it is extremely resistant to both rot and drought. One dead cedar found at the base of a cliff on Flowerpot Island, off the tip of the Bruce Peninsula, was determined to be 3,000 years old

Cones: 8–13 mm (0.3–0.5 in) long, in dense bunches at tips of branches, especially near treetop, pale green at first, turning brown as they ripen by end of summer, dropping most seeds mid-Sept. to Nov., the rest through winter; big crops every 2–5 years; first cones produced when trees 15–20 years old

Seeds: Light chestnut brown, encased in two wings, landing 45–60 m (150–200 ft) from parent tree

Annual seedling growth: Avg. 8 cm (3 in)

Roots: Shallow, thick, extensive on wet and rocky ground; deep taproot formed on thicker, drier soil

Wood: Light yellowish-brown heartwood and thin, whitish sapwood, soft, weak, brittle, 304 kg/m³ (19 lb/cu. ft), non-resinous, aromatic; snaps, crackles and pops when burned

Heat equivalent of 1 m³ (35 cu. ft) of wood: 98 L (21.5 gal) of oil

Companion trees and shrubs: Balsam poplar, fir, black ash, white spruce, tamarack, black spruce, and red maple in wetter areas and swamps; yellow birch, hemlock, white birch, aspens on drier upland sites

Associated plants: Canada mayflower, false Solomon's seal, miterwort, lady ferns, northern beech ferns, oak ferns, raspberry, black currant, violets, sedges

Common nesters:
Blackburnian, Cape May
and black-throated green
warblers, robins, blue
jays, grackles, song
sparrows, cedar waxwings,
golden-crowned kinglets,
house wrens

Frequent diners: Deer, hares,
porcupines, red-backed
voles and moose browse foliage; red squirrels, mice,
goldfinches, pine siskins and
crossbills eat seeds; pileated
woodpeckers, winter wrens
and yellow-bellied flycatchers also forage on trees

Insect inhabitants:
Carpenter ants, leaf miners

Range: From just north of
Lake Erie to James Bay and
Kenora in northwest; also in
Manitoba, Quebec, Nova
Scotia, New Brunswick and
Prince Edward Island; plant-
ed in other provinces

**Number of Cyprus family
species native to Ontario:**
4

**Number of Cyprus family
species worldwide:** About
60

Also see: White-tailed Deer,
Canadian Shield, Limestone

and bore 1,890 annual growth rings. In 1993, a Canadian Navy mini-sub exploring a flooded canyon in waters nearby found cedar stumps that are more than 9,000 years old. The tree's dura-bility made it the wood of choice in Canada's early history for palisades, log cabins, split-rail fences, shingles and posts. Having the lightest wood of any tree in Ontario, much less than half the density of oak, it has always been popular for canoes and boat frames.

Acidic soil is anathema to cedar. In the Canadian Shield, cedar is restricted mostly to lakeshores and bog edges, where moving groundwater can provide nutrients not available in the rocky, acidic ground. Farther south, cedar thrives in dense stands on thin soil over lime-stone bedrock and in wetlands. Deer, which love browsing on cedar foliage, often make their winter yards in the shelter of such stands.

WHITE PINE
Towering Above All Others

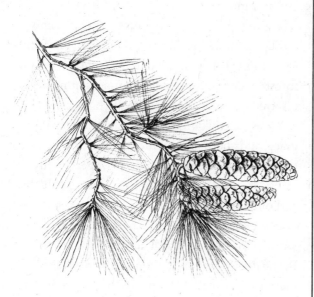

Canada is the scent of pines.
I left my land and returned
to know this and become
Canadian.
    – Milton Acorn, "Poem for the Astronauts"

Among his many feats, Napoleon Bonaparte had a profound and lasting influence on the forests of Ontario. In November 1806, after defeating Prussia and becoming master of northern Europe, he closed the Baltic seaports, cutting off Britain's biggest source of lumber. With supplies dwindling, the huge British Baltic trading fleet sailed to Canada in 1809, sparking a logging

Mature height: Avg. 15–30 m (49–98 ft)

Trunk width: Avg. 60–90 cm (2–3 ft)

Ontario giants: More than 45.7 m (150 ft) tall, in Gillies Grove, Arnprior; 45.1 m (148 ft) tall, 1.7 m (5.6 ft) thick, in Cardiff Township, Haliburton Co.

Tree weight: Can be more than 60 tonnes (65 tons)

Growth rate: 30–45 cm (1–1.5 ft) per year when young; 100-year-old trees up to 25 m (82 ft) high

Average age of a Temagami pine when it reaches the height of an 80-year-old Algonquin Park pine: 120 years old

Lifespan: Often 200–250 years, maximum more than 450 years

Age of second-growth trees cut by logging industry: 60–100 years

Alias: Eastern white pine, yellow pine, Quebec pine, Weymouth pine, majestic pine, cork pine, pattern pine, pumpkin pine, *le pin blanc*, *Pinus strobus*

Whereabouts: Along lakeshores and points, islands, hillcrests, moist, sandy outwash plains, in pure stands or mixed with hardwoods and other conifers

Needles: 5–15 cm (2–6 in) long, in bundles of 5, soft, flexible, with finely toothed edges; turn yellow and fall after 1–4 years

Bark: Smooth grey-green when young, with age becoming deeply furrowed, with wide, rough, frosted grey-brown ridges

Sex: Small, light green, male flower conelets appear in bunches near branch tips in May and disintegrate in early summer after releasing yellow pollen to the wind; female flower conelets pink or purplish, at ends of new shoots, mostly near top of tree; puberty at 5–10 years

Cones: 8–20 cm (3–8 in) long, slender, light green at first, turning woody and tan-brown as they mature over 2 summers, opening in Sept. to release seeds, then falling off during winter; big seed crops every 3–5 years with up to 400 cones per tree

Seeds: With wing about 2 cm (0.8 in) long, averaging 70 per cone, 60,000 weighing 1 kg (2.2 lb)

Roots: Widespread, moderately deep, with 4–10 often visible, thick main roots reaching out from base of tree

Wood: Pale to reddish-brown heartwood, creamy white to yellow sapwood, soft, strong, clear, with straight, even grain, 415 kg/m³ (26 lb/cu. ft)

Heat equivalent of 1 m³ (35 cu. ft) of wood: 103 L (23 gal) of oil

Time a mature white pine log takes to completely decay: About 150 years

boom that quickly spread up the Ottawa Valley and through rich green veins of white pine deep in the interior. Within a year, wood surpassed furs as Canada's biggest export, with tens of thousands of pines cut annually.

White pine, with its layers of long, sweeping, wind-sculpted branches, was the focus of logging for almost 100 years. Central Ontario's virgin forests were dominated by ancient pines that towered more than 10 storeys high, making surrounding hardwoods look like shrubs. Its size and grace, and the many medicines it yielded, made the white pine the Iroquois tree of peace. But its thick, straight trunk, tapering very gradually and often free of branches for 25 metres (82 feet) or more, made it ideal for the masts of Britain's world-dominating naval and merchant fleets. Royal Navy warships required main masts 37 metres (120 feet) high and a metre (3.3 feet) thick, previously supplied by heavy, pieced-together trunks of smaller Scots pine from the Baltic. In 1811, 23,000 Canadian pine masts were shipped across the Atlantic. Even larger numbers of pines were cut into square timbers 12 to 18 metres (40 to 60 feet) long, tied together and floated down the Ottawa and St. Lawrence rivers in huge rafts, bound for the saw pits of Britain. Protected by high tariffs on non-Empire imports, Canadian lumber provided 75 per cent of Britain's lumber needs by the 1820s.

The lumberjacks followed the tributaries of the Ottawa and Trent rivers far into the headlands of Haliburton and what is now Algonquin Park in the 1830s and 1840s. They spawned legends, such as those of Joe Montferrand – "Joe Mufferaw" of the Stompin' Tom Connors classic

– which many believe to be the basis for the American tall tales of Paul Bunyan. Montferrand, though, was a real person, the champion of Québécois *bûcherons* against the Irish in the Shiners' War brawls around the swampy little logging settlement called Bytown, later re-dubbed Ottawa.

As the lumberjacks pushed farther into the interior, the rapidly expanding U.S. construction market gradually replaced Britain as the major destination for Ontario pine. As logging reached Muskoka and the east shore of Georgian Bay in the 1870s, the large-toothed, two-man crosscut saw began to replace the axe, doubling the cutting speed of two axemen. Logging continued up the North Channel of Lake Huron, finally reaching Temagami in the 1920s and the Chapleau-Mississagi River region in the 1940s.

Though most of the great stands of white pine were gone by the Second World War, the mechanization of the logging industry has since allowed companies to get at many of the remnants. Bulldozers, trucks and logging roads replaced horses and rivers for transporting logs out of previously inaccessible high country. Chainsaws and giant cutting machines replaced the crosscut. Today, there are only 10 known stands exceeding 500 hectares (1,235 acres) of old-growth white pine left in Ontario. The logging industry wants those too, labelling them "overmature" or "decadent."

Many scientists counter industry claims that old pine forests need catastrophic disturbances such as cutting or fire to bring in enough sunlight and prepare the soil for regeneration. Some mature pine stands have gone 1,000 to

Companion trees and shrubs: Red pine, hemlock, sugar maple, yellow birch, white spruce, balsam fir, aspen, beaked hazel, chokecherry

Associated plants: Canada mayflower, blueberry, wintergreen, moccasin flower, wild sarsaparilla, jack-in-the-pulpit, large-leafed aster, partridgeberry, strawberry, bracken ferns

Common nesters and inhabitants: Ravens, goshawks, broad-winged and sharp-shinned hawks, osprey, bald eagles, great horned owls, crows, blue jays; blackburnian, pine and yellow-rumped warblers; red squirrels, flying squirrels, mother bears and cubs

Frequent visitors: Seeds eaten by evening and pine grosbeaks, chickadees, nuthatches, red crossbills, red-backed voles and mice; porcupines and hares eat twigs and bark

Tiny nibblers: Pine loopers, false loopers and many other moth caterpillars, white admiral butterfly caterpillars, white-pine weevils, bark beetles, sawyer beetles

Biggest fungal threat: Blister rust fungus

Range: Southern Ontario to about Timmins and Wawa and west from Lake Superior to Kenora; also in all other eastern provinces, a tiny portion of Manitoba and planted in British Columbia

Portion of Ontario's forest that is white pine: About 2%

Ontario's largest remaining old-growth white-pine stand: Obabika, Temagami, 2,400 ha (6,000 acres)

Specialty products: Doors, window casings, trim, cabinets, furniture, panels

Price of a white-pine mast in colonial times: About £100

Aroostook War: Disputes over rival logging claims brought American troops to the New Brunswick–Maine border in 1839 before the U.S. and British governments negotiated a settlement

Origin of word *lumber*: From "lumber room" for odds and ends, originally "lombard room," where the bankers of Lombardy, Italy, stored unredeemed pledges

Also see: Mushrooms, Red Pine, White Spruce

2,000 years without major disturbances. Instead, new trees sprout up when an old one dies or a small fire has burned, opening up space in the canopy and on the forest floor. Young white pines can grow in as little as 20 per cent of full sunlight. In fact, if white-pine seedlings are subjected to more than 40 to 50 per cent full sunlight, the likelihood of being preyed on by pine weevils – beetles that eat new shoots – increases significantly.

Ancient pine forests with natural gaps are very complex, with greater biological diversity than even-aged forests. The gaps provide a varied habitat for many plants and animals. Naturalists hold that modern science can never hope to fully know or recreate the immensity and minutiae of vital interrelationships that have been developed and fine-tuned over thousands of years in such a forest. There is even great genetic diversity within the pines of a single stand, unlike the homogeneity of replanted trees, which are more vulnerable to the spread of disease and insects. Diversity supports ecosystem stability with a complex web of interactions.

WHITE SPRUCE
Canada's Most Widespread Tree

The dense, sweeping boughs that give white spruce its beauty were long used by Native people, trappers, lumberjacks and campers as comfortable and springy wilderness bedding. The same qualities that make it a great mattress suit spruce to northern environments that few other trees could survive. Flexible, curving branches bend under the weight of heavy snow, which is held in place by dense, thickly needled layers of twigs, insulating the tree from cold winds. Spruce and fir trees, in fact, brace for the weight of heavy snows by contracting – closing the space between their branches – when the atmospheric pressure drops. In Switzerland, cut,

Portion of Ontario's forest that is spruce: 42%

Mature height: Avg. 18–25 m (60–82 ft)

Trunk width: Avg. 30–60 cm (1–2 ft)

Ontario giant: 39 m (128 ft) tall, 79 cm (2.6 ft) thick, in McClure Township, Hastings Co.

Lifespan: Commonly 100–250 years, up to 300 years

Age of spruce Christmas trees 2 m (6.6 ft) high: 7 years

Alias: Canadian spruce, cat spruce, skunk spruce, *l'épinette blanche, Picea glauca*

Name origin: From Old English *Pruse,* meaning "Prussia"

Whereabouts: Cool, moist, commonly rocky soils, along shores and on uplands

Needles: 1.5–2.2 cm (0.6–0.9 in) long, 4-sided, often with a bluish tint; shed after 5–10 years

Bark: Light grey and smooth when young, turning darker and scaly or flaky with age

Sex: Male flower conelets 1.5–2 cm (0.6–0.8 in) long, red at first, turning yellow; green to deep red female conelets, 2–2.5 cm (0.8–1 in) long, high on trees; appear in May; wind-pollinated

Cones: About 5 cm (2 in) long, with thin, light brown scales, dropping most seeds Sept. to Oct., but continuing winter and spring; big crops every 2–6 years

Seeds: Attached to round, fan-shaped wings, 4–8 mm (0.15–0.3 in) long, 30–140 per cone

Roots: Usually shallow, wide-spread, but putting down deep taproots in well-drained soils

Wood: White or yellowish, soft, smooth, straight grained, durable, 415 kg/m³ (26 lb/cu. ft)

Heat equivalent of 1 m³ (35 cu. ft) of wood: 98 L (21.5 gal) of oil

Special wood qualities: Resonance favoured for pianos, guitars and violins; used for food containers because of lack of taste and odour

Companion trees and shrubs: Balsam fir, aspen, white birch, black spruce, pine, red maple, cedar, chokecherry, red osier dogwood, beaked hazel

Associated plants: Feather moss, bunchberry, twinflower, wood sorrel, raspberry, violets

Common nesters: Red squirrels, blue jays, grackles, olive-sided flycatchers, evening grosbeaks; yellow-rumped, blackburnian, Cape May, bay-breasted and black-throated green warblers

Frequent diners: Chipmunks, mice, voles, chickadees, red-breasted nuthatches, white-winged crossbills, kinglets and pine siskins all eat seeds; spruce grouse eat needles

Y-shaped fir branches are used as barometers, the two ends drawing close before rain or snow.

White spruce can hold its own in moderate climates as well. It is the most widespread tree in Canada. Logging, however, has made white spruce less common in many areas, often replaced by aspen, birch and fir. As the red- and white-pine forests fell to the axe in the late 1800s, loggers turned to the next best thing that floated (in log drives). White spruce, with its tall, thick trunk and strong, durable wood, was soon a mainstay of the sawmills feeding a great building boom across North America.

The discovery of efficient techniques for making paper from wood fibre in the 1860s redoubled the economic value of spruce. Paper, invented by the Chinese 1,900 years ago, was previously made from straw or rags. Spruce, even spindly black spruce, was ideally suited to the new process because its wood is long-fibred, light-coloured and less resinous than other conifers. As supplies of prime lumber trees, 30 centimetres (one foot) or more in diameter, dwindled around the turn of the century, the lumber barons gradually sold their cutting rights to the new pulp and paper companies, which thrived on smaller trees. By the 1930s they were penetrating deep into the boreal forest, and today an area three times the size of Metro Toronto is cut every year in Ontario, the majority for pulp and paper. White spruce, though, also continues to be the biggest source of two-by-fours and other construction lumber, though commonly sold as pine, a general softwood group label.

Large tracts of forest are also eaten up each year by tiny brown caterpillars called spruce budworms. Forest-industry efforts to poison the caterpillars with pesticides may ultimately be counterproductive. Budworms actually prefer balsam fir to spruce needles, but the pulp mills and sawmills favour spruce. Fir, being the more shade-tolerant of the two species, tends to grow faster and crowd out young spruce in the forest understorey. With prolonged budworm outbreaks – which can last seven to 10 years – fir dominance in the understorey can be drastically cut back. The budworms, by providing nutrients to spruce seedlings in their droppings and decaying fir trees, act as intermediaries in what has been called an "energy transfer pulse" from fir to spruce.

Another infamous nibbler, the forest tent caterpillar, also ultimately benefits spruce, as well as fir, by defoliating aspens and other broadleaf trees, providing more light and nutrients for understorey evergreens. White spruce saplings can long persist in as little as 15 per cent of full sunlight beneath taller trees. A one- to two-metre (3.3- to 6.6-foot) spruce in the forest shadows can be 40 to 50 years old. The tree, in fact, can bide its time for a century or two in the understorey and then accelerate growth when a space opens in the canopy.

Range: From about Kingston, Peterborough and Bruce Co. north to tree line, though planted in southern Ontario; also in all other provinces and territories

Size of Ontario's commercially productive forest: 425,000 km² (164,050 sq. mi), 40% of province

Area infested by spruce budworm 2004–2007: 2,800–8,500 km² (1,080–3,280 sq. mi)

Area infested by spruce budworm at peak in 1980: 190,000 km² (73,360 sq. mi)

Average time between outbreaks of spruce budworm over a large area: 20–60 years

Average natural fire frequency in spruce forests: 60–200 years

Accolades: Provincial tree of Manitoba

Number of spruce species native to Ontario: 3

Number of spruce species worldwide: 35–40

Also see: Balsam Fir, White Pine

YELLOW BIRCH
Big, Tough and Animated

Mature height: Avg. 18–23 m (60–75 ft), up to 31 m (102 ft)

Trunk width: Avg. 60–90 cm (2–3 ft)

Ontario giant: 1.7 m (5.7 ft) thick, 24.7 m (81 ft) tall, at Lorimer Lake, Parry Sound District

Lifespan: Commonly 150–300 years; maximum more than 370 years

Alias: Sweet birch, gold birch, red birch, curly birch, hard birch, tall birch, Newfoundland oak, *le bouleau jaune, Betula alleghaniensis*

Whereabouts: Deciduous and mixed forests on moist, rich soil, especially on the lower slopes of hills

Bark: Shiny bronze or yellowish silver with numerous horizontal lines; smooth, soft and paperlike, usually shredding, curling and hanging in fringes; trunks of old trees develop rough, grey irregular plates; shiny, dark purple-red on saplings

Leaves: Oval with a pointed tip and serrated edges, 7–13 cm (3–5 in) long, dark green on top, lighter on bottom, turning yellow in fall

Sex: Dark male catkins stand 2 cm (0.8 in) long in fall and winter, opening before leaves in early spring to

Bronzed, shaggy yellow birch trunks add colour and animate beauty to the dark reaches of the forest interior. The trees' thick, flexing roots clutch the ground, stumps and boulders like giant birds' claws, making the birches look as if they're picking up and moving through the woods. Whole trunks may also bend and contort around rock outcrops or similarly snaking cedars. Though often toppled by the wind, yellow birches refuse to die, with upturned branches growing to become new trunks.

A great many yellow birches, though, go completely unrecognized by passersby at their feet. Unlike white birch, they can live a very long time, with the smooth, papery bark of their youth greying and cracking into deep fissures separating large, rough plates. They take their place among the mature maples, beech and hemlocks to become thick-bodied, towering monarchs.

Yellow birch has to be long-lived to hold its own in the mixed and hardwood forest. Opportunities for its seeds to get a start are few and far between, so year after year the tree must keep producing them. Although the tree is much more shade-tolerant than white birch, it still needs small openings in the forest to grow. And when they germinate in spring, its tiny, thin seeds – blown far and wide over the snow surface in winter – cannot produce root sprouts strong enough to break through the leaf litter to reach down to the mineral soil. Slope erosion or light autumn brush fires that burn away the duff layer create good conditions for yellow birch seeds over a wide area. The seeds also survive where the wind has taken down one or more trees, settling either in soil exposed by an uprooted trunk or in the decaying wood of an old stump or log. In later years, those that have grown out of stumps are often on stiltlike roots left after the rotted wood disintegrated beneath them.

Once established, yellow birch sprouts are adept at filling the gap in the canopy, growing up to three metres (10 feet) in their first six years. Many saplings, however, meet an early end in areas with lots of deer, who love the sweet wintergreen flavour of the trees' buds and twigs. Broken twigs give off the aromatic bubblegum scent. Moose, ruffed grouse and red squirrels are also common nibblers.

hang from twig tips like yellow caterpillars, 7.5–10 cm (3–4 in) long; green female catkins, 1.5–2 cm (0.6–0.8 in) long, stand erect farther back on twigs; puberty at about 40 years

Seeds: Confetti-sized, with wing flakes, start dropping from upright, oval cones, 2.5–4 cm (1–1.5 in) long, in late Aug., with most falling from Oct. into winter; big crops, every 1–4 years, usually produce 2.5–12 million seeds per ha (2.5 acres)

Buds: Chestnut-brown, 6 mm (0.2 in) long, pointed, slightly sticky

Roots: Thick, strong, extensive, usually shallow, sometimes more than 1.5 m (5 ft) deep

Wood: Reddish-tinted, golden-brown heartwood and light yellow or white sapwood, hard, strong, with fine and often wavy grain, 670 kg/m³ (42 lb/cu. ft)

Heat equivalent of 1 m³ (35 cu. ft) of wood: 174 L (38 gal) of oil

Companion trees: Sugar maple, hemlock, beech, white cedar, white pine, basswood, red pine, white spruce

Cavity dwellers: Heart-rot in large old trees commonly provides homes for yellow-bellied sapsuckers, porcupines, raccoons and fishers

Common diners: Deer, moose, beavers, porcupines and hares browse leaves, buds or bark; red squirrels, chipmunks, grouse, chickadees, goldfinches, pine siskins and redpolls eat seeds; sapsuckers tap tree

Honours: Provincial tree of Quebec

Range: Southern Ontario to Lake Temiskaming and Wawa; also in all other eastern provinces

Also see: Wintergreen, Sugar Maple, White Birch, White Cedar

The shiny bark of younger trees burns almost as well as white birch bark, but tends to be shed in only narrow shreds on the trunk, rather than in large, loose sheets. It's extremely durable, sometimes holding together the rotted wood of dead trees for many years. When dried, such soft, crumbly "punkwood" was ideal lighting material for the friction-started fires of Native camps.

In pioneer Ontario, yellow birch wood was popular for sled frames, ox yokes and especially wheel hubs, because it never released its grip on wooden spokes. But because the dense wood, when green, doesn't float, it wasn't widely cut in the days of the big river log drives. Demand zoomed during the Second World War, when Ontario yellow-birch plywood was added to British Columbia sitka spruce and balsa wood in Canadian-built Mosquito fighter-bombers, the fastest and most versatile Allied aircraft of the war. Today, yellow birch, used for floors, furniture, veneer, doors and trimmings, is second only to sugar maple in Ontario's hardwood lumber industry.

THE
HEAVENS

DAY SKY

*M*alls, offices, cars and subways conspire to make weather irrelevant to city living. But in the outdoors, weather is everything. It regulates the ebb and flow of life, from the sex lives of all animals to the date of the local regatta.

After a while, those living outdoors become, like animals and plants, attuned to every change in the day sky: shifting wind, falling or rising temperature, varying cloud cover that announces the arrival of a new weather system. A fun game is to try to guess the time by the position of the sun. It doesn't take long to become good at it.

Like the starry night sky, the day sky is a repository of human myths and legends. Sun gods, thunder gods and wind gods all made their home in the sky. As the habitat of such seemingly supernatural forces, the sky is an obvious place for heaven.

In a way, though, we have hell to thank for heaven. Ancient volcanoes spewed gases from deep inside the planet to form the early atmosphere. Later, plants provided the oxygen necessary for life as we know it.

The weather does its thing at night as well as during the day, of course. But for simplicity, we've grouped all the weather-related topics in this section.

CLOUDS
Exploring the Skyscape

Hamlet.   Do you see yonder cloud that's almost in shape of a camel?

Polonius.   By th' mass and 'tis, like a camel indeed.

Hamlet.   Methinks it is like a weasel.

Polonius.   It is backed like a weasel.

Hamlet.   Or like a whale?

Polonius.   Very like a whale.

— William Shakespeare, *Hamlet,* III, ii

Cloud watching is an old pastime that even Shakespeare obviously enjoyed. While his Hamlet took up the activity as a device to feign madness, cloud watching can't be beaten as a salve for modern stress. Up north, the ideal perch for cloud watching is a warm slab of rock jutting into a lake on the Canadian Shield. The patient observer is often entertained with other diversions, too. A merganser mom and her obedient brood may paddle by only metres away. A tiny song sparrow may land in nearby bushes and boom out its distinctive gurgled call. An osprey halfway down the lake may dive into the water for a bass snack. Perhaps a nosy mink will drop by to watch the cloud watcher.

The main atmospheric attraction on days like this are cumulus clouds, the familiar giant cotton balls with flat bases that metamorphose into camels and weasels and whales. Cumulus — *cumulus* is Latin for "heap" — is one of 10 main cloud types described in 1803 by English pharmacist Luke Howard, a part-time naturalist who

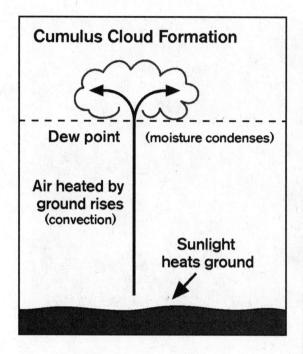

Cumulus Cloud Formation

Dew point (moisture condenses)

Air heated by ground rises (convection)

Sunlight heats ground

spent many hours flat on his back looking at the sky. Before his time there was no specific system for classifying cloud types. He came up with one, using Latin words in the scientific way adopted by Linnaeus, and it remains in use today. The German poet Goethe was so impressed with Howard's system that he wrote four poems to the man.

Clouds are airborne reservoirs of water. All air carries water in an invisible form called water vapour. For a cloud to form, there must be enough water in the air, and the air must cool past a certain relative temperature, called the dew point. At this point, tiny water droplets condense around bits of dust in the air. Billions upon billions of these droplets form visible clouds. When it's cold enough, the water droplets freeze into small, six-sided ice crystals.

compare pre– and post– Sept. 11 weather records.

Carl Linnaeus: Swedish scientist, 1707–1778, who developed and popularized the modern hierarchical system of classifying plant and animal species, with "kingdoms" at the top level and individual species at the bottom. He also adopted the idea of using double-barreled Latin names for species. He named and classified thousands of species, and often referred to himself as Carolus Linnaeus in his writings.

Relative humidity of clouds and fog: 100%

Ontario's cloudiest city: Owen Sound, with an annual average of 4,980 hours of overcast skies

Head in the clouds: Join fellow cloud watchers at cloudappreciationsociety.org

Also see: Groundhog; Mist, Dew and Fog; Rain, Thunder and Lightning, Wind and Weather Systems

Cumulus: the classic summertime cloud type

Nimbostratus: rain clouds spell indoor days

Stratus: for the Latin word for *layer*

Cumulus congestus: may become a thunderstorm

Cumulonimbus: an approaching thunderstorm

Cirrocumulus: high, rippled clouds of ice crystals

Cirrus: "mares' tails" formed by jet stream

Altocumulus: significant moisture at mid-levels

Cumulus clouds are created when air, heated near the ground, rises and then cools again at higher altitudes. Moisture-laden air moving over mountains also cools as it rises, and clouds may result. Large cloud banks occur along weather fronts, where a parcel of warm air meets a parcel of cold. Exhaling on a cold day produces a mini-cloud as warm, moist breath heated by the lungs hits the cold air outside. Contrails from high-flying jet aircraft are artificial cirrus clouds. As hot, moisture-laden exhaust from the jet engines cools, the water vapour condenses into ice crystals.

The presence of certain cloud types in the sky is useful for predicting weather. Wispy cirrus clouds, including the type known as "mares' tails," often precede a storm front by a day or so. Veil-like cirrostratus clouds also usually mean poor weather is on the way. When these clouds obscure the sun or the moon, they may produce faint halos around the heavenly bodies, leading to the old saying "A ring around the sun or moon brings rain or snow upon you soon." Sky-covering altostratus clouds are another sign of rainy weather.

Cumulus clouds usually don't appear in winter, because snow reflects sunlight that would otherwise heat the land and cause air to rise. That's why winter days often have clear blue skies, and why summer is supposed to arrive early when it's cloudy on Groundhog Day.

The most depressing clouds are unbroken, low-lying nimbostratus clouds associated with weather fronts. When they roll in, it usually means a day or two of rain and dreariness. Cloud watching then is an exercise in hope.

HOWARD CLOUD CHART

CLOUD NAME	DESCRIPTION	AVG. HEIGHT
Cirrus	Wispy, feathery, very high	8–12 km
Cirrocumulus	Blotchy cirrus clouds, may be rippled	8–12 km
Cirrostratus	Thin veil, doesn't block out sun, may cause halo	7–9 km
Altostratus	Thicker than cirrostratus, midlevel, partially blocks sun	2–6 km
Altocumulus	Puffy midlevel clouds; small puffs	2–6 km
Cumulonimbus	Giant cumulus clouds; thunderheads, maybe anvil top	450 m–15 km
Stratocumulus	Expansive, puffy clouds	150 m–2 km
Cumulus	Low puffy clouds, detached, flat bases	450 m–2 km
Nimbostratus	Grey layer of solid or almost solid cloud; rain	1–2 km
Stratus	Low-lying dull clouds; may drizzle	0–450 m

MIST, DEW AND FOG
Variations on a Theme

It's early morning. Down by the lake the air is still. Golden sunlight bathes the scene in a bright, purifying glow. A lone duck disappears into the soft white mist that lingers peacefully over the mirror-smooth water.

There's a good reason why mist is associated with such tranquil moments: it usually appears when the weather is calm and clear. The process begins at night, when the darkened Earth cools. As night swimmers know, the air cools faster than water. When water vapour from the warm lake rises into the cool air, it soon condenses into tiny water droplets, forming the mist that hangs just above the surface. Mist vanishes when the morning sun heats the air and vaporizes the water again. If it's overcast at night, mist will usually not occur, because the air doesn't cool enough. Similarly, wind turbulence disrupts the steady cooling process.

Fog is the same thing as mist, although meteorologists define fog as any bank of mist that reduces visibility to less than one kilometre (3,300 feet). Fog that rolls in off large lakes or the sea is created in a slightly different manner than mist over small lakes. In summer, water vapour in the warm air over land tends to condense as it hits cooler air over water. A fog bank appears. In winter, water vapour in warm sea air condenses when it moves across the cool land.

Dew is simply water vapour that condenses along surfaces that cool overnight. Sometimes, usually during the summer, only grass will be

Mist name origin: The ancient Indo-European word *migh* or *meigh*, meaning "mist," has evolved into our modern English word; similar in other Indo-European languages, including *migla* in Lithuanian and Latvian, *mgla* in Russian, *omíkhlé* in Greek and, like the English, *mist* in Dutch and Swedish

Dew: Also Indo-European roots, from *dheu*

Frost: Old English word, from the root *freusan*, for "freeze"

Fog: No clear origin for the English word, but may come from the Danish *fog*, for spray or shower

Water vapour: Air is composed of up to 4% invisible water vapour at any given time. Warm air can contain more vapour. When air cools, excess water vapour condenses into visible water droplets.

Also see: Clouds, Rain

dewy, while nearby objects such as stones will not be. Dew forms more easily on grass because the plant's large surface area, relative to its mass, gives up heat quickly. Stones retain much of their heat overnight, so the air surrounding them doesn't cool as much.

Because dew, like mist, occurs when the weather is good, the following old saying is fairly accurate:

When the dew is on the grass
Rain will never come to pass.

RAIN

Step on a Spider, and It Will Rain

Much of our old weather lore is about as accurate as a weather forecaster on a bad day. Long-range forecasts, especially those that predict next year's or next season's weather, are pure superstition.

But like the home remedies that scientists later discover have a basis in fact, some rhymes and sayings about short-term weather – especially rain – have good reason to be true. The Roman poet Virgil noted that "when swallows fly low there will soon be rain," or Latin words to that effect. This happens to be the case, because certain insects the swallows eat hang low just before a storm. One of the characteristics of a storm front is that the air is more humid higher up. Water vapour tends to condense on the little bugs and make them less airworthy, so they stick closer to the ground.

Many other animals and plants react to subtle atmospheric changes before rainfalls. Ants may be more active just before it rains because the relatively warmer temperature of a low-pressure rain system heats up their blood. Likewise,

Rain name origin: From Old English and Old Norse *regn;* Old High German, *Regen*

Maximum falling speed: 30 km (18 mi) per hour; air friction prevents faster velocities

Falling speed of snowflakes on calm days: 6 km/h (3.7 mph)

Raindrop size: 0.5–5 mm (0.020–0.20 in) in diameter; avg. 2 mm (0.075 in)

Cloud droplet size: Typically 0.001–0.05 mm (4/100,000–2/1,000 in) in diameter

Number of droplets to make a raindrop: Estimated 30,000–1 million

Average Canadian precipitation that falls as snow: 36%

Average worldwide precipitation that falls as snow: 5%

The walk-or-run debate: Scientists have proven that a runner stays drier (or, more accurately, less wet) than a walker while getting to shelter during a rainstorm. Although a runner does run into more raindrops than a walker in the same unit of time, the greater time a walker is out in the rain means a worse soaking. The only exception is when rain is falling on a slant in a

Orographic Rain

Heavier rain on west side of highlands

Dew point (moisture condenses)

Westerly winds

Air forced to rise over the highlands

tailwind. If this is the case, running faster than the wind would mean catching up to raindrops that would otherwise fall in front of the runner. But one mathematician has calculated that if the rain were falling at a 45° slant, this would entail running faster than the 4-minute mile.

How radar tracks rainstorms: Radar waves are sensitive enough to bounce off raindrops

"I smell rain": Several theories try to explain this phenomenon; water itself has no odour. Among the theories: Fungal earth odours in moist soil, triggered by lower barometric pressure, produce the so-called rain smell; plants give off more volatile substances when humidity is higher; lightning rips apart air molecules, releasing odorous ozone.

Most rainfall recorded in one hour in Ontario: 8.7 cm (3.4 in) in Fergus, June 10, 1967

Most rainfall recorded in 24 hours in Ontario: 26.4 cm (10.4 in) in Harrow (south of Windsor), July 19–20, 1989

Also see: Clouds; Mist, Dew and Fog; Thunder and Lightning, Wind and Weather Systems, Granite, Lakes

spiders pick up the pace in fixing and reinforcing their webs just before poor weather. Pine cones, as they absorb the moisture of an oncoming rain front, close up and become more supple. And the leaves of some deciduous trees, such as poplars, often turn bottom side up just before rain. Moisture-laden air softens the stems, and strong updrafts associated with thunderstorms rustle the leaves. "When the leaves show their undersides, be very certain that rain betides," as one saying goes.

Most rain betides when heated air rises and then cools at higher altitudes. Water vapour in the air condenses into microscopic water droplets around dust, soot and organic particles always present in the sky. As these droplets are tossed about in the cloud, they may collide and grow bigger. Eventually, the raindrop becomes heavy enough to fall to the ground. Contrary to popular depiction, they are not shaped like teardrops. "Instead, they are shaped like tiny hamburger buns, with the flat side down," Terence Dickinson, a noted Ontario skywatcher, has observed.

Often temperatures inside a cloud are cold enough for the water droplets to freeze into six-sided ice crystals, even in summer. These form the nuclei of snowflakes, which grow as other water droplets condense along their sides. If the air beneath the cloud is warm, the snowflakes will melt and fall as rain. If it's Canada, they'll fall as snow.

An average 700 to 1,000 millimetres (28 to 39 inches) of rain and snow falls across Ontario each year, a layer of life-giving rain about equal to the depth of the shallow end of a swimming pool. (The B.C. coast gets the most rainfall in Canada, with some locations receiving more than 3,000 millimetres, or 10 feet, of water.) The west sides of highlands receive greater amounts of precipitation because the prevailing winds force air up over them. Water vapour is then more likely to condense and fall as rain. This is called orographic precipitation, from the Greek root *oros,* or "mountain" (orography is the study of mountains). The west side of the Algonquin highlands receives more than 1,000 millimetres (39 inches) of rain and snow. Burk's Falls, located in this zone between Huntsville and North Bay, holds an Ontario record for having the third-most wet days in a year of any location in the province: 232 days, in 1980. The east side of the highlands lies in a rain shadow and thus receives less precipitation, averaging about 700 millimetres (28 inches).

Normal annual precipitation levels, from Environment Canada's Canadian Climate Normals 1971–2000

LOCATION	RAIN (mm)	SNOW (cm)
Barrie	700	238
Exeter	806	183
Gore Bay	625	267
Haliburton	747	262
Huntsville	746	286
Kingston	795	181
London	818	202
North Bay	775	273
Ottawa	733	202
Owen Sound	753	347
Peterborough	682	162
Renfrew	616	196
Sault Ste. Marie	634	303
Thunder Bay	559	188
Timmins	558	313
Toronto	710	133
Las Vegas*	11	0

*not monitored by Environment Canada. It has snowed seven times in Vegas since 1939, including 9 cm (3.5 in) on Dec. 17, 2008.

RAINBOWS
Covenant with Humanity

Rainbow name origin: From the Old English *regnboga;* in French, *arc-en-ciel*

Why rainbows are semicircular: Rainbows are actually circles, which can sometimes be seen from airplanes. From the ground, only the top portion of the circle is visible because of the angle of view. The bottom portion is below the horizon. A low sun produces taller rainbows, and vice versa.

Why rainbows appear in only late afternoon or early morning: Sunlight

If the Milky Way is the nighttime path of souls travelling from Earth to the heavens, rainbows serve the same function in daytime. To the Babylonians, the rainbow was a bridge formed by the necklace of the goddess Ishtar, linking Heaven and Earth. Similar descriptions exist in Norse, Persian and Japanese mythologies, and in Buddhist scriptures.

The rainbow is rich in other meanings for humans. Perhaps the most famous rainbow in history is the one that appeared to Noah after the Great Flood had cleansed the world of sin – and pretty well everything else. God, who was feeling kind of sorry for what he had done, sent the

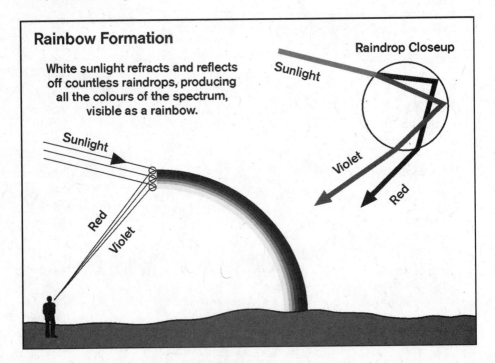

Rainbow Formation

White sunlight refracts and reflects off countless raindrops, producing all the colours of the spectrum, visible as a rainbow.

Raindrop Closeup

Sunlight

Violet

Red

Sunlight

Red

Violet

rainbow as a promise that "never again will the waters become a flood to destroy all creation."

In a Cree story, rainbows were said to be made of flowers. A young girl who loved rainbows was carried up to one by a Thunderbird, and she sent some of the flowers back to Earth to beautify the land. In Ireland, leprechauns liked to bury their pots of gold at the end of rainbows, probably because it is impossible for a mortal to get there. The ancient Greeks were among the few to look upon rainbows with trepidation. Iris, the rainbow goddess, was a messenger of the gods. But she was usually dispatched when the news was bad: impending war, or perhaps the death of a loved one.

Though rainbows don't lead to gold, they usually signify improved fortunes, at least as far as the weather is concerned. A rainbow needs two ingredients, sunlight and raindrops. The sun must be located low in the sky and behind the rainbow watcher. The raindrops must be in the air in front of the observer. Late-afternoon rainbows may foretell good weather because it means the sun is unobstructed in the west. Since weather systems generally come from the west, clear skies are probably on the way. And since the rain in the east is moving away, the bad weather has probably passed. For the same reasons, the opposite is true of an early-morning rainbow. The clear skies have already passed to the east, and the rain in the west is bearing down upon the observer, to dampen the day.

Rainbows are created by sunlight penetrating billions of falling raindrops. Most of the light passes straight through the drop; however, a small amount of light is bent as it enters the

reflects off each raindrop at angles between 42° (red) and 40° (violet). When the sun is higher than 42° in the sky, the colours reflected from a rainbow pass over an observer's head and are not visible. Generally, rainbows appear in a 3-hour period before sunset or after sunrise

Moonbows: The light from a full moon can sometimes produce a dim rainbow, if the same conditions that create a normal rainbow are in place

Iris: The name for the coloured circular ring around the pupil of an eye comes from the Greek word for rainbow. Iris was also the Greek rainbow goddess.

Rainbow Country: The tourism region running from Parry Sound to north of Sudbury; presumably named for the relatively frequent appearance of rainbows due to higher precipitation levels in this part of the province

Most rainbows in the world: Honolulu

Also see: Clouds, Rain

drop and refracts into the seven main colours that make up the visible spectrum: red, orange, yellow, green, blue, indigo and violet. The back of the raindrop acts like a mirror to reflect these colours out the front of the drop, towards the observer.

A rainbow watcher sees only one colour from each raindrop. But because the sunlight is refracting and reflecting off countless raindrops, the full spectrum is visible in the beautiful arc of a rainbow. Red is always the outside colour, and violet the inside. Because each observer is positioned at a different angle to the raindrops, each sees his or her own rainbow.

The most brilliant rainbows usually appear after a thunderstorm, because the large raindrops of that type of storm reflect more light. But rainbows can appear through the mist of a waterfall or the spray of a lawn sprinkler. All it takes are water droplets and the sun at the right angle. Sometimes double rainbows are visible, with the secondary outer rainbow much fainter. This occurs when sunlight reflects off the interior of raindrops twice. Each reflection dims the intensity of the light. The order of colours in the secondary rainbow is reversed.

SUN
The 0.7 Per Cent Solution

The source of almost all life on Earth begins with a slim surplus of mass deep inside the sun. Under pressure 250 billion times greater than the atmospheric pressure on the Earth's surface, and in 15 million °C (27 million °F) heat, four hydrogen nuclei fuse into one helium nucleus. But the helium does not equal the mass of the hydrogen parents; a tiny amount, 0.7 per cent, is left over. This missing mass, according to science, is converted into energy that ultimately becomes the heat and light that bathes our planet and all the other worlds in the solar system.

Scientists continue to unlock the secrets of nuclear fusion, as this process is called. But most ancient cultures understood that the sun is the giver of life, and had a sun deity or being who played a prominent role in their mythology. Shamash was the sun god of Babylonia; he was responsible for justice. The Egyptian Ra was the great creator and the defender of goodness. Helios, of ancient Greece, rode his sun-chariot across the sky and lived in a magnificent palace where darkness never fell. Apollo was also identified as a Greek sun god, although more properly he was the god of light and truth. The sun in Ojibway stories was a symbol of the Great Spirit or Kitche Manitou; sometimes it was referred to as the Great Spirit's wigwam. An Inuit fable describes the sun and the moon as brother and sister who committed incest while they were humans. In the sky they were to be forever parted. Nearly all cultures identify the

Historic expedition: In 1768, the English dispatched astronomer Charles Green and Cpt. James Cook – the latter of whom had distinguished himself in the Gulf of St. Lawrence during the English conquest of Canada – to Tahiti to record the transit of Venus across the face of the sun. The measurements were to be used to determine the distance of the sun from Earth. On his way back from Tahiti, in 1770, Cook became the first European to encounter eastern Australia. His ship sailed into Botany Bay and changed the history of that continent forever.

Period of rotation (the sun's "day"): About 25 Earth days at the equator

Diameter: 1,400,000 km (840,000 mi), or 109 times Earth's diameter

Mass: 333,000 times Earth's

Temperature: 15,000,000°C (27,000,000°F) at core, 5,500°C (9,900°F) at surface

Age: 4.6 billion years

Composition by number of atoms: 92% hydrogen, almost 8% helium, heavier elements the remainder

Magnitude: −27, (see page 502)

Closest distance between the Earth and sun: 147

million km (88 million mi) at
perihelion, early Jan.

Farthest distance: 152 million km (91 million mi) at
aphelion, early July

Vernal (spring) equinox:
Mar. 20–22 (exact date
changes from year to year)

Summer solstice: June
20–22

Autumnal equinox: Sept.
21–23

Winter solstice: Dec. 20–22

**Time it takes for sunlight to
reach Earth:** 8.3 min

Speed of light: 299,792 km
(186,282 mi) per sec

**Solar radiation reaching
Earth that is absorbed
into the ground and converted into heat:** About
50%; half the radiation reflects off clouds and the
Earth, or is absorbed by the
atmosphere

UV Index: Search
Environment Canada's UV
Index on the Internet for

sun with the masculine or fatherhood, perhaps because Earth and the moon are so closely associated with the feminine, and sunlight is the agent that fertilizes life.

Great festivals, such as the rowdy Roman Saturnalia, often marked significant solar events. Saturnalia was held around the winter solstice in December. At that time, the north pole is tilted away from the sun because of the Earth's 23.5-degree axial tilt to its orbital plane around the sun. At the summer solstice in June, after the Earth has travelled halfway around its orbit, the north pole is tilted towards the sun. The northern hemisphere thus receives the sun's warming rays at a more direct angle in summer. In December, when shadows are longest because the sun is low, the northern hemisphere receives the rays at an oblique angle. In other words, the same amount of sunlight has to heat a far greater area of land in the winter than it does in the summer. The seasons are reversed in the southern hemisphere.

On the summer solstice, the sun rises at its most northerly point along the northeastern

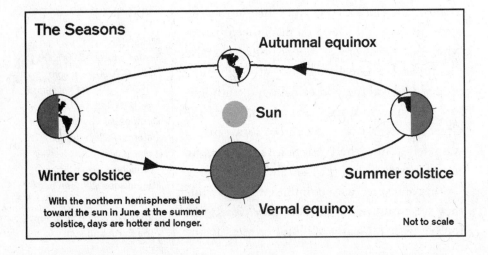

The Seasons

Autumnal equinox

Sun

Winter solstice

Summer solstice

Vernal equinox

With the northern hemisphere tilted
toward the sun in June at the summer
solstice, days are hotter and longer.

Not to scale

horizon and traces its highest arc of the year across the sky. This is the longest day of the year. The opposite occurs on the winter solstice, when the sun rises in the southeast and loops low across the southern sky. On the vernal and autumnal equinoxes, the sun rises and sets midway between the points demarcated by the solstices, which happens to be due east and due west. On the equinoxes, the hours of the day are split into roughly equal amounts of light and darkness, hence the name.

In addition to providing heat and the light for photosynthesis, solar radiation includes ultraviolet rays. UV rays interacting with the skin produce vitamin D, which helps prevent cancer and bone disease. It typically takes only 10 minutes of exposure two or three times a week to receive the beneficial effects of UV. (Canadians have been urged in recent years to supplement their vitamin D intake during the winter.) However, too much UV causes sunburns, which in the long term can lead to skin damage and skin cancer. Most UV rays are absorbed by ozone, a form of oxygen, in the atmosphere. But artificial chemicals have eaten away at the ozone layer in recent decades, allowing more UV radiation to reach the surface. In 1992, Canada became the first country in the world to issue a daily ultraviolet radiation index; Environment Canada later adopted a new UN standard that rates UV exposure on a scale of 1 to 11+. The higher the number, the greater the danger, with "cover up" prescriptions beginning at level 3.

Our sun is in comfortable middle age. Now and then the photosphere, the sun's roiling surface, erupts with violent flares and enormous

up-to-date forecasts and information

Sun: From ancient Indo-European *sau* or *su;* some groups of sun-related words adopted an *i* suffix, including *soleil* in French, and *helios* in Greek; others adopted the *n* suffix, including *sun*, *sonne* in German and *zon* in Dutch

Artificial star: The human effort to create nuclear fusion energy continues with the ITER reactor in the south of France; visit www.iter.org

Why the sky is blue: Air is transparent, which is why we can see the stars at night. The daytime colour comes from the complex interaction of sunlight striking gas molecules, moisture and dust particles. White sunlight is actually composed of the seven main colours of the spectrum. During the day, all these colours except blue travel directly to the Earth's surface. The blue light is scattered by gas molecules throughout the sky. The sun, which is white when viewed from outer space, appears yellow from the Earth's surface – all the colours of the spectrum minus blue. Space is black because there is no atmosphere to scatter the light.

Also see: Milky Way, Moon, Northern Lights, Stars, Planets and Comets

UV INDEX

UV Index	Category	Sun Protection Actions
0–2	Low	Minimal protection for normal activity
3–5	Moderate	Cover up. Wear hat, sunglasses, sunscreen if outside for 30 min.
6–7	High	Protection required. Reduce time in sun between 11AM and 4PM
8–10	Very High	Take full precautions and avoid sun between 11AM and 4PM
11+	Extreme	Take full precautions and avoid sun between 11AM and 4PM

Proper sun protection includes wearing a broad-rimmed hat, a shirt with long sleeves and wrap-around sunglasses or ones with side shields. Choose sunscreen with 15+ SPF (sun protection factor) that offers protection against both UV-A and UV-B rays. Apply generously before going outside and reapply often, especially after swimming or exercise.

Source: Environment Canada

gas prominences, but that's normal for a Class G2V nuclear-fusion reactor, as astronomers categorize our star. The flares are associated with sunspots, which are cooler areas of the photosphere caused by fluctuations in the sun's powerful magnetic field. These fluctuations have an 11-year cycle, so that every 11 years solar flares seem more pronounced.

But like all living things, the sun's time will come. In another five billion years or so, the engine of our solar system will be running on empty. Shortly afterwards, the sun will swell into a red giant that will engulf Mercury, Venus and Earth. Immense gravitational forces will then cause the sun's matter to contract into a small, dense star called a white dwarf. The stored-up heat from its previous processes will radiate away, and our sun will die.

Approximate sunrise and sunset times for the Muskoka, Haliburton, North Bay regions of Ontario. For other locations and dates, see notes below.

DATE	SUNRISE	SUNSET
Jan. 1	7:49 a.m. EST	4:52 p.m. EST
Jan. 15	7:47	5:08
Feb. 1	7:37	5:28
Feb. 15	7:15	5:50
Mar. 1	6:57	6:05
Mar. 15	7:30 a.m. DST	7:24 p.m. DST
Apr. 1	7:00	7:45
Apr. 15	6:34	8:02
May 1	6:08	8:23
May 15	5:50	8:39
June 1	5:35	8:56
June 15	5:30	9:07
July 1	5:43	9:01
July 15	5:52	8:56
Aug. 1	6:08	8:39
Aug. 15	6:22	8:22
Sept. 1	6:38	7:50
Sep. 15	6:57	7:28
Oct. 1	7:16	6:59
Oct. 15	7:32	6:36
Nov. 1	7:56	6:07
Nov. 15	7:15 a.m. EST	4:50 p.m. EST
Dec. 1	7:36	4:38
Dec. 15	7:50	4:36

For dates between the chart dates, take an average. For other locations, add or subtract the number of minutes as indicated: Kapuskasing: +12, Kingston: -12, Ottawa: -15, Peterborough: -5, Sudbury: +6, Thunder Bay: +39, Timmins: +8. Daylight Saving Time starts on the second Sunday in March and ends on the first Sunday in November. This chart has been adjusted to account for DST.

THUNDER AND LIGHTNING
Flashes Hotter than the Sun

Temperature of a lightning bolt: 10,000–40,000°C (18,000–72,000°F)

Temperature of the sun's surface: About 5,500°C (9,900°F)

Average current of a lightning bolt: 20,000 amperes

Typical speed of a lightning bolt: 150,000 km (90,000 mi) per sec

Speed of light: 299,792 km (186,282 mi) per sec

Anyone who has experienced the full fury of a thunderstorm, especially from inside a tent, has an idea of how our ancestors must have felt during one of nature's most awesome shows. The howling winds, the crashing thunder and the alien lightning bolts seem like a backdrop to the end of time. Perhaps that's why the thunder gods of many ancient civilizations were supreme beings, even more than sun deities. Zeus of Olympus and Thor of Valhalla hurled thunderbolts with impunity. Marduk, the supernatural

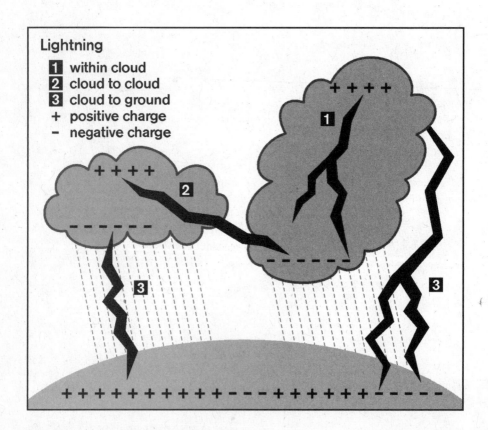

Lightning
1 within cloud
2 cloud to cloud
3 cloud to ground
+ positive charge
− negative charge

hero of ancient Babylon, was also a thunder god. One of the manifestations of the Semitic god Baal was a storm god with an arsenal of thunderbolts. Maybe they're all the same god – one story passed down through the millennia.

Native peoples of Canada also respect thunderstorms. To the Ojibway and many other nations, mythic Thunderbirds, or *pinesi* – important beings who play roles in many old stories – brought thunderstorms. When storms were raging, the Thunderbirds were said to be hunting. Thunder came from the flap of their wings, lightning from the flash of their eyes. Although *pinesi* had no definite shape, they are associated with hawks, undoubtedly based on the observation that hawks and thunderstorms appear about the same time each year, in April, and fade away at the same time, in October.

Another Ojibway conception of thunderstorms linked them to grandfathers. Because grandmothers were traditionally closer to their children and grandchildren than granddads, they were given a more regular, symbolic presence in Grandmother Moon. Grandfathers, angry at this lack of attention, returned as thunder, or Grandfather Thunder. Families offered tobacco in thunderstorms to appease the old grouch.

The classic thunderstorm occurs on hot, humid summer afternoons, when massive amounts of heated air rise to form huge cumulonimbus clouds. Scientists are still uncertain about the exact causes of lightning. Somehow, the air is ionized into negative and positive charges. One theory suggests Earth's magnetic field plays a role, another theory proposes that gamma rays from outer space trigger the charge

Speed of sound: 0.332 km (1,085 ft) per sec

Typical width of a lightning bolt: 2 cm (¾ in) at point of strongest current

Length of a lightning bolt: From 50 m to 35 km (55 yd to 22 mi), which is why a "bolt from the blue" can sometimes strike ahead of or behind storm clouds. Safety gurus recommend staying indoors if thunder can be heard within 30 seconds or less of seeing distant lightning, and for 30 minutes after a storm ends

Maximum height of a thundercloud: 20 km (12 mi)

Height of Mt. Everest: 8.8 km (5.3 mi)

Height of Ishpatina Ridge, the highest point in Ontario, in the Temiskaming area: 693 m (2,275 ft)

Distance to lightning strikes: To determine the distance to a lightning bolt, count the number of seconds between a lightning flash and its resulting thunder. Each second is about 300 m (1,000 ft).

Maximum distance thunder travels: About 40 km (24 mi)

Estimated number of thunderstorms occurring at this moment: 18,000 around the world

Estimated number of lightning bolts striking the ground every second: 100

Average number of times the CN Tower gets hit every year: 75

Tennyson's description of lightning: "Flying flame"

Ben Franklin's kite: In 1752, Benjamin Franklin supposedly flew a kite in a thunderstorm to prove that lightning was caused by electricity; he invented lightning rods. A Prof. Georg Richmann of St. Petersburg attempted Franklin's experiment the following year but unfortunately was electrocuted, thus also proving the theory.

Average annual lightning casualties in Canada: 6–10 people killed, about 120 injured

Chances of ever being hit by lightning: 1 in 350,000–600,000

Chances of winning the jackpot in Lotto 6/49, per play: 1 in 13,983,816

Fear of thunder and lightning: Brontophobia, from the Greek *bronte*, meaning "thunder"

Lightning and trees: Most healthy trees can withstand a direct lightning strike without serious damage, their moisture conducting the charge down to the ground, leaving perhaps a 1 cm–wide entry hole in the bark. Trees that come down are usually dead or dying, with rotting wood, or are very dry

Speed of falling hail: 160 km/h (96 mph)

separation. A common theory suggests that within the thunderheads, powerful downdrafts ionize the air by stripping molecules of electrons, similar to the way rubbing a balloon gives it an electrical charge. The top of a thunderhead is thus positively charged, while the base is negatively charged. The ground immediately below a thunderhead is positively charged too. Nature seeks to correct the electrical imbalance by transferring electrons from the positive ground or positive cloud top to the negative cloud base. Most lightning occurs within a cloud or between clouds. Only 20 per cent is cloud-to-ground lightning.

Lightning forms along a route called a tunnel or channel. In cloud-to-ground lightning, one end of the tunnel (called the leader) starts at the cloud base and moves downwards, while the other (called the streamer) starts on the ground – generally from a tall point such as a tower or tree – and moves upwards. The two meet, usually at a spot close to the ground, and the circuit is completed. The visible lightning bolt emanates from this point, moving up and down the tunnel in about 1/10,000 of a second. The explosive bolt heats the air instantly, up to seven times the temperature of the surface of the sun, and the resulting air expansion vibrates as thunder.

Sheet lightning is not another form of lightning but simply the glow of lightning bolts that occur within a cloud. Contrary to popular belief, lightning often hits the same place twice, especially tall towers.

Buildings and hard-top cars are the safest places to wait out thunderstorms. Appliances should be unplugged because electrical charges can sometimes surge down power lines. Standing under tall trees, in the middle of open fields or atop hills or ridges is dangerous. Swimmers and boaters should head for shore as soon as they hear thunder. Woods are relatively safe, but don't set up a tent beneath the tallest tree. If you're caught in the open, the "golfer's crouch" can prevent serious injury or death: kneel on the ground with hands on knees and bend forward. If a lightning bolt strikes nearby, the charge should pass under you without striking vital organs. Don't lie flat. Lightning strikes are lethal about 20 to 30 per cent of the time, when the charge passes through the heart or spinal cord.

Another hazard associated with thunderstorms is hail. These ice balls can kill animals, damage cars and wipe out fields of crops in seconds. Usually they are the size of peas, but grapefruit-sized monsters have been recorded in Canada. Hail occurs when ice crystals in a thunderhead are carried up and down by violent air currents. The crystals grow along the way as more moisture condenses and freezes on their surface. When they are too heavy to be supported by air currents, they fall explosively out of the bottom of the cloud.

Tornadoes may also accompany the biggest thunderstorms, and are usually preceded by heavy hail. Tornado winds can reach 500 km/h (300 mph), about twice as fast as the worst hurricane winds. Waterspouts are similar to tornadoes but not as violent, with winds approaching 80 km/h (48 mph). Both are rare in hilly Shield country but relatively common in southwestern Ontario, where about 25 tornadoes are reported each year.

Winter thunderstorms: The flash of lightning in a snowstorm can be spectacular, but winter thunderstorms are rare, because there is not as much heating of air (convection) in winter as in summer

Forest fires caused by lightning: About 35%

Forest fires caused by human activity: About 65%

Maximum length of a thunderstorm: About 2 hours

Thunderstorm travelling speed: Up to 100 km/h (62 mph)

Typical size of a frontal thunderstorm: 10–15 km (6–9 mi) wide, 200–300 km (124–186 mi) long

Time it takes a fluffy white cumulus cloud to turn into a thundercloud: 20–30 min

Also see: Yellow-bellied Sapsucker, Red Oak, Clouds, Rain

WIND AND WEATHER SYSTEMS
A Blow-by-blow Account

Wind is essential for life on Earth. Trees and plants owe their existence to winds that carry pollen and distribute seeds. Wind transports moisture around the world, bringing life-sustaining rains. Tailwinds and vertical air currents called thermals enable birds to migrate thousands of miles. Worldwide wind patterns distribute heat more evenly across the planet. The profound importance of wind was not lost on the ancients: wind is one of the four elements of antiquity, along with fire, water and earth.

The science of wind is complex. Many questions about its behaviour still stump researchers, not to mention novice sailboarders. But the basics are well understood. Put simply, wind occurs when air rushes from a high-pressure zone to a low-pressure zone, answering nature's call for equilibrium. A vacuum cleaner uses the same principle. A powerful fan creates an artificial low-pressure zone. Air outside the vacuum cleaner, now suddenly under higher pressure, swooshes up the nozzle towards the low-pressure area, carrying dust, dirt and lost Rummoli chips along with it. The greater the difference

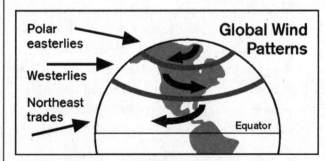

Global Wind Patterns

Polar easterlies

Westerlies

Northeast trades

Equator

in pressure, the faster the wind. Hurricanes and tornadoes are like enormous vacuum cleaners: both are extreme low-pressure systems, sucking deadly winds towards their centres and picking up everything in their paths.

Typical low-pressure systems aren't as violent, but they generally bring bad weather. In a low, the inward-rushing air is warm and moves upward as it converges towards the centre. As the moisture-laden air ascends, it cools. Water vapour condenses into cloud banks, and it often rains.

High-pressure zones are characterized by heavy, cooler air that sinks as it moves outwards. Cool air contains less moisture; therefore, the air is sometimes cloudless. A high-pressure system in the winter brings cold, clear air. In summer, the air in a high-pressure system doesn't seem so cool because it heats up during the day as intense sunlight warms the ground. Both high-pressure and low-pressure systems generally move westward across the continent because of prevailing westerly winds.

Boaters use a system called "the crossed-winds rules" to help predict weather, at least for the short term. They observe which direction the lower wind is travelling by watching the low clouds. They face that direction. Then they observe which direction the upper wind is travelling by carefully watching the high clouds (obviously, this works only if there are low and high clouds in the sky). If the upper wind is coming from the left, this means a low-pressure system is approaching and the weather will usually get worse. If the upper wind is coming from the right, the weather should improve. If

the father of dangerous winds

King of the Winds: In Greek mythology, Aeolus ruled the 4 winds; *Aeolian* means "pertaining to the winds"; the north wind was Boreas, the west Zephyr, the south Notus, the east Eurus

Wind power: Electricity-generating windmills produced about 1.3% of Ontario's power supply in 2009. Nuclear reactors produced 36%, the largest single source. Ontario wind power output is expected to grow more than 10 times by 2025.

Danish wind power: Scandinavian winds produced 25% of Denmark's power in 2009

Why wind feels cool or cold against skin: Wind evaporates moisture in the skin, removing heat energy. Thus, in summer, a gentle breeze will cool us down. In winter, a breeze freezes, and reminds us of our northern heritage.

Wind and canoe routes: Avoid adversity by taking prevailing westerlies into consideration when planning circuitous canoe routes. Plan eastward sections of the trip along lakes to take advantage of tailwinds, westward sections along narrower bodies of water and rivers, which are more protected from the wind.

Also see: Broad-winged Hawk, Mosquitoes, Clouds; Mist, Dew and Fog; Rain; Thunder and Lightning

the lower and upper winds are travelling parallel to each other, either in the same direction or in opposite directions, then the weather probably won't change. These forecasts are generally good for the following few hours or half day.

In the summer, gentle winds die down at night because their creator – the sun – disappears. During the day, the sun heats the ground, which then warms the air. As the warm air rises, other air rushes in to take its place, creating wind. Once the sun is gone the process stops.

BEAUFORT WIND SCALE

Named after Francis Beaufort, a British admiral, who invented the scale in 1805

NUMBER	WINDSPEED (km/h)	DESIGNATION	CHARACTERISTIC
0	up to 1	Calm	Smoke rises vertically
1	1–5	Light air	Smoke drifts, leaves rustle
2	6–11	Light breeze	Wind on face, small wavelets
3	12–19	Gentle breeze	Flags flutter
4	20–29	Moderate breeze	Dust blows, branches move
5	30–38	Fresh breeze	Flags stretched, trees sway
6	39–50	Strong breeze	Wires hum, wind whistles
7	51–61	Moderate gale	Walking is impeded
8	62–74	Fresh gale	Twigs break off, high waves
9	75–86	Strong gale	Branches break, tiles are blown
10	87–101	Whole gale	Trees uprooted, damage
11	102–120	Storm	Widespread damage
12	over 120	Hurricane	Major destruction

NIGHT SKY

*W*hen the precursor to this book was published in 1993, Pluto was the ninth planet, there were no known planets outside of our own solar system, and the International Space Station was five years away from the first module being launched. Now, Pluto has been officially demoted to a "dwarf planet," more than 350 planets have been discovered orbiting other stars in the Milky Way, and the International Space Station is permanently inhabited with a multinational crew, orbiting Earth 15 times a day. Astronomical knowledge has increased, well, astronomically in just a few years thanks to powerful new telescopes, nimble space probes and the inquiring minds of scientists poring over data and pictures.

So much change. Yet the fundamental allure of stargazing surely remains the same today as it was for our earliest ancestors in Africa. This section of The Complete Up North *is intended to enrich primal awe by providing a basic understanding of the major constellations and heavenly phenomena that, along with our myths, populate the night sky.*

If the grandeur of a planetary world in which the earth, as a grain of sand, is scarcely perceived, fills the understanding with wonder; with what astonishment are we transported when we behold the infinite multitude of worlds and systems which fill the extension of the Milky Way!
– German philosopher and part-time astronomer Immanuel Kant, 1755 (translated by W. Hastie)

BIG DIPPER
The Universal Bear

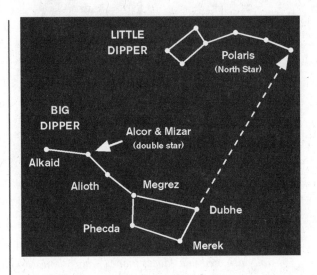

Through the millennia, people in the northern hemisphere have gazed into the night sky and connected the same starry dots to form what we now call the Big Dipper. It's the constellation we learn first because it's easy to pick out, it's promi-nent in the sky on summer nights and two of its stars conveniently point to the North Star, Polaris.

In fact, long before the Golden Arches came to exist, the Big Dipper was a touchstone for many civilizations. A surprising number of myths from Europe, Asia and North America refer to the Big Dipper as a bear. It's thought that the bear story originated in prehistoric Asia and travelled both eastward and westward with various human migrations.

The Mi'kmaq of Nova Scotia have just such a story, in which the four stars making up the cup of the Big Dipper represent a bear. The three stars of the handle, plus other nearby stars, represent birds. When spring came, the hungry birds hunted the bear. From high in the sky, they chased it closer to Earth. In autumn, the lead bird, Robin, shot an arrow at the bear. Blood splashed Robin, giving the bird its red breast. Blood also dripped onto the leaves below, giving them autumn colour. The hunt's cycle is repeated every year, with the position of the constellation serving as a calendar to record the seasons. The motion of the bear through the sky during the night also serves as a clock.

The Greeks, as always, saw in the Dipper constellations a star opera of love and jealousy. In one version of the legend, Zeus seduces the nymph Callisto. Zeus's betrayed wife, Hera, retaliates by turning Callisto into a bear. Out of compassion, Zeus transforms Callisto's son Arcas into a bear too, to keep her company, placing both of them in the heavens to protect them from hunters. There they are known by their Latin names Ursa Major, the greater bear, and Ursa Minor, the lesser bear. Zeus's manner of delivering both bears to the heavens – a cosmic heave – explains their stretched tails.

Another story also refers to the tail or handle of the Dipper, though it doesn't involve a bear. In an Ojibway legend, the Big Dipper is a fisher, a member of the weasel family. One year, the story goes, summer did not arrive. A certain hunter, named Fisher after the animal spirit that inhabited him, concluded that someone had captured the migratory birds that brought good weather. The culprit was Fisher's selfish cousin, Cruel-Face. After a skirmish, Fisher was able to release the birds of summer. Cruel-Face chased

some very bright stars now have negative values, while stars invisible to the naked eye but apparent in telescopes have values greater than 6.

Namesake spacecraft: The European Space Agency's *Hipparcos* satellite measured the distances and motions of more than 100,000 stars between 1989 and 1993

Double-star names: Mizar (larger star) and Alcor. This pair is called an optical double, because they are close to each other only by virtue of our line of sight from Earth. They are not gravitationally linked to each other like a true double-star system. Telescopic observations show that many stars are actually double stars, also called binaries. Mizar itself appears as a double star in telescopes.

Also see: Robin, Black Bear, Muskrat, Weasel, Boötes, North Star and Little Dipper, Star Charts

Fisher up a tree, where the hero's only escape was to follow the advice of the stars and leap into Sky Country. He did, forming the constellation. But as Fisher leapt, Cruel-Face fired off his last arrow, wounding Fisher in the tail. To this day, Fisher's injured tail – the crooked handle of the Big Dipper – attests to Cruel-Face's desperate shot. And to this day, the freed birds bring summer every year.

Like the Ojibway, other cultures saw unique shapes in the Dipper con-figuration. The Saxons called it a wagon, as did the Babylonians. In Britain it is still sometimes called the Plough. Ancient Egyptians looked up in the sky and saw a bull's thigh. In the pre-emancipation U.S., slaves called it a drink-ing gourd, because it resembled the shape of gourds they hollowed out for drinking cups. The celestial drinking gourd became a navigational beacon pointing northward as slaves fled under the cover of night along the Underground Railroad in the mid-1880s. Popular folk songs contained coded lyrics with instructions to "follow the drinking gourd" for getting north to Canada and other safe areas.

The official constellation Ursa Major, as defined by the International Astronomical Union, actually includes many more stars than just those in the Big Dipper. For this reason, the Big Dipper portion is technically called an asterism. It includes some notable astronomical features. The star at the crook of the Big Dipper's handle appears as a double star, for example. It is barely perceptible with the naked eye, which is why it was used as an eye test by many peoples, including Native North Americans, before wall charts were invented. One of the stars in the double star is itself a double star, the first ever discovered through a telescope, in 1650.

BOÖTES
Ice-cream Cone in the Sky

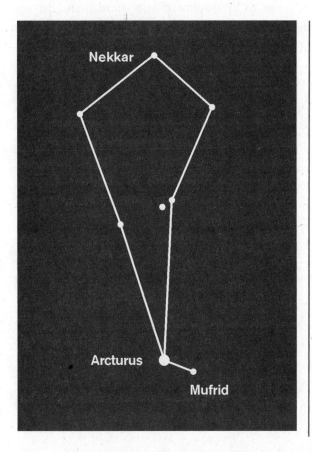

Nekkar

Arcturus

Mufrid

How Arcturus lit up Chicago: At the 1933 World's Fair in Chicago, organizers used the star's light to turn on the fair's floodlights. The starbeam was focused through a telescope onto a photoelectric cell, which generated the voltage to flip the switch. The starlight hitting the cell would have begun its journey to Earth in 1896, since Arcturus is about 37 light-years away.

Brightest star in Boötes: Arcturus, magnitude −0.04

Star closest to Earth: Arcturus, 37 light-years away

Star farthest from Earth: Nekkar, 219 light-years away

Also see: Big Dipper, North Star and Little Dipper, Star Charts

The constellation Boötes contains the brightest star of the summer sky, Arcturus. This giant nuclear furnace is about 120 times more luminous than our own sun and 25 times wider. The only star to outshine Arcturus in the northern hemisphere is brilliant Sirius, the "dog star" of winter that burns low in the southern sky.

Arcturus has great significance for northern peoples. It is the harbinger of spring, a signal to start thinking about planting crops or opening up the cottage. Arcturus climbs over the horizon into the early evening sky around the time of the spring equinox in late March.

Arcturus means "guardian of the bear" in Greek. The star was thought to herd Ursa Major, the Great Bear or Big Dipper, around the North Star. At some point in history, this notion was extended to include the entire constellation of Boötes, which means "ploughman" or "herdsman." In the Mi'kmaq myth of the Big Dipper, Arcturus was an owl in the group of birds hunting the celestial bear, while for thousands of years the Chinese have thought of Arcturus as one of the horns on a great sidereal dragon.

To find Arcturus and Boötes (pronounced *bow-OW-tays*), follow the curve of the handle of the Big Dipper to the next bright star – the famous "arc to Arcturus." Boötes extends out from Arcturus in the shape of a giant ice-cream cone; some people prefer to think of it as a kite. Continue the arc through Arcturus to find another bright star, Spica. Spica is the other horn on the Chinese sky-dragon. As summer progresses, Arcturus moves high across the night sky. It is almost directly overhead as darkness descends in late June and early July.

CASSIOPEIA
Stairway to Heaven

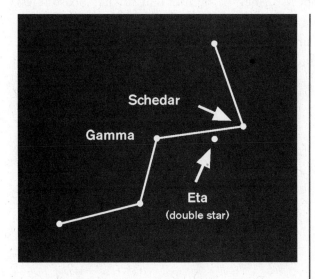

Schedar

Gamma

Eta
(double star)

The Sea Monster: Cetus, sent by Poseidon to terrorize Cassiopeia's subjects, took its name from the Greek word for "whale," *ketos.* The modern word *cetacean* refers to the order of animals that includes whales, dolphins and porpoises; *cetology* is the study of whales.

Closest star in Cassiopeia to Earth: Eta Cassiopeiae, 19 light-years away

Farthest star from Earth: Gamma Cassiopeiae, 613 light-years away

Brightest star: Schedar, magnitude 2.2

Double star: Even small telescopes reveal Eta Cassiopeiae, which lies between Schedar and Gamma Cassiopeiae, as a double star

Also see: Milky Way, Pegasus, Star Charts

Cassiopeia, queen of Aethiopia in Greek mythology, easily calls attention to herself from her heavenly perch. For many stargazers the Cassiopeia constellation is the one they learn right after the Big Dipper. Like the Dipper, it is circumpolar, revolving around Polaris and never setting below the horizon.

Northern cultures gave various meanings to Cassiopeia's distinctive shape. When it is low in the sky it looks like a giant W. As it moves higher it turns upside-down to become an M. To the Inuit this outline reflected the pattern of stairs cut in snow, an astral stairway connecting Earth to the sky country. The ancient Egyptians called it the Leg; to the Chinese it was the charioteer Wang Liang.

But it is the Greco-Roman tale that gives us the constellation's name. Cassiopeia, the Queen of Aethiopia, married to King Cepheus, was an unpleasant woman, apparently. She bragged that she was more beautiful than the sea nymphs – not a smart move, since the nymphs were the offspring of the mighty sea god Poseidon. The enraged god dispatched the monster Cetus to attack Aethiopia's coast. An oracle advised Cepheus that the only way to save his citizens was to sacrifice his daughter Andromeda to the briny beast. This he reluctantly did, although Andromeda was rescued by Perseus before Cetus could get his flippers on her. As punishment for her boastfulness, Cassiopeia was strapped to a chair and placed in the heavens. The other characters in this myth, including Cepheus, Andromeda, Cetus and Perseus, have nearby constellations named after them.

FALLING STARS

Anything to Worry About?

A paddle dips languidly into the ink-black water. A loon laughs. The night sky is a treasure chest of sparkling stars, reflected on the still lake. Every few minutes, high overhead, blue-green light streaks across the heavens. Sometimes there is a trail of sparks, like fireworks. In mid–August, to a human lying back in a canoe in the middle of a dark lake, the Perseid meteor shower entertains like no other show on Earth.

Meteors are reminders that the space between the stars and planets is not completely empty. "Falling stars" are caused when rocky particles called meteoroids enter Earth's atmosphere. Nearly all meteoroids are the size of a grain of sand or smaller. But every once in a while a big sucker gets through. Imagine how surprised the grazing dinosaurs of ancient Mexico must have

Favourite target of mete-
orites: Wethersfield, Conn.;
2 meteorites have smashed
into homes in this town, one
in 1971 and the second in
1982

Close calls: An Alaskan
woman suffered injuries to
her arm when a meteorite
slammed through the roof of
her house in 1954. In 1991,
a meteorite crashed into
Arthur Pettifor's garden in
England. He was quietly
planting onions about 18 m
(59 ft) away. In 1994, a
1.4 kg meteorite smashed
through a Spanish couple's
car windshield, narrowly
missing them. A meteorite
smashed the windshield of a
parked SUV in Grimsby,
Ontario, in 2009.

Bull's eye: A dog in Egypt
was struck dead by a meteorite in 1912

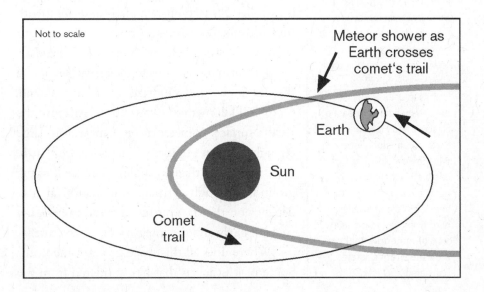

Not to scale

Meteor shower as Earth crosses comet's trail

Earth

Sun

Comet trail

Word origin of *meteor*: From the Greek *meta*, "beyond," and *eora*, "suspension"

Estimated number of meteorites heavier than 100 g (3.5 oz) landing on Earth's landmass each year: 5,800

Estimated weight of space dirt bombarding Earth each day: About 91 tonnes (100 tons)

Number of meteorite craters on Earth: About 160

Number of craters on the Canadian Shield: 24

Notable Ontario craters: The Brent Crater in northern Algonquin Park was discovered by aerial photography in 1951. It is a circular depression 4 km (2.4 mi) wide that now contains lakes Gilmour and Tecumseh. The crater was gouged into the Canadian Shield about 400 million years ago by a meteorite about 150 m (492 ft) in diameter. The mineral-rich Sudbury Basin is also the legacy of a meteorite that hit Precambrian Ontario 1.7 billion years ago. Other impact sites include the Slate Islands in Lake Superior, Lake Wanapitei northeast of Sudbury, and Holleford, north of Kingston. Some think the circular shape of eastern Hudson Bay suggests a massive crater, but detailed geologic studies have disproved that notion.

Force of meteorite that created the Brent Crater: Estimated 250 megatons

been when a boulder perhaps 10 kilometres (six miles) wide came out of nowhere and wiped out the neighbourhood. The collision, which scientists believe occurred 65 million years ago in the Yucatán (then under a shallow sea), would have thrown up an enormous cloud of dust, blocking out the sunlight for years. It seems certain this is what killed off the dinosaurs. Chicken Little has run scared ever since.

In fact, the fate of the dinosaurs has led some scientists and leaders to wonder if a giant asteroid has the name *Homo sapiens* written on it. In 1989, an asteroid about one kilometre (0.6 miles) wide crossed a spot in the Earth's orbit some six hours before the planet was there. About 1,000 asteroids larger than one kilometre in diameter cross Earth's orbit, and NASA's Near Earth Object program tracks potentially dangerous asteroids for an incoming apocalypse, with daily updates on its website. Spacecraft called gravitational tractors could deflect a rogue asteroid's orbit just enough to make it miss Earth, and scientists have urged the UN to prepare a plan for dealing with the unthinkable. But so far, preventing death from space has ranked low on political agendas.

The term *meteor* refers to the actual flare in the sky. The meteoroid vaporizes in about a second, 65 to 160 kilometres (40 to 100 miles) above the Earth's surface. A meteorite is a meteoroid large enough to survive the scorching descent to Earth. Anything bigger than an apple will make it to the ground, although a meteoroid's survival also depends on the speed it hits the atmosphere, the angle of entry and the integrity of its structure.

Where does all this space gravel come from? Some of it is debris that has wandered from the asteroid belt between Mars and Jupiter, destined to evaporate in a blaze of glory. Meteorites that hit Mars and the moon blow fragments into space that may also head our way – a meteoroid domino effect. Stray meteors appear at an average rate of about three to 12 an hour, and cannot be predicted. But look for them after midnight, because by then Spaceship Earth has spun so that we are looking "forward" into our orbit. The planet is now motoring into the path of any nearby meteoroids, so more meteors occur. Astronomers often compare this effect to a car travelling through a snowstorm: it collects more snow on the front windshield than the rear.

Regular meteor showers are a different phenomenon. Most occur when Earth intersects the path of a comet that's gone by. As a comet rushes towards the sun, it slowly disintegrates, leaving behind a concentrated trail of dirt. Because the trail is located along a specific line in space, a meteor shower occurs each time Earth crosses it; in other words, at the same time each year. The trail of the comet Swift-Tuttle causes the Perseid meteor shower. The rate of observable meteors may vary from year to year, sometimes wildly. Most years the Leonids in November produce about 15 meteors an hour under the best conditions. But every 33 years or so a spectacular Leonid shower may occur, with tens of thousands of meteors falling each hour as Earth crosses through a dense clump of debris from the comet Tempel-Tuttle, which has a 33-year orbit. The next Leonid blast is expected around 2033. Such showers have knocked out satellites and pose a danger to astronauts; cosmonauts heard Perseids pinging their *Mir* space station in 1993.

Largest nuclear explosion ever set off: 50 megatons, by the Soviet Union in 1961

Why the moon has more impact craters: The moon has no atmosphere to burn up incoming meteoroids. Also, geophysical forces on Earth erode crater features; no such forces exist on the moon.

Age of meteorites: About 4.6 billion years old

Age of solar system: About 4.6 billion years old

"Go and catch a falling star": The famous first line of John Donne's poem "Song," written in 1633, in which he suggests that fantastic feats such as catching a falling star are all easier than finding "a woman true, and fair"

1998 disaster-movie plots: Earthlings prepared for two comet strikes by building underground bunkers for 1 million people in *Deep Impact*, starring Robert Duvall. In *Armageddon*, a team of astronauts led by the Bruce Willis character flies shuttles to an asteroid streaking towards Earth; they attempt to bury a nuclear bomb in the asteroid to blow it up before it smacks the planet.

Falling star updates: Log on to www.spaceweather.com

Close-call updates: Log on to neo.jpl.nasa.gov

Also see: Fireflies, Planets and Comets, Canadian Shield, Limestone

Keeners will note that each meteor in a shower emanates from approximately the same point in space, called the radiant. Meteor showers are named after the constellation in which the radiant is located, the radiant of the Perseids being the constellation Perseus, for example. The Perseids is one of the best showers to enjoy because of the high intensity – about 50 an hour – and the fact that it's not –40°C outside.

In the old days, storytellers concocted all sorts of explanations for meteors. In Islamic folklore, meteors were missiles hurled by angels at evil spirits lurking around the gates of Heaven. English peasants in the Middle Ages believed a falling star was a soul passing from Heaven to Earth at the birth or conception of a new person – the reason they were wished upon. An Ojibway story describes meteors as demons sent to Earth by an idle sky spirit who wished to perplex the people living in the meteor's target zone; another tale says falling stars represent gifts of Kitche Manitou, the Creator, to someone on Earth. Pliny the Elder, a Roman philosopher and naturalist, thought a falling star marked someone's death, as every person had his or her own star in the sky. That raises the question: Did a meteor appear the day Pliny died? There should have been thousands, because the poor man went to Pompeii to study the eruptions of Mount Vesuvius in AD 79 and got caught in the most famous eruption ever. There were no reports of unusual meteor showers at the time.

MAJOR METEOR SHOWERS

SHOWER	DATE (PEAK)	RADIANT	RATE/HOUR*	SPEED HITTING EARTH (km/s)
Quadrantids	Jan. 4	Draco	40	41
Lyrids	Apr. 21	Lyra	15	48
Eta Aquarids	May 4	Aquarius	20	65
S. Delta Aquarids	July 28	Aquarius	20	41
N. Aquarids	Aug. 12	Aquarius	20	42
Perseids	Aug. 12	Perseus	50	60
Orionids	Oct. 21	Orion	25	66
S. Taurids	Nov. 2 or 3	Taurus	15	28
Leonids	Nov. 17 or 16	Leo	15	71
Geminids	Dec. 13	Gemini	50	35
Ursids	Dec. 22	Ursa Minor	15	34

* Single observer under exceptional conditions. Most observers will see far fewer.

LEO
The Pouncing Spring Lion

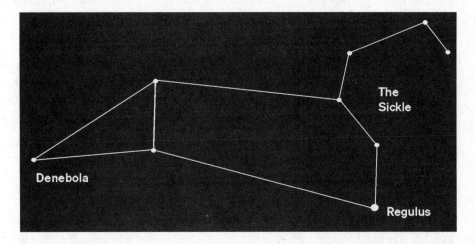

Novice stargazers often remark on how little the constellations resemble the mythological figures they're named after; the ancients stretched the limits of poetic licence when they imagined a charioteer in the winter constellation Auriga, for example, or a herdsman in the great summer constellation Boötes. Of the exceptions to this rule, Leo is one of the most striking. The stars in this zodiacal constellation clearly resemble the king of the beasts, pouncing across the dark spring skies.

Leo has three chief features. The famous "sickle," which also resembles a backwards question mark, defines the lion's head, mane and chest. The constellation's brightest star, the brilliant Regulus, lies at the bottom of the sickle, and is Leo's heart. A triangle of stars with its apex at the bright star Denebola outlines the lion's hindquarters and tail. *Denebola* is Arabic for "lion's tail," while *regulus* is Latin for "little king."

Best viewing time: Leaps head first across the southern night sky from about mid-Jan. to late June; most prominent in the evening sky by mid-Apr.

Location: Find the Big Dipper, then draw a line extending south from the two "bowl" stars closest to the handle. This line points to Regulus.

Regulus: Magnitude 1.3, distance 69 light-years; located almost exactly on the ecliptic, the line in space defined by Earth's orbit, along which all the planets travel and all the zodiacal constellations lie

Denebola: Magnitude 2.1, distance 40 light-years

Astrological period: July 23–Aug. 22; Leo is said to rule the heart

Also see: Sirius and Procyon, Star Charts

This stellar suite has been described as a lion since at least 3500 BCE. All the major Western cultures, from the Sumerians to the Romans, saw a lion. One ancient tale says Leo is the soul of the Nemean Lion, strangled by Hercules as the first of his 12 labours to atone for killing his own wife and children. (He didn't mean to, but Zeus's vindictive wife, Hera, had cast a spell of madness over Hercules because he was the son of Zeus by one of his many mistresses.) Several Mediterranean cultures associated Leo with the sun, because from approximately 2500 BCE to about the year 1, the sun was in Leo during the hottest days of summer. Nowadays the July sun is one zodiacal constellation over, in Gemini, a shift due to a wobble in Earth's rotation called precession. If precession didn't exist, perhaps we'd call the scorching summer season "the lion days of summer," rather than "the dog days." (For that story, see Sirius and Procyon on page 556.)

Within the official boundaries of Leo are several galaxies visible through a backyard telescope but not to the naked eye. Also invisible to the naked eye is a star called Wolf 359. It is notable as the second-closest star to Earth in our northern skies, and the fifth-closest neighbour overall, at 7.7 light-years. (The closest star in the northern hemisphere is Bernard's Star in the dimmer constellation Ophiuchus, at six light-years away.) Wolf 359 is a dim red dwarf, only 10 per cent the mass of the sun, and about 0.00002 times as bright. Modern spacecraft could reach Wolf 359 in about 262,000 years, making dreams of interstellar travel seem – at least with current technology – impossibly quaint.

MILKY WAY
The Path of Souls

The Milky Way, obliterated by city lights, glows to life in the dark night sky of the countryside and wilderness. Its horizon-to-horizon span suggests a pathway to the stars, a notion that ancient cultures fixed upon. In' many mythologies, humans and their spirits ascended this path to the heavens, or gods and sky creatures descended it to join mortals on the ground. The Ojibway called the Milky Way the Path of Souls. As part of the Ojibway burial ritual, a campfire is lit near the death-post marking a grave. The fire is kept burning for four days to light the way for the soul-spirit, which must travel the Path of Souls to reach the Land of Souls.

Diameter: About 100,000 light-years

Thickness: About 12,000 light-years including the gaseous outer layer

Travel time to leave the Milky Way galaxy in our fastest spacecraft: About 570 million years

Age: Uncertain, but probably 10 to 15 billion years old

Number of stars: Uncertain; probably 200 to 400 billion, maybe 1 trillion

Closest large neighbour: Andromeda Galaxy, 2.4 million light-years away

Collison course: Andromeda Galaxy and the Milky Way are moving towards each other at about 100 km/sec, but the anticipated collision won't happen for another 3 billion years

Number of galaxies in the universe: Uncertain, but likely 50 to 100 billion

Time it takes for our solar system to orbit the Milky Way: About 220 million years

Speed of our solar system as it orbits the Milky Way: About 250 km/sec (150 mi/sec)

Distance travelled while reading this sentence: About 1,250 km

Number of dry vodka martinis in the Milky Way: There are enough vodka molecules – composed of water, ammonia and ethyl alcohol – in interstellar gases to fill 10,000 glasses the size of Earth, according to some thirsty scientists, but because the water content is so high, the vodka is only 0.002 proof. Also, a Milky Way martini would be spiked with hydrogen cyanide.

Other names for the Milky Way: Many peoples from India to Scandinavia thought of the Milky Way as milk from the moon-cow goddess; worlds and creatures were created from the curdled milk, including a moon of green cheese. Celts

In classical Greek mythology, the whitish band is said to represent a stream of milk from Rhea's breast as she suckled her son Zeus. Another story says the milk came from Hera, Zeus's wife. (The word *galaxy* comes from the Greek word for "milk," *gala* or *galaktos*.) An account is also found in the myth of Phaeton, son of Apollo. One day Phaeton persuaded his dad to let him take the sun chariot for a spin. Apollo, wary as any father lending his car to his young son would be, told Phaeton to steer a middle course between Heaven and Earth. But Phaeton ended up an insurance statistic. The young driver lost control of the chariot, flew too high and scorched the sky, creating the Milky Way. Then he swerved back to Earth and burned the vegetation off the Sahara. Zeus ended the joyride with a fatal thunderbolt.

Pythagoras and other scientific Greeks theorized that the glow from the Milky Way came from a multitude of stars. But it took Galileo and his telescope to prove this conclusively. Modern science has shown that galaxies are the basic building blocks of the universe. Colossal agglomerations of stars, they come in four basic shapes: elliptical, spiral, barred spiral and irregular. The Milky Way, our own galaxy, is a relatively large spiral galaxy with several arms of superbright and many less bright stars. Our solar system is located in the Orion Arm, towards the edge of town, cosmically speaking.

For people of the northern hemisphere, the Milky Way is more prominent in summer than winter. This is because of the solar system's position about two-thirds out from the centre of the galaxy. On summer nights (winter in the southern hemisphere), the Earth is positioned so that we look into the dense middle of the galactic disc. In winter, all we see is the final one-third of the galaxy and the dark, deep space beyond. The vast swath of the Milky Way arcs across the celestial dome from north to south on early-summer evenings. It twists in the sky as summer progresses, until in mid-November it reaches from the eastern to the western horizon.

The spout of the famous "teapot" constellation, Sagittarius, which appears low over the southern horizon in the summer, points to the hub of the Milky Way. This is where the Milky Way is at its most luminous. But the galaxy's central nuclear bulge, a region where older stars are densely packed, is not clearly visible. Vast clouds of interstellar dust and gas block the view. These same clouds are responsible for visible rifts in the Milky Way. One of these dark patches cuts through the Summer Triangle.

Several constellations are located along the Milky Way, including Cassiopeia, Cepheus, Cygnus and Aquila. Both Cygnus the swan and Aquila the eagle fly in the direction of the astral belt. Ornithologists speculate, and Native peoples traditionally believe, that migrating birds use the glimmer of the Milky Way as a navigational aid – making it truly a path in the heavens.

called the Milky Way *Bothar-Bo-Finne,* or Track of the White Cow – the source of the story about the cow jumping over the moon. The Egyptians called it the Nile of the Sky, which flowed from the udder of the moon-cow Hathor-Isis. Other names include Irmin's Way, Anglo-Saxon; *Hiddagal* or River of the Divine Lady, Akkadian; *Umm al sama* or Mother of the Sky, Arabic; *Manavegr* or Moon Way, Norse; Silver Stream of Heaven, Chinese.

Galileo: Florentine astronomer and physicist, 1564–1642, condemned by the Inquisition for his support of Copernican theories, which placed the sun, not the Earth, at the centre of the solar system; the Vatican acknowledged its error 359 years later, in 1992

Also see: Yellow-rumped Warbler, Moon, Pegasus and Andromeda, Star Charts, Stars, Summer Triangle

MOON
The Original Timepiece

Selected Moon Landmarks

Human Sites
1. *Luna 2*, first on moon (September 13, 1959)
2. *Apollo 11* (July 20, 1969)

Seas (Mares)
3. Sea of Rains
4. Sea of Serenity
5. Sea of Tranquility
6. Ocean of Storms
7. Sea of Clouds
8. Sea of Crises

Craters
9. Tycho (rayed crater)
10. Plato
11. Copernicus
12. Schickard

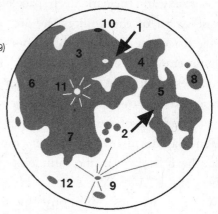

Number of one-way trips between Toronto and North Bay it would take to travel the mean distance between Earth and the moon: 1,148

Distance from Earth: 363,000 km at closest (perigee); 406,000 km at farthest (apogee)

Diameter: 3,476 km (2,085 mi)

Gravity: About 1/6 Earth's gravity

Age: 4.6 billion years old

First lunar probe to land on the surface: The Soviets' *Luna 2*, crashed Sept. 13, 1959

First man on the moon: Neil Armstrong, *Apollo 11*, July 20, 1969

Last man on the moon: Eugene Cernan, *Apollo 17*, Dec. 11, 1972

If the sun stands for permanence, the moon is transience. Our nighttime companion transforms itself every night; it appears and disappears, dies and is resurrected. For this reason the moon is powerfully connected with the rhythms and mysteries of life and the passage of time.

The first calendars were based on the phases of the moon. There is evidence that cave-dwellers in France recorded the lunar cycle with notches in animal bones and antlers 25,000 years before the first writing in Mesopotamia. It would have taken a few years, but eventually cavemen or cavewomen must have figured out that the seasons repeated themselves every 12 full moons or so.

In Europe the year was based on a lunar calendar until 45 BCE – an imperfect system because 12 lunar months do not add up to a solar year of 365 days. Julius Caesar, with the help of an Egyptian astronomer, resolved the problem when he ditched the idea of lunar months and divided the year into 12 independent calendar months, with a leap year every four years. The month of July is named after him. Later, in 1532, Pope Gregory XIII refined the Julian calendar because it was coming up short one day every 128 years. Gregory artificially shortened October that year – October 5 to 14, 1532, do not exist in history – and made other changes that were eventually adopted in most places, so that the calendar is now accurate to within one day every 3,200 years.

Although the Julian/Gregorian calendar has been adopted almost worldwide, some cultures retain the lunar calendar for religious, festive and day-to-day use. Moslem countries use a lunar calendar that began the day Mohammad was chased out of Mecca by unruly citizens enraged by his preachings (on July 16, 622, by the Gregorian calendar). The Moslem year of 12 lunar months makes no provision for the solar year. Every year the seasons begin earlier, until, in 32½ years, the cycle starts repeating. The Jewish calendar is also based on the lunar month, beginning with the biblical moment of creation (3761 BCE Gregorian time). It is adjusted for the solar year, however, with the addition of a 13th month every three to four years. Another lunar calendar, the Chinese, has been abandoned for civil use, but important Buddhist and Taoist festivals are still held around new and full moons.

The lunar cycle was of great importance to Native peoples in Ontario, who also used it as a calendar. Full moons were often named after natural events occurring around the same time,

Next visit: Possibly as early as 2018; as the space shuttle fleet is retired, NASA is turning its attention to a possible manned station on the moon as a prelude to a flight to Mars, under the project name Constellation

Magnitude: −12.7 at full moon

Why we see only one side of the moon: Just as the moon causes tides on Earth, the Earth's gravity causes "tides" on the moon. There is no sea, of course, but the landmass does shift. Over time, friction caused by the shifting land has slowed down the moon, so that the period of rotation on its axis – its "day" – matches the 27.3 days it takes to orbit Earth. In other words, Earth's gravity has locked on to the moon so that only one side ever presents itself to us. Tides on Earth are also slowing down our planet. The day is getting longer by one second every 60,000 years; when Earth was first formed, a day used to be 22 hours long.

Tides on lakes: Even a cup of tea is affected by the moon's gravity, but the lake tides are imperceptible to all but the most sophisticated equipment

Once in a blue moon: There are two popular explanations for this expression. The second full moon in a month with two full moons (it happens twice every five years or so) is said to be a blue moon. Also, the full moon sometimes appears blue because of atmospheric conditions created by high dust content after volcanic eruptions or large forest fires. Huge fires in Canada in Sept. 1950 created stunning blue moons.

Harvest moon: The full moon closest to the autumnal equinox, occurring in either Sept. or Oct.; owing to the alignment of Earth, moon and sun at this time of year, the bright moon before, after and during the Harvest Moon stays in the night sky longer than at other times of the year – ideal for farmers harvesting their crops at night

Why the moon seems bigger when it's close to the horizon: The best explanation for this illusion is that the full moon seems large near the horizon because the eye can easily compare its size with other objects, such as buildings. To check the illusion, hold an Aspirin tablet at arm's length and place it over the moon. It covers the moon whether it's near the horizon or higher up.

Moon goddesses: Artemis, the Greek goddess of hunting; Selene, a Greek Titan sometimes associated with Artemis (*selenology* is the study of the moon); Hecate, the Greek goddess of the new moon (and thus

and were sometimes associated with human activities such as hunting, fishing or food-gathering. The Ojibway call the full moon in May the Sucker Moon – that is the month suckers spawn up Ontario streams. June is the Blooming Moon, July the Berry Moon, August the Grain Moon and September the Leaves-Turning Moon. The Ojibway in more southern latitudes have given the moon names related to other natural events.

The rhythms of the moon are also deeply linked to fertility. The 29½-day period between full moons closely matches the average female menstrual cycle. The word *menstruation* comes from the Latin word for "monthly." Charles Darwin suggested that since humans ultimately evolved from the sea, it followed that menstrual periods were a distant echo of the tides. Whether the female and lunar cycles have a rational connection is a matter of debate. The menstrual cycles of other mammals, for example, do not match the average 28-day human one. But the fact that the lunar and human periods do coincide may have had a profound impact on the development of civilization. Some feminist scholars believe the earliest timekeeping evolved through the need of women to know the season of birth of their children, which would have required a knowledge of the link between menstrual and moon phases, and the nine-month or nine-moon gestation period. This could have led to the first calendars, perhaps those same cave calendars of France.

Symbolically, the fact the moon is "reborn" each month has led to its deep association with women since ancient times. Many mythologies and religions have moon goddesses; the most famous is probably Artemis, the Greek goddess of hunting, whose Roman equivalent is Diana. The Ojibway think of the moon as Grandmother Moon, the first mother in the creation myth, who still keeps watch over her offspring. The Sioux call it the Old Woman Who Never Dies.

The moon is related to another aspect of the human condition: madness. Lunacy, from the Latin *luna,* or "moon," has been attributed to a mysterious connection between the full moon and our mental state. It is traditionally thought that lunar gravity – the same force that causes the tides and probably earthquakes – somehow pulls our psyche out of kilter, perhaps in the same way it starts the menstrual flow. There is little proof for this, although there is no doubting the fact that 200 years ago, inmates in English lunatic asylums were flogged just before the full moon to deter violent behaviour. Who was actually mad in this case is another question.

One moon mystery remains unsolved even after visits to the silvery orb by several well-educated, middle-aged American men: How was it that Earth came to have a companion in the first place? Scientists have a few theories. The moon may have formed close to Earth at the same time Earth condensed out of the cloud of dust and gas that became our solar system. Alternatively, the moon may have formed elsewhere in the solar system but was somehow captured by Earth's gravitational field. A more recent and generally accepted theory proposes that a huge asteroid smashed into Earth early in the planet's evolution, and threw up debris that eventually coalesced into the moon. No one knows for sure.

darkness); Diana, the Roman goddess of hunting; Mama Qilla, the Inca moon goddess; Isis, the mother of Egypt; Galata, the Celtic moon goddess; Hina, of Polynesia

How to tell if the moon is waxing or waning: If the right-hand side of the moon is illuminated, the moon is waxing – heading towards full moon; if the left-hand side is illuminated, it is waning – past full moon and heading into new moon

Also see: Milky Way, Planets and Comets

NORTH STAR AND LITTLE DIPPER
The Peg That Fastens the Universe

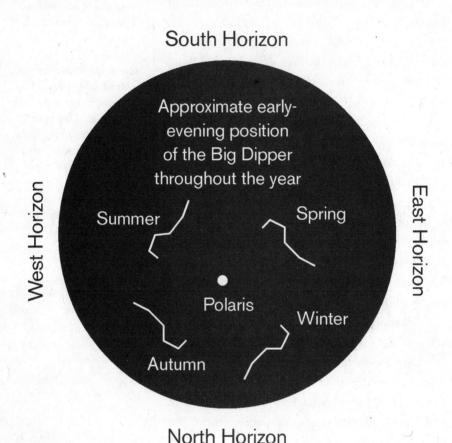

South Horizon

West Horizon

East Horizon

North Horizon

Approximate early-evening position of the Big Dipper throughout the year

Summer

Spring

Polaris

Winter

Autumn

Cynosure: The Greeks also called Polaris the Dog's Tail, or *Kynosaura;* this is the root of the word *cynosure,* meaning "a centre of attraction"

Distance of Polaris from Earth: 431 light-years away

How to determine latitude: At the North Pole, Polaris is directly overhead, or 90°

The North Star, Polaris, is the most important star in all the heavens. It is not the brightest star in the night sky, but by dint of its fixed location almost exactly over Earth's north pole, it has assumed a prominent role in civilization. It was the star by which early mariners navigated their way about the treacherous seas. It was central to the cosmology of many cultures. It remains a powerful metaphor for the constant – the truth.

As Hitler was consolidating his forces and civil war broke out in Spain in 1936, the American poet Archibald MacLeish wrote in his poem, "Pole Star for This Year,"

> We too turn now to that star:
> We too in whose trustless hearts
> All truth alters and the lights
> Of earth are out now turn to that star . . .

Because of the rotation of the Earth, all the northern constellations appear to revolve counterclockwise around Polaris. The observation of this movement as well as the cycles of the moon, sun and planets, gave the ancients their sense of time. People of many old cultures believed the appearance of specific stars at certain times of the year actually caused events, such as the flooding of the Nile. This is the origin of astrology.

The North Star appears in all mythologies. Its apparent immobility in the whirling procession of the stars must have been observed by the earliest cave-dwellers. The Moguls called it the Golden Peg that fastened the universe together. In Scandinavia's violent mythology it was the World Spike, the *Veralder Nagli*. (The Norse gods constructed their sky out of the chopped-up bits of adversaries; the nail in the centre of the universe finished off the job.) In an Arab myth, the Big Dipper was a coffin that held the body of a great warrior killed by the evil North Star. The stars that revolve around the North Star, including the Big Dipper, formed a funeral procession. Chinese stories about the North Star relate it to T'ai Chi, the great Absolute or Unity; it was the perfect union of the yin and yang principles.

straight up. The star is at a 45° angle to a viewer at 45° latitude, and so on. A sextant measures the angle. Early navigators who sailed below the equator got lost because Polaris disappeared over the horizon.

Precession: Gravitational forces of the moon and sun affect the spinning of the Earth, causing our planet to wobble on its axis like a spinning top as it slows down. Called precession, this wobble has a cycle of about 26,000 years. Because of precession, the star marking the celestial north pole changes over the millennia. The Babylonians observed the phenomenon 5,000 years ago; the Greek astronomer Hipparchus recorded this effect in the 2nd century BCE. Hipparchus also invented the system of magnitude for classifying the brightness of stars.

The south pole star: There isn't one; the spot in the sky marking the south celestial pole is not occupied by a convenient star

Also see: Big Dipper, Star Charts

The North Star was also a symbol for the emperor, representing permanence in a transient world. The Pawnee called it the Star That Does Not Walk Around.

An Ojibway story of two male cousins describes the origins of the North Star and the echo phenomenon. The cousins were great friends and hunters. One day their grandmother introduced them to two women who were to be their companions. But the cousins were suspicious and thought the women might form a wedge in their friendship. Sure enough, one cousin fell in love with his chosen mate and neglected his buddy, who remained the better hunter because his mind was not distracted. The hunter left his friend and ascended into the stars to become the North Star, *Ke-wa-den-ah-mung,* where he still pursues the bear. His love-struck cousin stayed on Earth and cried in the forest for his lost friend. He became known as *Bah-swa-way,* or Echo.

The pole star has actually changed over the millennia because Earth wobbles slightly on its axis, a phenomenon known as precession. Four thousand years ago, the pole star was Thuban, in the constellation Draco. Archeologists have discovered that Egyptian pyramids were built to align with Thuban. Polaris will be nearest the spot that is the true celestial north in the year 2100. Astronomers predict the bright star Vega will become the pole star 12,000 years from now.

In modern astronomy, Polaris is placed at the end of the constellation Ursa Minor, the lesser bear, commonly called the Little Dipper. Ursa Minor is a dim constellation, several of whose stars are at the limits of naked-eye visibility. Polaris is usually the only star visible from a city. Ursa Minor is, of course, related to Ursa Major, the great bear hauled into the heavens by Zeus in the Greek myth. One way to remember the arrangement of the two Dippers in the night sky is to think of them pouring their contents into each other.

NORTHERN LIGHTS
Ghostly Illuminations from Solar Wind

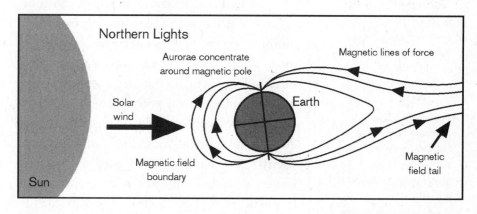

Northern Lights

Aurorae concentrate around magnetic pole

Magnetic lines of force

Solar wind

Earth

Magnetic field boundary

Magnetic field tail

Sun

The Inuit call them the Dance of the Dead. Poet Robert Frost likened them to "tingling nerves." Astronomers describe them as ionospheric gaseous luminations triggered by precipitating energetic particles. But to most people they are the northern lights, among nature's most stunning creations.

Northern lights are usually seen as a shimmering white or greenish glow just above the northern horizon. At first they may be mistaken for the haze of city lights, or even the glow of a gibbous moon before it rises over the horizon. But dark-adjusted eyes soon detect the telltale pulses of vertical shafts of light which intensify, then fade seconds later in a wavy, ethereal curtain. Sometimes a ray will shoot high into the sky, then dissolve into the blackness. In an intense display, the curtain rises higher, until it appears directly overhead like a surreal tunnel of light reaching to the zenith. This is called the aurora's corona. Magnificent streams of light cascade up and down the crown, accompanied

Aurora borealis name origin: From *aurora*, Latin for "dawn" (Aurora was the Roman goddess of dawn), and *boreas*, Greek for "north wind"

Speed of solar wind: 1.8–3.6 million km/h (1–2.2 million mph)

Next peak of the 11-year solar cycle: Estimated March–April 2013

Geomagnetic updates: Visit www.spaceweather.ca for auroral reports. In addition to producing aurora, solar wind storms can damage spacecraft, knock out GPS systems and even induce corrosion on long pipelines.

Solar wind forecasting: A NASA satellite launched in 1997 is "locked" in space at a point where Earth's and the sun's gravity exert equal force on it. It is measuring solar wind storms and can alert authorities when one is on the way.

Jupiter's northern lights: Telescopes have spotted aurorae above Jupiter; but unlike Earth's displays, which are generated by solar wind, Jupiter's appear to be caused by charged particles spewed by volcanoes on one of the Jovian moons, Io

***Waussnodae*, Ojibway northern lights:** The Ojibway believed northern lights were torches lit by the grandfathers to illuminate the Path of Souls for soul-spirits ascending to their final home. The Path of Souls was the Milky Way.

Best place in the world to observe northern lights: Northern Canada, because the north magnetic pole is located in Canada's Arctic archipelago; Yellowknife gets northern lights about 100 nights a year, attracting aurora-starved tourists from around the world; central Ontario gets an average of 20 displays a year

Best viewing time: Between 11 p.m. and 2 a.m.

Aurora australis: The southern lights are rarely seen except by penguins (and the occasional researcher). Of the populated continents, only the tip of South America extends into the prime viewing zone.

Artificial northern lights: The U.S. Air Force has built a giant "ionospheric heater"

by eerie pulses of white light unlike anything concocted in a sci-fi movie.

Northern lights are the result of solar wind entering Earth's magnetic field. Solar wind comprises millions of tonnes of electrons and protons emitted by the sun every minute. When these atomic particles enter the magnetic field surrounding Earth, they are separated, creating a vast store of electrical potential high above the ground. The magnetic field, in effect, becomes a 20,000- to 150,000-volt battery of static electricity. Observations from specialized satellites launched in 2007 suggest that an event called a magnetic reconnection triggers a burst of this energy along the lines of Earth's magnetic field, towards the north or south magnetic pole. The energy excites oxygen and nitrogen molecules, at altitudes of 100 to 400 kilometres (60 to 240 miles), into a gaseous glow: the northern lights, or aurora borealis.

Although it's almost impossible to predict exactly when northern lights will occur, or their intensity, some things are known about their behaviour. In years when the solar wind blows stronger, the northern lights are more intense. "Gusts" of solar wind are caused by sunspots and solar flares, which intensify approximately every 11 years. Northern lights thus tend to put on greater displays every 11 years or so, according to this solar cycle. The peak may last for two or three years. On March 13, 1989, during a peak period, a spectacular and rare display of red northern lights was seen as far south as the Caribbean. The energy storm was so powerful it knocked out the Hydro-Québec power grid, putting six million people in the dark.

Just as different gases in "neon" light tubes produce different colours, different gases in the atmosphere produce the varied colours of the northern lights. Green, the most common auroral colour, is produced by excited oxygen atoms about 110 kilometres (66 miles) above Earth's surface. Blue comes from high-level nitrogen molecules. Red light, a special treat, is produced by traces of oxygen between 200 and 400 kilometres (120 and 240 miles) up. Because the gas is so thin at that altitude, red light is rare and occurs only when great quantities of energy flow along the magnetic-field lines. Another type of red aurora, sometimes seen fringing other colours, occurs through a slightly different interaction lower in the atmosphere. Common white aurorae are simply northern lights of such low intensity that the eye cannot discern colours.

Some people claim they hear northern lights as a soft crackling. Skeptical scientists tend to discount this possibility, because the aurora occurs far above Earth in the thin atmosphere. But so many people have reported hearing the "murmurings of the spirits" that the jury is still out.

array of antennas that shoots electromagnetic energy into the sky to create artificial glows like the northern lights

ORION
The Spoke-too-soon Hunter

Best viewing time: Stands indelibly in the southern sky throughout most winter evenings, moving from east to west as the night progresses. At due south around 9 p.m. by late Jan. and early Feb.; early risers can catch a glimpse by mid-Aug. about 2 hours before sunrise

Location: Virtually impossible to miss in the southern winter sky; look for 3 belt stars close together in a straight line. Like the Big Dipper, Orion serves as a "pointer" constellation to other stars. The belt stars point north-westward to the bright star Aldebaran and, beyond that, to the Pleiades star cluster. The belt stars point the other way to Sirius, the brightest star in the sky. (See the star maps on page 560, 562.)

Orion's origins: Some say he was the son of the sea god Poseidon, but others say he emerged from the hide of an ox upon which Poseidon, Hermes and Zeus had peed (leading to his original name, Urion, meaning "urine") – which goes to show that even the gods had to go to the bathroom

Mintaka: Westernmost belt star, a double-double star, magnitude 2.2, distance

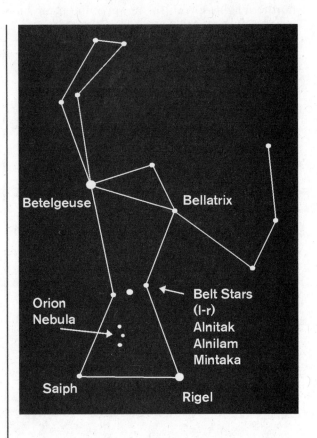

Betelgeuse

Bellatrix

Orion
Nebula

Belt Stars
(l-r)
Alnitak
Alnilam
Mintaka

Saiph

Rigel

Mintaka, Alnilam, Alnitak: the names aren't terribly familiar, but they are perhaps the three most famous stars after Polaris. These are the "belt stars" of mighty Orion, aligned in such a tight, unmistakable formation that they have probably captured the gaze of every human who's peered into the night sky.

Orion is such a celebrated constellation because not only is it composed of this stellar trio and other brilliant astral beacons – Betelgeuse and Rigel in particular – it can also be seen around the world. Orion bridges the celestial equator, the projection of Earth's equator into space, and so is visible to inhabitants of both the Southern and Northern hemispheres. During our winter, Orion commands the southern night sky. Meanwhile, it is summer in the Southern Hemisphere, where Orion struts across the northern night sky. Constellations closer to the North Star, such as Ursa Major (the Big Dipper), aren't visible to southerners – just as bright southern constellations like the Southern Cross are beyond our range.

With such a prominent perch, it's no wonder that cultures spanning the globe have told stories about Orion. Many focus on the belt stars. The Chumash and Shoshoni First Nations of western North America, among others, called the stars "Three in a Row." The Tachi Yokut Native people of California told a parable of how a selfish wolf, married to a crane, never brought food home for his wife and two sons. A terrible domestic fight ensued, during which the crane killed the wolf and escaped with her children to become the belt stars. People on the Indian sub-continent saw a stag shot with an arrow; a more elaborate story recounts how the incestuous lord of creatures chased one of his daughters (repre-sented by the star Aldebaran in Taurus) and was shot with an arrow by a character represented by the star Sirius. (Aldebaran, the belt stars and Sirius form an almost straight line.) In Brazil, the three stars were a caiman, an alligatorlike reptile. The Maoris of New Zealand saw a canoe. The Inuit looked upon three hunters.

Orion is famous in Egypt for representing the soul of the god Osiris, ruler of the afterlife

about 920 light-years; its name is from the Arabic for "belt"

Alnilam: The middle belt star; magnitude 1.7, about 1,400 light-years away; from the Arabic for the entire belt, which translates as "string of pearls"

Alnitak: Easternmost belt star, magnitude 2.0, distance 826 light-years; also derived from the Arabic for "belt"

Betelgeuse: Pronounced *bet-el-jooz,* a red supergiant that may be in its final stages of life; magnitude 0.5 (varies), distance 570 light-years; astronomers believe it has used up its main hydrogen fuel and is now "burning" other elements, causing it to expand and contract, a phe-nomenon visible in the star's varying brightness, not de-tectable with the naked eye; 2 companion stars too faint to see.

Rigel: Brightest star in Orion; magnitude 0.1, distance 860 light-years; 2 companion stars too faint to see

Nebula: From the Latin *nebu-la,* meaning "cloud" or "mist"; An interstellar nebula is vastly less dense than an Earth cloud, but does mark an area more gaseous than "empty" interstellar space

Fire of creation: The ancient Maya of Mexico believed the Orion Nebula was the smoke from the fire of cre-ation at the heart of the uni-verse; the fire's hearth was

defined by the triangle created by the stars Alnitak,
Rigel and Saiph

M and NGC: Celestial sights
denoted with an M are those
plotted in the late 18th century by Frenchman Charles
Messier, a comet hunter who
wanted to mark all the fuzzy
nebulae and star clusters
that could be mistaken for
comets. NGC stands for
New General Catalogue, a
much more extensive record
of thousands of deep-sky
objects, first established at
the turn of the 20th century.

Also see: The Pleiades, Sirius
and Procyon

and brother of Isis. Some modern Egyptologists
have determined that tunnels in the renowned
pyramids at Giza aligned with the stars in Orion
and with Thuban, the north star at the time,
when they were built about 4,500 years ago.
They apparently served as conduits to the
heavens for the pharoah's spirit. Robert Bauval,
in his book *The Orion Mystery,* has observed that
the arrangement of the three main pyramids at
Giza matches almost precisely the three belt
stars in alignment and relative size. Aerial photos
of the pyramids compared with astrophotos of
the stars reveal astonishingly similar patterns.
(Many scholars take issue with this conclusion,
however.) The pyramids were built west of the
Nile to reflect the fact that the afterworld was
associated with the west, where the sun sets.
Osiris-Orion is also located west of that great
river in the sky, the Milky Way.

The idea of these stars as a "belt" comes to
us, of course, from Greek mythology. Orion was
the great Boeotian hunter, and it's easy to
discern his form in the stars. The belt stars define
his waist. Below them, another string of dimmer
stars make up his sword or scabbard. To the
upper left of the belt stars shines the unmistakable Betelgeuse, a red giant about 50 times the
size of the sun and perhaps 15,000 times brighter.
Betelgeuse is usually translated from the original
Arabic as "armpit of the great one," and, indeed,
marks the right armpit or shoulder of the hunter
in many ancient sky maps. His other shoulder is
marked by Bellatrix, somewhat dimmer but still
easily visible to the naked eye, even in light-polluted urban areas. Kitty-corner from Betelgeuse,
on the other side of the belt stars, is Rigel – from

the Arabic for "foot" – one of the earliest-named stars. Rigel is the seventh-brightest star seen from Earth and one of the true powerhouses of the galaxy, with a luminosity estimated at 60,000 times that of our sun. Orion's right foot is pinpointed by Saiph, though in some old maps Saiph and Rigel mark the hunter's knees. Other stars in the constellation show Orion holding his shield towards next-door Taurus, the bull, whom he hunts, while his right hand wields a club.

Most of the Greco-Roman myths focus on Orion's death, and there are at least seven versions of his demise, falling under two broad types: he was either killed by the goddess Artemis or her brother Apollo or stung to death by a scorpion. The scorpion tales are the most intriguing, because they involve another constellation, Scorpius. Orion was a hunter, who boasted that no animal could get the better of him. As usual with the Greeks, this hubris proved fatal. The spiteful goddess Hera sent a tiny scorpion to deliver a mortal, mocking sting. Orion was placed in the heavens as a lasting warning to all, and opposite Scorpius so that the two constellations would never appear together in the night sky. His two hunting dogs – the constellations Canis Major and Canis Minor, notable for their stars Sirius and Procyon – were placed near their master. Orion was said to have coveted the Pleiades, the daughters of Atlas, and they became the famous star cluster near Orion – but always out of reach.

An Iroquois story also features a great hunter, and relates to his position in the sky. A noble hunter, the story goes, climbed a mountain to prepare for death. When the end came, he ascended the heavens where, remarkably, he recovered his powers. He was assigned a new job, to carry the sun high in the sky during summer. (Orion is, indeed, located in the day sky during the warm months, its presence blotted out by the glare of the sun.) But as winter approached, the hunter grew tired again, and had to pass the job to his son. The indolent son shouldered his responsibilities poorly, and barely managed to carry the sun above the horizon, bringing cold, wintry days. His father, meanwhile, rested in the winter night sky, gaining strength to resume his role in the summer.

Like many stars and constellations, Orion is a harbinger of the changing seasons. It is first visible to early risers by mid- to late August, clambering over the dark eastern horizon about an hour before the sun. It rises earlier every night as autumn progresses. "Its arrival is an announcement that the outdoor season is past, that the nights are becoming more and more frosty, and that the gorgeous tapestry with which the autumn hills seem covered will soon fall away and give place to the lovely low tones of winter," wrote the late Martha Evans in her popular book *The Friendly Stars*. By mid-December, the hunter is rising over the eastern horizon shortly after sunset.

On a clear winter night, take a close look at Orion's "sword." It contains one of the most studied celestial bodies: the Orion Nebula, known officially as M42 or NGC1976. The middle star in a band of three small stars defining the sword roughly marks the centre of the nebula, and a faint but distinct hazy patch can be seen with the unaided eye and through binoculars. The bright star here is, in fact, a quadruple star system known as the Trapezium. The four separate stars are just visible with a small backyard telescope. They are among the youngest stellar furnaces in the galaxy, perhaps 100,000 to one million years old, much younger than the billion-year-old rocks of the Canadian Shield in cottage country. The Trapezium's blazing thermonuclear starlight illuminates the surrounding nebula, a wispy cloud of mostly hydrogen gas estimated to be 56 trillion kilometres wide. Throughout the cloud, new stars and perhaps entire solar systems are being born. The Hubble Space Telescope has returned stunning astrophotographs of this marvellous Milky Way region. Perhaps one day, intelligent creatures on a planet in M42 will take pictures of us. Say cheese.

PEGASUS AND ANDROMEDA
The Steed and the Princess

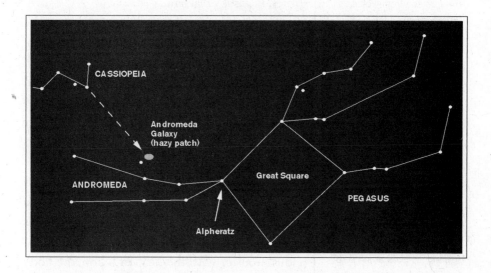

CASSIOPEIA

Andromeda
Galaxy
(hazy patch)

ANDROMEDA

Great Square

PEGASUS

Alpheratz

Late-night cottage or campfire gatherings are ideal occasions to watch the grand procession of constellations across the night sky. One of the greatest sights is the flight of the legendary winged horse Pegasus. In mid-July this majestic constellation soars above the eastern horizon at about 10 p.m., and by 4 a.m. it is high in the southern sky. (The later in the year, the earlier it rises; add about one hour for every two weeks.) Pegasus's most famous feature, the Great Square, is like a huge window into the inky depths of the universe.

In Western culture, the ancient Mesopotamians first construed these stars as a heavenly horse. Its form, like Hercules, is upside-down: the head and neck are the suite of stars along the bottom, while the two prongs coming from the top right of the Great Square are the horse's

Plot of 1971 B-movie *The Andromeda Strain*: A lethal virus from deep space arrives in the U.S.; scientists race against time to save the world

Number of stars in Andromeda Galaxy: Uncertain, perhaps 300 to 500 billion

Distance of Alpheratz, the shared star in Andromeda and Pegasus, to Earth: 97 light-years away

Medusa: The only mortal of the Gorgons, 3 mythical monsters with hair of serpents. Medusa's countenance was so horrible to behold that viewers were immediately turned to stone. Perseus, in killing Medusa, avoided this fate by using his bronze shield as a mirror. Shortly afterwards he used Medusa's head to help save Andromeda from Cetus. Perseus waved the head in front of Cetus, and the sea monster fossilized instantly.

Chimera (pronounced *kuh-MIR-ah*): This monster's name entered the English language with several related meanings – *chimera* is an absurd creation of the imagination, or any grotesque, fantastical creature; a hybrid organism with mixed characteristics; and the genus of fishes that includes sharks and rays

Homer: Scholars aren't sure whether a person named Homer actually existed, but the *Iliad* and the *Odyssey* are traditionally attributed to him. Part of Pegasus's story is contained in the *Iliad*. Homer, if he lived, probably wrote in the 9th century BCE.

Hesiod: Greek poet of the 8th century BCE who told the story of the Chimera

Also see: Deer Flies and Horse Flies, Cassiopeia, Milky Way, Star Charts

forequarters. The hindquarters are missing; one theory is that the nearby constellation Aries was formed with stars that may have been, in ancient times, Pegasus's rear end.

Greek poets wrote various episodes in the story of Pegasus. He was born when drops of blood from the head of the Gorgon Medusa fell into the sea foam. Medusa had been decapitated by Perseus, who used the head as a novel wedding present for his mother, Danaë, and her lover, King Polydectes. The sea foam accounts for Pegasus's whiteness.

Another story concerns Bellerophon, a young man whose greatest desire was to tame and ride Pegasus. As a pair, their most famous adventure was the slaying of the Chimera, a ferocious monster with the head of a lion, the body of a goat and the tail of a serpent. Bellerophon was actually sent on the mission under false pretences. He had spurned the love of Queen Anteia, and in her bitterness she set in motion a chain of events that was supposed to lead to the death of Bellerophon by the Chimera. But astride Pegasus, Bellerophon was invincible.

Almost. Success went to his head, and Bellerophon decided to ride up to Olympus to join the gods. Pegasus thought better of the idea and threw Bellerophon to the ground below. (In another version, Zeus sent a horse fly to sting Pegasus, causing the steed to buck his rider.) Pegasus ascended with the permission of the gods, to become a member of the Olympian stalls – and a constellation in the heavens.

Alpheratz, the top-left star in the Great Square, is officially a member of the constellation Andromeda. The two constellations are connected in mythology as well as in form. It was during his journey home after slaying the Medusa that Perseus spotted Andromeda chained to rocks in the sea off ancient Aethiopia. Perseus rescued Andromeda before she was assaulted by the sea monster Cetus, and later the two were married. Perseus also lies next to Andromeda in the night sky.

The famous Andromeda galaxy is so named because it is found in the vicinity of the constellation. The galaxy is the farthest object from Earth detectable with the naked eye, about 2.4 million light-years away. The light we see today left the Andromeda galaxy just as our species was evolving in Africa. On a dark night the galaxy is visible as an oval smudge; through binoculars it's possible to see a brightening in the middle that is the galaxy's central nuclear bulge. To find the Andromeda galaxy, imagine that the brightest star in Cassiopeia, Schedar, is the point of an arrow aimed directly at our galactic neighbour.

PLANETS AND COMETS
Wanderers of the Night Sky

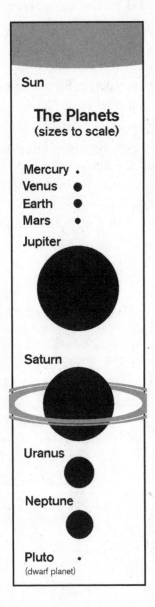

Sun

The Planets
(sizes to scale)

Mercury .
Venus ●
Earth ●
Mars .
Jupiter

Saturn

Uranus

Neptune

Pluto .
(dwarf planet)

Four and a half billion years ago, in this particular corner of the universe, there was no sun, no Earth, no solar system at all. But there was matter – a vast, churning cloud of gas and dust. Gravity caused this cloud to begin contracting, until internal heat from the great inward pressure ignited a powerful nuclear-fusion reaction in the centre of the nebula. The sun was born.

Leftover material was blown away from the solar furnace, but remained trapped in the sun's gravitational grasp. Over eons, this rotating matter coalesced into asteroids and comets, and eventually into the eight planets that today make up our cosmic neighbourhood.

As the planets move along their orbits around the sun, they appear in different positions against our night sky. Hence, the word *planet* comes from *planetes,* Greek for "wanderer." All the planets rotate around the sun in the same direction and on a rough plane called the ecliptic.

MERCURY, the Messenger

The naked eye can detect Mercury, Venus, Mars, Jupiter and Saturn, the planets (plus Earth) known to the ancients. Mercury is the most difficult to observe, because of its small size and its orbit close to the sun. However, it can be seen skimming the western horizon at dusk or the eastern horizon at dawn at certain times of the year. This scorched, cratered planet has virtually no atmosphere, owing to the sun's blazing heat.

It is named after the Roman god Mercury, the messenger with winged sandals, winged hat and winged magic wand who faithfully delivered Jupiter's memos. The planet is appropriately named: Mercury has the fastest orbit, taking only 88 days to circumnavigate the sun.

VENUS, the Goddess of Love and Beauty

Venus, in contrast with Mercury, is the easiest planet to observe. After the sun and the moon, it is the brightest object in the sky, a radiant jewel in the early evening or early-morning darkness. It is observable for about six months out of every 18, and travels closer to Earth than any other planet. Venus shines brilliantly because three-quarters of the sunlight hitting the sphere reflects off the dense, white, sulfuric-acid clouds that enshroud the planet. Lovely from a distance, Venus is in fact a greenhouse hell, with a surface temperature of 465°C (870°F) and a carbon dioxide atmosphere. Had they known the astronomical truth about this nightmarish world, the Romans might have been disappointed. Venus, after all, was their goddess of love and beauty. (The Greeks called her Aphrodite.) But in Mesoamerican societies of the central U.S. and Mexico, the planet Venus played a major role in rituals of war and sacrifice. Scholars believe the appearance of Venus regulated the timing of military raids and wars.

MOTHER EARTH

Nearly Venus's twin in size, but in all other respects completely different, is our own world. Earth is the only planet to support life, thanks to miraculous circumstances such as its distance

Planetary and night-sky updates: Try these sites for daily, weekly, or monthly updates on celestial attractions:
www.skynews.ca: The Canadian astronomy magazine; click on "This Week's Celestial Highlights"
www.rasc.ca: From the Royal Astronomical Society of Canada; click on "The Sky This Month"
amazing-space.stsci.edu: From the folks who run the Hubble Space Telescope; click on "Tonight's Sky"
www.skyandtelescope.com: Click on "This Week's Sky at a Glance"
Also see: Falling Stars, Milky Way, Moon, Northern Lights

MERCURY ☿
Distance from sun: 58 million km (36 million mi)
Diameter: 4,879 km (3,032 mi)
Length of day: 59 Earth days
Length of year: 88 days
Surface temperature: 450°C (840°F) day-side, −170°C (−275°F) night-side
Moons: 0
Magnitude: 1 to 2
Successful probes: *Mariner 10,* 1974; *Messenger,* 2008–2011
Day of the week: Wednesday, from *Woden,* Norse for Mercury; *mercredi* in French
Notable: Craters on Mercury are named after men and women of the arts, including

Rubens, Dickens and Beethoven. Mercury has a highly elliptical orbit. From Earth, the planet shows "phases" like the moon.

VENUS ♀

Distance from sun: 108 million km (67 million mi)

Diameter: 12,100 km (7,520 mi)

Length of day: 243 Earth days

Length of year: 225 days

Surface temperature: 465°C (870°F)

Moons: 0

Magnitude: −4.0 to −4.1

Successful probes: U.S. *Mariner* program, 1962 to 1974; *Pioneer Venus 1 & 2*, 1978; *Magellan*, 1990–92; Soviet *Venera* program, 1966 to 1984, including landings in 1970, 1975, 1982

Day of the week: Friday, from Old English *Frigg* or Norse goddess Freya, translation of Latin Venus; *vendredi* in French

Notable: Venus's day is longer than its year. The planet spins in the opposite direction from Earth and most other planets. Venereal diseases are "diseases of Venus." Surface features are named after famous women, both real and fictional. Like Mercury and the moon, Venus shows "phases" to an observer on Earth. The surface pressure is 90 times greater than Earth's.

from the sun and the 23.5-degree tilt that produces the seasons. These conditions give Earth its ability to produce and hold water, which covers 70 per cent of the planet.

The Earth's surface is divided into six or seven major crustal plates and many smaller plates that move about on the slippery mantle. Plate movement is caused when convection currents formed deep within the planet rise to the surface along mid-ocean ridges. This upwelling of hot magma pushes the ridges apart, creating new crust and shoving the plates outward; Europe and North America are moving about 25 mm (one inch) farther apart each year. At the other edge of the plates, such as in California, old crust descends back into the interior under overlapping fault lines. Earthquakes and volcanoes occur along mid-ocean ridges and faults. Mountain ranges may be formed where continents collide; the Himalayas are the result of the Indian subcontinent crashing into Asia.

This idea of moving plates was first considered when Europeans noticed that the shapes of the two sides of the Atlantic seemed to fit together. At the time, Europeans thought Earth was only 6,000 years old, according to biblical reckoning. Recent scientific inquiry, dating only from the 1960s and including advances made by Canadian J. Tuzo Wilson, proved the theory of plate tectonics. Plates have been moving about on the surface of the Earth for at least 2.5 billion years in a process dubbed the Wilson cycle, and as little as 200 million years ago all the continents were attached in a supercontinent called Pangaea. Old granitic rock such as that forming the Canadian Shield is less dense than the new rock on ocean floors, and thus remains atop plates as a sort of "granitic scum," as Wilson has called it. Earth is very much alive.

MARS, the God of War

Until recently, hopeful (or fearful) humans thought there was intelligent life on Mars, our closest neighbour after Venus. Evidence was supposedly found in 1877, when Italian astronomer Giovanni Schiaparelli reported seeing channels on the planet's surface, and others mistook this to mean artificial canals were present. Reputable scientists dreamed up various schemes for communicating with Martians, including a giant mirror to engrave words on the Martian desert with the focused rays of the sun. On Halloween in 1938, Orson Welles caused widespread panic in the United States when his Mercury Theatre of the Air broadcast an adaption of H.G. Wells's *War of the Worlds*, a story about an invasion of Earth by Martians. The fanciful idea of intelligent life on Mars was finally put to rest in 1976, when two *Viking* landers failed to meet any welcoming committees.

Yet the question of life on Mars – primitive life that may have gone extinct, or primitive life that continues to this day – remains one of the most compelling questions in astronomy. What keeps the quest alive is the proven presence of frozen water, found in the polar caps and also discovered underneath the surface in some regions. In 1996, some NASA scientists also announced they had discovered evidence of microscopic life in a meteorite that had made its way to Earth after being blown off Mars's surface by another meteorite impact on that planet, like

EARTH ⊕
Distance from sun: 150 million km (93 million mi)
Diameter: 12,756 km (7,654 mi)
Length of day: 23.9 hours
Length of year: 365.2 days
Spinning speed: 38,400 km/h (23,040 mph)
Orbital speed: 105,600 km/h (63,360 mph)
Surface temperature: Avg. 15°C (59°F)
Moons: 1
Atmosphere: 77% nitrogen, 21% oxygen; traces of carbon dioxide, methane, neon and other gases
Notable: Earth was the centre of the universe until 1543, when Polish astronomer Nicholaus Copernicus pointed out that we circle the sun, not vice versa. (Some early Greek astronomers also thought this, but, like Copernicus, they had a hard time convincing people.) Earth is considered a double planet because of its relatively large single satellite. Its name comes from the Old English *oerthe,* meaning "dry land." It is the only planet with a name not derived from Greco-Roman mythology.

MARS ♂
Distance from sun: 228 million km (137 million mi)
Diameter: 6,787 km (4,072 mi)
Length of day: 24.6 hours
Length of year: 687 days

Surface temperature: Avg. −30 to −40°C (−20°F to −40°F) during the day

Moons: 2, Phobos ("Fear") and Deimos ("Panic"), Mars's dogs in Roman mythology

Magnitude: 1.1 to 1.4

Successful probes: *Mariner 4*, 1965; *Mariners 6 & 7*, 1969; *Viking Landers 1 & 2*, 1976; *Mars Global Surveyor*, 1997; *Pathfinder/Sojourner* rover, 1997; *Odyssey*, 2001– 2002; *Express*, 2003; *Opportunity* & *Spirit* rovers, 2004; *Reconnaissance Orbiter*, 2006–2009

Day of the week: Tuesday, from Old English *Tiw,* equated with the Roman Mars; *mardi* in French

Notable: Mars has polar caps like Earth, but they are composed of frozen carbon dioxide and water. They advance and recede with the planet's long seasons.

Mars Mission: Visit nasa.gov and search for "Constellation"

JUPITER ♃

Average distance from Sun: 778 million km (483 million mi)

Diameter: 142,900 km (88,800 mi)

Length of day: 9.9 hours

Length of year: 11.9 Earth years

Temperature at cloud tops: −145°C (−230°F)

Moons: Dozens, but 16 larger than 10 km in diameter; largest, Ganymede

interplanetary dominoes. While robot landers have proven that water exists on Mars, the question of life remains hotly debated – and is one of the mysteries prompting humanity to consider a manned flight to the red planet before the middle of this century. Because of its Mars-like qualities, the Haughton Impact Crater on Devon Island in Canada's arctic is the site of a research station contributing to the Mars project.

Mars's thin atmosphere of mostly carbon dioxide has less than one per cent the barometric pressure of Earth's, and the surface is covered in red, iron-oxide dust that is sometimes blown into huge dust storms. The red dust accounts for Mars's appearance from Earth. Mars's bloodlike colour explains how the planet got its name. Mars was revered as the Roman god of war. (The Greeks called him Ares.) The red star Antares in the constellation Scorpius looks a lot like Mars. *Antares* is Arabic for "rival of Mars."

ASTEROIDS, the Minor Planets

There is a vast gap in space between Mars and the next planet, Jupiter. In 1800 a German astronomer, Johann Schröter, formed a group called the Celestial Police to find what was thought to be a missing planet in this gap. The group, along with other astronomers, soon found instead the asteroid belt. There are more than 3,000 identified asteroids in the belt, but millions more smaller ones, down to the size of a pebble. But why didn't Schröter and gang find a major planet in the asteroid belt? Astronomers theorize that the disruptive gravitational forces of nearby Jupiter prevent the space gravel from agglomerating into a planet.

JUPITER, the King

Jupiter is immense. It contains 70 per cent of the mass of the entire solar system, excluding the sun. Though not as brilliant from Earth as Venus (because of its great distance), through binoculars Jupiter appears as a distinct white disc against the starry dots in the blackness. Some of those nearby dots are Jupiter's moons. Four of its 16 satellites – Io, Europa, Ganymede and Callisto – are easily visible through a small telescope or binoculars mounted on a tripod. Viewing Jupiter and its moons is one of the most thrilling nighttime pastimes for a cottager or camper. Each night the moons are in a different position, aligned along an orbital plane; these are the moons Galileo first saw when he trained his new telescope upon the heavens, consequently destroying 2,000 years of prevailing wisdom in an evening of stargazing. More powerful backyard telescopes can detect the dark storm bands across Jupiter's face, and Jupiter's famous Great Red Spot, a 300-year-old storm in the planet's swirling hydrogen-rich atmosphere.

As befitting its size, Jupiter is named after Rome's supreme god, who was fashioned after Zeus, the chief Olympian in ancient Greece.

SATURN, the God of Agriculture

Spacecraft have determined that Jupiter has faint rings, thought to be dust blown off a quartet of small inner moons struck by meteorites and grabbed in orbit around the giant planet. But these rings are nothing like the great rings of Saturn. The first sight of Saturn's rings through a backyard telescope is unforgettable.

Magnitude: −2.1 to −2.3

Successful probes: *Pioneer 10*, 1973; *Pioneer 11*, 1974; *Voyagers 1 & 2*, 1979; *Ulysses*, 1992; *Galileo*, 1995

Day of the week: Thursday, from the Norse god Thor, equated with the Roman Jupiter; *jeudi* in French

Notable: The surface area of the great Red Spot is larger than Earth's. The Chinese studied Jupiter at least as far back as 1000 BCE, when the 12-year orbit was observed. Jupiter spins faster than any other planet. Scientists observed the collision of Comet Shoemaker-Levy 9 and Jupiter in 1994.

SATURN ♄

Average distance from sun: 1,427 million km (856 million mi)

Diameter: 120,600 km (74,900 mi)

Length of day: 10.7 hours

Length of year: 29.5 Earth years

Temperature at cloud tops: −175°C (−285°F)

Moons: Dozens, but 25 larger than 10 km in diameter; largest, Titan

Magnitude: 0.7 to 0.6

Successful probes: *Pioneer-Saturn*, 1974; *Pioneer 11*, 1979; *Voyager 1*, 1980; *Voyager 2*, 1981; *Cassini-Huygens*, 2004–2010

Day of the week: Saturday

Notable: Saturn's moon Titan is bigger than Mercury and

Pluto and has a dense nitrogen atmosphere; it can be seen with a backyard telescope. The *Huygens* probe landed on Titan.

URANUS ♅

Average distance from sun: 2,872 million km (1,784 million mi)

Diameter: 51,100 km (30,760 mi)

Length of day: 17.2 hours

Length of year: 84 Earth years

Temperature at cloud tops: −215°C (−355°F)

Moons: 21; largest, Titania

Magnitude: 5.7

Successful probes: *Voyager 2*, 1986

Notable: Uranus spins "horizontally" on a 98° tilt, while all other planets spin more or less "upright"; scientists speculate that a gigantic passing object may have knocked Uranus on its side

NEPTUNE ♆

Average distance from sun: 4,497 million km (2,698 million mi)

Diameter: 49,528 km (30,775 mi)

Length of day: 16.1 hours

Length of year: 165 Earth years

Temperature at cloud tops: −200°C (−328°F)

Moons: 11; largest, Triton

Magnitude: 7.9

Successful probes: *Voyager 2*, 1989

Notable: Neptune's moon

Suddenly, the solar system is tangible, and no longer just a picture in a book.

The rings themselves are composed of billions upon billions of icy particles, ranging in size from dust flakes to garages. There are thousands of separate rings. The whole system, perhaps as little as 10 metres (33 feet) thick by current reckoning, revolves precisely around Saturn's equator. No one knows for certain why Saturn alone has rings so pronounced, but it is thought the rings may date from the birth of the planet itself and may be the remains of a moon or moons that couldn't hold it together.

Not only is Saturn beautiful, for the ancients it had certain pleasant associations. Saturn was the Roman god of agriculture, and every December a great festival called the Saturnalia was held to mark the solstice. Businesses and public institutions were closed, citizens exchanged presents, wars were interrupted and slaves were freed. In other words, the people partied.

URANUS and NEPTUNE, the Distant Planets

Of the final two planets in the solar system, only Uranus can be seen with the unaided eye. But it is extremely dim, and an observer needs to know its exact location in order to spot it. The planet was discovered in 1781 by English astronomer William Herschel, and was named Uranus after the Greek father of heaven, king of the Titans.

Neptune, the last of the gas giants, was mathematically predicted before it was finally seen from the Berlin Observatory in 1845. It was named after Jupiter's brother, the god of the sea. To the Greeks he was Poseidon.

DWARF PLANETS and KUIPER BELT

In a controversial 2006 decision that made headlines around the world, the International Astronomical Union demoted lonely Pluto from a planet to a new category called a dwarf planet. Pluto shares more characteristics – such as puny size and funky orbit – with fellow objects in the so-called Kuiper Belt region of the solar system than it does with the other eight planets. It cannot be seen without a telescope. Pluto was first seen in 1930 by American Clyde Tombaugh, is smaller than the moon, and actually has its own moon, Charon, about half Pluto's size. Pluto was the Roman god of the underworld, who rarely left his dark kingdom. Charon was the boatman who ferried the dead across the river Styx.

The Kuiper Belt, discovered and studied only since the early 1990s, is a vast region of space beyond Neptune that may contain as many as 70,000 or more objects larger than 100 kilometres (60 miles) in diameter. It may be the source of so-called "short-period" comets that orbit the sun once every 200 years or less.

THE OORT CLOUD

Pluto's mean distance from the sun is 5.9 billion kilometres (3.7 billion miles). But our solar system may extend out as far as 18.8 *trillion* kilometres (11.7 trillion miles). This is estimated to be the edge of the Oort Cloud, named after Dutch astronomer Jan Oort, who proposed in 1950 that comets are born in a distant ring of primordial matter that encircles the sun. Every once in a while a gravitational bump knocks a comet out of the cloud. The comet then begins its long trek towards the sun.

Triton has nitrogen geysers and revolves around the planet in the "wrong" direction. *Voyager 2* passed only 4,900 km (3,063 mi) above Neptune's north pole, a cosmic pool shot of unbelievable accuracy.

PLUTO ♇

Average distance from sun: 5,900 million km (3,540 million mi)

Diameter: 2,300 km (1,380 mi)

Length of day: 6.4 Earth days

Length of year: 248 Earth years

Surface temperature: −230°C

Moons: 3; Charon, Hydra, Nix

Successful probes: NASA's *New Horizons* probe is scheduled to buzz Pluto in 2015

Notable: Dwarf planet Pluto has an exaggerated elliptical orbit. From 1979 to 1999, it was closer to the sun than Neptune.

OORT COMET CLOUD

Distance from sun: About 9,600,000 to 18,800,000 million km (1–2 light-years, or 6–12 trillion mi)

Estimated number of comets in cloud: Billions

Probes: *Voyager 2* should pass through the Oort Cloud around the year 60,000. On board is Chuck Berry's record "Johnny B. Goode," among other artifacts of human achievement.

Comet Halley: Named after English astronomer Edmond Halley, who in 1682 noticed its regular return; it was last seen in 1985–1986, and will reappear in 2061. The Chinese have records of Comet Halley dating before the birth of Jesus.

The average comet is composed of a rocky nucleus about a kilometre or two (3,300 to 6,600 feet) in diameter. An icy layer around the nucleus is warmed as the comet approaches the sun. The ice vaporizes into a cloud called the coma. Solar radiation blows some of the material away, creating a tail that can be hundreds of thousands of kilometres long. The tail gets bigger as the comet approaches the sun (the word *comet* comes from the Greek *kometes,* "long-haired").

Some "long-period" comets have such huge orbits that they are seen once and never again. Others, thought to be those from the Kuiper Belt, develop orbits within the inner solar system and return regularly, such as Comet Encke every three years and Comet Halley every 76 years.

In 2006, NASA's *Stardust* probe collected evidence of amino acids in a comet's tail, suggesting that comets bombarding Earth during the birth of the solar system may have brought the building blocks for life.

THE PLEIADES
Merry Siblings of the Night Sky

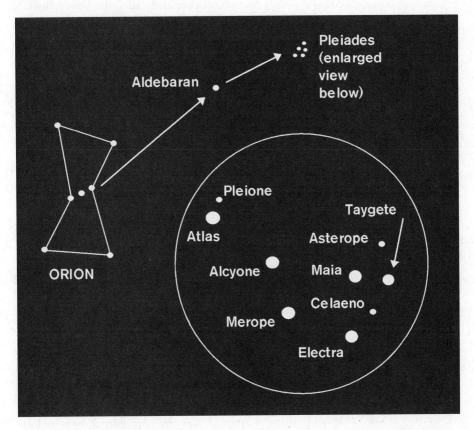

Aldebaran

Pleiades (enlarged view below)

ORION

Pleione

Atlas

Alcyone

Merope

Taygete

Asterope

Maia

Celaeno

Electra

The glittering Pleiades star cluster lies within the boundaries of the zodiacal constellation Taurus. Yet, like a brilliant child who has soared higher than her parents or siblings, the cluster's fame outshines that of its home constellation. "Minstrels and poets of the early days sang of their bewitchment and beauty," wrote the popular astronomy writer Roy Gallant of the cluster's stars, "and many of the great poets, from Homer and the author of Job down to Tennyson and the men of our own day, have had their

Best viewing time: Notable in the southern night sky throughout winter, moving east to west as the season progresses

Location: The cluster forms one end of an almost straight line running from the brilliant star Sirius in the southwest, up through the 3 belt stars in Orion, on to the bright star Aldebaran in Taurus and then to the Pleiades (see the star chart page 562)

Distance: About 440 light-years

The Seven Sisters: In Greek mythology, Alcyone, Merope, Celaeno, Asterope, Electra, Taygeta and Maia

Homer's *Odyssey*, Book 5: Odysseus, returning home to Ithaca after helping to destroy Troy, "sat at the helm and never slept, keeping his eyes upon the Pleiads." The irony is that Electra was mother of Dardanus, founder of Troy.

Job 38: God, demonstrating to the self-righteous Job that he knows nothing of the Lord's way, rhetorically asks the unfortunate farmer, "Can you bind the cluster of the Pleiades or loose Orion's belts? Can you bring out the signs of the zodiac in their season or guide Aldebaran and its satellite stars?" The satellite stars are the Hyades star cluster.

Alfred, Lord Tennyson's two bits: "Many a night I saw the Pleiads, rising thro' the mellow shade / Glitter like a swarm of fireflies, tangled in a silver braid"

Australian Aborigine view: The earliest Aussies saw a cluster of young girls serenading the Three Young Men (the belt stars of Orion)

Star fragments: A Polynesian myth says the Pleiades were once one bright star that boasted of its beauty. But gods disapprove of boasting. The god Tane fixed things by

fancy enlivened by them, and in one form or another have celebrated their sweetness and mystery and charm."

The Pleiades are also called the Seven Sisters, after the seven daughters of Atlas and Pleione in Greek mythology. Casual stargazers sometimes mistake them for the Little Dipper, for the shape is similar. But the Little Dipper, or Ursa Minor, is much larger and dimmer and is located in a different part of the night sky. The North Star, Polaris, marks the end of the Little Dipper's handle, and is therefore visible all year long from northern latitudes. The compact, sparkling Pleiades, on the other hand, are best viewed on a clear winter's evening. They rise in the evening in mid-October, reach their highest point in the southern sky by chilly early January and set close to the western horizon by late March.

There is nothing in the sky quite like this tight formation of bright stars. A pair of binoculars will startlingly reveal dozens of jewels in the cluster, which, for most people, appears as only six stars to the naked eye. This has given rise to the mystery of the lost Pleiad: Where is the seventh sister? Curiously, several ancient cultures, including some in North America, refer to seven stars in the group, but by the time of the classical Greeks, one seems to have vanished. The storytellers of the day suggested one of the daughters, Merope, may have hidden in shame because she married a mortal, the unfortunate Sisyphus, who was condemned by Zeus to spend eternity pushing a boulder uphill only to have it forever roll down again. Or perhaps it was Electra, who retreated in mourning over the devastation of Troy, which had been founded by her son Dardanus. Some astronomers suggest one formerly bright cluster star may have dimmed at some point, but there is no conclusive answer to the puzzle. It is still common for stargazers to compare how many stars they can see unaided; some have claimed they can discern as many as 11.

It is no doubt because the Pleiades are so compact that virtually all myths about them involve a group of siblings, often children. An Iroquois star parable, for example, recounts how a group of braves ignored their chores and danced instead. Elders warned that bad things might happen if they continued their merriment; the braves paid no heed and danced away. Soon they grew lightheaded and, frightened, began to rise into the sky. In one version of the story (these tales, remember, were all passed on orally and elaborated upon constantly), one of the eight braves recognized his father below, and became a falling star to reach him. That left the seven Pleiades, called Oot-kwa-tah by the Onondaga Iroquois.

The Kiowa people of Wyoming tell one of the most memorable Pleiades myths. Seven young sisters were playing in the woods when a bear found and chased them. They leapt onto a large rock and prayed to it to protect them. The rock responded, and grew to such a height that it was able to place the girls safely in the heavens as a star cluster. The bruin clawed madly but impotently against the rock, leaving deep grooves. That rock stands today as Devil's Tower in northeast Wyoming.

The Greek myth also involves pursuit and escape. Orion desired the seven nymphs born of Atlas and Pleione, but Zeus denied the hunter

throwing the nearby star Aldebaran at its neighbour, smashing it into smaller, dimmer pieces.

Brightest Pleiad: Alcyone, magnitude 2.9

Dimmest named Pleiad: Asterope, magnitude −5.8

Subaru logo: Subaru is the Japanese name for Pleiades; the Subaru car company uses the cluster as its logo

Also see: Orion, Star Charts

his quarry by turning the nymphs into doves and placing them among the stars. They remain in the celestial realm just out of his reach.

The Greeks called the Pleiades the "sailing stars," and seamen were said to set sail when the Pleiades were in the night sky. This calendric use of the Pleiades was common to many cultures. North American Native groups, including the Iroquois, timed their plantings with the setting of the Pleiades in the western sky in spring twilight. The star group even resembles a small packet of seeds, following the fertilizing sun into the ground. Earlier in the year, when the Pleiades reach their highest point in the night sky in January, the dancing braves are situated appropriately over the Iroquois Long House, where the new year's celebration called Ganahaowi takes place.

The Pleiades assume a notable role in astronomy as well as mythology. Officially known as M45, the Pleiades are young stars born from the same interstellar nebula of gas and dust. Sometimes a faint blur is visible in the region on a dark, clear night. Astronomers count about 400 stars in the family. The youngest stars are estimated to be about 20 million years old. By comparison, our sun is a 4.5-billion-year-old fogey.

SAGITTARIUS

The Teapot Pointing the Way Home

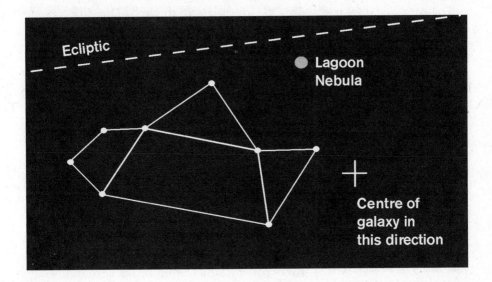

Ecliptic

Lagoon
Nebula

+

Centre of
galaxy in
this direction

When is a constellation not a constellation? When it's an asterism. Asterisms are groups of stars connected to form what are popularly called constellations but not officially recognized as such by the pooh-bahs at the International Astronomical Union. The Big Dipper is the most famous asterism; it's part of the official constellation Ursa Major, the Big Bear. Another asterism – also from the kitchen, curiously enough – is the Teapot, found in the constellation Sagittarius.

The Teapot is one of those constellations – sorry, asterisms – that shines brilliantly in the inky-black skies of the wilderness but is difficult if not impossible to see in light-polluted areas. It's a summer treat, positioned just over the southern horizon on mid-August evenings, as if it were pouring its steaming contents onto the ground below. The star that serves as the tip of

Best viewing time: Summer constellation. Prominent before midnight

Location: Low in the southern sky, to the east (left) of Scorpius

Planet zone: The ecliptic, the path of the planets, cuts across the sky just above the top of the Teapot. Look for planets in this zone; they make a fine sight with the Milky Way as a backdrop

Lagoon Nebula: About 4,500 light-years away; second only to the Orion Nebula in brightness

Milky Way: About 100,000 light-years across, with up to a trillion stars

Black hole: The collapsed corpse of a mammoth star.

Its gravity is so powerful even light can't escape, hence its name.

The Muses: Nine daughters of Zeus and Mnemosyne (memory), patron goddesses of the arts; they were Calliope (muse of epic poetry and eloquence), Euterpe (music and lyric poetry), Erato (love poetry), Polyhymnia (oratory or sacred poetry), Clio (history), Melpomene (tragedy), Thalia (comedy), Terpsichore (choral song and dance) and Urania (astronomy)

Astrological period: Nov. 22–Dec. 21. Sagittarius was said to rule the thighs

Also see: Milky Way, Orion, Scorpius

the spout is astronomically notable: think of it as a gunsight, targeting the centre of the Milky Way. On dark nights the ghostly swath of the Milky Way clearly bulges in this area. The galactic core lies about 30,000 light-years away in this direction, teeming with billions of stars. Evidence suggests a massive black hole is the central gravitational spike holding the galaxy together.

This prime patch of celestial real estate is excellent for binocular-assisted viewing. Through the glass, thousands of stars are seen to share the neighbourhood with dozens of deep-sky objects: open star clusters, globular star clusters and interstellar nebulae. The Lagoon Nebula, located above the Teapot's spout, is visible to the unaided eye on a dark night as a fuzzy patch distinct from the background Milky Way. But it's a better sight with binoculars.

Sagittarius is the mythological archer, half-man, half-horse, but his origins are murky. Sometimes he is identified with Chiron, ancient Greece's best-known mythological centaur. But another constellation, Centaurus, is usually said to be Chiron. (Centaurus is in the southern sky and hidden from our northern view.) Other theories suggest he represents Nergal, a Sumerian archer deity, or Crotus, the mythological founder of archery who lived with the nine Greek Muses. Old star maps depict Sagittarius firing his arrow at Scorpius to the west, but the reason for his enmity – other than the fear of getting stung – is not known.

SATELLITES
Smile! They're Taking Pictures

Iridium

The world entered a new era on October 4, 1957. On that date the Soviet Union launched *Sputnik,* the first successful spacecraft. Now nearly every industrialized country has a satellite orbiting the planet, and several nations have sent probes to the moon and beyond.

It's usually possible to spot an Earth-orbiting satellite within minutes of gazing into the early-evening sky, even from urban areas. Although the sky appears black, sunlight is still streaming high overhead for a few hours after sunset (and a few hours before dawn). Satellites soaring through space as they orbit Earth reflect these sunbeams. The artificial stars travel in all directions. They don't blink like aircraft, but some satellites seem to pulsate slowly. This is caused by a satellite's spin: as it revolves, it may present more surface area – such as the large solar

First Canadian satellite: *Alouette,* launched Sept. 29, 1962, making Canada the third country in space after the U.S.S.R. and U.S.; Canada was the first country to have a domestic satellite-communications system, with the launch of the *Anik* satellites in the early 1970s

Pieces of artificial space junk orbiting Earth: The U.S. Space Command tracks more than 12,800 pieces of non-functioning space junk, including 1,600 pieces created by a Chinese anti-satellite weapon collision in 2007. Large quantities of space junk fall back to Earth and burn up in the atmosphere, to be replaced by new trash.

Satellite sizes: *Sputnik* was about the size of a basketball. The International Space Station is about as wide as a football field; construction started in 1998 and will finish in 2011.

Iridium: The multi-satellite system used for satellite phone service; visible "Iridium" flashes are caused by reflected sunlight

Also see: Stars

"wings" that generate electrical power – towards the sun. Visible satellites orbit Earth at altitudes of 200 to 500 kilometres (120 to 300 miles). The International Space Station is highly visible when it passes overhead about 350 kilometres (217 miles) high; through steady binoculars, it's possible to make out its irregular shape.

Smile as a satellite passes overhead: it could be taking pictures. The low-flying birds are either spying, mapping, collecting weather information or performing scientific experiments. Navigation satellites in the Global Positioning System, used for military and commercial purposes, circle Earth almost 18,000 kilometres (10,800 miles) above the surface and are not visible. Farther out at 36,000 kilometres (21,600 miles) are communications satellites. At that altitude, a satellite's orbital speed precisely matches the speed of the rotating Earth, about 38,400 kilometres (23,040 miles) per hour. This is called geosynchronous orbit, because a satellite appears fixed over one spot on Earth. Arthur C. Clarke, the British science-fiction author who wrote *2001: A Space Odyssey*, first conceived the notion of geosynchronous orbit in 1945. Satellites parked 36,000 kilometres high are said to be in the Clarke Belt. Satellite dishes in backyards and atop taverns point towards distant spacecraft in Earth's artificial ring system.

SCORPIUS
The Celestial Stinger

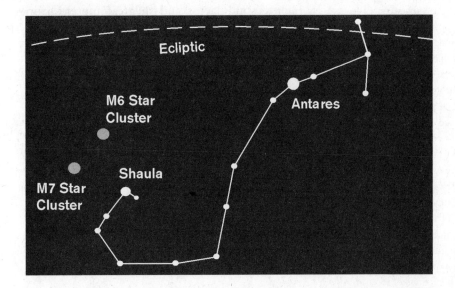

Scorpius has an evil reputation in some quarters, but the scorpion's appearance in the night sky is really a welcome sight. He moves to the beat of our brief summers. Come late May, he pokes his head above the southeastern horizon after sunset, as if sniffing the evening air for signs of Orion, his legendary quarry. By mid-July the astral arthropod is due south at 10 p.m., just over the horizon, as high in the sky as he'll get. Then, as summer turns to autumn, Scorpius scrambles below the western horizon in the evening twilight. He holes up for winter just as the leaves turn colour.

In classical mythology, Scorpius's notoriety derives, no doubt, from that of his earthbound relatives. Most of the approximately 1,000 species of scorpions worldwide are, in fact, harmless, but some deliver a painful toxic wallop with their

Best viewing time: Any dark summer night

Location: Skitters above the treetops along the southern horizon from east to west during the course of a night; just west (right) of Sagittarius

Antares: The 15th-brightest star, magnitude 0.9, distance about 550 light-years; slightly variable because it's a double star with a dim companion

Shaula: Magnitude 1.6, a triple-star system, distance disputed, between 365 and 700 light-years

Navajo Coyote star: A Navajo myth says the trickster Coyote spoiled the Black God's careful creation of all the major constellations by stealing magic crystals and scattering them in the sky. They became all the other dimmer stars that clutter up the heavens. The Coyote then placed his own wandering red star (Antares) in the sky as a counterpoint to the fixed North Star.

Astrological period: Oct. 23–Nov. 21; said to rule the "secrets" (genitals)

Chinese zodiac: Scorpius was a hare in the ancient Chinese zodiac. Later it became known as the Azure Dragon, a sign of spring. Because of the effects of precession (a slow wobbling in Earth's rotation), Scorpius is now a summer rather than spring constellation. In 4,000 years it will become a fall constellation.

Arthropod: The huge phylum that includes insects, arachnids, centipedes, millepedes, crustaceans and other exoskeletal creatures. Scorpions are arachnids, a class that also includes spiders. Only one scorpion species is found in Canada, in southern Saskatchewan, Alberta and British Columbia. Scorpions are among the oldest land creatures, dating back 400 million years.

Other celestial invertebrates: Cancer the crab, a dim constellation between Leo and Gemini, and Musca the fly, visible from the Southern Hemisphere

Also see: Orion, Sagittarius

sting, which in a few cases can be fatal. In Greek myth, scorpions were the instruments of evil (if not inherently evil themselves) in the deaths of Helios's son Phaeton and the great hunter Orion. Phaeton lost control of Helios's sun chariot, one version of the myth goes, because a scorpion stung one of the horses. (The careening chariot scorched the night sky, creating the Milky Way, then burned all the vegetation off the Sahara.) And the gods proved Orion's mortality by sending a tiny scorpion to kill the hunter, who had foolishly claimed he was invincible. In the afterlife, the Olympians placed the scorpion and Orion in opposite parts of the sky, one pursuing and one fleeing the other.

The constellation's famous bright star Antares also has sinister overtones. Some myths say the Greek god of war, Ares (Mars to the Romans), was forged from the flames of Antares, which translates as "rival of Mars." The connection is visual; the brilliant red star looks a lot like the planet Mars from our point of view on Earth. The pair sometimes appears together in the night sky, because Antares lies just below the ecliptic, the path of the planets across the celestial dome. Astronomically, of course, they couldn't be more different. Rocky, dusty Mars is smaller than Earth and never more than 378 million kilometres (235 million miles) away. Antares, on the other hand, is a red supergiant, one of the biggest stars in the galaxy, about 800 times the diameter of the sun, and 550 light-years, or 4,938 trillion kilometres (3,068 trillion miles), distant. Appropriately, the red star marks the scorpion's heart. The Chinese worshipped Antares as the "fire star."

Scorpius is among the original zodiacal constellations described by the Sumerians about 5,000 years ago. Its shape easily suggests a scorpion with its curled tail, and the names for some of its stars are in keeping with this. The tip of the tail, for instance, is called Shaula, Arabic for "stinger." For reasons that aren't entirely clear, however, the scorpion's claws were long ago separated from the constellation to form another, dimmer zodiacal constellation, Libra. The two brightest stars in Libra, Zubeneschamali and Zubenelgenubi, mean "northern claw" and "southern claw" respectively in Arabic, but now they represent the two pans of Libra's scales.

Another common description for the stars of Scorpius has more resonance for Ontario's cottagers and campers. Pacific cultures thought of Scorpius as a giant celestial fishhook. A Maori story from New Zealand recounts how a young man named Maui was given a magical fishhook by the goddess of the underworld. Maui used it to hook an enormous fish, which when brought to the surface turned out to be the islands of New Zealand. Pleased with this tremendous catch, Maui hurled the fishhook into the heavens, where it became the constellation we call Scorpius. The Hawaiian island chain was similarly formed, according to another myth.

Scorpius, like its next-door neighbour Sagittarius, lies partly across the Milky Way. On pleasant July nights, after the mosquitoes have gone to bed, Scorpius makes a good target for binocular-equipped stargazers. It's home to dozens of deep-sky objects, the brightest being M7, a cluster of about 80 stars that looks like one out-of-focus star to the naked eye. A good set of binoculars reveals about 15 brighter stars arranged in a pinwheel-shape. The so-called Butterfly Cluster, M6, is also located in Scorpius. Good binoculars and small telescopes indeed reveal a delicate sidereal butterfly. It's hard to believe Scorpius bespeaks evil when it offers such lovely sights.

SIRIUS AND PROCYON
The Dog Stars of Orion

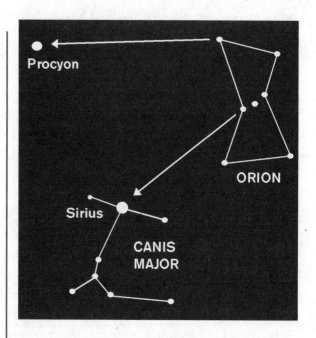

Of all the hounds in heaven, Sirius barks loudest. The famous Dog Star is the brightest star in the night sky, a brilliant white point piercing the black velvet of a winter's evening. His companion, Procyon, less bright but still ranked eighth in the astronomical Top 20, shines to the northeast. Sirius is the alpha star of the constellation Canis Major, the Great Dog, and Procyon is the alpha of Canis Minor, the Little Dog. The two canines are the hunting dogs of Orion, winter's mightiest constellation, who lies just to the west. When the Greek gods placed Orion among the stars after he was fatally stung by the scorpion, they thoughtfully elevated his best friends along with him.

Sirius, Procyon and Orion command the

southern night sky in winter. Six months later, these stars occupy the same area of the day sky. The ancient Egyptians believed the heat from Sirius was added to that of the sun, thus producing the "dog days of summer." Sirius is derived from the Greek word *seirios*, meaning "hot" or "scorching." (Procyon means "before the dog," because it rises before Sirius.) During the Mediterranean dog days, hounds were said to go mad, food and drink spoiled, lethargy reigned and everyone went just a little bonkers in the oppressive heat. The modern dog days are roughly July 3 to August 15.

To the ancient peoples of the Nile, Sirius was the most important star. About 4,500 years ago, Sirius appeared briefly in the dawn sky before the sun in mid-July, just as intense summer rains in the Nile's headwaters brought the floods that lasted until October. The overflowing Nile irrigated and fertilized the croplands along its banks, sustaining the entire Egyptian civilization. So important was this event that Sirius's sighting marked the beginning of the year in the Egyptian calendar. This led the Egyptians to devise a 365-day calendar as early as 3000 BCE, while other cultures used a lunar calendar. The Egyptians still had 12 months, of 30 days each, but tacked on five days at the end to equal 365. Later observations of Sirius revealed the year actually comprised 365¼ days.

Sirius is bright because it's a big brute and is nearby – indeed, the closest star to our own sun visible to the naked eye from the Northern Hemisphere. Astronomers reckon it's about twice the diameter of the sun, and 23 times as luminous. It is 8.7 light-years away – a hop and

between Ursa Major and Gemini. A French astronomer once proposed a domesticated cat, Felis, as a constellation, but kitty was never officially adopted.

Winter views: It's popularly thought that clear winter air makes it possible to see more stars. The air is, in fact, no clearer in winter than in summer. It just so happens there are more bright stars in winter than in summer skies.

Twinkle, twinkle: Stars located close to the horizon often seem to twinkle. The effect is caused by air turbulence, and is more apparent with stars near the horizon because our oblique view cuts through more of Earth's atmosphere.

Archibald Lampman: Poet, columnist, wilderness canoeist, post-office clerk, born 1861 in Morpeth, Ontario (then Canada West), died 1899 in Ottawa; influenced by Keats and Tennyson, preoccupied with nature and its healing powers

Also see: Orion, The Pleiades

a skip in cosmic terms, but still distant enough that it would take our fastest spacecraft about 300,000 years to get there.

Once the spaceship arrived, its occupants would see that Sirius is a double star. The companion star, dubbed the Pup by some wag after its discovery in 1862, is a so-called white dwarf, a burnt-out star radiating its remnant heat like an ember. It was the first white dwarf discovered, and astronomers now know the universe is full of them. They are small, having collapsed after the main hydrogen fuel ran out, but are super-dense. The Pup is perhaps only twice the size of Earth or smaller, but is as dense as the sun.

A mystery surrounds Sirius. Virtually all the ancient writings about the star, including those by Virgil, Seneca and the renowned Alexandrian astronomer Ptolemy, refer to Sirius as a fiery red star, when today it is clearly white or blue-white. Theories explaining this anomaly range from atmospheric phenomena turning the light red to a suggestion that the Pup was once a red supergiant star before it became a white dwarf.

Sirius's mystic allure (if not its astronomical mystery) has captured the imagination of poets and writers around the world. Ontario's great poet of the late 19th century, Archibald Lampman, wrote often about the stars, and in his sonnet entitled "Sirius," he dreams about Hathor, the Egyptian sky, joy and fertility goddess, whose temple at Denderah still stands:

> The old night waned, and all the purple dawn
> Grew pale with green and opal. The wide earth
> Lay darkling and strange and silent as at birth,
> Save for a single far-off brightness drawn
> Of water gray as steel. The silver bow
> Of broad Orion still pursued the night,
> And farther down, amid the gathering light,
> A great star leaped and smouldered. Standing so,
> I dreamed myself in Denderah by the Nile;
> Beyond the hall of columns and the crowd
> And the vast pylons, I beheld afar
> The goddess gleam, and saw the morning smile,
> And lifting both my hands, I cried aloud
> In joy to Hathor, smitten by her star!

STAR CHARTS

Navigating the Night Sky

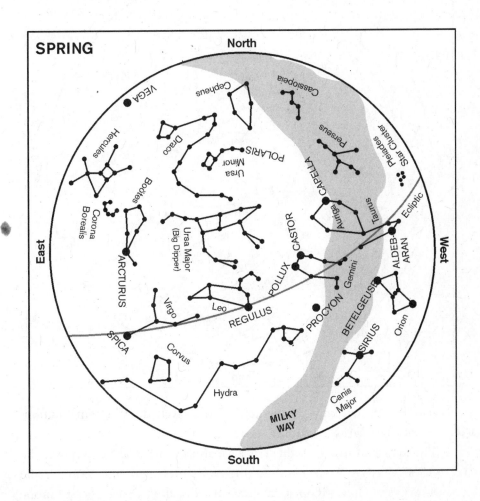

For thousands of years, different cultures around the world had their own
ways of organizing the heavens. The first printed star map was produced by
German painter and engraver Albrecht Dürer in 1515, a few decades after the
invention of the printing press. But it wasn't until 1930 that the International
Astronomical Union agreed on a common set of names and boundaries for
the 88 modern constellations. Of those, 48 were descended from the
Almagest, a star catalogue hand-produced by the Alexandrian astronomer

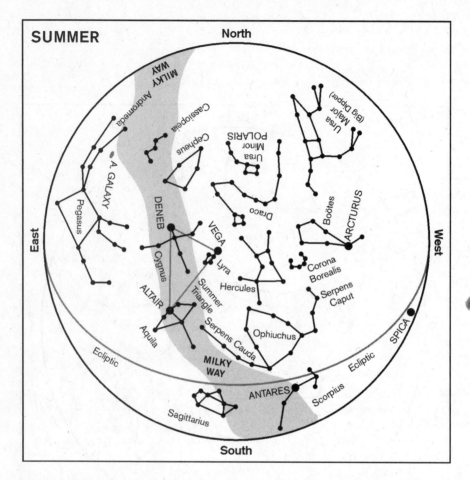

Claudius Ptolemy around 150. His constellations were derived from traditions dating back to at least 2000 BCE.

The names of many bright stars have also been handed down over the centuries. Most are Arabic, because the Arabs preserved and translated the classic works of Greco-Roman civilization while the barbarians cast Europe into the Dark Ages. In 1603, the German astronomer Johan Bayer took a scientific approach to naming stars. He named the brightest star of each constellation "alpha," after the first letter of the Greek alphabet. The second-brightest star was named "beta," and so on. (There are a few exceptions to this scheme.) Thus, astronomers refer to the brightest star in Lyra as Alpha Lyrae, although it also has an ancient Arabic name, Vega.

The rotation of Earth makes it appear as if all the stars are circling Polaris,

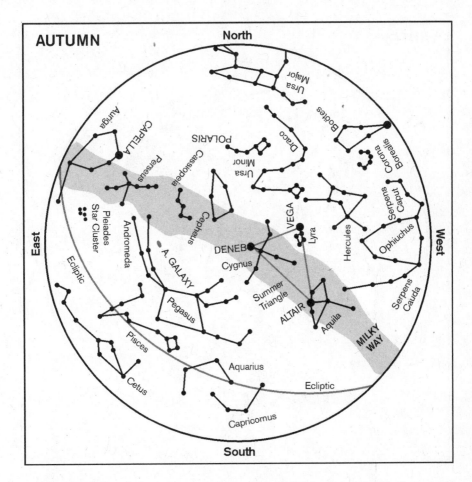

the North Star, in a counter-clockwise direction. Because of this motion, the star charts reproduced here are not exact for every time of night, every night of the year or every location in the Northern Hemisphere. But they are good guides to the heavens shortly after nightfall in the middle of each season in central Ontario.

To use a chart, hold this book upside down, hold it over your head and face north. The side of the chart marked "north" should point towards the north, the side marked "east" should face the east and so on. The position of the constellations in the night sky will roughly match those in the chart. Find the most prominent features first – the Big Dipper, Summer Triangle or Orion in winter – and use them as guideposts to the other constellations. Star names are printed in UPPERCASE, while constellation names are

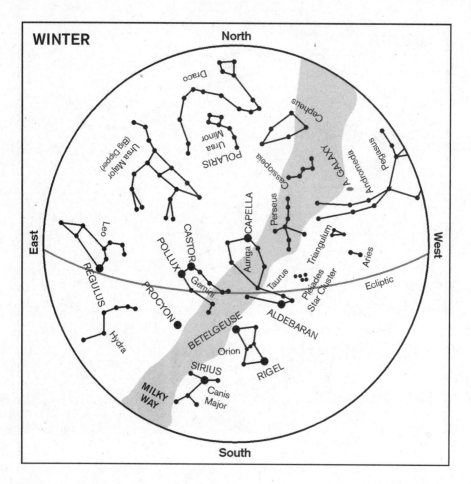

WINTER

North

Draco

Cepheus

Ursa Minor

Ursa Major (Big Dipper)

POLARIS

Cassiopeia

A. GALAXY

Andromeda

Pegasus

East

Leo

CAPELLA

Perseus

West

CASTOR

Auriga

Triangulum

Aries

REGULUS

POLLUX

Gemini

Taurus

Pleiades Star Cluster

Ecliptic

PROCYON

Hydra

BETELGEUSE

ALDEBARAN

Orion

RIGEL

SIRIUS

MILKY WAY

Canis Major

South

printed in Upper and lowercase. If you're under clear, dark skies in a wilderness area, you'll see many more stars than are indicated here. If you're in a light-polluted urban area, you'll see fewer.

To find planets, look for what appear to be bright stars along the ecliptic. Planets travel along this imaginary line in space. The ecliptic roughly defines the plane of the solar system – technically, it's the plane defined by Earth's orbit around the sun. Many constellations have their own entries and star maps in this book.

To help your eyes adjust to the dark, use a flashlight with red cloth or red paper wrapped around the light. After a while, you will become familiar with the night sky, and will be able to follow the march of the seasons by simply gazing into the starry depths – repeating a habit formed by our earliest ancestors.

SUMMER TRIANGLE
The Swan, the Eagle and the Vulture

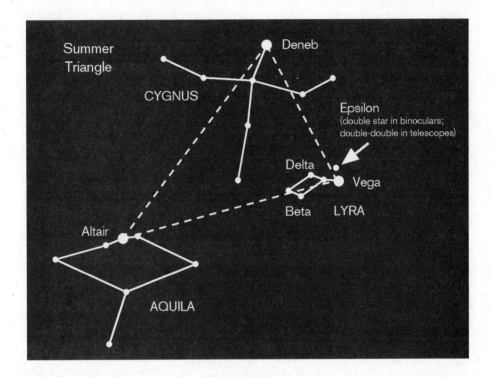

Three brilliant stars dominate the heavens from June to September. They are Vega, Deneb and Altair, and together they form the unmistakable Summer Triangle. Over the course of a summer night, the Triangle flies high across the sky like an enormous celestial kite, passing almost directly overhead. The formation is called an asterism because it is not an official constellation. But its prominence makes it one of the first groupings of stars introduced to novice stargazers.

Vega, Deneb and Altair are, however, members of their own constellations. Vega, the brightest of the three, is the lucida of the constellation Lyra. It is named after the lyre the

Scan zone: The Summer Triangle is one of the best areas of the sky to scan with binoculars. One of the thickest parts of the Milky Way runs through this part of the skydome, and hundreds of stars invisible to the naked eye materialize.

Look for: Delta and Epsilon Lyrae are double stars visible through binoculars. Epsilon Lyrae is actually a double-double, visible through telescopes. Beta Lyrae is an eclipsing double star: 2 orbiting stars that

563

eclipse each other from our vantage point, producing what seems to be a star of variable brightness; its luminosity changes over a period of about 13 days. The 2 stars in Beta Lyrae are so close to each other that astronomers believe superheated gas is flowing between them at a rate of 1.6 million km/h (1 million mph).

Distance of Vega from Earth: 25 light-years

Distance of Altair from Earth: 16 light-years

Distance of Deneb from Earth: About 1,500 light-years

Magnitude of Vega: 0.0

Magnitude of Altair: 0.8

Magnitude of Deneb: 1.3

Lucida: The brightest star in a constellation, from which we get the word *lucid*

Also see: Milky Way, Star Charts

Greek musician Orpheus used to enchant listeners during his various adventures. The most famous story concerns his attempt to rescue his wife, Eurydice, from the underworld of Hades. Orpheus took his lyre and entered the gates of hell to bring her back to life. His beautiful music so charmed Hades that the god granted Orpheus's wish, but with one condition: he must not look back as his wife followed him to the land of the living. Orpheus obeyed until, just as he stepped out into the sunlight, he could resist no longer and glanced back. It was too soon, and Eurydice disappeared. Orpheus was later reunited in death with his wife, and Zeus placed the lyre in the heavens to commemorate the musician's sweet melodies.

Asians also have a well-known myth for Vega, which the Chinese call Chih Nu, the Spinning Damsel or Weaving Sister. In one version of the story, Chih Nu was sent to Earth by her father, the Lord of Heaven, to marry and look after a poor servant. The servant did not have any paper money to place in the grave of his dead father, as required by ritual and still practised today. But the devoted Chih Nu wove her husband beautiful tapestries that brought him great wealth. Before her powers on Earth expired, the Lord of Heaven returned Chih Nu to the skies.

Vega is an Arabic word meaning "the stooping one," or "vulture" – the ancient conception of the constellation before the Greeks. The other two constellations of the Summer Triangle, Cygnus and Aquila, represent birds to this day. Cygnus looks much like its namesake, the swan. It is easy to imagine the outline of the great white swan as it flies along the shimmering path of the Milky Way. Deneb marks the tail of Cygnus; the word is Arabic for "tail of the hen." Christians also gave their own name, the Northern Cross, to Cygnus.

One of the Greek myths for Cygnus is said to explain the origin of the expression "swan song." Phaeton, the young man who created the Milky Way during a wild ride in his dad's sun chariot, had a close friend named Cycnus. When Zeus struck Phaeton dead with a thunderbolt, the mortal fell into a river. Cycnus tried several times to retrieve the body of his friend for burial, but his dives were unsuccessful. As he sang songs of grief along the riverbank, the gods took pity on him and placed him in the heavens as a swan. Thus was born, supposedly, the superstition that swans sing sad songs before they die.

Aquila, the constellation that includes Altair, was another bird of Greek mythology – the eagle that transported Zeus's thunderbolts. *Aquila* is Latin for "eagle," and the modern word *aquiline* means "of or like an eagle." *Altair* is Arabic for "the flying one." In Hindu mythology, Altair and the two bright stars nearby were thought of as the footprints of Vishnu, the preserver spirit.

A comparison of Deneb and Vega gives a good idea of how difficult it is to judge the size of stars and their distance from Earth. To the naked eye, Vega is slightly brighter than Deneb. Yet Deneb is, by astronomical reckoning, almost 60,000 times more luminous than Vega. The explanation, of course, is distance. Vega is only about 25 light-years from Earth, while Deneb, a colossal star possibly 200 times wider than our sun, is about 1,500 light-years away.

MOTHER
EARTH

MOTHER EARTH

*T*he geological drama takes place over such a long period of time that it is almost impossible to comprehend. If the history of our planet were condensed into one year, the entire evolution of our species would have taken place over the last four hours. The rocks of the Canadian Shield, meanwhile, would be as old as 314 days. Indeed, there's a good chance the rocks around your campfire are older than many of the stars overhead.

Though it's slow moving, the drama is very real. The Earth is constantly changing, evolving, alive with transformation. The signs of this continuous metamorphosis are all around us, from devastating earthquakes in faraway lands to the erosion of rock into sand down at the lakeshore. Some think of Earth as a single living organism called Gaia, the ancient Greek name for Mother Earth, who with Father Heaven begat the first creatures.

In central Ontario, the Canadian Shield is never far beneath the soil, influencing everything on it. The hard rock outcroppings are the remnants of ancient granitic intrusions, exposed by glacial erosion. Shield outcrops are the visible portions of the basement of the North American continent. The Earth's all-powerful forces can be seen in the lines, layers and shapes of the bedrock breaking the surface.

Photo credit: Karuppasamy.g /Dreamstime.com

CANADIAN SHIELD
The Basement of the Continent

Total area of Shield: 4.6 million km² (1.84 million sq. mi)

Total area of Canada: 10 million km² (4 million sq. mi)

U.S. Shield: The shield extends into northern Minnesota, Wisconsin, Michigan and New York, where it becomes the Adirondacks

Age of oldest Shield rocks: 4.28 billion years, discovered in 2008 on the eastern shore of Hudson Bay by McGill University researchers. These are the oldest known "whole rocks" in the world. Acasta gneiss from Northwest Territories is dated at 4 billion years old.

Age of Earth: 4.6 billion years

Shield name origin: Austrian geologist Eduard Suess coined the word *shield* in 1892 to describe the bedrock that seemed to form the foundation of each continent; other continents have shields, too, but they are mostly buried under younger rock

Precambrian: Cambria was the Roman name for Wales. Sedimentary rock from the area, about 600 million years old, seemed to contain the oldest-known fossils. Older rock didn't appear to have fossils and thus was called "Precambrian."

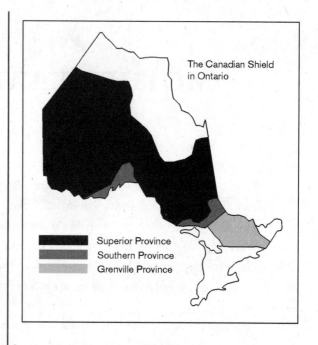

The Canadian Shield in Ontario

Superior Province
Southern Province
Grenville Province

A bush plane dips and soars above the rich expanse of pungent green forests and clear blue lakes. Highways carve their way through magnificent pink granite outcrops. The female loon ululates longingly across a moon-drenched lake. A solitary white pine clings to the tip of a wind-blown island.

This is the Canadian Shield, an ancient expanse of land that has shaped our national identity as solidly as the glaciers shaped the primal bedrock. "Like the sea, some landforms have a metaphysical force," wrote the late journalist Barbara Moon in 1970. "There are a number of people who believe that the Canadian Shield is such a landform. Certainly something in the country's geography has a grip on the subliminal consciousness of all its citizens."

The Shield derives much of its mystic power from sheer age. It contains the oldest rocks in the world, about four billion years old. These rocks were formed when the hot young Earth, covered in roiling molten magma, began to cool in space. A hard crust developed, like the scum that forms on thick soup when it has been removed from heat and left standing. Ancient volcanoes poked through the crust and spewed lava and ash, while mineral–rich asteroids plowed into its surface, concentrating valuable metals that would enrich Bay Street mining barons eons hence.

This was just the beginning of the Canadian Shield. Over the following billions of years, the land that is now a mecca for peace-seeking urbanites was subjected to powerful geological forces. Cottage country as we know it today was once a mountain range as high as the Rockies. Later the area was repeatedly submerged under vast seas. Long after the seas retreated, wave after wave of glaciers, some of them four kilometres (2.5 miles) thick, bulldozed the land. Only when the last glacier retreated, about 10,000 years ago, did the first humans battle the traffic to spend a weekend in the area.

Today the oldest volcanic rock is found in a region geologists call the Superior Province. Ancient rivers and glaciers eroded the Superior Province and dropped sediments around its fringes, forming the Southern Province. The Grenville Province comprises the 1.4- to 1.8 billion-year-old Central Gneiss Belt underlying

Precambrian fossils were found later.

Valuable metals found in the Shield: Gold, silver, nickel, zinc, uranium, copper, iron, platinum, selenium, cobalt, lead; the Sudbury nickel belt is thought to be the site of an ancient asteroid impact

Igneous rock: Molten rock, called magma, under the Earth's crust, forces its way to the surface along cracks and weak points. Some escapes to the surface as lava. Some, such as granite, hardens before it reaches the surface. Both are called igneous rock, from the Latin word for "fire," *ignis.*

Sedimentary rock: Composed of particles of eroded rock and chemicals from the skeletal remains of marine animals and from plant matter; laid down at the bottom of seas

Metamorphic rock: Originally igneous or sedimentary rock that has been altered by heat and pressure; gneiss, a metamorphic rock, makes up a large portion of the Shield

First appearance of humans in Shield country: About 10,000 years ago, as the last glacier retreated

Invention of birchbark canoe for traversing Shield lakes: At least 7,000 years ago

Ancient Shield life: Woolly mammoths, mastodons and giant beavers weighing

200 kg (440 lb) once roamed cottage country. They all died out by the end of the last ice age, about 10,000 years ago. Changing climate and, in the case of woolly mammoths, human predation, sealed their fate.

Main years of CPR construction across the Shield: 1882–1884

Number of men needed to build the CPR across the Shield: Almost 15,000

Number of horses: 4,000

Number of dogsled teams: 300

Number of dynamite factories built for railway construction across the Shield: 3

Also see: Painted Turtle, Birch, Falling Stars, Planets and Comets; Eskers, Moraines and Other Glacial Features; Granite, Lakes

Algonquin Park and Muskoka and the 1.2- to 1.3 billion-year-old Metasedimentary Belt, stretching from Haliburton to Gananoque.

After the Precambrian Era, when all this activity took place, seas advanced over the land and completely submerged the proto–North American continent. Sediments deposited at the bottom of the sea developed into a thick rock cover over the Precambrian Shield. When the waters retreated, the forces of erosion took over again. During the ice ages, glaciers scraped away the softer sedimentary rock, exposing the Shield in the contours we see today. Where the sedimentary rock was too thick to be removed entirely (such as in southwestern Ontario), or where glaciers didn't reach, the Shield remains hidden. It actually extends underneath most of North America, lying at the bottom of the Grand Canyon in Arizona. The Colorado River has cut through the sedimentary rock there just as the glaciers cut through to the Precambrian basement throughout much of Ontario.

ESKERS, MORAINES AND OTHER GLACIAL FEATURES
Landscaping on a Grand Scale

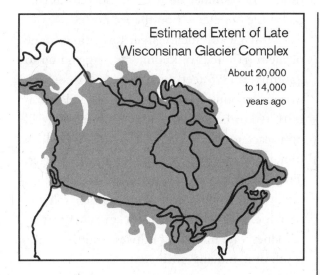

Estimated Extent of Late Wisconsinan Glacier Complex
About 20,000 to 14,000 years ago

Esker: From the Irish *eiscir*, "ridge"

Some eskers in Ontario: Balsam Lake Provincial Park (near Kirkfield), Esker Lakes Provincial Park (Kirkland Lake), south of Deux-Rivières (Mattawa), Madawaska (8 km [5 mi] west of town, on Highway 60), White (Lanark Co.)

Current extent of glacial coverage over world's land surface: About 10%, mostly in Antarctica and Greenland

Maximum extent of glacial coverage over entire planet at height of the Ice Age: 30%

Maximum extent of glacial coverage over Canada: 97%

Maximum extent of glacial coverage over Ontario: 100%

Recent ice ages: Began up to 2.5 million years ago. Four main glaciations are recorded in Ontario; the most recent is called the Wisconsin stage. Each glaciation lasted about 100,000 years, with warm periods in between. Many scientists believe we are still technically in an ice age evidenced by the ice sheets in Greenland and Antarctica, though we may be experiencing an interglacial period.

Winters today can get pretty cold up north, but they're nothing compared to 14,000 years ago. At that time Ontario was frozen solid all year round. The land that would become the province sat under a gigantic ice sheet up to four kilometres (2.5 miles) thick.

But over the next 4,000 years, the world heated up, the ice receded, plant and animal life began to flourish and humans moved into the area from the warmer south. The glaciers, as they melted, left behind vast lakes, millions of tons of rubble and the exposed bedrock that underlies the modern Ontario landscape.

The rubble, or glacial till, is composed of clay, sand, gravel and boulders, and is found in several types of formations across the province. Eskers are sinuous ridges typically a few kilometres (miles) long and 10 to 45 metres (33 to 150

What causes ice ages: The exact sequence of events is unknown, but Earth's 26,000-year wobble on its axis, volcanic activity, the re-arrangement of the conti-nents over millions of years, and other factors are be-lieved to interact to cause ice ages. Volcanic ash spewed into the atmosphere can dramatically cool the planet in a relatively short period of time. The location of large masses of land in polar and temperate regions is a prerequisite for conti-nental glaciation.

Oldest glacial till found in Ontario: 2.4 billion years near Cobalt; the Don Valley Brickworks in Toronto is fa-mous for its exposed record of recent glaciations over the last 135,000 years

Last time Ontario was com-pletely covered by glaciers: About 14,000 years ago

Last remnant of the Ice Age in Canada: Barnes Ice Cap, Baffin Island, 6,000 km² (2,300 sq. mi)

Speed of advancing ice flow: Varies greatly, depend-ing on climatic conditions and terrain. Mountain gla-ciers in cold climates may move as slowly as 1–4 m (3.3–13 ft) a year; warmer climates speed up this rate to about 300 m (984 ft) a year, but some "outlet" gla-ciers may temporarily surge at rates up to 7 km (4.3 mi) a year

feet) high. They are the deposits left by ancient glacial streams. These meltwater streams ran along the top of glaciers, in crevasses or through tunnels in or under the ice. The streams usually ran in the same direction the ice flowed.

Moraines are much larger formations, some of them hundreds of kilometres long and up to 250 metres (825 feet) high. A moraine contains massive amounts of till, released from a glacier as it melted or bulldozed by the front or side walls of a glacier as it ploughed forward. A terminal moraine marks the farthest advance of a glacier. The Oak Ridges Moraine north of Toronto is an unusual type called an interlobate kame moraine, formed between the margins of two ice lobes, one moving southwest and the other, south of it, moving northwest.

Far from being pristinely white, glaciers consist of dirty ice packed full of debris. The embedded debris causes glaciers to act like enor-mous sheets of sandpaper scraping the under-lying rock. Evidence of this is seen in scratches across polished rock faces or in smoothly gouged or furrowed rocks, often found around campsites. The direction of the markings generally indi-cates the direction of the ice flow.

Other glacial features include drumlins, kames, kettles and erratics. Drumlins are humpy hills sometimes called "whalebacks," which tend to occur in groups. The steeper side of a drumlin faces the glacial advance, while a gentler slope points in the direction the glacier travelled. A large drumlin field is found in the Peterborough area; they also occur along the south shore of Georgian Bay. Cone-shaped kames mark the bases of old waterfalls. Kames are made of debris carried by a meltwater stream over the edge of a glacier or a crevasse in the ice. They may also be formed of debris that accumulated in a depression in the ice. There is a kame field in the Tim River area of Algonquin Park. Kettles are small, round depressions usually occupied by a lake or a bog. They are formed when a block of ice is trapped underneath till and later melts. The collapse of the covering layer creates the depression. Erratics are boulders moved far from their place of origin by the Herculean forces of an ice sheet, some carried as far as 1,000 kilometres (600 miles), though usually no more than 100 kilometres (60 miles), and deposited randomly as the ice melted. Sometimes erratics assume bizarre perches atop smaller rocks.

Glacial deposits are enormously important to modern humans, because they provide the sand and gravel used in construction and road building. Gravel pits are often dug into the sides of kames or eskers. Many old eskers also form natural pathways. Portages, hiking trails, roads and railways sometimes run along the tops of eskers, which nature so conveniently placed thousands of years ago.

Speed of melting ice due to global warming: Not uniform depending on year and local conditions; however, most glaciers around the world are in retreat, and the Arctic Ocean ice cap has on avg. declined 10% per decade, or 72,000 km² (28,000 sq. mi) per year, measured from Sept. to Sept., from 1979 to 2007, according to the U.S.-based National Snow and Ice Data Center

GRANITE
Rock of Ages

Muskoka name origin: The word *Muskoka* may be derived from a combination of two Huron words, *musquash,* "it is red," and *ooka,* "large rocks." Thus *Musquash ooka* meant "large red rocks," or granite slabs. The more likely origin is the name of two local Ojibway chiefs, father and son, spelled variously as Musquedo, Misquuckky, Mesqua Ukie or Mesquakie. Both fought in the War of 1812 for the British, and they oversaw the cession to the British of land to the south and west of Muskoka.

Feldspar content of granite: 50–72%

Quartz content of granite: 25–40%

Mica and other dark mineral content of granite: 3–10%

Content of silicon dioxide, contained in feldspar and quartz, in most granite: 64–76%

Proportion of the Earth's crust made of silicon, oxygen and aluminum: 82%

Average hardness of granite on the Mohs scale of 1 to 10: 5.5

Size of granite crystal grains: 1.6 to more than 13 cm (0.6–5 in)

Aluminum content of granite: 8–16%

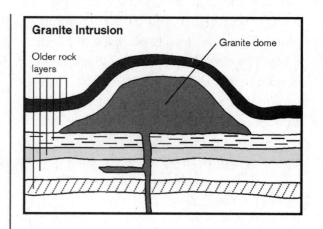

Granite Intrusion

Older rock layers

Granite dome

South-central Ontario's granite reveals the molten, creative forces of the Earth, for it crystallized deep beneath huge mountains 1.1 to 2.2 billion years ago – when single-cell bacteria and algae ruled the world. Time, wind, water and ice eventually swept the mountains away, leaving the Canadian Shield's harder, weather-resistant granite domes. When a canoe lands on the granitic shore of a lake in Shield country, it scrapes along the ancient foundation of the continent.

Granite is an easy rock to read. Its three main minerals can be picked out among the grains. The black specks are usually mica or hornblende, while about a third of the crystals are transparent or white quartz – pure silicon dioxide. The rest, more than half, is feldspar – silicon dioxide with a dash of aluminum. A topping of potassium produces the familiar red or pink feldspar, while sodium or calcium yields grey or white granites.

Wherever it occurs, granite holds clues to countless ages. Varying coloured bands reflect the direction its parental magma oozed into place, often in successive waves, with different minerals hardening at different temperatures. The result is like an imperfectly blended cake, with the most compatible elements crystallizing together first and the heavier contents settling to the bottom. The deeper beneath the Earth's surface the granite forms, the more slowly it cools, producing larger grains.

The largest crystals are in pegmatites, veins that contrast strongly in colour, texture and grain with the rock they run through. These veins, formed as the finishing touches of igneous-rock creation, are an amalgam of leftover, often volatile, ingredients that crystallized only after the more compatible elements of cooling magmas bonded and solidified. Squeezed into crevices created by the contraction and splitting of the host rock as it cooled, miscellaneous magmas, gases and water combined very slowly to form large, imperfect but often spectacular crystals.

At the other end of the scale, gneiss (pronounced "nice") often looks like granite but has smaller crystals in much finer, more distinct bands, sometimes in patterns that curl and loop like the fine lines of a fingerprint. At first glance the bands in gneiss may be mistaken for familiar sedimentary layering. But gneiss is a metamorphic rock. Under unimaginable heat and pressure, older rock deep below the surface becomes plastic. Different minerals in the rock align themselves into fine, thin layers, typically a few

Potassium content of granite: 2.7–6.5%

Sodium content of granite: 2–6%

Calcium content of granite: 0.1–3%

Other trace elements present: Iron, magnesium (about 2%, with oxides)

Main ingredients of pegmatite: Potassium feldspar, quartz, mica

Other minerals found in pegmatite: Calcite, garnet, pyrite, hornblende, chlorite, sericite, tourmaline

Size of pegmatite crystals: At least 5 cm (2 in) wide

Average length of a pegmatite dike: 30–300 m (100–1,000 ft)

Average width of a pegmatite dike: 1.5–30 m (5–100 ft)

Longest pegmatite dikes: More than 2 km (1.2 mi)

Hardness of pegmatite on the Mohs scale: Avg. of 6

Temperature at which pegmatite crystallizes: 500–900°C (932–1,652°F)

Meaning of Greek root words for *pegmatite*: "Solid mass"

Estimated portion of Canadian Shield made up of gneiss: Up to 80%

Gneiss: From the Slavic for "rotted" or "decomposed"

Metamorphic: From the Greek *meta*, "beyond," and *morphe*, "form"

Also see: Lichens, Canadian Shield, Quartz

millimetres wide, that bend and swirl according to the pressures acting upon them. The patterns are fixed as the rock cools. Gneiss may be metamorphosed granite or sedimentary rock, and comes in many varieties. Zircon, a trace mineral that contains uranium and is sometimes found in gneiss, allows geologists to date the rock by measuring its radioactive decay.

The rock has often folded, buckled and slid along fissures in the moving crust. Most recently, a million years of advancing and retreating glaciers sculpted and polished the granite and gneiss surface and deposited a thin granitic soil from the constant grinding. Granite yields acidic soil, making it largely unsuitable for farming even where it is thick. The countless lakes filling granite depressions, left by melting glacial ice 10,000 years ago, are also more acidic and harbour less vegetation than those farther south, making them especially susceptible to acid rain. From these conditions, all things in the ecosystem spring forth.

LAKES
A Fragile Abundance

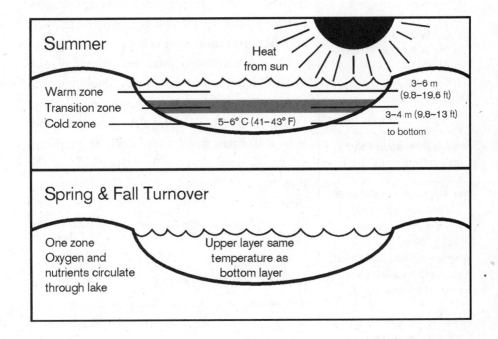

Across the face of the Canadian Shield, deep, rugged depressions in the Earth's bedrock crust have been filled with cool, fresh, clear, dark water. Rock and water, together with climate, determine the nature of all life in the ecosystem. Even humans, consisting of about 70 per cent water, become part of whatever lake they drink.

Most of the lakes puddling the Shield were formed by huge blocks of glacial ice that, as they melted, filled up the pockmarks and gouges in the eroded surface. Because there are so many lakes, especially in headwater areas such as the Algonquin and Temagami highlands, many have small drainage basins around them, with short,

Number of lakes in Ontario: About 250,000

Average time taken by water flowing into upper Lake Superior to reach the St. Lawrence River: 329 years

Deepest lake in southern and central Ontario: Mazinaw Lake, north of Kingston – more than 100 m (330 ft) deep

Maximum depth of Lake Superior: 410 m (1,323 ft)

Maximum depth of Lake Huron: 229 m (750 ft)

Height of the CN Tower: 553 m (1,815 ft)

Largest freshwater lake (by surface area) in the world: Lake Superior

World's largest island within a lake: Manitoulin Island, 2,800 km² (1,068 sq. mi)

Largest lake-within-a-lake in the world: Manitou Lake, on Manitoulin Island, 103 km² (41 sq. mi)

Origin of *Ontario*: Iroquoian for "beautiful lake" or "beautiful water"

Most popular sport-fishing lake in Ontario: Lake Simcoe

Average production of trout per hectare (2.5 acres) in Algonquin Park lakes: 560 g (1.25 lb)

Average production of trout per ha (2.5 acres) in the Kawartha lakes: 10,000 g (22 lb)

Sunlight that reaches 5 m (16.5 ft) below the surface of a clear lake: 20%

Temperature at which water is heaviest: 4°C (39°F)

Number of lakes in Ontario, Quebec and the Atlantic provinces threatened by acid rain: About 95,000

pH (potential hydrogen) of distilled water: 7

pH of normal rain: 5.6

Average pH of rain falling on Ontario: 3.5–5

Natural pH of a Canadian Shield lake: 6.5

pH of highly acidic lakes (30–40% above normal): 4.7

pH of lemon juice: 2

fast-running streams. The abundance of lakes and connecting rivers has long provided ideal, often circular transportation routes, with relatively short portages, for the Shield's first peoples, followed later by European explorers, trappers and modern canoe campers.

With their often small watersheds of thin soil and hard, acidic rock, most Shield lakes do not receive nearly as many nutrients as those farther south. Much of the plant debris that does wash into them sinks to the cold, deep bottom where bacterial decay is very slow and circulation is limited to spring and fall, locking up their nutrients for much of the year. Low nutrient levels curtail algae growth, the base of the aquatic food chain.

Circulation within lakes is limited because cold water is heavier than warm water. During the summer a warm layer, three to six metres (10 to 20 feet) deep, floats on top of a much colder transition zone of a few metres. After that, all the way to the bottom, the lake is about 5° or 6°C (41° to 43°F) all summer and never mixes with the top layer. In autumn, however, the upper layer cools till it reaches the same temperature as the lower, cold zone, eliminating the barrier and allowing water, oxygen and nutrients to circulate through the entire lake body. Though vital to the health of the aqueous system, the fall turnover, as well as that of early spring, can be a dangerous time to canoe, since the free flow of water allows winds to stir the whole lake, not just the top five metres, creating much bigger waves.

Ice in winter cuts the entire lake off from its oxygen supply, which is captured from the air by wave action. With spring breakup, the whole reservoir again circulates until the upper layer warms and reestablishes the temperature barrier, first in the shallows, then radiating to the centre of the lake.

Unfortunately, with the oxygen and nutrients that come in the spring, lakes can also receive an acid shock from the runoff of melting snow. Precipitation is naturally more acidic than lake or ground water because it reacts with nitrogen in the air. Rain or snow contaminated with sulphur dioxide and nitrogen oxides from industrial emissions is four to 400 times more acidic than normal precipitation. Canadian Shield lakes are especially vulnerable because the region's granite-based soils and coniferous forests make them more acidic than southern lakes, and they have few nutrients to neutralize acid rain.

Massive acid loading in spring runoff can push many organisms over the edge, especially those near the base of the aquatic food chain such as freshwater shrimp and stonefly larvae. It can also strike early-spawning fish, including pike, pickerel, minnows and white suckers, that congregate near inlets, where the acid infusion is greatest. In highly acidic conditions, some die in 24 to 36 hours. The eggs of fish and amphibians, especially spring peepers and salamanders, can also be severely affected. Compounding the damage, acidic runoff may leach natural toxic metals such as mercury, zinc and aluminum out of the soil.

People who study lakes, ponds and streams: Limnologists

Reason water feels warm to humans swimming in the rain: The body has already adjusted to coolness caused by rain, so blood vessels do not suddenly constrict upon submersion in lake water, as they do on a hot day

Also see: Brook Trout, Granite, Limestone

LIMESTONE
Ashes to Ashes, Life to Limestone

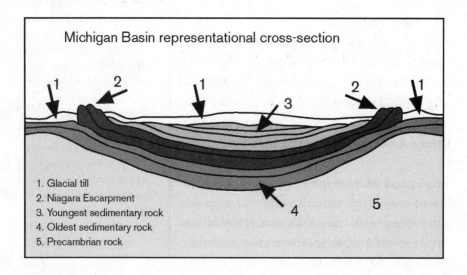

Michigan Basin representational cross-section

1. Glacial till
2. Niagara Escarpment
3. Youngest sedimentary rock
4. Oldest sedimentary rock
5. Precambrian rock

Limestone monuments:
  Pyramids of the Egyptians
  and Mayans, plus many
  other ancient wonders, were
  built of this soft, easy-to-
  work stone so abundant in
  many parts of the world
Alias: Calcium carbonate,
  calcite
Crystal shape: Hexagonal
**Hardness on the Mohs
  scale of 1 to 10:** 5.5
**Height of the Niagara
  Escarpment:** Up to 250 m
  (825 ft)
**Portion of the Earth's sur-
  face rock that is lime-
  stone:** 20%
**Portion of the Earth's crust
  that is limestone:** 8%
**Amount of carbon dioxide
  emitted into the**

A steep, towering, limestone cliff can be seen as a monument to life on Earth. All limestone is formed from accumulating layers of marine plants and animals, combining and solidifying with calcium, or lime, on shallow sea floors. Together with the world's deposits of petroleum and coal, which form in deeper seas or on land, limestone stores much of the carbon that made past life possible.

Carbon is the material of all life because its atoms have unique abilities to form extensive and varied stable chains, which can build living tissue and store energy chemically. The first living cells, three billion years ago, probably obtained carbon from the Earth's then-poisonous atmosphere. While carbon atoms have been continuously recycled from dead plants or animals back into the air ever since, time has frozen beneath the Earth's surface huge stores that have escaped decomposition.

But limestone erodes more quickly than most rocks and, after perhaps hundreds of millions of years, eventually does return to the carbon cycle. Much limestone once covering the Canadian Shield – built up on top of the ancient, eroded continent while it was submerged 450 to 250 million years ago – has since been washed away. To the south, limestone forms the backbone of Manitoulin Island and the Bruce Peninsula. The spine is part of the Niagara Escarpment, which runs in an arch 2,300 kilometres (1,400 miles) long from near Rochester, New York, to central Wisconsin. The escarpment exposes the outer rim of an 800-kilometre-wide (480-mile-wide) expanse of sedimentary bedrock called the Michigan Basin, with the state of Michigan at its centre. Some 600 million years ago, the basin was the broad bay of a shallow, tropical sea lapping the southern shores of the continent of Laurentia, today's Canadian Shield. There was no life on dry land at the time. The first multicellular marine organisms were just beginning to appear.

Over the next 300 million years, layers of sand, mud, algae, coral and primitive life forms accumulated in the Michigan Basin, up to 12,000 metres (7.2 miles) thick at its centre. Gradually, as the sediments collected, the centre of the basin began to sink, creating a saucer shape. Then, over the next 200 million years, deep-Earth forces pushed the entire basin upwards out of the water, like a raised bowl, until the rim finally broke free of the surrounding land, forming a continuous, rocky cliff. The escarpment's edge has since

atmosphere each year by humans burning fossil fuels and making cement: 7.7 billion tonnes (8.5 billion tons) in 2007, increasing by about 3.5% each year according to the Global Carbon Project

Amount of carbon dioxide removed from the atmosphere by natural sources such as trees, soil and oceans each year: About 4.3 billion tonnes (4.8 billion tons)

Portion of the atmosphere that is carbon dioxide: 0.03%

Amount of carbon dioxide in the atmosphere: About 2 trillion tonnes (2.2 trillion tons)

Increase in atmosphere's carbon dioxide content since 1850 chiefly due to the burning of fossil fuels: About 37%

Dolomite: Very hard limestone, tempered with magnesium, that caps the Niagara Escarpment

Chalk: Very soft limestone

Also see: Ferns, White Cedar, Falling Stars, Canadian Shield

eroded steadily inwards, 80 kilometres (48 miles) from the original cleavage, around Port Hope and Madoc in Ontario, towards the centre of the basin. The fallen rock has dissolved, crumbled or been carried away by glaciers.

Limestone also slowly dissolves into any lakes that rest upon it, releasing bicarbonate, which neutralizes acid rain. This buffering capacity has been a lifesaver for many sport-fishing lakes, especially on Manitoulin Island, while Shield lakes have suffered. Two exceptions in the Shield are lakes Gilmour and Tecumseh, which lie in a crater four kilometres (two and a half miles) wide gouged into the ground by a meteorite that struck the northern Algonquin Park area about 400 million years ago. Limestone subsequently accumulated within the crater while later seas covered the Shield.

Some areas, especially near the edge of the Shield, also feature limestone that has been recrystallized through heat and pressure beneath the Earth's surface to become the rock's metamorphic form, marble. Native peoples carved numerous mythological figures in the marble rockface at Petroglyphs Provincial Park, near Peterborough, more than 500 years ago. After finishing his or her work, each carver would cover it with leaves, preserving the site from weathering and from outsiders until its discovery by non-Native people in 1954.

QUARTZ
Crystals Harder than Steel

The Canadian Shield is a treasure trove of one of the oldest, most valuable gemlike stones known to humans. Quartz in its many forms and colours has been used to make tools throughout the world for more than 100,000 years. Coloured, banded quartz called agate was used to make beads and other jewellery in Mesopotamia and Egypt. Long before people of Near Eastern cultures learned to mould or blow glass, they were painstakingly chipping and polishing plates up to 70 centimetres (27 inches) wide and cups and urns as much as 25 centimetres (10 inches) deep out of solid pieces of quartz, sometimes from a single giant crystal. Glass itself was – and still is –

Alias: Silica, silicon dioxide, SiO_2

Hardness on the Mohs scale of 1 to 10: 7

Hardness of diamond: 10

Hardness of gold: 2

Portion of the Earth's crust composed of silica: About 60%

Portion of the Earth's crust composed of quartz uncombined with other rocks: 12%

Crystal shape: Hexagonal

Number of varieties of quartz: More than 200

Ontario's official mineral: Amethyst, a purple quartz,

coloured by a rare alignment of iron atoms, mined around Bancroft, Lake Nipissing and Lake Superior

Other semi-precious forms of quartz: Rose quartz, smoky quartz, opal, onyx, tiger eye, citrine; variously formed by characteristics of temperature, pressure and trace impurities at the time of crystallization

Quartzite: Sandstone composed of at least 95% white quartz that has recrystallized and hardened through heat and pressure beneath the surface

Famous quartzite formations: The white ridges of Killarney Provincial Park (pictured on previous page), which were quarried by Native people up to 10,000 years ago, when the crests were islands inundated by the meltwaters of a receding glacier then only 150 km (90 mi) to the north

Melting temperature: 1,723°C (3,133°F)

Minimum temperature oxygen needs to combine with silicon: 400°C (752°F)

Temperature at which quartz usually forms: Less than 800°C (1,472°F)

Temperature at which amethyst forms: 90–250°C (194–482°F)

Quartz wristwatches: Quartz has a property, called piezoelectricity, which makes it vibrate at a very precise frequency in an electronic

made mainly from quartz sand grains melted into liquid and cooled too quickly to allow crystals to re-form, essentially freezing the liquid configuration.

There is an abundance of quartz in sand and granite, and in its pure state around the world, because it is composed of the two elements that make up three-quarters of the Earth's crust. Some 90 per cent of all rocks contain both oxygen and silicon. Quartz is pure silicon dioxide, known as silica. Most pure quartz rocks are thought to form from groundwater that becomes supersaturated with silica it picks up from rocks as it moves deep into the increasingly hot nether regions of the Earth. Evaporation or a change in temperature causes the solution to crystallize in subterranean cavities to form quartz, later exposed on the surface as it is pushed up with the surrounding igneous rock.

Because oxygen and silicon form such a stable bond, quartz is harder than steel. Flint, a type of quartz tinted dark by fossilized marine microorganisms, is so hard and brittle that Stone Age humans shattered it to make tools and weapons from its shards. By hitting it together, they produced sparks to start fires. The word *silica* is derived from the Latin *silex,* meaning "flint." Living things also incorporate silica to give strength to their tissues, such as in tree trunks. The abrasiveness of a grass blade's sharp edge, which can in certain species cut a finger, is due to tiny bits of quartz in the plant.

Clear, colourless quartz, known as rock crystal, is common in Ontario. The word *crystal* comes from the Greek *krustallos,* meaning "ice," because the ancients believed quartz was ice frozen at such a low temperature that it could not melt. The belief persisted even into the 18th century, when Carl Linnaeus, Swedish father of the modern scientific system of classifying species, wrote that sand was caused by raindrops that had fused and permanently solidified. The ancients used rock-crystal lenses as magnifying glasses to start fires, especially ceremonial blazes. Large crystal balls of transparent quartz, which would take many months to make, have been used by seers in India and Europe for thousands of years. In Rome and Japan, the rich rolled the cool surfaces of small, sculpted crystal spheres over their skin for refreshment on hot, sweaty days.

Another form of silica rock that is especially abundant in the Canadian Shield is called milky, or white, quartz. Numerous microscopic cavities filled with liquid carbon dioxide or water within the rock cause its whiteness. Milky quartz is the most common rock appearing in seams that shoot through other igneous or metamorphic bedrocks. Most gold and other precious metal deposits in Ontario are contained within milky-quartz veins. Native peoples commonly used this quartz for spear- and arrowheads, since flint and chert (another form of quartz) were rare in Ontario and usually had to be obtained from elsewhere through trade.

circuit. This precision is used to keep accurate time.

Largest quartz crystals ever found: 6.1 m (20 ft) long, 1.5 m (5 ft) across, 39,916 kg (44 tons), from Brazil, which supplied much of the vital quartz for crystal oscillators used in military radio equipment in World War II. Giant crystal clusters have also been found in Namibia.

Percentage of quartz in sand used to make glass: 95–99%

Date of oldest-known human-made glass: About 2500 BCE

Date of oldest-known moulded glass: About 1500 BCE

Date of oldest-known blown glass: About 200 BCE

Also see: Canadian Shield, Granite

WETLANDS
Mother Nature's Kidneys

Bog formation in a kettle lake

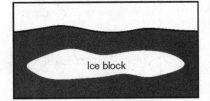

Retreating glacier leaves an ice block covered by glacial till.

Ice block melts, forming a kettle lake with no natural outlet.

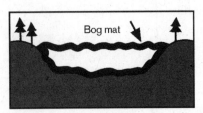

Over time, sedges, sphagnum moss, and other plants form a bog mat across the still water, with peat accumulating on the bottom and possibly filling the entire kettle lake. Trees invade from the edges.

The vapours and gases that sometimes rise from swamps and other still bodies of water were once believed to be the cause of many of the contagions that long plagued humanity. Even after the discovery of microbial pathogens in the past century, the popular bias against wetlands generally held sway. Only now are wetlands coming to be recognized by the public for the vital roles they play, including actually purifying water and providing hatcheries, food and habitat for a vast array of species.

Ontario's wetlands can be divided into four main categories: swamps, marshes, bogs and fens.

Swamps, often located along the edges of rivers, are wetlands specifically featuring trees. Usually sitting on top of clay or other nonporous material, swamps are flooded or wet all year long, though standing water sometimes dries up in summer. Because swamps are undefined collecting basins, their water levels may fluctuate significantly. They slow down the flow of water, helping prevent flooding and erosion. During dry spells, they are reservoirs, their soaked soils keeping the water table close to the surface while releasing water slowly into outflowing streams. The abundant dead trees in swamps are mined by woodpeckers, which in turn provide cavities for many songbirds. The relative inaccessibility of swamps also makes them favoured locations for heron rookeries and wolf dens.

In more open areas near the mouths of rivers, in shallow bays and around ponds, marshes form. Marshes are the richest of all habitats, forming where silty, organic sediments collect in calm water. They teem with life. The still water, filled with insects, pollen, algae and bits of organic matter, allows cattails and other water plants to sink roots and take advantage of the superconcentration of nutrients in the muck. Fast-growing marsh plants are far more efficient than most others at capturing nutrients and quickly turning them into living tissue. The rich plant life in turn supports high densities of insects, snails, fish, frogs, birds and mammals.

With their absorbent plants, marshes effectively filter silt and other contaminants. They have been dubbed "Mother Nature's kidneys." Creating marshes, which use less land than municipal water-treatment lagoons, has been suggested as the best means of cleaning up water pollutants, including sewage.

At the opposite end of the scale, bogs are the most nutrient-poor wetlands. With no drainage outlets, their water becomes stagnant. Many were formed 10,000 years ago by chunks of glacial ice that left depressions when they melted. Bogs maintain cold microhabitats because cold air settles in low pockets of land in summer. Dead vegetation tends to accumulate in bogs rather than decompose, because the cold, acidic, low-oxygen conditions are inhospitable to bacteria and most fungi. Sphagnum moss, which thrives

Area in Ontario covered by wetlands: 290,000 km^2 (116,000 sq. mi)

Portion of Ontario covered by wetlands: 33%

Portion of Canada covered by wetlands: About 14%

Portion of Southern Ontario's original wetlands that still remain: 32%

Area in Ontario covered by peat: 260,000 km^2 (104,000 sq. mi)

Energy equivalent of Ontario's peat stores: 72 billion barrels of oil

Portion of the world's peatlands possessed by Canada: 40%

Portion of the world's peatlands possessed by Russia: 35%

Number of years required to form 1 cm (0.4 in) of peat: 20

Common swamp vegetation: Red maple, white cedar, black ash, silver maple, white elm, speckled alder, white cedar, black spruce, fir, dogwood, naked mitrewort, bitter cress, duckweed, enchanter's nightshade, raspberry, jewelweed, northern green orchid.

Swamp dwellers: Swamp sparrows, barred owls, great blue herons, turkey vultures, woodpeckers, deer, wolves

A swamp with mainly shrubs: Carr

Marsh vegetation: Cattails, water lilies, horsetail, water-arum, water-shield, wild iris,

grasses, rushes, pickerelweed

Marsh dwellers: Red-winged
blackbirds, swamp sparrows,
marsh wrens, herons, bit-
terns, ducks, rails, osprey,
muskrat, water snakes,
snapping turtles, painted turtles, frogs, minnows, large-
mouthed bass

Bog vegetation: Sphagnum
moss, black spruce, tama-
rack, insect-eating sundew,
pitcher plants, orchids,
Labrador tea, bog laurel,
leatherleaf, crowberry, cran-
berry, bog rosemary

Bog dwellers: White-throated
sparrows, Wilson's warblers,
hawks, foxes, weasels, lynx,
bobcats, pickerel frogs

Fen vegetation: Sedge,
grasses, reeds, shrubs,
tamarack, cedar

Also see: Beaver, Cattail,
Black Ash, Black Spruce, ,
Red Maple, Tamarack

in bogs, intensifies the condition by drawing atoms of calcium, magnesium and other mineral nutrients from the water in exchange for hydrogen ions, making the bog even more acidic.

Compressed, unrotted vegetation piled up over the centuries in bogs, called peat, can be used as a long-burning fuel. The species succession of plant life after the retreat of the glaciers can be traced and dated from well-preserved pollen grains extracted from peat-bog layers. Intact prehistoric animals and 3,000-year-old human bodies have been unearthed from bogs in various parts of the world.

Fens are somewhat like bogs, though they are not as acidic and are dominated by sedges – grasslike plants with unjointed, three-sided stems. Peat builds up at the bottom of fens, also. Large areas of bogs and fens, called muskeg, cover much of northern Ontario.

ACKNOWLEDGMENTS

Many naturalists, scientists, friends, family, and publishing professionals contributed invaluably to the creation of *The Complete Up North* and its predecessors, *Up North* and *Up North Again*. We sincerely thank them here:

Richard Aaron • Jack Alex • Bob Alexander • Allen Alsop • Robert Anderson • Mark Bacro • Ken Barbour • Spencer Barrett • George Barron • Jim Bendell • G. Bennett • Michael Berrill • Roy L. Bishop • T. J. Blake • Chris Blomme • Jim Bogart • Bob Bowles • George Boyko • Marc Branham • Ron Brooks • Judy Brunsek • Ian Buchanan • Ron Burrows • Michael Cadman • Rob Cannings • Luca Cargnelli • John Carnio • John Cartwright • John Casselman • Paul Catling • Ted Cheskey • Charles Churcher • Nancy Kay Clark • Francis R. Cook • Paul Cooper • William J. Crins • Doug Currie • Geoff Cutten • Helene Cyr • Aruna Dahanayake • Kenneth Dance • Chris Darling • Don Davis • Nancy Dengler • Jim Dick • Terence Dickinson • Tim Dickinson • Jason Dombroskie • Charles Dondale • Bruce Duncan • R. Michael Easton • J. E. Eckenwalder • Judith Eger • Ken Elliott • J. B. Falls • M. B. Fenton • J. Donald Fernie • Jean Ferron • Don Filman • Dinah Forbes • David Francey • Henry Frania • W. G. Friend • Fuzz • David L. Gibo • Alan G. Gordon • Karen Graham • Premek Hamr • Alan J. Hanks • John Harcus • David J. Hawke • Robert Hawkes • Chris Hayden • Bernd Heinrich • Fred Helleiner • Tom Herman • Chris Heydon • James Hodgins • Anne Houtman • Brad Hubbly • Patrick Hubert • Don Huff • David J. T. Hussell • Robert R. Ireland • Ross James • Basil Johnston • Bob Johnson • David Johnson • Joe Johnson • Colin D. Jones • Ellie Kirzner • Jaime Kirzner-Roberts • Michael Kirzner-Roberts • Jackie Kaiser • Kathleen Kemp • Henry Kock • George Kolenosky • Donald Kramer • John Krug • Carole Ann Lacroix • Don Lafontaine • Lawrence Lamb • Doug Larson •

Anna Leggatt • Jacqueline Litzgus • Harry G. Lumsden • Ross MacCulloch • Stuart Mackenzie • G. L. Mackie • Jacquelyne Madill • David Malloch • Steve Marshall • Dave Martin • Lubomir Masner • Tom Mason • Michael May • Chris McCall • Jon McCracken • W.D. McIlveen • Margaret McLaren • Peter L. McLaren • Nora McLoughlin • Don McNicol • A. L. A. Middleton • Jack Millar • Sharmila Mohammed • Ted Mosquin • Jim Mountjoy • Philip Mozel • Ted Mumford • Erica Nol • Norm North • Milan Novak • Martyn Obard • Mike Oldham • Judi Orendorff • Ike Osmani • Mark Peck • John Percy • Larry Petrie • David Phillips • Andrew Podgorski • Michael J. Power • James S. Pringle • Rob Purdie • Peter Quinby • Norm Quinn • George Rason • Pete Read • John W. Reynolds • James D. Rising • Rick Rosatte • Bill Rose • Mike Rosen • Heather Sangster • Taylor Scarr • Frederick Schueler • Carolyn Seburn • John C. Semple • Sandra Shaul • David Sherry • Ann Shier • Howard Smith • Susan Smith • Kirk Sobey • Mark Stabb • Jocelyne St. Onge • Kenneth Story • Dan Strickland • Dan Stuckey • Don Sutherland • Gary Teeter • Ian Thompson • Victor Timmer • Tim Timmerman • Ron Tozer • Nick Tzovolos • V. R. Vickery • Dennis Voigt • Allan Wainio • Caren Watkins • Alan Watson • Patrick Weatherhead • Ron Weir • Wayne F. Weller • D.V. Weseloh • Terry A. Wheeler • Jan Whitford • Glenn Wiggens • Jane Young • and Soonki Schaub, Ben Schaub and Nik Sheehan, who were on that fateful canoe trip.

We would also like to acknowledge the following organizations, to which many of the above individuals are attached:

Canadian Forestry Service, Canadian Museum of Nature, Canadian Wildlife Service, Cornell University, The Friends of Algonquin Park, Environment Canada, Global Carbon Project, Laurentian University, National Oceanic and Atmospheric Administration (U.S.), National Snow and Ice Data Center at University of Colorado, Natural Resources Canada, NASA, Ontario Ministry of Natural Resources, Ontario Nature, The

Royal Astronomical Society of Canada, Royal Ontario Museum and the ROM Herbarium, Trent University, University of Guelph and the U of G Arboretum, University of Toronto, Westwood Creative Artists, *Wildflower* magazine

A very special thank-you to Marta Lynne Scythes, whose wonderful illustrations have contributed so much to the enjoyment of this and all earlier *Up North* books.

RECOMMENDED READING

For those interested in delving in more detail into various subjects we have touched upon in this guide, we recommend the following books:

Legacy (McClelland & Stewart), edited by John Theberge, is a thick, comprehensive compendium of the natural history of Ontario, written by the province's leading naturalists and featuring some of the best colour nature photography.

The Royal Ontario Museum has published three detailed ROM field guides (McClelland & Stewart) on the birds, wildflowers, and reptiles and amphibians of Ontario, with colour photos and range maps.

The Friends of Algonquin organization publishes a series of excellent booklets on the trees, flowers, mammals, birds, fish, reptiles and amphibians found in Algonquin Park, as well as **The Raven**, an enlightening natural history newsletter, all available at Park gate stations and outfitting centres or from the Ministry of Natural Resources.

Peterson's Field Guide to the Birds of Eastern and Central North America (Houghton Mifflin), by Roger Tory Peterson, is perhaps the best field guide for Ontario birds, complete with detailed colour illustrations, brief descriptions and range maps.

Bugs of Ontario (Lone Pine Publishing), by John Acorn, is a field guide to some of the most common insects and spiders in the province, with good colour illustrations and amusing natural-history notes.

The Encyclopedia of Canadian Fishes (Key Porter Books), by Brad Coad, is a thick tome with black and white illustrations and detailed accounts of all of the country's fish.

Wild Mammals of Canada (McGraw-Hill Ryerson), by Frederick Wooding, provides popular accounts on all of Ontario's common mammals.

Familiar Amphibians and Reptiles of Ontario (Natural History/Natural Heritage), by Bob Johnson, provides good accounts of all of the province's frogs, salamanders, turtles and snakes, along with illustrations and range maps.

Forest Plants of Central Ontario (Lone Pine), by Brenda Chambers, features brief accounts of almost 700 of the region's herbs, shrubs, trees, ferns, mosses and lichens, with both colour photos and illustrations.

Trees in Canada (Fitzhenry & Whiteside), by John Farrar, is the definitive text on identifying Canadian trees, featuring colour photos of leaves, seeds, flowers, buds and bark for each species.

The Audubon Society Field Guide to North American Weather (Alfred A. Knopf) is a comprehensive and useful guide to observing and forecasting the weather, with a large section of sometimes spectacular colour photographs.

Nightwatch: A Practical Guide to Viewing the Universe (Firefly Books), by Terence Dickinson, is an excellent guide to observing the night sky, with everything from superb star maps to advice on how to take pictures of the heavens.

The Observer's Handbook (The Royal Astronomical Society of Canada) is an annual publication containing a huge amount of information about stars, planets, eclipses, sunrises and sunsets, meteor showers and so on, most of which is accessible to the average reader.

Ontario Rocks: Three Billion Years of Environmental Change (Fitzhenry & Whiteside), by Nick Eyles, is a comprehensive, well-illustrated review of the geological history of Ontario.

The Audubon Society Field Guide to North American Rocks and Minerals (Alfred A. Knopf) provides colour photos and good thumbnail accounts of just about any chunk of geological curiosity you can stumble upon.

On Nature (the magazine of Ontario Nature) and **Canadian Geographic, Cottage Life** and **Wildflower** magazines are all excellent sources of ongoing information on nature in Ontario.

RESOURCE GUIDE

Bruce Trail Association, P.O. Box 857, Hamilton, Ont., L8N
3N9, (905) 529-6821, 1-800-665-HIKE; e-mail,
info@brucetrail.org; website, www.brucetrail.org

Canadian Parks and Wilderness Society, 506 – 250 City Centre
Ave., Ottawa, Ont., K1R 6K7, (613) 569-7226,
1-800-333-WILD; e-mail, info@cpaws.org; website,
www.cpaws.org

Paddle Canada, P.O. Box 20069, RPO Taylor-Kidd, Kingston,
Ont., K7P 2T6, (613) 547-3196, 1-888-252-6292; e-mail,
info@paddlingcanada.com; website, www.paddlingcanada.com

Earthroots, 401 Richmond St. W., Suite 410, Toronto, Ont.,
M5V 3A8, (416) 599-0152; e-mail, info@earthroots.org;
website, www.earthroots.org

Federation of Ontario Cottagers' Association, 201–159 King
St., Peterborough, Ont., (705) 749-3622; e-mail,
info@foca.on.ca; website, www.foca.on.ca

Friends of Algonquin, P.O. Box 219, Whitney, Ont., K0J 2M0,
(705) 633-5572; e-mail, info@algonquinpark.on.ca; website,
www.algonquinpark.on.ca

Girl Guides of Canada, 50 Merton St., Toronto, Ont., M4S
1A3, (416) 487-5281; website, www.girlguides.ca

Ministry of Tourism, 900 Bay St., Hearst Block, 9th Flr.,
Toronto, Ont., M7A 2E1, (416) 326-9326, 1-800-ONTARIO;
e-mail, General_Info@mtr.gov.on.ca;
website, www.tourism.gov.on.ca

Ontario Heritage Foundation, 10 Adelaide St. East, Toronto,
Ont., M5C 1J3, (416) 325-5000; website, www.heritagefdn.on.ca

Ontario Nature, 366 Adelaide St. West, Suite 201, Toronto,
Ont., M5V 1R9, (416) 444-8419; e-mail,
info@ontarionature.org; website, www.ontarionature.org

Ontario Parks, 6th Flr., 300 Water St., P.O. Box 7000,
Peterborough, Ont., K9J 8M5, (705) 755-2000,
1-800-667-1940; website, www.ontarioparks.com

The Royal Astronomical Society of Canada, 203–4920 Dundas
St. West, Toronto, Ont., M9A 1B7, (416) 924-7973, 1-888-924-
7272; e-mail, nationaloffice@rasc.ca; website, www.rasc.ca

Scouts Canada, 1345 Baseline Rd., Ottawa, Ont., K2C 0A7,
(613) 224-5131; e-mail, helpcentre@scouts.ca;
website, www.scouts.ca

Wildlands League, 401 Richmond St. W., Suite 380, Toronto,
Ont., M5V 3A8, (416) 971-9453, 1-866-510-WILD; e-mail,
info@wildlandsleague.org; website, www.wildlandsleague.org

World Wildlife Fund (Canada), 245 Eglinton Ave. E., Suite 410,
Toronto, Ont., M4P 3J1, 416-489-8800, 1-800-26-PANDA;
e-mail, panda@wwfcanada.org; website, www.wwf.ca

INDEX